Justinian II

The Roman Emperor Who Lost his Nose and his Throne … and Regained Both!

Peter Crawford

PEN & SWORD
HISTORY

First published in Great Britain in 2021 by
Pen & Sword History
An imprint of
Pen & Sword Books Ltd
Yorkshire – Philadelphia

ISBN 978 1 52675 530 8

A CIP catalogue record for this book is
available from the British Library.

Typeset by Mac Style
Printed and bound in the UK by
CPI Group (UK) Ltd, Croydon, CR0 4YY.

Pen & Sword Books Limited incorporates the imprints of Atlas,
Archaeology, Aviation, Discovery, Family History, Fiction, History,
Maritime, Military, Military Classics, Politics, Select, Transport,
True Crime, Air World, Frontline Publishing, Leo Cooper, Remember
When, Seaforth Publishing, The Praetorian Press, Wharncliffe
Local History, Wharncliffe Transport, Wharncliffe True Crime
and White Owl.

For a complete list of Pen & Sword titles please contact

PEN & SWORD BOOKS LIMITED
47 Church Street, Barnsley, South Yorkshire, S70 2AS, England
E-mail: enquiries@pen-and-sword.co.uk
Website: www.pen-and-sword.co.uk

Or

PEN AND SWORD BOOKS
1950 Lawrence Rd, Havertown, PA 19083, USA
E-mail: Uspen-and-sword@casematepublishers.com
Website: www.penandswordbooks.com

Queenie:	'Just tell me one thing. Is her nose as pretty as mine?'
Blackadder:	'Oh, no, no … ma'am.'
Queenie:	'Oh good, because otherwise I would have cut it off. And then you would have to marry someone without a nose and that wouldn't be very nice, would it?'
Blackadder:	'No, ma'am.'
Queenie:	'Imagine the mess when she's got a cold! Yuck!'
Blackadder:	'Well, quite ma'am.'

Blackadder II: Episode 1 'Bells'

Contents

Acknowledgements

I would like to give thanks to the established team of contributors who have played some part in the production and publication of this book.

To Phil Sidnell and Pen & Sword for once again giving me the opportunity to write about ancient history. Or are we into the medieval period now? These timelines are so confusing ...

Also to Matt Jones and his production team at Pen & Sword who turned this gather-up of text, photographs, diagrams, maps and drawings into this colourful tome.

To my sister, Faye Beedle, for making sense of my vague instructions and outlines to present such excellent maps and diagrams, and then inexplicably volunteering to draw an emperor without a nose ...

To Noble Numismatics for once again granting me access to their excellent archive of images, particularly as coinage played such a major role in the reigns of Justinian II and Abd al-Malik.

To the historians, writers, artists and photographers whose work has been consulted, digested, detailed and cited within. I hope to have done you all justice.

To Dr John Curran, whose fault this all remains ...

To the Classical Association in Northern Ireland for providing me with useful distractions.

To all the staff, past and present, at Queen's University, Belfast, and Dalriada School, Ballymoney, for all the time and effort you have put in to get me this far.

To the 'DRINK' chat for all the much-needed distractions and 'did ye ayes?'

To the innumerable cups of tea.

And to Mum ... those bookcases are starting to overflow a little.

gratias vobis ago

Introduction: A 'Tweet' and Treasure

There is no way to avoid this, so I will just come out and say it: the idea for this book largely came from the composing of a tweet; a tweet that was never actually sent!

'Justinian II: the Roman emperor who lost his throne and his nose, only to somehow regain both … and then lose his head.'

As the summing up of around forty-three years of Roman imperial history, I do not think that there are too many people out there who would not be at least somewhat interested in the story encapsulated in that tweet's 120 characters. I am sure that plenty of other Roman historians have raised an eyebrow when confronted with the spectacle of a Roman emperor with no nose. This unsent tweet became the basis for a pitch, leading eventually to what you have in your hand/on your screen.

I have investigated parts of the seventh century AD before, but in a previous literary outing for Pen & Sword I found it difficult to come to a natural end point. This was largely my own fault, for unlike my other books, I had not set out to follow the life of a specific emperor – in hindsight I should have focused on Heraclius. Another part of this inability to come to any chronological conclusion was my fascination with various aspects of the second half of the seventh century. In particular, it was the sheer extent of the Arab conquests, not just at the expense of the Romans, but also the North African Berbers, Iberian Visigoths, Gallic Franks and those living from the Central Asian Steppe to the boundaries of Chinese influence and parts of the Indian subcontinent. Perhaps more fascinating still was the mixed Roman response to the appearance of existential threats to their empire in the east and north.

At times, an empire with such a rich history of militarism just seemed to be completely 'fought out'. Important provinces like Syria, Thrace and Egypt were given up without much of a fight. There was to be no grand campaign of attempted reconquest in the mould of Justinian I in the West or Heraclius against the Persians in the East. Perhaps even more surprising was the Roman inability to make any sizeable gains against the disparate Bulgar and Slav invaders of the Balkans. It would be 200 years before any substantial reclamation of territory was achieved. This might seem like an immense amount of time for the Roman Empire to either be on the back foot or merely holding its own; however, it is perhaps not so surprising given the massive shock to the Roman system that the Arab conquests and the collapse of its Danube frontier had been. Centuries of dominance in the Mediterranean had been washed away in little more than a decade, with long-established military, administrative and economic structures no longer fit for purpose. Indeed, at least the first century after the initial wave of Arab conquest was spent in a transition from scrambled, improvised defence to something approaching a new administrative and military system, punctuated by two decades of what is dubbed 'military anarchy'.

And yet, despite my personal interest in these events, that inability to find what felt like a natural stopping point prevented me from continuing to look at the seventh century for literary inspiration for a few years. What actually brought me back to this period after looking into other emperors – Constantius II and Zeno the Isaurian – was a piece of serendipitous shopping. In my favourite little second-hand bookshop in Belfast – Self Help Africa on Botanic Avenue – I found a copy of Harry Turtledove's translation of the years 602–813 of the *Chronicle* of Theophanes the Confessor for the monstrous price of 50p. You have to take advantage of such good fortune!

Armed with such a combination of tweet and treasure, I dived back into the story of the Roman Empire in the second half of the seventh century and quickly latched on to the story of the 'emperor without a nose': Justinian II. His was a life lived at a time when the Roman Empire was starting to realize that the Arab conquest was not necessarily one to be overcome with a single great military action; the loss of the eastern provinces was becoming a little less impermanent. In the past, this had not been a period covered in much detail in the pages of history, although more recently, attention has been paid to the emergence of Islam, the subsequent conquests made under its banner across three continents and how the reeling Roman Empire reshaped itself into a bulwark against further Arab expansion into Anatolia. However, while there has been growing interest in this period, with some pieces on his edicts, coinage and religious policies, the life and reign of Justinian II usually gets tucked away as a curiosity in more general histories of the 'Byzantine' Empire.

Constance Head is the most prolific writer on Justinian II, starting with several articles surrounding his restoration and a re-evaluation of his second reign, culminating in a biography in 1972. While that was and still is a fine piece, replete with summations that – as will be seen throughout this work – make it eminently quotable, it did not illicit the reformation of Justinian's tarnished reputation that might have been aimed for, nor a significant increase in his historical profile. This is seen in the fact that Head's biography, which while still very readable, is nearly fifty years old, and there has been little move to replace or update it.

It is surely surprising that such a colourful character as Justinian II has not attracted more direct attention. Expanding briefly on the aforementioned non-tweet summary, Justinian II was the last of the Heraclian dynasty, which had saved the empire from the Persians and struggled valiantly against the Arab tide. After a reign of ten years involving military achievement and reverse, administrative expansion and innovation and religious debate, he lost his throne – and his nose. He then spent ten more years in exile, where he survived two plots to kill him, before returning home to regain the throne through barbarian help, only to again lose it, along with his head. As will be examined below and throughout this work, a major part of such a colourful and intriguing character being sidelined is due to the nature and perhaps paucity of the sources, but even this is an assumption that, as Head points out,[1] requires some careful examination.

This work largely follows a similar chronological layout to Head's biography, along with a couple of thematic sections. The opening chapter will look at the state of the Roman Empire at the time of Justinian's birth in around AD 668. With the contraction of imperial territory and the expansion of the Arab caliphate to encompass much of the Mediterranean coastline, it might be expected that the list of Roman opponents also contracted. However, if anything, that list expanded, or at least there was more variety in the sources to provide a better look at the number of imperial opponents – Arabs, Avars, Lombards, Slavs, Bulgars and Khazars. This is shown in my decision to gather that list into a single chapter of introductions for those various enemies rather than interrupting the narrative flow of the main text on several occasions to present an outline of various imperial opponents.

Such was the timing of his birth that the life of Justinian II encapsulated the controversial end of the reign of his grandfather, Constans II, and the entirety of his father Constantine IV's time on the throne. These periods were not only important to the survival of the empire, but also as Justinian's formative years. While following the chronological progress of Justinian's first reign, chapters will be given over to his imperial administration and religious policies, which will take in various developments throughout this period. We will then return to the chronological progression, with some focus on specific geographic areas, following Justinian's exile and restoration, his actions in the Balkans, the East, Italy and then Cherson, before his final deposition and demise. Throughout this book, we will also be introduced to various individuals whose careers coincided with that of Justinian II, such as the men to claim the imperial throne during his lifetime – Leontios, Tiberius III and Philippikos Bardanes. Significant time will be given to aspects of the reign of the Umayyad caliph Abd al-Malik, as well as the Bulgar khan Tervel and the Khazar khagan Busir. There will also be a look at various religious officials, including several popes, patriarchs and bishops.

I had originally planned to have this work take in not just the life and reigns of Justinian II, but also the reigns of his immediate successors – Philippikos Bardanes, Anastasius II and Theodosius III, culminating in the climactic defence of Constantinople by Leo III against the Arabs in 717–718. However, adding that would have made this book too long, bursting at the seams as it already is. Instead, the continuation of the 'Twenty Years of Military Anarchy' after Justinian II's demise is addressed in a brief epilogue, perhaps providing a taster for a future title focusing on the life and reign of Leo III.

Sources

Reflecting the dire situation the Roman Empire found itself in, the seventh century AD and on into the early eighth is usually considered a period of poor source material for virtually all of the Mediterranean. A particular issue is the lack of a surviving contemporary secular history in the mould of Procopius or any of his continuators: Agathias, Menander Protector or Theophylactus Simocatta. It seems to be because of this that, despite the clear importance of this century to the Roman Empire, the lands around the Mediterranean and world history in general, historians have largely accepted the surviving material with an uncritical eye and even neglected the entire period as 'a veritable Byzantine Dark Age'.[2] More recently, however, the fantastic work of James Howard-Johnston in *Witnesses to a World Crisis* (2010) has helped to demonstrate that while certain periods of the seventh century may be lacking a contemporary historian of the standard of a Tacitus, Ammianus Marcellinus or Procopius, it is still possible to reconstruct a workable chronology from the various sources of material that do survive.[3]

For Justinian II, it is the lack of criticism of the Eastern Roman source tradition that has led to his prevailing depiction as 'irresponsible, intensely cruel, devoid of any redeeming features'.[4] The oddity of Justinian's deposition, mutilation and exile may also have encouraged history writers – contemporary and later – to accept the monstrous depictions exaggerated/invented of him. This is seen in what is perhaps the only significant work on Justinian II before Head's biography in 1972: Charles Diehl's 1923 article 'L'Empereur au nez coupé' ('The Emperor with the cut nose'). While pioneering, Diehl took much of the material hostile to Justinian at face value, with limited criticism of what they were saying and why, propagating the almost entirely negative portrayal of Justinian. We must look beyond that historiographical hostility, the incredulity his reign might spark and the morbid fascination inspired by his *rhinokopia* and reclamation of the throne to investigate who Justinian might have been, what he did during his reign and why, and what effect he had on the Roman Empire and its neighbours.

The most important contemporary source for the life and times of Justinian II is possibly the so-called *History to 720*, which focuses on the period from just before and after the assassination of Constans II through to the early years of Leo III's reign.[5] While usually listed as 'anonymous', there has been some suggestion that the author of this chronicle is recorded in other historical material. The tenth-century Roman encyclopaedia known as the *Suda* mentions a 'Trajan the Patrician' as a contemporary of Justinian II and the author of a 'remarkable short chronicle'. Such praise could reflect the importance of his work in filling a gap in the historical record.[6] This identification seems to fit with what can be discerned about the writer of the *History to 720*, although there is some cause for caution. It may even be that the author was more a contemporary and even close associate of Leo III, or perhaps even Leo himself.[7]

Whoever the author of the *History to 720* was, 'his work is the ultimate source of most of what we know about internal Byzantine politics in the late seventh and early eighth centuries'.[8] The writer appears to be an office-holder who took care to present Leo III in a positive light, while destroying the reputation of Justinian II with 'a grim tale … well told'.[9] He compiled his chronicle from his own experiences, rather than from extensive research, bolstering it with the knowledge of his contemporaries and government, which can give good information but also skewed propaganda. In this, the author of the *History to 720* was 'not a true historian'.[10] He fails to analyse his sources, contemporary or otherwise, and when lacking evidence, he did not go looking for it. Consequently, the work seems more like a 'collective memoir', providing a 'history' of what he and his contemporaries remembered; or perhaps more crucially, how he and his contemporaries thought Leo III might want the reign of Justinian II remembered.

Of course, the strange thing about this *History to 720* with its pivotal role in the story of Justinian II is that none of it survives as a separate work. Its importance stems from the fact that it is considered the source of information for the reign of Justinian II used by later writers, most importantly Patriarch Nikephoros and Theophanes the Confessor. This led to the distaste for Justinian II expressed by the *History to 720* – actual or propagandist – shining through in a large section of the Eastern Roman historical tradition, going a long way to perpetuate and exaggerate the negative portrayal of Justinian throughout the ages.

Patriarch Nikephoros I came from an iconodule* family native to Constantinople, but nonetheless continued in service to the iconoclast Constantine V, who had banished his father. His support for icons saw him serving as an imperial commissioner at the Second Council of Nicaea in 787, where the first wave of Iconoclasm was overturned. Over the next twenty years, he resided at a cloister along the east coast of the Bosphorus and served as the director of a poor house in the capital, only to suddenly be chosen as patriarch of Constantinople by his imperial namesake, Nikephoros I, on 12 April 806. This caused some problems with the Church establishment, as the now-Patriarch Nikephoros had not been part of the clergy, marking his accession as uncanonical. However, the support of the emperor retained Nikephoros in his patriarchal place. That was until the restoration of Iconoclasm by Leo V. Forced off the patriarchal throne, Nikephoros was sent to the monastery of Agathias and then that of St Theodore, where he continued his writing until his death in 828. Despite his iconodule beliefs, Nikephoros was well-enough thought of for his tolerance to be put forward as a candidate for the patriarchate again in 820 during the transition to the reign of Michael II.

---

* Iconoclasm was the great religious dispute of the eighth and ninth centuries, initiated by Emperor Leo III in the 720s. He felt that in their excessive reverence for religious icons, Christians were breaking the Second Commandment against graven images and perhaps had been punished by God through the Arab conquests. In a series of edicts, Leo seemingly forbade the veneration of religious images, creating a schism in the Church between his supporters – iconoclasts ('breakers of icons') – and his opponents – iconodules ('lovers of icons').

This tolerance and non-partisanship can be seen in parts of his *Historia Syntomos/Breviarium*, which covers the period 602–769. However, that non-partisanship is not extended to the depiction of Justinian II, which is heavily influenced by the negativity presented in the source material of Justinian's successors. Constance Head, following Louis Orosz, suggests that Nikephoros used a '*713 Chronicle*' compiled during the reign of Philippikos Bardanes, who would have required that the historians of his time 'reflected the "official" view that Justinian had fallen because of his misdeeds and that Vardan, who played so large a role in the coup that dethroned him, was justified'.[11] Such an approach has Theophanes using an even more hostile source from the reign of Leo III; however, it has been suggested that 'the differences between the two accounts ... are not nearly as significant as Head suggests; it appears that they merely reproduce slightly different sections of the same narrative'[12] – i.e. the *History to 720*.

Nikephoros appears to use just the *History to 720* for Justinian's reign, which not only explains the anti-Justinian bias but also may reflect the general lack of sources available for parts of the seventh century. This is also demonstrated in the significant twenty-seven-year gap in Nikephoros' history between events surrounding Heraklonas, Martina, Valentinus and Constans II in October 641 and the assassination of Constans in 668. Theophanes uses his Syriac source for this period, so 'we can hardly avoid the conclusion that there was almost no "Byzantine" historical material for that period'.[13] Furthermore, Nikephoros' classicizing style may make his work succinct and easily digestible, but the removal of dates and the lack of critique of the events recorded reduces the overall usefulness of the *Breviarium*. This frequently leaves him in the shadow of Theophanes, who records all the same information and more,[14] even if the latter is not necessarily as reliable as Nikephoros. And yet, when these drawbacks and the bias provided by the *History to 720* are taken into account, Nikephoros' *Breviarium* 'remains an extremely valuable source of information'.[15]

As well as following the tradition set out in the *History to 720*, Theophanes the Confessor also shared a similar background and life path to Nikephoros: Constantinopolitan origin, iconodule family and the son of an imperial official. After his father's death, Theophanes was educated at the imperial court of Constantine V, at odds with his iconodule beliefs, and yet he served in various official positions under Leo IV. Theophanes then embraced religious life but without joining the clergy, entering the Polychronius Monastery near Cyzicus and then serving as abbot of a new abbey nearby.

This saw him present at the Second Council of Nicaea in 787 in support of the icons. Leo V attempted to convince him to embrace Iconoclasm, first through argument and then through two years of imprisonment and physical torture. When this failed, Theophanes was exiled to Samothrace in 817, but the extent of the torture had undermined his health, and he died mere days later.

Theophanes' *Chronographia* came into being between 810 and 815 through the request of George Syncellus as a continuation of George's own chronicle, which covered the period from the Creation to the accession of Diocletian in AD 284. Theophanes freely admits that George had provided him with the material to complete the work that now bears his name, which raises the question of exactly how much of the writing of the *Chronographia* Theophanes did? Could it be that he merely collated the material that George had already collected to bring his chronicle from 284 up to their modern day in the early ninth century? It would seem likely that the *Chronographia* of Theophanes should perhaps be regarded as a collaboration between Theophanes and George Syncellus, with the latter having gathered a significant amount of the material, while the former stitched the material together and collected materials himself.[16]

Covering the period from the accession of Diocletian in 284 to the fall of Michael I in 813, Theophanes' *Chronographia* is made up of two parts: the first is a year-by-year account, while the second is a series of chronological tables which contain numerous errors and may not have been completed by Theophanes. Further confusion arises from Theophanes' attempts to label each year with the regnal years of emperors, kings, caliphs and patriarchs. Despite these issues, and others such as a lack of critical insight, Theophanes' work is extremely useful for the seventh and early eighth century due to the lack of other source material. Theophanes' work was well-regarded enough in the ninth century to be used as the basis of a tripartite Latin compilation, along with George Syncellus and Nikephoros, by the papal librarian Anastasius in 873–875. Theophanes also eventually received his own continuation in a series of works known collectively as *Theophanes Continuatus*, commissioned by Constantine VII to chronicle the period from 813–961.

Through their usage of the *History to 720*, Theophanes and Nikephoros share a similar chronological order of events and include similar specific information through a similar vocabulary; however, both give information the other does not.[17] Furthermore, despite sharing the same background, beliefs, timeline and source, Nikephoros and Theophanes were seemingly unaware of each other's work, which seems peculiar. The dating of the *Breviarium* is unclear, but seems likely to be either a product of the 780s or the 820s. If the former, why is there no evidence that Theophanes used it for his *Chronographia*? If the latter, why is there no evidence that Nikephoros used the wealth of information presented by Theophanes? The answer may be in their shared iconodule beliefs, which might have seen their works kept out of circulation until the final defeat of Iconoclasm in 843. Iconoclasm and the reaction to it may in general have seen considerable information lost.[18]

Also in spite of their shared source, Theophanes is even more prejudiced against Justinian than Nikephoros, frequently providing more depth/exaggeration on unfavourable incidents. It could be that Theophanes was making up these extra details either to sensationalize his account or due to his personal opposition to Justinian; however, such intentional fabrication would be against Theophanes' own claim to have not added to the reports he was using and the usual treatment of their sources by Roman historians.[19] This suggests that Theophanes had other sources for the era of Justinian II not used by Nikephoros. He may have had access to an iconodule chronicler who began his history in *c.*720, perhaps something of a continuation of the *History to 720*.[20] The potential work of Trajan the Patrician is not the only source of uncertain name and authorship to be used by Theophanes and others. Along with the likes of Agapius of Hierapolis, Michael the Syrian and the *Chronicle of 1234*, Theophanes seems to have used a now lost Syriac source from around 750, the author of which has been frequently investigated and postulated as Theophilus of Edessa.[21] The origin of many of these works under the Isaurian dynasty could explain their anti-Justinianic leanings. Not only was there the need to make a previous dynasty look bad in order to present a legitimate basis for its overthrow and replacement by a new dynasty, but there were several political, religious and personal reasons for Leo III to have sought the destruction of Justinian's reputation.

There is a section of Theophanes' *Chronographia* under AM6177 (AD 685–686) which has been expanded upon after Theophanes' death in 818 as it knows the length of several patriarchates which took place after that year: Theodotus (815–821), Antonius (821–834) and John VII Grammaticus/Lekanomantis (834–843). Indeed, as the additions record that Lekanomantis had only been patriarch for six years and one month and it is known that he would be patriarch for another three years, this would seem to date these Theophanic additions to the year 840. Such additions highlight the care that needs to be taken with primary sources. Copyists and revisionists can have little compunction with changing the text of the works they are dealing with, which can cause problems for the historian looking to rely on the information stored within.

Due to such inherent biases, problems and the way its author presents material, Theophanes' *Chronographia* must be used with care, particularly for the period of Justinian II where his use of two sometimes overlapping and contradictory sources creates issues. However, Theophanes' style of reporting – stitching together rather than blending material – allows for some useful disentangling of his source material.[22] By using other sources, such as Theophilus for information on Umayyad Syria and perhaps the city chronicle of Constantinople, "Theophanes has left much the fullest and most useful account of Roman history'[23] for the period around Justinian II's lifetime. Without his work, the period of 669–720 would be much the darker.

Another ninth-century source to have used the *History to 720* is George Monachos. He presents some information not in Theophanes or Nikephoros, but such 'embellishments' seem more like extra detail rather than invention. Through the combination of Theophanes, Nikephoros and George Monachos, the anti-Justinianic hyperbole of *History to 720* does reach a wide audience; however, even at its times of greatest exaggeration, there is a more positive presentation of Justinian lurking within their words, a reflection of their inability to hide the positives. That said, while the extent or intent of some of Justinian's actions may have been embellished for propagandist aims, it is unlikely that they were all complete inventions. Therefore, while we might find that Justinian was a courageous, intelligent and able emperor, that should not obscure the man of short temper and impatience.

Many of the other Eastern Roman histories to survive in any useful form derive their information either directly from Theophanes or his sources, and therefore 'add scarcely anything to our knowledge'.[24] The Spanish *Chronicle of 741* relies either on the Syriac source used by Theophanes (possibly Theophilus) or on the Greek work used by said Syriac source for much of the seventh century.[25] As well as commissioning the *Theophanes Continuatus*, the tenth-century emperor Constantine VII oversaw the publication of *De cerimoniis aulae Byzantinae* – 'On Ceremonies', describing court ceremonies and protocol – and *De administrando Imperio* – 'On the Governance of the Empire', which gives useful information on domestic and foreign policy. These may not be histories, but they do provide anecdotes and insights into various areas of the empire important during the reign of

Justinian II. As already mentioned, the tenth-century Agapius of Hierapolis used the Syriac work of Theophilus of Edessa, although he also used other Greek and Syriac sources. This sees his *Kitab al-Unwan*, while surviving in patchy form, record some useful information about the Later Roman Empire and its interactions with the Arabs.[26] The likes of the late eleventh/early twelfth-century *Compendium Historiarum* of Kedrenus also drew heavily on Theophanes and George Monachos.[27]

It is perhaps not until the twelfth century that the considerable dependence on Theophanes for the later Heraclian dynasty slackens a little with the publication of the Syriac chronicle of Michael the Syrian. This patriarch of the Jacobite Church was a prolific consumer of source material, which is seen not just in the number of genres he addressed in his writing – canonical, theological, liturgical, historical – but also how his twenty-one-book history used at least 150 different sources.[28] A century later, another prominent Jacobite bishop, Gregory Bar Hebraeus, produced a combined world and church history in Syriac. It focused on the Near East and can provide some useful extra information about the period, such as the presence of several imposters claiming to be Justinian's son during the reign of Leo III in both Roman and Arab territory.[29]

While the majority of the historiographic focus for the reign of Justinian II falls on the sources from within the Roman Empire or following its literary tradition, there are other traditions from which to gather useful information. It was long held that the perceived distortion of Muslim sources rendered them supposedly useless for events relevant to the Roman Empire of Justinian II. It has taken something of a leap of faith to trust aspects of the Islamic historical tradition for the first century of Muslim history, which was not formally recorded until the later Abbasid period. Straightaway, this presents a non-contemporary element to these sources, with the most prominent Muslim writers, al-Baladhuri and al-Tabari, coming from the ninth and tenth centuries respectively. Then again, this is no different than having to rely on Nikephoros or Theophanes as 'primary' sources. Many of the Muslim sources act as compilers of other Muslim works, whether they be poets, historians or recording oral traditions. Again, this is not all that different from how we use the Roman source tradition, with various types of source material used to build the narrative picture. Indeed, the Muslim sources are frequently much better at identifying where they are getting their material from, while Roman sources merely record the material with little reference to its origin, leaving historiographical investigation to uncover their sources.

However, the Muslim sources focusing on the events of the late seventh/ early eighth century frequently concentrate on internal affairs, with foreign matters 'covered usually in brief notices, which simply round up the news at the end of a year-entry'.[30] Many of these reports are also lacking context, with even some internal affairs such as the outbreak of the First Fitna – Islamic civil war – 'attributed entirely to internal causes'[31] without reference to external pressures. Reverses suffered against various opponents – Romans, Mardaites, Berbers or Khazars – are frequently passed over either in total silence or it is merely stated that the battle took place without any reference to its result. But even with these problems, the internal affairs recorded by Muslim sources can provide useful context to Romano-Arab conflict. As will be seen, the distraction of the Second Fitna played a critical role in allowing Justinian II's reign to get off to a good military start. And while context and detail can be lacking in Muslim reports, they can help provide some clarity or backing for aspects of the Roman record which seem unclear, such as the target of a Roman or Arab attack under a certain commander or into a certain region.

Looking west, there is a cadre of sources which can provide somewhat alternative views on Justinian II. Through the compilation work of Louis Duchense in the late nineteenth century, and itself likely a compilation of various authors over time, the section of the *Liber Pontificalis* – 'Book of Pontiffs' – covering the late seventh/early eighth century appears to be contemporaneous with the reigns of Constantine IV and Justinian II. While unsurprisingly partial to the papacy, the *Liber Pontificalis* provides a good look at imperio-papal relations from the period. Along with the preserved records of the church councils – *Acta Conciliorum Oecumenicorum* – it chronicles important aspects of the controversy over Quinisext, such as the presence of papal representatives and their signing up to its decisions, the journey of Pope Constantine to the imperial capital and Justinian's intervention in the Romano-Ravennate feud.[32]

Another contemporary of Justinian II to record information about him is, perhaps somewhat surprisingly, the Venerable Bede in far-off northern England. His various works present how even three centuries after the end of Roman Britain, the empire still had an influence on the island. Bede also records the Western Christian response to Quinisext and even aspects of Justinian's Chersonite exile which other sources like Nikephoros and Theophanes seem to get a little incorrect. These earlier western sources are also less hostile to Justinian II than the eastern tradition, passing over the period of the emperor's supposed brutal reprisals in silence.

However, within a century, other western sources were starting to present a darker picture of Justinian, perhaps becoming infected with the bias promoted by the Isaurian dynasty. The eighth-century historian Paul the Deacon presents useful information on the Lombards from their legendary Scandinavian origins through their migrations to the death of Liutprand in 744 in his *Historia Langobardorum*. Despite using the *Liber Pontificalis* and Bede as sources, Paul is much more willing to buy into the anti-Justinian rhetoric, describing him in bloodthirsty terms.[33] Even more tainted by anti-Justinian bias is the ninth-century *Liber Pontificalis Ecclesiae Ravennatis* – 'Book of the Pontiffs of the Church of Ravenna' – of Andreas Agnellus. In terms of characterization of Justinian, Agnellus is much closer to Nikephoros and Theophanes than the earlier western sources. He is frequently so 'imaginative',[34] even Virgilian, in his recording as to undermine the value of his specific details. He may even devolve into intentional disinformation, such as the motives about Justinian's attack on Ravenna. He is one of the sources that records Justinian's wearing of a false gold nose.[35]

On the subject of gold, numismatics can also provide valuable information about the state of the empire at a particular time and place. The circulation of coins can imply how well the Roman economy was operating, while a large amount of coins in a particular area is a good indication of a strong imperial presence at a particular time. Most importantly for political disruption and usurpation, coins can demonstrate who held power at certain times, as well as the outward appearance presented by the imperial court. Furthermore, it will be seen that during the late seventh and early eighth centuries, numismatics represents a considerable source of information for various political, religious, artistic and even foreign policies not just of Justinian II but also of Abd al-Malik's caliphate.

One substantial issue with many of the sources is the matter of dating. By the late seventh century, along with *Anno Mundi* – 'World Year' measured from the Creation based on the Septuagint text of the Bible – the Romans were using a fifteen-year indiction cycle. This saw the year begin on 1 September, which can cause problems when attempts are made to equate such dates to the modern Gregorian calendar. For example, Theophanes places Constans II's assassination and Justinian II's birth in AM6160, which equates to a period of 1 September 668 – 31 August 669. Therefore, without a specific date or an indication of season, there would be a lack of certainty of the year of Constans' murder without outside help. And when there is no outside help forthcoming, we are left with a date of 668/669, as is the case with Justinian II's birth year.

This indiction trouble finds little solution when looking to the Muslim sources; indeed, it may even be exacerbated. This is because the Islamic calendar, usually denoted as 'AH' – *Anno Hegirae*: 'in the year of the Hegira', which starts in 622 – is based on the lunar cycle. Consequently, it is always considerably out of sync with the calendars of today and of the seventh/eighth century. This means that when combined, these Roman indiction and Islamic Hijri calendars can produce substantial dating problems, such as the likes of Theophanes and al-Tabari dating the same events a couple of years apart. This can make building a secure chronology for certain periods of Justinian II's life quite difficult.

Indeed, it was long thought that the likes of Theophanes had 'systematically misdated'[36] virtually every major event during the reign of Justinian II. This was largely accepted by academia, only for more in-depth looks at dating systems, events and other sources to suggest that Theophanes is more correct in his dates than usually supposed. There are still some errors, such as with the death of Abd al-Malik being dated to AM6197 rather than AM6198 – October 705 – or with events between 699 and 704 being a year too late; however, these may show 'that Theophanes like the rest of us had trouble converting eastern sources' years of the Hegira into ordinary solar years'.[37] You might think to look to Nikephoros for some help with these dating issues, but he simply avoids adding to this specific problem by not recording many dates at all. 'They are casualties of the classicizing makeover given to his sources',[38] although the order of his events is largely chronological.

As can be seen from the extensive, yet not exhaustive, secondary bibliography attached at the end of this work, there has been plenty of modern material to digest regarding the life and times of Justinian II; however, there are a few specific historians I would like to highlight. The various articles of E.W. Brooks from the late nineteenth and early twentieth centuries might seem a little dated, but several remain of considerable use to this day. As already mentioned above, the 1972 biography of Justinian II by Constance Head came in very useful to the creation of this book, as did her articles on various aspects of Justinian's reigns. Similarly prolific and useful on Justinian II is James Breckenridge, with his short book of 1959 on Justinian's coinage particularly valuable, a subject bolstered by Mark Humphreys' 2013 article on the supposed 'War of Images' between Justinian and Abd al-Malik. Andrew Ekonomou's 2007 work on the supposed 'Byzantine Papacy' provided an avenue into the western outlook on Justinian II, especially over Quinisext. Finally, any writer on the Roman Empire of Late Antiquity or the Early Medieval period almost certainly makes good use of the various books and articles of John Haldon.

Spelling Conventions

Given the various languages that sources for the seventh and eighth centuries were written in – Latin, Greek, Armenian, Syriac and Arabic – as well as the other peoples and languages those sources talk about – Germanic, Avar, Slavic, Bulgar, Khazar Turkic, Berber – it becomes important for the sake of clarity to establish spelling conventions. As I freely admit to having almost no knowledge of any of these languages, I have endeavoured to maintain consistency with what are essentially personal choices, rather than any sort of linguistic principles. But with the amount of names that do appear in this work and my direct quotation of numerous different sources, there is likely to be some disparity in the spellings employed. Hopefully, this does not create any difficulty in the identification of an individual or place. More prominent Anglicized versions of personal names will be used over Latin or Greek, so for the most part we will be in the realms of Justinian, Constantine and Leo, rather than Ioustinianos, Constantinus and Leon. On occasion though, due to the number of individuals sharing the same name, different spellings may be employed to differentiate them, such as 'Heraclius' and 'Herakleios'.

The eastern and northern neighbours of the Roman Empire present trickier problems, as the same name can have many different spellings in their transliterations into Latin/Greek and then into English. For example, the name of the first caliph of the Umayyad dynasty has been transcribed in various ways – Muawiyah, Mu'awiya, Mu'awiyah, Muawiya, Mauias. I have tried to use versions which are more obviously Arabic in origin, Muawiyah and Abd al-Malik, rather than some of the 'butchered' transliterations of Roman sources. There are similar issues with other names of non-Mediterranean origin, such as Tervel, Busir and perhaps Apsimar.

The Anglicized ancient name of an existing town, city or region prevails in the text, such as Constantinople over Istanbul, Antioch over Antakya or Anatolia over central Turkey. Roman-era provincial names will also be used over modern equivalents, although on many occasions, a lesser-known place name will be accompanied by its more modern equivalent or a more famous nearby location to aid in its identification. As for the empire as a whole, while some trace the beginning of the 'Byzantine Empire' to the refounding of Constantinople by Constantine I in AD 330, I am of the opinion that the empire based on that new imperial capital and the eastern provinces remained recognizably and lineally the Roman Empire until at least 1204, if not all the way to 1453. Therefore, apart from in quotations from other historians, throughout this work, the realm of Justinian II will be named as the 'Roman Empire' and its inhabitants will be known as 'Romans'. As for its neighbours, the name 'Umayyad caliphate' and 'Arab caliphate' will be used largely interchangeably, except when some differentiation is required during the Fitnas, where there was more than one Arab faction to identify. The semi-nomadic proto-states of the Danube delta and the northern Caucasus also require some appellative definition. While there were other Bulgar groups across various parts of Europe and the Eurasian steppe, those who settled around the Lower Danube are to be referred to either as the 'Danube Bulgars' or the 'Bulgar Khanate', with their ruler known as the 'khan'. The Turkic realm of the northern Caucasus will be referred to as the 'Khazar Khaganate', with its ruler the 'khagan'.

Any errors in continuity and consistency remain my own.

List of Illustrations and Maps

All maps, plans and diagrams were drawn by Faye Beedle

Geographical Maps

Strategic Maps

Tactical Diagrams

List of Plates

Coins
Courtesy of Noble Numismatics (http://www.noble.com.au/), unless otherwise stated

HERACLIUS, CONSTANTINE III AND HERAKLONAS: gold *solidus*, issued between 635 and 636 from Constantinople mint. Obverse: Heraclius centre, Constantine III left and Heraklonas right, cross above. Reverse: cross on steps, monogram of Heraclius left, *VICTORIA AVGUE CONOB*.

CONSTANS II AND CONSTANTINE IV: gold *solidus*, issued between 654 and 659 from Constantinople mint. Obverse: crowned Constans left, Constantine right, *DN CONSTATINUS C CONSTI*. Reverse: cross on steps, *VICTORIA AVGUE CONOB+*.

CONSTANTINE IV, with Heraclius and Tiberius: gold *solidus*, issued between 674 and 681 from Constantinople mint. Obverse; three-quarter facing bearded bust of Constantine IV in military garb, *dN CONST ANUS P.* Reverse: cross on steps, between Heraclius on left and Tiberius on right, each holding cross on globe, *VICTOA AVGU**Q*, CONOB*.

JUSTINIAN II (first reign 685–695): gold *solidus*, issued between 687 and 692 from Constantinople mint. Obverse: bust facing of Justinian with short beard, wearing chlamys and crown, holding cross on globe, *D IUSTINIA NUS PE AV*. Reverse: cross on steps, *VICTORIA AVGU H CONOB Γ*.

JUSTINIAN II (first reign 685–695): gold *solidus*, issued between 687 and 692 from Constantinople mint. Obverse: bust facing of Justinian with short beard, wearing chlamys and crown, holding cross on globe, *IUSTINIA NUS PE AV*. Reverse: cross potent on three steps, around *VICTORIA AVGUI CONOB*.

LEONTIOS: gold *solidus*, issued between 695 and 698 from Constantinople mint. Obverse: bust facing of Leontios, bearded, wearing crown and loros, holding akakia and cross on globe, *D LEON PE AV*. Reverse: cross on steps, *VICTORIA AVGUS, CONOB*.

TIBERIUS III: gold *solidus*, issued between 698 and 705 from Constantinople mint. Obverse: cuirassed bust of Tiberius facing with short beard, wearing crown and holding spear, *d TIbERI US PE AU*. Reverse: cross on steps, *VICTORIA AUGU CONOB*.

JUSTINIAN II (second reign, 705–711): gold *solidus*, issued in 705 from Constantinople mint. Obverse: facing bust of Christ, with cross behind head, curly hair and close beard, wears pallium and colobium, raising hand in benediction, *dN IhS ChS REX REGNANTIUM*. Reverse: crowned facing bust of Justinian, wearing loros and holding crosses, *DN IUSTINIA NUS MULTUS A, PAX*. (Courtesy of Classical Numismatic Group, Inc. http://www.cngcoins.com)

JUSTINIAN II AND TIBERIUS: gold *solidus*, issued between 705 and 711 from Constantinople mint. Obverse: facing bust of Christ, with cross behind head, curly hair and close beard, wears pallium and colobium, raising hand in benediction, *dN IhS ChS REX REGNANTIUM*. Reverse: facing and crowned busts of Justinian on left and Tiberius, cross between them, *[D N IUSTINIA]NUS ET TIbERIUS P P A*.

PHILIPPIKOS BARDANES: gold *solidus*, issued between 711 and 713 from Constantinople mint. Obverse: facing and crowned bust of Philippikos, *DN FILIPICUS MUL TUS [AN]*, facing bust, wearing crown and loros, holding cross globe and eagle-tipped sceptre. Reverse: cross on steps, *VICTORIA AVGU Z/CONOB*. (Courtesy of Classical Numismatic Group, Inc. http://www.cngcoins.com)

ABD AL-MALIK: *AE fals*, issued between 685 and 693 from Hims/Emesa mint. Obverse: crowned facing imperial bust, holding crossed globe, *KA**L* ON* (= 'good'). Reverse: large M, star between annulets above, *EMI-CHC*, below *'tayyib'* (= 'good').

ABD AL-MALIK: *AE fals*, issued in early 690s from Halab/Aleppo mint. Obverse: caliph standing facing, hand on hilt of sword. Reverse: transformed cross, *'waf'* to left, *'bi-halab'* to right.

ABD AL-MALIK: gold aniconic dinar, issued in 699–700 from Damascus mint.

Al-WALID I: gold aniconic dinar, issued in 713 from Damascus mint.

Pictures

All in the public domain, unless stated otherwise

List of Emperors, Caliphs, Popes and Patriarchs

List of Emperors

Phocas	23 November 602–5 October 610
Heraclius	5 October 610–11 February 641
Heraclius Constantine III	February 641–May 641
Heraklonas	February 641–April/May 641
Constans II	September 641–15 September 668
Constantine IV	15 September 668–14 September 685
Justinian II	14 September 685–695
Leontios	695–15 February 698
Tiberius III	15 February 698–21 August 705
Justinian II	21 August 705–4 November/11 December 711
Philippikos Bardanes	4 November/11 December 711–3 June 713
Anastasius II	3 June 713–November 715
Theodosius III	May 715–25 March 717
Leo III the Isaurian	25 March 717–18 June 741

List of Umayyad Caliphs

Muawiyah I	661–29 April/1 May 680
Yazid I	26 April 680–11 November 683
Muawiyah II	11 November 683–684
Marwan I	June 684–12 April/7 May 685
Abd al-Malik b. Marwan	12 April/7 May 685–9 October 705
Al-Walid I	9 October 705–25 January/11 March 715
Sulayman b. Abd al-Malik	25 January/11 March 715–24 September 717
Umar II	24 September 717–4 February 720

List of Popes

Vitalian	30 July 657–27 January 672
Adeodatus II	11 April 672–17 June 676
Donus	2 November 676–11 April 678
Agatho	27 June 678–10 January 681
Leo II	17 August 682–28 June 683
Benedict II	26 June 684–8 May 685
John V	23 July 685–2 August 686
Conon	21 October 686–21 September 687
Sergius I	15 December 687–8 September 701
John VI	30 October 701–11 January 705
John VII	1 March 705–18 October 707
Sisinnius	15 January 708–4 February 708
Constantine	25 March 708–9 April 715
Gregory II	19 May 715–11 February 731

List of Patriarchs of Constantinople

Pyrrhus I	20 December 638–29 September 641
Paul II	late 641 (?)–December 653
Pyrrhus I (restored)	early 654–1 June 654
Peter	654–666
Thomas II	667–15 November 669
John V	669–675
Constantine I	675–9 August 677
Theodore I	Late 677–679
George I	679–January/February 686
Paul III	687–693
Kallinikos I	693–705
Cyrus	705–early 712
John VI	Early 712–715
Germanus I	715–730

Heraclian Stemma

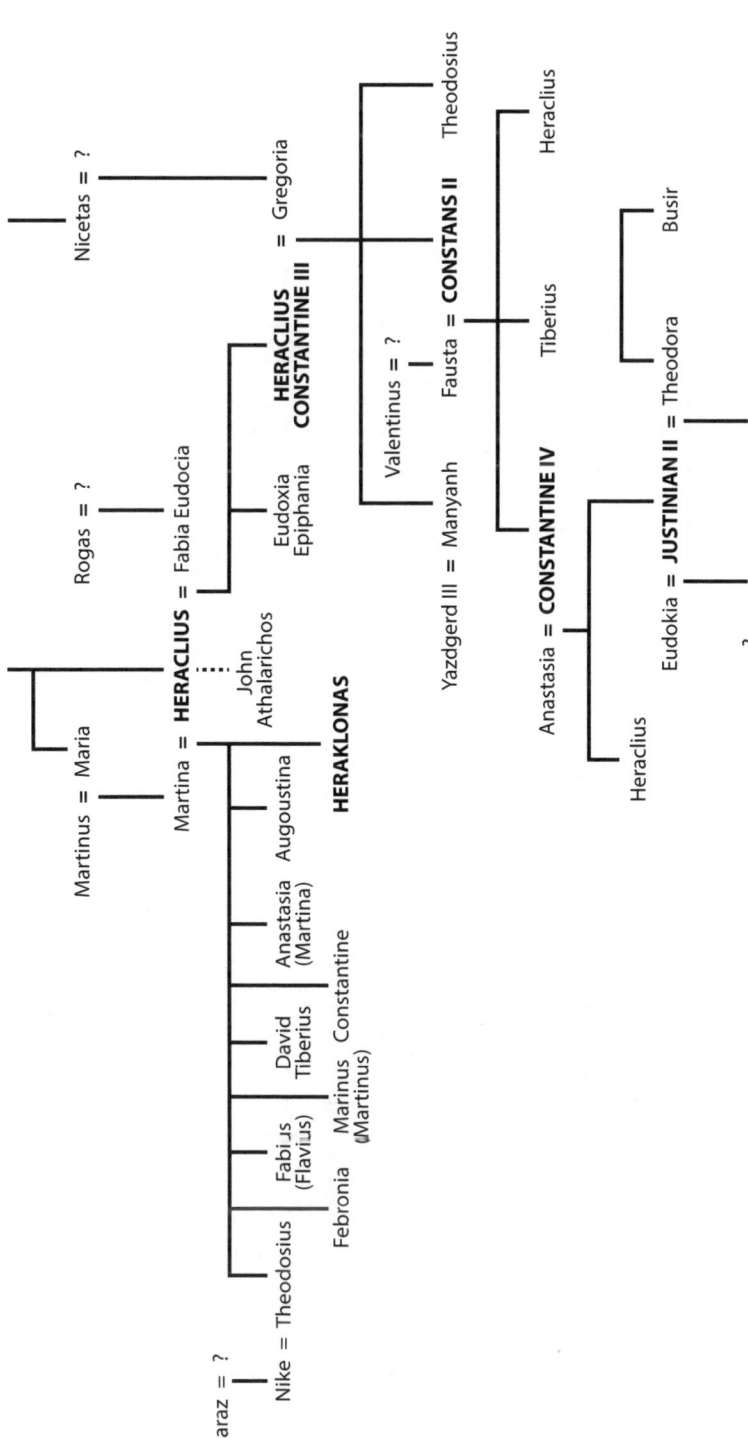

Umayyad Stemma

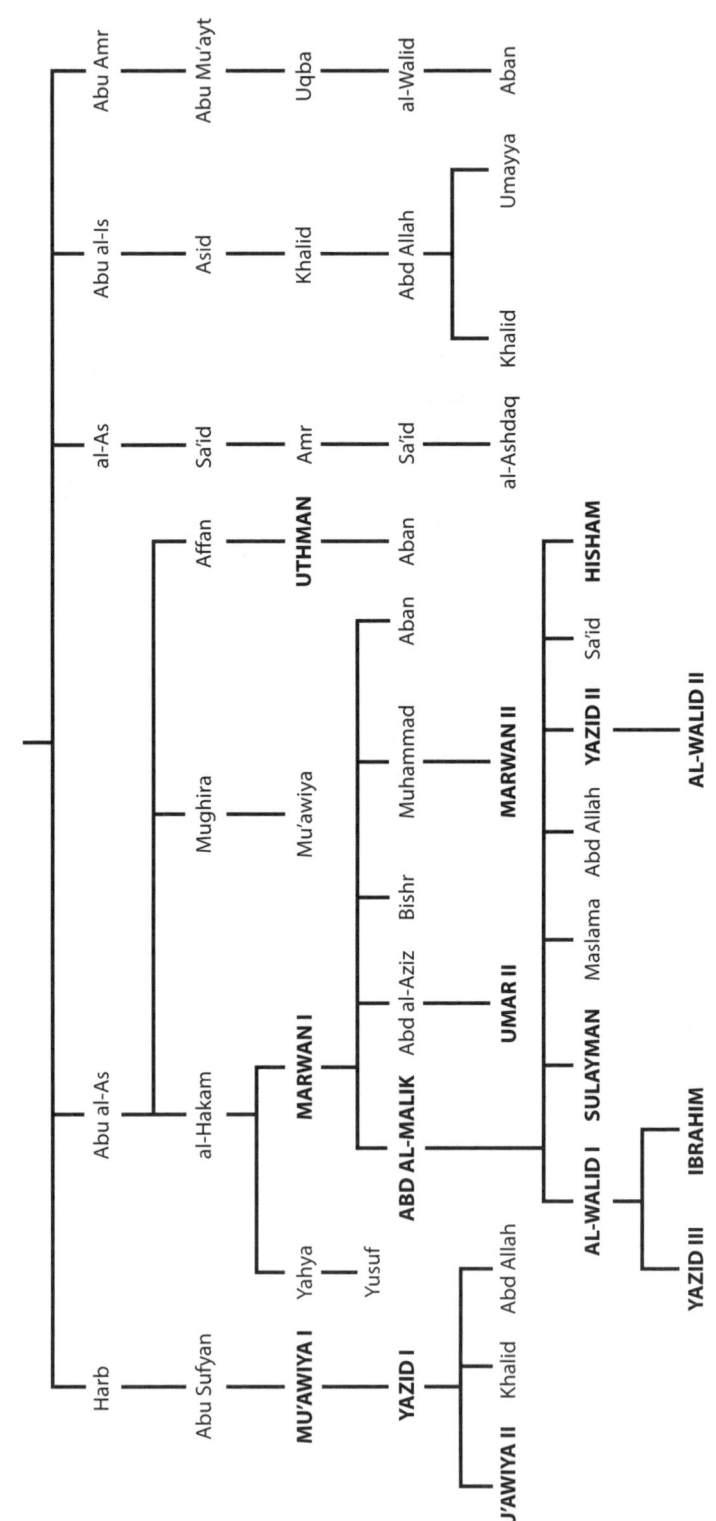

Chapter 1

The Roman Empire of AD 668

'The popes in Old Rome on the far western fringe of the Empire, the kings of the barbarian West, monks in cloisters as far away as Britain – all dated important events by the reigns of the emperors in Constantinople. Diminished though its territorial sway might be, Constantinople was still center of the world in the mind of the Early Middle Ages.'

Head (1972), 6

A Century is a Long Time in Geopolitics...

The seventh century AD had not been kind to the Roman Empire.[1] At its outset, things had looked rather rosy. The reconquests under Justinian I (527–565) in Africa, Italy and Spain had made it to the end of the sixth century largely intact. The emperor Mauricius (582–602) was in the midst of what looked like a successful campaign to restore large sections of the Danube frontier, and the Romans held a dominant position in the East due to the Sassanid Persian 'King of Kings' only being on his throne through Roman intervention. Indeed, a quick glance at a map of the Roman Empire of 600 would seem to present a strong, powerful state, capable of dealing with whatever challenges its opponents could muster.

But such a map hides numerous significant problems. The combination of those Justinianic reconquests and a devastating outbreak of plague had overstretched the capabilities of the empire. In the West, Italy was under pressure from the Lombards and the reconquered Spanish province was in the process of being ground out of existence by the Visigoths. Despite Mauricius' efforts, the Danube was much less secure than the position of the official frontier would suggest. Furthermore, the circumstances of Mauricius' murder combined to bring about significant instability and played a major role in instigating the first of two earth-shattering conflicts to rock the Roman Empire in the seventh century. By 602, Mauricius' Balkan campaign looked to be nearing total victory as the Avar Khaganate began to lose control of its Slavic and German underlings in the face of repeated Roman offensives; however, the emperor had pushed his forces hard to achieve that success, all the while reducing military expenditure. Ordering his Balkan forces to spend the winter of 602/603 in enemy territory proved the last straw for a disgruntled military. Mutiny became usurpation, with a certain Phocas replacing Mauricius on the imperial throne before 602 was out.

This seismic shift at the top of the imperial hierarchy was capitalized upon by the Persian king, Khusro II, who used the murder of his imperial benefactor as a *raison de guerre*, initiating what would become the last Romano-Persian War of 602–628. In this quarter century of conflict, the Persians managed to conquer Roman Mesopotamia, Syria, Palestine and Egypt, and make considerable advances into Anatolia. Only a last desperate counter-invasion into the Persian heartlands wrestled Roman victory from the jaws of catastrophic defeat. While this last Romano-Persian war contained more territorial exchange than perhaps the previous 400 years combined, the shifting frontiers and grand campaigns of emperors, kings and generals can obscure what was really happening in this titanic struggle – 'the two powerhouses of the Ancient World bludgeoning each other almost into mutual submission'.[2]

Other powers in the Mediterranean were not slow to take advantage of this imperial distraction. In the West, the last Roman foothold in Spain was eliminated by 621 and the African frontier came under pressure from Berber tribesmen, while the Lombard kingdom and outlier duchies tightened their grip over the Italian lands they had claimed. Proving that the job along the Danube had not been completed, the Avars and Slavs were able to undo Mauricius' successes within a decade of his murder. It got bad enough that at the nadir of Roman fortunes in 626, an Avar army with Persian connivance laid siege to Constantinople. Meanwhile, the Slavs roamed far and wide across the Balkans, escaping the control not just of the Romans but of the Avars as well.

However, nowhere did the Romano-Persian distraction allow for more radical developments than on the Arabian Peninsula. Ancient Arabia was a melting pot of polytheistic, Jewish and Christian tribes: some who traded with the major empires, some who fought proxy wars for them and others who remained detached. Essentially, Arab tribesmen were either useful allies or temporary nuisances. This was until the early seventh century, when Arab society underwent a revolution. The focus of this revolution was one of those merchants who had trekked the trade routes and was now finding life hard with the constant disruption of warfare. 'Wandering disconsolately among the grim hill-tops'[3] outside Mecca in 610, Muhammad b. Abd Allah b. Abd al-Muttalib was struck by a series of visions regarding the end of the world and man's judgement by Allah. In compiling his teachings on how man's entry into Heaven could only be achieved through regular prayer, benevolence, restraint and submission to the will of Allah into the *Qur'an*, Muhammad became the Prophet of Islam.

Muhammad and his followers quickly faced opposition from those elements in Arabia keen to maintain the religious and social *status quo*, and by 622, Muhammad had been forced to leave Mecca for Medina.[4] There, he found that his teachings were more widely received, and within a year Muslim-led Medina was coming into conflict with Mecca. Battles at Badr in 624 and Mount Uhud in 625, followed by the successful resistance to a siege of Medina in 627, so shattered the opposition to Islam that by the first weeks of 630, Mecca had accepted Muhammad as its leader. This was something of a breaking of the dam, for when Muhammad died on 8 June 632, much of Arabia had accepted Islam. A series of military strikes across the peninsula in 632/633 – the so-called Ridda Wars, or 'Wars of Apostasy' – only confirmed the military strength of this new Muslim state. It was not long before these forces, so successful in Arabia, were looking further afield for more lands to conquer. Their targets were the war-weary empires of Rome and Persia.

In 634, victories at Dathin and Ajnadayn established the Arab presence in Palestine, before the decisive defeat of the main Roman army at Yarmuk in 636 unlocked virtually all of the Levant to Arab conquest. Major cities such as Damascus, Jerusalem and Antioch had fallen before the end of 637. Perhaps only some Roman strategic regrouping and the mountainous terrain of Armenia and the Taurus Mountains stopped the Arabs sweeping up all Roman possessions in Asia. But it was not just Rome's Asian provinces that were under threat. In late 639, Arab forces drove into Egypt, with victories at Heliopolis and Babylon breaking Roman resistance. Within two years, the Roman Empire had lost its most valuable province forever.

Throughout the 640s, the Arabs continued to advance into Roman territory, although while Cyrenaica was conquered by 643 and Anatolia and Tripolitania were being raided, the scale of conquest was not of the same order of magnitude. The Romans established a defensive position in Asia Minor, while Arab energies were directed elsewhere. Significant attention was paid to the East. While the Romans had to face the ignominy of watching as those

Syrian, Palestinian and Egyptian provinces 'so painfully won back from the Persians were lost again to the Arabs',[5] it was certainly not the same extent of ignominy that their Persian counterpart faced. Yazdegerd III saw Arab victories at Qadisiyyah (636), Jalulah (637) and Nahavand (642) leave him as the last Sassanid 'King of Kings', his kingdom dying with him in 651. The Arabs were also beginning to face some of the political ramifications of their empire-building. Plans to strike at Constantinople in the mid-650s were put on hold by the growing discord within the caliphate after the assassination of caliph Uthman. Nevertheless, it had been an explosive arrival on the world stage for the Islam-inspired Arabs, and the Roman Empire was changed forever by it.

The Heraclian Dynasty

Through this drastic transition and change, there was one constant that had brought some consistency and resilience to the Roman resistance: their ruling dynasty, the Heraclians. While seemingly of Armenian origin, the Heraclian dynasty emerged from Roman Africa in 608 when the exarch Heraclius the Elder renounced his allegiance to the increasingly unpopular Phocas. This Heraclius already had a successful military career behind him,[6] hence his entrusting with the African exarchate by Mauricius, but it was to be his son, also Heraclius, who was to reap the imperial rewards of their revolt. The younger Heraclius' early life is clouded by poor sources, but he is likely to have served as part of his father's staff during his military activities in the East and Africa.[7] This was experience enough for him to lead the Heraclian revolt against Phocas. A two-pronged attack on Egypt and Constantinople was enough to secure the throne for Heraclius in 610, establishing a dynasty that would rule the Roman Empire for a century.

But a change of dynasty did not mean an immediate change in fortunes for the empire; indeed, the first decade of Heraclius' reign was marked by a string of disasters. Heraclius persevered, taking command of the last Roman army, building its confidence with limited actions and victories before launching a dynamic thrust into the heart of Sassanid Persia which ended the war and restored the lost territories by 628. While Heraclius proved unable to prevent the Arab onslaught taking all of the lands he had reclaimed from the Persians, he was the instigator of the policy of strategic withdrawal which allowed the empire to establish a somewhat defensible position centred on the highlands and cities of eastern Anatolia. And it was not just in the realm of defence that Heraclius had a long-term benefit. The importance of the political stability his thirty-one-year reign provided at a time of tremendous geopolitical upheaval should not be underestimated. Without that prolonged reign, the Roman Empire may well have fragmented in the face of the Persian and Arab attacks of the first half of the seventh century.

That is not to say that the reign of Heraclius and the dynasty he founded was free from internal squabbles. In 635 or 637, a nascent coup centred on Heraclius' illegitimate son, John Athalarichos, was uncovered, and in the last years of Heraclius' life, the succession became the focus of an increasingly hostile struggle. Normal procedure would have seen Heraclius' eldest son by his first wife Eudokia, Heraclius Constantine, succeed as emperor. However, Heraclius' second wife, Martina (who also happened to be his niece), persuaded him to elevate their son Heraklonas as well. Heraclius failed to do anything about the growing animosity,[8] so when he died on 11 February 641, power passed to both Heraclius Constantine III and Heraklonas, with Martina elevated to *Augusta*. When Heraclius Constantine died in late May 641 of tuberculosis, it seemed that supreme power had passed to Martina and Heraklonas. However, Heraclius Constantine had written to the generals and asked them to protect his children in the event of his death. In the face of Martina's unpopularity as a woman in a position of power, having married her own uncle and with rumours of poisoning her stepson, the army chose to back Heraclius Constantine's young son, Constans.[9] By late September 641, a combination of army, Senate and popular support had forced Martina and Heraklonas to accept the elevation of the 10-year-old as Constans II. This marked a dramatic shift in power, and when Martina attempted to promote another of her sons, David Tiberios, to co-emperor, the Senate, people and army of Constantinople deposed her and Heraklonas.

Initially, the sole rule of Constans II did not fix anything in the corridors of power at Constantinople, for like Heraklonas he was still a minor. Indeed, his advent to sole rule may have initially made things worse because it had only been achieved through the involvement of the army in succession politics. While the regency was technically under patriarch Paul II and the Senate, Constans was married to Fausta, daughter of Valentinus, the army leader who had forced Constans' elevation and deposed Martina and Heraklonas. As head of the imperial bodyguard, Valentinus appeared every bit the most powerful man in the empire, but one defeat by the Arabs in 643/644 quickly saw things unravel. With Constans nearing the end of his minority, the general tried to improve his position by marching troops on

Constantinople and 'suggesting' that he be made co-emperor. However, the popular and senatorial factions who had helped the general against Martina were firmly behind Constans II, dooming Valentinus to failure and death.

The end of Constans II's minority by late 646 steadied the dynastic ship after five years of discord, leaving the Heraclians to guide the empire through the next half century. Constans would try to take the military initiative on several fronts, but it was not exactly plain sailing. There were some hints of success in North Africa, with the recovery of Alexandria and Africa Province in 645 and 647 respectively; however, the former success failed to turn into the reclamation of Egypt through the commander's alienation of the locals, while the latter was in the aftermath of a rebellion by the exarch, Gregory the Patrician, who was defeated by Arab invaders rather than loyal imperial forces.

Things were even worse in Asia Minor, where the Arabs launched strikes into Armenia, Cappadocia and even Phrygia, and naval expeditions against both Cyprus and Crete before the decade was out, expanding to include Rhodes and the Aegean in the early 650s. This forced Constans to confront the Arab fleet at Phoenix off Lycia in 655; unfortunately for the emperor, this Arab fleet contained not only the ships of Syria but also those of Egypt, making it a much more dangerous opponent. And so it proved at the subsequent Battle of the Masts, where the Roman imperial navy was heavily defeated, with Constans barely escaping with his life.[10] It is at this point that Arab plans to attack Constantinople were interrupted by the growing discord surrounding caliph Uthman and his subsequent assassination in 656, although it is recorded by the Armenian source, Sebeos, that the Arab attack did go ahead, only to end in failure.[11]

The internal distractions of the Arab caliphate allowed Constans to take the offensive again, with a potential raid deep into Arab territory in 659 bringing about a favourable treaty with Muawiyah, the governor of Syria, who was well on his way to establishing the Umayyads as the ruling dynasty of the caliphate.[12] This windfall and closing down of the Asian frontier allowed the emperor to look to other troubles. He defeated some Slavs in the late 650s, forcing some Slavic recognition of Roman suzerainty. Then in the early 660s, Constans led an expedition to Italy, with the plan of re-establishing imperial control of the peninsula at the expense of the Lombards. He had some success against the duchy of Benevento, but his forces also saw some setbacks.

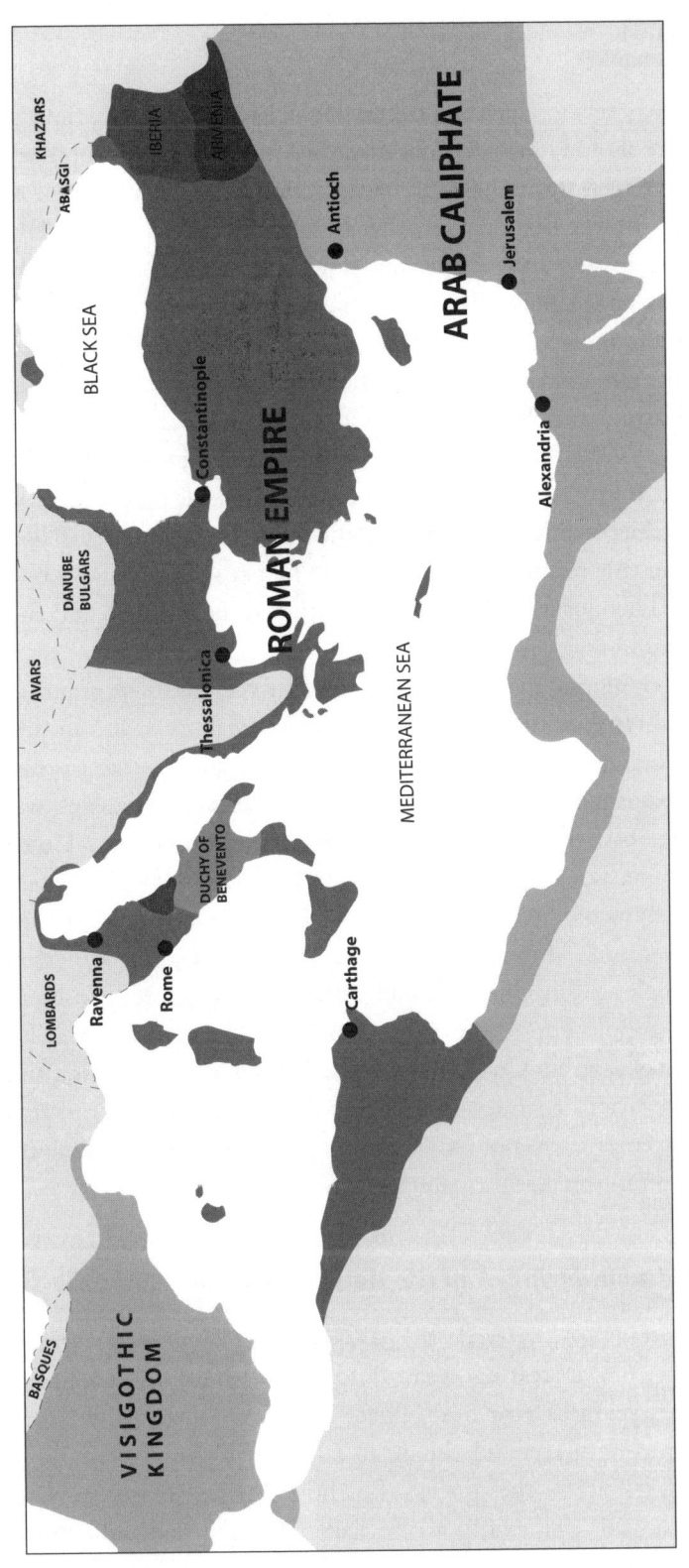

The Roman Empire in c.668.

His military record since the Battle of the Masts against various enemies of the empire should have seen Constans become a relatively popular Roman emperor; however, throughout the same period he made a series of religious and political moves that ensured that he was anything but popular. In the religious sphere, his attempt to shut down Christological debate between the orthodox and Monothelites with the *Type of Constans* edict in 648 had been both unpopular and unsuccessful. Instead of pulling back, Constans escalated the situation by attacking the most prominent anti-Monothelites – Pope Martin I and Maximus the Confessor, subjecting both to kidnap, torture and exile. The emperor made things worse for himself in Italy by following such brutal ecclesiastical repression with the stripping of multiple regions of valuables, including the Pantheon in Rome. Constans also added kinslaying to this résumé of unpopularity: he became suspicious enough of his brother Theodosius to first force him to take holy orders and then have him executed in 660.

That unpopularity manifested not only in ecclesiastical opposition but also political revolt with the Armeniac *strategos*, Saborius, and in the source material. The latter is perhaps best seen in the only source to record the emperor's plans post-668 – Theophanes.[13] Through whatever writer he used for the 660s, Theophanes would have it that in 661/662 Constans II abandoned Constantinople as the capital of the Roman Empire, establishing himself in Syracuse, with the objective of making Rome the imperial capital once more. This move reputedly involved sending a messenger to Constantinople, calling his wife and three sons to join him in Sicily, only for the city populace to refuse to let them go. This rumour must be taken with a pinch of salt, but Constans' extended absence from Constantinople at a time when various enemies and rebels were increasing the pressure on the centre of the empire was not only unpopular, but likely led to rumours of his supposed plan to transfer the capital.[14]

Was it the *Cubicularius* … in the Bath … with the Bucket?

When Constans II entered the Daphne bathhouse in Syracuse on 15 September 668 to rest his weary body, how would he look back on his twenty-seven years as emperor? There had been some bright spots. He could claim to have stymied the Arab advance in Asia Minor, extracting a substantial tribute in the process. But he must have been vexed, because stemming the tide was really all he had done. He had not pushed back against the various invaders the empire faced, beyond a limited success against the Slavs. Reconquests in Egypt and Armenia had proven extremely fleeting,[15] while his campaign against the Lombards had yet to bear any significant fruit. Having said that, checking the Arabs in Anatolia, the Slavs in the Balkans and the Lombards in Italy could be seen as building regional confidence and a firm basis from which to begin the reclamation of the occupied territories.

Furthermore, it seemed like time was on the emperor's side. In 668, Constans was still just 37 years old; a man in his physical prime. With him at its head, the Roman army could build on this firm basis, thwart the Arab advance on Carthage and perhaps eliminate a Lombard duchy or two. The victorious forces could then return east and square up to the chiefs, khagans and caliphs striking at the imperial heartlands. Constans' confidence could only have been helped by the dynastic security provided by his family. His son and heir, Constantine, was proving himself a capable leader in his father's absence, standing up to the rebel Saborius and the intermittent Arab raids. On top of that, Constantine's young wife, Anastasia, was likely already pregnant, so along with Constans' other sons, Heraclius and Tiberius, the future of the Heraclian dynasty seemed secure. But whatever confidence Constans II had in his own abilities and those of his sons, whatever cautious optimism he had for his campaigns against the Lombards and the defence of Carthage, and whatever long-term religious, political, military and social plans he might have had in mind were about to be replaced by a single thing … the bucket wielded by his *cubicularius*, Andrew, son of Troilus.[16]

With the emperor felled by this fatal blow, power transferred to his eldest son, Constantine IV, who was in Constantinople and who, much like his father, had grown up holding an imperial position from an early age. Indeed, he had been co-emperor since he was about 2 years old, but now in 668, he had just entered adulthood. More than that, he had recently or was just about to become a father for the first time with the birth of his son. If dealing with the murder of his father, parenthood and acceding to the imperial throne was not enough, Constantine IV also inherited all of the religious, political, military and social problems Constans II had faced. He and his advisors can have been under few illusions over the enormity of the task he, his brothers and his newborn son faced. There were just too many internal and external problems for them to reign comfortably and peacefully for long.

That said, Constantine clearly had high expectations for his heir. This is demonstrated in his choice of name. Rather than following the family tradition of the firstborn being either a 'Heraclius' or 'Constantine', the boy was christened Justinian after the emperor under whose auspices the Roman Empire had reconquered Africa, Italy and a large part of Spain in the mid-sixth century. Given the territorial losses Rome had suffered in the middle decades of the seventh century, Constantine IV may have thought that the empire needed the galvanising symbolism of a great conqueror, someone whose armies had been successful in the imperial battlegrounds of the late 660s. If that was the case, Justinian II had some pretty large shoes to fill before he could walk or perhaps even open his eyes. Such expectation, together with the example of his Heraclian predecessors, would influence Justinian's actions towards the denizens and enemies of his Roman Empire.

The State of the Imperial Union

But in what shape was the Roman Empire to be ruled over by Constantine IV at the time of his accession and the birth of Justinian II? Despite being faced with one of the most dire periods in its history, the Roman Empire still stretched from Gibraltar to Georgia, holding significant territories in Africa, Italy, the Balkans, Asia Minor, the Caucasus and around the Black Sea. That is not to say that the Roman Empire of 668 was not different from its earlier self; so different that many view it as a completely different 'Byzantine' entity, despite the unbroken line of Roman emperors tracing back through Theodosius and Constantine to Augustus. There were some significant changes to the make-up of that state, beyond it being smaller. The reduction of the empire largely to the Greek-speaking provinces of Greece and Asia Minor meant that Greek language and culture was becoming more prevalent in the empire as a whole; however, that is not to say that the Roman Empire of the late seventh century was a definitively Greek state. Instead, it was well on the way to transitioning from a Romano-Latin empire to an amalgam of Roman, Greek, oriental and Christian civilization.[17]

This transition is seen in the Roman army and its terminology. The late sixth-century military handbook, Mauricius' *Strategikon*, while written in Greek, has a substantial mix of Latin and Greek terminology, with the likes of *arithmos*, *moira*, *meros* and *strategos* balancing out *bucellarius*, *comes*, *defensores*, *dux* and *numerus*. The *Strategikon* also legislated for the singing of the *Trisagion* hymn in the morning and the evening, while the tactics may demonstrate eastern military influences too.[18] Similarly, Roman law was transitioning from the Latin codices of Theodosius II and Justinian I to Greek compilations such as the *Nomos Georgikos* and the *Ekloga*,[19] although the fact that this 'Byzantine' law-making included commentaries and summaries suggests that Romano-Latin law still played a major role in imperial rule.

This multifaceted synthesis is perhaps best seen in the depiction of the Roman emperor. As the seventh century progressed, it became more frequent for him to be presented as βασιλευς (*basileus*), instead of the traditional *Augustus*. And yet on imperial coins, Latin continued to be used throughout the seventh and on into the eight century, with the emperor still styled as *Dominus Noster* and *Augustus*, as well as the use of reverse legends such as *Victoria*. The emperor also remained an autocrat in the eastern, absolutist mould, and while a Christian Roman emperor could no longer claim to be divine, he had increasingly become depicted as the temporal representative of God.[20] This fusion of various civilization traits may not have been complete by the Heraclian dynasty, but it was already clear that whatever this 'Byzantine' identity was going to look like in its final medieval form, it was going to permeate large sections of Roman society.

Exarchates and Themes

While the emperor of Constantinople continued to exemplify 'the theory of absolutism par excellence',[21] the late sixth and seventh centuries saw developments in the hierarchies of command which actually undermined the absolute position of the Roman emperor in parts of his empire. The origin of this seeming dilution of imperial power came with Mauricius' reaction to the increasing pressure on the empire's western extremities, while he was distracted by Avars and Persians. The Lombard invasion of Italy had found the peninsula poorly defended and sapped of military zeal and resources after a generation of fighting between imperial and Gothic forces. Before the Romans could respond in any meaningful way, large swathes of Italy had fallen to the Germanic invaders, including major cities like Milan and Pavia. This left the remaining Roman possessions on the peninsula, besides a corridor through the Apennines from Rome to Romagna, as detached coastal regions.

Mauricius had these organized into a series of duchies[22] and placed under the overall command of the exarch of Ravenna, who was to be the emperor's representative in Italy, holding civilian and military authority, overturning the clear separation of these powers established by Diocletian in the late third century.[23] While Constantinople viewed all of Italy as being part of the

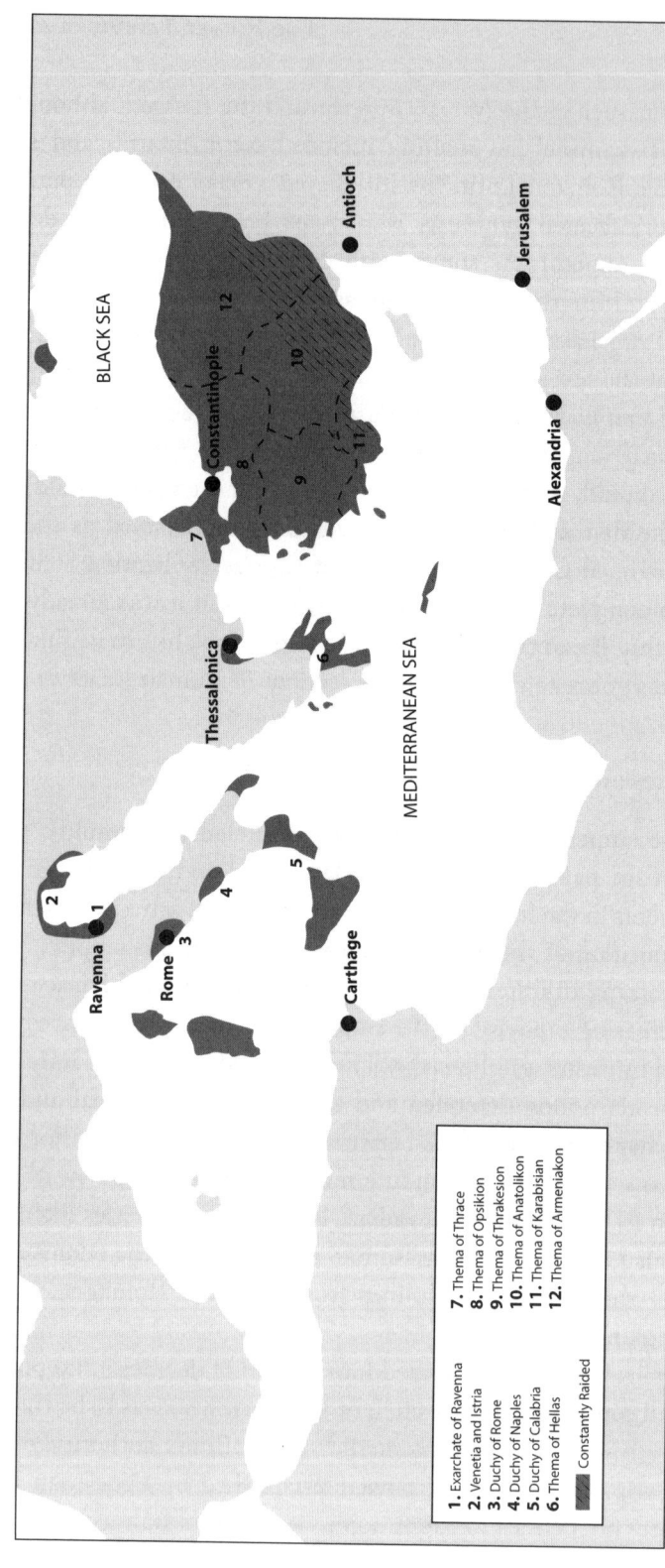

1. Exarchate of Ravenna
2. Venetia and Istria
3. Duchy of Rome
4. Duchy of Naples
5. Duchy of Calabria
6. Thema of Hellas

7. Thema of Thrace
8. Thema of Opsikion
9. Thema of Thrakesion
10. Thema of Anatolikon
11. Thema of Karabisian
12. Thema of Armeniakon

░░░ Constantly Raided

BLACK SEA

MEDITERRANEAN SEA

Ravenna
Rome
Carthage
Thessalonica
Constantinople
Antioch
Jerusalem
Alexandria

Themes of the Roman Empire in c.717.

exarchate, the reality was much different. Not only were there significant chunks of Italy under the control of the Lombards, but the various Roman *duces* and *magistri* were not to be always agreeable to Ravenna. The foremost of those recalcitrant underlings was the pope, who was in the process of becoming increasingly independent from his imperial master. Sicily remained a province and later theme unto itself.

The other major islands in the western Mediterranean – Corsica, Sardinia and the Balearics – were part of the other Roman exarchate, that of Africa and centred on Carthage. Encompassing virtually all of North Africa west of Cyrenaica,[24] the exarchate of Africa was established by Mauricius by the early 590s. While there was initially some confrontation with the Visigoths over the Roman province in Spain, the pressure on this exarchate came from the indigenous Berber peoples, whose raids wore away at the Roman frontiers along the length of North Africa, with areas such as Mauretania largely lost by the early seventh century. That was until the Arab conquests of Egypt and Cyrenaica brought Roman Africa into the firing line.

It is difficult to judge whether or not these exarchates really provided any substantial benefit to the empire. The nature of the sources and the largely outlier status of the exarchates meant that they only appear in the record when something drastic had happened – an invasion, a usurpation etc. Does that mean that the intervening periods of quiet were just that? Or would such an argument of silence mask the ongoing trouble both Ravenna and Carthage faced? The latter seems more likely. Perhaps the only benefit from the exarchate system was to relieve some of the pressure on the central government to get directly involved. Indeed, the extent of these exarchate powers was an admission that Constantinople viewed Italy and Africa not as useful assets but more as obligations that redirected imperial resources and attention away from the more important central provinces. The sheer fact that an autocratic emperor would be willing to give up even a modicum of direct control over some of his imperial territory may be very telling.

And what would the exarchs do with that local authority? Such a combination of civilian and military power could easily allow an ambitious individual to follow his own agenda, a path which could be quite distinct from that of the central government. In a sense, this subdivision of sovereignty provided another avenue to challenge the emperor. Most famously, the Heraclian dynasty itself had emerged from the exarchate system, something which it and perhaps much of the empire would consider a positive, but it does not hide the fact that this was an instance of the exarch rebelling against Constantinople. And it was not the only instance of a Heraclian exarch doing so; the aforementioned Gregory the Patrician, who rebelled in 646, was a kinsman of Constans II, with the suggestion being that he was a son of Niketas, cousin of Heraclius.[25]

Focusing on the success of Heraclius is to overlook the poisoned chalice that being exarch was. The social, political, religious and military vicissitudes that Mauricius and his imperial successors were taking a step back from by empowering their exarchs did not suddenly disappear. Indeed, without direct imperial involvement, it could be that central control in Ravenna and Carthage was only further weakened with troublemakers emboldened to take on the exarch because they thought the emperor unlikely to respond. The troubled nature of the exarchates can perhaps be seen in the multitude of those who held the Ravennate office. Over the course of its 170-year history, nineteen men served as exarch of Italy, a tenure which included at least four extended periods where the position appears vacant – 619–625, 652–653, 666–678 and 711–713 – and saw perhaps half a dozen exarchs killed in battle, by rebels or whilst rebelling. The exarchate of Africa would seem to be more secure, with only eight men listed as holding the position during the course of over a century; however, this more likely reflects a poor source record, with the dates of these men's tenures being uncertain, along with doubts over some of them actually serving as exarch at all. Therefore, while on the surface the power of the exarch might seem significant, in reality he was only as strong as the regions under his command allowed him to be. And in Italy and Africa, that may not have been all that strong, with war exhaustion, poor administration and constant fighting meaning that these regions had trouble looking after themselves.[26]

The Ravennate exarchate had the added problem of its incongruent shape, which hindered the centralizing of resources and saw many of the local dukes acting, and perhaps needing to act, more on their own initiative. This was seen most prominently with the growth of local militias and the increasing independence of the most prominent of the exarchate 'dukes' – the pope. Relations between the pope and the exarch could be a help or a hindrance to the empire. In the good times, the pope could be a unifying force, helping the exarch and therefore the emperor in times of trouble; however, the papacy could be a vehicle for local discontent, particularly as the exarch was frequently an eastern appointee and therefore regarded as something of a foreigner. These potentially mixed relations between the pope and the exarch would be demonstrated during the reign of Justinian II.

While it may seem like the subdivision of sovereignty involved in the position of exarch did little to help the empire, and may even have hindered it through an increase of potential internal strife, the Heraclian dynasty built on this provincial policy in the mid-seventh century. It must be said, however, that the circumstances for this expansion in numbers of powerful provincial commanders were hardly ideal. The loss of territory and the retreat of the imperial field armies in the face of Arab, Avar and Slav advances saw the need for drastic provincial reorganization forced on the empire, rather than being by choice. This led to the development and adoption of the theme system.

A 'theme' was essentially a region made up of several provinces, which hosted, provided and provided for its thematic army. The leaders in these thematic regions – the *strategoi* – were civilian governors and commanders-in-chief.[27] While perhaps initially paid in cash, thematic soldiers were eventually given plots of land to farm for the support of their families and the army. This allowed the empire to reduce a soldier's pay, while still keeping ownership of the land. Thematic service was also to be inherited, which reduced the need for conscription while reducing military expenditure.[28] Unfortunately, the sources provide little information about the development of the theme system and its inner workings, leaving certainty impossible. Even this general layout may contain anachronistic depictions, as sources such as Theophanes may have had to fill gaps in the contemporaneous record by projecting the fully formed thematic system of his day in the late eighth/early ninth century back onto the mid-seventh.

One of the significant issues over the origins of the themes is the word itself – θέμα, pl. θέματα (*thema*, pl. *themata*). While its etymology is uncertain, it seems to have had two distinct meanings – a military unit/army and a geographic district, with the latter developing out of the former as army occupation of certain regions became increasingly permanent. As these regions could incorporate several provinces, they came to be recognized as the area of that 'theme', with the district taking the name of the army that was stationed there.[29] The problems with the dual meaning of 'theme' bleeds into the arguments over the date of their creation. It was long thought that Heraclius was the originator of the theme system, with a seemingly significant piece of evidence being Theophanes mentioning Heraclius arriving 'in the lands of the themes'[30] in 622. This was taken as showing 'that the process of establishing troops (themes) in specific areas of Asia Minor has already begun at this time'.[31] However, this overlooks the likelihood that the term 'theme' was already established as meaning 'military unit' or 'army' before its association with the new 'thematic' province. It also does not appear that the development of the themes was well-planned, but rather something that gradually coalesced out of the chaotic reaction to the Arab conquests in the Middle East, the retreating of the field armies to Anatolia and the need to form some kind of defensive position.[32] Some, if not all, of the armies who were to give their name to the themes they occupied were probably stationed in those areas before the death of Heraclius in 641 or soon after. But while there may have been aspects of what became the theme system present during and even before the reign of Heraclius,[33] it seems more likely that the official establishing of the themes as permanent structures did not happen until the reign of Constans II (641–668) or later. It could perhaps be linked to the period after the advantageous and lucrative peace treaty the emperor won from Muawiyah in 659, giving the empire time to reorganize itself.[34]

Unfortunately, the source record of the period is decidedly poor, with many of the first mentions of individual themes coming years and perhaps even decades after their official establishment. The earliest recorded is the Armeniac theme (Θέμα Ἀρμενιάκων, *Thema Armeniakōn*), which is attested in 667. Born out of the army of the *magister militum per Armeniae*, from its capital at Amaseia, it covered the territories of Pontus, Armenia Minor, eastern Paphlagonia and northern Cappadocia. It formed the bulwark of Roman defence against Arab invasions alongside the Anatolic theme (Θέμα Ἀνατολικῶν, *Thema Anatolikōn*). First mentioned in 669 and born from the army of the *magister militum per Orientem*, the Anatolic theme covered lands in Lycaonia, Pisidia, Isauria and much of Phrygia, with its capital at Amorion. Perhaps the most prestigious of the early themes was that of the Opsikion (Θέμα Ὀψικίου, *Thema Opsikiou*). Attested from 680 and covering Bithynia, western Paphlagonia and parts of Galatia from its station at Nicaea, its prestige stemmed from its proximity to Constantinople and the fact that its origins were in the *Obsequium*, the imperial retinue that surrounded the emperor on campaign. It may even have been initially stationed in the imperial capital before its move to Nicaea. Unlike the other themes, its commander retained the title of *comes*, rather than *strategos*.

Of what is now considered the core four early themes, the most historiographical dispute comes with the Thrakesian theme (Θέμα Θρακησίων, *Thema Thrakēsiōn*). With a name like that, it might be expected that it was focused on the provinces of Thrace; however, instead it was centred on the Asia Minor provinces of Ionia, Lydia and Caria, with its capital probably at Chonae. Its name comes from the Thracian field army that was stationed there. This multiplication of regions and forces with the name 'Thracian' affected the proposed first attestation of the Thrakesian theme. It was long held that it was not until 711, when Justinian II sent Christopher, the Thrakesian *tourmaches* – a high-ranking thematic military commander – to Cherson. Indeed, the Thrakesian *strategos* is not attested until the then holder of the office, Sisinnios, supported Constantine V against Artabasdos in 741. This led to the idea that the provinces of Ionia, Lydia and Caria were initially part of the Anatolic theme and were perhaps not raised to the status of their own theme until the early eighth century. However, it has become more regular to identify the '*Thracianus exercitus*' recorded in a *iussio* of 687 as an army not of geographic Thrace but of the Thrakesian theme, placing its establishment before that date and perhaps even as early as those of the Armeniac, Anatolic and Opsikion themes.[35]

Besides these four original Asian themes, there may also have been other areas of Roman territory that received thematic reorganization, even if they did not yet receive the name. The geographic region of Thrace that remained under Roman control may have been ruled like a theme, but it appears to have been under the command of the Opsikion *comes*.[36] The Arab expansion onto the waves also saw the establishment of the Karabisiani (Καραβησιάνοι, *Karabēsianoi*) as a permanent naval corps by 680.[37] While the first definite reference to the Karabisiani is during the Slav siege of Thessalonica in *c*.680, it has been speculated that such a naval establishment may have been instituted after a significant naval failing, such as the Battle of the Masts in 655[38] or the first Arab attack on Constantinople, where the Arab fleet appears to have advanced through the Aegean largely unhindered.[39] There is also argument over the intended scope of the Karabisiani. Was it just another provincial fleet, tasked with defending the Aegean and the coast of Asia Minor,[40] or was it a much more wide ranging fleet, taking in most if not all Roman navies and charged with defending imperial waters from Gibraltar to Georgia?[41] Regardless of its date or extent, on the surface, it appears to be a theme like the others. While there is dispute over its exact origins – the Illyrian field army or *quaestura exercitus*[42] – it would seem to be from the consolidation and stationing of previous units in a specific area. In the case of the Karabisiani, that area was the southern coast of Asia Minor and the Aegean Islands, with its capital possibly at Attaleia.[43] However, despite these similarities and that it is frequently referred to as the 'Carabisian theme', the lack of specific land divisions and it remaining a purely military establishment seems to differentiate the Karabisiani from the actual themes, at least in its earliest iteration.[44]

No matter who was the main instigator of its development or how that development took place, the theme system 'worked well in the perennial crisis situation of the seventh century and played a vital role in preserving the Empire from total absorption by the Arabs and the barbarians'.[45] However, it shared the one significant negative of the exarchate – it increased the possibility of rebellion by provincial governors who held both civilian and military power. The reign of Heraclius might have seen the overturning of 250 years of the emperor not leading the army, restoring martial respect to the imperial position, but the empowering of the exarchs and *strategoi* provided the emperor with more potential internal opponents. The threat posed by the regional power of exarchates and themes was exacerbated by the military, political and religious troubles overtaking the empire. With the prioritizing of the emperor's attention and the empire's resources to any specific crisis, Roman forces who felt ignored increasingly looked to their regional commander to provide on-the-spot leadership. This in turn led to rivalry between regions and with the emperor. With the theme system, this negative was compounded by their proximity to the seat of power. While in theory that proximity would mean that the emperor could keep a much closer eye on his subordinates, in practice it tempted an ambitious *strategos* or unhappy thematic army to make a quick strike against the emperor in Constantinople.

Imperial recognition of this temptation may be seen in the frequency of generals and politicians being transferred to different positions. Perhaps the emperor did not want skilled individuals gaining a foothold in certain military/political hierarchies through prolonged tenures. That said, it could reflect the emperors making good use of skilled manpower, transferring competent commanders to positions where they were needed. This in turn may suggest that there was a dearth of skilled manpower and/or a dearth of manpower that the emperors felt they could trust. In rotating positions of power and influence amongst a select few, the emperors were limiting that power and influence to a tight, select group, which they could more easily stock with men whom they trusted and could keep an eye on.[46] However, such measures were not entirely successful. As we have already seen, even before the assassination of Constans II in 668, the African exarch, Gregory the Patrician, and the Armeniac *strategos*, Saborius, had rebelled against the central government. And as will be seen, exarchate and thematic forces would repeatedly play leading roles in opposition to the imperial incumbent throughout the late seventh and early eighth centuries.

The Jewel in the Eastern Crown

While the Heraclian dynasty had seen the emperor restored as an active army commander, the collapse of the Danube and eastern frontiers and the growth in potential for internal revolt raised the importance of that one great edifice of the Roman Empire – the city of Constantinople itself – to an even greater height. Traditionally founded as Byzantion by Megarian colonists in the seventh century BC, its position along east/west lines of communication and on an outcropping surrounded by water on three sides saw the Romanized Byzantium chosen by Constantine I in 330 to be his new imperial capital. This prominent position straddling the frontier between Europe and Asia, along with imperial sponsorship, saw Constantinople quickly become the centre of the Roman world. By the end of the fifth century, it had overtaken Rome as the biggest city in the Mediterranean; by the seventh century, perhaps only Chang'an in China was bigger, with both pushing towards a million inhabitants.[47] Such rapid expansion in population was facilitated by Roman logistics, with open-air reservoirs, subterranean cisterns and aqueducts bringing and storing water for the city and numerous harbours bringing in food from across the empire to feed the multitudes. These harbours were also the destination for the many wares of the empire and beyond; although Constantinople was not just the consumer of many of these products. It was also a major trade hub, redistributing the wares of the world to all points of the compass.

Being a focal point of Roman administration and the imperial residence meant that Constantinople was not just a population and trade centre. Stretched across its seven hills was some of the world's most spectacular architecture. As a visitor walked along the main thoroughfare, the Mese, they would have been confronted with a vast array of different but nonetheless remarkable buildings: from the aforementioned cisterns and aqueducts through vast forums such as those of Constantine, Arcadius, Theodosius and the Ox, past celebratory and decorative columns such as those of Constantine, Marcian and the Goths, the Egyptian obelisk brought from Karnak and the Serpentine Column from Delphi, to the administrative centre of the Great Palace. This imperial residence was littered with important edifices, such as the ceremonial square of the Augustaion, the enormous Baths of Zeuxippus and the immense Hippodrome. It is from this imperial heart, with all its interconnecting, labyrinthine passages and tunnels primed for intrigue, that the term 'byzantine' gets its negative connotations. As a Christian capital, Constantinople was also dotted with

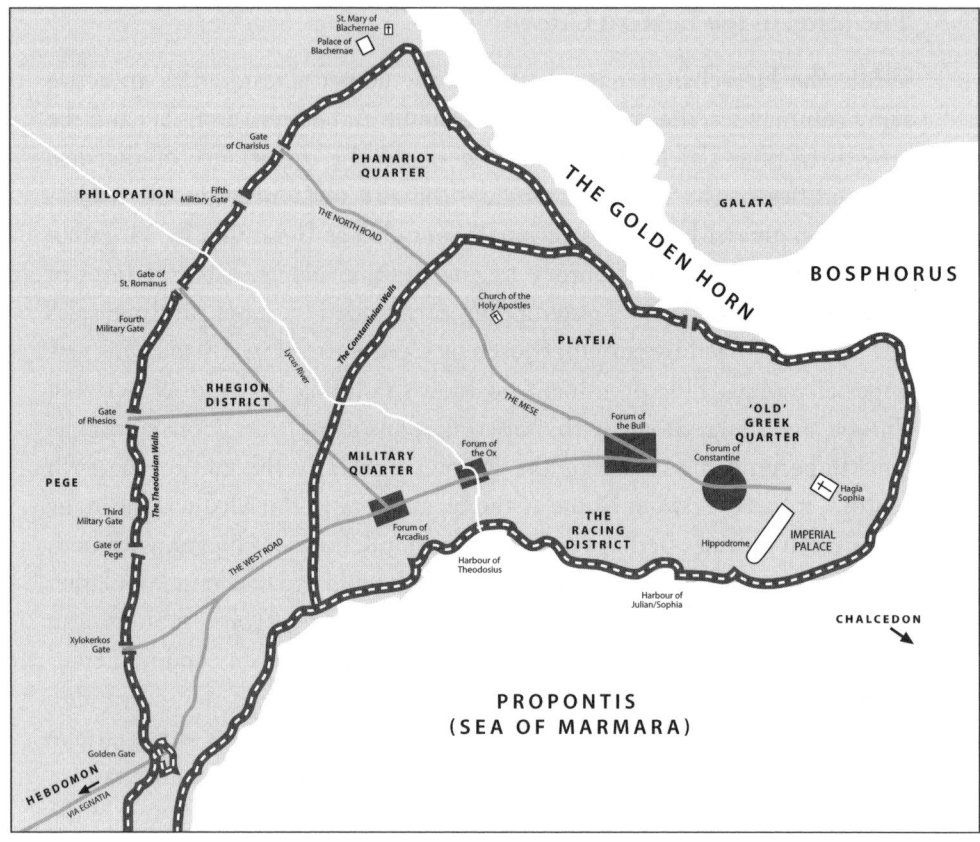

Constantinople, city plan.

many magnificent churches. To name but a few, the Church of the Holy Apostles was the burial site of numerous emperors and held the relics of many saints, while the gravity-defying dome of Hagia Sophia, the biggest church in the world for a millennium, and the splendour of Hagia Irene still decorate the cityscape of Istanbul to this day.

While Constantinople had grown into an imperial, administrative, cultural and religious centre that most of the world would envy and respect, in the seventh century, its most important features lay not in its size or symbolic status but in its defences, both natural and man-made. The same peninsula that gave it access to the sea lanes also provided the city with a highly defensible position. The open waters of the Bosphorus and the Sea of Marmara to the east and south, along with the magnificent natural harbour of the Golden Horn inlet to the north, provided natural maritime defence. Furthermore, the entrance to the latter could be blocked by raising a massive chain between Constantinople itself and the neighbouring suburb/city of Sykai/Galata, while massive seaward walls and the imperial navy ensured that attacking Constantinople from the sea was going to be a virtual non-starter for any opponent.

With the northern, southern and eastern approaches protected by the sea, an enemy army would have to approach from the western landward side. They would not have liked what met them. The Romans had made sure that the landward approaches to Constantinople were equally, if not more, uninviting to an attacker. Ever since its original foundation, the inhabitants had walled off the landward side of the city with ever-increasing defences, from the original wall of Byzantion to the expanded Severan Wall and the Constantinian Wall. However, after the walls started by Constantine were outgrown by the expanding city within a century of its refoundation, they were replaced by truly monumental defences begun under Theodosius II (or his father Arcadius).

By the time these Theodosian Walls were complete, they had more than doubled the amount of land encompassed by the defences and presented an obstacle to make any army think more than twice about attacking. Just to reach the first outer wall, an enemy would have had to cross a 20m-wide, 10m-deep moat and then a 20m killing zone. The outer wall itself was 8.5m high and 2m thick, with ninety-six towers placed at 55m intervals.[48] If that was not enough, after another 20m terraced killing zone, the main inner wall was 12m high, 5m thick and also crowned by ninety-six towers. These land and sea fortifications posed a formidable obstacle to any would-be conqueror. It would not be until the early thirteenth century that the sea walls were breached by force of arms, while it would take the invention of the cannon to finally see the Theodosian land walls broken through in 1453. Large sections of the Theodosian Walls still stand today.

But even with such immense and verging-on-impregnable defences, such was the stature and importance of Constantinople in the seventh century that no rebel *strategos* or would-be conqueror could ignore the city. It was not just a symbol of Roman power and authority; Constantinople had become its greatest and perhaps even at times its last bastion. Indeed, the defences had already facilitated the survival of the Roman Empire in the seventh century. As already seen, a combination of Avars, Slavs and Persians had besieged the city in 626 while Heraclius was campaigning in the East. The combination of the imperial navy keeping Persian forces from crossing to Europe and the massive land walls holding the Avar khagan at bay saved Constantinople, and potentially the Roman Empire too.

So, while various Roman regions were facing raids, invasions and even conquest, the Constantinopolitan core of the empire refused to buckle, preserving the Roman Empire, when it might otherwise have been washed away by the Persian, Avar or Arab threats of the seventh century. And as will be seen later, during the lifetime of Justinian II, these defences were to be further bolstered by an invention that made the Roman navy an even more deadly foe for those trying to approach Constantinople by sea. This was much-needed, for during the second half of the seventh and the early eighth centuries, Constantinople would be faced with numerous attacks, culminating in a year-long Arab siege in 717/718.

The threat of attack was not the only effect the seventh century had on the imperial capital. The loss of territory and constant raids by Avars, Slavs and Arabs may have actually seen the population of cities like Constantinople grow as people from the provinces fled the invaders for safer places to live. This in turn increased the pressure on the imperial grain fleet to feed the capital, pointing to why the loss of Egypt was so drastic and perhaps why the Roman presence in the Crimea, another grain-producing region, was increased. This would further explain the importance Constans II placed on blunting early Arab naval operations and potentially his drastic reaction to the defeat at the Battle of the Masts and the loss of Roman domination of the seas by thinking of moving the capital to Italy.

Any increase in population at a time of diminishing resources may also have fed that other great enemy of the empire in Late Antiquity – plague. The seventh-century Mediterranean was still in the throes of the plague cycle that had begun with the Justinianic outbreak in 541. Densely packed and undernourished populations would have been particularly susceptible. Initially, the Arabs appear to have been sheltered from the plague by its failure to breach the Arabian Peninsula, which could be part of the explanation for their successes against the Romans and Persians.[49] However, once they were established in the plague-ridden lands, the Arabs proved no less susceptible. It could be that the stutters in the Arab advances were as much to do with plague as they were Roman resistance and internal trouble.

'Byzantine' Religion

The wars of the first half of the seventh century also had a significant effect on aspects of the religion of the Roman Empire. It might be expected that that change would come in the form of religious doom and even a decline in faith, with the immense territorial losses to the emergent Arab caliphate viewed as punishment from God for the sins of the Roman people. Contemporary Christian writers certainly thought so, while early Muslim historians viewed their success as a reward for their piety.[50] But rather than some definitive, irreversible judgement, the Christian populations of the empire saw this as a challenge to redouble their faith. Heraclius had not seen any decline in the religious fervour of his empire, and he set about capitalizing on it by re-energizing the religious significance of the imperial position.

The position of Roman emperor had had a religious significance since Augustus took up the title of *pontifex maximus* in 12 BC, meaning that every emperor up to the late fourth century had also been 'chief priest'. The Christianization of the empire had seen opposition to certain paganistic traits of the imperial position, and by the fifth century, it appears that the Roman emperor was no longer the *pontifex maximus*, reducing the symbolic religious significance of the position somewhat.[51] While he was not the first to do so (for example, the patriarch of Constantinople is recorded crowning new emperors by 473), Heraclius set about restoring the religious significance of his position as a focus of solidity in the Roman state. He incorporated religious ceremony and belief into the fabric of his imperial office, presenting himself and his successors as God's deputy. Surrounded by non-Christian/non-orthodox enemies, it was no surprise that the emperor at Constantinople wrapped himself up in the cloak of the protector of Christendom. Not only was it a traditional role of the Roman emperor, it was now largely factual. The West was busy organizing itself into the medieval Christian kingdoms, while the papacy was still trying to find its feet in the morass of Lombards and local Roman governors. It was not only the position of emperor which was imbued with religious significance. Religion was 'an element of vital importance in the daily lives of everyone from the *basileus* down to his poorest subjects'.[52] This was demonstrated in the prevalence of icons in virtually every household. The continued growth in importance of these icons and the influence of the neighbouring and increasingly aniconic – opposed to icons and images – Islam would have significant repercussions for the Roman Empire in the eighth century.

This is not to say that Heraclius' rejuvenating of the religious symbolism around the Roman emperor had succeeded in subjecting the Christian Church to the whim of the *basileus*. Indeed, the Donatist cry at the outset of the Christianization of the imperial hierarchy – 'What has the emperor to do with the church?'[53] – still rang as true in the mid-seventh century as it had done in the early fourth. Furthermore, the imbuing of the imperial position with religious significance did not prevent holders of that office from sporting what were to be considered unorthodox and even heretical religious views. This was because Christianity itself, even within the empire, was not a united faith. The doctrines encapsulated in the official Nicene/ Chalcedonian Creed were not shared by all Roman Christians, with much of the focus falling on the nature of the Trinity and how Jesus of Nazareth could be both divine and human. This seems unnecessarily pedantic to the modern reader, but in antiquity it enflamed religious passions, sparking numerous disputes between individuals, groups and even entire patriarchies throughout the first three centuries of imperial Roman Christianity. The calling of local assemblies, region-wide synods and even full ecumenical councils usually failed to fix the problems they were called to address; and if they did, they usually sowed the seeds of the next great doctrinal or hierarchical issue.

These issues could be long-lasting. Church politics in the early seventh century were still dealing with the decisions taken at the Council of Chalcedon in 451. The papacy saw Chalcedon's elevation of the patriarchate of Constantinople to a position second only to Rome as a challenge to the Eternal City's supremacy, while the Alexandrian patriarchate rejected Chalcedonianism altogether and, in an example of the emperor possibly being considered a heretic, so did Anastasius I. In trying to balance these two sides with an open-ended compromise, Constantinople alienated both, leading to schism between Rome and the imperial capital. While this schism would be healed in 519, it showed that there was some divergence of doctrine and practice between East and West. This divergence was also seen in the 'Three Chapters' controversy, which stemmed from Justinian I's attempt to reconcile non-Chalcedonians. His anathematizing of certain writings of Theodore of Mopsuestia, Theodoret of Cyrrhus and Ibas of Edessa in 543–544 was largely accepted in the East, but faced considerable opposition in the Latin Church. This East/West divergence would provide a substantial problem for Justinian II.

While the 'Three Chapters' would linger on throughout the seventh century, that specific controversy drew much less attention than the continued dispute over the canons of Chalcedon, particularly in Egypt, Syria and Armenia. Given the importance of these regions to the empire, it is unsurprising that Heraclius and his Constantinopolitan patriarch, Sergius I, sought a way to bridge the doctrinal gap between Chalcedonians and non-Chalcedonians. Sergius hoped that while they disagreed on will and nature, they might agree on the idea that Christ had a singular 'energy' (Monoenergism). Initial signs were good, with agreement in all the major sees – Rome, Constantinople, Antioch and Alexandria – except one. Sophronius, patriarch of Jerusalem, expressed concern that doctrinal orthodoxy was being compromised for the sake of ecclesiastical unity, championing the cause of 'dyothelitism' – the doctrine of the two wills of Christ. In the face of a doctrinal alliance between emperor, patriarch and pope, the opposition of Jerusalem should have been brushed aside, but Sophronius was made of stern stuff. He succeeded in undermining Monoenergism by highlighting how it was inconsistent with Chalcedonian orthodoxy and was accidentally opening the door for Monophysitism – the non-Chalcedonian doctrine of Christ's single nature.

This failure of Monoenergism refocused discussions on the will of Christ. In 638, Heraclius and Sergius released the *Ecthesis*, which forbade debate on Christ's 'energy', whilst promoting that he possessed two natures but only one divine will. This proposed compromise was christened Monothelitism, and when it was widely accepted in the East, Heraclius and Sergius must have felt they had achieved unity. Instead, they were merely attracting Christological opposition from the papacy and Maximus the Confessor. The ramping up of tensions eventually saw Constans II intervene. His imperial edict called the *Type of Constans* made further discussions regarding Christ's will and energy illegal, demanding that the whole controversy be forgotten. This was wishful thinking. Not only were church authorities never keen on imperial interference in doctrinal matters, but the Monothelite genie was out of the bottle. The Lateran Council of 649 condemned the *Ecthesis* and the *Type*, with Pope Martin I writing to Constans asking him to condemn Monothelitism and his own *Type*. This was a direct affront to imperial authority – the *Type* had been an edict – and Constans was not the sort of emperor to accept such a rebuke.

Acting through his newly appointed exarch of Ravenna, Olympius, Constans was determined to see his *Type* followed in Italy, even if it required force. The new exarch attempted to win the support of the citizenry of Rome and Italian bishops to oppose the pope. He is even thought to have considered assassinating Martin. All of these efforts met with little to no success and may have encouraged Olympius to defect to the papal cause. This betrayal was only a brief interruption, as Olympius' replacement as exarch, Theodore I Calliopas, carried out Constans' orders to impose the *Type*. In

653, he marched to Rome, burst into the Lateran Palace and abducted Pope Martin, dispatching him on a ship to Constantinople. Constans sought to execute Martin as a disobedient subject, although Patriarch Paul convinced him that exile was more appropriate, with the pope sent off to the Crimea, where he died on 16 September 655. Maximus the Confessor was also tried for his 'heresy' of dyothelitism, as well as facing accusations that he had aided the Muslim advance in Africa. He too was sent into exile, before being tried again in 662. Again, he refused to accept Monothelitism, leading to his conviction for heresy once more. Before being exiled to Lazica, Maximus was brutally maimed – his tongue was cut out and his right hand cut off so he could no longer speak or write his heresy. Such brutality was not limited to Martin and Maximus, with other opponents of Monothelitism and the *Type* cowed into silence, although not necessarily obedience, throughout the remainder of Constans' reign.

The loss of many of the non-Chalcedonian provinces of Egypt, Syria and Armenia may have reduced the need for the Monothelite compromise, but at the time of Constans' assassination in 668, Monothelitism and the *Type* was imperial religious policy. Any attempt to enforce that policy would be met with the same opposition that the Heraclian emperors had signally failed to get to grips with so far, with the reactions of Heraclius and Constans II getting them both labelled as heretics. Would the succeeding generations do any better in dealing with doctrinal disagreements? And what of the papacy? These repeated doctrinal problems were demonstrating that for all the notions that he remained an imperial subject, the pope in Rome was becoming increasingly independent from the emperor of Constantinople. But while the seventh century saw a significant weakening of Roman control over Italy, it was still strong enough for the exarch to strike at the pope on several occasions. Constans II's arrest of the holder of the papal throne would prove an example that Justinian II would attempt to replicate.

Of course, it is a supreme irony that this burgeoning religious and temporal independence of the papacy only came about through the breaking of Christianity's centuries-long dominance over the Mediterranean. Not only was there a growing divide between eastern 'Orthodox' and western 'Catholic' Christianity, there were Arian heretics ruling most of Italy; the Balkans were overrun by largely pagan Avars, Slavs and Bulgars; the Black Sea was threatened by pagan Khazars; while the Middle East and Egypt had been lost to Islam. That said, this pressure from pagans, heretics and

Muslims allowed Christianity in general to be a rallying call for the defence of imperial territory in the Balkans, Africa and Anatolia.[54]

The Roman Empire of 668 was one very much in transition. It had been chastened on the battlefield, reduced in territory, reformed in make-up and remained divided in religion; problems which it was still in the process of either coming to terms with or finding solutions for. But for all of these setbacks, teething problems and distractions, the Roman Empire still remained a formidable state, the most advanced of the Mediterranean, even if no longer the biggest. In the hands of capable leaders, its armies could still resist and even defeat the best its many enemies could send against it. And even if those enemies got past the Roman armies in the field, there was still the immense bastion of Constantinople to (fail to) overcome. Even the seemingly inexorable forces of the Arab caliphate found the Roman Empire and its capital a daunting prospect. The Roman emperor was still a man to respect and fear within and without his borders.

In short, the Roman Empire was not going anywhere.

Chapter 2

Imperial Opponents: Arabs, Avars, Lombards, Slavs, Bulgars and Khazars

'If you believe you are the city on the hill, the world's best hope, it is tempting also to believe that outside your boundaries are barbarians.'

Linda Colley

The Umayyad Caliphate and the First Fitna

That the Roman Empire of 668 continued to be a potent force can be best demonstrated in the number, extent and relentlessness of the opponents it had survived in the previous century. The Persians may have gone, but they had been replaced by a far more dangerous, existential threat in the form of the Islam-inspired Arab caliphate in the 630s. By the time of Constans II's assassination in 668, the Arabs ruled a block of territory that stretched from Cyrenaica in the west to Pakistan and Afghanistan in the east, and the Caucasus in the north to the Gulf of Aden in the south. Northern India, the Central Asian steppe, North Africa and the Iberian Peninsula were next on the agenda. It might be imagined that for the Arabs to conquer an empire to match any of its ancient predecessors in just a generation took a series of inexorable advances; however, it had not all been smooth sailing.

The very nature of Islam as a 'revealed religion' had caused problems regarding the succession to the Prophet Muhammad as the temporal and spiritual head of the new Muslim state; problems which were exacerbated by the rapid expansion that state underwent in the middle decades of the seventh century.[1] A conclave of leading Muslims chose Abu Bakr, one of the Prophet's earliest followers, to lead the caliphate upon the Prophet's death, but this was not universally accepted. Some felt that the Prophet had chosen his cousin and son-in-law, Ali b. Abi Talib, to succeed him. Even though they seem to have accepted Abu Bakr's leadership for the time being, this dispute was to bubble away just under the surface and have long-term effects

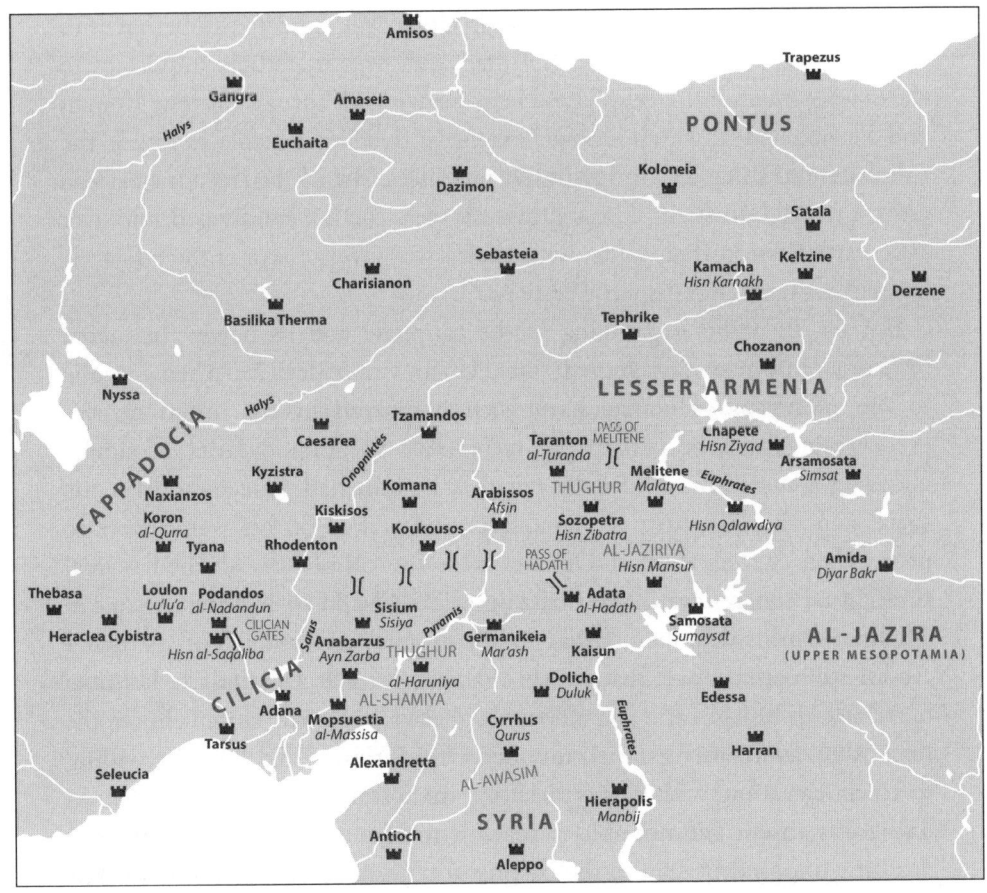

Romano-Umayyad Frontier Zone.

on not just the leadership of the caliphate but for Islam as a whole. This power struggle between those who initially felt that the caliph should be chosen or elected by representatives of the Muslim community and those who felt Ali and his descendants were the rightful heirs to the Prophet developed into a religious schism, rending Islam into separate denominations – Sunni, Shia and Kharijite.

The second caliphal succession was particularly controversial. After a reign of just over two years, dominated by the Ridda Wars and then the initial strikes into Persian and Roman territory, Abu Bakr's demise did not see a large communal meeting choose a follower of Muhammad as caliph. Instead, before his death, Abu Bakr merely appointed Umar as his successor, reputedly to avoid dissension. The unpopularity of this stemmed not just from the lack of input from the community and the ignoring of

Ali's claim once more, but also because Umar was expected to be harsh in his rule. However, the decade of Umar's rule was incredibly important to the development of the caliphate. He oversaw major thrusts into the Roman and Persian states, which were so extensive that he was able to divide the caliphate into thirteen administrative provinces, stretching from the eastern Sahara to Afghanistan.[2] These provinces were further subdivided into over 100 districts and urban units, with their own governors to enforce Islamic law, collect taxes and dispense justice.

But for all of his organizing of the caliphate and its newly conquered territories into a well-governed state, Umar was indecisive when it came to the succession. He may have been hampered by his initial choices predeceasing him, or perhaps he recognized the unpopularity of simply choosing a successor. And if he felt that he still had time to address the succession, the fallout of the conquests undertaken on his watch were to prove Umar wrong. On 31 October 644, the caliph was stabbed several times by a Persian slave called Firuz in the Al-Masjid an-Nabawi mosque in Medina. On his deathbed, Umar finally nominated a council of six men – Abdur-Rahman b. Awf, Saad b. Abi Waqqas, Talha b. Ubaidullah, Uthman b. Affan, Ali b. Abi Talib and Zubayr b. al-Awwam – who would choose the next caliph from amongst their number. Only Uthman and Ali were willing to accept elevation, with Zubayr backing the former and Saad the latter. As Talha was absent and not able to make it to Medina within the three-day deadline imposed by Umar, the casting vote went to Abdur-Rahman. His choice, and therefore the caliphate, fell upon Uthman.

This third caliphate saw Arab territorial acquisitions continue. In the East, the Persian Empire was virtually extinguished, save for a strip of territory along the south coast of the Caspian Sea; rebellion was suppressed in Fars, Kerman, Sistan and Khurasan, while probes were sent into what is now Pakistan and across the Oxus River.[3] In the Mediterranean, Uthman's governors resisted Roman attempts to retake Egypt and Syria and continued raids into Anatolia, whilst establishing a firmer grip on Cilicia and Isauria. A new front was opened by taking to the waves, defeating Constans II at the Battle of the Masts, attacking islands such as Cyprus and possibly planning a strike at Constantinople. An Arab army marched into Tripolitania and squared up to the forces of the rebel exarch, Gregory the Patrician, defeating and killing him at Sufetula in 647. Some later sources would claim that Uthman's forces followed up the defeat of the exarch by conquering most of North Africa and even crossed to Spain, with Uthman possibly linking this European invasion to his proposed attack on Constantinople.[4] However, there is not only no evidence of an Arab attack on Spain in the 650s, but the Exarchate of Africa continued to exist until the last years of the seventh century. This 'conquest' of Africa could be a reading of the new exarch, Gennadius, buying off the Arab raiders with a tribute payment.[5]

With more territory came greater need for governance, and in that, Uthman built on the administrative and infrastructural successes of his predecessor. He then used that platform and his own background as a trader to bring economic prosperity to the caliphate by expanding agriculture and trade through deregulation, selling off land, giving out loans and building canals. This prosperity in turn allowed Uthman to further solidify the caliphate by expanding the army, beautifying existing holy sites such as the Kaaba and the Al-Masjid al-Nabawi, building many more new mosques and centralizing Muslim worship through the providing of hundreds of copies of the *Qur'an*. When it came to his governors, Uthman favoured a policy of delegation, giving them more authority to deal with opposition and continue the expansion of the caliphate. On the surface, this seems like a legitimate course of governance, especially as the caliphate had grown to a size where seeking caliphal backing for a decision on the frontiers became less practical. However, there is more than a hint of suspicion about Uthman's choices of advisers and governors – they were all of his Umayyad clan.

The Banu Umayya were part of the Quraysh tribe, sharing an ancestor with Muhammad; however, as powerful traders, they were initially staunch opponents of the religious revolution. They led the Meccan armies against Muhammad at Uhud and the Trench, only embracing Islam on the eve of Muhammad's capture of Mecca in 629. Despite this, the Umayyads retained a prominent position in Arab society; prominent enough for one of their number, Uthman, to be chosen as caliph in 644. It was under Uthman that the seeds of a caliphal dynasty were planted. Within five years of his elevation, the caliph had appointed members of his clan to the four major governorships of the caliphate – Egypt, Kufa, Basra and Syria.[6] Uthman also surrounded himself in Medina with cousins as advisers. The most important Umayyad governor was actually not an appointee of Uthman. Muawiyah b. Abi Sufyan had been governor of Syria since 639 and had proven himself a capable administrator and leader. Uthman still managed to enlarge Muawiyah's sphere of control and provide him avenues to increase his power within his province. The caliph added Upper Mesopotamia to Muawiyah's domain in 645/646 and granted him permission to take direct possession of conquered Roman land to pay his troops.[7] It was under his leadership that the Arabs first employed a fleet and began the conquest of Mediterranean islands. His prolonged tenure as Syrian governor allowed Muawiyah to build a strong, disciplined and personally loyal Syrian army.

These appointments, when coupled with Uthman's relaxing of central control on the governors, only increased the power of the Umayyads at a time when the caliphate had to decide where to draw their leaders from as companions of the Prophet died out. This nepotism seems to have stemmed from a 'conviction that the house of Umayya, as the core clan of Quraysh, was uniquely qualified to rule in the name of Islam'.[8] Uthman may well have been completely earnest in his belief that the caliphate needed a strong core of connected men to run it. However, any thoughts of altruistic nepotism were scuppered by what seemed like Uthman's growing acquisitiveness. Taxes from Kufa and Egypt were funnelled to Medina for his caliphal use, frequently as rewards to his fellow Umayyads. Rich lands in Iraq were also transferred to the caliphal estate, taking them away from providing directly for the army.[9]

Therefore, Uthman was growing increasingly unpopular. So, when the rebels struck in mid-656, they were met with the support or neutrality of the majority. This was most dire for the caliph in Medina, where the population largely watched on as the rebels besieged his house and, on 17 July, snuck in and killed Uthman.[10] This ignominious end for Uthman had drastic consequences for the caliphate, but perhaps not with the most obvious result. While Uthman's economic successes strengthened the resilience of the caliphate, his 'doting love for a corrupt and rapacious kin'[11] severely undermined the meritocratic heart of the caliphate, paving the way for dynastic rule.

Immediately, Uthman's assassination brought about the election of Ali as caliph.[12] This should have seen some unification at the top of the caliphate, but Ali squandered that opportunity by proving completely uncompromising towards the Umayyads, who in turn were keen to use any way they could to maintain power.[13] The caliph looked to remove all Umayyad governors, and was largely successful aside for one rather important exception -- Muawiyah refused to step down from his position in Syria. This was not just because Ali sought to deprive him of his governorship, but also because the caliph had failed to punish the assassins of Uthman. The situation quickly escalated, with the caliph's willingness to take a military stance against Muawiyah met with disdain by other Muslims. This led to the already mutinous triumvirate

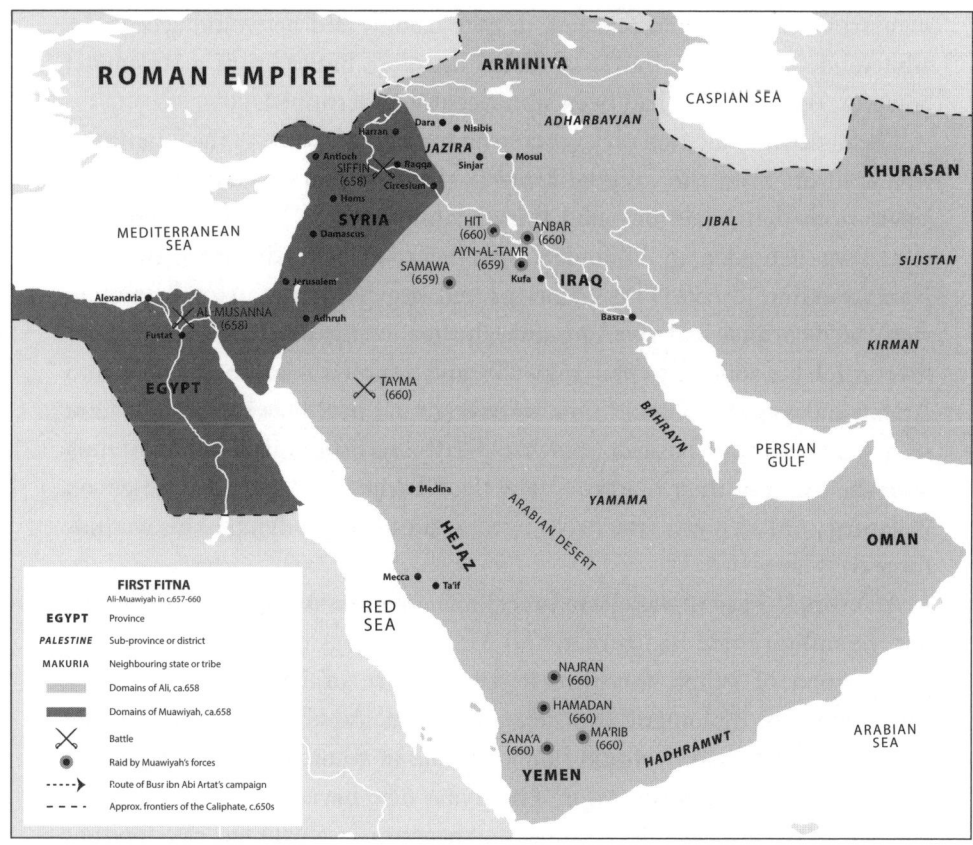

First Fitna.

of Zubayr, Talha and Abu Bakr's daughter, Aisha, taking up arms against Ali. While the caliph defeated this revolt at the Battle of the Camel, it represented the first time Muslims had fought one another and ignited a civil war – the First Fitna – which was to last the duration of Ali's caliphate (656–661).

This continuation of the First Fitna after Ali's victory over Zubayr, Talha and Aisha was because Muawiyah refused to bow to the caliph's diplomatic overtures and pressure. The armies of the caliph and the Syrian governor met at Siffin, near modern-day Raqqa in Syria, in late July 657. The dismay caused by the subsequent three-day mutual slaughter led to both Ali and Muawiyah agreeing to arbitration of their dispute. Ali's agreement to enter arbitration caused great dissension in his camp, especially when the caliph's representative was tricked into pronouncing that both the caliph and the governor should stand aside in favour of the election of a new caliph; a suggestion that Ali then rejected, despite having said he would accept the arbiters' decision. The Battle of Siffin therefore broke up as a stalemate; however, Ali's position had been significantly undermined.

The dissension focused on a group which became known as the Kharijites, who split off from the caliphal army as they felt that all parties at Siffin (apart from them) had deviated from Islam. As these Kharijites retreated east, it was beholden on Ali to deal with them, which he did at the Battle of Nahrawan in mid-659. This victory proved largely pyrrhic. Ali's distraction with the Kharijites had given Muawiyah time to expand the territory under his control. He added Egypt in mid-658, and by 660 was advancing deep into Arabia and towards Kufa.[14] This warmongering by Muawiyah might have seen Ali rebuild his position, but his '[fertilizing] the soil of Mesopotamia with the blood of their martyrs'[15] saw the Kharijites exact their revenge: on 26 January 661, Ali was attacked by a Kharijite assassin, dying of his wounds three days later.

Ali's son, al-Hasan, was elected as caliph by the remaining Alid supporters, but the military tide had turned and Muawiyah was now intent on taking the position of caliph for himself. In the face of Muawiyah's military superiority and diplomatic overtures, al-Hasan chose to capitulate on the promise that Muawiyah would rule justly and in accordance with Islam and not seek to choose his successor. There may also have been some hint that Muawiyah would back al-Hasan as his successor in a caliphal election, but for now the Arab caliphate had a new leader in the form of Muawiyah I. It cannot have escaped the notice of many that the caliphate had gone from an elective theocracy to the rule of a leader whose strength stemmed from his political and military successes. It would be nearly two decades before that promise of a free election upon Muawiyah's death was tested and proven to be false, leading to an even longer Second Fitna (680–692), with the religious factionalism revealed and instigated by the war between Ali and Muawiyah much to the fore once again.

It was the internal dissension of the First Fitna that prevented the Arabs from delivering the final hammer blow to Roman Anatolia and perhaps even the empire as a whole. Muawiyah had agreed to a truce with Constans II in 657/658 in order to confront Ali, which allowed the Romans to reorganize Anatolia along the lines of what became the theme system. Umayyad distraction also allowed the Armenians to install pro-Roman leaders, while Constans moved against some of the Slavs in northern Greece, conducted raids into northern Mesopotamia and Media and planned his campaign in

Italy. But with the capitulation of al-Hasan, Muawiyah was now able to re-establish firm rule, incorporate the populations of the caliphate into its hierarchies and armies,[16] colonize other areas such as Khurasan and then look to continue the expansion of the Arab realm. He focused particular attention on his Roman frontiers. He had already achieved the initial captures of Rhodes and Crete, and not long after his victory in the First Fitna, Muawiyah was looking to build on this string of victories against the Romans. He forced the recapitulation of Armenia in 662 and reinitiated the frequent raids into Roman Anatolia.[17] Some of these raids were of particular size and depth, with one perhaps winning a significant victory over a Roman army in 662/663 and another reaching as far as Chalcedon, directly across the Bosphorus from Constantinople, in 663/664. Muawiyah's Egyptian forces were also making raids into Roman Africa. Advancing through Tripolitania, raiders reached Byzacena (modern southern Tunisia) and struck into the Fezzan region, bringing some of the local Berber tribes under control through the mid-650s. It was these Arab raids into Roman Africa that Constans II thought to oppose from his base in Sicily at the time of his assassination in 668.

In the Roman psyche, these Arab conquests were still thought of as fleeting; a test from God to overcome, the same way the Romans had overcome or outlasted every other major threat that had presented itself in the past. But any such thoughts were based on previous experience, not the immediate situation. The administrative and infrastructural achievements of Umar and Uthman survived the First Fitna intact enough for Muawiyah to restore and then build upon them. Umayyad control may have eventually focused Arab rule on a minority within a minority, but Muawiyah was careful to continue the integration – or at least the neutrality – of non-Arab and non-Muslim populations within the caliphate. This allowed for strong administrative control of all the core provinces, providing stable governance and tax revenues. This in turn enabled Muawiyah and his governors to build a loyal, varied and less-ephemeral army, capable of advancing in multiple directions simultaneously. This successful implementation of 'government by the minority' firmly established the Arab caliphate as a state rather than a collection of territories conquered by a religiously driven army; one that was not going to be overthrown by a single military defeat or the death of a particular caliph.

Heirs to Attila? The Avars

While the Umayyad caliphate may have been the biggest and most grave threat to the Roman Empire by the mid-seventh century, it was by no means the only opponent Roman armies faced. Along the Danube, the most important event in the previous century had been the arrival of the Avars in the 550s.[18] Who exactly these people were is disputed, but it may be that they were a polyethnic group of Mongolian, Turkic, Chionite and Hephthalite tribes fleeing from various defeats on the Central Asian steppe, perhaps most recently by the emerging Turkic Khaganate: Menander Protector refers to the Avars as 'escaped slaves of the Turks'.[19] In 557/558, an Avar delegation arrived in Constantinople, with Justinian I deciding to use them in the latest episode of the well-established Roman policy of playing barbarian opponents off against one another. In return for payments in gold, the Avars agreed to deal with unruly tribes of Kutrigurs, Sabirs and Antes for the empire. They proved too successful in their task, absorbing the defeated Huns and Slavs. This meant that by 562, the territory controlled by the Avars may have stretched from the Lower Danube to the borders of the Caucasus.[20]

Justinian continued to employ the Avars as his Danubian troubleshooters, perhaps hoping that the lure of his gold, the strength of his armies and his diplomatic contacts with the Turks would be enough to keep his new ally in line. On the emperor's instigation, the Avars intervened in the war between the Lombards and Gepids around the Danube bend and Pannonia. Within a year, the Avars had destroyed the Gepid kingdom and forced the Lombards to migrate, leaving them as the undisputed masters of the Danube and the biggest threat to the Roman Balkans since Attila the Hun. Diplomacy seems to have redirected Avar aggression against the surrounding tribes for the duration of the 570s. But by 580, the Avar khan had established firm control of his newly conquered lands. These victories over Huns, Germans and Slavs had seen the Avar Khanate expand in numbers drastically from what was originally perhaps a strike force of around 20,000 horsemen to a much larger, more multifaceted military threat. It was also a rapacious one. Having seen the depth of the empire's pockets, and perhaps also its inability to confront them, the Avar war machine started to probe imperial territory.

Pannonia and Dalmatia felt the force of Avar raids, with Sirmium (modern Sremska Mitrovica, Serbia) captured by 582, and when the empire refused to increase its already sizeable tribute payment, further Avar attacks captured other major cities such as Singidunum (modern Belgrade) and Viminacium

(Kostolac). This loss of virtually the entire Danube focused the attention of the Romans, with Mauricius launching a series of strikes into Avar territory throughout the 590s. While they may not have had a long-term effect on the position of the Romano-Avar frontier due to the increasing neglect of his successors, Mauricius' Avar campaigns should not be underestimated as a success for the Roman military and may have had a significant impact on the khanate itself. The Roman strikes deep into the Avar heartlands may have severely undermined the power of the khan over the constituent tribes of his empire. Slavic colonization of areas that the Avars had conquered surely demonstrates the lack of numbers and direct control the Avar khan had over vast swathes of his territory. Unlike the Arabs, the Avars do not seem to have built any significant administration or infrastructure in their core lands, which is likely a reflection of both their nomadic origins and the lack of pre-existing organization in the transdanubian lands they had conquered. Perhaps, therefore, while it might seem like the Avar Khanate at the outset of the seventh century stretched from the frontiers of the Frankish kingdom to the Caucasus, the writ of the Avar khan may have only been law in his core Hungarian lands and where his army happened to be campaigning at the time.

This does not mean that the Avar Khanate stopped being a substantial threat to the Romans as the seventh century began. The revolt against Mauricius had given them a much-needed respite, and by 610 they were on the rampage again, striking into the Balkans and even Italy with impunity. In 617, they struck at Constantinople, overrunning the suburbs and almost capturing Heraclius. Increasing raids saw the Avars extort their record sum of tribute by 626.[21] In that same year, the Avars launched their most ambitious endeavour yet – a siege of Constantinople. However, it is here that their lack of siege warfare experience showed as the immense Theodosian Walls proved much too strong, particularly once their Persian allies failed to move armed support across to Europe.

In the aftermath of the failed siege, the Avars found that they were losing control of their erstwhile underlings. Many Slavic tribes and clans had followed the Avar advances into the Balkans, but were now increasingly out of reach of Avar suzerainty. By 631, the Avars had also lost a sizeable chunk of their northern and western territory, as well as population, to the Slavic alliance of Samo.[22] Around the same time, a Bulgar rebellion under Kubrat of the Dulo tribe removed any remaining Avar control of the lands north of the Black Sea to a new Bulgar state. These newly independent tribes formed something of a buffer between the Avars in the Alfold and the

Balkan territory still under Roman control, which at this point amounted to coastal cities around the peninsula and eastern Thrace.

This geographical detachment not only saw Romano-Avar interactions decrease, but also direct Avar mentions in Roman historical material. We are increasingly reliant on tangential mentions of Bulgar dealings that just happen to involve the Avars, archaeology to see Slavic and Bulgar influences on Avar development and later western sources. There is evidence that the Avar Khanate retrieved some Wend territory by the 660s after the death of Samo and took in some immigrants from the steppe on the death of Kubrat the Bulgar. Archaeological finds in the Carpathian Basin in the late seventh century show some development and structure in these core lands of the Avar Khanate, as well as perhaps some influence from these recent arrivals and the increasingly influential Slavic population.[23]

While there are a lot of questions that could be asked and investigated about the Avars of the late seventh/early eighth centuries, this separation from Roman affairs means that they play little role in the events of the life and reign of Justinian II beyond the long-term effects of their previous actions. Indeed, the empires that increasingly took up the attention of the Avars in the next century were not those of the Romans or Arabs but of the Bulgars and the Franks, whose authority was extending along the Danube throughout the seventh and eighth centuries. It would be a combination of the Franks of Charlemagne and the Bulgars who would destroy the Avar Khanate in the early ninth century.

The Last of the *Volkerwanderung*: The Lombards

While the Avar Khanate may have been removed as a major threat to the Roman Empire as the seventh century progressed, the impact it had on providing the empire with other threats cannot be overlooked. Indeed, the four other major opponents of the Romans in the late seventh century beyond the Arabs and Avars – Lombards, Slavs, Bulgars and Khazars – and their circumstances of imperial opposition had some connection to the Avars. Aside from their own raids, conquests and extortion, perhaps the biggest impact that Avars had on the Roman Empire was the reaction they instigated in the Lombards following their victory over the Gepids in 567. Rather than accept the Avar yoke as various Huns, Slavs and Gepids had done, under King Alboin, the Lombards migrated *en masse* west through the Julian Alps into northern Italy in 568.[24]

Lombard Italy.

This was not the first migration that the Lombards had undertaken in their history, a history which is recorded in the anonymous seventh-century *Origo Gentis Langobardorum* and the eighth-century *Historia Langobardorum* of Paul the Deacon, himself a Lombard. Together, these sources record stories which may appear largely mythological, but could contain some kernels of historical truth. Their origin story posits the proto-Lombards in southern Scandinavia as a scion of the Winnili tribe that migrated across the Baltic to the area around the mouth of the Elbe River. This is a similar origin to the likes of the Goths, suggesting perhaps that both moved to Germania at a vaguely similar date in the last century BC/first century AD and did so for similar reasons of overpopulation. This could also link to the migration of the Cimbri and the Teutones in the late second century BC.[25]

Arriving at the mouth of the Elbe, the Winnili migrants came into confrontation with the Vandals, during which comes the 'silly story'[26] of how the Lombards got their name. In consulting Odin, the Vandals were told that victory would go to those whom Odin saw first at sunrise. The

Winnili consulted the goddess Frea, who encouraged the Winnili women to tie their hair across their faces to look like the beards of their husbands and to then march with the men to increase their number. Frea then turned Odin's bed towards the east so that when he woke, he saw the bolstered, bearded Winnili first. The god exclaimed, 'Who are these long-beards?', to which the goddess replied, 'My lord, thou hast given them the name, now give them also the victory ... From that time the Winnili were called Langobards',[27] Anglicized as 'Lombards'. Modern theories surrounding the name 'Lombard' also focus on their taking of Odin as their chief deity. Odin was also known as *Langbarðr* and was frequently depicted with a long or grey beard.[28]

A Lombard presence astride the Elbe is attested in imperial Roman sources, and they already had something of a reputation. Tacitus remarks that the Lombards were 'famous because they are so few',[29] while Velleius Paterculus called them 'a race surpassing even the Germans in savagery'.[30] Both Tacitus and Strabo regarded the Lombards as being connected to the Suebi.[31] The German campaigns between 11 BC and AD 16 all involved crossing the Weser River and perhaps also the Elbe, which likely brought them into contact with the Lombards.[32] After the Roman withdrawal from Germania, the Lombards overthrew Suebi suzerainty in AD 17 and grew in stature enough to interfere in the internal politics of the neighbouring Cherusci by AD 47.[33] However, after that, information about the Lombards becomes more scarce. Archaeology around the Elbe has been considered 'Langobardic'[34] and has seen the Lombards considered practitioners of both crematory burial and agriculture.[35] It is not until the prelude to the outbreak of the Marcomannic Wars in 166 that we hear about the Lombards again. Cassius Dio records them taking part in a strike across the Danube into Pannonia, where they were defeated by local Roman forces.[36]

It is difficult to determine with certainty how the Lombards faired in the growing Germanic tendency towards larger confederations. Were they far enough away from Roman territory to escape notice or had their hard-won freedom from the Suebi been lost, subsumed by one of the growing unions, quite possibly the Saxons by 300?[37] Ostrogothic propaganda would have it that at least some of the territory of the Lombards on the east bank of the Elbe was under the control of Ermanaric by the mid-fourth century.[38] Poor harvests and pressure from neighbours may have seen the Lombards gradually migrate south along the Elbe towards the Middle Danube in the late fourth century. However, if there was any notion that the Lombards were looking to escape the control of others by traversing the Elbe and Oder,[39] they were in for a rude awakening. For the best part of a century, the Lombards will have been subsumed to some extent by the Hunnic empire of Attila, until the Battle of the Nedao River in 454.[40] While they are not listed in the sources as doing so, it could be that there were Lombards in the armies of Attila that raided the Roman Empire, approaching Constantinople and fighting at the Battle of the Catalaunian Fields.

Aside from some regal chronology in Paul the Deacon and these assumptions of subservience to the Huns, little is known of the Lombards between their migration from the Lower Elbe and their establishment along the Middle Danube by the last years of the fifth century.[41] With the Roman reconquest of Italy in the 530s and 540s, more of a light is shone on the Lombards. They took advantage of the defeat of the Gothic kingdom by occupying the former Roman provinces of Noricum and Pannonia. Rather than try to oust them, Justinian I employed the Lombards as allies. In 552, the Lombard king, Audoin, sent 5,500 men to join the Roman army of Narses at the Battle of Busta Gallorum.[42] Justinian also paid the Lombards to act as a counterweight to the troublesome Gepids, hoping that by having these two tribes fight each other, they would have been in little mood to raid Roman territory.

By the mid-560s, Paul the Deacon would have it that the new, energetic Lombard king, Alboin, had subjugated the Gepids and then chosen Italy as a new home for his people.[43] There was a victory or two over the Gepids, one of which may have involved the death of the Gepid king, but this is usually thought of as the doing of the Avars, not the Lombards. Paul the Deacon even tries to suggest that Alboin bestowed Pannonia upon the Avars in some sort of negotiation on the condition that should the Lombards ever return to Pannonia, they would be given back their lands.[44] The reality is that even if the Avars did intervene against the Gepids as allies of the Lombards and at the instigation of Justinian, the Avars were so overwhelmingly victorious that they took over all Gepid territory and then bullied the Lombards into vacating their lands along the Middle Danube.[45]

The timing and destination of this Lombard migration proved serendipitous. Italy may have been the original heartland of the Roman Empire, but it had fallen out of the imperial orbit by the late fifth century. The forces of Justinian I had succeeded in reclaiming the peninsula, but Gothic resistance proved stubborn, and together with Frankish and Alamanni invasions, final Roman victory did not come until 562. By that time, over a quarter century of incessant and attritional warfare had devastated and depopulated the Italian countryside, severely depleted local imperial finances, exhausted the local Roman garrisons and sapped enthusiasm for fighting. It was into this war-weary Italy that the Lombards arrived, and any thought of seeking accommodation was quickly set aside as Alboin realized that there was no Italian force capable of standing against him. The Lombards benefitted not just from the poor state of Italy but also from the distraction of the Roman Empire with war in the East and the Balkans, with the latter distraction ironically caused by the Avars.

Within a year of their arrival, the Lombards had taken Milan and begun a three-year siege of Pavia. Once it fell in mid-572, Pavia was made the capital of a new Lombard kingdom.[46] Against this onslaught, the Romans could only rely on their coastal defences supplied by the navy and hope that the Lombard thrust petered out. As it was, the latter did occur to some extent. Not long after his capture of Pavia, Alboin was assassinated on the connivance of his Gepid queen and possibly the Roman exarch.[47] His successor, Cleph, ruled for just eighteen unpopular months before he too was assassinated. What followed was a period of at least a decade where the Lombards had no king, a period known as the 'Rule of the Dukes'.

On the surface, this looks like a collapse of Lombard central authority that the Romans could take advantage of. However, when they tried, Baduarius, son-in-law of Justin II, was defeated and probably killed by the Lombards in 576.[48] Polycephalic ducal rule may actually have increased the threat of the Lombards as the dukes sought to secure their own positions and perhaps make a case for their election as Lombard king by attacking the Romans. This interregnum also allowed other enterprising Lombard leaders to set out on their own, with the two most prominent driving south through the Apennines to establish the largely independent duchies of Spoleto and Benevento in central and southern Italy respectively.

Once the Romans regrouped in their reduced territory and behind their coastal defences, the lack of unity engendered in ducal rule began to tell on the Lombards. Without a central authority to bring together larger armies to take well-defended forts and cities, the Lombard advance ground to a halt. The shutting-off of avenues of advance against their non-Lombard neighbours may well have seen an increase in disorder and violence between the duchies. This disorder also brought down potential disaster upon the Lombards when an invasion of Provence in 584/585 sparked a furious counter-invasion by the Franks. This forced the dukes to elect a new king in the form of Cleph's son, Authari. He thwarted the proposed Franco-Roman alliance and managed to re-establish a somewhat strong central kingship, although the allegiance of many of the dukes was frequently suspect.

There was a serious ducal revolt in the early seventh century, but overcoming such obstacles strengthened the central Lombard monarchy and enabled it to resist significant political complications, such as the regency of a Bavarian queen Theodelinda, the rule of an increasingly unstable young king[49] and the division of rule into two kings in the 660s. It also meant that under strong kings such as Rothari (reigned 636–652) or Grimuald I (662–671), the Lombard kingdom could resist Roman attempts at reconquest – such as that of Constans II – and even continue their own expansion.

While the Franks and later the Slavs as well as the imperial remnants provided problems, perhaps the biggest issue for the Lombards in the mid-seventh century was the growing religious schism within their realm. While at least nominally Christianized during their time astride the Danube, it was not until they moved to Italy that the majority of the Lombards converted to Christianity. Unfortunately for Romano-Lombard relations, the version of Christianity the Lombards converted to was an obstacle to integration. As with many of their fellow Germans, the Lombards converted to Arian Christianity, which subordinated the Son to the Father within the Trinity because Jesus Christ had been born and was therefore created and inferior. This put them at odds with the Trinitarian orthodoxy of the empire and the papacy. While the Lombards would gradually Catholicize once they were established in Italy, it would not be until the 650s that the Lombard kingdom was nominally Catholicized, and probably not actually until the last decade of the century.

By the mid-seventh century, the Lombard kingdom covered the entirety of the Po Valley, Tuscany and Liguria, while the independent Lombard duchies of Spoleto and Benevento had lifted virtually all of central and southern Italy from the Romans. While this represented the vast majority of the Italian peninsula, strong city defences and rivalry between the king and the dukes allowed Constantinople to maintain control of the hinterlands around major cities such as Ravenna, Rome and Naples, as well as the heel and toe of the Italian boot. There were also nominally subordinated Roman *duces* in Venice and along the Adriatic coast. The maintaining of so many coastal cities also suggests that for all their success, the Lombards had made little headway in challenging Roman naval superiority. This is also seen in continued imperial control of the islands of Sicily, Sardinia, Corsica and the Balaerics. This naval superiority perhaps even maintained the Roman presence in Italy beyond the capabilities of the land forces available to the exarch. Coupled with the increasing religious problems between Rome, Ravenna and Constantinople, the forces of Justinian II were going to have a tough time if they were to turn back the clock and repeat the Italian successes of his imperial namesake.

A Great Leap Forward: The Slavs

While the initial dominance of the Avars largely obscured the movements of some Germans and Huns, there was a far larger and more widespread movement of peoples going on behind that Avar screen: the Slavs. This latest threat to Roman territory was of somewhat enigmatic origins. Slavic literature was non-existent until the mid-ninth century, and it was not until the early twelfth century that the Slavs generated their own accounts of their past. And when they did, the *Chronicle* of Cosmas of Prague (*c.*1120), the Polish *Gallus Anonymus* (*c.*1115) and the *Russian Primary Chronicle* in Kiev (1116) focused on the origins of their immediate Slavic states in Bohemia, Poland and Kiev respectively rather than the rapid dispersion of Slavs in the sixth and seventh centuries. This leaves us reliant on Roman, Italo-Lombard and Frankish sources for early Slav history, where they are depicted as invading barbarians, stunting the usefulness of the information recorded about them. But this reliance is even more troublesome because these sources do not record an awful lot about the Slavs, reliable or otherwise.

On the surface, it appears that 'there is no mention of "Slavs" in any Roman source – Greek or Latin – written before the deposition of the last Western Roman Emperor Romulus Augustulus',[50] but even such a statement is not without controversy. The focus of that controversy forms around the sixth-century historian Jordanes' claim that the Slavic Sclavenes and Antae were scions of the Venedi from along the Vistula.[51] The potential historiographic importance of this comes from the Venedi being recorded by the first/second-century Roman historians Pliny the Elder, Tacitus and Ptolemy. Pliny called them the *Sarmatae Venedi* and situated them along the Baltic coast, which is echoed by Ptolemy, who placed the *Vouenedai* along the southern shores of the Baltic, east of the Vistula and in Sarmatia. In his *Germania*, Tacitus says that he does not know whether to list the Venedi (along with the Peucini/Bastarnae and Fenni) as either Germanic or Sarmatian and records them having traits of both – Sarmatian-style plundering raids but a more settled

Germanic lifestyle and focus more on infantry rather than cavalry. Such Tacitean difficulty in Slavic identification could be connected to the modern problems of identifying proto-Slavs in the archaeological record.[52]

This would seem to provide an historiographic anchor for proto-Slavs in the form of the Venedi along the Vistula and Baltic coast, with them migrating south to eventually appear along the Danube by the early sixth century. However, the veracity of Jordanes' Venedi-Slav connection has been questioned.[53] It could be that Jordanes has relied on Tacitus' *Germania* to anchor his own work, inventing this connection in 'a further example of a documented tendency for Roman writers to claim that there were no "new barbarians", merely old ones by new names'.[54]

Even with the potential story provided by Jordanes, 'so deficient is the coverage provided by the written sources that the creation of Slavic Europe had to be studied as virtually a prehistoric subject, using almost entirely archaeological evidence',[55] as well as some linguistic analysis. Unsurprisingly, this source combination has its own problems. If they did originate in the area of the Tacitean Venedi, then perhaps proto-Slavs are to be more closely associated with the Przeworsk and Zarubintsy cultures; however, archaeologists face difficulties in distinguishing Slavic and non-Slavic findings, and due to the wide area they expanded into, there are multiple other cultures that could be included in Slavic archaeology. Such a wide variety also highlights the ability of Slavs to assimilate aspects of other cultures and peoples. Any such ethnogenesis, along with the lack of certainty over their homeland, makes it very difficult to associate the various Slavic groups or their progenitors with any one cultural origin.[56]

One linguistic suggestion is that the Slavs were not derived from the Baltic Venedi because the Slavic vocabulary shows no evidence of early exposure to either the sea or amber, two things that a people on the Baltic coast should have spoken of.[57] But even if the specific connection to the Tacitean Venedi is disbelieved, it could be that there was a connection to the Baltic region for 'Slavic languages as a whole are most closely related to those of Europe's Baltic-speakers'.[58] Indeed, it would seem that the Slavs and Balts were scions of a shared Indo-European ancestor who did not migrate from the Baltic region.[59]

Whether highlighting the influence of Jordanes' Venedi connection or possibly showing an influence on him, the names used to identify various groups of Slavs are similar to the name 'Venedi'. Western sources such as Jonas of Bobbio, Fredegar and Boniface called the Slavs 'Venethi/Veneti', although Jonas also referred to them as 'Sclavi', while Martin of Braga wrote of the 'Sclavus'. Furthermore, Fredegar and other Frankish and Lombard sources wrote of the 'Wenden/Winden' and the 'Windische'.[60] By the reign of Justinian II, sources such as the *Miracles of Saint Demetrius* were starting to name specific Slavic tribes rather than the more general 'Sclaveni' or 'Antae'. This may reflect closer interaction with these pre-existing subtribes rather than a recent development within the Danubian Slavs. For the Romans, 'Sclavene' was 'an umbrella term for various groups living north of the Danube frontier, which were neither "Antes", nor "Huns" or "Avars"'.[61]

This lack of historiographic and archaeological clarity is perhaps best displayed in the sheer number of proposed original homelands for the Slavs in academic circles – Bohemia, Cernjachov, Polesia, Kievan, Przeworsk, Pannonia, the Carpathians and the Danube region. Many of these proposals are surely influenced by 'nationalist rivalries ... rooted in the demands of contemporary politics'.[62] Such ideas following narrow agendas giving the Slavs a millennia-long origin story where they were frequently depicted as a 'submerged' majority below a thin ruling tribal elite have increasingly lost their credibility.[63]

The proto-Slavs could be a creation of socio-political and economic contact with the Roman world;[64] but while there is no record of Slavs in the Danube region during its rule by Romans, various Germans and Huns, positing their creation along the late fifth-century Lower Danube, may be taking things a bit too far. It could be instead that the Venedi/Sclavenes/Antae/ proto-Slavs migrated south into Transdanubia over the course of decades or even centuries. Along the way, they interacted with various cultures long enough to be influenced by them, dividing into numerous groups through military encounters, internal politics or geography. Perhaps they then arrived north of the Danube just before or after the fall of the Attilan empire, to be significantly changed again by contact with Romanity.[65] The economic and agricultural impact of meeting the Roman world may have seen a significant population boost for the Slavs, enabling them to roam so widely after escaping the Avar yoke.

Despite considering them 'undisciplined and disorganised',[66] the *Strategikon* found the Slavs to be 'populous and hardy, bearing readily heat, cold, rain, nakedness, and scarcity of provisions',[67] and well-suited to the raiding and guerrilla tactics they employed both on foot and on horse.[68] The Roman inability to subjugate the mass of Slavs may also have been due to their seeming dislike of being ruled, with the *Strategikon* claiming that 'the Sclaveni and Antes were both independent, absolutely refused to be enslaved or governed, least of all in their own land'.[69] Procopius even went as far to say that the Sclaveni and Antes practised democracy,[70] which while used in a denigrating tone suggests that they lived in a decentralized tribal society. Whatever the case, 'Without kings or large-scale chieftains to bribe or defeat, the Byzantine Empire had little hope of either destroying them or co-opting them into the imperial system.'[71]

Left largely unhindered by the distracted Romans and free from the Avars, these small, scattered Slavic settlements were able to grow in size through intermarriage with other neighbouring Slavs and the locals. This in turn saw their consolidation into larger tribal groups and gradual coalescence into proto-states 'which form the framework of the ethnic make-up of modern eastern Europe'.[72] Reputedly, this first happened with the Wends of Samo in the early seventh century, but this proved short-lived. Slavic states with any longevity did not appear until the ninth century with the likes of Moravia, Serbia, Croatia and a Slavicized West Bulgarian Empire.

In terms of religion, the Slavs of the late seventh century remained by and large animistic polytheists, with concepts of spirits, demons, gods and even a supreme deity. Indeed, much of Slavic Europe would not be Christianized until the late ninth century, while Kievan Russia would not convert until a century later. Along with other imperial opponents like the Avars, Bulgars and Khazars, the Slavs' continued paganism provided an obstacle to peace and integration, something which was much more of an issue for the Romans because there were significant numbers of Slavs on imperial territory.

Jordanes' mention of the Gothic Vinitharius' defeat of the Antae would seem to be the earliest chronological note of a definitively Slavic people in the historical record;[73] however, there are considerable issues in the Gothic genealogy, with Vinitharius appearing in both c.375 and c.450.[74] At best, it could suggest that the Antae were in or near the eastern Carpathians in the mid-fifth century. The earliest Slav appearance in Roman sources may be that of the Antae during the reign of Justin I (518–527), when their raid of the Balkans was heavily defeated by the *magister militum per Thracias*, Germanus.[75] A generation later, the Sclaveni and Antae drove as far as Dyrrhachium on the Adriatic in 547/548 and showed some aptitude for taking well-defended positions.[76] An ambitious raid in 550 was seemingly only hindered by the defences of Naissus and Thessalonica and the appearance of a Roman army marching west to fight the Goths in Italy.

The raiders quickly regrouped and won a further victory at Hadrianople, and then struck to within a day's march of Constantinople. Despite these wide-ranging raids, there appears to have been little Slavic intent as yet to transform these attacks into settlements on Roman territory.

The Antae made peace with the empire in 545 and were employed to distract and hinder their Slavic brethren and Hun neighbours, a role they fulfilled until at least 602, when they were targeted for destruction by the Avars for their Roman alliance.[77] However, the Sclavenes, while seen serving in the Roman army, remained such a thorn in Justinian's side that the emperor may have had them in mind as much as the Gepids and Lombards when it came to channelling the newly arrived Avars as a transdanubian police force in the 560s.

As already mentioned, the Avar subjugation of the tribes north of the Danube may not have been as complete as it first seems. Indeed, rather than keep the Sclavenes under control, the umbrella of the Avar Khanate may have increased the Slavic threat to the Balkans. Some Slavic clans and tribes had escaped the Avar yoke by crossing the Danube into Roman territory, but the bulk of the Slavs came to make up a substantial part of the Avar army. In the 580s, while Mauricius was embroiled in the east, in the wake of several large Avar columns, various Sclavene tribes hit Thrace and Illyricum, threatening Thessalonica again in 586 and seemingly reaching the Peloponnese in southern Greece. However, the Roman riposte in the 590s was a marked success, defeating the Avars, eliminating the nascent Slavic settlements south of the Danube and then striking across the river into the Avar heartland and crushing several Slavic tribes.[78]

Unfortunately for the Roman Balkans, Mauricius was murdered by his mutinous army before a decisive conclusion to his Avaro-Slav campaigns could be reached. By the time the Avars and Slavs recovered a decade later, they found the Romans teetering on the brink of catastrophic defeat by the Persians in the 610s, with virtually all Roman military resources removed from the Balkans. This allowed the Avars and Slavs to strike across the Danube in increasingly spectacular scale. Thessalonica only just held out, but several important cities like Naissus, Serdica and Salona were all lost. The Slavs again reached the Peloponnese, and in the wake of the Avar failure at Constantinople in 626, these Slav raiders increasingly escaped the control of their erstwhile Avar masters, avoided or defeated the heavily depleted Illyrian and Thracian armies and began to settle more permanently. The emergence of Islam hot on the heels of the end of Heraclius' Persian war meant that there was little time for the Romans to respond to the growing Slav presence in imperial territory.

Archaeology and historiography can be used to present areas of Slavic occupation in the Balkans – between the Danube and the Haemus Mountains, Macedonia, Thrace, Thessaly, along the Strymon River to Thessalonica, the Peloponnese and parts of Greece. These may have been joined slightly later by the progenitors of the Serbs and Croats, who defeated some of the Avars and moved into the western Balkan lands they are associated with to this day. It must be said that these origin stories do have 'a distinctly legendary tone',[79] even in their recording by the *De Administrando Imperio* of Constantine VII. This does not preclude a basis in fact that the Serbs and Croats followed their fellow Slavs in moving into imperial territory in the wake of the collapse of the Danube frontier in 614 and the Avar failure at Constantinople in 626.[80]

As already mentioned, the Balkans were not the only destination of Slavic migration during the sixth and seventh centuries. They were also establishing themselves along the Elbe in Germany, across much of Central and Eastern Europe and into what would become Russia. Perhaps only the presence of the Avars in the Alfold, the convergence of the Bulgars north of the Black Sea and the continued ability of the larger, coastal Roman settlements to resist prevented something of a Slavic clean sweep from Italy and Germany to Russia and Ukraine. The focus here, however, will be on those Slavic tribes in the Balkans that Justinian II had to deal with, and for the most part that will be those settled in Macedonia and Thessaly.

Given how widespread it would seem to have been across large sections of the Balkans, it might be questioned how well Roman forces would have dealt with this influx of Slavs even if they had no other distractions. As will be seen, when the likes of Justinian II was able to gather a Roman army of some strength, the Slavs proved resilient even after defeat. Indeed, lasting success against the Slavs in the Balkans would elude not only Justinian II but successive Roman emperors until the early ninth century, and even then Nikephoros I only succeeded in re-establishing imperial control of peninsular Greece. More extensive reclamation of Balkan territory would not come until the early eleventh century.

One of Five Brothers: the Danube Bulgars

To make matters worse for the Roman Balkans, the Avars and Slavs were not the only peoples probing Danubian lands. By the mid-seventh century, the Lower

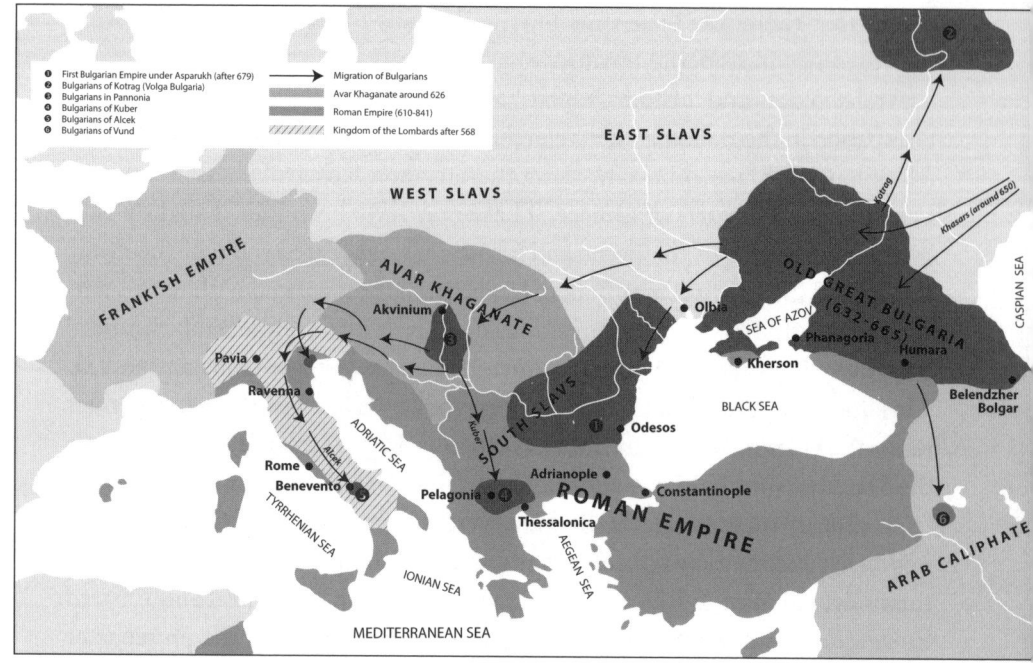

Fall of Old Great Bulgaria (665) and the Migration of the Bulgars.

Danube was also coming under pressure from a people called the Bulgars. As with the Avars and Slavs, the origins of these Bulgars are unclear. The lack of clarity in the evidence – historiographic, archaeological or etymological – is displayed in the sheer number of proposed origins of the name 'Bulgar' itself. It is difficult to trace back earlier than the fourth century,[81] and may well predate the appearance of the people who became exclusively associated with it. There may also be the additional issue of that name being used anachronistically to describe past peoples or for potentially invented connections. It has become most common to see 'Bulgar' deriving from the Turkic *bulğha*, which meant 'stir', 'mix', 'disturb' or 'confuse'. This in turn raised the idea that other Turkic peoples saw the 'Bulgars' as a mixed confederacy and/or 'disturbers' of the peace.[82] The Chinese record a potentially Turkic people called the *Buluoji* as one of their opponents during the fourth century, whom they described as 'mixed' and 'troublemakers', a description quite similar to this Turkic *bulğha*.[83] Another potential Bulgar origin in Chinese sources comes in the form of the Turkic Pugu, who were possibly connected to the Bulgars through a later shared home north of the Caucasus.[84]

A Turkic origin of the Bulgars may be seen in the frequent Roman association of them with the Onogurs or Unogundurs, who are some of the first Turkic tribes to appear north of the Black Sea in Late Antiquity, even if the reason for this Roman historiographic connection is unclear.[85] A Bulgar connection to some of the steppe inhabitants such as the Kutrigurs and Utigurs beyond etymological associations could require a slight rethinking of the idea of Turkic origins of the Bulgars. This is because both the Kutrigurs and Utigurs were regarded by various Roman sources as Hunnic.[86] If this is the case, it could be that long before they became Slavicized, the Bulgars had already been a mixed tribal confederation of Turks, Huns and others. However, the likes of Procopius may have used 'Hun' in the same way that previous historians used 'Scythian' as an all-purpose name for steppe barbarians. The name 'Bulgar' may have been used in a similar manner. The twelfth-century Syriac patriarch Michael the Syrian records 'Bulghars' entering Thrace during the reign of Mauricius (582–602), which is either a mistaking of the Avars for these 'Bulghars' or an example of such anachronistic, all-purpose usage.[87] This potential mislabelling does not eliminate the idea of the Bulgars being at the head of a union of tribes including the Kutrigurs and Utigurs. It may even make such a confederacy more likely if they were all Turkic in origin.[88]

Could the word 'Bulgar' even be of Latin origin? It has been suggested that it derives from '*burgaroi*' – a Roman term for mercenaries stationed in frontier forts called *burgi* – or a Germanic translation of the Latin *homo pugnax* – 'combative man'.[89] Or could it be from a more straightforward derivation from the Latin *vulgaris*, meaning 'usual' or 'of the common people'? Certainly, some of the likely anachronistic attempts to anchor the Bulgars in a Biblical or historical context before their first appearance along the Danube in 480 do at least appear etymologically similar to the Latin *vulgaris*, although this is by no means proof. This could more simply be a Latinization of the Turkic *bulğha*. The *Chronology of 354* seems to link the 'Vulgares' back to the Biblical Shem through an individual called Ziczi, while Movses Khorenatsi may record the Armenian rulers, Varazdat and Arshak III, facing two separate Bulgar migrations during the fifth century. Paul the Deacon also suggests that an early fifth-century Lombard king, Agelmund, was defeated and killed by 'Vulgares' in the Carpathians. In revenge, the new Lombard king, Laimicho, defeated these 'Vulgares' to such a degree that they were still Lombard subjects upon Alboin's migration to Italy in 568.[90] Again, much like with Michael the Syrian, we may be seeing these writers calling a section of Avars or Huns by the name 'Vulgares'. However, it could also be that as a migrating people, the Bulgars were spread out over a wide area across the steppe, through the Caucasus and into the lands north of the Danube, swept along and largely hidden by the western movements of the likes of the Huns or Avars.

One of the more well-informed sources of barbarian affairs in the mid-fifth century, Priscus, is rather conspicuous in his lack of mention of the Bulgars, even when discussing an array of tribes living on the Ponto-Caspian steppe. He has Saragurs, Ogurs and Onogurs visiting Constantinople to appeal to the emperor Leo I (457–474), to whom they explained how they had been harassed from their homelands by Sabir Huns, who had in turn been forced to move west through attacks by the Avars. The Bulgars are not mentioned in this procession of advancing tribes, but individual clans or entire tribes could be hidden under the various tribal names like the Onogurs, confederations like the Avars or as part of the initial advances of their fellow Turks such as the Saragurs.[91]

Perhaps even more telling regarding the potential lack of Roman contact with the Bulgars before the seventh century is their non-appearance in the pages of the *Strategikon*. While the authorship and date of that military treatise are disputed, if it is to be linked to the campaigns of Mauricius, the almost total absence of the Bulgars as an imperial enemy is striking. The only seeming direct mention of them comes in a section on the clothing to be worn by Roman infantry, with a Roman soldier's mantle said to be 'simple, not like a Bulgarian cloak'.[92] However, again showing the potential problems with nomenclature in identifying barbarian tribes, the *Strategikon* does mention Turks on a couple of occasions, but without any clear indication of which 'Turks' these are.[93] Furthermore, it lumps the Turks together with the Avars in a section titled 'Dealing with the Scythians, That is, Avars, Turks and Others Whose Way of Life Resembles that of the Hunnish Peoples'.[94]

It is usually taken that the first definitive mention of the actual Bulgars is in 480 when they were paid by Zeno to distract the Goths by invading Roman territory, a somewhat dubious action that he repeated in 486, before they appear again seemingly as allies of the Gepids in 488.[95] Even with this apparently sure historical footing, it is unknown if these fifth-century 'Bulgars' were the same people who would become a significant problem for the Roman Empire by the late seventh century. Zeno's 'Bulgars' could easily have been a band of Kutrigurs from north of the Black Sea, proto-Avars or a remnant of the Attilan Huns, rather than the same people who would form the 'state' of Old Great Bulgaria and later the First Bulgarian Empire.

As has already been mentioned, the Bulgar progress across the steppes likely saw considerable integration with other Asiatic and Indo-European tribes. This means that even if the Bulgars were originally a Turkic people, by the time they came to be interfering in Danubian politics, they may have been much more of a 'confederation' of barbarians, including Onogurs, Kutrigurs, Utigurs, other Turks and Alans under Bulgar leadership, rather than a single tribe. Such assimilation could be part of the explanation of why many sixth-century historians identified the Bulgars as Huns. Some of them may even have served in Hunnic armies,[96] and through some limited Hunnicization, Bulgars may well have appeared and fought in a similar manner to the Huns.

While not overlooking the possibility for misidentification, the Bulgars are recorded along the Danube frequently during the late fifth/early sixth centuries. The departure of the Goths for Italy may have seen the Bulgars turn to raiding Roman territory as the emperor no longer had need of paying them.[97] A Bulgar force defeated and killed Julian, the *magister militum per Thracias*, in 493, while another drove deeply into Roman territory and defeated the forces of the *magister militum per Illyricum*, Aristus, on the banks of the Tzurta River in 499.[98] In 502, a Bulgar raid met little resistance in Thrace, perhaps a result of previous victories and the incipient Anastasian War with the Persians.[99] A generation later, the Bulgars inflicted a further series of defeats on successive Roman armies. In 528, Justin, *dux Moesiae Secundae*, and Baduarius, *dux Scythiae*, intercepted a Bulgar raid of their territories, with the former being killed. The Romans collected together a sizeable force under three men – Justin's successor, Constantinolus; Ascum, a Hun/Bulgar serving as *magister militum per Illyricum*; and Godilas, *magister militum per Thracias/vacans* – which defeated the same Bulgars who had moved on to raid Thrace. The three commanders had no time to celebrate their victory, as they were ambushed by another Bulgar column and taken prisoner. Godilas managed to escape, but Justinian I paid a ransom of up to 10,000 *solidi* to secure Constantinolus' release. There is no further record of Ascum. This Bulgar raid was not fully defeated until the following year by the Gothic general, Mundo, although there was still a further Bulgar raid in 535 which needed the attention of the *magister militum* Sittas, while the Hunnic raid that reached the outskirts of Constantinople in 539/540 likely contained significant Bulgar forces.[100] Unsurprisingly, the Romans were quick to enrol these marauders into their armies, with significant Bulgar contingents serving Sabinianus in 505 and Vitalian in 515.[101]

Strangely, after these frequent appearances in the record of the first half of the sixth century, the Bulgars largely disappear.[102] There were plenty of events north of the Black Sea to turn Bulgar attention away from the Danube. The political machinations of Justinian I seem to have encouraged a conflict between the Kutrigurs and Utigurs, which may have involved the Bulgars. This was also around the time that the Avars and their Turkic pursuers were appearing north of the Caspian Sea. The mutually weakened Kutrigurs and Utigurs found themselves at the mercy of the new arrivals, with the former being overwhelmed by the Avars and the latter perhaps accepting some form of suzerainty of the Turkic Khaganate.[103] It is difficult to see how the Bulgars could have escaped a similar fate, although defining which of these spheres of influence incorporated the majority of the Bulgars is difficult to assess. Mid-sixth-century sources Jordanes and Ps-Zacharias Rhetor suggest that the Bulgars were situated north of the Black Sea and north of the Caspian Gate respectively.[104] This confusion is even before the spectre of both of these writers potentially using their terms for 'Bulgars' to mean 'Huns', 'Turks' or more generally 'barbarians' is taken into account.

While there were Bulgars under the sway of both the Avars and the Turks, could it be that a Bulgar-led confederacy began to coalesce as a 'proto-nation' around this period north of the Black Sea in something of a 'no man's land' between the Avar and Turkic spheres? The Avars may have been unwilling to push back east for fear of conjuring up another defeat at the hands of the khaganate and were busy establishing themselves on the Hungarian plain. The Turks had reached the extremity of their western advance and were beginning to face internal trouble. Both Avars and Turks may have been feeling the strain of their empire-building too, with the Slavs poised to break free from Avar control by the turn of the seventh century, while the Turkic Khaganate split into western and eastern halves in around 582.

The retreat of Avar and Turkic influence from north of the Black Sea left a power vacuum, which was filled by Kubrat, a member of the Bulgar Dulo clan.[105] It is recorded that there was some kind of Romano-Bulgar alliance visible in his early life. It would not be surprising to see the Romans reaching out to the Bulgars in the early seventh century, as they were faced with the dual threat of the Avars and Persians. Heraclius came to an arrangement with the Khazars in the 620s, so the emperor was on the lookout for allies. While its exact date is unknown, this diplomatic contact reputedly saw Kubrat, either as a child or young adult, live in the imperial palace in Constantinople. Exactly what was happening amongst the Bulgars for them to send their potential leader to the imperial capital is open to speculation. If the example of the Goths sending Theoderic the Amal to Constantinople over a century earlier was a template,[106] then it could be that Kubrat was sent as a hostage and to remove him from the succession. Such an arrangement may have been orchestrated by the Ermi clan, specifically Kubrat's maternal uncle and regent, Organa, whose name may instead have been Gostun, with Organa being a title.[107] The Romans may also have hoped to at least partially Romanize their hostage, so he would then influence his tribe in a pro-Roman direction. Indeed, his time in Constantinople may even have seen Kubrat baptized as a Christian.[108] This was a long-standing imperial policy, but it could backfire with the returned hostages using their Roman education and training against the empire. Like Arminius, Tacfarinas, Alaric and Theoderic the Amal, Kubrat could prove an 'ungrateful' product of the Roman hostage system.[109]

Seemingly by 630, Kubrat was sent back to lead his people on the Ukrainian steppe. Over the course of the next five years, he and his Dulo clan led the Bulgars in the creation of a tribal alliance amongst the various Hunnic, Alan, German, Slav and Turkic tribesmen in the area. The retreat of the West Turkic Khaganate back to the Central Asian Steppe had allowed the Avars to restore some semblance of suzerainty north of the Black Sea, but the loosening of their imperial grip demonstrated by the scattering of the Slavs made them extremely vulnerable. Backed by Heraclius, Kubrat successfully rose in revolt against the Avar khan in 635, founding the 'state' of Old Great Bulgaria around the Sea of Azov and the northern Caucasus.[110]

While Kubrat may have reigned for over three decades and been an important ally of the Romans, little is known about his rule. Phanagoria on the modern Taman peninsula would seem to have been the initial 'capital' of this Bulgar state,[111] although there is some evidence that the focus moved west to Poltava on the Ukrainian steppe, as the Bulgars claimed some formerly Avar territory. Beyond this, there is little evidence that he succeeded in establishing 'Old Great Bulgaria' as anything approaching a state, with it remaining a loose confederation of tribes with the Bulgars as its leaders. Despite the reputed conversion of Kubrat, the Bulgar-led group remained largely shamanistic; indeed, the Bulgars would not convert to Christianity until the late ninth century. This failure to build a coherent and resilient state is best seen in its collapse not long after Kubrat's death.

It is not entirely clear from the historical record when Kubrat died. The *Nominalia of the Bulgarian Khans* records that Kubrat of the Dulo clan ruled for sixty years and was born under the sign of the ox in the Bulgar calendar, but without giving a firm anchor of the date. There is an interpretation that suggests that the *Nominalia* could mean that Kubrat lived for sixty years, having been the rightful ruler from his birth or perhaps the death of his father. Theophanes records that Kubrat died 'in the days of Constantine, who dwelt in the West',[112] with the name 'Constantine' seemingly linked to Constantine IV (668–685); however, Constantine IV never 'dwelt in the West'. Instead, this 'Constantine' should be identified with Constans II, whose regnal name was also Constantine. This may place Kubrat's death during Constans II's Italian campaign of 663–668.[113]

One rather spectacular archaeological find perhaps provides evidence of the Bulgar expansion into the Ukrainian steppe and the interactions between the Romans and the Bulgars in the mid-seventh century. In 1912, Ukrainian villagers discovered the Pereshchepina Treasure near Poltava, a stash of 21kg of gold and 50kg of silver artefacts. The most important of these are some Roman coins and a ring, which indicate the close relationship between Kubrat and the early Heraclian dynasty. The ring is inscribed with the Greek '*Chouvr(á)tou patr(i)k(íou)*', which has been suggested as reflecting not just Kubrat's name but also his position as *patricius*, leading to the treasure site becoming associated with the Bulgar leader's grave. The coins in the treasure date between the reigns of Mauricius and Constans II, with the latest-dated coin being from 646, suggesting that the treasure and therefore Kubrat's death is not from before that date.[114]

Kubrat himself seems to have recognized the potential for the disintegration of his fledgling 'state'. Not long before his death, he reputedly warned his five sons – Batbayan, Kotrag, Asparukh, Kuber and Alcek – 'not to depart under any circumstances from their common life that they might prevail in every way and not be enslaved by another tribe'.[115] They either could not or would not follow his advice. In the face of internal rivalries and pressure from the emerging Khazar Khaganate in the North Caucasus,[116] Old Great Bulgaria disintegrated within a couple of years of Kubrat's death. He was succeeded as leader of the nascent Bulgar-led state by his eldest son, Batbayan, who has been considered to be the Bezmer recorded after Kubrat on the *Nominalia*.[117] If this Batbayan/Bezmer connection is correct, then this second khan of Old Great Bulgaria only ruled for three years before being defeated by the Khazars, perhaps in around 668, living out his life as a subject of the Khazar khagan.[118] The group led by the second brother, Kotrag, possibly a 'personification' of the Kutrigurs, migrated north up the Volga River, settling around its confluence with the Kama River. This became the centre of what was known as the Volga Bulgars, a statelet that was to convert to Islam in the ninth century and survive down until the Mongol conquests of the mid-thirteenth century.[119]

However, while Batbayan likely continued to lead a Bulgar remnant under Khazar suzerainty and Kotrag laid the foundations for a Bulgar state on the Volga, it was the three younger sons of Kubrat who were to be obstacles for the Roman Empire. Two of the sons seem to have briefly ended up under the sway of the Avars along the Danube. The fourth son, seemingly called Kuber, led a mixed group of Bulgars, Slavs, Germans and Roman provincials to settle briefly around Sirmium as a vassal of the Avar khan.[120] After perhaps more than a decade, this Bulgar-led group rose in revolt, escaping south-east into Macedonia in the late 670s/early 680s.[121] There, he appears to have entered into negotiations with Constantine IV over some recognition of his position. These negotiations failed to appease Kuber, as he led his forces in an attempt to capture Thessalonica, which only survived through the intervention of St Demetrius. While this is the last direct mention of him, it could be that the Bulgars that Justinian II had to deal with during his Thessalonica campaign were those of Kuber.[122]

The second brother to fall under the sway of the Avars was Alcek. At some point, he too led his people away from the Avars, arriving in Italy, where he 'reached the Pentapolis, which is near Ravenna, and accepted allegiance to the Christian Empire'.[123] Paul the Deacon tells a slightly different story in that he has Alcek arriving in Italy to seek shelter with the Lombard king Grimuald I, who sent the Bulgars further south to the lands of his son, Romoald of Benevento. Whichever version of Alcek's arrival in Italy is nearer the truth, it would appear that these Bulgars were still a recognizable group by the late eighth century.[124]

While Kuber and Alcek would both have direct interactions with the Roman Empire, the most important of the sons of Kubrat was Asparukh. Crossing the Dneiper and Dneister in c.679,[125] he settled on the Oglos, which was either a river (south of the Danube) or a wedge-shaped strip of land north or at the mouth of the Danube, potentially named for its angular shape.[126] It may be what is now northern Dobruja, surrounded by the Danube to the west and north and by the Black Sea to the east.[127] Such a position would fit in with how Asparukh reputedly 'thought the location secure and invincible from all sides, for it was marshy ahead and surrounded by rivers in other directions. It provided his people, who had been weakened by their division, relief from their enemies.'[128] Asparukh might have thought he and his followers were safe at Oglos, but their arrival on the Danube and decision to raid beyond it was ill-timed. As will be seen, Asparukh's Bulgars drew the ire of Constantine IV. The imperial reaction to this Bulgar intrusion and the ability of Asparukh and his followers to deal with it would have a monumental impact on the future of this nascent Bulgar state.

While there is no clear record of the make-up of his group,[129] much like Kuber and Alcek, Asparukh probably came to lead a varied group of Bulgars, Slavs, Huns, Roman provincials and others. The Slavs in particular became increasingly influential as the decades and centuries progressed, with Asparukh seemingly stationing some of their more organized tribes on his western frontier with the Avars. This influence, coupled with perhaps the lack of Bulgar numbers, played a significant role in the eventual Slavicization of this new Bulgarian state.[130]

One Tribe Left Behind: The Khazars

The last of the threats faced by the Roman Empire in the late seventh century has been mentioned several times already: the Turks. That is because much of what happened along the Danube and in the Balkans with the Avars, Lombards, Slavs and Bulgars has at least some connection to the western advance of the Turks in the sixth and seventh centuries. The origin of this European influence was seemingly the overthrow of the Rouran Khaganate, centred on what is now Mongolia and stretching west towards the Pamir Mountains, by a combination of the Western Wei Chinese and the Turks in the mid-550s. The victorious Turks founded their own extensive khaganate and reputedly chased the Rouran remnant across the Central Asian steppe to the frontiers of Europe, proving a catalyst for many of the problems faced by the Romans in the century before the birth of Justinian II.

This western drive of the Turkic Khaganate to the northern Caucasus and its probing of the Ukrainian steppe likely swept along many of the constituent peoples of what would become the Avars, if they were not the Rouran themselves. As has already been seen, this in turn led to the migration of the Lombards and affected the southern movement of the Slavs. Before the Turkic Khaganate could further interfere more directly in the affairs of Europe, internal matters saw them pull back to the Central Asian steppe, where a civil war split the Turkic Khaganate into two separate halves. This Turkic incursion into Europe may have been short, but it had left a significant legacy in the form of the burgeoning Avar Khanate along the Danube and a single Turkish tribe in the Caucasus which was to have a significant role in the life and reigns of Justinian II: the Khazars.

Much like the majority of the tribes addressed already, there is great difficulty in presenting a clear picture of who these Khazars were. Were they 'an oriental race, with the slanting eyes, black hair, and dark skin typical of many of the peoples of Central Asia'?[131] Or was it that 'their complexions were white, their eyes blue, their hair flowing and predominantly reddish, their bodies large and natures cold. Their general aspect is wild'?[132] A major issue with any such descriptions of the Khazars is that while it may originally have been a single Turkic tribe or ruled by a Turkic clan,[133] what became the Khazar Khaganate encompassed various other tribes and peoples resident in the surrounding area – Kutrigurs, Utigurs, Bulgars, Sabir Huns, Alans and Caucasians, as well as any number of Central Asian, Turkic and proto-Mongolic peoples swept along by the western advance of the Turkic Khaganate.[134] Indeed, there could have been over two dozen ethnic or tribal groups encompassed in this Khazar Khaganate. As well as its various ethnic groups, there may also have been a political division in the top echelons of the khaganate in the form of the 'White Khazars' and the 'Black Khazars'. This may have encouraged some outside observers to see an ethnic division within the ruling Khazar tribe, but it seems that a political division into ruling 'white' warriors and ruled 'black' commoners was frequent in Turkic tribes.[135]

The polyethnic make-up of the nascent Khazar state also affects attempts to identify its predominant language. The language of the Khazars is now extinct, with few indigenous records surviving. It is therefore something of an educated guess that the Khazar elite spoke a form of Common Turkic, but this was not necessarily the main language of the khaganate as a whole. Alanic, proto-Bulgar, Hunnic, Iberian, Oguric and other forms of Turkic were also spoken in the region ruled by the Khazars.[136] There is also considerable discussion over the origins of the name 'Khazar' itself, with connections made to various Turkic roots, personal or tribal names, Chinese ethnonyms or even a derivation through Middle Persian of the Roman title of 'Caesar'.[137]

Another of the languages spoken in the lands of the khaganate reflects perhaps the most famous development amongst the Khazars: Hebrew. It appears to have arrived with various Jewish groups escaping persecution by Roman authorities throughout the seventh century and beyond. Their influence would seemingly see the Khazars convert to Judaism sometime in the eighth or ninth century. Doubts still exist about this conversion, or aspects of it,[138] but for the most part it has been accepted as having a basis in fact, even if it was just the Khazar court or elite who converted. By accepting Judaism, the Khazar elite 'may well have been trying to enjoy the benefits of a high religion without coming under the cultural influence of Byzantium or the Arabs'.[139] This Jewish conversion took place outside the chronological scope of this work, but it does present an interesting aspect of the potential contacts being made between this Turkic state and the ancient world.

Despite some success from Armenian and Albanian missionaries in spreading Christianity into Khazar lands,[140] before the Jewish conversion (and surely during it), the populations of the khaganate remained predominantly pagan. While direct information of the exact form Khazar religion took is fleeting, the likelihood is that they followed some form of shamanist worship of the sky god Tengri, which was prominent on the Central Asian steppe and with which the Ashina clan had a close association. There was also support for various cults – sun, trees, ancestors – and practices such as horse sacrifice and offerings to fire, water and the moon. Furthermore, it will be seen in their interactions with Justinian II that there was also a belief in the afterlife and the practice of human sacrifice...

The gradual move towards monotheism in some parts of Khazar society may be part of more general developments within the khaganate in terms of structure. Some Khazars and parts of the khaganate population remained nomadic, but some of the Khazar elite became more sedentary in reaction to their rise in status as rulers of a sizeable kingdom of some longevity. In particular, the ruling family is seen living in a palace. Despite such developments and the growth of the Khazar Khaganate into a power of some significance in eastern politics, they would still be regarded as barbarians two centuries after the time of Justinian II. The tenth-century emperor Constantine VII would advise his son to 'never marry a Khazar',[141] although this might be influenced by previous emperors having done so, including as will be seen, Justinian II himself.

Unfortunately, the position of the Khazars north of the Caucasus and hugging the coast of the Caspian rather than the Black Sea saw them removed from the general attention of the historical sources. They therefore drop in and out of view dependent on their direct interaction with the dominant peoples of the East – Romans, Persians, Arabs and their various Caucasian vassals. This leaves the timing of the establishment of the Khazar Khaganate open to speculation. The civil war that split the Turkic Khaganate seems to have occurred in the early 580s, but it is difficult to accept that Khazar control over the northern Caucasus was established straightaway. The West Turkic Khaganate may even have continued to exert some suzerainty over the Caucasus until its break-up under pressure in the mid-seventh century from the armies of Tang China.[142]

A continued West Turkic presence in the Caucasus until c.630 and beyond could affect the proposed initial contact between the Khazars and the Romans. In the midst of the last Romano-Persian War, Heraclius, desperate for allies, reached out to the Turkic overlords of the northern Caucasus through a diplomat called Andrew. This embassy bore fruit in 626 as a raiding party burst through the Caucasian passes and swept across Persian territory, carrying off significant booty and captives. The identity of these raiders is the crux of the problem. They are identified as the Khazars by the likes of Theophanes, but in the mid-620s, they may not as yet have established their prominence, so it could have been some of the other Turkic tribes or even the West Turkic Khaganate itself.[143]

The Turkic/Khazar khagan felt that his 626 raid had been profitable enough to accept Heraclius' invitation to join him on campaign in 627. To meet up with the Roman emperor and his army near Tiflis (modern Tblisi), the khagan had his forces capture Derbent, gaining control of the pass through the Caucasus along the western coast of the Caspian Sea. The meeting between the khagan and Heraclius saw much ceremonial exchanging of gifts, swearing of allegiance and even the proposing of marriage between Heraclius' daughter, Eudocia, and either the khagan or his son.[144] This Romano-Turkic army forced the retreat of the local Persian army but then failed to capture Tiflis from its pro-Persian garrison, causing most of the Turks to return home, leaving some cavalry to join Heraclius' army. These Turks also took advantage of Heraclius' defeat of Persia by attacking Tiflis again in 628/629. This time, the khagan's men were able to storm the walls, and 'a dark shadow of dread came upon the pitiful inhabitants of the city … the wailing and groaning ended and no one was left alive'.[145] This success emboldened the Turks to invade Armenia, forcing the newly enthroned Persian king, Shahrbaraz, to dispatch a force of 10,000 men, only for it to be lured into a trap and destroyed.[146]

Despite their roles in jump-starting Heraclius' victory and undermining Shahrbaraz's reign, there is almost total silence from Roman sources about the Khazars for the next half-century after 630. It was during this period, if they had not already by the time of Heraclius' Turkic dealings, that the Khazars established their dominance in the northern Caucasus and laid the foundations of their khaganate.[147] As already seen, the Khazar state was likely well-enough established by the late 660s to break up Old Great Bulgaria and perhaps impose some suzerainty over the Bulgars who remained north of the Black Sea and along the Volga.[148]

However, it was not until their interactions with Justinian II that Roman attention turned back to the Khazars, with Justinian's time in Khazaria giving the clearest insight into Khazar culture and politics to this point. He would find a well-established khaganate ruling over the territory north of the Caucasus between the Black and Caspian Seas, pushing its suzerainty onto the Ukrainian steppe and even interfering in Roman Crimea. The Khazars seemed to follow a dual kingship, with a lesser king – *îšâ* or *bek* – leading the army, while the greater Khazar – *xâqân* – was a more sacral position, seemingly detached from daily rule.[149] With the sacral position of the khagan came significant court ceremony, although it must be asked if the Khazar ceremony was influenced by their contacts with the Romans, Persians and Chinese. Part of the khagan's initiation ritual was to be strangled until he declared how many years he wanted to reign (seemingly with an upper limit of forty years), at the end of which period, his nobles would kill him. Entering the presence of the khagan involved barefoot prostration and purifying fire, while there were significant rituals attached to a khagan's burial, including the site being obscured from view during construction and then covered over by a redirected river.[150]

It was not just the Khazar court that demonstrated significant development. The khagans may have been protected by a field army called the *Ursiyya*, of between 7,000 and 12,000 men at its height, while calling in retinues, reserves, tribute and hiring mercenaries could see a Khazar central army of double or even treble that. However, it must be noted that while it has been suggested that this unit originated amongst the khagan's Alan subjects, there is little evidence for it before the tenth century, where it appears to be a unit of Muslim origin.[151] The Khazar army also had some leadership infrastructure beyond being under the purview of the *îšâ*/*bek*, as there are subordinate officers called *tarkhans* mentioned. Similarly, the Khazar government appointed an administrative official called a *tudun*, one of whom will be seen operating in Roman territory, suggesting that he could be something of a diplomat.

This administrative control of their lands allowed the Khazars to exploit their position along the northern routes of the Silk Road. The relative peace and stability their dominance brought to the region likely encouraged the growth in import and export trade through Khazar lands, which they then benefited from by taxing transit. They also developed quite a diverse economy, employing both pastoralism and agriculture, extensive fishing of the Volga and some local manufacturing, which further bolstered the Khazar export market. The Khazars would also become a major player in the slave trade. Such an extensive and varied trade network along important east–west and north–south routes was reflected in not just the duties and tithes exacted on merchants and tribes, but also in the need for a commercial tribunal to be established to deal with trade disputes.[152]

While the focus on Justinian II means that Romano-Khazar relations are to the fore, it must be remembered that their position in the northern Caucasus meant that the Khazars also had to confront the advancing power of the Arabs. Muslim forces were probing the Caucasian passes perhaps as early as 642, before striking through the mountains to Khazar territory by the end of the decade. This campaign culminated in an attack on the Khazar capital at Balanjar in 652, where the Arabs under Abd ar-Rahman b. Rabiah were heavily defeated. The Khazars repelled a further Arab invasion three years later, although they felt that the lure of Balanjar was such that they moved their capital further north. These reverses and their subsequent distraction with internal struggles meant that the Arabs held back from further Khazar attacks throughout the remainder of the seventh century. The Khazars did not respond in kind. A minor raid was resisted by the Albanians in 661/662, while a much larger attack between 683 and 685 cut a significant swathe across the region, with princes of Iberia and Armenia killed in the process and large amounts of treasure and prisoners taken back north. It would not be until after Justinian II's death and the tightening of Umayyad control over Armenia that Arab-Khazar conflict would begin again in around 713. It would then continue intermittently throughout much of the eighth century, characterized more by raids back and forth through the Caucasus rather than large battles or any definitive territorial acquisitions.[153]

The Roman Empire may have shrunk in size as the seventh century progressed, but if anything, that reduction in territory was accompanied by an increase in enemies. The largely tripartite division of opposition in c.600 that encapsulated the Avars, Lombards and Persians expanded to include the Arabs, Bulgars, Slavs and Khazars by the middle of the century. This longer list of enemies was no longer merely nibbling at frontier territories of the empire, such as the African desert, Spanish coast, Danubian bank or

Mesopotamia. The 'zero-sum game' that was Romano-Persian warfare had been replaced by the increasingly permanent losses of important provinces like Syria and Egypt. Much of the Justinianic reconquests were also under severe and ultimately irresistible pressure. But even the now core Balkan and Anatolian provinces were not safe, with Slavs, Bulgars and Arabs wearing away at Roman control.

The Roman ability to respond to this cavalcade of catastrophes had not been helped by many of these problems being interrelated. The Roman-sponsored actions of the Avars had led to the Lombard invasion of Italy and the Slavic settlement of much of the Balkans, while the westward moves of the Avars and then the Bulgars had been instigated by the Turkic tribes of the Central Asian steppe. It must be remembered that while the barbarian opponents of the empire in Europe are labelled as 'Avar', 'Lombard', 'Bulgar' and 'Slav', their actual make-up was far more varied as migrating tribes swept up other peoples as they passed by and integrated locals when they arrived. Paul the Deacon's pronouncement about the Lombards of Alboin likely speaks to the multiculturalism of many of these barbarian 'nations': 'It is certain that Alboin then brought with him to Italy many men from various peoples who either other kings or himself had taken. Whence, even until today, we call the villages in which they dwell Gepidan, Bulgarian, Sarmatian, Pannonian, Suabian, Norican, or by other names of this kind.'[154] Such variegated groups may have seen them fight with a form of combined arms, as different tribes could have different skills in the waging of war. This could make it more difficult for the kings, khans and khagans to lead, but if they succeeded in forging a coherent force, the Romans would find such multi-faceted warfare from militarized peoples very difficult to resist.

This incidental 'combined arms' of Roman opponents highlights that these barbarian confederations should not be thought of as bands of marauding horsemen spreading out across formerly imperial territory or squashing infantry-based Roman armies. While there were important horse elements of varying sizes within all of the opponents of the Roman Empire in the seventh century, the imperial military nadir is not to be explained solely as the triumph of cavalry over infantry. Not only did the infantryman remain the core of the Roman army, he was also a central figure amongst its enemies. While the Roman army may have taken on tactics, attributes and personnel from their Germanic, Hunnic and Turkic neighbours, the opposite will also have been true in order for them to fight in, capture and rule over the kind of terrain that the Roman legionary had for centuries. Certainly, several of the tribes faced by the Romans, particularly the Germans and Slavs, had little experience with horses and therefore fought mostly on foot. However, the best example of this continued preference for infantry is amongst the Arabs. A general assumption about the Arab conquests is that they came on the back of a horse (or even a camel), but while the great Arab armies who defeated the Romans and Persians at Yarmuk, Qadisiyyah, Nahavand and elsewhere contained strong cavalry corps, those victories were built on platforms provided by steadfast Arab infantry. This infantry bulwark would be continued in the Umayyad army, particularly that of Syria, where it was confronted by a Roman army and mountainous terrain.

Under such relentless pressure from all directions and in various forms, it is unsurprising that the Roman Empire was in considerable trouble in the mid-seventh century. Indeed, it is a testament to the infrastructure, organization, belief in tradition and sheer bloody-mindedness of the Romans that they did not allow their empire to be swept away by the twin barrage of the collapse of the Danube frontier and the Arab conquests. While it would not all be plain sailing, significant aspects of the Romans living in an 'empire that would not die'[155] were established during the lifetime of Justinian II.

Chapter 3

Before Power: The Early Life of Justinian II

'By ancestry, I was born to rule.'

Nelson Mandela

In Proud Imperial Purple? The Where and When of Justinian II's Birth

It was into this severely chastened Roman Empire faced with almost relentless pressure on all sides that Flavius Justinianus was born to the emperor Constantine IV and his wife, Anastasia. However, such is the paucity of the source record for the late 660s that the exact date and place of birth for the new imperial heir is not firmly attested. The patchy source record and the indiction dating system employed by the likes of Theophanes means that Justinian's birth can only be placed between 668 and 669. On the surface, this somewhat vague dating might not seem to be of too much importance, as there is no hint of his legitimacy or parentage being tied up in when he was born; however, there is one potential consequence of the exact date of Justinian's birth: whether or not he was a *porphyrogenitus* – 'born-in-the-purple'.

While this title would grow to encapsulate being born in a porphyry-lined bed chamber set aside for the birth of imperial children,[1] before then it would apply to those born during the reign of their father. This seems like it must have been a usual occurrence in Roman dynastic affairs; however, while there were some sons born to reigning *Augusti* during the first century – Britannicus to Claudius and the unnamed son of Domitian – it was not until 180 that a 'born-in-the-purple' son came to the throne when Commodus succeeded his father Marcus Aurelius. It was another 157 years before it happened again when the sons of Constantine I succeeded him in 337. While there would be three more during the late fourth/early fifth century – Valentinian II, Honorius and Theodosius II – it would not become a regular occurrence, not happening again for another 233 years when Heraclius was succeeded by Heraclius Constantine III and Heraklonas in 641.

There is also little evidence that this status had become an important, official measure of a claim to the throne. While the term *porphyrogenitus* was mentioned during the sixth century, it was not securely used until 846 and not made common until the accession of Constantine VII in the early tenth century.[2] That said, the fifth century usurper Flavius Marcianus tried to bolster his claim to the imperial throne by highlighting that his wife, the imperial princess Leontia, had been born after her father, Leo I, had come to the throne in 457. The imperial incumbent, Zeno, was married to Leontia's older sister, Ariadne, who was born before Leo I's accession. In opposition to the primogeniture case for Ariadne and therefore Zeno, Marcianus could suggest that Leontia was the preferred candidate of God and so he had a superior claim. The term *porphyrogenite* is not used in the sources with regard to the status of Leontia, but this incident does show that the idea of prevalence based on being 'born-in-the-purple' was around as early as 479.

It must also be noted that while it was not a generally frequent occurrence for sons to be born and then succeed imperial fathers, by the time of Justinian II's birth, it had become something of a family tradition for the Heraclian dynasty, with each emperor so far succeeded by a son born during his reign – Heraclius > Heraclius Constantine III > Constans II > Constantine IV. Perhaps for some it was becoming a status tied up in Heraclian legitimacy, or at least in the superstition surrounding the rule and good fortune of the dynasty. It may therefore have been dynastically useful for Justinian to be viewed as *porphyrogenitus*, particularly when his reign came under threat. If being 'born-in-the-purple' was an important part of the imperial Heraclian claim, the biggest threat came in the form of Justinian's younger brother, Heraclius. While there is little definitive information about him, Heraclius was definitely born after Constantine IV's accession, making him a *porphyrogenitus*. If there were doubts over Justinian being 'born-in-the-purple', it could have been an avenue of support for Heraclius against his brother.

So, was Justinian 'born-in-the-purple'? His father, Constantine IV, became emperor on the murder of the bathing Constans II on 15 September 668, so to be *porphyrogenitus*, Justinian would need to have been born after that date. Given that his birth is usually recorded as either 668 or 669, and that the indiction year used in the recording of the dates involved began on 1 September, the likelihood, statistically at least, is that Justinian's birthday was after 15 September 668, therefore making him 'born-in-the-purple'. Sources like Theophanes do not mention Justinian being a *porphyrogenitus*, but this does not negate the probability. As already mentioned, Theophanes was relying on sources which were likely to present Justinian in the least legitimizing terms possible – perhaps intentionally leaving out any status he had as *porphyrogenitus*, if it was thought of as being of any importance in the early eighth century. Theophanes was himself writing before being *porphyrogenitus* became more important in the mid-ninth century. It is more likely that the absence of mention of Justinian as a *porphyrogenitus* is a reflection of the lack of importance of that status in the late seventh century, rather than any source cover-up or Justinian being born before 15 September 668.

As for exactly where Justinian was born, there is little direct information, but there is enough to make an informed deduction through the attempted actions of his grandfather. As already mentioned, Constans II tried to get his wife and children to join him in the West, an action that fuelled speculation that he was planning to move the imperial capital to Sicily or Italy. Because the Constantinopolitan public and probably some of the imperial court refused to allow this, it can be conjectured that Fausta and her children remained in the imperial capital.[3] And while Constantine IV himself may have ventured out beyond the city walls in his role as co-emperor, the threats faced by the empire in the late 660s will have made it more than likely that his pregnant wife, Anastasia, would not have joined him. This makes it likely that the future Justinian II was born within Constantinople and probably in the imperial palace.

However, in later centuries, a legend grew up that Justinian was born on the island of Cyprus.[4] Certainly, Cyprus was a focus of imperial attention as Arab incursions saw it become something of a 'no man's land'; for example, Muawiyah had led a sizeable attack on the island in 648/649, reputedly with 1,700 ships, capturing the city of Constantia and sacking much of the island, only to be forced to retreat back to Syria by an expedition led by the *cubicularius* Kakorizos.[5] As will be seen, Justinian himself would have positive dealings with the Cypriots, which no doubt coloured their perception of him and encouraged their building upon any rumoured connection he had with the island to claim him as one of their own. However, the exact status of Cyprus in 668/669 is uncertain, but it does appear that the Arabs had obtained some kind of hold over the island in the 650s and there is no record of Constantine IV or his wife, Anastasia, campaigning or visiting the island. This suggests that this 'tradition is in all probability groundless'.[6]

While there is plenty of information about Justinian's father, there is a significant lack of information about his mother, Anastasia. Indeed, there is nothing known about her early life. She only enters the historical record upon the assassination of Constans II and the accession of her husband as Constantine IV, with very little known of her origins. She is likely to have been of a young age when she bore Justinian, as Constantine was only 17. The aforementioned claim that Justinian II was born on Cyprus could hint at Cypriot origins for the empress, but just because this is the only suggestion from the ancient sources regarding Anastasia's origins does not mean that this wild premise recorded nearly three centuries later should be accepted. It could be that this supposed Cypriot origin of Anastasia and therefore Justinian II stems from similar rumours surrounding Theodora, empress of Justinian I. Perhaps Constantine IV's reverence for the first Justinian, an error made by other sources or a kernel of truth/rumour helped form this imperial Cypriot tradition, however erroneous it may be.[7] The likelihood is that Anastasia came from a high-ranking Roman and even Constantinopolitan family, although there were plenty of instances of empresses from beyond the capital and even of not completely Roman origins. Some of the Eastern Roman emperors since 395 had had wives from regional nobilities, the pre-existing imperial family or some mixed heritage, but few if any had married out and out foreigners – it would be Justinian II who 'shattered the tradition'.[8]

As mentioned above, Justinian was not the only child born to the union of Constantine IV and Anastasia. They had a second son, given the dynastic name of Heraclius, but almost nothing is recorded about him. He was still alive in 684/685 to be mentioned in the *Liber Pontificalis*, so it might be assumed that he outlived his father, who died in 685, but even that is speculative, along with anything else beyond. If Constantine and Anastasia had any other children beyond Justinian and Heraclius, male or female, there is no record of them, whether they lived to adulthood or not.

That is not to say that the imperial family was limited to the emperor, empress and their two sons. Constantine IV had two brothers – technically co-emperors – Heraclius and Tiberius. It also appears likely that their mother, Fausta, was still alive upon the assassination of her husband. Apart from them being younger than Constantine IV, there is little evidence of the exact age of these two younger sons of Constans II. They had both been born by the time Constans II left for Italy in 659, as they are recorded being elevated to co-emperors, a position Constantine IV had held since 654. All this can tell us about Heraclius and Tiberius is that they were both at least

8 years old but no more than 16 by the death of their father and the birth of Justinian II in 668/669. This could have seen Heraclius and Tiberius be more like elder siblings or cousins to Justinian and Heraclius than uncles. That said, the later actions of Constantine IV in his zealous guarding of his own imperial seniority may have seen any interaction or influence of his brothers over his young sons carefully monitored, with the emperor watching 'his brothers closely as they grew to maturity, lest they display signs of undue ambition'.[9]

Limiting any undo influences from family or others will have encouraged tight control of the education of the imperial children. While there is little information of what an imperial education looked like in the second half of the seventh century,[10] the Romans continued to place a high value on learning, so Justinian and Heraclius will have been well-educated. Given his name, it can be imagined that Justinian was given a thorough education in the history of the Heraclian and Justinianic dynasties. The great campaigns, law-giving and building that took place under Justinian I will have stoked the imagination and ambition of the young Justinian II. This was surely what Constantine IV, himself no stranger to the pressures of a name heavy with historical significance, intended in breaking with the family custom of calling the eldest son Constantine, Heraclius or a combination of both.[11] The military successes of the Heraclian dynasty were perhaps not as spectacular as the reconquests of Justinian I – certainly not since Heraclius' victory over Persia – but they were no less important to and had more direct involvement in the shaping of Justinian II. Not only had they produced the world that he lived in and his right to the imperial throne, they were his example to follow in leading the embattled bulwark of political, social and religious civilization that the Roman Empire had become in the face of the Muslim caliphate and pagan tribes. Making him think it was his duty and even birthright not only to safeguard the Roman Empire but to reclaim lost lands does seem to have had an influence on Justinian II, although not always for the better.

An Imperial Countenance and Character?

While the making of imperial busts seems to have fallen out of artistic favour or to have been beyond the abilities of Roman sculptors during the fifth century, there is one sculpture that has been identified by some to be of Justinian II. This is the so-called 'Carmagnola', a porphyry head located on the south-western corner wall of the treasury of St Mark's in Venice.

Despite its Venetian surroundings, it is of Constantinopolitan origin and was likely looted in the sack of Constantinople during the Fourth Crusade in 1204. The name 'Carmagnola' stems from the nickname of the Venetian *comandante di ventura* Francesco Bussone, who was beheaded in St Mark's Square on 5 May 1432. But in an era not known for its imperial busts, why then is it suggested that the 'Carmagnola' is of Justinian II? Beyond its likely Constantinopolitan origin and sporting of an imperial diadem, the basis for this Justinianic identification focuses on the statue's mutilated nose. It is hardly surprising to see an ancient statue missing its nose, as this kind of *rhinokopia* was hardly rare; however, it has been proposed that the 'damage' to the 'Carmagnola' is not the result of later mistreatment/mishandling, but was a feature of the original sculpture. As this statue's nose was not as badly mutilated as Justinian's, it was further proposed that Justinian attempted to have his nose repaired through some primitive corrective surgery.[12] There is no backing for such a proposal in the written sources and it does not synchronize with traditional depictions of Roman emperors. Would a sculptor really have risked his head by portraying Justinian in a less-than-perfect way? It seems far more likely that the rounded edges of the displaced 'Carmagnola' nose come from polishing or weathering since its initial damaging.

Aside from the mangled nose and the diadem, there is little to associate the 'Carmagnola' with Justinian II. The statue is beardless, which in itself does not disqualify it as being Justinian, for while that emperor was usually depicted as sporting a thin beard, his earliest coins have him without one. The short hair of the 'Carmagnola' is also not much of an obstacle to a Justinianic identification. However, a facial hair issue arises with the suggestion that the 'Carmagnola' emperor appears to be much older than Justinian II when he was beardless. Another more problematic issue is with the shape of the head of the 'Carmagnola'. It has a somewhat square, rounded face, which is slightly asymmetrical, possibly meaning it was meant to be viewed from an angle rather than straight on. Justinian II is frequently depicted on his coins and mosaics as having a narrow face and pointed chin. While there could have been some change in Justinian's countenance as he aged, it is hard to shake the thought that the 'Carmagnola' looks nothing like Justinian II.

So, if the 'Carmagnola' is not Justinian II, who might it be? While there is no definitive identification, it could be that the statue head belongs in the early fourth century. The large frog-like eyes of the 'Carmagnola' are similar to those of some Constantinian statues and coins. Also, while it was used in imperial buildings since its first discovery in the early first century, the use of porphyry in statues was more prevalent in the late third/early fourth century – such as the Porphyry Tetrarchs, which are also in St Mark's Square, near the 'Carmagnola'. It could be then that the 'Carmagnola' was part of the enthroned statues of Constantine's sons 'in the region of the so-called gate of Philadelphion',[13] targeted by the Crusaders in 1204, but survived in some form to become known as the 'True Judges' by the fifteenth century. However, caution should be urged that 'there are too many discrepancies between those groups and *Parastaseis*'s descriptions here to permit any certainty'.[14]

If Justinian II looked nothing like the 'Carmagnola', what exactly did he look like? Thankfully, there are some hints of his appearance in surviving sources. While sculpture may have fallen out of favour, coins continued to depict the emperor, and the sixth and seventh centuries saw mosaic grow as a medium of imperial propaganda. As already mentioned, the coins from the earliest part of his reign depict Justinian with a beardless, youthful face, 'yet his hollow cheeks and very pointed chin lend a certain air of distinction'.[15] His hair is curled and hung at ear length, with his fringe visible across his forehead. Within a year of his accession, the numismatic Justinian began to sport a thin beard. This could be a personal fashion choice, but could also demonstrate a need to not appear as young and inexperienced as he still was. The curled hair and fringe remained a feature of his coins throughout his reign. It does seem that within a year, Justinian had chosen to appear increasingly like his father on his coins, with perhaps the exception of a slightly narrower face.

As for mosaic, the Justinianic focus falls on the imperial mosaic in Sant'Apollinare in Classe, Ravenna, which depicts the granting of *privilegia* by Constantine IV to a representative of the Archbishop of Ravenna. The presence of Constantine's brothers on this mosaic presents another level of importance to be looked at later, but it is the figure to the extreme left that demands attention here. It is Justinian II himself. His portrayal is idealized, for while he does appear youthful, he has been made to look older and taller than he really was – as the mosaic was from 681 at the latest, Justinian will have been a maximum of 13 years old:

'Clad in a short brown tunic with elaborate embroidery on the sleeves and around the skirt, Justinian stands clutching a model church building, symbolizing, no doubt, his father's benefactions to the bishopric of Ravenna. The young prince's legs are encased in white stockings, and on his feet are black shoes with pointed toes exactly like those worn by his uncles. A small circlet indicating his princely rank rests on his light brown hair. He is a handsome boy, in spite of the fact that his youthful gaze stares out at the world with a somewhat furtive expression.'[16]

His dress is so different from that of both his father and uncles that it raises questions about its meaning and even the suggestion of whether Justinian was originally part of the mosaic scene. If Justinian was depicted on the original mosaic during the reign of his father and made to look older, then why was his younger brother Heraclius not similarly depicted?

Another avenue of evidence of what Justinian II might have looked like comes from his being the latest in a line of emperors from the same family. Any descriptions of his imperial predecessors might contain some family traits. The founder of the dynasty, Heraclius, is described as 'handsome, tall, braver than others and a fighter'[17] and 'robust, with a broad chest, beautiful blue eyes, golden hair, fair complexion and wide thick beard'.[18] The golden hair appears to be something of a Heraclian family attribute, with both Constantine IV and Justinian II depicted with similar-coloured hair on the Sant'Apollinare in Classe mosaic. Might this have seen Justinian also as handsome, broad-chested, tall, brave, robust and of fair complexion? Sporting a beard appears to have been something of a family fashion/traditional choice as well, although there are some differences. Numismatically, Heraclius and Constans II are depicted with much bushier beards than other Heraclians. Could this bigger beard be part of an attempt to highlight their seniority? That said, when Justinian II started to have his own son, Tiberius, depicted on coins, he does not have a bushy beard, but the young co-emperor is of a similar size, merely lacking the thin beard.

Given that several of its members suffered from *rhinokopia* during the seventh century, could it be that the male line of the Heraclian dynasty all had a prominent proboscis? This is likely looking for a connection between the prominence of the Heraclians and the rise in *rhinokopia* that is not there. At the very least, it would be expected that any such 'Heraclian nose' would be featured in the sources. Of course, it must be remembered that it was not just the mosaic in Sant'Apollinare in Classe that provided an idealized depiction of Justinian. His coins and any other propaganda represent an ideal rather than a realistic representation. This is a phenomenon that exists throughout all imperial depictions, but is perhaps exemplified with Justinian II in particular as the coinage of his second reign continued to depict him with a nose, despite the *rhinokopia* inflicted upon him at his first deposition.

The imperial heritage that may have bestowed physical traits upon Justinian II will also have influenced various aspects of his personality, either through genetic predisposition or the surroundings of his upbringing. It could be that Justinian II's interest in building and theology was influenced by that of Justinian I;[19] however, Justinian II aimed to be much more hands-on than his namesake, who had rather effectively delegated political, religious and military affairs. In this aim, Justinian II showed himself not only a worthy successor to the name 'Justinian' in religion and architecture, but he also lived up to the example established by his great-great grandfather, Heraclius. In squaring up to the rampaging Sassanid Persians, Heraclius 'revived the old Roman tradition of the emperor as personal commander of his forces in the field, a practice that Justinian's more immediate predecessors had continued',[20] and one that Justinian himself was to follow, marking him as potentially brave.

Merely being a Heraclian will have influenced Justinian's mindset. With the repeated succession of fathers and sons during the seventh century on the backdrop of external pressures and internal ructions,[21] 'the Heraclians seemed destined to reign forever'.[22] Any such propagandist crowing cannot have deflated 'Justinian's already abundant self-confidence'.[23] It must be asked if this prolonged dynastic rule could have bred complacency and/or arrogance in Justinian, something potentially exacerbated by his being handsome. While a certain haughtiness was to be expected in the occupant of the Roman imperial throne, it could be that Justinian took it to a level that some found unacceptable, or at least that is what the negative sources might want believed. The potential for Justinian to succumb to the emotional outbursts that he was accused of could also have been a family trait, as Heraclius and Heraclius Constantine III are recorded crying in each other's arms upon the former's return to Constantinople after the war with Persia.[24] All of this may have moulded a man with 'considerable self-assurance ... [who was] undeniably intelligent and possessed of a genuine interest in affairs of the state'.[25] It may also have made him arrogant and so wrapped up in his right to rule that it blinded him to his own mistakes and incited his rage and vengeance if and when he thought his 'divine right' was being challenged.

Moulding a Young Mind: The Reign of Constantine IV

Given that there is little known about the day-to-day upbringing of Justinian II, it is difficult to state with any certainty the level of parental influence the heir to the throne was under. However, as Justinian spent the entirety of his life up to his accession under the reign of his father, who was a dynamic and active emperor, Constantine IV and his actions surely had a significant impact on Justinian II. Therefore, it is necessary to look at Constantine IV's time as emperor not just due to the effect it had on the empire that Justinian was to inherit, but also for its potential direct or indirect impact on the young Justinian. And the near seventeen-year reign of Constantine IV was certainly littered with several important events.

From its very outset, Constantine's reign began with significant pressures on the imperial family. It had only come about through the murder of Constans II, which, despite the unpopularity his six-year absence from Constantinople and other policies had caused, would still have been a tremendous shock to the Heraclian system. There was also Constantine's relative youth, being just 16 years old upon his accession, and the myriad problems he inherited from his father. Even before his accession, Constantine was having to take on a leadership role at Constantinople through not just Constans' absence in the West but also the incipient revolt of Saborius in the East. Upon hearing of the Armeniac *strategos*' reaching out to Muawiyah, offering to subject the Roman state to the caliphate in return for Umayyad aid, Constantine and his advisors responded quickly and effectively. The eunuch *cubicularius* Andrew was dispatched to Damascus to treat with the caliph, and while he was put under pressure to match the outrageous demands agreed to by Saborius' representative, Sergios, Andrew held his own. He ridiculed Sergios and Saborius, reminding Muawiyah of the respect, tradition and remaining strength of the empire before departing.

This might not seem like any kind of victory for Andrew and his imperial master, but the *cubicularius* was not finished yet. While Sergios agreed to supply Muawiyah with financial control of much of Asia Minor in return for military aid, Andrew headed north to Melitene and Arabissos, finding many of the passes were under the command of loyalist officers. He organized for Sergios to be imprisoned and brought to him. Remembering an insult about his eunuch status made in the presence of the caliph, Andrew had the rebel castrated and impaled on a stake. The *cubicularius* had also been sure to report the movements of Saborius and the Arab army of Fudhala to Constantine, who responded by sending a force under Nikephoros the *patricius* to intercept the rebel *strategos*. This rapid action brought an end to the revolt, although not quite in the way that might be expected. Saborius moved to Hexapolis in Bithynia to give battle, but during his preparations, his horse bolted and he smashed his head on the city gate, killing the rebel and the rebellion before it had faced its first military test.

While the Armeniac forces returned to their imperial loyalty, there was still the substantial Umayyad force of Fudhala in Roman territory. Rather than order a retreat, Muawiyah sent reinforcements under his son, Yazid. This combined Arab force marched as far as Chalcedon, taking numerous prisoners and then moving on to Phrygian Amorion, which they captured and garrisoned with 5,000 men before returning to Syria. However, Fudhala and Yazid did not count on Constantine and Andrew being willing to campaign in the dead of winter. Even in heavy snow, Andrew got his army to Amorion and then over its walls, massacring the entire Arab garrison.[26]

If the dealing with Saborius was something of an imperial audition, as soon as he became Constantine IV, he was to be confronted with a similar obstacle. The soldiers who had signally failed to protect his father decided to raise their own emperor. Their choice fell on an Armenian called Mezizios, supposedly because 'he was very handsome and in the full bloom of youth'.[27] It is more likely that he was a high-ranking member of Constans' army. In a letter to Leo III, Pope Gregory II referred to Mezizios as the *comes* of the Opsikion, which in 668 was the emperor's personal army rather than a thematic force. Even later sources such as Michael the Syrian and the *Chronicle of 1234* list Mezizios as a *patricius*.[28] There is some suggestion that Mezizios was elevated against his will or that he took action at the behest of Sicilian bishops who viewed Constans as a Monothelite heretic. However it came about, the rebellion lasted up to seven months,[29] although the source material is divided on how it ended. Theophanes has Constantine lead a large naval expedition to Sicily, where he defeated and killed Mezizios and the murderers of his father (the use of the plural, 'murderers', suggests that Andrew, son of Troilus, had not acted alone) before returning east to be crowned emperor.[30] The likes of the *Liber Pontificalis* have it that loyalist troops from the Italian and African exarchates, along with Pope Vitalian, defeated and killed Mezizios, sending his head to Constantinople.[31] If Constantine had had to campaign in Sicily, it could be that he missed the birth of Justinian or at the very least was not around in the early months of his son's life.

Another potential obstacle for Constantine to deal with early in his reign was a protest amongst the Anatolic army at Chrysopolis in 669/670. They complained over how Constantine had severely limited the imperial power of both of his brothers, Heraclius and Tiberius, despite all three sons of

Constans II being crowned. The Anatolic officers proclaimed, 'We believe in a Trinity! Let us crown the three!', suggesting that at the very least Heraclius and Tiberius had no authority and perhaps had not been crowned at all. Constantine decided that he could not accept an army command attempting to influence the imperial throne. Therefore, while the patrician Theodore of Koloneia was sent to harangue the soldiers, Constantine met with some of the leaders on the promise that he would take their grievances to the Senate – instead he had those leaders hanged at Sykai. While Theophanes records that Constantine had the noses of his brothers slit in connection with this Anatolic protest, it will be seen later that the argument over the position of Heraclius and Tiberius would rumble on for more than a decade.[32] It should be noted, though, that Theophanes' dating of any such Anatolic protest and even parts of the story itself can be called into question through the record of Michael the Syrian, as will be seen below on Constantine IV's relations with his brothers.

The 'First Arab Siege of Constantinople'

Within months of his accession, Constantine IV had seemingly faced three rebellions against his authority and had succeeded in facing them all down. The revolts in the provinces will not have had much impact on the young Justinian as he grew up in the splendour of Constantinople, surrounded by its culture, status, architecture and politics; however, the tension between Constantine and his brothers may have had more of an effect on Justinian. And any internal disagreement was about to be put under even more pressure as there was something much more dangerous on the horizon. This was because the strikes of Fudhala and Yazid deep into Roman territory in support of Saborius had not occurred in a vacuum. Throughout the 660s, Arab raids struck into and even wintered on Roman territory virtually every year,[33] and were ultimately a prelude to the most important event of Constantine IV's reign: the 'First Arab Siege of Constantinople'.[34]

The traditional interpretation of this 'first' Arab attack on the imperial capital, based almost solely on the account of Theophanes, saw Muawiyah build on the repetitive success of his raiders, the ability of Fudhala and Yazid to penetrate as far as Chalcedon and perhaps even words of discontent amongst the Anatolic army. By the winter of 670/671, Fudhala was able to winter in Cyzicus, a major town on the Sea of Marmara, adding further impetus to Muawiyah's plan to strike at Constantinople.[35] This was not to be an opportunistic raid. The caliph organized a series of advances by land and sea to set up a string of supply bases. By 673/674, a squadron under Qais had wintered in Cilicia and reached Lycia, while that of Muhammad b. Abd Allah had occupied Smyrna; Busr raided Roman territory, perhaps to keep Roman forces distracted, allowing Khalid to lead another overland expedition in support of these naval advances.[36]

By the outset of the campaigning season of 674, there was an Arab flotilla anchored on the European side of the Bosphorus and a Muslim force had landed at Hebdomon and was probing the defences of the Golden Gate at Constantinople. Throughout the summer, there was fighting before the Theodosian Walls, only for the Roman garrison to stand firm, forcing the Arabs to retreat to their winter base at Cyzicus in September.[37] Constantine's forces were able to stave off this initial Arab attack because it seems that the Romans had recognized Muawiyah's intention and made the appropriate preparations: gathering forces and supplies into the capital, carrying out any repairs needed to the land and sea walls and marshalling the imperial fleet. However, traditionally, the most important step taken at Constantinople for its defence was the employing in *c.*672 of a certain inventor/engineer/architect Kallinikos of Heliopolis (now Baalbek in Lebanon).[38] A refugee from Arab Syria, Kallinikos reputedly brought with him an invention that was to help protect the imperial capital for centuries: Greek fire, a 'napalm-like substance that burned in water and could be projected great distances from the bows of ships'.[39]

The Romans themselves recognized the opportune timing of this invention, attributing its appearance and subsequent role in the saving of Constantinople to divine intervention. This is shown in the advice that Constantine VII gave to his son Romanus II in *De Administrando Imperio*. He told his heir to keep the composition of Greek fire secret because it was 'shown and revealed by an angel to the great and holy first Christian emperor Constantine ... [who was] not to prepare this fire but for Christians, and only in the imperial city'.[40] Constantine VII even provides the example of a Roman official who was bribed to hand over the secrets of Greek fire to imperial enemies, only to be struck down by 'flame from heaven' as he was about to enter a church.[41]

According to Theophanes, Constantine IV's initial deployment of this new secret weapon came in preparation for Muawiyah's attack (coincidentally, a year before the historian records Kallinikos' arrival in Constantinople), with 'huge, two-storied [*sic*] warships equipped with Greek fire and siphon-carrying warships' being sent to anchor in the Proklinneasian harbour of the Caesarium, a small harbour just east of the Eleutherios/Theodosian harbour.[42] Despite the presence of this secret weapon, as already seen, Theophanes would have it that the Umayyads did manage to establish a bridgehead on the European side of the Bosphorus and probe the defences of the Theodosian Walls from the direction of Hebdomon. This may highlight that Greek fire was not the all-conquering weapon that it might otherwise be thought as. Certainly, while the combination of the Theodosian Walls, imperial forces and Greek fire may have thwarted the initial Umayyad attempt on Constantinople in c.674, it did not deter the Arabs from continuing to threaten the imperial capital for the next four years from their base at Cyzicus.[43]

But in this Theophanic version of events, the c.674 landing at Hebdomon and probing of the Golden Gate was the zenith of Umayyad achievement during this 'first siege'. So condensed is this account that it would appear that the 'siege' regressed to a series of sea-battles between the Arab and imperial fleets in the waters surrounding Constantinople, although further Arab landings in Europe cannot be completely excluded. It would seem that each time the Arab fleet set out from Cyzicus over the next four campaigning seasons, it faced mounting damage and casualties inflicted by the Greek fire-wielding Roman fleet. After one final naval defeat, possibly with Constantine IV overcoming the Arab admiral Yazid b. Shagara, the Umayyads decided to cut their losses and retreat from Cyzicus and some of their other forward bases. As the Arab fleet retreated home, a violent storm smashed into it off Syllaion in Pamphylia (southern Turkey), destroying it almost completely. At some point during the 'siege' or in this aftermath, the Romans also won a significant victory on land when a force under the command of Florus, Petronas and Kyprianos defeated the Arab army of Sufyan b. Auf, reputedly inflicting 30,000 casualties.[44]

It was long accepted that this record represented the four years (or seven years according to Theophanes[45]) of the 'First Arab Siege of Constantinople' of 674–678; however, in more recent times, this 'siege' has become something of a bone of contention in academic circles, with its date, narrative, extent and even very existence coming into question. Looking beyond Theophanes and the Roman literary tradition can provide a substantially different account of events surrounding Constantinople early in the reign of Constantine IV. A poem by Theodosius Grammaticus which celebrates the successful defence of Constantinople has been linked to Muawiyah's foiled attempt. It speaks of a decisive naval victory before the walls of the city and hints that these Arab attacks had been a recurring feature, which may reflect Constantine IV's naval victory and the Arab raids from their base at Cyzicus.[46] It must be said, however, that, aside from positing Arab raids on Constantinopolitan waters, this poem does not give any real idea of a prolonged siege or of any specific dates. A seemingly tangential piece of evidence emerges from the declaration of George the *chartophylax* at the Sixth Ecumenical Council on 28 March 681. He suggests that an Arab incursion against Constantinople encapsulated the patriarchate of Thomas II, which is securely dated from 17 April 667 to his death on 14/15 November 669. The intimation is that Thomas could not send his synodical letter to Pope Vitalian throughout his patriarchate due to the Arab blockade. George also called the incursion 'long-lasting', which he is unlikely to have done had it been 'followed by an even longer siege of Constantinople in the 670s'.[47]

Such a shorter and much less involved blockade or series of raids would seem to fit in with the Arabic and Syriac sources, as they do not record a siege at all, only a number of raids that perhaps peaked between 668 and 670.[48] However, just because the Arab sources do not attest some kind of attempt on Constantinople in the late 660s or 670s does not mean that such an action did not happen at all. As whatever took place between the forces of Constantine IV and Muawiyah ended in the defeat of caliphal forces – a fact highlighted by the significantly pro-Roman peace treaty that followed – Umayyad propaganda would be keen to downplay the extent of Muawiyah's aims in the Sea of Marmara. The caliph does seem to have initiated a more ambitious naval policy in the Mediterranean by the late 660s, repopulating Levantine coastal cities, fortifying Alexandria and sending raids along the Anatolian coast to Rhodes, Crete, the Aegean and even Sicily.[49] There have been attempts to associate Muawiyah's naval raids with not only the Arab land advances through Anatolia, but also the revolts of Saborius and Mezizios in building a coherent narrative surrounding a grand plan by Muawiyah to pressurize the Roman imperial capital.[50]

Such is the lack of clarity surrounding aspects of this 'First Siege', it could even be that Greek fire was not the great game-changer in the waters around Constantinople that it was traditionally thought to be. Any suggestion that the entire Umayyad fleet was destroyed would seem to be undermined by Abd Allah b. Qais and Fudhala being able to land in Crete in 675/676. Perhaps the real difference-maker during this first Arab action against the Roman capital was merely the return of the military and naval forces that had comprised Constans II's western campaigns. Certainly, in the early 670s, the Romans appear far more active militarily in response to Umayyad raids and advances. Any such return of imperial forces likely stiffened resolve in the Sea of Marmara and facilitated a more widespread Roman counteroffensive, with raids on Egypt, a possible victory off Syllaion, the defeat of Sufyan b. Auf by the three patrician commanders, raids along the Levantine coast and perhaps even the encouraging of revolt in Umayyad territory.[51]

As can be seen, even with a re-evaluation of the sources, what exactly happened during the period recorded as the 'First Arab Siege of Constantinople' is difficult to ascertain. The very idea of a 'siege', with Umayyad landings in Europe and probing attacks on the Theodosian Walls, seems like a later interpolation, influenced by the events of the Second Arab Siege of Constantinople in 717–718, by the sources used by Theophanes or a 'historical misunderstanding' created by Theophanes' attempt to meld together the records of the *History to 720* and Theophilus of Edessa.[52] However, to write off the whole idea of a blockade as a myth seems a little drastic.[53] There is too much from all sides of the historical record that points to something happening in the waters around Constantinople. Their occupation of Cyzicus must have seen the Arabs do something in the Sea of Marmara, even if it only amounted to raiding the Roman sea lanes. It could even be that there had been an informal blockade of Constantinopolitan waters since 657, with an attempt to make more of it in the late 660s by landing troops in Europe. This leads to further speculation that it could have had an influence on the assassination of Constans II. Perhaps the ministers behind Andrew and his bucket were encouraged to act due to the emperor's failure against the Arab blockade of the imperial capital.[54] Indeed, looking west provides potential backing for the idea of a prolonged Roman distraction with events at the heart of their empire, siege or not, in the success achieved by their other enemies. The Lombards were able to strike deeply into Calabria and take the major Apulian cities of Tarentum and Brundisium, while the Slavs blockaded Thessalonica, raided the Aegean and even made an appearance in the Sea of Marmara.[55]

Fortunately for the subject at hand – the life and reign of Justinian II – it is sufficient to know that *something* took place in the waters around Constantinople during his early years. Even if not exactly besieged and taking place before he was of an age to understand what was happening, Justinian's formative years will have been spent under the threat of impending Arab attack. This may have had a detrimental impact on the young prince's temperament and psyche. It could be imagined that Justinian watched some of the naval encounters between the imperial and Arab fleets from the walls of the capital, which could have imbued in him an understanding not just of the persistence and threat of the Umayyads, but also the importance of the Theodosian Walls, the imperial fleet, its chemical flame-thrower and of Constantinople itself as both a symbol and bastion of the Roman Empire.

Justinian will also have come to recognize the benefit of direct and decisive leadership in watching, listening to and hearing of his father's exploits. Constantine's example may also have highlighted the usefulness of striking back into territory seemingly lost to the Arabs, either by raiding or through encouraging insurgency. The benefits of such action were displayed in the aftermath of the 'First Arab Siege of Constantinople' as the Roman counteroffensive across various parts of the eastern Mediterranean brought Muawiyah to the negotiating table. Constantine IV received the caliph's envoys and sent his own representative, the *patricius* John Pitzigaudis, to Damascus to thrash out a peace treaty. The result was a rather spectacular diplomatic coup for Constantine and the empire. Muawiyah agreed to pull back from any remaining forward bases in Roman territory and pay an annual tribute of 3,000 *nomismata*, fifty prisoners and fifty high-bred horses in return for a thirty-year peace.[56]

What lessons could Justinian have learned from this seemingly serendipitous 'treaty of 678', beyond the aforementioned willingness to take the fight to the Umayyads when possible? This requires a brief look at the potential reasons behind Muawiyah's willingness to agree to such an inordinately disproportionate treaty. Beyond the ultimate failure to gain any new territory in Anatolia, the damage wrought by the Greek fire-wielding imperial fleet and the weather, the defeat of Sufyan b. Auf and insurgency in the Levant, the caliphate of the late 670s may have been facing some political and religious trouble rooted in the Umayyad dynasty itself. Indeed, the sheer act of it becoming a dynasty at all was unpopular with certain elements within the caliphate. All told, this made closing down the Roman frontier, even at a financial cost, a prudent move on the part of Muawiyah.

The Second Fitna to Late 685

Despite any assurances he might have made during the culmination of the First Fitna, it seems that Muawiyah had every intention of nominating his son Yazid as his successor, perhaps as early as 666.[57] While potentially a decade in the making (and longer in the planning),[58] it may not have been until 675/676 that Muawiyah announced his decision to have his son succeed him as caliph.[59] Any attempt to tie this announcement to the 'First Arab Siege of Constantinople' is beset by the problems of its dating. The traditional dates of 674–678 could have it that Muawiyah was acting on the succession from a position of power as the 'siege' was ongoing, but any revision to the late 660s reduces the likelihood of any connection. The reversal of fortunes involved with Constantine IV's counteroffensives may have seen Muawiyah act to bolster his succession. It must also be noted that by 678, Muawiyah was at least into his mid-70s and would be dead within two years of the 'treaty of 678'. Perhaps he was feeling unwell or at least felt that time was not on his side.

The nomination of a son as successor was without precedent in the Arab caliphate. Previous caliphs had all been close to Muhammad, while Muawiyah himself could at least point to his long career as governor of Syria as a basis for his rule at a time of internal strife. But now the caliph was trying to establish his own family as the only dynasty to rule the caliphate. Through careful promotion and positioning of supporters in important roles, giving Yazid opportunities to show his not inconsiderable leadership skills against the Romans and a liberal use of threats and bribes, Muawiyah had succeeded in limiting opposition to his dynastic plans to a select few; unfortunately, that 'few' incorporated several prominent sons of caliphs or companions of the Prophet, such as Husayn b. Ali, Abd Allah b. al-Zubayr, Abd Allah b. Umar and Abd al-Rahman b. Abu Bakr. Muawiyah tried to persuade them to accept his replacing of the caliphate's elective theocracy with a hereditary monarchy, but he enjoyed such little success in this that it seems that by the time of his death in 680, the caliph had been planning to deal with these opponents.

Whatever he had planned, Muawiyah's death and the succession of Yazid sparked the Second Fitna within the Arab caliphate, with opposition to the Umayyad dynasty centring on Abd Allah b. al-Zubayr, son of a companion of Muhammad, and Husayn b. Ali, the younger son of caliph Ali, both of whom had support in the Hejaz.[60] While Abd Allah b. al-Zubayr established himself in Mecca, Husayn was invited by the people of Kufa to lead the city in revolt against the Umayyads. However, Yazid was quick to counter this Alid-Kufan threat, with the Umayyad loyalist Iraqi governor, Ubayd Allah b. Ziyad, intercepting Husayn and his retinue as they made their way to Kufa. The subsequent Battle of Karbala on 10 October 680 saw the death of Husayn and most of his male relatives. This significant defeat actually helped galvanize the Alid faction into becoming its own religious denomination, with Karbala taking its place as a vital historic and theological event in Shia Islam.

In the immediate political situation, Karbala and the massacre of Husayn and his followers bolstered opposition to the Umayyad caliphate of Yazid. By 684, the Alid remnant in Kufa had coalesced around Sulayman b. Surad as a group calling themselves the Tawwabin, meaning 'penitents' because they felt that their failure to help Husayn was a sin that needed to be absolved through vengeance on his Umayyad murderers. While popular, the Tawwabin lacked any political programme, and despite being heavily outnumbered, they marched out to face Ubayd Allah. The three-day Battle of Ayn al-Warda in January 685 saw the Tawwabin getting what they wanted: their almost total destruction. Despite this brutal defeat, there was still support for the Alid cause in Kufa, and it was Mukhtar al-Thaqafi who harnessed it in the aftermath of the Tawwabin massacre.[61] A controversial character – he is viewed variously as a sincere Alid, a ruthless opportunist or even a false prophet[62] – Mukhtar led the Alid faction to take control of Kufa in late 685, where he still ruled by the time Justinian II was ascending the Roman imperial throne.

However, while the Alids were trying to establish themselves again in Kufa, the main focus of the Second Fitna fell upon the struggle between Abd Allah b. al-Zubayr and the Umayyads. The killing of Husayn bolstered not only opposition to Yazid at Kufa but also in the Hejaz, centring on al-Zubayr and the cities of Mecca and Medina. After months of diplomacy failed to get al-Zubayr to recognize him as caliph, Yazid dispatched an army to force compliance. The initial contest came at the Battle of al-Harrah on 26 August 683, where the Umayyad army defeated the forces of Medina, thereafter occupying that city. The Umayyad force then subjected Mecca to a siege throughout the autumn and into the early winter of 683. While important sites like the Kaaba suffered damage during this siege, the city was saved from further destruction by the unexpected demise of Yazid on 12 November 683.

The Umayyad court at Damascus was quick to institute Yazid's succession plan in declaring his teenage son, Muawiyah II, as the new Umayyad caliph. This rapid transfer of caliphal power to someone of little or no leadership experience and who may already have been showing signs of fatal illness, greatly undermined Umayyad authority across Muslim lands. Throughout his caliphate, Muawiyah II would not be recognized anywhere outside Syria, and sometimes not even there. This may have encouraged the Umayyad commander at Mecca, Husayn b. Numayr, to enter into negotiations with al-Zubayr, reputedly offering to accept him as caliph if he would march with Husayn to Syria. Al-Zubayr rejected this overture, as moving to Syria might expose him to treachery, but the subsequent departure of the besieging Umayyad force left him in command of the Hejaz. Furthermore, with the weak rule of Muawiyah II and the general unpopularity of the Umayyads, al-Zubayr was quickly recognized as caliph by almost all of the Muslim world.

Perhaps somewhat serendipitously for Umayyad prospects in the Second Fitna, Muawiyah II's reign did not last long – anywhere from twenty days to four months – with something like jaundice or plague being blamed. Unlike with his father and grandfather, he had not designated a successor and his brothers were too young, leading several local Syrian leaders to throw in their lot with al-Zubayr. Fortunately for the future of the Umayyad dynasty, a prominent scion of the main Sufyanid branch of the family stepped forward to provide much-needed military leadership. Marwan b. al-Hakam, cousin of Uthman and second cousin of Muawiyah I, had served several caliphs as a secretary and cavalry commander before he emerged as a candidate for Umayyad caliph. It seems that he too almost capitulated to al-Zubayr, only for the Iraqi governor, Ubayd Allah, to encourage him to claim the caliphate for himself. Marwan was able to rally enough support to be elected by the Umayyad loyalists, and then secured his position by defeating pro-Zubayrid forces at the Battle of Marj Rahit in August 684.

The reunification of Syria under central Umayyad control enabled Marwan to begin to reclaim other areas of the Muslim world from al-Zubayr and Mukhtar. Alongside one of his sons, Abd al-Aziz, the new caliph had recovered Egypt and thwarted a Zubayrid attack on Palestine by early 685. It was not all positive for Marwan, as an attempt to retake the Hejaz was defeated near Medina and the doomed Iraqi expedition of Ubayd Allah was also launched. Even less positive for Marwan was that after just nine months as caliph, he died sometime in the late spring or early summer of 685. The suddenness of his demise led to rumours of murder, although it could be that plague accounted for him as well as Muawiyah II. Unlike his predecessor, Marwan had established a line of succession through his eldest son, Abd al-Malik, who had held important positions under both Muawiyah I and Marwan.[63] While the reign of Abd al-Malik would see the full restoration of Umayyad rule over the Arab caliphate, it was not something that would happen overnight. Large sections of the Arab world still recognized Zubayrid, Mukhtar or Kharijite rule, and it would be deep into the reign of Justinian II before the Second Fitna was to be settled decisively in Umayyad favour. In the few months that remained of Constantine IV's reign, Abd al-Malik focused on securing his rule and that of the Umayyads in the territories they controlled in Syria and Egypt, with the caliph appointing his brothers Muhammad and Abd al-Aziz as governors.[64]

What Justinian learned from the Second Fitna, which was still ongoing at his accession, was that after just half a century, Islam was not a unified faith, religiously or politically. This provided opportunities for the Roman Empire, whether it be a caliph's need for peace in Anatolia or striking against a distracted caliphate through direct military action on land or sea, supporting the likes of the Christian Mardaites or even hinting at backing a caliphal contender. Indeed, as will be seen, taking advantage of the Second Fitna in an effort to improve the terms of the already pro-Roman treaty between Constantine IV and Muawiyah was one of Justinian II's first major military decisions.

Constantine IV's War with the Bulgars and the Sixth Ecumenical Council

Another lesson for Justinian to learn from Constantine's actions was to take advantage of peace with the Arabs to concentrate on other opponents. It even seems that many of those opponents – Avars, Slavs, Lombards – felt that that was how the empire was going to act following the 'treaty of 678', as several sent envoys to Constantinople seeking confirmation of their own treaties with Constantine.[65] As it was, the imperial focus fell upon the Bulgars; more specifically, the Bulgars of Asparukh, who were seemingly established at the mouth of the Danube. Either too desperate, too ignorant or too arrogant to heed any warnings about how the emperor might react, Asparukh's Bulgars 'sallied forth to ravage the land near the Danube'.[66] Freed from the Anatolian front, Constantine IV gathered a vast force comprising 'all the thematic armies'[67] in Thrace and marched on the Danube, with a fleet in support.

Despite this initially strong showing, things started to go wrong almost immediately for Constantine IV. It may be that this Roman army was too large, as the Bulgars refused to fight, withdrawing to their marshy stronghold in the Oglos. This forced the Romans to resort to an incomplete blockade, and after a few days, Asparukh and his men began to realize that the imperial demonstration was more toothless than it first appeared. The Bulgars took further courage from the withdrawal of the emperor himself, who left his army for treatment on his gout. While he had left instructions for the blockade to continue, Constantine's departure had a devastating effect on the morale of the Roman force, with some misconstruing this imperial departure as an imperial flight. Once a section of the Roman cavalry decided to withdraw, the Roman army as a whole broke off its blockade and began a retreat south.

While there had been no great battlefield victory, the demonstration of a vast imperial army marching to the Danube may have been example enough to curb the Bulgar raids; however, Asparukh grasped the strategic opportunity presented to him. As the Romans moved away, the Bulgars burst out of the Oglos and fell upon the thematic forces, turning what was a disorderly retreat into a rout and seeing a large number of Bulgars strike deeply into Roman lands, with many refusing to leave.[68] Having lost a significant portion of his army, Constantine was left with no option but to negotiate, concluding 'hostilities by granting these newcomers a subsidy; and thus, ironically, much of the annual income from the caliph's tribute was in turn handed over, year by year, to the Khan of the Bulgars'.[69] Perhaps more important was that this treaty gave tacit acknowledgement to Asparukh's independent presence on formerly Roman territory. The year 680/681 would effectively become the traditional founding date of the Bulgarian state that would survive in some form for over three centuries.[70] Constantine's Bulgar war not only provided Justinian with a further example of the active emperor and using peace with the Umayyads as an opportunity to deal with other problems, but also provided him with a historical wrong that had to be righted; a humiliation that could not be left unavenged, as 'folk far and near were amazed to hear that the emperor, who had subjected everyone to himself, had been beaten by this newly arrived loathsome tribe'.[71]

Another such 'wrong' to be righted for Justinian II came in his father's religious policy. More detail on the religious policies and doctrinal issues of the Heraclian dynasty will come later, but it may be that the defeat by the pagan Bulgars and his own ill-health encouraged Constantine IV to abstain 'from all warlike activity until his death'[72] and concentrate on religious matters, specifically efforts 'to unite God's holy churches everywhere'.[73] The focus of these unifying efforts was the divisive doctrines of Monoenergism and Monothelitism. These had been promulgated during the reign of Heraclius under the Constantinopolitan patriarchs Sergius and Pyrrhus and supported by Constans II, despite significant opposition from within the Church as a whole. To deal with these problematic doctrines, Constantine IV and his religious allies called the Third Council of Constantinople in 680. Unsurprisingly, an ecumenical council called by the emperor and held in his imperial capital ratified the doctrines he supported – those of Jesus' two wills and energies, a complete turn away from Monoenergism and Monothelitism, which were both proclaimed as heresy.

The unfinished business for Justinian was not any divergence from his father's doctrinal beliefs, but more an opportunity presented to him by a procedural oversight by both the Fifth and Sixth Ecumenical Councils in not drawing up disciplinary canons. This allowed Justinian to call his own council and therefore present himself as both an arbiter and champion of orthodoxy. Justinian may also have felt compelled to intervene in religious politics and doctrinal issues due to the burden of his name. The first Justinian had called the Second Council of Constantinople in 553, while he may have taken a further cue from his father as Constantine IV had an even more illustrious name to live up to in regards to Roman religious policy.[74]

Paving the Way? The Deposition of Heraclius and Tiberius

While the political, military and religious events of Constantine IV's reign affected Justinian's life and the empire he was to inherit, the event to have perhaps the most direct, personal effect on Justinian II came sometime after mid-681. With all of the dynamic and decisive leadership Constantine IV had shown throughout his reign, you would be forgiven for thinking that his imperial position was undisputed; however, this was not the case. While he had been raised to co-emperor by his father in 654 and had provided some semblance of leadership during the western campaigns of Constans II, upon the murderous intervention of Andrew and his bath bucket, Constantine IV acceded to the throne alongside his two younger brothers, Heraclius and Tiberius. Indeed, these two had been co-emperors with Constans and Constantine since 659, with their elevation known from coins.[75]

This division of authority seems to have caused trouble amongst the imperial family. As already seen, there had been some idea that Constantine IV had moved to limit the power of his brothers either before or just after their accession, with it being public enough to stir a protest from the Anatolic army. Constantine not only rejected such a three-way sharing of power, he had the leaders of the protest hanged,[76] although this could be more to do with Constantine not wanting to bow to the demands of a rebellious army rather than specifically limiting the authority of his brothers. The emperor had certainly demonstrated his unwillingness to accept any rebellion from his military forces in his dealing with Mezizios and Saborius. Theophanes claims that in the aftermath of this Anatolic protest, 'the emperor slit his brothers' noses'.[77] Such drastic action does not tabulate with his later pronouncement that 'Constantine removed his brothers Heraclius and Tiberius from the imperial power'[78] in 681/682, for *rhinokopia* in 669/670 would have already removed the brothers from power. It could be that Theophanes' recording of the mutilation and later deposition of Heraclius and Tiberius was 'merely a duplicate of the earlier notice'[79] as he juggled eastern and western sources of varying standard, while the total silence of Nikephoros on the depositions may be to do with him not wanting to present the doctrinally orthodox emperor in a poor light.[80]

This contradiction in the two notices of Theophanes about Heraclius and Tiberius highlights the more general problem Theophanes seems to have had with his sources over the treatment of the brothers of Constantine IV. It may even be that 'no satisfactory solution has yet been found'[81] because it is not just the contradictory nature in the twelve-year gap between *rhinokopia* and deposition of Heraclius and Tiberius that may be a consequence of Theophanes' juggling of separate sources. The *Chronicle* of Michael the Syrian gives a substantially different account of Constantine's dealings with his brothers. He has Constantine, at the outset of his reign, demand that his brothers be recognized as emperors alongside him, and that 'all the heads should be placed upon the coins and that all should receive equal honour'.[82] This may well reflect the idea that Constantine's seniority and the leadership he had shown in his father's absence had seen him expected to succeed alone, only for him to enforce the 'trinity'.[83]

However, Michael the Syrian has it that after the defeat of Mezizios and the Arabs, Constantine removed his brothers from power in order to make Justinian the clear heir. The cries regarding an imperial Trinity – 'A Trinity reigns in Heaven, and a Trinity reigns on earth. I will not deny the Trinity in Heaven, and I will not reject the Trinity on earth'[84] – are put in the mouth of a certain Leo the patrician, who was condemned to having his tongue, hands and feet removed for opposing the depositions. Before the Senate, which had been bought off, Constantine asked his brothers whether they saw him as their brother or their emperor? They answered that while he was their 'elder and superior', he was not their emperor as they were emperors too. Constantine therefore dubbed them his enemies and had them deposed, with Agapius of Hierapolis suggesting that they were banished to an island.[85]

A further source showing that Constantine did not completely sideline his brothers from the very outset of his reign is the great imperial mosaic in Sant'Apollinare in Classe near Ravenna. It depicts not only Constantine IV, the future Justinian II, an envoy of the bishop of Ravenna and his retinue, but also the two co-emperors. While their attire – their white cloaks lack purple and gold, and their shoes are black instead of imperial red – and position behind and below Constantine place them in a subordinate position, their names and imperial rank are recorded at the top of the mosaic – '*HERACLII ET TIBERII IMPERATOR*', a rank further borne out by their halos. This suggests that at the time of the mosaic's creation the two brothers were still recognized as co-emperors and at a higher rank than Justinian. Unfortunately, the mosaic cannot be firmly dated. The Bishop of Ravenna, whose envoy is receiving the *privilegia*, is not identified,[86] and as mentioned earlier, inferences on how old Justinian looks in the mosaic are hindered by him surely being made to appear older than he really was. The best that can be done is to place it between the joint accession of the three sons of Constans II in 668 and the events of late 681.

With neither Theophanes nor Michael the Syrian giving a concrete dating for the deposition of Heraclius and Tiberius, evidence must be sought elsewhere. One of the aforementioned major events of the reign of Constantine IV would appear to provide just such evidence. The synodal acts of the Sixth Ecumenical Council list Constantine, Heraclius and Tiberius as emperors, so the deposition had not happened by 16 September 681. Furthermore, the edict of confirmation of the council dated 13 December 681 only has Constantine listed as emperor.[87] Such a period for the deposition would synchronize somewhat with Theophanes, albeit potentially because he compounded one error with another.[88]

The doubting of Theophanes' record, any preference for that of Michael the Syrian and the potential dating of the deposition in late 681 would seem to eliminate the idea of an Anatolic thematic protest altogether, but this is not necessarily the case. It could just be that Theophanes has misdated the protest to 669/670, which seems like an inopportune date for the Anatolic army to detach itself from the Anatolian frontier. At the very least, it was after the 'treaty of 678' and probably should be pushed back to late 681/early

682. Any protest was surely demanding the reinstatement of Heraclius and Tiberius after the deposition was announced, either out of loyalty to them or worry over a young boy being the lone imperial heir, rather than demanding their elevation, which had already happened.[89] It could be that Leo the patrician was an otherwise unknown Anatolic *strategos*, whose trinitarian cry was reflective of Anatolic demands and whose mutilation – there is a good chance he died following the removal of his tongue, hands and feet – was the basis for Theophanes' recording of Anatolic officers being executed in the capital on Constantine's order.

The importance of any Anatolic protest may not just be the willingness of thematic forces to get involved in imperial politics, but perhaps the effect it had on the treatment of Heraclius and Tiberius. Given the muddled nature of the source material, it could be that Constantine had just deposed his brothers in order to secure the succession of Justinian (possibly encouraged by his success against the Arabs or his failure against the Bulgars[90]). The protest of Leo and/or the Anatolics then forced him into mutilating and banishing Heraclius and Tiberius to prevent them being a focus for opposition to his rule and that of his son. An island banishment would certainly explain why the brothers disappear from the imperial record, and would be in keeping with the Heraclian policy of mutilation and exile, something which Justinian II himself would fall victim to.

The historical sources give no real reaction of Justinian to the deposition, mutilation and exile of his uncles, but there are some inferences that can be made. Given the possibility that Justinian was quite close to one or both of his uncles in age, it could be expected that he had some affection for them like elder brothers; however, as already mentioned, if Constantine had any inkling to limit their authority and influence, Justinian may have been kept away from Heraclius and Tiberius, and therefore would have little to miss of them. Even if he did, Justinian may have been ruthless enough to see the deposition as being good for the imperial family and for him in particular. Certainly, there is no hint that he made any attempt to reverse the actions of his father, repair the reputation of Heraclius and Tiberius or even recall them from any island exile they had faced (if they still lived post-685) once Justinian acceded to the throne. As will be seen below, rather than react with revulsion, Justinian may instead have seen his father's actions against his brothers – and indeed that of his grandfather, Constans II, against his brother Theodosius – as a blueprint for his own fraternal dealings. That said, a willingness to potentially repeat such familial brutality could demonstrate the psychological impact of a 12/13-year-old boy being privy to the *rhinokopian* fates of his uncles; fates that would have come flooding back to him in 695.

Imperial Deaths and the Accession

One peculiarity surrounding the removal of Heraclius and Tiberius is that if it was carried out by Constantine IV to facilitate the clear succession of his son, it would be expected that the emperor would make some move to present Justinian as a junior or co-emperor. Indeed, this was generally assumed to be the case; however, while Theophanes claimed, somewhat absurdly, that after deposing his brothers, Constantine 'ruled alone with his son Justinian',[91] it seems more likely that this is a misunderstanding of how the fraternal deposition was meant to secure Justinian's status as heir, not his immediate accession. Furthermore, the legal, epistolary and numismatic record gives little hint of Justinian ever being co-emperor alongside his father. A letter from Justinian II to Pope Conon dated 17 February 687[92] speaks of it being his second year as emperor, and co-emperors usually counted periods of joint rule as part of their full reign. Consequently, it would seem that there could only have been a co-rule between February 685 and Constantine's death in July 685, if there was one at all. There are also no coins depicting Justinian as co-emperor from his father's lifetime, unlike those which had both Heraclius and Tiberius on them. The aforementioned mosaic in Sant'Apollinare in Classe does depict Justinian II alongside his father and uncles, although he is not listed as *IMPERATOR* as they are.

The question then may be asked of why Constantine did not raise his son to an overt joint rule as his own father had done with him in 654, particularly if he had gone to the lengths of the deposition, mutilation and exile of his own brothers. Unfortunately, the only potential answers are all supposition. Perhaps he wanted Justinian to prove his worth before giving him an overt imperial position, or he did not feel it necessary as the elimination of Heraclius and Tiberius made the imperial succession obvious. It must also be noted that by the end of 681, Constantine IV was maybe still only 29 (he was 31 at most); a man very much in his prime, and he likely felt no need to rush promoting his designated heir into the limelight.

This focus on the deposition of Heraclius and Tiberius being a move to establish Justinian as the heir to the throne overlooks another individual within the imperial family – Justinian's younger brother, Heraclius. Perhaps

Constantine's hesitation to elevate Justinian openly was linked to some procrastination 'over what to do about his second son'.[93] Similar to Justinian, the young Heraclius does not appear on any of his father's coins, but unlike Justinian, he also does not appear on the imperial mosaic of Sant'Apollinare in Classe. That is not to say that Constantine completely overlooked his younger son. The *Liber Pontificalis* records an interesting 'incidental glimpse'[94] of not just an imperial ceremony and imperial-papal relations under Constantine IV, but also of the young Heraclius too. As part of his cultivating of the good will of the papacy, sometime in 684/685, Constantine sent a package to Benedict II. The pope must have known of the contents of the gift, as upon its approach to Rome, he, along with the clergy and soldiers, processed out to meet it. The contents were locks of Justinian's and Heraclius' hair. The significance of this peculiar gift was that the emperor's sons were now 'spiritual sons' of the pope.[95]

There is something else important about this 'spiritual adoption' of the imperial sons by the pope in 684/685 – it is the last record of the young Heraclius. Perhaps he died around the same time as his father in *c*.685. It might also be tempting to posit some kind of brotherly removal by Justinian after the death of Constantine IV to secure his own sole accession, following the examples of both his father and grandfather.[96] While there might be room for such speculation, this is based on the nefarious depiction of Justinian in later sources. The Justinian appearing in the pages of Nikephoros and Theophanes would certainly seem capable of fratricide or brotherly mutilation, but this is not necessarily a fair reflection of the man, particularly early in his first reign. Furthermore, if there was any hint that Justinian had been behind the disappearance of Heraclius, surely Nikephoros and Theophanes would have openly accused him of such actions, and maybe even presented his kinslaying as the undisputed truth. The loss of potentially three close family members in quick succession must have had an impact on Justinian. He may have felt lonely and abandoned, even within the vast metropolis of Constantinople, and possibly even a little paranoid that his own imperial rank did not shelter him from political and familial machinations. It may also have made him increasingly reliant on the presence of his father, even if there was any resentment regarding the deposition of his uncles. But if that was the case, then Fate was about to intervene cruelly once more.

Death stalked the imperial family in the first half of the 680s. The removal of Heraclius and Tiberius through mutilation and the apparent disappearance of Justinian's brother Heraclius seemingly not long after

684 were followed rather quickly by the sudden death of Constantine IV on 14 September 685.[97] The cause of death is given as dysentery, common in the ancient world, and it must also be remembered that Constantine, despite being active and in his prime at 33–35 years old in 685, had suffered from gout. Perhaps for all his relative youth and activity, Constantine IV was not a particularly healthy individual. Despite the poor depiction of his son Justinian, the assassination of Constans II and the unpopularity of his removal of his brothers, there is no inference of Constantine's death being unnatural or orchestrated by anyone who may have held a grudge or sought to benefit from his demise.

This untimely death meant that in the summer of 685, with apparently no uncles or brother to share the burden of imperial power, the 16/17-year-old Justinian II acceded to the throne alone. While inexperienced and young, he was thought of as being of age and therefore not in need of a regent. There is no record of Justinian's coronation, although some inferences at what might have occurred can be made from the record of other Heraclian emperors and the *De Caermoniis* of Constantine VII, which provides official records of the coronations of fifth-century emperors. It might be expected that the coronation of Heraclius by patriarch Sergius in the chapel of St Stephen[98] would most closely resemble that of Justinian II, but the former was against the backdrop of internal rebellion and Persian invasion, perhaps leaving little time for what would have been a full ceremonial coronation. Looking to *De Caermoniis* and other sources alongside those for Heraclius' coronation provides some suggestion of the potential extent of the ceremony involved in the coronation of Justinian II, which came at a time of relative peace at the heart of the empire. Justinian may have enjoyed an acclamation by the army at Hebdomon (complete with the promise of an accession donative), followed by a ceremonial procession through the streets of Constantinople, a meeting with and acclamation by the Senate, presentation with a gold crown and, perhaps after some kind of *refutatio imperii* – a deferential show of reluctance to accept imperial power – a final acclamation by a congregation of officials, soldiers, ambassadors and the general population in the Hippodrome, before his crowning by patriarch George.[99]

If Justinian had made any attempt to follow aspects of Heraclius' coronation, one of the first things he may have done was to get married.[100] Given the importance placed on the Heraclian dynasty, Justinian must have felt the need to establish some form of succession, particularly if his brother Heraclius had been disposed of, had died or seemed to be ill. The empress had become increasingly important during Late Antiquity: the Theodosian women, the prominent Leonids – Verina and Ariadne – through to Theodora being an almost imperial equal of Justinian I, Sophia aiding Tiberius II in their regency for the ailing Justin II, and Heraclius' second wife, Martina, holding a considerable amount of power.

However, very little is known about Justinian's first wife, beyond her being called Eudokia. Indeed, her existence is only recorded on the inscription of her tomb; there is only silence from the literary sources.[101] This name might hint at high rank, as various empresses of the previous three centuries had similar names. If Justinian found himself in a rush to marry and secure the succession upon the unexpected death of his father, it could be that he looked for a wife in the most immediate vicinity – the Constantinopolitan aristocracy, and perhaps more specifically, the imperial court. Eudokia is thought to have died while still quite young during Justinian's first reign, and was buried in a rose-coloured marble tomb in the Church of the Holy Apostles. Her burial in one of Constantinople's most famous churches would certainly suggest that she died in the city before Justinian's deposition in 695.

Dying at such a young age might suggest that Eudokia perished during pregnancy or childbirth. Justinian and Eudokia are known to have had at least one child, a daughter, probably named Anastasia after Justinian's mother. While little else is known of her, Anastasia lived long enough to become a valuable negotiating tool in the political machinations surrounding Justinian's restoration in 705. Justinian and Eudokia's first child being female might increase the likelihood that the empress died during pregnancy, particularly if Justinian played into the perpetual nature of the Heraclian dynasty and its so far unbroken succession of sons succeeding fathers. In order to not be the one to break that line, Justinian needed a son, so it will have been behoven of Eudokia to provide him with one, perhaps to her eventual demise. Eudokia could even have died giving birth to Anastasia very early in Justinian's reign, although this would raise the question of why it took him almost two decades to marry again when he did not have a male heir.

The lack of information about Eudokia, Anastasia and Justinian's personal life in general raises questions of the sources. Given the tendency of the likes of Theophanes and Nikephoros to portray Justinian in a negative light whenever possible, the lack of information on Justinian's family may suggest that the emperor's private life, at least in the early stages, did not provide much ammunition for scandal-mongers. It could even be that an unwillingness to present a story which might illicit sympathy for the emperor was behind the lack of information about potential tragedies regarding Eudokia and Heraclius. This might seem like exaggeration, but Theophanes and Nikephoros were willing to present much more information on Justinian's military, political and religious policies, likely because they felt that there were opportunities to besmirch the emperor.

Now that Justinian II was secured upon the imperial throne, with his wife by his side and a child on the way, he would have plenty of opportunity to act on his military, political and religious policies. But he had some pretty large shoes to fill, with the substantial expectations provided by the example of his Heraclian predecessors, his imperial position and his name, all while still a recently bereaved teenager, who should be forgiven for any mental scarring he had endured even before he took the reins of imperial power. The pressures of these expectations, having an empire to protect and a young family to raise would influence Justinian's actions towards the denizens and enemies of *his* Roman Empire – for good or ill.

Chapter 4

Justinian's First War with the Umayyads

'Wars not make one great ...'
Yoda (*Star Wars Episode V:
The Empire Strikes Back*, 1980)

Taking Advantage: An Initial Strike Eastwards

Eager to show that he was worthy of the position of Roman emperor, Justinian II looked to win some military renown for his fledgling reign. As with his personal life, care must be taken in evaluating the emperor's military career from the hostile sources. As will be seen, the likes of Theophanes are not beyond passing overly negative comment on actions and motives which do not particularly deserve it. That said, such hostile writers inadvertently present 'something of the extent of [Justinian's] ambitions. Other sources help to place Justinian's military policy in clearer perspective and show that his accomplishments were by no means as disastrous as the hostile chroniclers would have us believe.'[1]

Justinian's first military action was initially a somewhat indirect strike at the Umayyads. In so doing, Justinian risked undoing a period of prolonged Romano-Arab calm that had perhaps not been seen since the first Arab eruptions in the 630s. The Roman resistance to whatever pressure comprised the 'siege' of Constantinople and the subsequent raids on various Arab-held territories by land and sea had brought about the significant success that was Constantine IV's favourable thirty-year treaty with Muawiyah I.[2] And in 685, that treaty still had twenty-three years to run, with all of its Umayyad tribute flowing into Roman coffers. However, both the signatories of that treaty were now dead, and while Constantine's dysenteric death had resulted in the orderly succession of Justinian II, as already seen, the demise of the elderly Muawiyah had led to increasing disorder within Arab territory, with significant regions refusing to recognize the Umayyad succession. This was exacerbated by the short-lived reigns of Muawiyah's successors – his son, Yazid I, lasted only three-and-a-half years; his namesake grandson,

Muawiyah II, died childless after less than a year; then Marwan I, whose reign began the stabilizing of the Umayyad position, only lasted between six and ten months. Marwan's eldest son, Abd al-Malik, ascended the Umayyad throne in mid-685, facing the continuation of the Second Fitna with the Zubayrids and Mukhtar.

Faced with civil war, unifying Syria, plague and Mardaite raids, the new caliph was keen to maintain the peace in Anatolia. The last thing he needed when trying to deal with his rivals was a Roman invasion threatening Syria. It is not surprising then to find Theophanes recording Abd al-Malik sending envoys to Constantine IV, seeking a similar treaty to that which the emperor had signed with Muawiyah I.[3] The terms that Theophanes claims the caliph agreed to in early 685 – an annual payment of 360,000 *nomismata*, 365 slaves and 365 high-bred horses – are the same he later lists as being agreed between Abd al-Malik and Justinian in 686/687.[4] Overlooking the fact that Theophanes' date for the treaty between the caliph and Justinian is incorrect – it belongs in 688/689 – *and* the terms themselves seem to be incorrect, the similarity of these caliphal agreements rouses suspicion.

Finding Abd al-Malik, mired in internal troubles, reaching out to Constantine IV in 685 for reassurance that the 'treaty of 678' still held is perfectly reasonable and likely did happen in some diplomatic form. But would he really offer to increase Muawyiah I's annual payment of 3,000 *nomismata*, fifty prisoners and fifty high-bred horses[5] without any further defeat at the hands of the Romans in the interim? Theophanes may well be attempting to shift credit for the increase in the Umayyad tribute payment to the empire from Justinian II to his father, or he might have just made a mistake on the level of tribute paid by the Umayyads in the last months of Constantine's reign. Another aspect of Theophanes' dating is that when Abd al-Malik reached out to Constantinople early in his reign, he may have found Constantine already unwell or perhaps even dead, although there were five months between the accessions of Abd al-Malik and Justinian.

Regardless of who was on the imperial throne at the time the caliph's envoys arrived in Constantinople, their very presence and hope to reaffirm the 'treaty of 678' could have been taken by Justinian II as a sign of continued Umayyad weakness. This may have encouraged the new emperor to target the first military action of his reign against lands under Arab control. However, there may have been other reasons that encouraged Justinian to turn his military focus on Anatolia. The crumbling of Umayyad central control in the aftermath of Muawiyah I's death not only saw large Arab-controlled regions back rival caliphs, but may also have seen smaller tribal confederations and subject peoples look to strike out on their own and gain their independence. The disruption Abd al-Malik was faced with in Syria could easily have spilt across the frontiers into Roman territory, requiring a military response.

Others such as the Armenians and Iberians may also have looked to take advantage of the turmoil of the Second Fitna, perhaps even looking for help from the Romans. Any such call would have further encouraged Justinian to launch a campaign into eastern Anatolia, as the locals could provide aid to his imperial forces, help get his reign off to a positive start with an important military victory and better enable the empire to maintain any reconquests. There could also be an ulterior motive to moving into eastern Anatolia. There was considerable territory in Armenia, Iberia and the Caucasus that was technically independent of both the empire and the caliphate, so the Romans could act against at least some of those regions without engaging in a direct conflict with the distracted Umayyads.

Whatever the reasons behind his choice, it was across eastern Anatolia and into Armenia that Justinian chose to launch the first military strike of his reign. To lead this endeavour, the emperor selected Leontios, an old friend and comrade of his father, who was currently serving as *strategos* of the Anatolic theme. A skilled general, Leontios led a successful campaign into Armenia, defeating its Arab garrison and reputedly reclaiming the region for the empire. Perhaps due to the success and seeming ease of this initial move, Leontios, almost certainly with Justinian's acquiescence or foreknowledge, seems to have struck further east into 'Iberia, Albania, Boukania and Media'.[6] This attack brought considerable prestige, plunder and perhaps territory in the form of conquest or tributary status to the new imperial regime.

While Theophanes seems to present this conflict as centred on one dramatic strike across Arab territory from eastern Anatolia to Iran, the war lasted three to four years. This gives plenty of time for there to have been numerous Roman strikes into the caliphate and its tributaries. Indeed, an expedition that expelled Arab garrisons from and recovered territory in Armenia, Iberia, Albania, Azerbaijan and Media would have required a circuitous route, which would have been difficult to achieve in a single campaigning season. There is also evidence that Justinian's first war with the Arabs was more wide-ranging than the actions carried out by the Anatolic *strategos*. The *Liber Pontificalis* has the Romans achieving some success in rolling back Arab advances in North Africa,[7] while the sticking points of the subsequent treaty between Abd al-Malik and Justinian hint at other areas of conflict. The prevalence of Cyprus, along with Armenia and Iberia, in the treaty would suggest that the Roman navy had made some inroads against any Umayyad control of the island, while the caliph's use of the Mardaites as part of the negotiations could suggest that he felt there was some Roman involvement in their ongoing raids.

Care must be taken in accepting the extent of the success of Justinian's first war with the Umayyads due to the problems with the record of Theophanes. There is some corroboration from the *Liber Pontificalis* over North Africa, while the eighth-century Armenian chronicler Ghevond records Roman success in Armenia at the time, but it is unlikely that Leontios' forces actually conquered territory as far east as Iran. While Theophanes is unlikely to have presented the campaigns of an emperor he disliked as being more successful than they really were, the historian or his sources have already been seen to not be above making substantial errors of fact and logic, on top of intentional misinformation. In recording these early campaigns of Justinian against caliphate targets, Theophanes is certainly far from complimentary towards the young emperor, complaining that 'as he was but sixteen, Justinian was not one to follow traditional practice. He ran things without advice.'[8] However, as mentioned above, not only does Theophanes perhaps inadvertently record the extent of the strikes achieved under Justinian – possibly reaching Iran – he also makes a mess of the chronology of this Romano-Arab conflict. He has Abd al-Malik's suing for peace in not just the wrong year (it happened in 688/689 rather than 686/687), but even before Leontios' Armenian campaign, which was the catalyst for the war the treaty was bringing to an end.[9]

The Treaty of 688/689: Tribute, Shared Territory and Transplanting Populations

Even though there is room to doubt the exact extent of the Roman successes won in Justinian's first war against the Umayyads, the four years of fighting do seem to have gone well for the Romans. They were successful enough for Abd al-Malik to send envoys to Justinian suing for peace. The emperor was encouraged enough by the caliph's offer, perhaps keen to shut down the Anatolian front and move against another imperial enemy, that he sent a representative, the *magistranos* Paul, to thrash out a treaty with Abd al-Malik. The terms of the subsequent treaty are well-recorded in the sources and demonstrate the extent of Justinian's achievement, particularly if Theophanes' claim of an attempted caliphal restructuring of the 'treaty of 678' in the last months of Constantine IV's reign are rejected.[10] The tribute to be paid by the caliph was increased from the annual 3,000 *nomismata*, fifty slaves and fifty high-bred horses of Muawiyah I to 1,000 *nomismata*, one slave and one horse per week.

Even here, in the same section where Justinian is being denigrated for being young, inexperienced, hard-headed and of poor judgement, Theophanes and/or his source mistakenly suggest that this payment was to be made on a daily basis, suggesting that Abd al-Malik was forced into paying a colossal 365,000 *nomismata* to the Constantinopolitan treasury, as well as 365 slaves and 365 horses, every year. It must be said that the Spanish *Chronicle of 741* also suggests that the tribute was to be paid daily, and adds in a silk garment and a duration for the tribute payments – 'the quantity of one thousand gold *solidi* of proven weight, one girl, one hairy Arab mule, and a silk garment daily without interruption for 9 years in succession'.[11] This could suggest that any mistake in listing this tribute payment as 'daily' was not of Theophanes' making but of a shared Syriac source, such as Theophilus of Edessa.[12] The ninth/tenth-century Iranian scholar, al-Tabari, suggests more reasonably that rather than 'each day', this tribute was to be paid 'every Friday', which would equate to every assembly day. Unfortunately, al-Tabari does not provide any more information on the conflict, merely stating that 'the Byzantines arose and gathered an army against the Muslims in Syria. For fear of what he might do to the Muslims, Abd al-Malik made peace with the Byzantine emperor.'[13]

While the source record regarding this new treaty in 688/689 may encourage focus on the size and regularity of the tribute payment, the treaty also contained some rather inventive solutions to the problems of the spheres of Roman and Umayyad influence. Rather than assign the disputed territories of Armenia, Iberia and Cyprus to one power or the other, or divide them up to be disputed over at a later date, Justinian and Abd al-Malik decided not to claim any sovereignty over these territories. Instead, they came to a condominium arrangement whereby they would share the tax revenues of these three regions. That the emperor and the caliph would give up any portion of the revenues of these territories suggests that neither had particularly strong control over any of them. This in turn highlights the patchiness and even weakness of Umayyad power beyond its northern Syria frontier, while also downplaying the success of the Roman 'subjugation' of these regions in the previous three years.

On the surface, this does not seem like an agreement that would last for any period of time, as there were too many parties – Romans, Arabs, Armenians, Iberians and Cypriots – who might take issue with the arrangement at some point. The subjugated locals in particular would surely rankle under the 'spurious independence of a no-man's land'[14] while paying tribute to both Constantinople and Damascus. And so it would prove for the Armenian and Iberian condominiums, as sovereignty over those regions would be a focus of trouble throughout the rest of Justinian II's reign.[15]

Cyprus was another story. The condominium, along with Arab raids, was regularly seen as having placed the island in 'a political and administrative limbo'.[16] However, this may reflect the dislike of the Roman sources for Justinian himself and the whole idea of the condominium, with its incumbent idea of the 'giving up' of formerly imperial territory, rather than the reality of Cyprus' position. An inspection of usually overlooked archaeological evidence – ceramics, coins, seals – shows that Cyprus seems to have enjoyed 'an unsuspected economic soundness … with local elites manning their part in a sophisticated regional economy'[17] in which the island played an important commercial link. This success could reflect the benefits of a connection to both the Arabs and Romans, with the silence of the sources regarding the specifics of Cyprus perhaps reflecting the stability of the island instead of its decline. This is surely reflected in the fact that the Cypriot condominium essentially lasted for 260 years. If it had been as useless as the sources initially suggested, why would it have endured so long?[18] Perhaps it was out of gratitude for being the emperor behind their 'local autonomy and unusually stable government'[19] that Cypriots sought to incorporate Justinian directly into the history of the island as being the son of a Cypriot mother or as a native himself.

Beyond the Friday tribute and tax condominiums, the treaty between Justinian and Abd al-Malik also addressed another flashpoint between the two powers – the Mardaites. These were a group who inhabited the Amanus Mountains, now known as the Nur Mountains on the western side of the Turkish-Syrian border. Who these people were and how they came to be in northern Syria is the source of considerable academic argument, with various ethnic and political origins being put forward. It was usual to refer to the Mardaites in ethnic, even tribal terms, perhaps through some influence from the likes of the Isaurians of Cilicia or the Arab tribes prominent in Syrian politics during the Second Fitna. However, little is known about Mardaite ethnicity, with various origins being proposed – Persian, Armenian, Levantine or Arabian – through different geographical and linguistic reasons, but using either of these determining factors may well be unsound. Just because they appear with Syriac and Arab-based names and in a Syrian area does not mean that they originate from lands where such languages predominate. The Mardaites were also known as the *al-Jarajimah*, which could suggest a connection to the Cilician town of Jurjum, but the Arab name translates to 'sick' or 'insane', which may derive from their predatory raids, fierce fighting style or general disloyalty. The name 'Mardaite' itself 'seems to be a Graecized form of the Syriac "maridoye" meaning "rebel"',[20] while they are also called 'lipure', which could be a transliterated version of the Greek words *laphyra* – 'plunderers' – or *leipo* – 'deserters'.[21] However, there is a considerable difference between being considered a 'plunderer' or a 'deserter'; a difference that plays out in the proposals over where these Mardaites came from.

Both of these conflicting views suggest that, rather than see the Mardaites as an ethnic group, they were initially a military corps of Roman origin which found itself in Umayyad territory by the 670s. The difference is in how they came to be there. The first proposed Mardaite origin was as a commando strike, involving only a few hundred men, which landed on the Levantine coast between Tyre and Sidon as part of the Roman counteroffensive during the Umayyad 'siege' of Constantinople, the dates of which, as already seen, are far from clear – any time from the late 660s to the mid-670s. The plan behind this strike was for the 'proto-Mardaites' to establish themselves in Umayyad territory in a defendable position and, through insurgent attacks on Arab possessions, attract local peasants, slaves and former Roman provincials to their camp. That they are thought to have been Christians also suggests recruitment amongst local populations. A most important group – perhaps even the original *al-Jarajimah* who had possibly been employed by the Umayyads as border guards – to join up may have come from the lands to the north of Antioch in the Amanus Mountains, which, along with perhaps the Lebanon Mountains, became a centre for Mardaite action. This would suggest that the Mardaites were so successful that they soon numbered in the thousands and took control of the upland territories stretching from the Amanus Mountains, down through western Syria and into Palestine, even reaching Jerusalem itself. 'From their strongholds, they ranged over the surrounding lowlands, causing extensive damage and, in due course, inducing real apprehension at the highest level in the new Arab regime. Its hold on the former Roman provinces of the Middle East was imperilled.'[22]

This painting of the Mardaites as a substantial, Roman-directed threat to the Umayyad Levant makes them an important factor in the treaty negotiations between Constantine IV and Muawiyah I and then Justinian II and Abd al-Malik. While the record of the 'treaty of 678' sees the Mardaites as a catalyst for the Umayyad suing for peace, it does not mention any agreements made regarding them, although 'Constantine must have been required to cut off support for the insurgents and to do what he could to restrain them'.[23] Either Constantine could not (or would not) do anything about the Mardaites or Justinian initiated another wave of their insurgent attacks after 685, as Abd al-Malik had their removal from Umayyad territory be a condition of the treaty of 688/689. Justinian agreed to remove 12,000 Mardaites to Roman territory, a figure which – if to be believed – demonstrates the potential problem they posed.[24] Thousands of insurgents within Umayyad territory, even if they were not under the control of the Roman emperor, could cause serious issues and would help explain the caliph's willingness to substantially increase the tribute payment to Constantinople, on top of Leontios' campaigns and his internal problems.

Theophanes has Justinian receive the returning Mardaites in person in Armenia.[25] While it might be feasible that Justinian would want to tour any new conquests won by the campaigns of Leontios, this does little to bolster either argument of the Mardaites being successful Roman insurgents or returned captives/deserters. There is also no confirmation of Theophanes' imperially overseen Armenian repatriation of the Mardaites from other sources. It would seem that he again attempted to fill a gap between his Syriac and Constantinopolitan sources with a somewhat logical but unsupported assumption.[26] Upon their 'repatriation' in the Roman Empire, the Mardaites seem to have been settled in several places, or at least came to be posted in various maritime locations such as Attaleia in Pamphylia, the Peloponnese, Epirote Nicopolis and Cephalonia. Certainly, by the early tenth century, the Mardaites retained an important naval and even regional influence in Pamphylia, with a *katepan* (a senior Byzantine military rank) commanding them at Attaleia, while there were enough of them to provide 5,000 marines for an expeditionary force in 911.[27] However, it may be that by this time, any connection to the 'original' Mardaites apart from the name had been lost.

But what if the 'lipure' name for the Mardaites derives from the Greek *leipo* – 'deserters' – and it is not a general disparaging remark? Given that it is thought that various escaped slaves and peasants joined the Mardaites, the Arabs could have seen them as 'deserters' and 'rebels'. However, it has been surmised that the Mardaites had their name from before they arrived in Umayyad territory,[28] so if they were called 'deserters' or even 'rebels' before appearing in northern Syria and it was not something of a call to arms to the locals, who exactly had they deserted from or rebelled against? There is really only one other option if the Umayyad caliphate is discounted; could the Mardaites have been 'deserters' or 'rebels' against the Roman Empire? There were plenty of opportunities for Roman citizens to be carried off to Arab territory courtesy of the persistent Umayyad raids of Anatolia throughout the 660s and 670s; however, if they were captives, they would not be considered 'deserters' or 'rebels' by the Romans. Furthermore, if they were sold off as slaves, it is unlikely that they would have been settled as a group on Umayyad territory. Their limited numbers would also have undermined the sort of group dynamic the Mardaites seem to have managed.

However, there is one such group which could fit the bill as an imperial 'deserter'/'rebel' and was in a position to be settled on Arab lands: the supporters of the rebel Armenian *strategos* Saborius. As seen above, Muawiyah I had agreed to give Saborius support in his rebellion against Constans II, and even when the rebel smashed his head on the gate of Hexapolis, the remaining rebels may still have thrown their lot in with the Arabs, recognizing that they had no future in Roman territory. As Hexapolis was in Bithynia, this could suggest that the rebel *strategos* had already moved west towards Constantinople, although the fact that Fudhala found out about the death of Saborius in what is likely to be the Armenian Hexapolis, centred on Melitene, may place the rebel's death much closer to Armenia. Of course, Saborius dying either in Armenia, Cappadocia or Bithynia does not make that much difference to the potential for his supporters to have joined Fudhala and Yazid as they advanced to Chalcedon. The Saborian loyalists could have joined them at any point from their entry into Roman territory, and then stayed with the Arab commanders throughout their expedition and followed them to Syria. It could be argued that the 5,000-strong garrison left in Phrygian Amorion by Fudhala and then massacred by Andrew the *cubicularius*[29] was comprised of these Saborian loyalists, but at least some are likely to have gone back east along with the 'many prisoners' the Arabs took during the campaign.

There is evidence that Muawiyah I and his successors settled such Roman defectors on Umayyad territory. In 664/665, Abd al-Rahman b. Khalid raided Roman territory and 'wintered there after devastating many towns'.[30] As he returned home to Syria, he was joined by 5,000 Slavs, who were either serving in the Roman army or had been planted in Anatolia to bring land back into use. Muawiyah I had these Slav defectors 'settled in the village of

Seleukobolos near Apamea',[31] just to the south of Antioch. As will be seen later, Abd al-Malik came to settle another band of Slavic defectors in 692, and it would appear that he chose the same region of northern Syria that the Mardaites vacated upon their 'repatriation'.[32] This could infer that the Umayyads saw these Slavs and the Mardaites in similar terms – defectors from the Roman cause. The *Chronicle of 741* also refers to the release of deserters as a vital part of Justinian's negotiations with the 'king of the Saracens'[33] in 688/689.

Jumping to the conclusion of the Mardaites being defectors seems like a stretch. Would the Romans really have taken back such defectors and settled them in Pamphylia to use as a vital component of their naval forces? The initial answer may well be in the negative, but when it is highlighted that naval service was physically demanding and perhaps even more life-threatening than that in the army, it could be that the Mardaites were military men who 'deserved some form of punishment duty'.[34] Justinian and his advisers may have therefore seen the return of the Mardaite 'deserters' as an opportunity to teach them a lesson while also bolstering naval manpower. While initially serving as conscripts, as time passed, Mardaite naval service may have become an accepted and even hereditary status.[35]

However, the Mardaites being deserters settled in Umayyad territory would significantly undermine the reported trouble faced by Muawiayh I and Abd al-Malik. It would require a total rejection of a connection to any Roman landings along the Levantine coast near Tyre and Sidon, and even the entire notion of the Mardaites being an internal problem for the Umayyads. There is plenty of scope to doubt the sources of this period, particularly the imagination of Theophanes when he is faced with problematic sources of his own. However, it may be going a little far to suggest that he and/or his Syriac source either covered up or misunderstood a mass defection of Armeniac forces and instead invented a prolonged insurgency within Umayyad territory, complete with naval landings, based almost solely on a projection of the naval association of the Mardaites from the mid-eighth century back to the late seventh.[36] Rather than marking the Mardaites specifically as defectors like the Slavs of Abd al-Rahman, the Umayyad placing of the latter in the territory vacated by the Mardaites may just highlight that they were both foreigners being posited on vacant land, rather than running the risk of annoying other inhabitants of the caliphate by settling a band of foreigners amongst them.

The exact nature and origins of the Mardaites is not the only avenue of potential deviation from the source material. The sheer extent of their success in Umayyad territory is also to be questioned. From their mountainous holdfasts, the Mardaites reputedly 'controlled the heights from Galilee to the Black Mountain, sallying out all the time into Arab territory to plunder and destroy'.[37] Theophanes would have it that Muawiyah I was encouraged to sue for peace in 678 because Mardaite attacks had not only encouraged many slaves, captives and locals to join them, but had stretched from the Lebanon mountains to 'the Holy City'.[38] This suggests that the Mardaites were an enormous threat to the Umayyad Levant, capturing territory from the Amanus Mountains – also known as the Mauros/Black or Nur Mountains – in northern Syria all the way south to Jerusalem, the 'Holy City'.

While this would have been 'a stunning military achievement',[39] the idea of such a widespread success is hampered by the lack of corroboration. Had a Roman marine force succeeded in wrestling a coastal strip of 300 miles from the Umayyads, surely the sources would have made much more of it.[40] This may be another example of Theophanes trying to make sense of his sources telling him different things, and in the process, presenting an exaggerated story. The supposed extent of Mardaite successes seemingly stem from a misidentification of this 'Holy City'. Rather than meaning Jerusalem, this is probably Cyrrhus in northern Syria, which was also called Hagioupolis, literally meaning 'Holy City'.[41] Mardaite territory being limited to an area just north of Antioch, incorporating Cyrrhus and the Amanus Mountains, makes much more sense geographically and politically than pan-Levantine conquest.[42] Misidentification of the areas under Mardaite control may also be seen in the frequent associating of them with Mount Lebanon and Lebanon in general. Both Lebanese locations may be much too far south for the Mardaites to have gained control over. While there is room for Mardaite raids and outposts further south than Antioch, it may be prudent to downplay the connection between the Mardaites and Lebanon.[43] However, positing the Mardaites solely in northern Syria does not mean that they were not able to raid far and wide, generally making a nuisance of themselves for the Umayyad caliphate.

Any elimination of a Lebanese connection may undermine another possible identification of the Mardaites. Many adherents of the modern-day Syriac Maronite Church claim a connection to the Mardaites, through how the original followers of the fourth-century hermit St Maron migrated to Mount Lebanon from near Antioch. This connection relies on oral tradition and some geographic similarity centuries apart, rather than solid documentary evidence. This does not rule out a connection, but makes it difficult to corroborate. The Mardaites do seem to have been Christians, and the question could be asked as to why an isolated, mountainous Maronite people would make up such a connection with the Mardaites if there was not some sort of link.[44]

Such an array of possibilities requires some attempts at clarity, and some seemingly polar opposite ideas may not be as far away as first thought. Constantine IV sending a marine commando unit into enemy territory to inspire an insurgency seems like something much more akin to modern warfare, although this does not completely discount the idea. There is some hint that insurgent attacks did help the Roman cause during the 'siege' of Constantinople. It does make it difficult to believe that Constantine IV and Justinian II had much control over the Mardaites, even though Theophanes suggests that the treaty between Abd al-Malik and Justinian stipulated that 'the emperor would keep the Mardaites' troops out of Lebanon and stop their attacks'.[45] The idea that the area under Mardaite influence was largely confined to northern Syria, outside of some raids, is persuasive, particularly the identification of the 'Holy City' as Cyrrhus rather than Jerusalem. A Mardaite threat from the Romano-Umayyad frontier all the way south to southern Palestine seems too much.

While positing the entire Mardaite cause as merely a misunderstood deserter settlement that Justinian demanded be returned for 'punishment duty' in the Roman navy may require too much of a rejection of the source material, it does provide other useful ideas. The highlighting of the potential presence of former soldiers of a rebellious Armenian *strategos* in northern Syria could considerably bolster the extent of the threat posed to Umayyad authorities. Rather than just a small commando unit gathering escaped slaves, disgruntled peasants and tribesmen and former Roman provincials, these defections could have seen Constantine IV's insurgent force combining aspects of the opposing views on the Mardaites: a Roman-instigated insurgency bolstered by Roman defectors. If the emperor knew of these settlements in and around Cyrrhus, Antioch and the Amanus Mountains, they could even have been his target of insurgency. This would have been much more of a threat to the Umayyad Levant, one that Abd al-Malik would have been desperate to get rid of, with Justinian happy to take them back and put them to good naval use, even if there were some defectors in their ranks. The funnelling of the Mardaites into maritime colonies may not have been a punishment or simply a recognition of the need for naval manpower, but perhaps also an understanding that a group that had spent over a decade as raiders might need the discipline and distraction of military service to prevent them from inflicting similar damage on the Roman state.

No matter who these 'plunderers/deserters' were and how they came to be in northern Syria, by the time they were repatriated into the Roman Empire through the treaty of 688/689, the Mardaites had been in Umayyad Syria for at least a decade, if not two. In building their numbers up to be counted in the thousands by attracting various malcontents, there must have been women and children among them, even if the sources do not mention them. Certainly, there would need to have been intermarriage or connection to the local populations if any form of group integrity remained in the Mardaite colonies in Pamphylia, the Peloponnese and the Adriatic coast down to the tenth century.

It is also worth noting that while they may not have been an ethnic group,[46] the 12,000 taken into the empire by Justinian II does not seem to have been all of the Mardaites present in Umayyad territory, or the terms involved in their name survived the Justinianic repatriation. This is seen in the career of a certain Maiouma al-Gurgunami – 'Maimun the Mardaite'. Al-Baladhuri has Maimun originate as a slave of Muawiyah I's sister, only to escape and join the Mardaites. Evidently, Maimun did not partake in Justinian's 'repatriation', and seemingly continued the Mardaite insurgency until the forces of caliph al-Walid put an end to it by force and integration. Through either his Mardaite raiding or initial Umayyad service, Maimun caught the attention of the caliphate's foremost general, Maslamah b. Abd al-Malik, who had him promoted to emir of Antioch and prominent military command. Theophanes would have it that the 708 siege of Tyana by Maslamah and al-Abbas was launched partly in revenge for the defeat and death of Maimun at the hands of the Roman general Marianos during an Arab attack on Cilicia.[47]

Depending on the view taken, the treaty of 688/689 either saw Justinian reluctantly recall his insurgents from Umayyad territory or Abd al-Malik accede to imperial demands for the return of Roman defectors.[48] Whichever of these is closer to the truth, Theophanes saw their removal to Roman territory as a significant strategic mistake. He thought that it eliminated a valuable bulwark against the Arabs along the Romano-Umayyad frontier, allowing the caliphate to gain more direct control over those lands and therefore launch more attacks into Roman Anatolia.[49] It might well be that Arab raiding of Asia Minor increased in the 690s, but this is not necessarily anything to do with the removal of the Mardaites from Umayyad territory, and more to do with Abd al-Malik's success in unifying the Arab caliphate. Regardless of attempts by the likes of Theophanes to blacken the achievement of this treaty in order to make Justinian look bad, examining the terms agreed to by Abd al-Malik in 688/689, they seem a great success for the emperor and the empire. Perhaps the only real negative from this first squaring up to the Umayyad caliphate was that Justinian had been unable or unwilling to take greater advantage of the Second Fitna. Had the empire not been faced with problems on its other frontiers, the emperor may have been able to make more decisive interventions in Transcaucasia and even northern Syria. As it was, he was satisfied with the improved treaty and the closing down of the Anatolian frontier for now.

The Second Fitna up to the Treaty with Justinian

In all the focus on Justinian's reputed conquests in Armenia and the subsequent triumph that was the treaty of 688/689 with its condominiums and insurgent repatriation, it must be remembered that throughout this Romano-Umayyad conflict, Abd al-Malik was still mired in the Second Fitna. And even then, Theophanes has it that the Umayyad caliph was able to launch a counteroffensive against the Romans, capturing Circesium and Theopolis. However, this is an example of poor presentation by Theophanes or his source. Neither of these two cities were in the hands of the Romans at this time, and their recapture appear little to do with the campaigns of Leontios. Situated at the confluence of the Euphrates and Khabur rivers, Circesium was much too deep into Arab Iraqi territory to be in the hands of the Romans. It does seem to have rebelled against Abd al-Malik and submitted to him in c.690,[50] which would appear to be the military success that Theophanes is referring to here. Theopolis – 'City of God' – was the name given to Antioch by Justinian I, and while it may have been in range of an audacious Roman thrust, that Abd al-Malik 'subjected Theopolis' suggests that it was in revolt against him, rather than taken by Leontios. While there is no record of an Antiochene revolt at this time, the trouble Abd al-Malik was having within Syria makes it possible. It has also been suggested that these caliphal actions at Circesium and Theopolis were instead corrupt and misdated references to Abd al-Malik's settling of Slav deserters at Cyrrhus and Antioch.[51] It should also be pointed out that the outset of Justinian's first Romano-Umayyad war seems to have come hot on the heels of a Khazar strike through the Caucasian passes, which 'inflicted

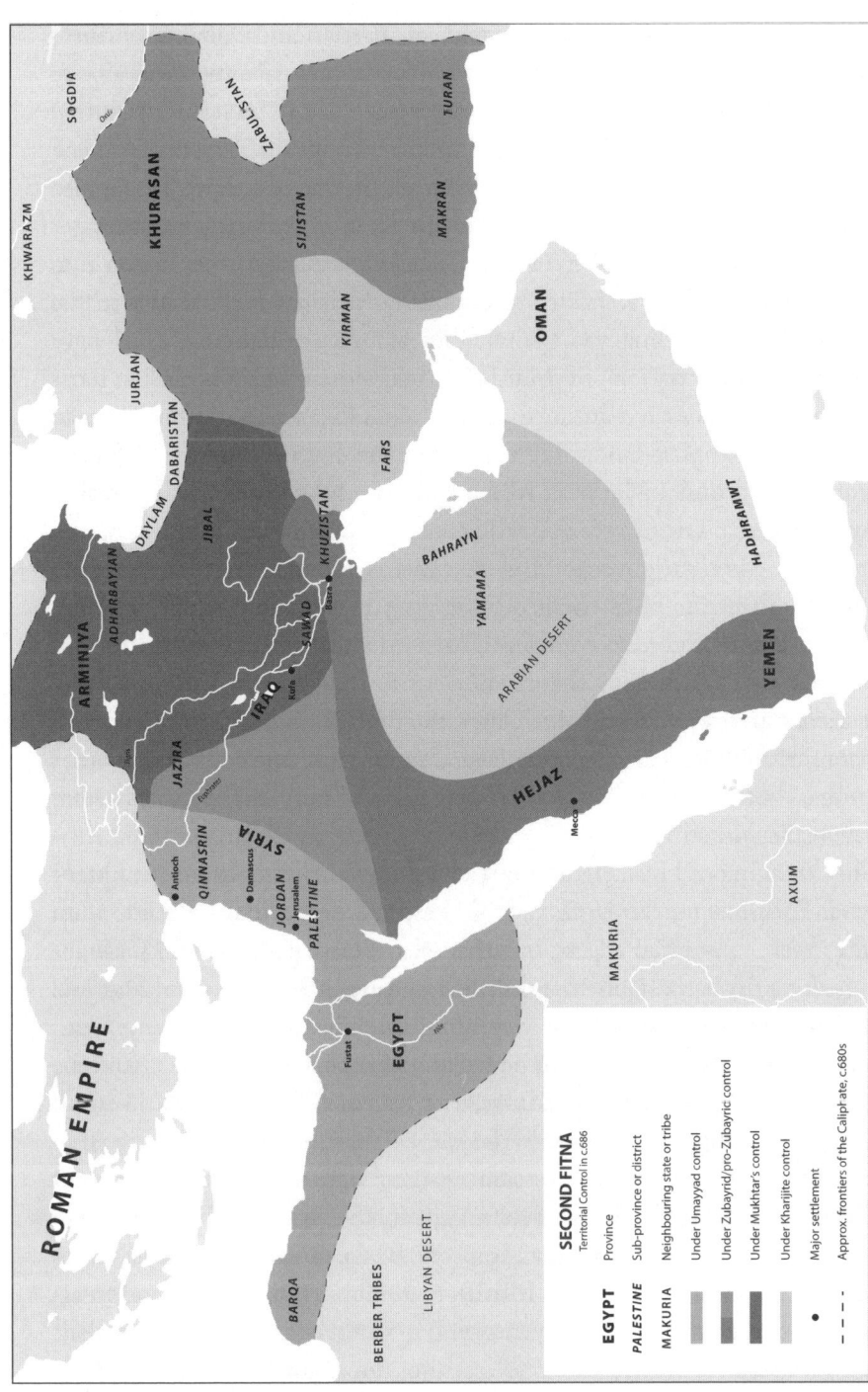

Second Fitna.

a serious defeat on a coalition of Armenian, Iberian and Albanian princes in August 685'.[52] Such damage may help explain how Leontios was able to range so widely when he struck east.

Within the caliphate, Abd al-Malik still faced opposition from al-Zubayr centred on the Hejaz (the eastern provinces beyond Kharijite Persia also recognized him) and Mukhtar centred on Kufa and Iraq. The successes of Marwan in reclaiming Egypt and defeating a Zubayrid incursion into Palestine enabled Abd al-Malik to establish much-needed stability in the Syrian core of the Umayyad caliphate, a stability which may well have involved the 'repatriation' of Mardaites to Roman territory. This focus on Syrian unity does not mean that Abd al-Malik was not attempting to reclaim other caliphal lands. He supported the Iraqi campaign of Ubayd Allah launched under Marwan, which had already defeated the Tawwabin at Ayn al-Warda, forced pro-Zubayrids onto the defensive and taken Mosul from its pro-Mukhtar governor. But that was as good as it got for Umayyad forces in Iraq in the 680s. Bent on avenging Husayn and the Tawwabin, Mukhtar sent his forces to confront Ubayd Allah. Despite being victorious in a skirmish in July 686, the Alids were forced to retreat by Umayyad numerical superiority; but a month later, the Battle of Khazir saw Mukhtar's forces rout the Umayyad army, killing Ubayd Allah. It would be another three years before Abd al-Malik would try again in Iraq and five years before he saw real success there.

This avenging of Husayn and the Tawwabin was the zenith of Mukhtar's success. Focusing on the Umayyads in Iraq had distracted the Alids from another more existential threat; one that was at least partially of Mukhtar's own making. When establishing himself in Kufa in late 685, Mukhtar had looked to widen his support by appealing directly to the *mawali* – local, non-Arab converts to Islam. This new manpower enabled him to expand the territory under his sway to include most of Iraq and some of north-western Iran. However, this reaching out to the *mawali* was unpopular with the Arab elite. Mukhtar's ruthless suppression of their opposition and subsequent execution of any suspected of involvement in the defeat of Husayn saw a significant exodus of prominent Arabs to Basra. The Kufan Arab elites persuaded the Basran governor, Mus'ab b. al-Zubayr, brother of caliph al-Zubayr, to strike at Mukhtar's territory. For all their exuberance over their defeat of Ubayd Allah, it all came crashing down for Mukhtar's Alids as Mus'ab's move against Kufa resulted in the annihilation of Mukhtar's army at the twin battles of Madhar and Harura by the end of 686. Mukhtar and his remaining supporters were subsequently besieged in the palace of Kufa for the next four months, until in April 687, Mukhtar himself was killed during a sortie, leaving his remaining supporters to surrender. This reduced the combatants in the Second Fitna to the Umayyads and the Zubayrids.

While the Muslim civil war was entering its final phase, the treaty of 688/689 between Justinian II and Abd al-Malik saw the attention of the Roman sources shift away from the Romano-Umayyad frontier for the next three years. This was because, seemingly even before the treaty had been finalized, Justinian and his advisers felt that the increased tribute and the batch of military recruits they had attained in negotiations with the caliph was sufficient to turn their attention to their Balkan problems. The emperor had a paternal humiliation to avenge.

Chapter 5

Saving the Second City: Justinian in Thessalonica

'the [Greek] peninsula was in fact lost to Byzantium'

Ostrogorsky (1963), 3

'A Roman Island in a Slavic Sea'?[1]

The humiliation that Justinian II sought to avenge was the defeat of the Bulgar expedition launched by his father in 680. The subsequent peace treaty of 681 had seen tacit Roman recognition of the nascent Bulgar state, with the empire paying out the tribute it had won from the Umayyads straight into the Bulgar treasury. Justinian could not let this blemish on his family's record go unchallenged. Even before the treaty with Abd al-Malik was signed, the emperor had refused to pay the annual subsidy to the Bulgars. This amounted to little more than an overt declaration of war. 'One might expect that so patriotic a move as the refusal of tribute to the barbarian Bulgars would win Justinian commendation from the chroniclers';[2] however, demonstrating the extent of the anti-Justinian bias of men such as Theophanes and Nikephoros, this breaking of Constantine IV's treaty was presented as a travesty. Overturning his father's peace, they said, was a sign of Justinian's poor judgement, completely ignoring the results of the campaign and the failure that had produced the treaty with the Bulgars in the first place.[3]

However, while Justinian may have hinted that his aim was all-out war with the Bulgars in revenge for the defeat of his father's army at the Oglos, his actual ambitions appear far more specific. The emperor was going to lead the army in person in order to show himself a military leader, just as the previous generations of his family had done. He was not marching north to fight the Bulgars of Asparukh along the Danube; indeed, while he would face some Bulgars in the course of the campaign, it may even be incorrect to suggest that Justinian was targeting Bulgars at all. Instead, Justinian marched out from Constantinople, likely with some pomp and ceremony, and headed west along the north coast of the Aegean into northern Greece, perhaps even along the *Via Egnatia*, with the objective of securing imperial territory there. The target was specifically the area around Thessalonica.

Founded on the Thermaic Gulf in around 315 BC and named after Thessalonike, half-sister of Alexander the Great and wife of Cassander of Macedon, Thessalonica had quickly grown to become one of the most important cities in Greece. Upon the Roman takeover, Thessalonica was made the provincial capital of Macedonia and its position along the *Via Egnatia* made it an important trade hub between East and West. It also lay at the southern end of the Balkan trade routes north to the Danube. While not one of the original four regional capitals of the Tetrarchy, Thessalonica became an important centre for the emperor Galerius, who contributed greatly to the architecture of the city, building a palace, a triumphal arch and the Rotunda. By the end of the fourth century, Thessalonica was the capital of the eastern praefecture of Illyricum and the second-largest city in the Eastern Roman Empire, behind only the imperial capital at Constantinople.

Thessalonica was also one of the early centres of Christianity; it was visited by St Paul, who later addressed two of his letters to its inhabitants, which became the biblical books of First and Second Thessalonians.[4] At some point in the fourth century, Thessalonica acquired St Demetrius as its patron saint, who had reputedly been martyred during the Great Persecution. It seems likely that this association was the result of the translation of the cult of Demetrius from Sirmium, probably around the time that Thessalonica replaced Sirmium as the main military base in the Balkans. It also highlights that Demetrius was not a Thessalonian native,[5] and yet he became an invaluable part of the Thessalonian mythos, fully embraced as a patron saint and interwoven into the hagiography and history of the city.

The prominence of Demetrius in the fabric of the Thessalonian mindset is seen during the city's response to the growing threat it faced from the Avars and Slavs during the last decades of the sixth and on into the seventh century. With Roman forces increasingly preoccupied with war in the East and 'imperial authority [varying] from weak to non-existent',[6] groups of Slavs settled unhindered in the region around Thessalonica, although perhaps not on the scale that the sources present.[7] In such a position, surrounded by barbarians who were in no way content with being just occasionally noisy neighbours, Thessalonica was transformed from one of the empire's great cities to one of its most fortified; an outpost almost completely surrounded by an enemy that made several attempts to capture the city. The surprise at the survival of the city against such repeated attacks may have encouraged the persistent attribution of saintly intervention by Demetrius.

This saintly appreciation amongst the Thessalonians is also highlighted in the most important of the sources for the history of the city in the seventh century – the collection of Greek homilies that comprises the *Miracles of Saint Demetrius*. As the name suggests, this collection recounts the miracles performed by the saint on behalf of the Thessalonians as they faced several sieges by the surrounding Slavic tribes. While caution is required when dealing with such material and its potential distortion of events to fit a hagiographic story, it does show the importance of Demetrius to the Thessalonian resistance. It also provides an insight into a part of the Roman Empire which the main sources had been unable to record.

According to *Miracles*, the first attempt against Thessalonica in the seventh century came in around 615 under the Slavic leader Chatzon. While the mass of his people blockaded the city by land, Chatzon's men attempted a naval assault in their rudimentary logboats. This failed due to poor weather, which was attributed to the intervention of Demetrius. The combatants then resorted to negotiation, with Chatzon entering the city in peace. However, this incited a riot, with the inhabitants venting their fury on the Slavic delegation. Despite the attempts of the city leaders to keep him safe, Chatzon was murdered by a mob.[8] This outrage saw the now leaderless Slavs call their erstwhile Avar overlords for help, enticing the khan with the wealth of the city and its importance to what remained of Roman influence in the Balkans.

The Avar attack came in 617/618 and met with little to no opposition as the khan had his siege engines brought to bear on the Thessalonian walls. Outside help amounted to a few supply ships sent by Heraclius. The Avars were far more proficient in siege warfare than the Slavs (indeed, than most barbarian tribes), and the siege lasted thirty-three days. That said, it was the failure of some key pieces of siege equipment that undermined their efforts against Thessalonica. The walls were too strong for their battering rams and a siege tower collapsed, killing its crew – shoddy building work, strong defensive counter-measures or saintly intervention? Eventually, the city leaders paid the khan to lift the siege.[9]

The next half-century of Slavo-Thessalonian relations appears to have been peaceful, perhaps even verging on the amicable. There may have been a failed Bulgar attempt under Mauros, a lieutenant of Kuber, to capture the city by a ruse in 640. Constans II reputedly dreamt he was in Thessalonica on the eve of the Battle of the Masts in 655, suggesting it was still in imperial hands.[10] There may be some hint that renewed imperial activity in the eastern Balkans under Constans II – who campaigned against certain Slavs in 658[11] – the weakening of the Avars and the arrival of the Bulgars may have encouraged the Slavs into a less confrontational stance towards Thessalonica. There is even some hint recorded by the *Miracles* in the form of Perboundos, leader of the Slavic Rhynchinoi, that some of the southern Slavs were becoming somewhat Romanized. Perboundos spoke Greek, dressed as a Roman and had good enough relations with Thessalonica that he had a residence within the city.[12]

Despite this amicable relationship, a Thessalonian governor heard a rumour that Perboundos was planning to attack the city. He sent word of this to Constantine IV, who ordered that the Slavic leader be arrested and sent to Constantinople. The Rhynchinoi, along with their Strymonitai neighbours and the Thessalonians, sent a delegation to the imperial court asking that clemency be shown (perhaps showing at Perboundos had done *something* wrong). This possibly unprecedented joint Romano-Slavic delegation succeeded in getting Constantine to defer judgement until after he had finished with the Arab conflict he was dealing with. The envoys returned home, apparently satisfied with that result. However, Perboundos then went some way to proving that the suspicions about him were correct, or that at the very least he did not expect the emperor to be clement. With the aid of an imperial translator, he escaped captivity and went on the run. It took forty days for imperial forces to find Perboundos, who was hiding in the translator's Thracian estate near Biyze. Brought back to the capital, the Rhynchinoi leader attempted to escape again, but upon his failure, he admitted to planning the capture of Thessalonica. With that, he was executed.

Upon hearing of Perboundos' death, the Rhynchinoi, the Strymonitai and another neighbouring tribe, the Sagoudatai, declared hostilities against the Romans and prepared to attack Thessalonica.[13] During the manhunt for Perboundos, Constantine had sent warning to the city, instructing it to prepare for a Slavic attack. By the time the renegade Slavic leader was recaptured and word of his execution had reached northern Greece, Thessalonica likely had several weeks if not months to prepare. Whatever preparations the Thessalonians made were overshadowed by their civic leaders selling off much of the city's grain stores cheaply just before the blockade was initiated. This might seem short-sighted – the author of the *Miracles* certainly thought so – but the previous Avaro-Slavic attacks on the city suggested that any blockade or siege would not last long and could be bought off with gold. The civic leaders may just have been filling the city treasury for such an eventuality.

However, any such gambit was to prove almost catastrophic because the Slavs seem to have learned something of the art of siege warfare from their Avar and Roman connections. This latest attempt on Thessalonica was 'better organized than in any of the preceding sieges, with an army of special units of archers and warriors armed with slings, spears, shields, and swords'.[14] The Slavic allies enforced a tight blockade of the city by land, the Strymonitai to the north and east, the Rhynchinoi to the south and the Sagoudatai to the west. Daily raids by land and sea removed any livestock and agricultural produce and destroyed any avenue of resupply. This tight noose and the selling-off of grain saw Thessalonica quickly face a famine, which was exacerbated by a lack of water. The situation was bad enough for some Thessalonians to defect to the besiegers. The numbers of defectors became high enough that the Slavs feared a revolt in their camp, so many of these citizens were sold as slaves to the other Slavic tribes.

The only real hope for the Thessalonians was the imperial fleet and army, but during the earlier parts of the siege, both were heavily deployed protecting the capital from whatever constituted the 'First Arab Siege of Constantinople'. Constantine IV did manage to dispatch a squadron of ten armed transports, which forced their way through the Slavic blockade of the Thessalonian harbour. However, these sailors were not numerous enough to tilt the balance in the favour of the besieged. They also sold the supplies they had brought at exorbitant prices and were enough of a nuisance to the citizenry that they voted to send them on a mission to obtain more food from the city's Belegezitai allies in Thessaly. Noticing the departure of the imperial squadron, the Slavs decided that now was the time to assault the city walls. They sought the assistance of the Drougoubitai, a neighbouring Slav tribe who were proficient in siege craft; the extent of the help they provided is unclear, but at least some engines and perhaps their crews arrived before Thessalonica for an attack to begin on 25 July of the 'fifth indiction'.

It is here that *Miracles* suggests that St Demetrius made his first intervention, supposedly causing the Strymonitiai to retreat before even reaching the city walls. It is speculative to try to extract any factual basis for this retreat beyond the hagiographic, although there could be some straightforward reasons for it. Perhaps they were bought off by the Thessalonians or heard of attacks on their own lands. Perhaps they were not even meant to be part of this assault at all. Whatever the reason, the Slavic assault on Thessalonica was left to the Rhynchinoi and the Sagoudatai. Over the course of three days, the waves of Slavic attacks were beaten back by the defenders, with Demetrius again intervening at numerous points to help. At one stage he repelled Drougoubitai attackers who seem to have gained entry to the city through a postern gate. At the end of the third day, the Slavs gathered up their dead and withdrew to their camps. A few days later, the imperial squadron sent to the Belegezitai arrived back with much-needed food.

The defeat of the landward assault and these new supplies may have released some of the pressure on the Thessalonian defenders, but it did not end the blockade. The Slavs continued to raid right up to the city walls, and now they looked to shut down any traffic reaching the city from the sea. A combination of primitive logboats and some actual ships saw the Slavs becoming increasingly piratical around the northern Aegean. While taking to the sea to cut off Thessalonica from the outside world was vital in forcing a conclusion to the siege, in the process the Slavs drew attention to themselves through their raids. In particular, at least one such raid struck into the Sea of Marmara, likely noticed by imperial forces, with word reaching Constantinople.

With the Arab attacks on the capital seemingly over, Constantine IV could now respond to Thessalonica's plight and the Slavic raids by sending a significant force through Thrace to attack the homes of the besieging tribes. The Slavs were able to mount a defence in the highlands, but the imperial army was victorious, scattering the tribesmen and relieving Thessalonica. In revenge, and likely with the help of the newly arrived soldiers, the Thessalonians launched an attack on several nearby Slavic settlements. An imperial fleet then arrived with a vast amount of wheat to help feed the city. The combination of imperial forces and their own military defeat caused the Slavic tribes to sue for peace. The outcome of this overture is unknown, but it could well be imagined that the Thessalonians tried to get the imperial army to make more decisive attacks against the local Slavic tribes. Conversely, they may also have been too exhausted for more warfare after their initial pillaging. It is likely that the imperial army, if the emperor himself was not present, was only to fulfil a specific order – defeat the Slavs besieging Thessalonica, relieve the city and carry out some mopping-up operations – which did not include a full-scale war against the entirety of the Slav peoples in northern Greece. If there had been a formal peace, Theophanes is likely to have made sure that Justinian got any blame for breaking it. Perhaps this is why the historian or his source focuses on the emperor's rejection of the treaty with the Bulgars, despite the focus of his campaign being the Slavs of northern Greece.[15]

As might be imagined about a historical outline reconstructed from the collection of homilies that is the *Miracles of Saint Demetrius*, there are chronological issues. Beyond the mention of 25 July of the 'fifth indiction' and the three-day assault, there is no definitive chronological marker within the *Miracles*. Even the emperor it mentions is not named. This has seen significant and broad speculation about when this siege actually took place, with various points and reigns during the seventh century being mentioned. T.L. Tafel placed it in 634 during the reign of Heraclius, which seems unlikely as the emperor was not in the capital at the time and war with the Arabs had yet to break out. Hélène Antoniades-Bibicou and Halina Evert-Kappesova placed the arrest of Perboundos in 644, the siege in 645–647 and the 'fifth indiction' assault in 647, followed by the relief of the city by imperial forces in 648/649. There was certainly war with the Arabs at this point, but would the *Miracles* have overlooked the youth of Constans II – he was only 14 in 644 – or the conflict with Valentinus? The aforementioned campaign of Constans II in 657/658 has also been suggested as involving the relief of Thessalonica. The imperial distraction could have been Muawiyah's preparations for an attempt on Constantinople and the subsequent Roman defeat in the Battle of the Masts, with Constans then able to turn against the Slavs due to the outbreak of the First Fitna.[16]

The entire Slavic siege of Thessalonica has also been postulated as belonging in the reign of Justinian II. Justinian did launch a campaign towards Thessalonica in 688, where he is well-remembered, which would be appropriate for an emperor who saved the city from attack. This would place the siege in around 685–687, a period when the empire was facing war with the Arabs; however, were the campaigns of Leontios enough of a distraction for Justinian to not send more than a token force to Thessalonica? There must have been some men available from Thracian and Asian units of the Opsikion theme, while the imperial navy does not appear to have been involved at all in the campaigns of *c*.685–688. A positing of the Slavic assault in 692 and therefore a siege covering 691–692 has also been made, but there was no Arab war to distract Justinian before 692.[17] It has also been suggested that the anonymous author wrote during the reign of his unnamed Roman emperor, and if it had been Justinian II, he would surely have mentioned him by name, given that that emperor visited Thessalonica in person.

The more widely accepted chronology (and the one followed here) connects the siege of Thessalonica and the inability of imperial forces to respond to the 'First Arab Siege of Constantinople'. It sees the arrest and execution of Perboundos sometime in early 676, with the Slavs then attacking Thessalonica during the summer. The 'two-year' siege would then involve the rest of 676 onto the assault on 25 July 677. The rest of 677 and early 678 would involve the return to a blockade and the piratical Slav attacks in the northern Aegean. The imperial relief expedition followed in summer 678, after the defeat of the Arab siege of Constantinople.[18] Of course, as already seen, the dating of this 'siege' of the imperial capital is problematic in itself, making any reliance on aspects of it to chronologically anchor the Slavic attack on Thessalonica similarly so. However, such problems should not discount a comparable dating and even a connection between the threats to Constantinople and Thessalonica during the reign of Constantine IV. They just reduce the ability to present as specific a series of dates as has previously been done. Whatever the 'siege' of Constantinople entailed, it was certainly an Arab war to take the attention of the emperor and – perhaps most importantly – it explains the lack of imperial moves to relieve Thessalonica, particularly the specific absence of the imperial navy.

To Hellas and Back: Justinian in the Field

The trouble dating the Slavic siege of Thessalonica is just one example of the poor state of the record of Roman counterattacks against Avars, Bulgars and Slavs in northern Greece. It could be that the very paucity of the material regarding the Balkans in the seventh century reflects the desperation of the situation there. Either there was little information preserved through choice or 'relatively little history was being written for the grim realities of life permitted little leisure for scholarly pursuits'.[19] While the chronology is not completely secure, it does seem that Thessalonica had been under direct Slavic threat during the 670s. And with Justinian's choice to march out towards Thessalonica, it might seem that any peace that was signed after the relief of the city by imperial forces had not held. Archbishop John II of Thessalonica was present at the Third Council of Constantinople in 680–681, which hints at the city still being connected with the outside world,[20] but this does not eliminate the idea of it coming under pressure again. Perhaps some of the Slav tribes seen off by the forces of Constantine IV had re-established themselves closer to the city or a combination of Bulgar and Slav tribes had cut the land routes east to Constantinople.

This could explain Justinian's choosing of the Slavs for his first venture into the field. Perhaps he felt that the recent defeat of the Slavs under his father's auspices would make them an easier target, although by 688, that defeat was at least a decade old. It may be that Justinian was not looking for any great military confrontation. If he was, it might have been expected that he would strike more directly at the Bulgars or drive deeper into Slav-held territory in northern Greece. Theophanes perhaps hints at this campaign being more for show than military success, with Justinian having 'ordered the thematic cavalry to cross to Thrace, as he wanted to take prisoners among the Bulgars and the Sklavinoi'.[21] Such an action would likely be to gather ransom funds, hostages or manpower, whilst providing a demonstration to Bulgars, Slavs and even Roman citizens that the new emperor was willing to take to the field. It is also worth repeating that in campaigning against the Bulgars and Slavs, Justinian II was following a course that both of his predecessors, Constans II and Constantine IV, had trod with varying degrees of success. This family heritage may have been as important as anything to the latest Heraclian emperor.

Theophanes presents Justinian's campaign in the Balkans as beginning with the emperor sending out the thematic cavalry into Thrace. This may have been a combined raiding/scouting party, gathering intelligence on the tribal forces he might face in marching west along the *Via Egnatia* and providing warning to any such tribes that imperial forces were active in the area once more. The dating system of Theophanes makes this seem like an advanced party headed out a year earlier than the main force, as his record of Justinian's Balkan campaign is split over two annual entries – AM6179 and 6180; however, it is likely that these took place in the same campaigning season – summer 688, which just happens to be divided in two by the indiction dating system. It may even be that this advance by the thematic cavalry and Justinian's own march to Thessalonica were one and the same action.

This advance along the *Via Egnatia* through the Rhodope Mountains saw Justinian come into conflict with 'groups of Bulgars'.[22] While the sources seem keen to paint this campaign as involving the Bulgars of Asparukh, who had signed the treaty with Constantine IV, it is more likely that these Bulgars are those linked to another of Kubrat's sons, Kuber. After living under Avar domination around Sirmium, Kuber had moved into this area of south-east Macedonia during the latter years of Constantine IV's reign, perhaps encouraged to do so by the success of Asparukh. It could be argued that the Romans or Theophanes recognized the familial connections between the Bulgars of Asparukh and those of Kuber, and therefore saw them as one entity, covered by Constantine IV's 'appropriate edicts'[23] that Justinian was now confounding. Instead, this could be a lumping together of all Bulgars of the eastern Balkans or a mistaking of Kuber's Bulgars for those of Asparukh. Given the late arrival of Kuber in the Rhopode Mountains, it could be that either Constantine IV or Justinian himself had negotiated some kind of treaty with Kuber in recognition of that position, only for one party or the other to renege on it. Whatever the background, that Theophanes has Justinian 'thrust back as far as possible the Bulgars he encountered'[24] may well lend some credence to the idea that the emperor sought to remove this Bulgar group from the lines of communication between Constantinople and Thessalonica.

The imperial army then forced its way into northern Greece, squaring up to significant groups of Slavs. It would seem that the emperor had to win more than one battle against these tribes as he forged his path towards Thessalonica. That even the anti-Justinian sources do not mention any sort of trouble on this outward march would suggest that the emperor had marshalled a sizeable force to undertake this campaign and/or that the numerous Slavs were not acting in concert against him. Theophanes also recounts that in his victories, Justinian captured significant numbers of Slavs, enough to establish a military colony in the Opsikion theme in Bithynia. But perhaps more surprisingly, as word of Justinian's transplanting of Slavs to new lands spread, there seems to have been a considerable number of Slavic volunteers from the unconquered tribes in the Balkans, 'attracted by the prospects of regular service in the imperial army and, perhaps, of land grants in their new location'.[25]

While the suggestion that Justinian relocated 100,000 Slavs[26] would seem exaggerated, it does appear that the emperor did transfer a significant number to Asia Minor, suggesting that 'Justinian was a firm believer in wholesale relocation as a cure for many of the Empire's ills'.[27] The people of Thrace, southern Macedonia and northern Greece likely noticed a reduction in Slav marauders, while imperial forces in Asia Minor will in time have felt the bolstering of new recruits to deal with the Umayyads. Of course, some locals in Bithynia may not have taken too kindly to the appearance of tens of thousands of non-Romans in their midst. Any conflict between locals and the new Slavic planters could have caused unwanted distractions for local thematic forces, with them having to act as a police force rather than a defence against Arab raids. It has been suggested that not only was Justinian willing to accept some local disgruntlement for the benefits of such a relocation, he may even have been actively targeting some of the local magnates for a chastening. The emperor was no friend of the landed aristocracy, so his relocation of thousands of Slavs, which will have involved the appropriation of large tracts of land, may have had the extra motive of reducing some of the power and influence of these local magnates.[28] Whatever the full circumstances of their transfer to Asia, the soldiers recruited from these Bithynian Slavs would play a significant role in Justinian's wars in Anatolia, while any disgruntlement of the landed aristocracy would lead to political problems for the emperor as well.

Despite their faith in the protection offered to their city by the saintly Demetrius and its increasingly impressive defences, it can be well imagined that the citizens of Thessalonica were overjoyed at the news of an imperial army marching through western Thrace into Macedonia. The defeats it then inflicted on the Bulgars and Slavs will only have heightened the sense of relief, particularly as numerous Slavs were to be transplanted away from the immediate area. To top off that joy, the new young emperor was at the head of this imperial army and he had now directed it towards Thessalonica itself by the end of summer 688. Indeed, so happy were the Thessalonians with the arrival of Justinian II that it has been suggested by some that they celebrated this great 'triumphal' entry with commemorative frescoes painted on the walls of the Church of St Demetrius.[29] However, the identification of the figure in these frescoes as Justinian II is not universally accepted.[30] Room for various interpretations of these frescoes is provided by the fact that they were covered over by other decorations – could that itself suggest that it 'was' Justinian, with a form of *damnatio memoriae* taking place due to his later political and religious reception? Uncovering the frescoes caused some damage and there is no identifying inscription to record who this bearded horse-rider actually is. He certainly looks like he could be a Heraclian emperor, with the white horse and attendants perhaps demonstrating his imperial status. Furthermore, the content suggests that the fresco was pre-iconoclastic, and as Justinian is known to have sported such a beard from his coinage and to have visited Thessalonica, he would seem a likely candidate.

It has been pointed out that the man in the fresco does appear considerably older than Justinian's 19 or 20 years of age in 688, but as has already been seen with the imperial mosaic of Sant'Apollinare in Classe, imperial propaganda was not above 'aging' a subject in artistic depictions to increase grandeur, wisdom and experience. Furthermore, the fresco was not necessarily painted in 688 during or immediately after Justinian's visit. It may therefore depict the emperor as he chose to be seen later in his reign, and he is known to have started sporting a beard from his coins in around 688.[31] 'In any event, if the fresco is a portrait of Justinian, it could help to explain why apparently some memory of him lived on in the city of St Demetrius, long after most of the Empire had forgotten he ever existed or knew him only as the villain of Theophanes' *Chronographia*.'[32]

That fond memory Thessalonica had for Justinian II may also be demonstrated in an inscription dating to the Palaeologan period, the last Roman dynasty to rule Constantinople. Inscribed on the silver frame of a mosaic originally part of a reliquary for the 'holy oil of St Demetrius', is the plea 'O great martyr Demetrius! Intercede with God that He may help me, thy faithful servant, the earthly Emperor of the Romans, Justinian, to vanquish my enemies and subjugate them beneath my feet.'[33] The initial thought may be that this is Justinian I, the sixth-century emperor whose armies had reconquered Africa, Italy, southern Spain and the western Balkans. Such a successful leader would be more than worthy of a plea of intercession. However, this plea seems more personal, asking for help from someone who perhaps had already provided direct, personal assistance to the city and people of Thessalonica. For all the reconquest carried out in his name, 'so far as is known ... [Justinian I] was never personally involved in warfare around Thessalonika'.[34] As there were no other emperor Justinians, that would seem to leave Justinian II as the only candidate. He had been involved in fighting near Thessalonica and had personally entered the city in triumph. This fits the mould of an emperor you might beseech for help at a time of crisis, alongside a saintly patron. 'The fact that Justinian's name is associated with that of Thessaloniki's beloved St Demetrius in this context is indeed an intriguing hint of the survival of historical traditions about him differing sharply from those preserved by Nikephoros and Theophanes.'[35] The only other option may be that by the time of the Palaeologans (1261–1453), the personages of Justinian I and II had somewhat amalgamated into a single character – a mighty emperor Justinian responsible for great conquests and the saving of Thessalonica from the barbarians, with none of the negatives of the latter being remembered.

On top of the frescoes and Palaeologan silver frame inscriptions, there is another epigraphic piece linked to Justinian's time in Thessalonica, or at least connected to his reign. An inscription on a marble tablet, rediscovered in the nineteenth century, preserves an edict of an emperor who 'renders thanks to St Demetrius for his recent victories and confers upon the saint's church the privilege of a *halike*'.[36] Unfortunately, the workmen who uncovered this inscription managed to break it into over seventy pieces and it was left to several scholars to try to reconstruct the text it contained.[37] Much like with the Palaeologan silver inscription, it appears that this edict belongs to Justinian II because he was present in Thessalonica, and 'as far as we know, Justinian I never visited Thessalonica, so … the inscription does not refer to him'.[38]

There is also some dispute over what exactly αλικη/*halike* means in this situation or period. It is certainly to be associated with salt, but in what form? It would appear to be one of three potential meanings: a salt tax; a salt works/pit/pan, where the salt was extracted or manufactured; or a salt shop/store, where it was sold. The Church of St Demetrius appears to have been exempt from paying tax on this αλικη/*halike*, so that would seem to make it unlikely that it was 'salt tax'. The edict seems to suggest that the αλικη was located in the city, which would seem to make it a place rather than a tax, and probably a building rather than a pit, mine or pan. A salt store within the city, possibly owned by the government, would make it easier for Justinian to give away and exempt from taxation.[39]

Regardless of what was being given over to the Church of St Demetrius, through whatever imperial official wrote the edict, Justinian displays his own considerable self-assurance and belief in how he was God's chosen champion both as emperor and saviour of Thessalonica, with the help of St Demetrius.

'We are convinced that God who has crowned us is always the benevolent champion of our piety and more abundantly grants victories to us … We have come to this city of Thessalonica according to the aid of God who had crowned us … We have obtained the helpful support of the holy great martyr Demetrius in various wars which we had made against his and our own enemies.'[40]

Could Justinian have taken Demetrius as his own protector/patron saint? Could that help explain the continued memory of Thessalonica if the emperor tied his fortunes to those of Demetrius? If he was willing to give up *halike* to the Church of St Demetrius, what else might he have provided?

Perhaps more revealing of Justinian's view of himself that he wished to project to the world are the epithets attached to his name within the edict. He appears as 'the lord of the whole universe, Flavius Justinianus, the God-crowned and peace-maker Emperor … the autocrat peaceable benefactor … the faithful Emperor in Jesus Christ the Lord'.[41] Not only was the enacting of the support and name of God and Jesus Christ an increasingly usual thing amongst Roman emperors at this time, but Justinian's presenting of himself as a peacemaker is even more applicable to the time and place where this edict was being issued. Thessalonica and the surrounding area had seen considerable warfare in recent decades and Justinian was keen to present his intervention as having ended the Slav menace in southern Macedonia. That said, there was a tinge of hypocrisy regarding such peaceful pronouncements, for Justinian himself may well have been the instigator of the latest round of war with the Bulgars and Slavs in breaking the treaty established by his father.

Having won, celebrated and then commemorated his victories *en route* to and around Thessalonica, Justinian then seems to have tried to use those victories to re-establish more direct governmental control on central Greece. This seemingly took the form of the θέμα Ἑλλάδος (*Thema Hellados*), more commonly known as the Hellas theme. The historical record does not specifically mention the establishment of this theme, but Leontios, the Anatolic *strategos* who led Justinian's first war against the Umayyads, is recorded as *strategos* of Hellas in 695. This at the very least suggests that the Hellas theme was founded during the first reign of Justinian II, and as he was in the region in late 688, this is usually thought to be the time of the foundation.

There is one last rather important addendum to Justinian's march to Thessalonica. For all it appears to have achieved militarily, territorially, governmentally and in terms of positive propaganda for Justinian, it may have culminated in almost fatal disaster. After he had finished with his celebrations and organizing in Thessalonica, Justinian and his army began the trek back to Constantinople. In the narrow mountain passes, they found themselves intercepted by what must have been a significant Bulgar force. Justinian 'was barely able to get through, and his army took many casualties'.[42] This almost total disaster in the Rhodope Mountains may demonstrate the young emperor's recklessness, impatience and inexperience. The way

Theophanes records this ambush suggests that the Bulgars had been lying in wait for the imperial army, which in turn implies that Justinian and his forces took the same route home as they had on their outward journey. This could have been a strategic mistake on the part of Justinian, as it not only gave the Bulgars the chance to set up an ambush, but may have seen the army unable to resupply as well as it might because the outward journey had denuded the route. But as these were narrow passes through mountains, it is likely that the Bulgars laid their ambush in a spot where they knew the emperor would have to pass through because it was the only option.

Instead, this disaster may display a more general Roman arrogance regarding the Bulgars and other barbarians. They may have seen the initial defeat as Justinian marched west as enough to prevent these Bulgars being a threat on the way home, leading to limited or no scouting missions ahead of the main column or for Justinian to race on ahead with the cavalry. It could also demonstrate the reach of the nascent Bulgar state if Asparukh had some part to play in this ambush. Perhaps more likely is that it shows that the initial Roman victory was a limited one against a small force of 'Kuber' Bulgars, and rather than receive aid from Asparukh, these local Bulgars found common cause with some of their Slav neighbours to ambush the emperor.[43]

However, there are grounds to doubt Theophanes' testimony here. Nikephoros, who would surely jump on any opportunity to denigrate Justinian, does not record his falling victim to a Bulgar ambush in 688. He does, however, have Justinian facing something of a Bulgar ambush during his second reign at the Battle of Anchialus in 708, but then Theophanes mentions this ambush as well.[44] Perhaps Theophanes has duplicated this military setback for the emperor accidentally, rather than merely inventing a defeat for Justinian in 688. Of course, it is also possible, if less likely, that it is Nikephoros who has made the mistake in missing the ambush in the Rhopode Mountains.

It must be noted that neither Theophanes nor Nikephoros give all that much detail about Justinian's campaign in 688. It could be because there was little to actually record, with Justinian's march west being uneventful aside from some limited skirmishes with first Bulgar and then Slav forces. However, the number of Slav prisoners taken, even if heavily exaggerated, suggests at the very least that the mere presence of Justinian at the head of an imperial army won a significant strategic success for the empire. It is more likely that there were some not insignificant victories won by

Justinian and his generals for so many Slavs to have been taken prisoner or volunteered for settlement in Bithynia. The physical evidence of frescoes and inscriptions suggest that Justinian II made a significant impact during his time in Thessalonica. While this could have been just because the emperor had visited the city, and the hint of religious propaganda is hard to shake, the Thessalonian adoration and the formation of the Hellas theme may suggest that Justinian II had done something worthy of military praise.

Even if there was some kind of Bulgar reverse in late 688, it was not severe enough to overturn the plans Justinian had implemented in Greece or to nullify what had been a strong military start to his reign. The first three years had seen victories over the three main enemies of the empire – the Arabs, Bulgars and Slavs. In the process of those victories, Justinian and his generals may have recovered territories around Thessalonica, along the *Via Egnatia*, in Armenia, Iberia, Azerbaijan and Media, while strengthening governmental control in central Greece. Certainly, in a political sense, the treaty with Abd al-Malik had been a great achievement. It also encompassed a much-needed financial boost through increased Arab tribute, revenues from Armenia, Iberia and Cyprus, and any booty taken from other caliphate dependencies in Transcaucasia and even Iraq and Iran. These revenues were added to by the stopping of the tribute to Asparukh's Bulgars and any spoils taken from the Slavs. There were also the expanded manpower resources of the defeated and volunteer Slavs and the returned Mardaites.

Justinian may have been 'barely able to get through'[45] the Bulgar-defended narrow passes of the Rhopode Mountains, but when he did reach the safety of Constantinople, he could look back on a good start to his reign. His armies and generals had proven capable, and with an expanded army, a bolstered treasury and the Umayyads still distracted with internal problems, Justinian II could look forward to building on this good start.

Chapter 6

A 'War of Images' all about The Money? The Romano-Umayyad War of 692

'thanks to a lack of good sense, Justinian broke the peace with Abd al-Malik.'

Theophanes, *Chron.* AM6183

Maskin and Mecca: The Culmination of the Second Fitna

If the sources had been lacking in detail for Justinian's first three years, they provide even less about the next three years. When dealing with the Romans, both Theophanes and Nikephoros (so it can be imagined that their shared source did likewise) jump from Justinian's success against the Slavs around Thessalonica and the aftermath in late 688 to the outbreak of war with the Umayyads in 692. Of course, that is not to say that nothing happened within the Roman Empire during this period. Justinian will have been hard at work consolidating his reign at home, informing his subjects of the success of his military campaigns, implementing infrastructural changes like his establishing of the Hellas theme and perhaps laying the groundwork for his church council. Furthermore, the Romano-Umayyad War of 692 did not just happen out of nowhere. There were considerable diplomatic, economic, religious and propagandist issues which seem to have driven this drift back to war in Anatolia. Before that though, while the written sources would claim that there was little to report about the Roman Empire internally during the period 689–692, there were significant developments within the Umayyad caliphate: 'the Arabs' civil war ended'.[1]

While the 'treaty of 688/689' had been a political, military and financial success for Justinian II and allowed him to turn his attention to Thessalonica, it was also a welcome development for Abd al-Malik. While it showed an unwillingness to continue the fighting and was set to cost his regime almost half a million *nomismata* over the course of the next nine years, closing down the Anatolian front allowed Abd al-Malik to focus on finishing the

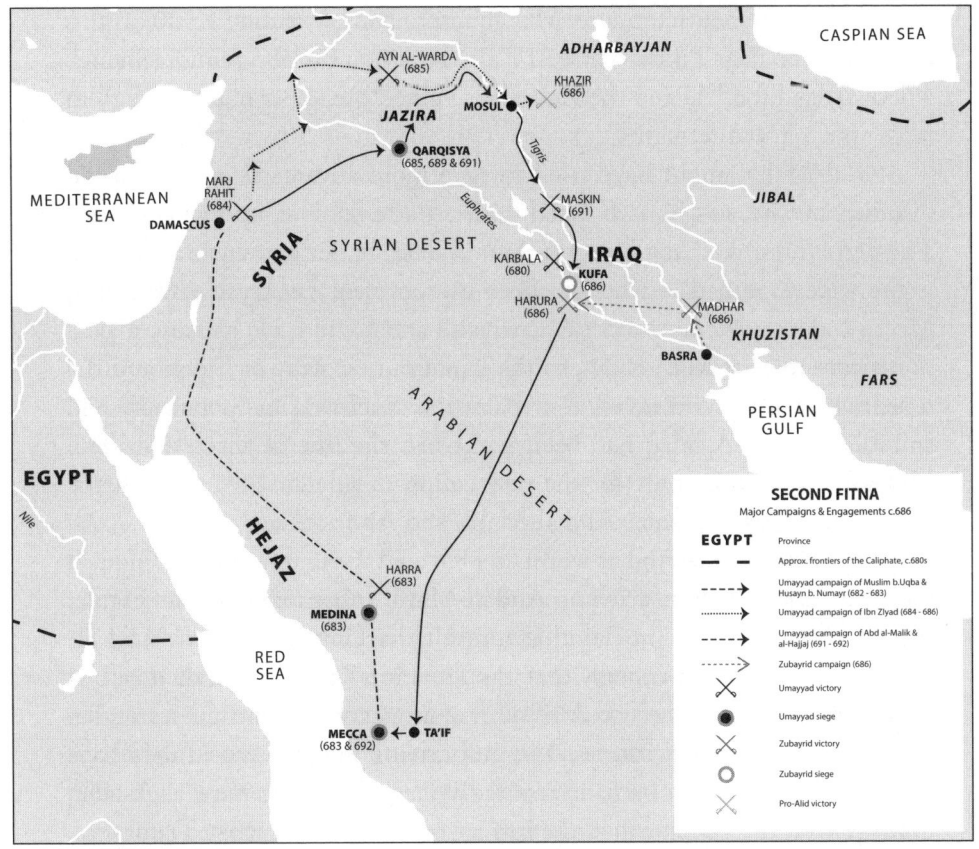

Second Fitna Actions.

Second Fitna. While there were still lands around the Persian Gulf under the control of the Kharijites, the death of Mukhtar at the hands of Mus'ab had left the fight for the caliphate a two-horse race between the Umayyads and the Zubayrids.

The cessation of hostilities with the Romans saw Abd al-Malik turn his attention to Iraq, where he had previously been foiled by Mukhtar's Alids. In 689, the Umayyad caliph led a force to the Syria-Iraq border, camping at Butnan Habib just east of Aleppo. Mus'ab responded by gathering his army near Tikrit. While the Umayyad and Zubayrid armies both sat astride the main road from Syria to Iraq, they were still some 350 miles apart, suggesting some mutual reticence. Rather than advance, Abd al-Malik tried to use the absence of Mus'ab from Basra to stoke anti-Zubayrid protests amongst its inhabitants. The caliph's kinsman, Khalid b. Abdallah, succeeded in raising a pro-Umayyad revolt in the city, leading to a series of clashes lasting a month or more. Mus'ab responded by sending 1,000 cavalry from his camp near Tikrit, while Abd al-Malik sent his own reinforcements. These arrived too late and the Zubayrids gained the upper hand, enough to force an Umayyad retreat.[2]

Abd al-Malik might have tried to take more advantage of this Basran disorder, but he was himself faced with an attempted coup in Damascus. The perpetrator was Abu Umayya Amr b. Said, better known as al-Ashdaq – 'the wide-mouthed' – who had been a prominent Umayyad governor in Mecca and then Medina under Muawiyah I and Yazid I. He had also played significant roles at Marj Rahit, in the Umayyad recovery of Egypt and the repelling the Zubayrid invasion of Palestine. Such was his popularity and ambition that al-Ashdaq had been named in the line of succession upon Marwan I's election, only for the new caliph to sideline him through the promotion of his own sons, Abd al-Malik and Abd al-Aziz.

On the accession of Abd al-Malik in 685, al-Ashdaq refused to relinquish his claim, and in 689 he acted on Abd al-Mailk's absence at Butnan Habib, seizing Damascus and proclaiming himself the Umayyad caliph. Abd al-Malik moved quickly enough that the situation had not spiralled out of control and al-Ashdaq accepted his offer of amnesty in return for surrender. The caliph proved more ruthless and unforgiving than the rebel might have thought. Acting on an oath he reputedly gave should he have al-Ashdaq in his power, the caliph called the former rebel to the palace of Damascus, assaulted him and had him beheaded.[3] It might not have truly threatened Abd al-Malik's reign, but the revolt of al-Ashdaq had hindered the caliph's efforts in the Second Fitna.

A further Iraqi campaign in mid-690 proved equally abortive for Abd al-Malik, with the Umayyad and Zubayrid armies again congregating at Butnan Habib and near Tikrit respectively, but making no move against each other before dispersing for the winter. A third Iraqi campaign in 691 appeared to be going poorly when Umayyad forces failed to take the pro-Zubayrid city of Qarqisiya; however, this is the Circesium that Theophanes records falling to Abd al-Malik,[4] so the caliph must have succeeded through negotiation. The Umayyad caliph was also aided by the actions of Mus'ab. In his brutal repression of the followers of Mukhtar and the Umayyads, the Zubayrid governor had made himself unpopular with certain sections of the Basran and Kufan leadership. This was not helped by the continued raids of the Kharijites requiring Mus'ab to keep a significant portion of his forces in Basra. Zubayrid forces in Iraq were therefore facing defections, unpopularity and conflict on two fronts when Abd al-Malik marched against Mus'ab in 691.

Al-Tabari records an anecdote regarding the make-up of Mus'ab's army, suggesting that the Zubayrid had made a critical error in the selection of his forces with which he planned to confront Abd al-Malik. The Zubayrid governor of Khurasan, Abd Allah b. Khazim al-Sulami, inquired who had joined Mus'ab in marching against the Umayyads. After hearing that all of the generals he considered competent (including himself) had been left behind to serve as governors of various Zubayrid regions under threat from Kharijite raids, Abd Allah despaired: 'Take me and drag me away, O she-hyena; rejoice over the flesh of a man whose helper was not present today.'[5]

By the autumn of 691, the Umayyad army had set up camp at Maskin, along the Dujayl canal just west of the Tigris and within striking distance of Tikrit and Mus'ab's base camp, which had been fortified with a trench that became known as the 'Ruins of Mus'ab'. Despite this defensible position, all was not well in the Zubayrid camp. The absence of Mus'ab's best soldiers and his repression in Basra and Kufa had greatly undermined the cohesion of the Zubayrid force. This was something that Abd al-Malik was quick to take advantage of, sending letters to all of the tribal leaders within Mus'ab's camp. One loyal Zubayrid commander, Ibrahim b. al-Ashtar, brought his letter to Mus'ab unopened for the governor to read himself. It contained an offer of the governorship of Iraq in return for defection to the Umayyad cause. Al-Ashtar warned Mus'ab that virtually all of his commanders had received similar letters and yet none had come to tell their governor, urging him to take drastic action:

> "'Heed me concerning them, and cut off their heads!" "Then," said Mus'ab, "their tribesmen will not be loyal to us." Ibn al-Ashtar said, "Then load them with irons, send them to the White [Palace] of Khusraw, and imprison them there. Put in charge of them someone who will cut off their heads if you are defeated. If you are victorious, you can bestow them on their tribesmen as a favour."'[6]

Mus'ab felt that he could not take the chance that his army would simply melt away if he executed or imprisoned many of its leaders on the eve of battle. It may be queried as to why Mus'ab would leave his entrenched positions to square up to Abd al-Malik when he clearly knew that the loyalty of significant numbers of his men was suspect. With the Umayyad forces so close, it could be that retreat was no longer an option. Mus'ab had to fight now before more of his men deserted or defected.

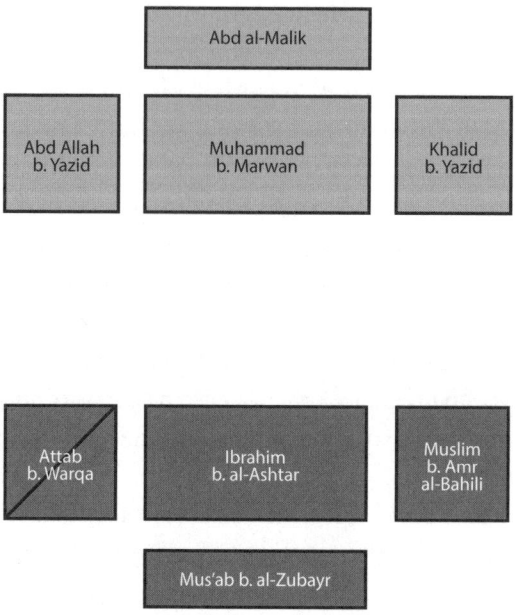

Battle of Maskin I: Initial Deployments.

As it was, the Zubayrid force marched out from its camp, squaring up to the Umayyad army at Dayr al-Jathaliq in the middle of October 691.[7] The exact deployment of Mus'ab's force is not completely clear, but al-Ashtar commanded the centre vanguard and Attab b. Warqa led a cavalry corps on the Zubayrid left. It would seem that the Zubayrid right was under Muslim b. Amr al-Bahili and Mus'ab himself led a reserve rearguard. In contrast to the divisions within the Zubayrid camp, Abd al-Malik had members of his family in command of his various divisions – his brother Muhammad commanded the Umayyad vanguard, Abdallah b. Yazid was on his right wing and Khalid b. Yazid was on the left. The caliph himself likely commanded a substantial reserve or even the main part of his army behind the vanguard.

Perhaps demonstrating his increasing need for a quick resolution, the outset of the battle saw Mus'ab throw his centre under al-Ashtar straight at that of Muhammad, with the Umayyads being forced back by the ferocity and surprise of such a direct attack. Abd al-Malik checked al-Ashtar's momentum by ordering Abdallah to attack his left flank and possibly committing some of his reserve to shore up Muhammad's ranks. The next actions within the battle are not recorded, but given that Muslim b. Amr al-Bahili then appeared in the thick of the action, it would seem that Mus'ab reacted to the check of his vanguard's advance by sending in his right wing.

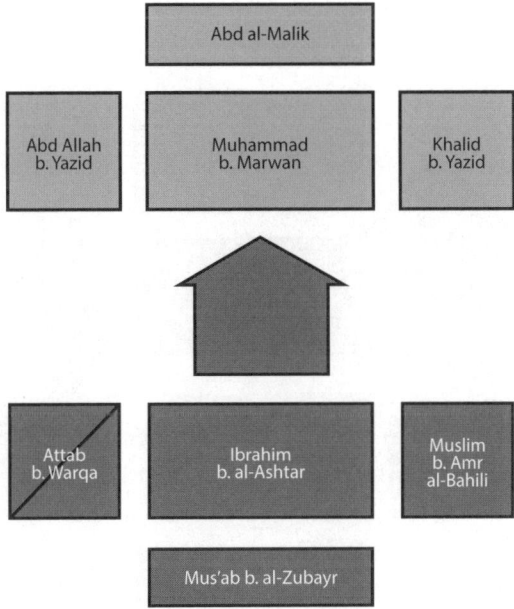

Battle of Maskin II: al-Ashtar's Attack.

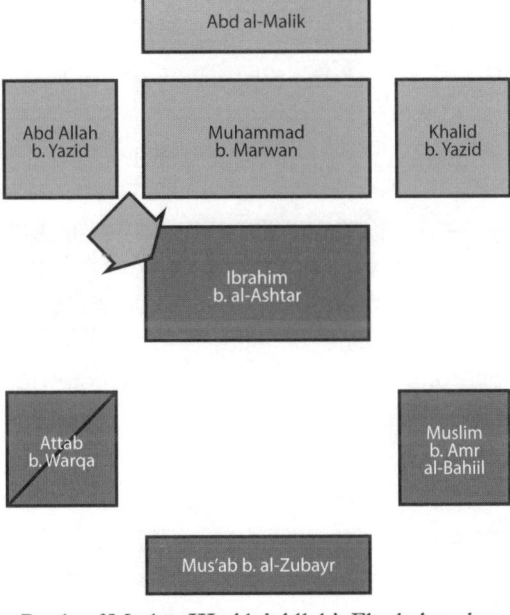

Battle of Maskin III: Abd Allah's Flank Attack.

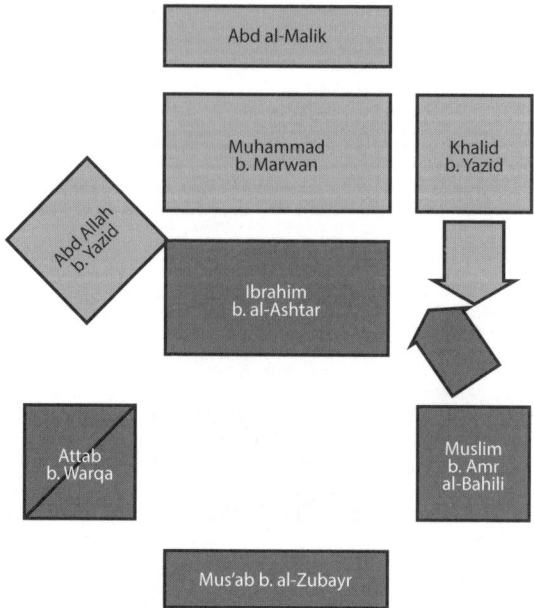

Battle of Maskin IV: Attack of Muslim b. Amr and Khalid.

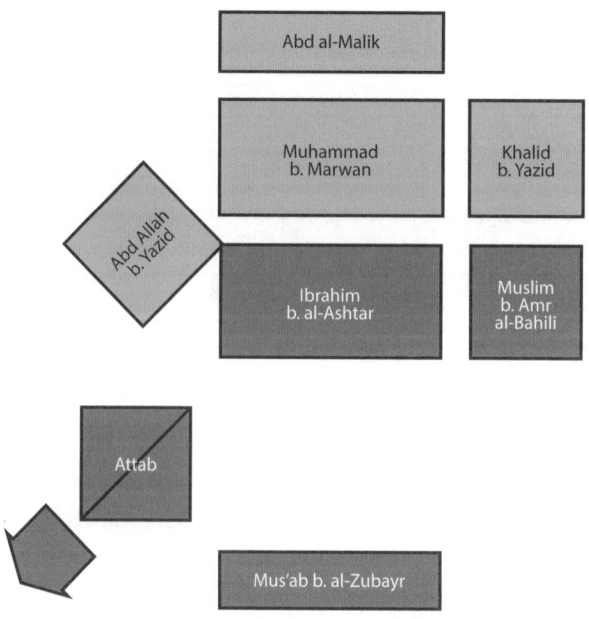

Battle of Maskin V: Deaths of al-Ashtar and Muslim b. Amr.

While it is also not recorded, it would seem logical for Abd al-Malik to have responded by committing his left wing under Khalid in direct opposition to Muslim.

Khalid's counter-charge/spoiling attack against the advance of Muslim, while possibly necessary to thwart al-Ashtar's reclaiming of the initiative, represented a significant opportunity for the Zubayrids. The Umayyad centre and both of its wings would seem to be committed fighting just the centre and right of Mus'ab's army, exposing the flanks of Abd al-Malik's force. Even if the reserve corps under Abd al-Malik's direct command had not been drawn into the fighting to help Muhammad's centre, any move to counter a Zubayrid flank attack would leave Mus'ab with the final card to play with his own reserve.

However, it was at this potentially pivotal moment that the Zubayrid cause was struck by three consecutive blows. In the midst of the fighting in the centre and on the Zubayrid right, both al-Ashtar and Muslim b. Amr al-Bahili were killed.[8] All need not have been lost, for the Zubayrid centre and right did not collapse upon the loss of their commanders, while Mus'ab still had his left-wing cavalry to throw into the fray. Or so he thought. It was with the deaths of two of the Zubayrid leaders that the embers of division within Mus'ab's ranks, fanned by Abd al-Malik's letters, burst out into the open. Rather than attack, Attab b. Warqa led his cavalry force in a mass desertion of the Zubayrid cause. This may even have been a pre-planned move, with Attab having already defected to the Umayyads and not showing his true colours until the worst possible moment for the Zubayrids.[9] The loss of his left wing was a heavy blow for Mus'ab, but it need not have been decisive. The Zubayrid governor may have lost the tactical advantage, but he still had his reserve force to commit to battle. A well-aimed and well-pressed strike, perhaps at the Umayyad right flank, might still salvage a draw or even better. He could even have retreated with his reserve to his trenches near Tikrit and held out until he could bring up his best troops from the Kharijite front. But for Mus'ab and ultimately the Zubayrid cause, the divisions wrought by his actions in Basra and Kufa, the promises of Abd al-Malik and the self-preservation instinct of many of the tribal leaders were too great. For many of Mus'ab's generals, the desertion of Attab's cavalry had left the battle a lost cause; any charge into the fray or retreat south now was a futile gesture of defiance.[10]

As his last corps refused to follow orders and melted away, Mus'ab recognized that the day was lost. It would appear to have been obvious enough

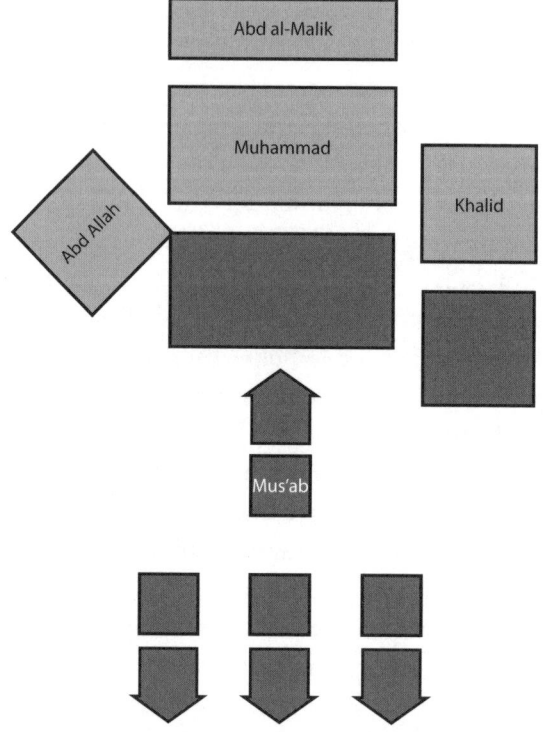

Battle of Maskin VI: The End Game.

that the battle was lost for the Zubayrids that Abd al-Malik sent a message via Muhammad to Mus'ab, offering him amnesty in return for surrender. Mus'ab responded that 'A man like me leaves this place either victor or vanquished.'[11] Muhammad then turned his entreaties to Isa, Mus'ab's son, offering him similar amnesty. Mus'ab also seems to have implored his son on two different occasions to either flee to Mecca or accept Abd al-Malik's clemency. On both occasions, Isa b. Mus'ab refused, choosing to die with honour like his father.[12] With a very limited escort, Mus'ab and his son charged into the fray. Wounded by an arrow, Mus'ab was knocked from his horse by a spear wielded by Za'idah b. Qudamah, a kinsman of Mukhtar, and then beheaded by Ubayd Allah b. Ziyad in revenge for having killed his brother. Ubayd Allah took Mus'ab's head to Abd al-Malik, who tried to reward him with 1,000 dinars, but he refused to take it: 'I did not kill him out of obedience to you; I killed him to avenge what he did to me. I do not take money for carrying a head.'[13]

Abd al-Malik's victory at Maskin gave him control over most of Iraq, but he must have felt wary of the Basran forces which had not been present at the battle due to their campaigning against the Kharijites. The caliph need not have worried, as al-Muhallab b. Abi Sufrah, a Zubayrid commander who might have made the difference at Maskin, upon hearing of the result of the battle, ordered his Basran forces to swear allegiance to Abd al-Malik.[14] This allowed the Umayyad caliph to enter Kufa and accept the allegiance of all of Iraq and the eastern provinces (aside from the territory in Fars and Kerman controlled by Kharijites). While Abd al-Malik oversaw the reintegration of Iraq into his realm, he dispatched his capable administrator al-Hajjaj b. Yusuf with an army to deal with al-Zubayr in the Hejaz.

It is worth querying where the Zubayrid caliph had been during this extended civil war. On the surface, he seems to have played little part in the battles to secure his caliphate, but when looking at the situation in the Arabian Peninsula, there was plenty to keep him occupied. Throughout the 680s, a Kharijite group striking out from the Persian Gulf had been making considerable headway in the agricultural centre of Arabia, particularly Yamama province. By 685, Najda b. Amir al-Hanafi had emerged as sole leader of what was swiftly becoming an independent Kharijite statelet. Najda continually proved himself a cunning and capable leader, out-thinking, outmanoeuvring and outfighting various Zubayrid generals and armies. Al-Zubayr and his sons proved increasingly incapable of not only controlling these Najdat Kharijites, but of confronting them at all. By 688, areas such as Bahrain, Oman, Yemen and Hadhramawt had been essentially lost, giving Najda control of virtually the entire Arabian Peninsula outside the Hejaz. This effectively cut off al-Zubayr from his forces in Iraq and the eastern provinces. Perhaps the true testament of Najda's power came in June 687 when he led a group of Kharijite partisans on the Hajj pilgrimage to Mecca; al-Zubayr was powerless to stop him, and it appeared that Najda was at very least an equal of the Zubayrid caliph, if not of Abd al-Malik as well.[15]

Even before Maskin, al-Zubayr was also not secure in the Hejaz. In 688, Najda had penetrated as far as Medina, before capturing Ta'if the following year. Therefore, when the expedition of al-Hajjaj arrived in the region in late 691/early 692, it found Zubayrid opposition to be lacking. The Umayyad general moved to Ta'if, his hometown, lifting it from whatever control Najda had over it. From there, al-Hajjaj launched a series of raids against Zubayrid forces, probing their strength. A second Umayyad force under Tariq b. Amr then appeared before the walls of Medina, capturing it from its Zubayrid garrison. Keen to follow Abd al-Malik's orders not to attack Mecca unless completely necessary, al-Hajjaj tried to negotiate an end to the Second Fitna with al-Zubayr, offering him safe conduct and amnesty. The Zubayrid caliph rejected any surrender, prompting al-Hajjaj to ask permission from Abd al-Malik to attack Mecca. That permission was granted.

The siege of Mecca began on 25 March 692, with Tariq b. Amr arriving from Medina with Umayyad reinforcements within a month. Al-Hajjaj had supplies cut off and bombarded the city with catapults, with the sacred Kaaba being damaged. But still the remaining Zubayrids clung on. It was up to seven months before the pressure finally told. Some 10,000 inhabitants and defenders, including two of al-Zubayr's sons – Khubayb and Hamza – took up al-Hajjaj's promise of amnesty in return for surrender. But al-Zubayr himself remained defiant to the end. Like his brother at Maskin, he chose death in battle, charging the Umayyad lines with only a few followers. His head was sent to Abd al-Malik and his body put on public display. His passing on 4 October/3 November 692 marked the end of the Second Fitna and the total victory of the Umayyads.

However, there was still the problem of the Najdat, and for all Abd al-Malik's proclamation of a 'Year of Unity',[16] he seems to have recognized this problem as he appointed al-Hajjaj not just governor of the Hejaz, but also of Yemen and Yamama, areas where the Najdat held sway. This Kharijite statelet could have been a serious problem for Abd al-Malik, particularly given the abilities Najda had been shown to possess. It appears, though, that the Umayyad caliph had already gone some way to undermining this threat through his cunning use of diplomacy. He reached out to Najda, offering amnesty and the Yamama governorship in return for recognition of his caliphate. Najda rejected the offer, but the sheer idea that he had been in contact with the Umayyad 'usurper' caused dissension in the Najdat ranks. Such internal trouble may explain the loss of some outlying Najdat territory such as Oman to a local revolt and why al-Hajjaj seems to have been able to focus solely on Zubayrid Mecca, despite operating from a city that the Najdat had controlled. This dissension grew into a full split, with some favouring a treaty with the Umayyad caliphate and hardliners who refused to deal with the 'usurpers'. This culminated in the murder of Najda in 691/692 by the radicals. The Najdat statelet did not last much longer, with a combined force of Basran and Kufan forces defeating the last Najdat army and capturing its holdout by mid-693.[17]

The end of the Second Fitna gave Abd al-Malik the opportunity to reshape much of the Arab caliphate. The most long-lasting of his developments were in the realm of building. The siege of Mecca had damaged the Kaaba, leading to repairs taking place under Abd al-Malik's auspices, although these were not without controversy.[18] It had of course been his forces who had caused the damage, and the caliph made the choice to have the Kaaba flattened and rebuilt as it had been in the day of Muhammad, removing additions made under the Zubayrids. It is this Kaaba that still stands today.[19] Abd al-Malik also oversaw the construction of what is perhaps the second most famous building of Islam: the Dome of the Rock in Jerusalem. Its chronology is uncertain, but it seems to have been completed by 692, which means it was being built during the Second Fitna. Perhaps Abd al-Malik was looking to create an alternative site for pilgrimage if the Zubayrids restricted access to the Kaaba.

Governmentally, the overreliance of personal connections to the caliph and the loyalty of the Arab nobility revealed throughout the Second Fitna encouraged Abd al-Malik to build a more centralized system of government. To enforce this, he expanded on the nucleus of a professional army in Syria, adding a fixed salary for soldiers. He also looked to reduce the reliance on pre-existing Roman and Persian infrastructure, administration and officials. Arabic became the official language of the caliphal government, more of the taxation raised in the provinces was to be sent to the caliphal treasury for redistribution and he initiated the minting of new Islamic coinage rather than relying on altered Roman or Persian issues. This numismatic development would seem to have a substantial effect on Romano-Umayyad relations even before the final defeat of al-Zubayr.[20]

Raisons de Guerre: Colonies, Condominiums and Coins

While the treaty of 688/689 was a great success for Justinian and had provisions – specifically the Cypriot condominium – which were to last for the best part of three centuries, the peace it established between Constantinople and Damascus lasted for less than three years. What seemed like an intricate treaty ultimately failed. The Arabs complained bitterly that it was Justinian who had broken the treaty, although it is likely that the emperor would claim that blame for the outbreak of war in 692 was at the very least to be shared, if not completely the fault of the Umayyads. Our main sources are not particularly helpful in discovering just who was to blame: 'Unfortunately, the chroniclers Nikephoros and Theophanes had such biased material to work with that they made no real effort to get to the roots of the conflict, and the disarmingly uncomplicated data they present as causes leave many questions unanswered.'[21]

They present what is essentially one core *raison de guerre* in 692 – as they had done previously, both Theophanes and Nikephoros blame the hubris and recklessness of Justinian II. This manifested in three specific ways. Firstly, both historians have Justinian being keen to test the forces raised from his new Bithynian Slav colony in battle against the Arabs. Theophanes then speaks of Justinian seemingly looking to build on the success of his Mardaite and Slav colonies by transplanting Cypriots from their island home to an Asia Minor colony, undermining the condominium agreement in the process. Theophanes also has Justinian being offended by the numismatic reforms of Abd al-Malik as a basis for the imperial treaty-breaking, with the added notion that the caliph had manipulated the emperor into either breaking the treaty himself or leaving the Arabs with a plausible pretext to declare the treaty void.[22]

Justinian's successes in southern Macedonia and northern Greece had provided significant Slav prisoners and volunteers for his new military colony in Bithynia. The question of the exact size of this new Slav population in the Opsikion theme has also already been raised, and will be raised again when it comes to their performance in battle and the aftermath. Both Theophanes and Nikephoros claim that Justinian was able to raise a force of 30,000 Slavs from his colonies, called the 'Chosen People' or 'special army' by the former and λαός περιούσιος – the 'Peculiar People' – by the latter.[23] It could be that this total involves other Slavs already settled in Asia Minor, with Constans II recorded defeating Slavs in 657/658 when 'he took many prisoners and brought many people under his control'.[24] Slavs in Asia Minor after this victory but before Justinian's transplanting numbered in the thousands; however, in a warning to Justinian, 5,000 Slavs settled in Asia Minor seemingly defected to the Arabs in 664/665.[25] The transplanting of populations and settling of refugees in places like Bithynia was perhaps not just Constans II and Justinian II establishing sources of military manpower, but also 'a clear indication of the damage inflicted by almost constant warfare on the indigenous populations'.[26]

The Quinisext Council provides evidence regarding Justinian's planting of other colonies in Asia Minor. Its canons record the presence of a certain Isidore, bishop of Gordoserba.[27] This is the first appearance of such a bishopric, and as it was not at the Sixth Ecumenical Council, it was likely founded sometime between these two councils in 680/681 and 691/692 respectively. The settlement's name appears to mean either 'city of the Serbs' or more likely 'the place of the Gordos Serbs'/'the place of the Serbs of Gordos'. While the presence of Slavs in Bithynia is borne out by the written sources and surviving official seals, were there also Serbs? There may have been Serbs settling near Thessalonica under Heraclius in an area called Serblia, which seems to have been named for them rather than them being named after it.[28] This puts them in the firing line of Justinian II's Thessalonian campaign, and it seems likely that Serbs were either amongst those taken prisoner or took up the emperor's offer of settlement in Bithynia, where they were given their own city of Gordoserba and a bishopric, probably because they were already Christians.

While there is no discounting that Justinian may have felt emboldened by his Thessalonian success, it should not be overlooked that if there were this many Slavs in Asia Minor and so many of them were soldiers, the emperor may not have just *wanted* to send them into battle, but felt he *needed* to. Part of the transplantation agreement may have involved the opportunity to fight and win rewards. If they were in any way permanent soldiers, the emperor may also have been obliged to pay them, and if they were present in such huge numbers, this could have been the equivalent of another thematic army to pay for. There could also be some hint of the well-established Roman policy of employing their enemies against one another. Having this new Slav corps battering against Umayyad walls or armies could be a 'win-win' for the Romans. Unfortunately for Justinian, there would be a third, much less appetizing option. If Justinian did pursue a war with Abd al-Malik in 692 for the purpose of testing his newly recruited Slav 'special Chosen army', he was about to be taught a grave lesson about having too much faith in the power of imperial victory.

The seeming extent of the recruiting power that the military colonies of Mardaites and Slavs provided Justinian may have encouraged him to look elsewhere for manpower with which to plant more of these colonies. Theophanes has Justinian 'foolishly anxious to resettle the island of Cyprus'.[29] As might be imagined from such a short summing-up and an historian using sources with an anti-Justinian agenda, this would appear to involve only a half truth. Much like with Gordoserba, the canons of the Quinisext Council provide corroboration that the transplanting of Cypriots did happen. In this case, it is the thirty-ninth canon where Justinian elucidates on his justification for relocating these Cypriots.[30] It is claimed that many Christian Cypriots were being harassed by their Muslim neighbours and were being moved for their own safety. Justinian felt that this harassment justified his interference in Cyprus, although there is some evidence that it was the Cypriots themselves who called upon the emperor to intervene, with John, metropolitan archbishop of Cyprus, visiting Constantinople. The Cypriots may well have been moved so they could be freed from 'the slavery of the infidel'.[31]

The region around Cyzicus was chosen as the new home of these transplanted Cypriots. In another instance of his unreliable sources and/or willingness to paint Justinian in a poor light, Theophanes records that 'a number of the Cypriots who made the effort drowned or died of sickness'.[32] The Quinisext canons and Constantine VII provide proof that this Cypriot colony was established at Cyzicus. The reason for the choice of Cyzicus was that it had been considerably depopulated during the 'First Arab Siege of Constantinople', when it was held by the Arabs as a naval base for repeated strikes against the imperial capital. It seemed a particularly good choice of position to plant a colony of able Cypriot seamen. Justinian was so happy with his new colony that he bestowed the name 'Nea Justinianopolis' – the New City of Justinian – upon it. It also seems that Justinian had his new colony given significant ecclesiastical benefits. It is recorded as having 'the right of the city of the Constantinians',[33] which if meant to be Constantinople is a spectacular position for this new colony to be promoted to; so spectacular in fact that it is undoubtedly incorrect: 'It is likely that this phrase contains a textual error and should read "the right of Constantia", i.e. the metropolis of Cyprus. If so, this is merely a further statement of the transfer of the archbishopric from the island to Nea Justinianopolis.'[34]

Despite the pride Justinian took in his new colony and his supposed excuse of Muslim harassment of Cypriots, there was no overlooking the fact that Justinian had intervened in the affairs of Cyprus without the permission of Abd al-Malik. This would seem in contravention of their joint control of the island. The caliph could have seen this interference in Cyprus in two ways. The removal of some Cypriots reduced the Christian presence on parts of the island, possibly giving Muslims more of a foothold going forward. Alternatively, he could have seen it in purely financial terms: in removing Cypriots from Cyprus and planting them at New Justinianopolis, the emperor was denying the caliph his 50 per cent share of the taxes these Cypriots would have paid to the Umayyad treasury as part of the condominium agreement.

While the Second Fitna might not have been over by the time Abd al-Malik turned some of his attention to Justinian's dealings with the Cypriots, the Battle of Maskin, the surrender of Iraq and the cornering of the Zubayrids in the Hejaz allowed the caliph to broaden his international horizons. If he was looking for a reason to declare the treaty of 688/689 violated and potentially void, Justinian's minor infringement in Cyprus provided one. At the very least, Abd al-Malik responded to Justinian's colony with a Cypriot plantation of his own, settling significant numbers of them in Syria. Of course, for all the distrust the likes of Theophanes have bred in their record, it must not be overlooked that Justinian was perhaps using the plea of the Cypriot metropolitan to test the resolve of the caliph. Interfering in Cyprus by removing Umayyad tax-payers to Roman territory and even treating Nea Justinianopolis as a special new city may have all been part of the emperor's plan to instigate a conflict, or at least to advance his objectives.

A Numismatic 'War of Images'?

Of all the reasons given for the outbreak of war in 692, Justinian being offended by numismatic reforms within the caliphate seems by far the most specious. At least the emperor wanting to test his 'Chosen' Slavs or interfering in Cyprus had hints of warmongering and treaty-breaking. However, the numismatic developments within the empire and the caliphate under Justinian II and Abd al-Malik respectively were heavily influential in the future of their respective coinages and even aspects of their art, culture and religion. This influence, together with Theophanes' assertion that numismatics played a role in Justinian's warmongering, has seen the Romano-Umayyad War of 692 labelled as a 'War of Images'.

On the surface, Abd al-Malik's currency reform seems like a rather peculiar thing for Justinian to get offended about – 'if true [it] would reveal Justinian as a very foolish young man'.[35] The focus of this reputed 'War of Images' were the new gold coinages of both the emperor and the caliph. More specifically, the proposed numismatic *raison de guerre* was the tribute payment that Abd al-Malik owed Justinian as part of the treaty of 688/689. From its inception, the Arab caliphate had not minted its own coins, relying instead on Roman and Persian issues. But now sometime during the reign of Abd al-Malik, the Umayyads began minting their own currency and then tried to pay their tribute to the imperial treasury with these new dinars. The Romans would have been accustomed to receiving their tribute in their own *solidi/nomismata*, complete with imperial portraiture, or slightly altered but still recognizably Roman coins. According to Theophanes, Justinian was deeply offended by being sent these new Arab gold dinars instead of Roman coins, complaining that because the dinar was minted to a lighter standard than the *solidus/nomisma*, Abd al-Malik was looking to get away with paying less than the treaty of 688/689 demanded, something that Theophanes seems to give tacit acceptance of. The emperor therefore sought to refuse this payment, only for the caliph to respond by 'begging' Justinian not to break the peace and promising that even with his new coins, he would still be sending the correct total weight of gold stipulated by the treaty.

Justinian took this pleading by the caliph as a sign of weakness and fear, which presented an opportunity to further build on his previous victories, using this attempted violation of the treaty through an unacceptable and/or underweight payment as his pretext. Unsurprisingly, Theophanes portrays this imperial action as the young emperor not only having 'a lack of good sense',[36] but also him being played like a fiddle by Abd al-Malik. The caliph had 'satanically dissembled'[37] over the payment in such a way that he now could 'break the peace with a pretext that seemed plausible',[38] looking like the injured party despite the outbreak of war being his aim from the very start.

There is another issue that Theophanes mentions regarding the outbreak of war in 692 which played a significant role in the linking of that conflict to any 'War of Images'. He states that 'the Arabs could not accept the Romans' impress on their own coins'.[39] This seems contrary to the importance of the *solidus* to the Umayyad caliphate. However, Theophanes is referring to a significant numismatic innovation under Justinian II which may have made it so that the Arabs were unwilling to use the *solidus*. Indeed, if there were any grievances about coinage to affect the outbreak of war in 692, it is conceivable that it was Abd al-Malik who was doing the complaining.[40]

While Constantine IV had had himself portrayed numismatically in military garb and in a pose copying that of his great hero Justinian I, Justinian II was far more original in his coin designs.[41] Employing a skilled die maker who had served his father,[42] Justinian upped the artistic style and innovative flair. There was to be little or no imitation in his coins. Rather than military garb, Justinian appears in civilian clothing, wearing a *divitision* tunic and a *chalmys* cloak. In one of the few nods to imperial fashion, his *chalmys* is fastened by a *fistula* pin with three jewelled pendants. Somewhat surprisingly, Justinian's crown is a simple cross-topped circlet. In some of his coins, Justinian had himself depicted in a full-length portrait, wearing a ceremonial scarf and holding a large cross. 'Although the emperor's effigy on these issues is so small that it gives little hint as to his actual appearance, it is an attractive and distinctive design.'[43] Some of Justinian's coins bore his monogram cipher, which contained each of the letters of his name in Greek.[44] Such imperial monograms had begun to appear on coins in the fifth century, late in Theodosius II's reign (c.445–450), and had become increasingly prevalent since, appearing not just on coins but also on bricks, monuments or imperial clothing.

None of these innovations or artistic choices had the potential to give offence to Arabs. They had been using coins bearing such imperial portraiture for centuries and even since the revelation of Islam. However, Justinian's more famous numismatic innovation could have provoked the disgust of the caliph and Muslims in general. The emperor began having the effigy of Christ depicted on imperial *solidi*. This was technically not the first Christ appearance on Roman coinage – a 'unique *solidus* of Marcian and Pulcheria' had depicted Christ in c.450[45] – but was the first to enter mass production. By this time, the *solidus* was only minted in Constantinople, so it was not only a lynchpin of the Roman and Umayyad economies, but was providing a direct look at imperial propaganda from the heart of the Roman imperial government: 'an inherently conservative medium … [so] any radical change was exceedingly rare and had to reflect deliberate imperial policy'.[46] These Christ coins were therefore to be thought of as carrying a significant imperial message, but what was that message?

The appearance of emperor and Christ together – 'literally forming two sides of the same coin'[47] – demonstrated the religious importance of the emperor as the earthly deputy of Heaven. This was a concept backed up by the inscriptions on the coins. Above Christ was inscribed *REX REGNANTUM* – 'King of those who reign' – while above Justinian's portrait was *D[OMINUS] JUSTINIANUS SERVVS CHRISTI* – 'Lord Justinian, Slave of Christ'. It has been suggested that this use of *SERVVS CHRISTI* was targeted specifically at the caliph because the name 'Abd al-Malik' literally meant 'slave of the king'.[48] Justinian might have known of this meaning of the caliph's name – perhaps highlighting that 'a slave of the King of Kings is better than one who rejects him altogether'[49] – but it is extremely unlikely that this was a central reason for the inscription appearing on imperial coinage. It seems quite the epithet for the Roman emperor to apply to himself, even if it was a concept from the earliest days of Christianity. However, this *SERVVS CHRISTI* is backing up the public presentation 'of the emperor as Christ's deputy and as the upholder of orthodoxy'.[50] That imperial subservience is also seen in the innovation of the emperor's portrait being moved to the reverse of the coin, 'though it is doubtful that Justinian's subjects paid as much attention to the distinction between obverse and reverse as modern numismatists do'.[51]

Rather than a calculated attack on the caliph specifically or Islam in general, his Christ coinage may just show 'Justinian's deep concern for the outward niceties of the faith'.[52] There may be some connection between these new coins and the Quinisext Council, which was 'replete with Christological allusions and it was clearly aimed at mobilising ecclesiastical support, and divine aid, in preparation for war with the Caliphate'.[53] It could be that canons 73 and 82 – no cross displayed on the ground and against the depiction of Christ as a lamb respectively – had some numismatic connections, which could date the Christ coins around the time of the council in *c*.691/692. However, connecting these canons to numismatics is a stretch, and 'the Trullan canon did not necessarily precede or directly lead to the Christ *solidus*'.[54] They likely reflect the 'internal theological politics of the imperial decision to abandon monothelitism and reaffirm a traditional dyothelete creed, and the use of imperial iconography as one element in this message'.[55] Indeed, the undraped Christ may be a new iconography created by Justinian II.[56] There are arguments that see iconoclastic aspects of Justinian's policies and actions,[57] but this is more of an eighth/ninth-century attitude coloured by Iconoclasm, something which the late Heraclian age would not have had.

The Christ coin and the Quinisext canons may also reflect a wider discussion over the depiction of Christ across the Mediterranean, particularly in the aftermath of Islam's arrival: 'the stage is the same, but all else, characters, scenery, dialogue, the whole frame of reference has changed immeasurably.'[58] There are other coins that demonstrate that Justinian's Christ coin did not develop in a vacuum. A contemporary Visigothic coin depicts Christ, 'probably predating Trullo, Justinian's coins and any Islamic innovation'.[59] A rare Sicilian copper *follis* of *c*.689/690 depicts Justinian wearing a *loros* – a long, narrow and embroidered cloth, wrapped around the torso and draped over the left hand, which was 'a crucial innovation of the reformed *solidi*'.[60] The use of the *loros* was also something of a harkening back to a traditional past, as it was part of the costume of Roman consuls, which had not been seen on coins for a century. The return of consular regalia to imperial coinage might demonstrate not only Justinian's use of tradition, but also his unifying of the office of consul with that of emperor.[61]

A similar depiction of Christ to Justinian's coinage – 'thin short beard, the curly crown of hair, and also it seems, the wide-open eyes'[62] – appears in the fresco *Adoration of the Cross/Crucified* on the triumphal arch of Santa Maria Antiqua in Rome. This image does not conform to the other depictions of Christ known from the papacy of John VII. Therefore, rather than reflecting a growing trend towards such depictions of Christ, which in turn influenced Justinian's Christ coinage, Santa Maria Antiqua's *Adoration* may reflect the impact of Justinian's numismatic reforms. Indeed, the fresco may date to Justinian's second reign.[63] Santa Maria Antiqua hints at the influence that Justinian's Christ coins would eventually come to have; however, it was a precedent ignored by his successors for nearly 150 years until the final defeat of Iconoclasm. But when Michael III (reigned 842–867) had Christ depicted on coins again, the design came from those of Justinian II, which in turn became a template for representations of Christ on imperial coinage and Christian art for centuries to follow.[64]

The *Adoration* fresco of Santa Maria Antiqua possibly getting its numismatic influence from post-705 raises the issue that if there is to be any influence on the outbreak of the War of 692 from Justinian's coins, a dating for their initial issue must be investigated. Unfortunately, Justinian's Christ coins have no dating marks, prompting some detective work. In the most general terms, the Christ coins were definitely from Justinian's first reign – 685–695 – and survive in such numbers that could suggest they were first minted a significant period before 695, although neither of these necessarily puts Justinian's new coins in a position to influence the outbreak of war in 692. Any connection to the Quinisext Council does not provide much dating aid as it cannot be determined if the council would have been reflecting or prompting a change in imperial numismatic trends.[65] While it might predate Justinian's Christ issues and therefore suggest that they were a reflection of a wider discussion over the depiction of Christ, the Visigothic Christ coin comes with little firm dating and does not help to pinpoint similar imperial issues.

However, there are some other numismatic and die developments which might help give a more specific date to Christ's appearance on Justinian's coins. The aforementioned Sicilian copper *follis* depicting Justinian wearing a *loros* would seem to be inscribed with the third indiction, which would date it to between 1 September 689 and 31 August 690.[66] Perhaps only a detailed die-study could give more clarity, but if this is a precursor to Justinian's Christ coinage then it provides a possible *terminus post quem* of 1 September 689 for the numismatic Christ. The designs present on Roman imperial coins were not just limited to numismatic issues. The images on official Roman seals were 'nearly always synchronised with that on the *solidi*',[67] and those of Justinian II were no different. Seals are frequently undated, but some officials had the indiction inscribed on them. The first seals recorded using the 'Christ coin' imagery of Justinian belong to Georgios the *patricius* and Theophylaktos, the *archontes* of the Blattion, which are dated to the fourth indiction: 1 September 690 – 31 August 691.[68] These two officials also had seals which used the pre-reform image.[69] Intriguingly, these seals contain two indictions – the third and fourth – suggesting they were appointed for at least a two-year period, taking in the dates 1 September 689 to 31 August 691. It may be more likely that it came from earlier in the fourth indiction, as 'otherwise its production would have been pointless'.[70] It could even have been from before the fourth indiction started, as the officials might have received their seals before the next indiction began. This could put the Christ seals and therefore the Christ coins pre-September 690 but post-September 689.[71]

Further narrowing of that period could potentially come from what these *solidi* were actually meant to be used for beyond imperial propaganda: payments to officials and the army. Information about how Roman forces were paid by the late seventh century is scant, but it is possible to surmise a payment schedule by working backwards from the issuing of the thematic cyclical donative – the *rhoga* – to the Armeniacs recorded in 811.[72] By the seventh century, Roman salaries were paid during Lent, and as the army was a significant receiver of cash payments, it would seem like a good time to introduce numismatic changes and the imperial propaganda they held.[73] The Anatolic and Armeniac thematic armies received their cyclical payments in 690 and 691 respectively, and as they were at the forefront of Roman military endeavours at the time, they may have been the first to receive *solidi* depicting Christ and the new imperial image during Easter 690.

Early 690 would certainly have seen Justinian II in a triumphal mood – he had already defeated the caliph and the Slavs, as well as receiving a hero's welcome in Thessalonica. His survival of the Bulgar ambush may also have made him thankful. These victories brought resources that could be used for new coins and a new triumphalist message, while perhaps paying the army with such Christ-emblazoned *solidi* at Easter encouraged it to prepare for a war against the dissension-ridden caliphate.[74] The overt Christian imperialism of Justinian's new Christ coin may have further highlighted the weakness of Abd al-Malik's position, undermining the caliph's claim to leadership of the *jihad*, while presenting an imperialistic view that the emperor claimed jurisdiction over all Christians. It must be said that despite their preponderance, none of these new Justinianic Christ coins have been found in Umayyad Syria; however, there are some other Justinian coins in Syrian hoards. The proximity to the imperial frontiers of the thematic forces likely to be issued with these new coins could have seen them, along with pilgrims to Jerusalem, being a conduit for the Christ coins to appear in Umayyad lands.

It therefore seems that Justinian's new Christ coinage may have been issued at a time that could have seen it affect Romano-Umayyad relations in the run-up to the 'War of Images' in 692; however, this does not prove that Abd al-Malik's numismatic reforms were also involved in that deterioration. It has already been mentioned how important the Roman *solidus* was to the economy of the Umayyad caliphate: 'the Muslim army and ruling elite drew their wealth overwhelmingly from the receipt of taxes paid primarily in cash, and as such had a vested interest in maintaining the tax system they had inherited, including the pre-eminence of the *solidus*.'[75] Indeed, pre-Umayyad Muslim numismatic policy has been summed up as 'importation and imitation',[76] with the caliphate rounding up any and all Roman coins – gold, silver and copper – to use as their own. Such was the extent of this importation that the Romans saw a way to benefit from it, selling their own copper coins to the Arabs. This move had not only a financial dimension, but also a propagandist one. This is because even more than a generation after they started, the Romans still viewed the Arab conquests as temporary 'and – if they had noticed the religious dimension at all – as an Arab heresy of Judaeo-Christian origin'.[77] Maintaining the Roman numismatic presence in territory lost to this Arab 'rebellion' was therefore a way to sustain a Roman ideology of world empire and control over their briefly lost provinces. Despite this early reliance on Roman issues, the importance of coins in the Arab caliphate should not be underestimated as they 'offer the only continuous and contemporary independent and primary source for the period of the genesis of the new religion and its empire from Spain to Central Asia'.[78]

While normally a status reserved for Abd al-Malik, it seems to have been Muawiyah I who first – but somewhat abortively – attempted to move beyond 'importation and imitation' with a policy that included 'appropriation' too. From his regional mints at Damascus, Tiberias and Emesa, Muawiyah issued his so-called 'Imperial Image' coppers. While these still depicted the Roman emperor and Christian crosses, they also had 'carefully prepared flans and well engraved dies',[79] many of which were better quality than those being produced in Constantinople. They also had both Greek and Arabic script, which was an attempt to establish the latter as a 'language of the validating authority'.[80]

Muawiyah did make some effort to remove the more overt Christian iconography on his 'appropriations': the prominent 'cross on steps' motif was transformed in various ways, such as a 'bar on a pole on steps' or 'sticks with a small pellet above'. It has also been suggested as being made into the *qutb* or *omphalos*, the lynchpin of the world, with a possible connection to the Bab al-'Amud, also known as the Damascus/Shechem/Nablus Gate, in Jerusalem: 'Such monolithic columns symbolizing urban and civic pride were a common feature in late Roman and even Umayyad cities, and therefore understandable even without a specific allusion to Jerusalem.'[81] Perhaps most importantly, this altered cross has been suggested as alluding to the *qadib*, the ceremonial staff of the Prophet, which was part of the Umayyad caliphal insignia.[82] But even with this suggestion of a Muhammadian *qadib* (which is admittedly not displayed anywhere else) and the range of appropriated and altered Umayyad coinage growing throughout Muawiyah's reign, it has been suggested that 'almost no attempt was made to represent the new state or religion on coins ... [with] none of the other subjects ... convincingly established as a religious Islamic symbol'.[83]

It appears that early Umayyad coinage and the mutilating of the cross was less about establishing Islamic symbology, and more about gradually moving away from Christian iconography and the Roman political propaganda inherent within it.[84] In this, the Umayyads were behind the curve within the Muslim world. During the Second Fitna, the Zubayrids and particularly the Kharijites had built more clearly on the numismatic foundations of others. They inscribed Sassanid coins with overtly Islamic ideas, projecting a pious Muslim identity that the Umayyads were signally failing to deliver by continuing to follow the Roman rules of numismatics.[85]

There is some suggestion that Muawiyah went a little further in his coinage beyond a de-Christianized/de-Romanized *solidus*. His reign may well have been the origin of the so-called 'Standing Caliphs' coin, using a Roman coin depicting Heraclius and his sons, Heraclius Constantine III and Heraklonas, with their imperial regalia changed. On the reverse was another 'pole on steps', but this time with the *shahadah* inscribed in Arabic – 'There is no god but God alone; Muhammad is the prophet of God'.[86] This could connect to the fact that Abd al-Malik's numismatic reforms were not just limited to his minting of a new coin, going through perhaps more than a decade of experimentation before coming upon his ultimate success – the aniconic dinar. Initial coins from his reign do seem to have been similar appropriations to those of Muawiyah. A 'Standing Caliph' type appeared at Gerasa in perhaps 685, possibly as something of an 'accession issue',[87] while a *follis*-based 'Standing Caliph' issued at Jerusalem might even depict the Prophet Muhammad, as its Arabic inscription read '*Muhammad rasul Allah*' – 'Muhammad is the messenger of God' – instead of using Abd al-Malik's name.[88] The only other similar coin found so far came from Mesopotamia, a region not controlled by Abd al-Malik until 691, which could put this 'Muhammad' coin from around this period. However, it has also been suggested that this 'Muhammad' looks like Justinian II, perhaps putting its date post-685 or even post-686 after Justinian began to appear bearded.[89]

These earlier dates and the Muawiyah issues would preclude any idea of Abd al-Malik's 'Standing Caliph' being a response to the numismatic innovations of Justinian II. Indeed, as these initial issues of Abd al-Malik were still in the Roman propagandist mould as well as being used for payment, it may be best to view them solely through the lens of internal Muslim politics, rather than as any response to Roman numismatic developments. Various forms of Abd al-Malik's 'Standing Caliph', *shahadah* or 'Muhammad' coins may have been issued in connection with important events within the caliphate, particularly when he felt that the loyalty of his army needed rewarding: his accession, the aftermath of the Umayyad reclamation of Egypt and before or after campaigns or battles in the Second Fitna – he seems to have struck coins at Damascus after the defeat of Mus'ab,[90] and perhaps after the defeat of various rebellions such as those of al-Ashdaq, the Najdat or the Kharijites. Abd al-Malik's reforms 'can be seen on the one hand as an attempt to integrate the defeated moderate Zubayrid movement, and on the other hand, as a forceful reaction to the ongoing and ideologically much more potent Kharijite challenge'.[91] Indeed, if there was a 'War of Images' in the late seventh century, it may well be more correct to view it as between the Umayyads, Zubayrids and Kharijites, rather than between Abd al-Malik and Justinian II.

Another detraction from the idea of a Romano-Umayyad 'War of Images' is that Abd al-Malik had much more important things to address when it came to his coinage than what the Roman emperor was putting on his. The annual tribute demanded by the treaty of 688/689 put pressure on the Umayyad exchequer. Even if it was 52,000 *nomismata* rather than 365,000, it was still a significant sum,[92] and that is even looking past the value of the fifty-two slaves and prize horses the tribute also entailed. This will have been an untimely drain on Umayyad finances, particularly when at the time of its agreement, the Umayyad caliphate only encompassed Egypt and parts of Syria and Palestine. There have also been doubts over just how much the Umayyads could extract from the Egyptian tax base, then how much of that actually made it to the Damascus treasury.[93]

The burden of the Roman tribute may therefore have fallen heavily on a portion of Syria-Palestine, a region which could pay one or two million *solidi* a year in the 500s, before the destruction inflicted upon it by a century of war and conquest.[94] Around fifteen years of paying tribute to Constantinople through the treaties with Constantine IV and Justinian II, even at the lower rates of 3,000 *per annum* and 1,000 per week, will have seen hundreds of thousands of *solidi* leaving the Umayyad economy. This is demonstrated in the sharp decline of *solidi* in Syrian coin hoards in the late seventh century.[95] This drain on the Umayyad exchequer was a significant threat to the entire caliphal system, not just in terms of pure financial underpinning, but also because the caliphate relied heavily on cash to pay its armies and officials. With such growing numismatic, propagandist and financial pressures, it is perhaps no surprise to see Abd al-Malik look to reform the Umayyad coinage, remove its reliance on Constantinopolitan gold and produce his own smaller, Islamic gold coin. It certainly appears more internally necessary and part of a grander programme of reform than any reaction to the numismatic innovations of Justinian II.[96]

The biggest impediment to Theophanes' attribution of Abd al-Malik's new dinar as part of Justinian's complaint in the countdown to the War of 692 is one of date. While there were some 'Islamified' coins issued by Umayyad caliphs and even perhaps some experimental pre-reform dinars early in Abd al-Malik's reign,[97] Arab sources state that more radical currency reform did not appear until post-692. This is after the outbreak of the war the Arab dinar was supposed to have caused.[98] But just what was Abd al-Malik's new dinar? For all the seeming independence of his initial coinage reforms, Abd al-Malik had still been playing by Roman numismatic rules and using Roman numismatic tools. The *shahadah* coins looked like *folles*, while his 'Muhammad' and 'Standing Caliph' still looked like Roman emperors and the 'pole on steps' was still a modified cross. That experimentation continued with various symbols and designs being deployed throughout the majority of the 690s, with the caliph trying to find the right formula for a wide-ranging and permanent reform. For example, the initial use of '*Muhammad rasul Allah*' was upgraded to an inscription of the full *shahadah* on gold and silver coins by 692–693. But for all of this experimentation, the lingering notion that the Umayyads were still playing by the numismatic rules of Constantinople would only be shaken off by a radical departure.

Abd al-Malik did not achieve this until perhaps 696, but in the process of doing so he established what became the definitive layout for Islamic coins, perhaps in the process laying the foundation of 'Muslim antipathy to figural imagery'.[99] This was because the new dinar that Abd al-Malik oversaw the minting of in Damascus, perhaps in 696, was completely aniconic. There were no figures or items to be mistaken for slightly altered Roman originals or ideas.[100] Instead of images of the Prophet, caliphs or various appropriated Islamic symbols, the dinar was only to 'bear the new religious symbols of Islam and its empire, the *shahadah*, encircled by the Qur'anic *risla*, the prophetic message of Muhammad (a shortened version of *Qur'an* 9.33), and on the opposite side of the word of God, the beginning of Surat al-Ikhlas (a shortened variation of *surah* 112), surrounded by the date of the striking'.[101] The dinar also differentiated itself from the *solidus/nomisma* by being smaller and therefore of a different weight system.

In just one single coin type, Abd al-Malik had a profound influence on various aspects of the Umayyad caliphate and Islam in general. Along with the silver dirham, the gold dinar broke the *solidus'* monopoly on the economy, putting an Arabic and Islamic 'face' on numismatics in Syria. Indeed, so successful was Abd al-Malik's breaking of the Umayyad reliance on Roman coinage for styles and cues that when Leo III came to introduce a new Roman silver coinage in 720, instead of using previous Roman issues – the *antoninianus* or *siliqua* – as a template, he used the dirham.[102] The inscribing of the *shahadah* and Qur'anic verses on the coins enshrined words as the medium of Islamic religion and Muslim propaganda, while the absence of the caliph saw the 'replacing of the regnal character of the Caliphal Image with a theocratic coinage that was appropriate for a ruler who defined his role as God's deputy'.[103] It is perhaps no coincidence that widespread minting and distribution of this new aniconic dinar came at a time when Abd al-Malik had just defeated the Kharijite caliph Qatari b. al-Fuja'a and the Najdat, potentially making the new coinage part of an attempt to 'legitimize

Marwanid rule in the entire empire with Islamic propaganda common to all Muslim factions'.[104]

Such unifying propaganda goes beyond the religious messages of the coin: 'By giving visible expression to the dominant role of Arabic in the administration of the state, it promoted the language reform which the caliph had initiated in his chancery.'[105] Much like Justinian's Christ had such an influence on Christian art, Abd al-Malik's 'new kind of nonfigurative image heralded Islamic art's break from the Greco-Roman representative tradition'.[106] It also fits in with Abd al-Malik's building programme. As already mentioned, he oversaw the rebuilding of the Kaaba, but he also initiated the construction of both the Dome of the Rock and the Aqsa Mosque in Jerusalem: 'the Islamic empire had finally found its distinctive symbolic form of representation.'[107]

This later date for the new Umayyad dinar does not completely disprove Theophanes' premise that new Arab coinage perturbed Justinian II in c.691. Even if the 'Standing Caliphs' coins of Muawiyah and the various experiments of Abd al-Malik were just prototypes, sparse in number, local in scope and even not made of gold,[108] it would only take one – with an Arabic inscription or obviously mutilated cross – to make its way to the emperor for Justinian to complain to Abd al-Malik about these 'Islamified' Roman coins. Furthermore, Theophanes does show knowledge of the new Arab dinar, stating that it bore 'a new type of stamp and had never been seen that way before'[109] and suggesting that it was lighter in weight than the *solidus*.[110] Perhaps Theophanes has conflated two potentially separate numismatic developments in the caliphate and formed them into a single Roman complaint and therefore a *raison de guerre* in c.691/692: 'Islamified' Romano-Umayyad coins and the later, smaller dinar.

Even if a Romano-Umayyad 'War of Images' influencing the War of 692 seems unlikely, there does appear to be some historical basis for imperial offence at Arab inscriptions beyond Theophanes. Since the Arab conquest of the Middle East and Egypt, the Romans had relied on Arab trade to provide them with papyrus. Just before his monetary reform, Abd al-Malik initiated reform of his caliphate's papyrus production, ordering all papyrus made for export to the Roman Empire to be marked with Muslim religious inscriptions.[111] It would be unsurprising for Justinian to be angry at this development, and he is recorded threatening the caliph that if he did not stop this religious inscribing of papyrus exports, the emperor would place an inscription insulting to Muhammad on imperial coinage.[112] No such offensive inscription ever appeared, but it could well be imagined that 'Islamified' papyrus and Justinian's threat could be taken by later observers as being part of a 'War of Images', with Justinian's Christ coinage and Abd al-Malik's new dinar just escalations in an iconographic struggle.

It is understandable to view the Romans and Umayyads making immensely influential innovations numismatically and artistically at around the same time as too much of a coincidence to not be related.[113] Certainly, it is impossible to rule out that Justinian II and Abd al-Malik had their attention grabbed by the numismatic developments occurring in each other's empires. But as has been seen, both the Christian and Muslim worlds were in the midst of deep political changes, far-reaching artistic choices and profound religious pressures that produced new numismatic thinking independently of Romano-Umayyad interaction. However, while a Romano-Umayyad 'War of Images' may be just the invention of an emperor or caliph looking for a pretext for war, or by later sources seeing a connection to a series of unconnected iconographic developments, 'new discoveries in this rapidly evolving field might significantly change the picture'.[114]

If it is accepted that there was no real tit-for-tat 'War of Images' between the Roman Empire and Umayyad caliphate, beyond perhaps both emperor and caliph looking to aspects of it as a propagandist pretext or explanation, then what did start the Romano-Umayyad War of 692? There are plenty of inferences to be made about the potential warmongering on both sides. Abd al-Malik will have been keen to overturn his tribute status, reclaim lost territories and revenues and avenge the defeat of 685–688. A war with the Romans also played into his unity propaganda as he restored Umayyad rule of the whole caliphate; after years of internal fighting, Islam could again unite behind the banner of fighting the infidel, with Abd al-Malik highlighting his leadership of the *jihad*. That said, there are some potential obstacles to an Umayyad thirst for war in Anatolia in 692. By the time of the outbreak of war, the Second Fitna was not yet complete. While the time of year of the Romano-Umayyad War of 692 is not recorded, the siege of Mecca continued until at least early October, if not early November, while operations against the Najdat dragged on into 693. Sparking or accepting a war against the Romans saw Abd al-Malik risk any war-weariness or continued disunity of the caliphal armies presenting the Romans with another victory.

As mentioned above, Justinian may have wanted to test his 'Chosen' Slavs, building on his successes in Anatolia and the Balkans, while his interfering with Cyprus may present him as looking to take advantage of the caliphate's continued internal distractions. Such was his confidence in his new Slav force that Theophanes has Justinian writing to tell the Arabs 'that he would not abide by the peace which had been agreed upon in writing'.[115] Theophanes then repeats his notion that while the Arabs themselves 'did not choose to break the peace … imperial guilt and indiscretion forced them to do so',[116] they were 'hypocritical' in their complaints, with Abd al-Malik having manipulated Justinian into a war.

Opposing the possibility of Justinian being the cause of war is the idea that the treaty he had attained from Abd al-Malik already provided a handsome boon to the imperial treasury – at least 250,000 *nomismata* – which may have enabled Justinian's aggressive stances, particularly once the empire stopped paying out tribute to the Bulgars.[117] It is unlikely that Justinian would reject such a sizeable tribute or seek to end the treaty altogether, as that would see the loss of 'a substantial percentage of the surviving annual imperial fiscal revenue'.[118] It is here that accusations of recklessness may ring true. Justinian would have only accepted an end to the treaty of 688/689 if he thought he could impose even harsher terms on his defeated caliphal opponent and perhaps reclaim more territory. But any overconfidence or opportunism bred by his previous victories, and any want to test his new Slavic soldiers, were to backfire significantly.

The actual first military move of the war of 692 would appear to have been made by the Umayyads with the central battle of the conflict, Sebastopolis, located within Roman territory. This suggests that Abd al-Malik was the aggressor and perhaps therefore the treaty-breaker; however, this would not make a great deal of sense if the caliph was portraying himself as an innocent party: 'If Justinian found that caliph's payment unacceptable and refused to receive it, it was hardly the Arab's responsibility to force it on him, but rather his problem to make them pay for it in the old style coinage.'[119] It could be that the movements in the lead-up to and the location of the Battle of Sebastopolis itself suggest that the Roman forces were returning from a foray into Umayyad territory, perhaps even towards northern Syria or Iraq, recently reclaimed by Abd al-Malik and the possible avenue of success in 685–688.[120] At the very least, Roman forces seem to have already congregated at Sebastopolis for Abd al-Malik to strike at, suggesting that if the caliph had not struck first, the emperor was going to do so, if he had not already.

In the end, it appears that both Justinian II and Abd al-Malik had their own reasons for wanting a war, or perhaps more accurately, not stopping one breaking out. The emperor had been seeing how far he could push the Umayyad distraction with his Cypriot interference and inscriptional complaints, and when the caliph finally pushed back, Justinian felt secure enough in his successful army and new Slavic allies to not back down. Similarly, Abd al-Malik, freed from his internal distractions, was now more willing to challenge and even manipulate Justinian's actions. Buoyed by his successes in Iraq and Arabia, he surely welcomed the opportunity to overturn the treaty of 688/689 with a brief war against the Romans. With two confident, propaganda-laden and religiously charged leaders, war was probably inevitable. It just so happened that it came at a time of mutual numismatic reform, rather than any real 'War of Images'.

Defections, Disaster and Dire Consequences?: The Battle of Sebastopolis 692

Such has been the build-up to the Romano-Umayyad War of 692 presented above, that you might be expecting it to be a titanic tussle with several skirmishes, large set-piece battles, strategic and tactical toing and froing, before a climactic showdown between imperial and caliphal forces. However, its very name intimates that this was not the case. Indeed, it did not even last the length of its eponymous year: it was a short, sharp conflict, perhaps reflecting how, while both were keen to test their forces against each other, emperor and caliph were far less keen to be dragged into an extended war. The sources do not provide much information beyond single sentence round-ups or inferences, with most of their focus falling on one specific action and the aftermath of the Battle of Sebastopolis.

Reputedly unwilling to listen to Abd al-Malik's claims to have not broken the treaty, Justinian levied an army of supposedly 30,000 men from his Slav colonists and placed this 'Chosen People' under the command of a certain Neboulos. Theophanes then has Justinian himself travel with this army and the thematic cavalry to Sebastopolis, which seems like a prelude to an invasion. There is some discussion over exactly where this Sebastopolis was. It is usually identified with Elaiussa Sebaste in Cilicia, now along the southern coast of Turkey near Mersin, but modern Sulusaray, some 250 miles to the north, was also called Sebastopolis in antiquity. The latter might seem attractive given its more central position in Anatolia, but the most decisive argument comes down on the side of Elaiussa Sebaste, with Theophanes recording that Justinian, his Slavs and thematic cavalry travelled to Sebastopolis by sea.[121]

While there is frequently room to doubt some of Theophanes' information when it comes to presenting evidence disparaging Justinian, there is little reason to accuse him or his sources of poor interpretation or bias invention over the identification of this Sebastopolis.

Could the position of Sebastopolis suggest any potential strategic aims of Justinian and his generals? Arriving by and staying close to the sea might highlight that the emperor aimed to use his fleet as part of his offensive. This could involve advancing east along the Cilician coast, sticking close to his fleet. Such a combined land and sea campaign would perhaps have seen Justinian reaffirming existing Roman control in the region around Tarsus and Adana, and perhaps looking to carry the fight into Umayyad Syria, possibly aiming to reclaim Antioch if things went well. The presence of the fleet could also hint that Justinian hoped to raid the Levantine coast, possibly recreate the previously successful Mardaite raids and claim full control of Cyprus. On the part of Abd al-Malik, that he moved straight for the congregated Roman forces at Sebastopolis would imply that his war aims amounted to bringing the Romans to battle and defeating them quickly.

Justinian's own presence in the field may be doubted, but it could be evidence of his growing confidence. He had not taken part in the previous Arab war, only for his success against the Slavs to have encouraged him to be much closer to the action this time round. That said, it is usually thought that even if the emperor was present with the army at Sebastopolis, he delegated command to a more senior general; in this case probably Leontios, the Anatolic *strategos* and leader of the previous successful strike against the Arabs.[122] Along with Neboulos, it is likely that the generals who had served Justinian well against the Slavs in 688 were also present with the thematic cavalry. The Roman congregation at Sebastopolis seems to have taken long enough for the Umayyads to have gotten word of their presence. Once Abd al-Malik had made his protest known, so he could claim not to be to blame for the war, he quickly got his forces into the field and struck towards Sebastopolis. That the Romans made no move from Sebastopolis may have been part of their initial plan to draw the Umayyads to them, or perhaps it became their plan after word of the approach of the Arab army reached them.

Upon taking the field, the Umayyad army, under the command of Muhammad b. Marwan, signalled their 'innocence' in the revoking of the treaty of 688/689 by reputedly marching with a copy of said treaty as a war banner, pierced full of holes and mounted on a lance – 'doth the lady protest too much?'.[123] Initially, it seemed as if the Arab claim that 'God would be the judge'[124] was going to have them found guilty as the Romans got the better of the initial exchanges once battle was joined. Unfortunately, none of the surviving material provides any information about the tactical moves that took place at Sebastopolis and whether it was a specific part of the Arab army or all of it that was feeling the pressure early in the battle; or even if it was perhaps all a ruse.

With the Arab forces under pressure and probably in some kind of retreat, Muhammad unveiled his master stroke and the scale to which Justinian II had been wrong about his new Slavic army and the ability of the empire to force loyalty on its defeated opponents. The Umayyad commander had somehow managed to suborn Neboulos 'with a purse loaded with *nomismata*, and deceiving him with many promises'.[125] Those promises likely included a new home for the commander and his men, coupled with better treatment and probably further financial rewards. It must be remembered that while some of the Slavs did join Justinian willingly in their transplanting to Bithynia, many were there by force and not enough time had passed to integrate these Slavs into the imperial hierarchies and breed any real loyalty. Furthermore, the Slavs will have been unused to the forced military service, taxes and requisitions expected of imperial subjects, coming from a 'democratic', decentralized tribal society.[126] Furthermore, in order to finance the war with the Umayyads, Justinian likely began increasing taxes and requisitions.

Whatever their motives, with victory seemingly within the grasp of Justinian and Leontios, Neboulos led up to 20,000 Slavs in a mass defection to the Arabs.[127] The opportune timing of this defection at the height of the fighting could suggest that Muhammad had not only bribed Neboulos before the battle started, but also that there was some coordination about when the defection should take place to cause maximum effect. In such a light, the initial Roman success could have been part of the plan by Muhammad and Neboulos to get Justinian and Leontios to fully commit their forces in pressing a retreating foe. In such a scenario, the defection of a large section of the Roman force would account for the sudden turnaround in the battle. Furthermore, the forces of Abd al-Malik and Muhammad have already been seen employing this tactic at the Battle of Maskin, while Slavic tribes had previously shown disloyalty to their Roman imperial masters.[128] A well-executed plan or not, the Slavic defection left the remaining Roman forces badly exposed. If Justinian's confidence in his 'Chosen People' was anything like what Theophanes claims, they may well have been placed in an important position in the Roman lines or given a vital role to play. With a significant hole in their lines and now almost certainly heavily outnumbered, the remaining imperial forces were dealt a significant defeat.

It is in the aftermath of Sebastopolis that 'Theophanes launches one of his gravest charges against Justinian II'.[129] Outraged by the betrayal of Neboulos and 20,000 of his 'Chosen People', Theophanes would have it that the emperor gave full vent to his rage, executing the remaining Slavs in his army, all of their wives and children living in the Bithynian colonies and any other Slavs he could get his hands on in and around the Opsikion theme. This slaughter of innocents was taken as a prime example of the monster that Justinian was; 'a black legend that grew up after the emperor's fall'.[130] It could well be imagined that Justinian was feeling a mixture of embarrassment and anger, particularly if he accepted or even pushed for war in order to test his 'Chosen People'. That decision not only humiliated him on the battlefield and considerably weakened the empire's strategic position, but likely had put his life in danger if he had travelled to Sebastopolis. However, as with any accusation against Justinian from the sources, especially the likes of Theophanes, there is room for considerable doubt regarding this Slavic massacre.

In terms of written accounts, no other source to mention anything about this battle recalls a vengeful imperial purge of the Slavs. Nikephoros, who might be expected to follow any path that makes Justinian look like a monster, does record the Slavic defection at Sebastopolis, although he has the entire Slavic corps desert the Romans and join the massacring of the imperial forces. Pointedly, he says nothing of a post-battle, vengeful massacre of their families. Michael the Syrian records a similar outline, with all of the Slavs defecting and no subsequent massacre. Perhaps more interestingly, Michael only lists 7,000 in the Slavic corps, a figure which might be more realistic. Muslim sources such as al-Tabari and al-Baladhuri are even more scant on detail, merely stating that a battle took place, with no mention of a mass Slavic desertion or subsequent massacre, although the latter states that it was Muhammad's attack that broke the treaty of 688/689.[131]

Archaeology also casts doubt on Theophanes' massacre, or at very least, its genocidal scale. In the late nineteenth century, the lead seal of an official in the Slavic military colony in Bithynia was discovered.[132] It not only displayed Justinian's portrait, but also listed its date as being of the '8th indiction'. The only '8th indiction' to occur during Justinian's first reign was in 694/695. Therefore, the seal posits the continued existence of a Slavic military colony a minimum of two years after its supposed annihilation following the defection at Sebastopolis.

This could completely undermine the very notion of a Justinianic massacre of the remainder of the Slavic corps and their families. However, there is something of a middle ground between total destruction and total invention.[133] Justinian could well have punished the 10,000 Slav survivors of Sebastopolis and even some of their families, but these could have represented only a portion of the population of the Bithynian colony – which was previously suggested as being up to 100,000 – with enough surviving to maintain the existence of the colony and its seal-holding officials. Furthermore, would the Bithynian Slavs have been so happy to maintain their allegiance to Justinian had he been responsible for a massacre of their friends and family?

Another mark against a genocidal Slavic massacre is the sheer logistical common sense against killing thousands of soldiers in the immediate aftermath of a crushing defeat at Sebastopolis. The empire had already lost a significant number of men to death and defection. The inherent stupidity of killing thousands more in a revenge mission and having to redeploy soldiers to carry out such a massacre at a time when the Umayyads may have been looking to capitalize on their victory would surely have stayed the hand of the emperor. Whatever the circumstances post-Sebastopolis, chastened by defeat, defection and perhaps massacre, the Slavic military colony continued to exist in Bithynia, and may have continued to do so into the ninth century.[134]

Despite their decisive victory at Sebastopolis, the Umayyads do not seem to have tried to capitalize on it immediately, settling for having made their point on the battlefield rather than attempting to occupy any imperial territory at this point. It might be pondered whether Muhammad was a little wary of his new Slavic troops – all 7,000–30,000 of them – who had already proven themselves to be untrustworthy. In the immediate aftermath of Sebastopolis, he may have felt obliged to return to Syria and see to the settling of his new allies. As has been seen above, it appears that these Slav deserters were settled between Antioch and Cyrrhus, a region vacated by the transplanted Mardaites.[135]

This is not to say that the Umayyads did not make some moves to follow up their victory at Sebastopolis. The damage Muhammad and the Slavs had inflicted on the Roman forces allowed a return to the almost annual Arab raids of Roman territory. According to Theophanes, every year remaining in Justinian II's first reign saw some kind of Arab attack on 'Romania'. In

693/694, he has the 'Agarenes' – 'the followers or descendants of Hagar'[136] – growing bolder after being freed from an internal revolt in Persian Khurasan under Sabinos and 'ravaging Romania'. In 694/695, Muhammad invaded Roman territory, bringing with him some of the recently defected Slavs because they knew the land, which could suggest that Muhammad aimed to strike as deeply as Bithynia and that maybe some of the prisoners taken were actually the surviving families of these Slavs. In 695/696, Muhammad then raided the region of Fourth Armenia.[137]

This was not the only recorded Umayyad action in Armenia following the outbreak of war in 692. The Roman defeat at Sebastopolis encouraged a rebellion amongst the Armenians ruled by the empire. Its leader was the patrician, Symbatios – also known as Sabbatios and Sembat Bagratuni – and his revolt allowed the Umayyads to re-establish control of southern Armenia.[138] It could be that this Umayyad takeover was referred to in Muhammad's raiding of Fourth Armenia. Muslim sources record not only Umayyad interjection in Armenia but also considerable Roman activity along the Syrian border. In the same year as Sebastopolis, al-Tabari records Uthman b. al-Walid invading Armenia and coming into conflict with a large Roman army. Suspicion is roused by his claim that Uthman's 4,000 men defeated 60,000 Romans; not just the improbability of such a miraculous victory but also of the Romans being able to put so many men in the field. Around the same time, al-Baladhuri has Dinar b. Dinar, a freedman of Abd al-Malik and governor of Qinnasrin, defeat a Roman force near Shimshat – Arsamosota – in Armenian Sophene near the Euphrates. A short while later, al-Baladhuri also records Muhammad b. Marwan subduing rebellion in Armenia, which could also be linked to Theophanes' account of the same general 'raiding' Fourth Armenia in 695/696.[139] Muslim sources clearly felt that the Umayyads were heavily active in parts of Armenia and had seemingly won a victory over the Romans there, perhaps the Armeniac thematic army, as part of the conflict that had broken out between Justinian and Abd al-Malik.

Al-Baladhuri goes further. In the aftermath of Sebastopolis, he records the advance of a large Roman force through Germanicia Caesarea – he hints at it being in Roman hands, but the likelihood is that by the early 690s, Germanicia Caesarea had been claimed by the Umayyads and become Mar'ash (now Kahramanmaraş in Turkey). This force was intercepted and defeated by an Umayyad army under Aban b. al-Walid.[140] There is no corroboration for this supposed victory in other sources, and it might well be imagined that Theophanes and Nikephoros would have been keen to highlight any further Roman defeat as evidence of the folly Justinian II had led his army and empire into. That is not to say that any such confrontation along the Romano-Umayyad border did not take place. The chronology of these potential battles, raids and rebellions in connection with the Romano-Umayyad War of 692 in Roman and Muslim histories is muddled enough that some important events could fall through the cracks and get reinterpreted or repositioned. A Roman advance through Germanicia Caesarea could connect with the proposal that the Battle of Sebastopolis came *after* a Roman incursion into Umayyad territory, in something of a repeat of Leontios' previously successful campaign.

The War of 692 had not gone well for Justinian or the empire. It went a long way to overturning the success of his father and his own victory that had brought about the treaty of 688/689. In the process of its undoing, the defeat at Sebastopolis revealed that that recovery had been built on rather precarious foundations, relying almost completely on the ability of the empire to concentrate its forces on one frontier and the distraction of the Umayyads. Muhammad b. Marwan inflicting defeat(s) on the Romans in 692 brought the whole house of cards down, with annual raids returning, Roman allies switching sides and the Umayyads regaining not just the initiative but also border territory. The imperial position in the Caucasus and eastern Asia Minor was undone much more quickly than its re-establishing.

It might be thought that the reason behind the overturning of a decade of Roman rebuilding was the extent of the losses inflicted at Sebastopolis. Unfortunately, the casualties endured by Justinian's forces are difficult to quantify due to the paucity of numbers mentioned in the sources, apart from the 7,000/20,000 Slav defectors. Certainly, Sebastopolis was not a complete annihilation, as important individuals such as Justinian and Leontios survived without being captured. If the Roman army at Sebastopolis – thematic cavalry, Anatolic army and perhaps other units from the Opsikion – had ceased to exist, it would have taken quite a display of iron discipline on the part of Muhammad b. Marwan to not follow up that victory with a major invasion of Anatolia, even if it had not been part of the initial plan. The ability of the Romans to field armies in Armenia, Anatolia and possibly probe the Syrian border near Germanicia Caesarea may also suggest that casualties in 692 were not that high. This would imply that Justinian's forces returned from the battlefield of Sebastopolis beaten, bloody and bereft of Slavs, but not completely broken.

However, it would not take heavy battlefield casualties to alter the balance of power on Constantinople's eastern frontier. Some of the manpower lost to the empire – Slavs, Armenians and possibly some prisoners taken during the raids – was now bolstering the ranks of the enemy, doubling the effect of their loss. There is also the psychological effect of Sebastopolis on both the victorious Arabs and the defeated Romans. All of a sudden, the Romans were on the back foot, cooped up in their cities and fortresses, while the buoyant Umayyads were sending multiple armies to their northern frontier. This in turn saw thematic garrisons faced with conflict on two fronts – the recurring raids into Anatolia and Arab conquest in Armenia. The Anatolic army had struggled to deal with annual Arab raiding in the past, when it might have been in a healthier state than post-Sebastopolis, so why would it now be expected to deal with the various incursions into 'Romania'? The Armeniac army, possibly undamaged due to its absence from Sebastopolis, can be excused not staving off the loss of southern Armenia against local rebellion and various Umayyad incursions under Uthman, Dinar and Muhammad, particularly if no reinforcement was available. And this was a situation that was only getting worse. Sebastopolis may not have been serious enough in itself in terms of casualties to prevent the Romans deploying armies, but taken together with the events it precipitated – defeats at Germanicia Caesarea and Arsamosata, losses of Slav and Armenian manpower and the damage done by annual Arab raids of Anatolia – it will have represented something of a repeated downward spiral for the Roman military position in Anatolia if it was not arrested somehow.

While Justinian had been keen to assert and then build on the dominant position recent Roman victories and Arab distraction had brought, his Romano-Umayyad War of 692, together with its peculiar origins, marked a destabilizing of relations between the empire and the caliphate. Or perhaps more accurately, it marked a return to the 'normalcy' of continual warfare along the frontier that had prevailed since Syria had first fallen to the Arabs; a normalcy punctuated only by brief periods of peace following the defeat of the 'siege' of Constantinople and Umayyad distractions with civil wars.

But while he may have failed to prove himself a great military champion, there was another arena in which the emperor had an opportunity to prove himself of champion material … Justinian II was going to try to deal with the Christian church.

Chapter 7

Justinian, The Orthodox Champion?

'What has the emperor to do with the church?'
Optatus, *Against the Donatists* III.3

'That Would be an Ecumenical Matter' – The Religious Policies of Constantine IV

The War of 692 may have reopened a can of worms in the military arena, but it was not the only avenue of incessant trouble revisited by Justinian II. While concurrently one of its great strengths, the Christianity of the Roman Empire could and did provide significant problems for imperial unity. The Arab conquests themselves had revealed the extent to which divisions within the Christian church could undermine loyalty to Constantinople. Substantial areas of Egypt, Syria, Armenia and Palestine had held to different doctrines than the imperial orthodoxy. This had made many of them more willing to accept Arab Muslim rule rather than Roman-enforced doctrine, as well as its heavy imperial taxes to maintain the army, navy and other amenities. As it was, the Arab conquests largely restored the Christian unity of the Roman state by removing the territories of those doctrinal dissidents, while to the north, the displacement of the Germanic tribes by pagan Avars, Slavs, Bulgars and Khazars gave more of a factual basis to the imperial claim to be the protector of Christendom. It also allowed Christianity in general to be a rallying call to defend imperial territory and, as already seen with Justinian's numismatic innovation, had become an integral part of Roman imperialist propaganda to be projected both within the empire's frontiers and beyond.

This intensified Christian identity of the Roman Empire and its *basileus* added to what was already a multifaceted civilization,[1] providing the state with extra layers of authority and mystique. However, this centrality of Christian thought added an extra dimension to potential disagreements. Following the Arab conquests in the Levant and Egypt, the focus of such potential differences of Christian opinion had fallen upon Italy. The largely Arian (although gradually Catholicizing) Lombards provided some Christological opposition, but it was the papacy and other Catholic bishops who provided an alternative view of who was the pre-eminent source of Christian orthodoxy in imperial territory. The final Great Schism between East and West was still several centuries away, but there had already been significant issues between eastern Christianity and the papacy. The latter felt that the Council of Chalcedon in 451 had questioned the supremacy of Rome through the elevation of Constantinople, an argument which grew into the Acacian Schism of 484–519. The 'Three Chapters' controversy may not have had the same vehemence to its disagreements, but again showed the doctrinal and practical divergence between East and West.[2]

Heraclian emperors had already dipped their toe in the pool of Christian doctrine, and none had faired well. Heraclius had failed spectacularly with first Monoenergism and then the doctrine of Christ's two natures and one divine will, Monothelitism. Constans II had not only failed to learn from these mistakes, but repeated and then doubled down on them with his horrendous treatment of Pope Martin I, Maximus the Confessor and others for their rejection of his *Type* and Monothelitism. His assassination in 668 was no doubt taken as evidence of divine wrath coming down on someone who challenged the Christian Church.

Despite this, by the time of Constantine IV's accession, the *Ecthesis*, the *Type* and Monothelitism were still the imperial orthodoxy. As a Heraclian, it could be expected that Constantine would follow the policies and approach of his dynastic predecessors. Such is the paucity of information from the 670s that Constantine IV's initial religious policies are almost impossible to assess. This should not be taken as a personal lack of interest in religion from the new emperor. Not only would such a supposition overlook the trouble facing the empire in the 670s, but it also ignores the prominent role that Constantine would play at the Sixth Ecumenical Council. He clearly took his role as protector of the Christian Church seriously. It is just that during the first decade of his reign, he had rather more pressing military matters to attend to, with the 'siege' of Constantinople and the arrival of the Bulgars.

It would seem that the *Ecthesis*, the *Type* and Monothelitism remained imperial policy throughout the 670s. This does not necessarily reflect any personal view of Constantine pro- or anti-Monothelitism, but at least represents a possible pragmatism in the face of increasing Umayyad pressure on the imperial capital. For Constantine to reignite a doctrinal dispute would be to risk discord within the city at a time when it needed to work together to repel the Arab raiders. However, Constantine also appeared in no mood to enforce these Monothelite stances in the same manner as his father. This is best demonstrated in his lack of action towards Pope Vitalian, who almost immediately upon the death of Constans, openly declared himself in favour of Dyothelitism, the opposing doctrine to Monothelitism. This was despite the patriarchs of Constantinople and Antioch, Theodore I and Macarius, pressing the emperor to punish the papal 'heretic'. That Theodore, a fervent Monothelite, was not patriarch until 677 backs the idea that Monothelitism remained the official imperial orthodoxy throughout the first decade of Constantine IV's reign.

It was not until after the defeat of Muawiyah's attempt on Constantinople that Constantine made a decisive move in religious politics. The appointment of Theodore, who not only sought imperial action against Vitalian but also had the pope's name removed from the Constantinopolitan diptychs, may also have helped bring things to a head. Again though, Constantine refused to follow the heavy-handed interventionist stance of Constans II. Instead of using Theodore, Macarius, the exarch Theodore II and the power of his imperial office to impose his will on the papacy, Constantine sought a more consensual remedy to the Church's internal divisions. He wrote to the pope, who by 678 was Agatho, to ask if he would be willing to send delegates to an ecumenical council to be held at Constantinople in 680 to deal with the question of Christ's will(s). This may signal that Constantine had come to recognize the ultimate failure of the *Ecthesis*, the *Type* and even Monothelitism itself in shutting down Christological dispute. However, to suggest that 'the provinces which had fallen to the Arabs had no longer to be reckoned with, and any further maintenance of monothelitism was therefore pointless'[3] is to go too far, particularly if the Roman Empire still viewed the Arab conquests as a rebellion to be weathered and then overcome. In imperial propagandist terms at least, Egypt and the Middle East were soon to be recovered. The patriarchates of Alexandria, Jerusalem and Antioch, which were all now outside the Roman Empire, were all represented at the resultant council, although probably by Roman appointees.

For Agatho to prove as receptive as he did to an ecumenical church council held under the auspices and in the presence of the emperor at Constantinople would suggest that the intervening decade since the death of Constans II had renewed some papal faith in the impartiality of Constantine IV. While there appear to have been a string of Monothelite patriarchs in Constantinople, it could be imagined that a lack of imperial strong-arming in Italy and possibly even some correspondence between emperor and popes was the basis of this positive reception. It may also be important to imperial-papal relations and the holding of the ecumenical council that Theodore's patriarchate was ended in 679 not by his death but by his replacing with George I.[4] Agatho was careful to bolster his own position by taking in the views of large sections of the western Church. A series of synods were held at Rome, Milan and Hatfield[5] to gauge opinion on the matters at hand – all three condemned Monothelitism, with their reports forwarded to the resultant Sixth Ecumenical Council at Constantinople in 680/681.

The council opened in the imperial palace in the presence of Constantine IV – he would attend twelve of the eighteen sessions, including the first eleven and the last – on 7 November 680, with representatives from all five patriarchies.[6] Over the course of almost a year, with sessions and negotiations behind the scenes, it became increasingly apparent that Monothelitism had had its day. A letter from Agatho was read out, asserting the traditional belief of the Christian Church that Christ was of two wills: divine and human. Macarius was allowed to defend Monothelitism, but quickly found that he had little support, perhaps revealing that Constantine had himself abandoned any backing for 'one will' and had even seen to the appointment of similar dyothelites to represent some of the patriarchies.

By the time the Sixth Ecumenical Council closed on 16 September 681 with Constantine IV's signing of the decrees, Dyothelitism was professed as true orthodox doctrine, with Christ possessing 'two natural wills and two natural energies, without division, alteration, separation and confusion'.[7] Monothelitism and Monoenergism had been almost unanimously condemned because they were thought to diminish Christ's humanity, and any clergy who had openly championed these heresies were condemned. Agatho did not live long enough to be presented with the decrees of the council, but his successor, Leo II, accepted them, even with the anathematizing of a previous pope, Honorius I. Almost unbelievably, a variety of theological, political and grammatical mistakes and disagreements were largely set aside and the dispute which had rocked the Church for the best part of half a century ended rather abruptly.

The Sixth Ecumenical Council and its repudiation of Monothelitism was not the only development in imperial-papal relations in the last five years of Constantine IV's reign. The emperor must have felt that Rome had proven its political and doctrinal loyalty, for during the papacy of Benedict II (684–685), he rescinded the need for imperial approval of papal elections – 'the one elected to the Apostolic See may be ordained pontiff from that moment and without delay'.[8] There might have been some untidy successions after Constantine's restoration of this 'ancient practice' of quick consecration without imperial acceptance, but ultimately, after Sergius I's election in 683, there would be fifty years of smooth papal succession. This improvement in relations between the papal and imperial palaces is also seen in the aforementioned honouring of the pope by the emperor sending him locks of hair from his sons Justinian and Heraclius, 'symbolically placing the young princes under the protection of both the Papacy and the people of Rome through a gesture which, in both East and West, was comparable to creating a bond as strong and inviolable as baptismal sponsorship, adoption and marriage'.[9] Constantine also rewarded the papacy, in the person of John V (685–686), by abolishing a significant portion of the taxes due on papal lands in Sicily and Calabria and removed a surtax on grain sale.[10]

There was something else happening within Rome itself that may have aided these improved relations with the eastern emperor: aside from Gregory II (715–731), from about 680 until the mid-eighth century, every man to sit on the papal throne was of eastern Roman descent, either having been born in the former eastern provinces or their parents had.[11] While names do not necessarily reflect ethnicity, the increasing popularity of oriental names must reflect oriental influence and perhaps even 'a radical transformation in the ethnic composition of the city'.[12] This was surely the result of the Arab conquest of the Levant, with various populations fleeing west in search of more peaceful, Christian homes. It is hard to imagine such an alteration of the lay and ecclesiastical populations of Rome occurring without at least some tacit agreement from the emperors in Constantinople. Such migrants will have been crossing their lands and/or using their ships to get from the East to Italy or Sicily.[13] The later Heraclian emperors may even have encouraged the 'easternizing' of the clergy and influential laity in Rome so as to increase their own influence over the papacy.[14]

It certainly seems then that through the abandonment of Monothelitism, respectful treatment, political and financial reward and perhaps some ethnic alteration in Rome itself, there had been a significant rapprochement between the papacy and Constantinople. As Justinian was to follow in the orthodox footsteps of his father, there was little to suggest that this rapprochement was not going to continue post-685. From what has been seen above of Justinian's reign, attributing religious sentiments to him may seem to modern eyes at odds with his militant actions in Anatolia and around Thessalonica. However, this would not have seemed out of place in Late Antiquity, particularly as Justinian was the temporal leader of a Christian empire. Because of that, while we might sneer at his use of religion as hypocritical or two-faced, there is little real evidence that Justinian was anything but genuine in his faith or that his faith was all that different from any other denizen of the Roman Empire of the seventh century – 'Justinian II was a typical son of Byzantium'.[15]

Demonstrating Orthodoxy

Justinian was keen to demonstrate his taking up of his father's mantle as a champion of orthodoxy, but such was the job that Constantine IV had done that there was no significant doctrinal dispute with which his son could make his mark. There were two situations that required some ecclesiastical attention. Firstly, Theodore I had become patriarch of Constantinople once more in 686, but given his Monothelite past, it was felt necessary for him to make a more public and synodal profession of his new-found Dyothelitism. This rehabilitation of a heretic provided a powerful symbol of the achievement of the Sixth Ecumenical Council. The second situation was the disappearance of one or more copies of the Acts of the Sixth Council, likely including the originals. The emperor complained that they had been removed from the official archives without his permission and then circulated through some unknown individuals before being returned. Justinian was not just angry at the impudence of those who had 'borrowed' such important documents; he feared they could have been copied and altered by Monothelites to suit their own beliefs. Therefore, Justinian called a synod at Constantinople early in his reign, likely mid/late 686, for Theodore to profess his orthodoxy publicly and to investigate whether or not the Acts of the Sixth Council had been tampered with.[16]

The actions of this synod are recorded in a *iussio* that Justinian sent to the pope dated 17 February 687.[17] This imperial report was addressed to John V, although he had died on 2 August 686, six months before – 'a vivid example of the slowness of communication between Rome and Constantinople in this era, a problem which rendered effective working relations between pope and emperor difficult even at best'.[18] Such sluggish communications may have encouraged Constantine to allow the consecration of the pope without imperial agreement. The Justinianic *iussio* was instead received by the new pope, Conon (686–687); unfortunately, the one surviving copy is a poor Latin translation of unknown origin.[19]

In it, Justinian explained how the Acts were read out and then signed off as authentic by the Church officials and dignitaries present, including the papal *apocrisiarius*/ἀποκρισιαριυς, a high-ranking diplomatic representative of the pope usually present in Constantinople. This office, also called *responsalis* ('he who answers'), had existed since the fifth century, but was only made official in law under Justinian I.[20] The Acts were then entrusted to the emperor, who promised to preserve them 'so that there will be no opportunity for those who do not wish to have fear of God to corrupt or change anything in them at any time it pleases them'.[21] The *iussio* also acted as a statement of Justinian's own acceptance of the Sixth Ecumenical Council and therefore his orthodoxy and willingness to act as God's representative, all witnessed by those same Church officials, dignitaries and soldiers present at the Constantinopolitan synod.[22]

There has been some suggestion that Justinian's synod was an early sign of his want of ecclesiastical independence from and then control over the papacy, which would manifest more clearly in succeeding imperial-papal relations.[23] However, Conon looked favourably upon the young emperor's intervention,[24] with no hint that he took Justinian's promise 'to guard and preserve forever unimpaired and unshaken' the Acts of the Sixth Ecumenical Council as infringing upon papal prerogative. For now, the pope felt that Justinian was building upon the foundations laid by his father in making the Heraclian dynasty a staunch defender of orthodoxy, with Justinian referring to the pope in respectful terms – 'universal pope' and 'the most holy and blessed father'. This, in connection with Justinian's profession of orthodoxy, got relations between Rome and Constantinople off to a positive start; a belief strengthened by two further imperial rescripts of 687. Again, following in the footsteps of his father, Justinian reduced taxes on papal territories, remitting 200 measures of the *annonae* levied on Bruttium and Lucania. The second rescript ordered local militias in Bruttium, Lucania and Sicily to send back papal peasants they were holding in pledge.[25]

Justinian upheld his claim as a champion of orthodoxy by targeting heretics within imperial territory. Despite his seeming fear of their tampering with the Acts of the Sixth Council, Justinian does not seem to have had many problems with Monothelites. This may demonstrate the lack of depth in belief in Monothelitism, although it would be a Monothelite, Philippikos Bardanes, who replaced Justinian in 711.[26] The emperor's more active anti-heretic activities centred on a group called the Paulicians. Originating in the second century, this was a Christian sect who followed adoptionism, the belief that Jesus was a mere man until God's Spirit had descended upon him at his baptism by John the Baptist.[27] This belief saw them place even more emphasis on the importance of baptism, while they held a firm opposition to the cult of saints and the veneration of icons. They may also have been dualist, non-Trinitarian and became a focus for 'local hostility and opposition to the state and its fiscal apparatus'.[28] Their exact date of origin is somewhat disputed, with initial links to the third-century bishop of Antioch, Paul of Samosata, and their condemnation at an Antiochene synod in 268 possibly the result of a misidentification with Paulianists. While taking influences from other beliefs – Manichaeanism, Marcionism, Gnosticism, etc. – the Paulicians may well be a new sect of the seventh century.

Their growth or even first appearance had drawn the attention of Constantine IV, with the Paulician leader, Constantine-Silvanus, being killed in *c.*681 during a persecution. However, this did little to deaden the zeal of the Paulicians. By 690, the leadership of Symeon-Titus had seen the Paulicians cause enough alarm for the bishop of Koloneia to complain to Justinian about their activities in Armenia.[29] Justinian ordered an investigation, with a persecution following. Immolation was prescribed for the most obstinate Paulicians, including Symeon-Titus.[30] While an horrendous action and reflecting poorly on Justinian in modern sensibilities, such rooting out of heresy was seen as a positive, even virtuous action for a Roman emperor. It should not be taken as part of the reasoning behind the negative portrayal of Justinian. Indeed, this positive reception is perhaps best displayed by the lack of mention of the Paulician suppression by either Theophanes or Nikephoros. There seems to have been no way to spin the destruction of heretics as any sort of negative to be held against Justinian. The only other explanation is that the Paulicians and their suppression by Justinian were far smaller in scale than Petrus Siculus would have it, small enough for it to escape the non-contemporary chroniclers' notice. This Justinianic attack quietened the Paulicians for half a century, but it did not break them. Indeed, they would not be fully dealt with in the eastern frontier until 872 by Basil I.[31]

Under the Dome: The Quinisext Council

His hunting of heretics and respectful dealings with the papacy may have got Justinian off to a good religious start, but he felt the need for a more grandiose display of his championing of orthodoxy. He needed his name attached to an ecumenical council, but there was no major doctrinal issue that required a full meeting of the Church for Justinian to preside over. The emperor found his reason in an oversight by both the Fifth and Sixth Ecumenical Councils (553 and 680/681 respectively): neither had drawn up disciplinary canons. In completing the work of these two previous councils, Justinian could continue to paint himself as following in the orthodox footsteps of not only his father, but also his own great namesake, Justinian I, who had called the Fifth Ecumenical Council. However, such was his desperation to present himself as a champion of orthodoxy like his father and namesake, Justinian II would end up replicating the actions of his grandfather with 'a spectacular attempt to arrest the pope'.[32]

Before the descent into that latest nadir in imperial-papal relations, Justinian's council met in the imperial palace at Constantinople, specifically the same Domed Hall that the Sixth Council had taken place in. This meeting place gave the council one of its names – the Council in Trullo, with τρουλος being the Greek for 'dome'. Rather than being the Seventh Ecumenical Council, Justinian's council also became known for its proposed finishing of the work of the two previous councils – the Fifth-Sixth, Penthecton or Quinisext Council. For such an important event in the reign of Justinian II, and indeed for the Christian Church, it is not completely clear from the sources exactly when the Quinisext Council took place. Even the exact year is somewhat difficult to nail down. This is due to a combination of copyist mistakes, the Roman indiction cycle and the fact that their year started on 1 September. The more usually accepted date is some time in the twelve months between 1 September 691 and 31 August 692.[33]

With 215 bishops in attendance, all from the East (which should raise some alarm bells), the opening address of the Quinisext Council used many of the usual appeals – the Church faced a period of moral decay and needed reform, perhaps even hinting that it needed imperial leadership to guide the Church into the future by seeing it back to the morality of the past:

> 'Christ our God, who steers this greatest of ships, the entire world, had now set you over us, the wise governor, the pious emperor, our protector indeed; you, who dispense your words in discernment, safeguard truth always, render judgement and justice upon earth and walk in the blameless path. Wisdom bore you in her womb and nurtured you well with virtues, she brought you up and educated you and filled you with the Spirit of God; she made you the eye of the universe, you who brightly illumine your subjects with the pureness and splendour of your

mind. To you, she has entrusted her Church and has taught you to meditate on her law, day and night, for the correction and edification of the peoples subject to you ... For this reason, then, we have assembled at your command in this God-guarded imperial city, and have drawn up these sacred canons. Wherefore ... even as you have honoured the Church with your letters of convocation, so may you finally confirm our resolutions through your pious signature.' (*Trullo* 49–50, 54)

There are similar ideas of divine imperial appointment in Justinian's *iussio* of 687 and the opening of the *Ekloga*, which 'imply an emperor who was both the divinely appointed and divinely guided ruler as well as the shepherd and defender of the Christian flock under God's divine protection'.[34] Even more than that, this opening and the pronouncements of the Quinisext Council take orthodoxy, the Church, the civilized world – *oikoumene* – and the Roman Empire as essentially being one and the same.[35] It is possible to see a significant amount of personal imperialism on the part of the emperor in these pronouncements. While in keeping with the Christianization of the imperial office, his presentation 'as the mediating authority between God and humankind, as the shepherd who guides the Christian flock, and in which canon law was effectively deployed as an aspect of the legislation of the state'[36] could be seen as the position of emperor being promoted to something more than just the leading lay person on the planet.

While the opening address spoke of Justinian in such glowing terms, it is difficult to ascertain how much of the council the emperor was present for, or even how much direct influence he had on its decisions. Given the fact that the emperor remained a layman in the face of a Church gathering, Justinian was supposedly unable to impose his will on the council. However, the example provided by Justinian I and Constantine IV was that emperors could influence an ecumenical council, 'and his attendance certainly would not have been at all unusual';[37] indeed, given the importance he placed in his 'orthodox champion' persona, Justinian likely made his presence felt in the Domed Hall, which was of course part of his palatial home. It is also rather telling that the Quinisext Council did not promulgate any canons that the emperor did not like. How much this demonstrates the shared orthodoxy of Justinian and the clergy gathered under the Dome or how much the emperor was able to influence their decisions is difficult to gauge. The poor reputation of Justinian in the sources and his upcoming showdown with the papacy could influence the depiction of how he directed the council.

The result of the deliberations of the Quinisext Council was the promulgation of 102 canons 'designed to upgrade the moral standards and practices of orthodox Christians, both clergy and laity'.[38] The first two canons presented Quinisext's endorsement of not only the six ecumenical councils, but also other collections of doctrinal practices such as the fourth-century Syrian *Apostolic Canons*, the Synod of Laodicea of 363–364, the Third Synod of Carthage and the 39th Festal Letter of Athanasius, which lists the books of the Bible he thought to be canonical, to be read and those to be rejected as apocryphal. After that, and cutting through their lack of order, there are some clear categories that emerge from the canons – 'uprooting of surviving pagan customs, much specific attention to marriage and celibacy laws, the attempt to secure empire-wide conformity in a number of liturgical and worship practices, and strict insistence on higher standards of moral conduct'.[39]

Canon 62 banned various practices considered to be pagan in origin: festivals like the Bota to Pan and the Brumalia to Bacchus, while invoking Bacchus, even in jest, during wine production was also banned, as were dances in honour of any old gods or goddesses, especially those that involved cross-dressing. The wearing of various types of mask – comic, tragic or satiric – were also banned as relics of the Ancient Greek theatre considered to have pagan overtones. Laymen found partaking in these now banned actions would be excommunicated, while churchmen would be deposed from their clerical position. Similarly, Canon 65 banned the lighting of a bonfire and jumping over it as part of the celebrations of the New Moon, while Canon 94 excommunicated anyone found to have sworn a heathen oath. In its warning to civil law students not to wear uncustomary clothing or to take part in theatrical, athletic or pagan events, Canon 71's 'concern about student behaviour has a strangely timeless tone'.[40] The council also issued stern warnings against fortune tellers, horoscopes, selling bear hair, magic amulets and other superstitious practices – the punishment was to be six years of penance (Canon 61). This was largely ignored, particularly the attempts to predict the future, which were popular at many levels of Roman society; even the sponsor of the Quinisext Council, Justinian II himself, is reported listening to the predictions of a monk called Cyrus.

Quinisext's attacks on theatrical performance is also seen with Canon 96's condemnation of wigs and hairpieces, whether male, female or clerical – one should 'adorn the inner man rather than the outer' – while Canon 57 forbade clerical participation in theatrical shows as actors, dancers and animal-fighters. However, 'it is doubtful how effective these stringent curbs on theatrical performances could have been in a city so noted for its love of spectacular entertainments as Constantinople was.'[41] Any attempts to enforce such restrictions will no doubt have affected the popularity Justinian experienced in the capital.

The mentioning of clerics with regard to wigs and performing was also just a small part of the significant section of the Quinisext canons which established a high standard of behaviour amongst the clergy. Canon 10 banned them from taking interest on loans; Canon 9 forbade clergy from working in a tavern; Canon 24 banned clergy from taking part in horse races and ordered that they leave a wedding should celebratory games begin. Canon 50 forbade clerics and laymen from playing dice. Numerous canons (86, 87, 98, 91, 92 and 100) addressed the morals of both clergy and laity. Many were restating rules regarding major issues, such as adultery, rape, abortion, brothel-keeping and pornography. There was also a sub-section on the treatment of churches, with singing not meant to be loud or rowdy (Canon 75), no eating or selling of food in church (Canon 76) and the banning of animals, except in emergencies (Canon 88). Old Bibles and Church Father writings were also not to be destroyed unless 'rendered useless either by bookworms or by water or in some way' (Canon 68).

Numerous canons also dealt with liturgical procedures and local customs at odds with central orthodox practices. The practices of the Armenians and the western church were of particular worry to the bishops in Trullo. Four canons focused on Armenian practices – offering communion with unmixed wine (Canon 32); ordaining only members of specific families (Canon 33); eating eggs and cheese on Saturdays and Sundays in Lent (Canon 56); and cooking meat to serve to priests inside church sanctuaries (Canon 99). Any clergy found to be contravening these canons were to be deposed, while laypeople would be excommunicated. While this seems like the central Church dictating to its constituent parts, it must be remembered that there were several Armenian bishops present at the Quinisext Council. That they signed up to these reforming canons suggests that there was at least some who thought reform was required. That said, the Armenian rebellion of Sembat in the aftermath of Sebastopolis could easily have been linked to resistance to any attempts to enforce these canons, which were going against accepted Armenian practice. It was not just sections of the Christian Church which were targeted by Quinisext. Canon 11 of Quinisext built upon the widespread anti-Semitism of the Roman Empire, banning any lay person from eating unleavened bread, being treated by Jewish doctors, sharing baths with Jews or having confidential dealings with Jews.

While it tackled an 'exceptionally broad spectrum of activities and practice',[42] the fact that the Trullan council sought to force traditional and practical uniformity was bound to cause trouble, particularly when the council settled on Greek customs without much countenance for other well-established traditions. This had its greatest impact when it came to the canons which targeted, directly or indirectly, the Roman West. Justinian and his clerical allies do seem to have recognized the potential discontent their forced uniformity would cause and attempted to display a 'great deference to the practice of the church of Rome'.[43] Initially, the Quinisext canons claimed to combine the traditions of Rome and Constantinople 'into one in a manner at once in keeping with the fathers and pleasing to God admitting neither unrestrained mildness nor harsh severity' (Canon 3). However, that mask slips with the prescribed use of Greek traditions and a general tone of eastern superiority, referring to certain western practices as 'barbaric'. It soon became obvious that the papacy was not going to accept canonical legislation that was in any way contrary to Roman practice.

Eastern Embrace and Papal Protest

Given the eastern/Greek traditional leanings of those in attendance at Quinisext and the canons they produced, it is unsurprising that the eastern church completely (aside from some probable Armenian resistance) embraced Quinisext as ecumenical.[44] This raises questions regarding the records of Nikephoros and Theophanes, or more accurately the lack thereof. Nikephoros, who was patriarch of Constantinople, makes no mention of this ecumenical council, while Theophanes, an orthodox monk, only presents 'a confused brief statement'[45] at the outset of Justinian's reign. It treats Quinisext as an addendum to the Sixth Ecumenical Council, but does not mention Justinian's involvement with it.[46] This could suggest that as early as the writing of the *History to 720*, the historical record was looking to denigrate Justinian or play down his successes at any opportunity. This tendency must have been particularly strong for an orthodox patriarch to ignore what was considered an ecumenical council. Justinian could not be associated with anything the Church approved of.

This denigration of Justinian may have become almost all-pervasive in the written histories, but there is some evidence that sections of the eastern

Church continued to recognize him for his championing of orthodoxy. Indeed, some Eastern Orthodox calendars listed him as St Justinian Rhinotmetos, with a feast day on 15 July. That his saintly name included the fact that he had had his nose removed shows that this sainthood lasted beyond his first deposition. It is in more modern times that, 'no doubt because the chronicler's evaluation of Justinian's misrule came to be almost universally believed, his name has been expunged from the Orthodox calendar'.[47] But even with this dropping of saintly praise by some, the sheer fact that the emperor had attained this position at all demonstrates 'that in bygone centuries there existed traditions about him far different from those recorded by his historiographical adversaries'.[48]

By far the most important reaction to Quinisext came from Rome. When Justinian put his red imperial signature to the six copies of the canons,[49] he did not expect any opposition from the papacy: there was a space left for the pope to sign below the emperor, before the four eastern patriarchs. Demonstrating Justinian's favouring of his new Cypriot colony, the emperor accorded John, archbishop of Nea Justinianopolis, the privilege of signing after the patriarchs, at the head of some 200-plus bishops and Church representatives who had been in attendance. All six copies were forwarded to Rome for ratification by the pope, who since 687 had been Sergius I.

While of Antiochene Syrian descent, Sergius was born in Palermo, Sicily, perhaps in 650. He is recorded as being a talented musician in his youth, which saw him become a choirboy, the entry point for his religious career.[50] When aged between 19 and 23, he moved from Sicily to Rome to serve as an acolyte during the pontificate of Adeodatus II (672–676). Pope Leo II appointed him cardinal-priest of Santa Susanna on 27 June 683, a position he held until his election as pope after the death of Conon on 21 September 687.[51] The succession to Conon was by no means a straightforward affair. Conon's archdeacon Paschal had reputedly bribed John II Platyn, exarch of Ravenna, to make him pope, while a large faction in Rome favoured the archpriest Theodore. This disagreement exploded into fighting within the Lateran Palace. To prevent further bloodshed, a large meeting of clergy, army officers, civic authorities and citizens was called to find a compromise. From this palatine meeting emerged a new papal candidate – Sergius. This mixed 'conclave' then marched on the Lateran, expelled the warring followers of Paschal and Theodore and forced the acceptance of Sergius as pope.

Despite his apparent capitulation, Paschal continued to intrigue against the new pope, sending messages to the exarch, offering gold in exchange for armed support. John Platyn soon arrived at Rome, but quickly realized that Sergius had been properly elected and had significant popular support. This saw the exarch accept Sergius' elevation, departing Rome after his consecration on 15 December 687. Paschal did not let this latest setback stop his intriguing, and he was eventually confined to a monastery on charges of witchcraft.[52] The importance of this disputed election of Sergius is that it provided the new pope with some confidence in his position. The inability of John Platyn to influence the papal election to any great degree showed some decline in Constantinopolitan control on the Italian peninsula in the face of the Lombards, an increasingly confident papacy and the growing local allegiance to the pope rather than the emperor.

Sergius demonstrated his increasing confidence in his reaction to the arrival of the *Tome* containing the Quinisext canons. He not only decided not to sign the canons, but refused to allow them to be read in public, supposedly exclaiming, 'I would rather be dead than to consent to the new errors they contain.'[53] The record does not go into any detail about what the pope considered to be 'new errors', leaving various historians to present their thoughts on what raised this papal opposition.[54] The very first Quinisext canon contains something that might be offensive to the papacy: the anathematizing of Pope Honorius I; however, the papacy had accepted this through the Sixth Ecumenical Council, and even if Sergius was inclined to reverse acceptance of this papal anathema, it would hardly be classed as a 'new error'. Another possible problem undermined by not being 'new' is Canon 36's reiterating of Constantinople's equal ecclesiastical privileges to those of Rome, while upholding the latter's primacy. This had been a sticking point between the two imperial capitals since the First Council of Constantinople in 381 and again at Chalcedon in 451, so it would be peculiar for Sergius not to voice his dislike of its reiteration. In the past, Canon 36 was viewed as something of a 'formal declaration of war'[55] by Justinian against the papacy; however, while it had not been pleased with such statements, the papacy, along with patriarchs and emperors, had managed to largely put this debate to one side for the past 300 years. It seems unlikely then that this was the problem over which Sergius chose to reject the council.

Another not 'new error' is the presence of the *Apostolic Canons* in Canon 2's list of accepted texts and synods. Quinisext accepted all eighty-five of the *Apostolic Canons*, while the papacy only recognized the first fifty. The *Apostolic Canons* were claimed to be a collection of governing and disciplinary decrees written for the Early Church by the Apostles, but their mentioning of decrees from the Council of Antioch in 341 suggests at the very least they were updated or altered in the fourth century. Any known connection to this Council of Antioch may not have gone down well with Rome, for the pope at the time, Julius I, was not represented, while it was held under the auspices of Constantius II, whose supposed Arianism made him unpopular. Of course, in the seventh century, the *Apostolic Canons* themselves were not to be considered a 'new error', but then Quinisext's full embracing of them may have been novel.[56]

What on the surface seems a general theme of clarification over various marriage and celibacy rules contained some significant divergences between East and West, specifically over clerical marriage.[57] Canon 3 went against the Roman practice of forcing all twice-married priests to choose between setting aside his wife or remaining a priest. Canon 13 allowed a married man to be ordained, although he would be required to continue to live with his wife – attempting to send her away was to be punished by excommunication. This ran contrary to western practice, which demanded celibacy from an ordained man; if married, man and wife would have to be permanently separated. Quinisext clearly realized that there would be some trouble with Canon 13, for while it highlighted that the Roman practice exceeded that legislated in the *Apostolic Canons*, it established something of a loophole. Canon 30 permitted clerics 'in the lands of the barbarians' to continue with those practices, 'but we have conceded this to them on no other ground than their narrowness, and foreign and unsettled manner'. Such patronizing language could well have irked Sergius, although the sheer presence of some idea of compromise, even if it was disparagingly worded, somewhat undercuts the attack and may even reflect the influence of 'papal' representatives at the council.[58] Furthermore, again, it could even be these marriage canons should not be considered 'new'. In 420, Honorius and Theodosius II issued a decree that allowed clergy to co-habit with their wives so long as the marriage took place before he entered the Church. It also made it illegal for married clergy to divorce. This suggests that clerical marriage was a historic division between East and West, which in turn may be reflected in the willingness of Quinisext to highlight its own compromise with western practice.[59]

One prohibition by Quinisext which might have annoyed Sergius on a personal level was Canon 82, which banned the depiction of Christ as a lamb, stating that he should always appear human. Sergius seems to have had a personal liking of that depiction, with his Syrian parentage likely playing a role. The exact timing is not completely clear but it would appear that in protest to this ban, Sergius added the *Agnus Dei* invocation – 'Lamb of God, you take away the sins of the world, have mercy on us' – to the celebration of Mass at the breaking of the Host. He also restored the damaged façade mosaic in the atrium of St Peter's that depicted the worship of the lamb.[60] It is unlikely that there was any personal targeting of the pope by Quinisext, even if the *Agnus Dei* addition and the mosaic repairs came before the council, but in that case what were Justinian and his allies attempting to achieve by such a prohibition? Canon 82 has been viewed as part of the iconographic policy that also produced Justinian's Christ coinage.[61] Together, the banning of Christ as a lamb and Canon 73's forbidding of the use of crosses in floor designs[62] represent a considerable action for Byzantine art and perhaps 'the most significant instance of imperial concern for proper use of icons in the pre-iconoclastic era'.[63] However, while the Heraclian dynasty as a whole attached importance to icon veneration, there is little evidence to connect Quinisext to the Christ coinage or an overall iconographic agenda, including any embryonic iconoclasm. Canon 82 may instead have been Justinian and the bishops trying 'to impose order on confusing iconography'.[64] For example, sheep were seen as weak, easily misled, stupid, defenceless, sacrificial animals; hardly a connection to be made with Jesus Christ.[65]

While some of the canons may spark more conversation than others, it could well be that attempting to find a single canon that encouraged Sergius' rejection of Quinisext is to dig down too far. The sheer fact that a substantial list of canons to irk the papacy can be rendered may be more to the point. One or two somewhat dubious canons could perhaps be overlooked, but when there were perhaps a dozen or more, that is much more difficult to ignore. Indeed, it may seem like an overt attack on western Church tradition. The combination of the departure from and censure of some Roman practices and the general disparaging and superior tone, labelling them as 'barbaric', likely made Sergius' rejection of Quinisext more likely than Justinian and the bishops of Quinisext anticipated.

One problem that Sergius' opposition to Quinisext faced, which in turn may give some substance to Justinian's angry response for having 'woefully misjudged'[66] the papal reaction, is the possibility that the papacy *had* been represented at the council. If there were no official representatives at Quinisext, that alone could have led the pope to complain over its ecumenical status, even before he read the canons. However, the *Liber Pontificalis* suggests that there had been papal legates present in Trullo and that they had even signed the canons.[67] This seems clear, but there is some question over the status of these supposed papal legates – were they dispatched to Constantinople to take part in the council, or were they permanent residents in the capital like the papal *apocrisiarius*? The *Liber Pontificalis* does not say, but it seems that the latter is more likely.[68] Whatever papal representatives were present in Trullo and whatever they were purported to have signed, their names do not appear on the official list of signees to the Quinisext canons. Did they agree to sign an earlier version? Or perhaps they were not included in the final list of signatories because they were not all bishops. Virtually all signatories, besides the emperor, were bishops, with only a few deacons deputized to sign on behalf of their bishop. No signatures of papal representatives appearing on the final drafts of the Quinisext canons may represent the confidence of the emperor, the patriarchs and the bishops in Trullo that the pope would sign up to their canons. Why have some low-level deputies sign when the pope himself was going to sign?

That these supposed papal legates gave any kind of consent to the Quinisext canons was problematic for the pope and for historians. The *Liber Pontificalis* suggests that they were 'deceived' into signing canons they did not comprehend the true, offensive meaning of. The truth is difficult to prove: 'Perhaps they did not dare to oppose the emperor's wishes, or perhaps they simply had no idea how vigorously Pope Sergius would react against the work of the Quinisext.'[69] However, the absence of any western signatures on the final drafts of the canons aided the pope's rejection, but there was one potentially significant problem: Bishop Basil of Gortyna had signed the canons. While not mentioned by the *Liber Pontificalis*, Basil not only signed his name, he added the peculiar 'holding the place of all the Synod of the holy Church of Rome'.[70] This could be very embarrassing for the pope, as it looked like a papal representative had given his backing to the Quinisext canons. However, 'apparently, Pope Sergius thought the best thing to do about Basil's signature was to ignore it.'[71] Yet that leaves the question of why Basil would claim such a position of papal representation. Basil's bishopric on Crete was part of the Roman patriarchate, so at the very least he was to be considered a western bishop. Furthermore, he had been assigned as a papal legate for the Sixth Ecumenical Council in 680, and it may be that at the very least Basil and others in attendance assumed that his presence at Quinisext allowed him to continue in that role. He may even have been there with the backing of the pope, only for the Holy Father to not like what he signed up to and then ignore Basil's presence and signature.[72]

The fact that Basil, the *apocrisiarius* and possibly other papal representatives do seem to have been present at Quinisext – even if they had no official right to speak for the pope – would have led Justinian and his priestly allies to think that the papacy had assented to the canons it had promulgated, making the rejection by Sergius all the more surprising. It also suggests that Justinian had not attempted to exclude the papacy, or at least not actively. It is true that the West was under-represented in Trullo, but this does not definitely mean that Justinian held any anti-papal feelings in 691. A small western contingent at ecumenical councils was probably par for the course when those councils were taking place in the East. The growing obstacles facing East-West communications – Bulgars and Slavs in the Balkans, Arab pirates in the Mediterranean and Lombards in the Italian hills – will only have made it more difficult for western representatives to travel to Constantinople. But whatever the reasons behind it, Justinian seems to have been given a false perception of papal acceptance.

Conversely, it must be said that Pope Sergius was presented with plenty of reasons to not accept Quinisext: under-representation (or even non-representation) of the West; various anti-western canons; 'erroneous' endorsements of other canons; the 'deception' of the papal representatives mentioned by *Liber Pontificalis*; and the general tone of eastern superiority towards the 'barbaric' West. The opposition of the pope to Quinisext was reflected in the writings of western ecclesiastics. Paul the Deacon wrote of it being erroneous, while Bede referred to it as a 'heretical synod'.[73] However, in Visigothic Spain, Quinisext and its canons were ratified by the Eighteenth Council of Toledo, seemingly at the urging of king Wittiza; however, he was lambasted for this decision and it would later be overturned by Fruela I of Asturias (ruled 757–768).[74]

A Leaf from Grandpa's Book ... Arrest the Pope!

Whatever his specific reasons, Sergius had rejected the canons presented to him, and without the pope's assent, there could be no unity of the faith expressed by Quinisext. This enraged the emperor. He would not allow one man to undermine his living up to the legacy of his father and illustrious imperial namesake. Rather than allow civil discourse and compromise to find common ground between Quinisext and the papacy, Justinian gave vent to his rage by following the example set not just by his grandfather, Constans II, but also by Justinian I: he would arrest prominent members of the Church.[75] The emperor's first targets were allies of Sergius. He sent a special envoy called a *magisterianus* (unhelpfully also called Sergius) to arrest John, bishop of Portus, who had served as a papal legate to the Sixth

Ecumenical Council, and an apostolic counsellor called Boniface, and bring them to Constantinople.[76] There was likely a dual intent in these arrests. It presented a warning to the pope that if he did not relent in his opposition to Quinisext, the forces of the emperor could reach him. Yet it could also be that Justinian thought that he could gain the support of John and Boniface, then have them persuade Sergius to accept the Trullan canons. Whatever plan the emperor had, it did not alter the position of the pope.

Therefore, Justinian decided to further up the ante. He sent his *protospatharios* (an officer in the imperial bodyguard), Zacharias, to arrest the pope and bring him to Constantinople.[77] The arrival of Zacharias in Italy caused rumours of his mission, leading the militias from Ravenna and the Pentapolis to band together and march to Rome in support of the pope. The *Liber Pontificalis* does not mention the militia of Rome itself supporting Sergius. This could be accidental or even an omission because the author felt there was no need to exclaim the papal leanings of the Roman militia. That it made no recorded attempt to oppose those who came to Pope Sergius' rescue suggests that at the very most, they retained a technical loyalty to the emperor.[78]

By the time the 'papal' militias arrived at Rome, Zacharias had made it to the city and closed its gates. However, the *protospatharios* quickly realized that there was no support for his mission and soon found himself trapped in Rome, with the Italian militias entering the city through St Peter's Gate and the Roman mob controlling the streets. Zacharias was left with only one potential safe haven – the Lateran Palace, where Sergius may have been briefly kept prisoner upon the *protospatharios*' arrival. The militias and mob marched on the papal palace, demanding the release of Sergius. Stoked by rumours that the pope had already been smuggled out of the city and put on a boat to Constantinople, the soldiers then threatened to destroy the Lateran Palace if they were not given entry. Suitably terrified, Zacharias reputedly hid under the papal bed! Recognizing the bloodthirstiness of the gathered crowd and the potential imperial reaction to the murder of Zacharias, Pope Sergius interceded on his behalf, quenching the hostility of the crowd. Moved by the compassion of the pope, the mob and the militias agreed to spare the *protospatharios* on the condition that he leave Italy immediately. Zacharias would have gleefully accepted his unceremonious ejection from Rome, but this reaction may have only seemed fleeting for now he had 'to face the dismal prospect of returning to Justinian with the report of his failure'.[79]

Care must be taken not to view this solidarity between Sergius and exarchate forces as anything other than 'exclusively spiritual'.[80] It was a not a display of political independence by either Rome or Ravenna;[81] indeed, the pope did the exact opposite. This is seen in his decision to mollify the irate militias and Roman populace and facilitate Zacharias' escape from Rome: 'a pontiff with a separatist political agenda would have acted otherwise.'[82] Even the pro-western *Liber Pontificalis* makes no mention of the papacy or Italy looking for independence from the empire during the late seventh century.[83] Sergius' opposition to Quinisext was focused on the treatment of the western Church by the council and its canons. He was not against the idea of a council to complete the unfinished business of the Fifth and Sixth Ecumenical Councils, and was not opposing the position of the empire or the emperor with regard to political or religious influence. He would protect the practices of the Roman Church if he felt they were under threat and would not be the emperor's 'captive in matters of religion',[84] but he would not 'reject those Eastern customs and practices that were part of his oriental heritage and that did not clash with Rome but instead enriched it spiritually … [The emperors] would remain his lords and sovereigns to the end.'[85]

But even if Sergius was able to communicate his continued imperial allegiance, Justinian may have found such a distinction between imperial and religious adherence incomprehensible. This was because the sacralization of the Roman Empire and the position of emperor in the East had been so successful that a clean separation between Church and state no longer existed. In contrast, the West was 'a thriving Christian community that did not require the existence of the Roman state'.[86] Even if some in the imperial court might have understood such a distinction, it is unlikely that Justinian would have been willing to listen to them. He had been angry enough at the pope's opposition and the failure of his arrests of John and Boniface. No doubt he would have been incandescent at the news of Zacharias' failure and any claim on the pope's part that the interference of the Italian militias and Roman mob in imperial business did not represent any form of treason. It could well be imagined that the pope and his allies were readying themselves for another expression of imperial outrage.

However, Sergius, Zacharias and Italy were spared the immediate consequences of another outburst of Justinianic rage, for not long after the *protospatharios* was forced to hide under the papal bed, the political situation in Constantinople changed dramatically. Justinian II had lost his nose and his throne, developments which saw the Quinisext canons forgotten. The pope was certainly willing to ignore them, while the men to sit on the imperial throne over the next ten years had little inclination to get involved in religious squabbles while their rule was unsure. But then Justinian II was not a man to let exile, losing his nose and being kicked off his throne stop him. Once he was back in the imperial purple, the canons of Quinisext would be back on the imperial-papal agenda.

Chapter 8

Administering an Empire in Transition: Forces, Furrows and Finances under Justinian II

'Many changes took place at this time; changes in the governmental machinery of the provinces, changes in the peasantry, and in the laws and customs of land-holding.'

Head (1972), 81

Justinianic Themes

The chronological story of Justinian II's first decade on the imperial throne may be taken up with his military, religious and even numismatic policies, but those are only part of the narrative of his reign. He also oversaw an expansion of the theme system, while his provincial administration saw significant land, tax and social reform. It is difficult to prove whether many of Justinian's policy initiatives were part of a more long-term plan, a series of reactionary changes reflecting regional developments, gradual evolution over the course of years that had to be accepted as a *fait accompli* or a tangled mess of all of the above in an attempt to bring governance to the new-look Roman Empire. It is even difficult at times to accredit some of the policies to Justinian himself, rather than other emperors. Various aspects of these policies may have been involved in the crisis that was to rapidly overtake Justinian's regime in 695.

The most prominent of such ill-defined developments in the late seventh century that Justinian found himself interacting with was the continued expansion of the theme system. Whatever it was and whoever was the main instigator of its development, the theme system, with its overturning of the traditional separation of military and civilian authority in the person of the *strategos*, 'worked well in the perennial crisis situation of the seventh century and played a vital role in preserving the Empire from total absorption by the Arabs and the barbarians'.[1] This success encouraged Justinian to build upon this system. Many of the same issues of a lack of detail and clarity persist with thematic developments attributed to the reign of Justinian II. Fortunately, the emperor himself furnished us with a list of themes in his *iussio* to the pope.[2] This provides something of a chronological anchor for some thematic developments – the *iussio* is dated 17 February 687. This list does add to the consensus about the Opsikion, Anatolikon and Armeniakon themes, but unfortunately, 'because of strange spelling and geographic uncertainties there has been considerable dispute as to precisely what areas the emperor was naming at one or two points'.[3] The specific troubles have already been explored above – the Thrakesion theme being based in Asia rather than geographic Thrace, and the location/nature of the Karabisiani. The list also suggests that while Justinian would make additions to the theme system, they were not established by early 687.

His earliest addition has already been touched upon, and while not recorded in the sources until 695 when the soon-to-be rebel Leontios was appointed as its *strategos*, the theme of Hellas likely dates to the aftermath of Justinian's successful Slav campaign in and around Thessalonica in 688. At the very least, this represents a hope or expectation that Roman control of at least part of the Greek peninsula had been restored. That said, the actual term 'theme' was not applied to Hellas in the surviving sources until over a century later. It was instead recorded as a στρατηγία/*strategia*, which does suggest that it was under the control of a *strategos* like a theme. Perhaps this lack of thematic formality reflects the fluid formation of these new politico-military land divisions, with the Heraclian emperors still coming to terms with what the 'theme system' and a 'theme' actually was, even by *c.*690. The question could also be asked whether the foundation of the Hellas theme as a '*strategia*' was a reflection of the actual situation on the ground. Could a *strategia* be more of a military arrangement than the governmental apparatus that the theme had come to encapsulate? Such a potential difference could highlight that while enough Roman control had been re-established over parts of northern and central Greece to impose some governmental restructuring, there were still continued military problems in the region. Could Justinian have been ushering in a phased thematic establishment in the area or was he merely demonstrating his aspiration for reintegrating central and southern Greece, where imperial control remained either weak or purely nominal?

Unfortunately, the lack of information surviving about the early Hellas theme makes it difficult to state much about it beyond the period of 688–695 for its foundation. It does seem that the Hellenic *strategia* was to have the

HERACLIUS, CONSTANTINE III AND HERAKLONAS: gold *solidus*, issued between 635 and 636 from Constantinople mint. Obverse: Heraclius centre, Constantine III left and Heraklonas right, cross above. Reverse: cross on steps, monogram of Heraclius left, *VICTORIA AVGUE CONOB*. (© *Noble Numismatics*)

CONSTANS II AND CONSTANTINE IV: gold *solidus*, issued between 654 and 659 from Constantinople mint. Obverse: crowned Constans left, Constantine right, *DN CONSTATINUS C CONSTI*. Reverse: cross on steps, *VICTORIA AVGUE CONOB+*. (© *Noble Numismatics*)

CONSTANTINE IV, with Heraclius and Tiberius: gold *solidus*, issued between 674 and 681 from Constantinople mint. Obverse; three-quarter facing bearded bust of Constantine IV in military garb, *dN CONST ANUS P*. Reverse: cross on steps, between Heraclius on left and Tiberius on right, each holding cross on globe, *VICTOA AVGU**Q**, *CONOB*. (© *Noble Numismatics*)

JUSTINIAN II (first reign 685–695): gold *solidus*, issued between 687 and 692 from Constantinople mint. Obverse: bust facing of Justinian with short beard, wearing chlamys and crown, holding cross on globe, *D IUSTINIA NUS PE AV*. Reverse: cross on steps, *VICTORIA AVGU H CONOB Γ*. (© *Noble Numismatics*)

JUSTINIAN II (first reign 685–695): gold *solidus*, issued between 687 and 692 from Constantinople mint. Obverse: bust facing of Justinian with short beard, wearing chlamys and crown, holding cross on globe, *IUSTINIA NUS PE AV*. Reverse: cross potent on three steps, around *VICTORIA AVGUI CONOB*. (© *Noble Numismatics*)

LEONTIOS: gold *solidus*, issued between 695 and 698 from Constantinople mint. Obverse: bust facing of Leontios, bearded, wearing crown and loros, holding akakia and cross on globe, *D LEON PE AV*. Reverse: cross on steps, *VICTORIA AVGUS, CONOB*. (© *Noble Numismatics*)

TIBERIUS III: gold *solidus*, issued between 698 and 705 from Constantinople mint. Obverse: cuirassed bust of Tiberius facing with short beard, wearing crown and holding spear, *d TIbERI US PE AU*. Reverse: cross on steps, *VICTORIA AUGU CONOB*. (© *Noble Numismatics*)

JUSTINIAN II (second reign, 705–711): gold *solidus*, issued in 705 from Constantinople mint. Obverse: facing bust of Christ, with cross behind head, curly hair and close beard, wears pallium and colobium, raising hand in benediction, *dN IhS ChS REX REGNANTIUM*. Reverse: crowned facing bust of Justinian, wearing loros and holding crosses, *DN IUSTINIA NUS MULTUS A, PAX*. (© *Classical Numismatic Group, Inc.*)

JUSTINIAN II AND TIBERIUS: gold *solidus*, issued between 705 and 711 from Constantinople mint. Obverse: facing bust of Christ, with cross behind head, curly hair and close beard, wears pallium and colobium, raising hand in benediction, *dN IhS ChS REX REGNANTIUM*. Reverse: facing and crowned busts of Justinian on left and Tiberius, cross between them, *[D N IUSTINIA]NUS ET TIbERIUS P P A*. (© *Noble Numismatics*)

PHILIPPIKOS BARDANES: gold *solidus*, issued between 711 and 713 from Constantinople mint. Obverse: facing and crowned bust of Philippikos, *DN FILIPICUS MUL TUS [AN]*, facing bust, wearing crown and loros, holding cross globe and eagle-tipped sceptre. Reverse: cross on steps, *VICTORIA AVGU Z/CONOB*. (© *Classical Numismatic Group, Inc.*)

ABD AL-MALIK: *AE fals*, issued between 685 and 693 from Hims/Emesa mint. Obverse: crowned facing imperial bust, holding crossed globe, *KA**L* ON* (= 'good'). Reverse: large M, star between annulets above, *EMI-CHC*, below '*tayyib*' (= 'good'). (© *Noble Numismatics*)

ABD AL-MALIK: *AE fals*, issued in early 690s from Halab/Aleppo mint. Obverse: caliph standing facing, hand on hilt of sword. Reverse: transformed cross, '*waf*' to left, '*bi-halab*' to right. (© *Noble Numismatics*)

ABD AL-MALIK: gold aniconic dinar, issued in 699–700 from Damascus mint. (© *Noble Numismatics*)

Al-WALID I: gold aniconic dinar, issued in 713 from Damascus mint. (© *Noble Numismatics*)

Kubrat and his Sons, Dimitar Gyudjenov (1926).

Imperial family, Sant'Apollinare in Classe. (*Reproduced with permission from Dr Marlena Whiting*)

Justinian II, Sant'Apollinare in Classe. (*Reproduced with permission from Dr Marlena Whiting*)

'Carmagnola', St Mark's Square, Venice.

Sixth Ecumenical Council, Constantine Manasses, *Chronicle* miniature 45.

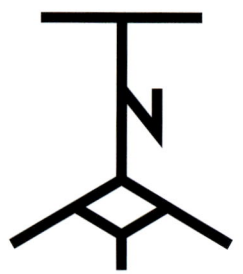

IOYCTINIANOC

JOUSTINIANOS

Justinian II's Monogram. (*Drawn by Faye Beedle*)

St Demetrius' Church, Thessalonica.

St Demetrius, Church of Protaton, Mount Athos.

Fresco of Justinian II's entry into Thessalonica (?), St Demetrius' Church, Thessalonica.

Crucifixion from Santa Maria Antiqua, Rome.

'Standing Caliph' coin of Abd al-Malik, modestly dressed and holding sword, surrounded by the Islamic profession of faith, the *shahahdah*.

Patriarch Kallinikos.

Pope Sergius I.

The Rebellion of Leontius, 695. Emperor Justinian is cut off his nose, and his servants are dragged to death.
Matthäus Merian the Elder (1630).

The Mutilation of the Byzantine Emperors Justinian II and Phillipicus, workshop of the Boucicaut Master in Paris, c.1413–1415.

Christ as a Soldier, standing on an asp and lion, St Andrew's Chapel, Ravenna. (*Author's collection*)

Tervel and Justinian II. (© *Astromentum 2018*)

СТЫН ТРИВЕЛІЙ   ЦРЪ ВОЛГЖСКІЙ

Tervel the Bulgar as St Trivelius.

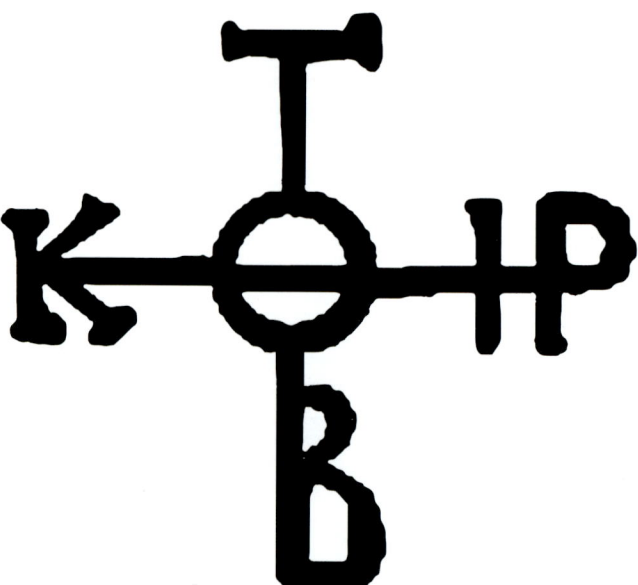

Tervel's Monogram. (*Drawn by Faye Beedle*)

Madara Rider, Bulgaria.

Pope John VII, mosaic in St Peter's, Rome.

Pope John VI, Chevalier Artaud de Montor, *The Lives and Times of the Popes*, New York (1911).

Pope Sisinnius, Luigi Tripepi, *Ritratti e biografie dei romani pontefici: da S. Pietro a Leone 13*. Rome (1879).

Pope Constantine, *Nuremburg Chronicle*, 1493.

Pope Gregory II, *Nuremburg Chronicle*, 1493.

Murder of Tiberios, son of Justinian II, under the orders of emperor Philippikos, Constantine Manasses, *Chronicle* miniature 46.

administrative infrastructure of the other themes, but the lands it actually covered is unclear. Much like the rest of the Balkans and Danubian provinces, there was likely a Roman propagandist notion that the entire Greek peninsula still belonged to the Roman Empire, with the Hellas *strategia* covering the old province of Achaea. However, the area still under direct imperial control was far more limited. The original Hellas theme was likely of a rather small size and mainly focused on the eastern coast of the peninsula, such as major islands like Euboea and historical regions like Boeotia and Attica, as well as some parts of southern Thessaly. It may also have incorporated some other western Aegean islands, Megara and Peloponnesian areas such as Corinthia and the Argolid. The thematic capital would seem to be either Thebes or Athens.

Conspicuous by their absence in the new Hellas theme were the lands in northern Greece that Justinian had recently visited – the area around Thessalonica, the Chalcidice and sections of the Strymon valley. It is difficult to garner the status of this region in the late seventh century. Could these regions have been part of the original Hellenic theme, only to be detached in the late eighth/early ninth centuries to form their own Thessalonian, Macedonian and Strymonian themes? It seems more likely that the still-limited Roman possessions in northern Greece and southern Macedonia made up an ill-defined but small region under the command of the Thessalonian eparch. It would not be until the conquests carried out under the later Isaurian emperors and Nikephoros I that the Greek peninsula would be fully under Roman control again. The limited manpower available in the small area covered by the Hellas 'theme' may explain why Justinian II and/or his successors chose to plant Mardaites in Greece to provide garrisons and naval manpower.

A second potential thematic foundation by Justinian II came in Sicily. Since its reconquest from the Goths by Belisarius in 535–536, the island had been governed politically by a *praetor* and militarily by a *dux*.[4] A dating of the establishment of the Sicilian theme during Justinian's first reign relies on the titles accorded to a certain Salventios, known only from two surviving seals.[5] One records him as a *patricius* and the other as a *patricius* and *strategos*. Unfortunately, there is no geographic identification or date on these two seals, so applying a Justinianic origin to the Sicilian theme relies on the style of Salventios' seals and his name. The seals are thought to be good seventh-century Roman examples,[6] while the name 'Salventius' is Latin and therefore suggests that he was a westerner, possibly of Roman senatorial origin. By this point in Roman history, western origin likely meant imperial service in the West, and as Sicily was the only western theme of any comparable time period, it seems likely that Salventios served as Sicilian *strategos*.

There was what appears to be a senatorial Salventius family in mid-sixth-century Rome prominent enough for two brothers, Praetextatus Salventius Verecundus Traianus and Salventius, to be appointed urban prefect in Rome under the Gothic king Athalaric in 533. The latter was the recipient of two letters from Cassiodorus.[7] If there was any connection between these 'Salventii', it could suggest that the choice of a senatorial *strategos* was Justinian compromising with the Italian elite or perhaps even attempting to gain their support in the face of internal Italian opposition.[8] The very creation of the Sicilian theme could be in part a response to any lack of trust Justinian felt for the Ravennate exarch, both militarily against the Lombards and in the religio-political fallout of Quinisext. It could also be that Justinian was taking some pointers from the extended campaign of Constans II, when a large imperial army was stationed in Sicily, providing a position to intervene in both Italy and Africa in support of (or even opposition to) the exarchs.

While somewhat circumstantial, taken together with the terminus provided by Justinian's *iussio* of early 687 and the recording of a certain Theophylact holding the position of *strategos* of Sicily just after the turn of the eighth century,[9] the information to be gleaned about Salventius suggests that the Sicilian theme was established sometime between 687 and 700, the majority of which is covered by the first reign of Justinian II, who we have already seen following a policy of expanding the theme system. Arab sources also suggest that Sicily was being governed by a *strategos* during Justinian's first reign.[10] The thematic capital was at Syracuse and the island itself was divided into districts called *tourmai*. As the Ravennate exarch declined in authority, the Sicilian *strategos* exerted more influence over the other Roman duchies of Calabria, Naples, Gaeta and Amalfi, although they were not incorporated into the theme system.[11] A similarly difficult thematic development to date is that of the Sardinian theme, a collecting together of many of the other western Mediterranean islands. If Justinian II had any role in its foundation, it is likely to have come in his second reign, as there was little need for a Sardinian theme until the Arab conquest of Carthage in 698.

Another 'theme' that Justinian may have had a role in establishing or altering is even less clear. The emperor's reference to the 'Cabarisiani' in his *iussio* would seem to refer to the Karabisiani fleet, 'but this identification has been questioned'.[12] Despite some seeming similarities, such as a base in the Aegean islands and the south coast of Asia Minor, the Karabisiani was not a theme in itself. It was a purely military formation with no civilian governor aspect and no land forces, plus there is a lack of clear detail about its size and scope. The development that the Karabisiani underwent seemingly during the first reign of Justinian II is cast as something of a prototype for the actual first θέμα ναυτικόν/*thema nautikon* – the Cibyrrhaeot theme. The source of Justinian's reputed expansion of the Karabisiani was his 'repatriation' of the Mardaites in southern Asia Minor to provide naval service as rowers and marines. However, rather than be raised to replace the Karabisiani, the Cibyrrhaeots seem to have co-existed with them. Indeed, it seems more accurate to describe the original Cibyrrhaeot group as a subordinate 'district' of the Karabisiani 'theme', and, like other smaller fleets and squadrons making up the imperial fleet, come under the command of a *droungarios*.[13]

The name Κιβυρραιῶται/*Kibyrrhaiōtai*, which meant 'men of Cibyrrha', demonstrates the southern Asian Minor origin of the Cibyrrhaeots, although it is not certain if their initial base was Cibyrrha the Great in Caria or Cibyrrha the Lesser in Pamphylia. The Cibyrrhaeots first appear in the sources in connection with the expedition to Carthage sent by Leontios in 697/698.[14] To have been picked for such an important mission would suggest that the Cibyrrhaeots were sufficiently established as a naval force by *c*.697. Their strong reputation and perhaps well-established existence by 698 are also demonstrated by the fact that it would be their *droungarios*, Apsimar, who would be chosen by the mutinous navy as their imperial candidate.

Given their geographic name and this chronological terminus, it may be more accurate to say that Justinian's 'repatriating' of the Mardaites expanded the Cibyrrhaeots specifically, laying the foundation for what would become the Cibyrrhaeot theme, if not actually founding it outright between 687 and 695. Perhaps the Mardaite infusion into the Cibyrrhaeot division of the Karabisiani proved so successful that the subordinate squadron outperformed the larger, more unwieldy naval corps, if the Karabisiani was such a thing. The spreading of 'Mardaite' colonies to Hellas and then later (perhaps under Nikephoros I by 809[15]) to the Peloponnese, Epirote Nicopolis and Cephalonia may well be a recognition of their success as part of the Karabisiani and then the Cibyrrhaeots.

However, the replacing of the Karabisiani by the Cibyrrhaeots appears to have been more of a gradual transition, rather than an immediate imperial *diktat* by Justinian II or one of his successors. The last mention of the

Karabisian *strategos* was not until 710/711, while the Cibyrrhaeot *strategos* does not appear in the sources until 732.[16] Of course, silence from the sources proves little, but this does highlight some significant overlap in these two military establishments. It could be that the final disbanding of the Karabisiani was a decision taken by Leo III, possibly due to poor performance against the Arabs or various revolts. It could even be that what was left of the Karabisiani naval corps proved a little too ready to support revolt against Leo, possibly in Sicily (717), Venice (726) or the Cyclades (726).[17]

Upon its constitution as a theme (or even before), the Cibyrrhaeots incorporated all of the coastal regions of Asia Minor south of Miletus up to the Cilician borderlands with Umayyad Syria, including Caria, Lycia, Pamphylia, parts of Isauria and the Dodecanese islands. These territories included some good farming, allowing for land grants to eligible men for the supporting of their families and the equipping of themselves, like in the other themes. Also like its land counterparts, the Cibyrrhaeot theme was commanded by a *strategos*, whose main base appears to have been at Attaleia. It was also divided into similar districts called *droungoi* and *tourmai*, commanded by *droungarioi* and *tourmarches* respectively, although the Cibyrrhaeots had the extra addition of the *katepano* of the Mardaites. Unfortunately, aside from the establishment of the Mardaite colonist rowers in southern Asia Minor, it is difficult to assess what direct impact Justinian II had on the development of the Cibyrrhaeots, even if it was likely in existence by the end of his first reign and he may have had some role in replicating the Mardiate aspect with the naval forces of his Hellas theme.[18]

Dealing with Revolting Themes

Justinian's willingness to build upon it would seem to suggest that the whole thematic reorganization was a dramatic success. It is true that the new-look armies played a significant role in saving the empire from the Arabs and then even providing some military pushback in Asia and Europe. However, there were a few teething problems and some pre-existing issues that the institution of the themes could not overcome. This is to be expected in a system that was largely improvised, unevenly deployed and still evolving. These issues may be best manifested in the military revolts within the themes. Justinian II being deposed by military revolt twice was traditionally seen as the outcome of his supposedly terrible behaviour squandering the goodwill towards his dynasty. This is to look back at the internal workings of the Heraclian dynasty and the attendant development of the themes with the erroneous assumption that with some military success came internal stability. In actual fact, even with its extended imperial tenure, 'the Heraclian dynasty had never enjoyed absolute security. It had frequently experienced abortive conspiracies, military insubordination and family rivalries.'[19]

This trouble was not limited to specific, seemingly unpopular emperors such as Constans II and Justinian II. Every Heraclian emperor experienced significant amounts of military and political opposition. Heraclius faced a military standoff with Comentiolus, the brother of Phocas; his own illegitimate son John Athalarichos was at the centre of a plot to overthrow him; and Vahan, Roman commander at Yarmuk, may have been declared emperor by his men in the prologue to that catastrophic Roman defeat in 636.[20] The brief reign of Heraclius Constantine III saw the confrontation with Martina and Heraklonas, and before he made himself unpopular with his religious politics, Constans II faced the attempted usurpation of Valentinus and then the rebellion of Gregory the Patrician in Africa. Even a seemingly popular emperor like Constantine IV had faced poor discipline amongst Roman forces, with at least four protests/rebellions from major armies – the army of his deceased father under the usurper Mezizios in Sicily, the Armeniacs under the rebel *strategos* Saborius, the 'protesting' Anatolics under Leo and the thematic forces that routed at Oglos upon rumours of his own 'flight'.

It might be thought that the haphazard development of the themes encouraged such a glut of military revolts, and 'in theory the fusion of civil and military powers in the hands of a *strategus* improved his ability to begin and accomplish a military revolt'.[21] Instead, it could well be that the themes had little effect on the frequency of military revolt.[22] While they increasingly became a focal point of internal trouble as the century progressed, this is less to do with any inherent flaw in thematic make-up and more about them becoming the make-up of the army. It could be that the themes merely represented the latest iteration of overly ambitious men being put in charge of large armies and therefore having an avenue to give rein to their ambitions or negative emotions towards the emperor.[23] However, if the themes and their armies being too big was a serious problem for the central government, why did it take until the aftermath of the defeat of Artabasdos by Constantine V in 743 for the biggest and most politically influential (i.e. interfering) theme, the Opsikion, to be divided into four separate units – the Bucellarian, Optimatoi and Opsikion themes and the *tagmata* imperial guard? Further evidence that the themes themselves were not the sole origin of military revolt is seen in several rebellions being focused on non-thematic armies: Gregory the Patrician was an exarch; the revolt of Leontios, while he was a previous Anatolic and current Hellenic *strategos*, was not focused on those thematic armies; and the Cibyrrhaeots were not a theme at the time of their revolt in 698, and technically neither were the Karabisiani they were a part of.

Indeed, rather than having a thematic origin, the revolts during the Heraclian dynasty hint at something much more endemic and long-lasting. Facing down military unrest was already on the empire's agenda before the first proto-thematic armies appeared. There was the revolt of Phocas against Mauricius in 602; the 'loyalist' revolt of the general Narses against Phocas in favour of the man claiming to be the slain Theodosius, son of Mauricius, in 603; and the revolt of Heraclius himself in 608.[24] Indeed, while the seventh century as a whole was perhaps a perfect storm of encouragement for revolt – military defeat, territorial losses, persistent incursions, religious dispute, growth in power of non-imperial individuals and firm/harsh rule of the Heraclian emperors – this kind of military unrest was nothing new. For example, Mauricius' replacing of his general Philippicus with Priscus in 588 sparked a year-long sedition amongst the troops at Monokarton, while Priscus faced a similar revolt amongst the Danubian troops near Dorystolon in 593. The reigns of Justin II and Tiberius II saw considerable disgruntlement amongst the soldiers of the Danube frontier, causing a significant defeat by the Slavs. Even the reign of the great Justinian saw considerable unrest amongst the soldiery. There was perhaps a barely broken trend of eastern Roman military unrest back to at least 471.[25]

Therefore, any perceived acceleration in military revolt under the theme system is not necessarily a reflection of the themes, *strategoi* or even the emperors themselves, but of an underlying, chronic and long-established military unrest, which was now exacerbated by a truncated empire lacking the resources it once had.[26] It could even be argued that the administrative make-up of the themes acted to reduce revolt as much as it increased it: every negative could also be a positive. The shrinking of the empire saw the thematic armies all geographically much closer to the imperial capital, politicizing them (the Opsikion in particular) more than in previous times. However, these armies were also now nearer to the emperor for him to exert his influence and closer to each other, making an individual thematic revolt more difficult if its neighbours stayed loyal: the themes acting as each other's deterrent. The smaller sizes of these armies reduced the ability to protect the empire, but also reduced their ability to replace the emperor. Alliances between themes could be dangerous for the central government, such as that between Leo the Isaurian of the Anatolics and Artabasdos of the Armeniacs in the 710s, although this example also showed the potential benefit of such an alliance to the defence of the empire, as Leo and Artabasdos combined well to hinder various Umayyad generals.

The position of *strategos* was similarly double-edged. As much as it provided the office-holder with military and civil power that could be turned on the central government as a lightning rod for soldierly dissatisfaction, the concentration of power in a single individual could give the emperor closer control of the themes, provided he selected loyal men. An extreme case of this is with Tiberius III, who not only chose his own brother Herakleios, but appointed him as *monostrategos* – 'solo general' – of the Asian themes.[27] Theophanes' declaration of this Herakleios as being 'quite competent'[28] might seem a little like damning with faint praise, either towards Tiberius III or a whole glut of Roman commanders in the age, but the troubles facing the empire necessitated the appointing of not only loyal but competent men to high offices. Mediocrity was not enough. Such was the need that several individuals who had proven themselves loyal and competent were rotated to various posts 'to carry out functions the emperors deemed necessary'.[29] Does this demonstrate a good use of skilled manpower or a *lack* of skilled manpower? An example of the latter may be Justinian's appointing of Leontios to Hellenic *strategos*. There may also be a hint of the emperors not wanting skilled individuals gaining a foothold of popularity and support in certain areas through prolonged service in one place.

Focusing power on a tight group would also have helped the emperors keep more of a handle on power, as they would appoint men they trusted. Furthermore, promoting competition for office on something of a meritocratic basis could increase not only the standard of service rendered, but also dependence on the favour of the emperor. However, there was a fine balance to be struck with such imperial manipulations. Encouraging competition could lead to infighting; dangling the carrot of promotion or frequent reposting could easily foster paranoia amongst the tight leadership group, while reliance on this cadre of officers could spark resentment from those on the outside who felt that their good service was not being suitably rewarded. Again, the revolt of Leontios and other aspects of Justinian's reigns provide examples of the trouble this could cause.[30]

The recombining of military and civil power in the *strategoi* may also have lessened bureaucratic decision-making and implementation, with grievances – particularly those of soldiers – more quickly addressed. This may be seen in some possible change in emphasis in the complaints of soldiers. Together with their settling on land within a theme, their dispersal to their homes when not on campaign and the focusing of thematic forces in a specific region, the elimination of some bureaucracy in the person of the *strategos* may have reduced military complaints over pay and rations. The sources do not mention such trouble amongst thematic forces post-641, despite it having been a major issue for Heraclius. Such a supposition might be relying too heavily on an argument from silence, but the thematic reorganization does seem to have made soldiers more self-sufficient, potentially reduced bureaucratic delay, expenditure and abuses, and shortened the lines of communication and logistics, enabling imperial government – thematic and central – to address problems more quickly.[31]

For all its potential benefits and possible reduction of the logistical basis for trouble, the theme system did not eliminate military revolt. The first decade of Justinian II's reign seems largely void of military trouble. His early successes against the Arabs and Slavs may have kept any issues at bay, but they were certainly still there under the surface, as they had been for most of the previous two centuries. Justinian's reign had not seen any revolutionary approach that could have rooted out any such systemic problems; problems which had reared their heads as recently as Constantine IV's failure against the Bulgars in 680 and would appear again with the Cibyrrhaeots and the Karabisiani in 698.

Justinian seems to have recognized the need to maintain a firm grip on the military and, in the form of his immediate predecessors, he had 'some forceful examples of effective methods'.[32] Such definitive action may have seen Constantine admired long after his death,[33] but he still faced poor discipline from his forces. Firm action was not a cure-all for the empire's military ills, and neither was it necessarily always appropriate. 'Simply continuing the stern, forceful methods that his father and grandfather had employed against suspicious military figures and their truculent soldiers'[34] might have seemed natural to Justinian; however, the potential reduction in unrest through his early military successes and the possible stabilizing of pay and rations may have made such harshness unnecessary and maybe even counterproductive. Certainly, part of Justinian's poor reputation and a major catalyst of his initial deposition stemmed from his harsh treatment of some of the military hierarchy.[35] This could be part of a wider policy to curb the excessive power of certain sections of the aristocracy. Adding a political dimension to firm or harsh treatment of the military leadership, not to mention the methods supposedly employed, which will be seen below, may have made it all the less tolerable. However, this idea of a targeted, aristocratic purge being part of his military policies is purely speculative, with the very notion of an attack specifically on the aristocracy not at all clear.[36]

This is not to say that Justinian resorted solely to the iron fist approach when it came to his relationship with the army. His *iussio* to the pope in 687 provides evidence of the emperor attempting to integrate soldiers and commanders into his 'scheme of authority'.[37] Their presence is noted at the synod of Constantinople in 686/687, and it is hinted that the exarchs and the *strategoi* were represented at important meetings of the imperial council. It is not certain if their involvement in the confirmation of the Acts of the Sixth Council was an exception rather than the rule. This makes it difficult to gauge how much influence or say the exarchs and *strategoi* had on imperial policy. It might very much depend on the specific emperor and any circumstances facing a particular exarch or *strategos*. It would be easy to suggest that Justinian II was a particularly headstrong emperor who would be less willing to listen to the advice of his subordinates, but care must be taken not to project the negative portrayals of the sources onto our own depictions of Justinian's potential actions.

Giving generals, officials and the soldiery any semblance of a say at important imperial events could be Justinian aiming to tie these men into his regime. However, in the case of the synod of Constantinople, the presence of military representatives may have been a specific reaction to army opposition to Constantine IV's shift in religious policy in 680–681. Justinian's inclusion of the army as a witness and even signatory to the decisions of the synod could be seen in various ways: the extension of a hand in cooperation in his still-new regime; a way to weed out opposition, with perhaps anyone who refused to sign up to the faith declared in the *iussio* to be demoted or removed from service; and perhaps handcuffing others in future, for with this confession, no commander could claim not to have agreed to it or to speak for the army as a whole with his own beliefs. If there were any such thoughts in play with Justinian's *iussio*, they would not take root to any great degree over the course of his life, as he would eventually be succeeded by Philippikos Bardanes, a staunch Monothelite. The failure of Justinian's attempts to shore up the loyalty of the thematic armies is also seen in the process of Bardanes' revolt.

The commitment of the Thrakesion and Opsikion themes to the Heraclian cause quickly melted away when offered safe passage and no repercussions for their initial backing of Justinian against Bardanes.[38] Personal recognition of some of these failings may have influenced some of Justinian's more 'reactionary' moves, particularly in his second reign.

It might even be argued that if Justinian was focusing his disciplinary efforts on the exarchs, *strategoi* and other military officers, he might have been looking in the wrong place. Actual revolt may have centred more on officers/commanders, but the rank and file soldiers were becoming increasingly important, along with the clergy, in '[representing] provincial opinion'.[39] A recognition of this new reality comes in the *Ekloga*, Leo III's updating of the Justinianic Code, with the ordinary soldiers singled out for a share of the spoils, reflecting 'the centrality of soldiers to both society at large and to the emperors'.[40]

Land and Tax

It was not only his dealings with the military hierarchies that may have seen Justinian undermine his own popularity with the elite. The transformation of the Roman Empire in the face of the Arab conquests and the Slavic invasion of the Balkans had led to significant developments in landholding, both forced and through imperial policies. This could raise the opposition of the aristocracy because, in spite of the efforts of the emperors, leading imperial officials and the elite in general had become large landowners, and lesser landowners were increasingly kinsmen or at least associates of these aristocrats. Such new allegiances intruded on the sphere of imperial administration and may explain why Justinian and other emperors attempted land reform.

Two aspects of land reorganization that took place under Justinian II and had military connotations have already been mentioned: his colonies and his expansion of the theme system. Settling Mardaites, Slavs and Cypriots on Roman territory may have been more military in nature, but the choices of where to settle them likely involved some consideration of bringing land back into use to provide produce and taxes. The Cypriot settlement in Cyzicus/Nea Justinianopolis perhaps involved more of such a consideration than the military colonies for the Bithynian Slavs and Mardaites. It must also be mentioned that virtually every emperor had partaken in such population transfers, although Justinian may have been more vigorous than most.[41] As there was a military motive involved in such colonies, it could well be imagined that some Roman citizens, of various classes, were made to give up some of their land to accommodate these new military resources. Even if they were compensated for this loss of land (which is by no means a certainty), there would have been ill-feeling about having to give up their property and homes.

Together with the theme system, these military colonies may also have seen the expansion of land granted to soldiers in return for their service. It was long thought that under the themes, 'the men who made up the armies of the themes were also farmers, free, independent, small landowners, cultivating their fields in peacetime and fighting the more zealously to defend them in times of invasion'.[42] This would make these military landowners a fundamental part of not only the empire's defence but of its supply chains. It is perhaps this perceived vitality of such thematic freeholders to the empire that has led to suggestions that this idea of 'farmers as soldiers' has been overplayed. Many recruits were likely from rural backgrounds, but as the Roman army, even in this new thematic form, remained a professional outfit, any of these farmers who enlisted would have quickly left their past lives behind and come to see the army as their career and life. This would not necessarily preclude the empire providing land grants for its soldiers upon their retirement, but it may be that the very idea of a theme-based growth of a small farming class under the Heraclians is incorrect.[43]

That said, even if it was not due to active soldier land grants, the number of small landowners did increase during the seventh century. Given its reduction in size and the retreating of some Roman armies and populations from the advances of the Arabs, Bulgars and Slavs, the population density of what remained the Roman Empire likely increased. This has been considered a driving force behind some of the changes to the peasant and landed classes, as in some regions 'the old Roman system of a peasantry bound to the soil of their master's estates was disappearing'.[44] The fragmenting of Roman landholdings into more small independent farms had considerable consequences for social hierarchies of the empire. Perhaps in a similar way to the growing importance of the ordinary soldiery, these small landowners became an important voice to be heeded and even courted by those in power. They, or more accurately their land, were much coveted. These new small landowners came under consistent pressure from the land-hungry nobility. This type of 'class conflict' provided the emperor with an opportunity to garner popularity with the masses by championing the rights of these small landowners, while also limiting the power of the aristocracy. Maintaining these independent farmers prevented more of the citizenry being tied to the land, making them largely unfree and therefore less available for taxation and recruiting. It also limited the ability of the super-rich to resist imperial orders, rules and laws.

While 'the evidence is both complicated and tenuous',[45] it seems that Justinian followed this socio-political route, backing small landholders against the landed aristocracy. This will undoubtedly have led to opposition to the emperor from those aristocrats, opposition which surely contributed to his deposition in 695. Part of this tenuous source record is the *Nomos Georgikos* – 'the Farmer's Law' – a document containing numerous laws and rules designed to help the farming class, concerning 'boundary disputes, property exchanges, leases, trespassing, hired labour, losses of livestock, theft, and related matters'.[46] This document was frequently identified as being compiled under Justinian II and therefore evidence of his support for small farmers and his attempts to limit the power of the elite, although some have cast doubt on this Justinianic attribution.[47]

A seemingly definitive piece of evidence regarding the authorship of the 'Farmer's Law' comes in the inscription presented at the beginning of the source – 'Chapters of the Farmer's Law according to an extract from the book of Justinian'. It was initially thought that this was Justinian I, suggesting that the 'Farmer's Law' was taken from the edicts of the great emperor of the sixth century. However, there were several issues which refute such an attribution. Significant sections of the *Nomos Georgikos* contradict agrarian policies and laws recorded in the Justinianic Code. Indeed, the general agricultural picture depicted in the 'Farmer's Law' does not match that recorded for the mid-sixth century. It deals not with local serfs or tenant farmers tied to the land by obligation to the landholder, but with small landowners in their own right, who were not a substantial group until the Heraclian age.[48]

The inscription at the start of the 'Farmer's Law' has also been considered to not be of the correct layout to be regarding Justinian I. It would surely have mentioned whichever book it was derived from if it was something like the *Institutes, Digests, Codex* or *Novella*, and/or talked about 'books' in the plural. It would also be likely that that emperor would be referred to as 'the great Justinian'. This would seem to eliminate Justinian I from being named at the outset of the *Nomos Georgikos* as an invocation of his authority as a lawgiver.[49] Justinian II may be the only real option as the object of the opening inscription. The lack of the regnal 'II' does not affect the arguments of identification, as such numerals were very rare in antiquity; Justinian never seems to have publicly referred to himself on coins, inscriptions etc. as 'Justinian II'.

This does not necessarily mean that Justinian II either wrote, oversaw or even ordered the compilation of this *Nomos Georgikos*. It could be a private compilation that 'merely reflects already established customs and practices of the time rather than imperial efforts to protect the rights of the small landholders'.[50] It could later have been associated with the *Ekloga* of the Isaurian emperors.[51] But then the naming of Justinian at the beginning suggests that the author wanted to associate the laws with the emperor in some way. As it is 'dedicated' as 'an extract from the book of Justinian', it would seem to, at the very least, partially reflect not only the world of Justinian II but also his own socio-political policies. Even the bare minimum association with Justinian II requires the taking of the *Nomos Georgikos* into account when looking at the nature of his support, and more importantly the opposition he was faced with.

While it might be possible to infer some potential disgruntlement amongst the aristocracy for his protection of small landowners and possible agrarian policies, the admittedly hostile pages of Nikephoros and Theophanes are far clearer on what stoked up the majority of the opposition to Justinian II – his financial policies.[52] Preventing the elite from gaining more wealth was not as bad as depriving them of some of their pre-existent fortunes. Unlike his possible involvement in the land question, the unpopularity Justinian incurred from the financial sphere was supposedly due to him *not* being involved directly. It is claimed that Justinian took little or no interest in imperial finances as he was focused too much on military and religious activities. This led to him doling out increasingly powerful positions to certain ministers of the imperial treasury.[53] It was these 'men of a cruel and exceedingly harsh character'[54] who were to breed increasing hatred for Justinian.

Chief amongst these unpopular finance ministers was Stephen the Persian, the chief eunuch of the imperial palace, who was appointed as *sacellarios* – 'keeper of the privy purse'. He is described as 'a lord and a powerful man, but bloodthirsty and cruel'.[55] Even without his apparent reputation, Stephen being a non-Roman foreigner and a eunuch set him up for a poor reception, as neither of these groups were particularly popular. This in turn would reflect poorly upon Justinian for appointing such a man. As for his actions as a finance minister, Theophanes and Nikephoros are united (likely showing the thoughts of their shared source) in claiming that Stephen 'worked many evils throughout the community'[56] and 'inflicted many punishments ... on those under his authority'.[57] As will be seen, Stephen's demise would suggest that his actions raised the ire not just of the aristocracy, but of the ordinary citizens of Constantinople.[58]

The sources are less forthcoming about what these harsh exactions actually were. Rather than focus on Stephen's specific financial policies, Theophanes and Nikephoros revel in the report that shows that the eunuch *sacellarios* had become increasingly powerful and arrogant. It went so far that he dared to whip Anastasia, Justinian's mother, with leather strips, 'as a school-master might whip a pupil!'[59] It seems that Justinian was absent at the time, although Stephen received no overt punishment for his deed.[60] There is no record as to what Anastasia might have done to incur the wrath of the *sacellarios*. However, it has been suggested that the presence of the strange term 'en schemati' in Nikephoros' account means that Stephen's whipping of Anastasia only happened 'in semblance'; perhaps he only mimed or just threatened such physical punishment.[61] Even if Stephen only motioned the whipping of the emperor's mother, the fact that he could do so without seeming repercussion might demonstrate the level of power he held. If he was willing to mimic beating Anastasia, what would he do to non-imperial individuals in order to achieve his financial ends? Of course, this entire 'whipping' story might be just that; a story made up to highlight the actual power and arrogance of Stephen or as a way to denigrate both the eunuch and his emperor.

Justinian compounded the unpopularity caused by Stephen by appointing the 'terrible and wild'[62] Theodotus, a monk at Stenon in Thrace, as general *logothete* – minister in charge of the imperial treasury. The sources give more specifics about his exactions than those of Stephen:

> 'This man not only exacted money with exceeding cruelty from those under his power, whom he suspended by rope and suffocated with smoking straw, but even confiscated [the property] of persons of high position and put them to death by inflicting unbearable torments on them.'[63]

> 'Theodotus rashly, vainly and unjustifiably put into effect schemes, confiscations, and tax assessments against a great many leaders of the state and important men, not only from the governing class, but also from among the property owners of the city. He hanged them and lit chaff-heaps under them.'[64]

His targeting of property owners in Constantinople would explain why Theodotus would suffer the same demise as Stephen.[65] Theophanes also suggests that under imperial order, the prefect of the city imprisoned many men of aristocratic background for prolonged periods – perhaps up to eight years – which was an uncommon practice amongst the Romans, stoking further opposition to the emperor.[66] Given their position in the chronicler's text, it could be that these imprisonments were in connection with the financial exactions carried out in Justinian's name. Perhaps many of these men were being imprisoned because they refused to pay their taxes and the *logothete* was holding them virtually for ransom.

This helped give the impression that these financial and various other imperial policies were targeting the nobility specifically, rather than as any sort of reform to aid the state. However, it must be remembered that most historical information comes from the aristocracy and they will have been keen to portray Justinian and his ministers as being the worst of the worst, potentially skewing the record of imperial reforms as being more a vindictive attack on the elite. That Bardanes enjoyed enough support from these πολιτων αρχαιογενων – old families – to be scheduled to dine with them on the night he was overthrown[67] suggests that any targeting of the aristocracy by Justinian had not led to a wide purge. Plenty of them may have faced prison, loss of land/earnings and influence due to Justinian's policies, but did he really execute any of them? Again, he may have been following the policies of his predecessors to limit the power of the upper classes.

With the sources not keen to provide any specific layout, the question must be asked as to what these policies might have been. Despite a lack of information, there has been support for the suggestion that a widespread tax reform was introduced under Justinian II.[68] Since Diocletian overhauled much of the Roman Empire following the Third Century Crisis, the two main taxes – the *capitatio* (head tax) and the *iugatio* (land tax) – had been collected together, a process which saw many effectively tied to the land in order to, or because they could not, pay it. This arrangement had been largely unchanged for 400 years. However, now in 687, we see what could be the last definite example of such a tax being levied, or in this case not being levied, as Justinian is recorded remitting Pope Conon's obligation to pay the *capitatio-iugatio*.[69]

Unfortunately, we are left foraging for hints of the replacing of this Diocletianic system, none of which give definitive information for the late seventh century. The *capitatio-iugatio* taxes had definitely been replaced by a combination of a hearth tax levied on families (*to kapnikon*) and a separate land tax (*he synone*) by the reign of Nikephoros I. Given that the first Nikephoros reigned between 802 and 811, this hardly seems like a useful date for a connection to Justinian II. That said, some of those hints from the sources can narrow down the foundation of this new tax system. The references to the *to kapnikon/he synone* taxes under Nikephoros suggest that they were well-established by the early ninth century. A more tenuous hint posits the existence of these new taxes under Leo III (reigned 717–741), bringing the reform much closer to the time of Justinian II. This in turn could be applied to some of the ambiguous terminology contained in the *Nomos Georgikos*. Certain readings could suggest that the old system was no longer in use, with the separate *to kapnikon* and *he synone* already existent.[70]

Of course, 'the scarcity of the evidence on the tax reforms means that the assignment of it to Justinian II must remain a hypothesis'.[71] But if Justinian did initiate these reforms, he will have been responsible for the expansion of peasant mobility and the acceleration of the end of tying people to the land in a version of serfdom. This was a process that was already underway in some regions before his reign, as it was viewed as being increasingly impractical. This would surely have also brought on the ire of the landed upper classes. An innately conservative group, they will have seen the reforming of a system over 400 years old as meddling with the traditional workings of the empire. This is even before looking at the idea that they saw some of their own wealth being drained through the loss of influence over land and the increasing of their tax burden, fervently exacted by the likes of Stephen and Theodotus.

Justinian II may have raised further anger by what he was seen to be doing with the windfall from his financial policies. Through personal and political taste or in following the example of his imperial namesake-predecessor, Justinian II embarked on an extensive building programme. 'But while many of the first Justinian's projects, including the magnificent Hagia Sophia, have survived through the centuries to ensure him undying fame as a patron of building',[72] it seems that no structure of the second Justinian survives. This leaves us to rely on the written sources for suggestions that Justinian II was an extensive builder, suggestions that also preserve further 'evidence' of the emperor and his ministers stoking their own unpopularity.

One of the earliest building projects attributed to Justinian was a series of additions to the Great Palace. These do not appear to be the same kind of superficial embellishments of his more recent predecessors – his 'creative projects rendered the court a center of revived artistic activity'.[73] The most prominent extensions were two massive reception halls called the *lausiacus* and the *triclinum*. The former seems to have been a connection between the imperial throne room and the Daphne section of the palace, while the *triclinum* was an imperial passage between the Great Palace and the Hippodrome. By the time of Constantine VII, the *triclinum* had become known to the denizens of the imperial palace as the 'Justinianos'.[74] The building of the *triclinum* gave Stephen the Persian another opportunity to demonstrate his cruelty, for having been appointed as an imperial adviser on the project, 'he was not content with mercilessly harassing the workmen, but even stoned them and their leaders'.[75]

Part of Justinian's building programme surrounding the imperial palace also raised the opposition of the patriarch of Constantinople. The emperor wanted to build a fountain and seating area where he could meet with representatives of the Blue circus faction.[76] It seems strange that Justinian would be looking to design a meeting place specifically for the Blues, as he is recorded as being a supporter of the Greens. Perhaps this comes from a period when Justinian was not so anti-Blue and was still willing to bridge the political gap to the faction that would play such a significant role in his first overthrow. This fountain/meeting place project hit a snag immediately as there was a church, possibly to Mary Theotokos, on the site the emperor sought to use. Unwilling to raise the ire of the church faithful, Justinian asked patriarch Kallinikos to perform a proper deconsecration of the site before the church was pulled down. The patriarch resisted, claiming: 'We have a prayer over the construction of a church, but we have not inherited a prayer over the demolition of a church.'[77] Justinian was not a man to take 'no' for an answer. Kallinikos was pressured into begrudgingly performing the ceremony, with a short, improvised prayer: 'Glory be to God, who is long-suffering now, always, and forever and ever. Amen!' With that, the church was torn down and the fountain constructed.[78] While the lost church was replaced with a new construction in the Petrion region of Constantinople, pressuring the patriarch to improvise a deconsecration prayer in order to destroy a church at the centre of the imperial capital cannot have helped Justinian's popularity.

Another likely part of Justinian's building programme not to survive was a set of golden plaques added to the Milion, the milestone at the centre of the city from which all distances were measured: 'These plaques depicted the Six Ecumenical Councils and were one of the marvels of the capital until destroyed by the bitter iconoclast Constantine V.'[79] It is not definite that Justinian was the originator of these plaques, but as it reflected six councils, it had to be post-681; and as Leo III grew more iconoclastic as his reign progressed, Justinian II, with his interest in councils and building, is the most likely candidate.[80] There are some other building works potentially linked to Justinian. He is credited with surrounding the entire Great Palace with a wall, or at least strengthening its pre-existing defences. There are also significant arguments over his involvement in the creation of some of the mosaics in the imperial palace, which – considering his building of the *lausiacus* and the *triclinum* – would not be out of the ordinary.[81]

There was nothing radical about virtually any of Justinian's administrative policies. Frequently, they come across as merely a continuation of or the next logical step in the development of the empire fostered by his Heraclian predecessors. This is seen most clearly with his establishing of themes in Greece and Sicily (and perhaps later in Sardinia) and his possible building of the foundations of an exclusively naval theme from the Cibyrrhaeot section of the Karabisiani. Even in his land and tax policies, which fostered so much opposition, he was still building on those who had come before him. Checking the power of the elite, promoting some meritocracy amongst high officials and protecting the independence of small farmers/potential military recruits seem to be trends of the Heraclians – sensible ones at that – rather than some radical departure by Justinian. Any role he had in the overhauling of the tax system should be viewed through a similar prism of the land reforms recorded in the *Nomos Georgikos*: a growing necessity in the new-look Roman Empire of the second half of the seventh century, with the possibility that the 400-year-old Diocletianic tax system was no longer fit for purpose. It could be argued that the explosion of opposition to Justinian in 695 and the subsequent denigration of his character as an unjust attacker of the aristocracy by the sources could suggest that he had been more successful in his reforms than his Heraclian forebearers.

However, even if it is decided that Justinian did not target the aristocracy for vindictive reasons, he must have overplayed his hand in some respects for the governing classes to rise in revolt against him and be able to carry at least part of the populace of Constantinople with them. Perhaps much like his dealing with military unrest, it was the attitude that Justinian took towards the aristocracy rather than his actual policies that caused friction. Decades of firmness from Constans II and Constantine IV may have seen the aristocracy somewhat used to curbs on their land ambitions and tax exemptions, only for Justinian to continue pressuring them, which only engendered antagonism and resistance. It may be that that resistance to the implementation of Justinian's policies did not lead to stonings, whippings, eight-year imprisonments and roasting of feet, but such stories are rarely complete invention, rather an exaggeration of a kernel of truth. The combination of protecting the small landowners, outbreaks of war, setting up of new themes and possible large-scale reform may have led to a considerable tax burden on specific groups of the citizenry, such as the upper classes and urban dwellers. When they voiced their opposition or even refused to pay, Justinian deployed more forceful means, which may have involved imprisonment, confiscations and even physical coercion through the offices of Stephen and Theodotus.

Even played down from the form it takes in the pages of Theophanes and Nikephoros, socio-political opposition from governing and urban classes towards Justinian's land and tax policies likely existed. Add it to religious opposition over his forceful reaction over Quinisext, the alienating of the patriarch over the church deconsecration, some inappropriate harshness towards the army and the defeat at Sebastopolis and the subsequent restarting of the annual Umayyad raids of Anatolia, and Justinian II had certainly managed to antagonize a significant cross-section of his people. At the very least he had bred such antipathy towards the Heraclian dynasty, that if someone was to try something drastic, there would be little fight to retain Justinian's throne. That someone did exist, but as of 695, he had been languishing in prison for up to three years.

Chapter 9

Mutilation and Exile: The Revolt of Leontios

'He that is taken and put into prison or chains is not conquered, though overcome; for he is still an enemy.'

Thomas Hobbes

A Caged Lion Bites Back

That languishing prisoner was the previously reliable former Anatolic *strategos* Leontios. For a man about to be catapulted to the highest position in the land, very little is known about his early life, aside from him being 'a native of Isauria'.[1] A reading of the *Chronicle of 1234* might suggest that Leontios had some Armenian origins, although this is unclear. This may just be a slightly confused passage highlighting that Leontios had recently campaigned in Armenia.[2] At some point, Leontios joined the Roman army and must have served with sufficient distinction to climb the ranks and come to the attention of Constantine IV. It could even be that Leontios had served long enough to have first come to the attention of Constans II. Nevertheless, it was Constantine who appointed him *patricius* and *strategos* of the Anatolic theme in *c*.682. Beyond that, any attempt to reconstruct Leontios' military career under Constantine is merely speculative. To be in a position to be appointed to one of the most important military commands in the empire might suggest service in the defence of Constantinople against Muawiyah's 'siege' and/or a leading position in the productive counterattacks in Anatolia and the Levant that produced the advantageous treaty of *c*.678.

That Leontios' lofty position was not just down to a personal friendship with Constantine, but based on a strong military reputation, may be seen in Justinian II's maintaining of him as Anatolic *strategos* in an age where leading commanders were liable to be transferred to various posts. It could be that Leontios served as Anatolic *strategos* for a full decade. Leontios repaid that trust placed in him by the new emperor by leading the successful Roman campaign of 686, driving into Armenia, Transcaucasia and possibly even into Umayyad Media. This brought about the even more favourable 'treaty of 688' with its condominiums and increased tribute payments.

But if the Anatolic *strategos* had provided such good service to the empire, how did he come to be languishing in a Constantinopolitan prison in 695? The sources do not mention why, but the timing would suggest some connection to the poor Roman showing in the war with the Umayyads in 692. His thematic command in Anatolia, proven track record and experience must have seen him given a prominent position – perhaps even general in command – in the force Justinian brought together at Sebastopolis. His previous success in taking the fight to the Umayyads would also have made Leontios a prime candidate to lead any Roman strike into Arab territory in the run-up to that battle. Whether he was present at the battle or absent on another raid, it would seem that Leontios' imprisonment was due to Justinian placing blame for the catastrophic defeat at Sebastopolis on his shoulders.[3] However, the extent of Leontios' imprisonment could suggest that there was something more to this punishment. Could it be that the experienced *strategos* criticized Justinian's strategy, tactics, reliance on the Slavs or the general acceptance of war altogether? Could he have been a victim of the emperor's financial officials for refusing to pay his taxes? Could there even have been something graspingly 'imperial' about Leontios' seeming transgression?

Whatever Justinian's reasons for imprisoning Leontios, the deposed general was to languish in the imperial prison of the *praetorium* for the next three years. Suddenly in autumn 695, the emperor not only had Leontios released, but appointed him to be *strategos* of the Hellas theme. Why the sudden change of heart? It is possible that the emperor recognized the need for experienced generals in the face of the Symbatios rebellion in Armenia and the incursions by Muhammad. Perhaps an Asian *strategos* had been killed in the fighting since Sebastopolis. But why then send Leontios to Hellas? Why not to Anatolia to help deal with the Arab incursions? This appointment could be construed in several ways. While recognizing his need for experienced generals, Justinian had not fully forgiven Leontios for his failure or slight and so he appointed him to the Hellas theme and perhaps promoted the previous Hellenic *strategos* (if there was one – Leontios is the first recorded holder of that post) to any vacancy amongst the ranks of the Asian *strategoi*. It could have been the Hellenic *strategos* who had died in 695. Alternatively, the appointment of Leontios to Hellas could suggest that Justinian *had* forgiven him. This was, after all, one of the emperor's new themes, so being picked to command it was something of an honour and Justinian may have wanted a man of proven ability to build on his successes on the Greek peninsula. It is more likely though that Justinian was somewhat desperate, suffering a dearth of skilled commanders to fill a vacancy somewhere in the ranks of the *strategoi* and was forced to turn to someone who had been locked away in prison for most of the last three years.

The newly freed and appointed Hellenic *strategos* was provided with a small force and three ships and orders to leave for Greece immediately. Such an order could suggest that Justinian wanted Leontios out of the capital as quickly as possible, although it could also be a reflection of potential trouble in Greece, with the emperor furnishing his new *strategos* with reinforcements for the thematic army and fleet. Leontios was reputedly none-too-pleased with his new position, mainly because he thought he was being sent to a dangerous frontier to meet his death at the hands of rampaging barbarians – saying 'as I depart hence, I shall be overtaken by a cruel death'[4] or 'in future I will constantly be expecting death'.[5] These do not seem like the words of a grizzled veteran of many a dangerous military campaign. It could be that his three years in prison had affected Leontios deeply, or perhaps rather than the Slavic barbarians waiting for him in Greece, he was thinking more of an imperial spectre looking over him. Perhaps he expected that his freedom was going to come at the cost of his life, a price extracted by an agent in imperial employ. On the contrary, you might imagine that Leontios would be happy enough to be out of prison and presented with a military position, even if it was a seemingly dangerous assignment. Besides, he was being presented with an imperial order. He could hardly refuse if he wanted to stay alive in the immediate future.

While Leontios was making his preparations in the Harbour of Sophia/ Julian to take ship for Greece, he was visited by two friends: Paul, a monk from the monastery of Kallistratos in Constantinople, and Gregory the Cappadocian, a former *kleisouriarch* (officer in command of a mountain pass) and now a monk/abbot at the monastery of Florus in the imperial capital. Both seem to have visited Leontios during his imprisonment, but rather than going to their friend to bid him farewell, they went to beg him not to go. Instead, they wanted him to make an attempt on the imperial throne. As well as being a monk, Paul was also an astrologer, a combination of pagan practice and Christian faith that was far more common than might be imagined. At some point, Paul used whatever celestial observances he studied to predict that Leontios would one day be emperor. Gregory agreed with this prediction wholeheartedly. These monks may have brought this prediction to Leontios before, only for the *strategos* to not act upon it. Rumours of such a prediction might have contributed to Justinian having Leontios imprisoned,[6] but such use of astrologers was a capital offence. Had the emperor heard of the prediction, Leontios would have been executed rather than imprisoned. That Paul was also still a free man would suggest that this prediction had not reached the ears of the emperor.

In response to the monks' pleading, Leontios initially scoffed at the prediction, saying 'in vain have you predicted that I would become emperor',[7] before decrying his transfer to a dangerous frontier away from the centre of power. The monks were not to be put off, urging the *strategos* that 'should you not hesitate, your bid for power will at once be fulfilled. Only listen to us, and follow us.'[8] The sureness of Paul and Gregory in the ultimate success of any bid for power by Leontios could be taken as evidence of the unpopularity of Justinian that they felt from within their monasteries and perhaps saw in the streets of Constantinople. However, it must be remembered that this is a story told from the benefit of hindsight. It not only knows the outcome, but may be trying to give the subsequent usurpation an air of divine favour by positing an astrological prediction of success and the backing of monks from two Constantinopolitan monasteries. Such a look was far more wholesome and defendable than what Leontios' bid for power really was – a military revolt within the walls of the imperial capital that proved correct any doubts the emperor had over the loyalty of his new Hellenic *strategos*. Of course, it could be that it was Justinian's unfounded doubt and the actions it predicated that fuelled Leontios' disloyalty.

Egged on by promises of support from the city and remembering his three years in prison, Leontios allowed himself to be talked into making an attempt to oust Justinian. That night, Leontios, Paul, Gregory and the soldiers under the *strategos*' command marched to the *praetorium*. There, they informed the prefect that the 'emperor' was demanding entry. Not waiting to confirm the legitimacy of this claim, the prefect had the prison gates opened. Leontios and his men stormed in, 'overpowered, clubbed down and bound [the prefect] hand and foot'.[9] They then began releasing the prisoners, many of whom were upper-class victims of Justinian's finance ministers, although Theophanes regards many as being soldiers. Whoever they were, unsurprisingly after so long locked away – some for as long as eight years – they proved ready recruits in the revolt against Justinian. Leontios then marched to the Forum and sent out messengers into the city to encourage the populace to rise against the emperor, proclaiming 'All you Christians, go to Hagia Sophia!'[10]

Theophanes would have it that while Leontios was emptying the *praetorium* and mobilizing support in the city, Justinian ordered Stephen Rhousios – 'Stephen the Red', patrician and *strategos* – 'to kill the populace of Constantinople',[11] starting with patriarch Kallinikos. This seems like a later invention, added by Theophanes or his sources – Nikephoros makes no such genocidal accusation – to further denigrate Justinian and/or to make Leontios' *coup d'etat* seem more necessary. It is notable that Theophanes presents Justinian's reputed order of city-wide massacre *before* Leontios' meeting with Paul and Gregory. A similar story would emerge in the run-up to Justinian's second deposition with regard to his order of execution for the people of Cherson. That said, if Justinian was sufficiently unpopular in the Constantinople of 695 and his ministers had been murderously over-zealous in their financial exactions, rumours of homicidal crowd-control could have spread through the city, possibly put about to fire opposition to Justinian.

Whether through this rumour of his impending grizzly murder,[12] religious disputes or personal dislike, patriarch Kallinikos was persuaded by Leontios and his allies to join the rebellion. This patriarchal backing allowed Hagia Sophia to be used as a focal point. Soon, hundreds if not thousands were gathered at the church. Before this congregation, Kallinikos proclaimed his support for the revolt and likely performed some sort of acclamation of Leontios as emperor, complete with the declaration that 'This is the day which the Lord hath made!'[13] With his military, religious and civilian support, Leontios marched on the Hippodrome before the night was out. This was accompanied by the chant of 'Let Justinian's bones be dug up',[14] a show of how much some had come to hate him; or at least a show of the kind of insult Theophanes might have felt was shouted. Nikephoros only records that 'the multitude, for its part, insulted Justinian'.[15]

'Thus far, the chroniclers' narrative of Leontios' coup are disarmingly straightforward';[16] Theophanes and Nikephoros would have it that Justinian's overthrow and indeed that of the Heraclian dynasty, was essentially a simplistic three-step plan, which roused the entire city of Constantinople:

1) two monks approaching a disgruntled general;
2) a prefect tricked into opening the prison gate;
3) a patriarchal call to arms.

There must have been more to it than that. Leontios and his allies must have tapped into some pre-existing resistance to Justinian amongst the upper classes and other groups. Indeed, Paul and Gregory could perhaps be viewed as the representatives of any such resistance movement, sounding out a general with whom they had a previous connection. The short record of the mid-ninth-century chronicler George Monachos provides some potential backing for there being more planning and a more specific opposition to Justinian than Nikephoros' 'multitude' or Theophanes' 'people'. George suggests that Leontios was publicly proclaimed *basileus* by the Blues.[17]

Any involvement of the Blues, perhaps even their primary involvement, in the elevation of Leontios may alter the view of this revolt and its proposed spontaneity. While usually listed as circus factions, the Blues and Greens were far more than supporters' clubs cheering on their teams from the stands. They represented varying political interests and opinions and formed part of the city militia. This combination of political, military and social representation gave these factions significant influence. They could voice their opinions to the emperor in the Hippodrome and receive immediate action. Many emperors would even openly align themselves with one of the factions.[18] The most infamous example of the potential power of these factions was the explosion of public anger at burdensome taxation and unpopular ministers, led by the uniting of the Blues and Greens, during the *Nika* riots of 532 against Justinian I. These saw the attempted coronation of a usurper, the destruction of maybe half of the imperial capital and the deaths of some 30,000 people.

The politics of the factions are a little less clear. They certainly were not split into aristocratic and common groups, as people of all backgrounds appear in both factions. It may instead be that the Blues were led by members of the landed aristocracy and senators of long-standing, while Green leadership appears to have been drawn from court officials, civil servants and businessmen. If this division in faction leadership is correct, then there should be no surprise to find the Blues providing Leontios with prominent support. After all, Justinian had seemingly made neutering the landed aristocracy a significant part of various policies of his reign. Those aristocrats, in their guise of leaders of the Blues, would surely rally behind any potential opponent to Justinian. It will have helped that Leontios was a patrician himself and likely had contacts with high-level aristocrats. Justinian was a strong supporter of the Greens, although it is not completely clear if they were correspondingly staunch partisans of the emperor.[19] That Leontios' collection of supporters is recorded marching from Hagia Sophia specifically to the Hippodrome could indicate some support for the presence of the Blues. Then again, the Hippodrome was connected to the imperial palace and was a space that could accommodate the seeming horde of rebels.

Backed by some combination of landed aristocrat prisoners, supporters of Kallinikos, answerers to the patriarchal call to arms, the Blue faction and his own thematic soldiers, Leontios took control of the Hippodrome and seemingly the adjacent imperial palace before the night was out. The exact circumstances of this apparent lack of resistance from the imperial regime is not recorded in the sources. It would be expected that any fighting would be written about, which could suggest that the imperial bodyguard recognized the futility of resistance and gave up their Heraclian ward before Leontios' men needed to initiate an attack on the palace. Any other garrison forces in Constantinople were either too slow to react to the rebellion, meagre enough in numbers that any resistance was futile or fickle enough to not give armed support to Justinian, if not actively support Leontios.

However it happened, Justinian II fell into the hands of the rebels and the next morning was paraded before Leontios' supporters in the Hippodrome. While stripped of his imperial position, Leontios had to decide what to do with Justinian himself. A deposed emperor was always going to be a source of trouble. Plenty of Roman emperors had christened their reign with the execution of predecessors or rivals. The most recent example had come at the establishing of the Heraclian dynasty when Heraclius had Phocas executed in 610, while Phocas himself had Mauricius and his sons executed in 602.

Before a baying crowd, Leontios must have been under pressure to provide a similarly bloody end for the Heraclians; however, he decided to show some mercy to Justinian. It was suggested that the new emperor decided against executing his predecessor due to the respect and admiration he held for Justinian's father, Constantine IV.[20] There could also be some aspect of the growing religiosity of the imperial position and therefore the man holding it at play here, although that had not prevented the murder of Constans II in 668. That is not to say that the mob in the Hippodrome were deprived of their opportunity to satisfy their bloodlust. Captured alongside the deposed emperor were his despised ministers, Stephen the Persian and Theodotus. The mob 'bound them by the feet, and dragged them through the Mese … carried them into the Forum of the Ox and burned them alive'.[21] While Justinian's life was to be spared, he was not to be spared physical discomfort because he had to be made ineligible for retaking the imperial throne; and in late seventh-century Constantinople, this meant mutilation.

A Brief History of 'Byzantine' Mutilation

Mutilation, even specifically nasal mutilation, as a punishment had a long and wide history before its introduction into Roman dynastic politics. Punitive mutilation must have been a prevalent practice in Middle Bronze Age Mesopotamia for it to be rather extensively prescribed as a punishment in the law code of the Babylonian king Hammurabi in *c.*1754 BC, which included the following:

> 192. If a son of a paramour or a prostitute say to his adoptive father or mother: "You are not my father, or my mother," his tongue shall be cut off.
>
> 194. If a man gives his child to a nurse and the child dies in her hands, but the nurse unbeknown to the father and mother nurses another child, then they shall convict her of having nursed another child without the knowledge of the father and mother and her breasts shall be cut off.
>
> 205. If the slave of a freed man strikes the body of a freed man, his ear shall be cut off.
>
> 218. If a physician makes a large incision with the operating knife, and kills him, or opens a tumour with the operating knife, and cuts out the eye, his hands shall be cut off.
>
> 226. If a barber, without the knowledge of his master, cuts the sign of a slave on a slave not to be sold, the hands of this barber shall be cut off.
>
> 282. If a slave says to his master: "You are not my master," if they convict him his master shall cut off his ear.[22]

The code's epilogue also invoked the god Nergal to 'cut off his limbs with his mighty weapons' of any successor to Hammurabi who would ignore his laws.

While Babylonian culture made room for the amputation of hands, ears, tongue and breasts in its laws, one appendage that is absent from the Code of Hammurabi as a target for punitive amputation is that which Justinian was about to lose in the Hippodrome: the nose. The nose is not only important as an olfactory organ, but also as an aesthetic element, for its symbolic value and as expression of the character of the subject.[23] It is thus unsurprising that it was targeted for punitive amputation long before the late seventh century, even if the Babylonians did not legislate for it. *Rhinokopia*, the removal of the nose, seems to have been a punishment for officials abusing their power and for adultery under the Egyptian pharaoh Horemheb (1319/1306–1292 BC). It was also a punishment for insurrection under Rameses III (1187–1156 BC), who had the noses and ears of several plotters from the 'Great Harem Conspiracy' mutilated. It was also a prevalent enough punishment in ancient India for medical skill and technological advances in nasal reconstructive surgery to be recorded in first-millennium BC Sanskrit texts.[24] Such punishment even appears in pre-historic Peruvian cultures, with ancient pottery suggesting examples of lip, leg, foot and nose amputations as penalties for bearing false witness, theft and laziness.[25]

Mutilation as a punishment does not seem to have been prominent in the Roman Empire until Late Antiquity, although it was not non-existent. Sections of Martial's *Epigrams* suggest that *rhinokopia* as a punishment for adultery was, while infrequent, at least thought of in the first century AD.[26] It might be expected that the Christianization of the empire did away with such brutal maiming as punishment; however, if anything, punitive mutilation increased under a Christian Roman Empire. While there is perhaps no correlation between these two developments, Christianized Romans could point to the Bible for justification of such brutality, with Matthew 5:29–30 proffering the advice to 'Cut your hand or your foot if it scandalizes you', and 'better being lame or crippled rather than able-bodied and damned'.

The increase in mutilation in the Later Roman Empire may even have been the result of a reduction in the severity of punishments. This may seem contrary, but physical maiming came to be seen as 'a merciful substitute for the death penalty'.[27] This trend had begun at least as early as the first half of the sixth century with the *Novels* of Justinian I, which also saw the downgrading of certain mutilation punishments, so there may have been a general lessening of the severity of legal punishments.[28] This 'lessening' of punishment/increasing use of mutilation continued throughout the seventh century and on into the eighth, when it was recodified in the *Ekloga* by the Isaurian emperors, Leo III and Constantine V. It is notable, although perhaps not surprising, that the doling out of physical punishment in the *Ekloga* depended on the financial means of the guilty. A rich person could pay a fine for their crime; a poor person was forced to pay with a part of their body. The *Ekloga* is also more likely to deal with crimes against the state, such as counterfeiting and forgery, which were punishable by losing a hand (a reduction from beheading), but that does not mean that it was only those types of public crimes that were to be punished by mutilation. The *Ekloga* may also have codified *rhinokopia* as the punishment for adultery,[29] while the

Nomos Georgikos records four different types of mutilation as punishment for crimes against the individual:

1) Blinding, for a third offence of theft (ch. 42, 68, 69).
2) Branding, for destruction of property (ch. 58).
3) Cutting out the tongue, for swearing falsely (ch.28).
4) Cutting off a hand(s), for more grievous destruction of property (ch. 44, 59, 65, 66, 80).[30]

It was not just in the Roman Empire that mutilation was employed as a legal punishment. The Frankish king Childebert II (*c*.570–595) is recorded condemning a group of plotters to various forms of maiming: 'Some were thrown into prison, some had their hands amputated and were afterwards released, some had their ears and noses cut off and were then let out as a subject of ridicule.'[31]

While mutilation may have been a well-established punishment in the Later Roman world, and much more so in the wider world by the late seventh century, political mutilation was a somewhat different aspect to this gruesome exaction. Rather than strictly a punishment for a crime, political mutilation was seen as an effective way to remove an individual from candidacy for the imperial throne. Physical imperfection as a potential disqualifier from rule was nothing new. The fourth-century BC Spartan king Agesilaus II was thought ill-suited to rule due to having been born lame, while the Roman emperor Claudius' various physical maladies were thought to not only rule out him as an imperial candidate, but even from a career in the public eye.[32] It must be said that these two examples of men with physical disabilities both enjoyed prolonged periods on the thrones they were supposedly disqualified from; Agesilaus was king of Sparta for nearly forty years, while Claudius was emperor for thirteen years. As will be seen, these two men would share this overcoming of seeming disqualification through physical impairment with Justinian II.

The Christianizing of the position of Roman emperor increased the need for the man sitting on the imperial throne to be physically unblemished. As a representative of God in the temporal world, the emperor had to be free from obvious imperfections, so the idea of physical mutilation increasingly became a political weapon. The focus for the origins of Roman political mutilation usually falls on the punishments of John Athalarichos and the *magister officiorum*, Theodore, the illegitimate son and nephew of Heraclius respectively, for their roles in a conspiracy against that emperor in 637. However, there are some earlier examples from Late Antiquity which might carry dynastic dimensions. A son of the emperor Jovian, probably Varronianus, who was passed over for the throne as being too young on his father's death, may appear in the writings of John Chrysostom, having 'had an eye put out, from fear of what was to follow, though he had done no wrong'.[33] This may have been a way to prevent him from challenging the Valentinian dynasty for the throne. In the early fifth century, there may be two further examples of political mutilation: Priscus Attalus, twice a Goth-backed usurper of the imperial throne, had his hand mutilated by Honorius after his capture in 416, while the usurper Ioannes, upon his defeat and capture, had his hand cut off.[34]

It is difficult to ascertain if any of these mutilations were meant to remove the victim from the line of succession or as merely punitive punishments. In the case of Ioannes, it was quickly followed by his execution, so his imperial candidacy was not a factor. While it could be that the 'necessary' physical perfection of the Roman emperor was in play by the late fourth century, these three incidents may be coloured by the future Roman tendency towards mutilation as a dynastic tool. Other men removed from imperial contention in the fifth century were either killed or made to enter the Church, rather than mutilated and exiled.

It is not even clear if the punishments of John Athalarichos and Theodore in 637 – both had their nose and hands removed, while the latter also lost a leg – were meant solely as punitive or had a dimension of removing both from imperial candidacy. Could the harsher treatment of Theodore reflect such dynastic considerations? Not only was the *magister officiorum* maimed to a greater degree, he was also exiled further away – Gaudomelete (possibly modern-day Gozo, part of the Maltese islands) compared to Prinkipo, off the coast of Constantinople. Could it be that as the legitimate son of Heraclius' brother, he was seen as more of a dynastic threat than the illegitimate Athalarichos? Or was there little to no dynastic aspect to these punishments, Heraclius merely finding it easier to treat his nephew more harshly than his son?

Whatever its meaning at the time, the mutilation and exile of John Athalarichos and Theodore proved something of a watershed for such dynastic maiming in the seventh century. Within four years it would be used again on more sons of Heraclius. This was because the death of Heraclius in 641 had exposed the trouble brewing between his chosen successors –

Heraclius Constantine III and Heraklonas – with the looming shadow of the empress Martina, mother of Heraklonas. Martina's meddling in politics and her incestuous marriage to Heraclius – she was his niece – made her and Heraklonas unpopular; so much so that when Heraclius Constantine died around four months after Heraclius, rumours abound that she had had him poisoned, rather than his dying of tuberculosis.[35] This led to the overthrow of her and Heraklonas by the Senate and army, in favour of Constans II.

Three of Martina's remaining sons – Heraklonas, David Tiberios and Marinus – were stripped of their imperial position and had their noses cut off, before being exiled to Rhodes. Her youngest son, possibly Marinus, was also subjected to castration 'through fear, as they said, of his becoming emperor when he grew up. But the child could not endure the great wound, and straightway died.'[36] The only one of Martina's sons to come out physically unscathed from their removal from power was Theodosius, who was already removed from the line of succession on account of being a deaf-mute. Martina herself also faced mutilation and exile to Rhodes, with John of Nikiu suggesting that she faced similar *rhinokopia* to her sons, while Theophanes proposes that her tongue was cut out. This latter idea would seem a more personal punishment, reflecting her involvement in imperial politics.[37]

The use of such dynastic mutilation seems to have jumped an Heraclian generation, for while Constans II is recorded tonsuring and then executing his younger brother, Theodosius, in 660, there is no mention of any political mutilation.[38] Constantine IV, however, did resort to *rhinokopia* when it came to removing his brothers, Heraclius and Tiberius, from imperial contention.[39] This meant that at least eight members of the imperial family, including one in Heraklonas who ruled as emperor, had faced some form of mutilation by 695. It was not a massive break with precedent then for Leontios to enact the same dynastic punishment on Justinian II. However, the failure of *rhinokopia* to conclusively disqualify Justinian from imperial contention may have seen it fall out of fashion, replaced instead by blinding. In the eighth century alone, a list of emperors, imperial candidates, patriarchs, generals and plotters running into the dozens are recorded being blinded, either as a punishment or to remove them from imperial contention.[40] It would continue as such a punishment and dynastic preventative throughout virtually the entire remaining life of the Roman Empire.

'Off With His Nose!'

Even if Justinian's example did encourage a change to punitive and political mutilation in the Roman Empire, that will have come as no comfort not only to the many future victims of blinding, but also to the deposed emperor himself in 695. Shorn of his imperial position and all overt support, before the baying crowd in the Hippodrome, Justinian II suffered the horrors of *rhinokopia* and *glossotomia* – the mutilation of both the nose and the tongue, which Agnellus of Ravenna describes as having 'reduced the excellence of his body'.[41] Despite the lack of a full description of the extent of the damage caused by this mutilation, there are some inferences that can be made. His *glossotomia* does not seem to have been too debilitating to his ability to speak, so perhaps his tongue was slit rather than removed. As for his nose, while he was fortunate to have the wounds heal without any serious infection, the mutilator's knife had not used any half-measures – Justinian's nose was gone. It was drastic enough that he would be remembered as *Rhinokopimenos* or *Rhinotmetos*, the 'slit-nosed'. Agnellus reports that Justinian had a prosthetic nose made out of gold,[42] although there is no information about where this prosthetic came from and how it was attached; 'As an exile, it seems rather unlikely that he had access to much pure gold, and perhaps this adornment came only later when his fortunes improved.'[43] The fate of Justinian's nose also brings us back to the proposal that he could have received some form of operation, and the result of that is depicted in the 'Carmagnola' porphyry in Venice.[44] As also seen above, reconstructive surgery was well-established in parts of India long before the seventh century,[45] so it is not completely out of the question for Justinian to have been operated on by an itinerant reconstructive surgeon during his exile or even upon his return to Constantinople. However, the sources give no hint at such a surgery, and surely even the most hostile of sources to Justinian would have found it hard not to comment on him having managed to have at least part of his nose reconstructed.

Even with him seemingly removed from imperial contention, Justinian still had to be dealt with. Although mutilated, the former emperor could still be a threat if left to his own devices close to the centre of power. Agnellus suggests that after Justinian was mutilated and relieved of his imperial position, he was left 'wandering, maimed, along the coast'.[46] However, in this short section, Agnellus is condensing the entire story of Justinian's deposition, mutilation, exile and return in order to explain his later actions against Ravenna and so must be treated with caution. It also refers to

Justinian's 'limbs' being mutilated and that his life was only spared due to his begging.[47] Weakened from blood-loss and likely in shock following the mutilation of his nose and tongue, the idea of even a fit and healthy 26-year-old Justinian begging for his life is not hard to understand. It could be that even if Leontios had no intention of killing his maimed predecessor outright, he may have hoped that the wielder of the knife would be heavy-handed and cut a little too deep, leaving this 'merciful' mutilation to become fatal. Leontios would then be free from a rival and from accusations that he had executed an anointed emperor. Agnellus' 'wandering, maimed, along the coast' may also be a misinterpretation or extremely short-hand version of Justinian's actual destination and future journey back to the imperial throne. As well as losing his nose and tongue, Justinian was exiled to one of the most remote Roman outposts: Cherson, 'a desolate port city in the Crimea, the veritable end of the earth'.[48]

One thing that seems not to have been part of Justinian's deposition along with mutilation and exile was the necessity that he enter the Church. It could be that the increased use of mutilation saw forced tonsure decline as a punishment or at least supplanted in the record. It could be that Constantine IV's brothers were mutilated and confined to a monastery, only for just their mutilation to be recorded. Had Justinian been forced to join a monastery, his opponents will have made much of his breaking of that vow when he began his scheming to reclaim the throne, but neither Theophanes nor Nikephoros make such an accusation. It could be that Justinian lived in a monastery in Cherson without becoming a monk, a somewhat solitary life befitting an exile. It was meant to be a lifelong exile, and as the last Heraclian, there was little hope of recall. Justinian almost certainly recognized this. Through his own force of will, perhaps some paranoia in Constantinople about his continued existence and the opportunism of the empire's barbarian neighbours, it was to be an eventful 'lifelong' exile that was to only last ten years.

Chapter 10

The Lion and the Snake:
The Reigns of Leontios and Tiberius III

'Traitors who prevail are patriots; usurpers who succeed are divine emperors.'

Gore Vidal

Unpeaceful Peace: The Reign of Leontios

With the mutilated Justinian shipped off across the Black Sea to Cherson exile, Leontios now looked to stamp his authority on the imperial throne. Yet this was to be no easy task. Despite the personal animosity Justinian had managed to build up against himself, the Heraclian dynasty had ruled the Roman Empire for eighty-five years and helped it navigate the most desperate period it had faced for at least four centuries. Any latent loyalty to the Heraclians from the various social, political, religious and military hierarchies within the empire (and even some without) could have made things incredibly difficult for the new emperor. However, according to Theophanes, Leontios was immensely successful during his first full year in office, maintaining 'a policy peaceful in all respects'.[1] Such grandiose claims of universal Leontian peace either reflect a lack of source record for Theophanes to work from or a conscious effort to further denigrate Justinian. This would make it seem that all the Romans needed to do to restore peace was to get rid of such an awful man. Unfortunately, the paucity of the source material leaves the record of the reign of Leontios lacking in detail and depth. But even with this dearth of information, it can be seen that it was far from being as 'peaceful' as Theophanes portrays it.

Some information about Leontios can be deciphered from his coinage. His appearance has been considered 'among the most life-like of Byzantine coin effigies',[2] but it was a familiar one to late seventh-century audiences. While not following the Christ imagery of his predecessor, the issues of Leontios do use the numismatic symbolism of the Heraclian dynasty. He continued the trend of sporting a beard, a crossed crown and a cross-globe, while the reverse side saw a return to a cross, either alone or on steps. Leontios will have hoped that his use of well-established numismatic trends could confer some form of legitimacy to his new reign. After all, while he may have retained part of his reputation as a skilled general, he was still sitting on the imperial throne as a military usurper.

Another aspect of this search for legitimacy may be seen in Leontios' choice of regnal name. On his coins he appears as *LEON*, which might just seem like a shortened version of his full name; however, instead, it reflects Leontios' choice to rule as 'Leo'.[3] Taking a name which had already been used – he would have been known today as 'Leo III' had it stuck – was an attempt to receive some latent legitimacy from the previous Leos. This was made doubly important by the only previous Leontios to claim the imperial throne having been a failed usurper in 484–488.[4] Various chroniclers such as Theophanes, Nikephoros and likely their sources steadfastly refused to follow this renaming. This is probably because Leontios' reign as the emperor 'Leo' would not be long enough to override the familiarity of sources with his longer military career as 'Leontios'. The twenty-four-year reign of Leo III the Isaurian which started just over a decade after Leontios' death also likely impacted on source unwillingness to identify Leontios as Leo. That said, the more geographically detached western sources such as the *Liber Pontificalis*, Bede and Paul the Deacon do refer to Leontios as 'Leo'.[5]

Theophanes' attempts to depict Leontios' reign as peaceful may reflect the more moderate approach he tried to take in political and military terms. In Anatolia, Leontios appears to have held the thematic armies back from confronting the annual Umayyad raids. In a time when a general had been made emperor largely on the strength of his military reputation, Leontios will have been wary of the results of any Roman action against the raiders of Abd al-Malik. In victory or defeat, a general may have decided to follow the former Anatolic and Hellenic *strategos* and make a play for the imperial throne. That said, restricting the actions of the army and focusing on the consolidation of his reign when Arab columns were striking into Roman territory could easily be seen as cowardly, stoking opposition from amongst provincial populations and armies.

The lack of revolt amongst the thematic forces on the ground in Anatolia might suggest that for the most part, Leontios' 'peaceful' policy was somewhat successful. This may be putting too much faith in Theophanes' reporting for

696/697. It could be that there was no Umayyad attack of any great size on Roman territory in that year, and as there had been a significant attack on Armenia by Muhammad the previous year – which succeeded in carrying off 'many prisoners'[6] – perhaps the Umayyads took time to rest. It should also be noted that the caliphate was facing some internal problems around 696/697. The appointment of al-Hajjaj b. Yusuf to the governorship of Iraq and the eastern provinces had revealed some considerable indiscipline in the garrison forces there. Al-Hajjaj's attempts to reassert discipline strained relations with the locals at a time when he needed their manpower to deal with the Kharijite leader Shabib b. Yazid b. Nu'aym al-Shaybani. This strain would eventually result in first mutiny and then open anti-Umayyad rebellion under Abd al-Rahman b. Muhammad b. al-Ash'ath. There was also trouble from the governor of Hamadan, Mutarrif b. al-Mughira, who tried to throw off Umayyad control.[7]

Alternatively, there being a successful Arab attack in 695/696 might make it more likely that there would be another attack the following year, to build on that victory. Theophanes' record for 697/698 would certainly suggest that the Arabs had no intention of extending any 'peace' beyond a year. An Umayyad general called 'Alidos' by Theophanes – this is considered a mistake for either 'Khalid' or 'al-Walid', the latter of which would probably be the caliph's son and eventual successor – led an attack on Roman territory, again taking many prisoners. More seriously, in Roman Lazica, a revolt broke out under the *patricius* Sergios, son of Barnoukios, which succeeded in handing the region over to the Arabs.[8] Any seeming reticence from Leontios to meet the Umayyads in battle may have emboldened Abd al-Malik to target one of the empire's overseas provinces: the Exarchate of Africa and its great bastion, Carthage.

Arab Advance into North Africa

Ever since their conquest of Egypt was completed in 641, the Arabs had made various attempts to strike west along the Mediterranean coast of Africa.[9] At the fall of Alexandria, the Arab general and governor of Egypt, Amr b. al-As, led his army into Cyrenaica. Capturing Barca, Amr used it as a base to spread Arab control into some of the Cyrenaican and Tripolitanian hinterlands to the south. He also looked to continue expansion to the west, targeting Tripoli. The city was well fortified by the Romans and had a naval squadron that could provide it with not just military defence, but also

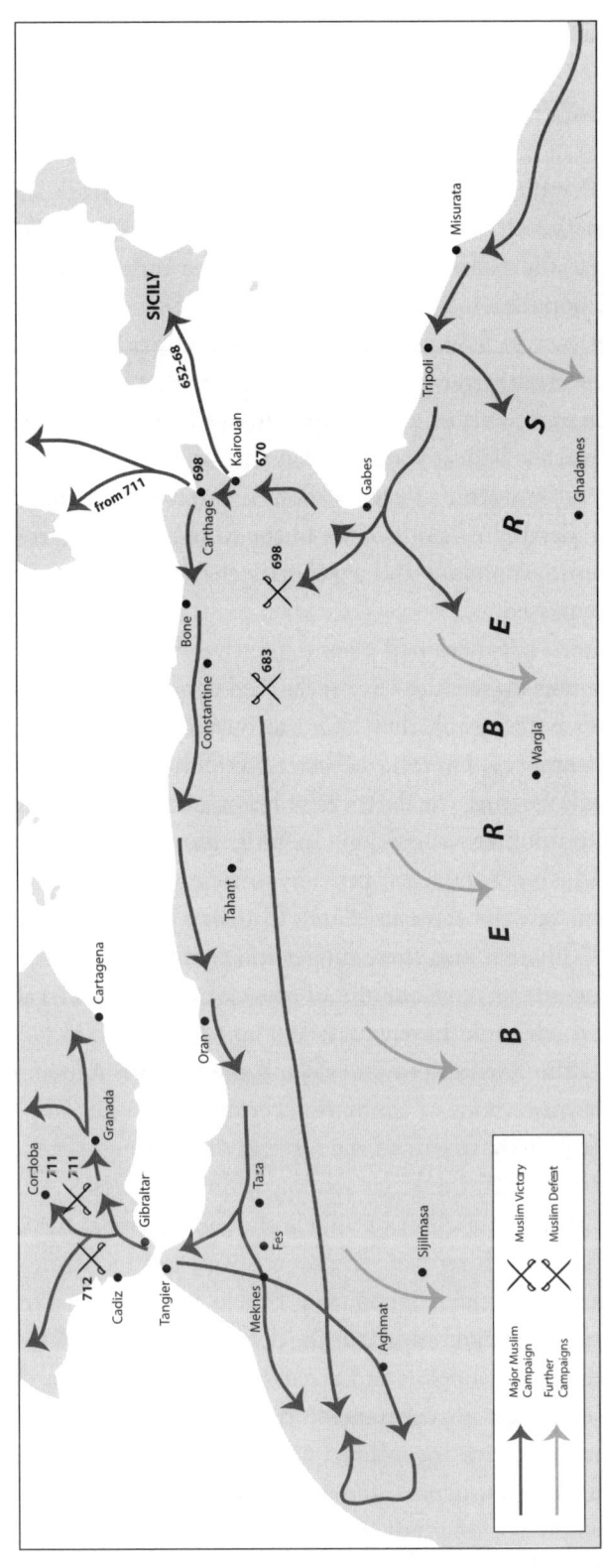

Arab Invasion of North Africa.

supplies to resist a prolonged siege. Lacking siege engines, Amr resorted to the same kind of blockade that had been so successful at Alexandria. After a month, and with no relief force having appeared, Amr's men managed to sneak into the city through a vulnerable section of its walls, although it appears that the Romans had undertaken an orderly evacuation of the garrison and population by sea. Amr followed up this success with another strike further west to Sabratha, which he captured without much resistance. From here, the Arab general planned to take the fight into the core provinces of the African exarchate, only for caliph Umar to recall him to Egypt for fear that he had overreached. It could be that the intervening years or even their retreat back east saw Amr's forces work to secure their control of Cyrenaica, capturing and destroying some of the major Roman coastal strongholds such as Paraetonium, Apollonia and Ptolemais that the advance to Barca and Tripoli had bypassed.

Amr's western advances had been a great warning to the exarchate. But while the Romans do seem to have reclaimed control of Tripoli within a few years of Amr's withdrawal, they failed to oust the Arab presence from the Cyrenaican Pentapolis, Fezzan and eastern Tripolitania. Furthermore, rather than focus on bolstering the defences of the region, the Exarchate of Africa played host to another usurpation. In 646, the failure of Constantinople to stop the Muslim conquests, provide sufficient aid to Africa and reject Monothelitism saw the African exarch Gregory the Patrician rebel against Constans II.[10] There is also some suggestion that the Africans rebelled after Constans demanded a huge amount of money from them; al-Tabari suggests 300 *qintars*, which could have equated to up to 30,000lb of gold.[11] A heavy tax burden on the African provincials and their imprisonment upon failure to pay being a major bone of contention certainly does not ring false.

Gregory seems to have gained the support of Maximus the Confessor and Pope Theodore I, with the latter sending word to Gregory of a dream had by Maximus that had a choir of angels showing support for Gregory over Constans.[12] The rebelling exarch also received support from the African populace and some of the neighbouring Berber tribes. Such a regional revolt was at best a double-edged sword for the defence of Africa. While not having to provide manpower, supplies and taxes to the central government will have enabled the exarchate to concentrate its resources on defending itself, it would in turn not receive any military aid from the central government while it was controlled by a usurper.[13] Circumstances would ensure that Gregory's usurpation would not only fail to threaten the regime of Constans II, but also ultimately fail to protect Africa.

This was because the first military test of Gregory's usurpation did not come from any imperial loyalist element within the exarchate or from Italy. It came instead through renewed Muslim attack. In 647, caliph Uthman ordered his new Egyptian governor, Abdallah b. Sa'ad, to invade the African exarchate with up to 20,000 men. The unpreparedness/distraction of Gregory, the damage done by Amr's incursion and the sheer size of Abdallah's army may be proven by the major battle against the Arab invaders taking place not near any of the fortress cities of Tripolitania, but at Sufetula (modern Sbeitla), just over 200km from Carthage. This was a first test that Gregory and his usurpation failed, as the Battle of Sufetula saw a comprehensive Arab victory and the death of the usurping patrician.[14]

Despite this heavy defeat, the remaining Roman forces managed to secure various fortresses against Abdallah's army. That the Egyptian governor felt the need to retreat back east suggests that once again an Arab army invading Roman Africa had come ill-prepared for siege warfare, and possibly that Gregory had invested some effort in building up the defences of the core African provinces. However, it is likely that Abdallah only agreed to withdraw on the payment of a vast amount of gold on top of all the plunder his forces had taken. While Gregory's death brought Africa back under central Roman control and circumstances within the caliphate meant that it would be nearly two decades before Arab attempts to conquer Africa were resumed, Abdallah's victory at Sufetula had done considerable damage to the exarchate, with many of the frontier regions and Berber tribes falling out of Roman control.[15]

It was not until Muawiyah I was secure on the caliphal throne that Arab attempts to spread into the western Mediterranean resumed, but it does not seem that the intervening years had been put to good use by local and imperial forces in Roman Africa. The threat to the African exarchate may have encouraged Constans II's prolonged campaign in Italy and Sicily, but it is difficult to know what aid he may have been able to provide before his assassination in 668. He could well have restored or bolstered some supply lines to Africa and even sent some troops, although such direct reconnection saw the resumption of the harsh taxation that so annoyed the African populace.

This imperial pressure had the new exarch, Gennadius, refuse to fulfil the increased payment demand and even expel the emperor's representative in 663. This had all the hallmarks of a repeat of the rebellion of Gregory; however, instead, the local citizens and military forces opposed the exarch and, under the leadership of Eleutherios the Younger, drove Gennadius from Africa in 665. Unfortunately for the Romans, Gennadius was driven right into the arms of the Umayyad caliph, arriving at Damascus to ask for aid in retaking the exarchate. Already emboldened by the ability of his raiders to land on Sicily in 663, even with Constans II possibly in the vicinity, Muawiyah saw the arrival of Gennadius at Damascus as perhaps the key to conquering the exarchate.[16]

While Gennadius himself died on the journey back west, the caliph's namesake, Muawiyah b. Hadayj, led a large army into the core lands of the exarchate in 665/666. This invasion further undermined Roman control of the African hinterland, capturing Gabes and threatening Hadrumetum. Its most impressive military achievement was a successful raiding of the city of Hippo, on the north coast of Africa, although it seems that even in the face of weakening Roman resistance, the Arabs were unable to as yet threaten Carthage itself. Perhaps the most important action of this 665/666 campaign was the identifying and brief garrisoning of the site of what would become Kairouan. The following year, the Arabs kept up the pressure by raiding the commercially valuable island of Djerba, while another Arab force under Uqba b. Nafi set out across the northern reaches of the Sahara. Along this route, Uqba set up various military posts to strengthen Arab control of southern Tripolitania and the Fezzan. In the process, he took over the Zawila oasis and Germa, the capital of the Garamantes, opening these regions to Muslim influence and eventually Islamification: an extremely important step in the next wave of Arab conquest in North Africa and beyond. By 670, Uqba had built on any foundations by Muawiyah b. Hadayj at Kairouan, establishing its first mosque; what is now the Great Mosque of Kairouan, sometimes known as the Mosque of Uqba. Over the course of the next decade, from this new base, Uqba staged a series of increasingly far-reaching raids across Numidia and Mauretania, dealing fatal damage to whatever Roman provincial administration remained in what is now Algeria and Morocco. He may even have reached the shores of the Atlantic, although there is considerable discussion over the historiographical accuracy on the career of Uqba b. Nafi and the progression of the Arab conquest of the Maghreb in general.[17]

Whatever the extent of Uqba's campaigning, the strike to the Atlantic was to be the end of that success. The city of Tingi (modern Tangiers) successfully resisted Arab attack, forcing Uqba to retreat into the Atlas Mountains. Worse still, the extent of the Arab raids had driven many Berber tribes back into alliance with the Romans. And so, in 682/683, as it returned east from its thwarting at Tingi, Uqba's column was ambushed by a Romano-Berber coalition commanded by the Berber king Kusaila/Caecilius near Vescara (modern Biskra in north-eastern Algeria). The subsequent Battle of Vescara was a disaster for the Arabs. Uqba himself was killed, his army largely destroyed and much of the territory it had acquired was lost. A remnant of Uqba's army made it back to Kairouan, but ultimately decided to retreat to more secure territory in Cyrenaica. The Romans and their Berber allies then took some advantage of this victory at Vescara and the distraction of the caliphate with the Second Fitna. Kusaila led his forces to claim control of Kairouan, while Roman forces raided Arab Cyrenaica. Such raids would be in-keeping with the successes that Constantine IV had achieved in the 670s, so for him and Justinian II to encourage their continuation would not be much of a surprise. Such was the success of this Romano-Berber coalition in defeating Uqba and overturning much of his gains that the *Liber Pontificalis*, likely echoing papal/imperial propaganda, proclaimed that by 685 'the entire province of Africa was again totally subjugated to the Roman Empire'.[18] Of course, while there may have been some idea that Kusaila was a Roman ally or even *foederati* subordinate, it was increasingly clear that he was acting independently.

Unfortunately for the Romans and Berbers, the Egyptian front of the Second Fitna was shut down rather more quickly than the rest of the flashpoints, with Marwan I establishing his second son, Abd al-Aziz, as governor in early 685. This allowed the Arab forces in Cyrenaica to try to reclaim Kairouan sometime before 688, under the command of Zuhayr b. Qais. Kusaila's Berbers retreated into the mountains before the advance of Zuhayr, leaving Kairouan to the Arabs. The subsequent Battle of Mamma saw the death of Kusaila, but the Roman attacks on Cyrenaica – and perhaps the extent of the casualties suffered in killing the Berber king – saw Zuhayr lead his men back to Barca. On this return journey east, Zuhayr was caught and killed in a Roman ambush.

The repulse and killing of a second Arab invader would seem to suggest that the African exarchate had had new life breathed into it. But looks can be deceiving. The Exarchate of Africa was in dire straits, undermined by years of incessant Arab raids and drained through heavy tribute paid to both Damascus and Constantinople. Its brief successes were also reliant on Arab distraction and military aid from elsewhere. The Roman forces that had staged the raids on Cyrenaica and killed Zuhayr may well have been reinforcements from the central government, which could not be relied upon to always be around, particularly once Justinian II had embarked on war with the Arabs, Bulgars and Slavs. Furthermore, the prevalence of the Berbers in the victories over Uqba and Zuhayr should not be overlooked. Even more detrimental to the future defence of Africa, perhaps, was the death of Kusaila. Without such a forceful Berber leader who recognized that the Arabs posed far more of a threat than the Romans, the Berbers lost their cohesion for the time being. With that, the Romano-Berber alliance lost its teeth at a time when an offensive against Arab positions in Tripolitania, Fezzan and even Cyrenaica may have borne fruit.

The Conquest(s) of Carthage: Hasan b. al-Nu'man, Dihya the Seer and John the Patrician

Having brought an end to the Second Fitna and won a significant victory at Sebastopolis, Abd al-Malik sent up to 40,000 of his freed-up forces under Hasan b. al-Nu'man to re-establish the Arab position in Africa. With the biggest Arab army yet deployed to Africa, Hasan was to accomplish much more than that. His military achievements and administrative institutions were to create the first real Arab government in Africa, making him 'in many ways, the real founder of Muslim North Africa'.[19] Unfortunately, the campaigns of Hasan in Africa suffer from the same historiographical issues as his predecessors, meaning that the dating of his adventures can be confused. This is best demonstrated by the lack of clarity over exactly when Hasan took control of Carthage for the first time. It could have been as early as 695 that the Arab commander marched into a poorly defended and sparsely populated Carthage, with many of its inhabitants possibly evacuated to Sicily.[20] Rather than defend Carthage, a Romano-Berber force had congregated near Hippo, but suffered a major defeat when Hasan squared up to them. This left Hasan in control of what had been Africa Province, largely equivalent to modern Tunisia.

This slightly earlier date for the first Arab capture of Carthage may help explain how Leontios managed to receive word of its fall, gather together and then launch an expedition to reclaim the city within his brief reign. It could be argued that Leontios might have planned the expedition to save the Africa exarchate in general, but it seems less likely that he would have mobilized such an expedition without the disastrous loss of Carthage to spur him on. To lead this African expedition, Leontios chose John the

Patrician, an experienced and 'competent man',[21] furnishing him with the 'entire Roman fleet'.[22] There is likely some hyperbole in this pronouncement of the size of the expedition, with only the Korykiote squadron of the Cibyrrhaeots actually recorded amongst the fleet to sail to Africa. At a time when Leontios was newly on the throne and faced with conflict against the Arabs in Anatolia, would he really have dispatched all of his naval forces to the western Mediterranean? However, it could be imagined that some squadrons from the various fleets – Karabisiani (if it still existed), the Hellenic theme, forces defending Constantinople (attached to the Opsikion) and more of the Cibyrrhaeots beyond the Korykiotes – were detached to join John's expedition. It might also be expected that various themes would have contributed land forces as well. Such Constantinopolitan expeditions to Africa tended to stop off in Sicily, so it could be that John did the same and picked up some Sicilian thematic forces. John may even have received some manpower support from Wittiza and Ergica, the kings of the Goths in Spain.

Whatever the make-up of John the Patrician's expedition, it was strong enough to immediately force its way into Carthage's harbour by severing the large chain across its mouth. The Roman expedition then defeated the garrison left behind by Hasan and established full control of the city. From his new base, John set about reclaiming large sections of the former Africa Province, defeating any Arab forces he found there and garrisoning it with his own men. He then sent word back to Leontios in Constantinople regarding his success and to ask for further instructions. The reply came that he was to winter in Africa, with the understanding perhaps being that he was to consider himself the new African exarch and prepare for the inevitable Arab counter-attack.[23]

The ability of John the Patrician to reclaim Carthage and much of Africa Province was due not just to the strength of his own forces, but also the distraction of Hasan. After his victory at Hippo, the Arab commander had turned his attention to his most powerful opponent left in North Africa, the Berber coalition in the Aures Mountains. There, Kusaila had been ostensibly succeeded by a queen called Dihya, but more widely recorded as 'al-Kahina' – 'the seer'. Unfortunately, al-Kahina's confrontations with Hasan not only suffer from poor historical reporting, but also the legendary nature of some of the achievements accredited to both. Thinking that killing the Berber queen would finish off any significant resistance to the Arab conquest of North Africa,[24] Hasan allowed himself to be lured into the Aures Mountains. At a wadi of Meskiana in modern Algeria, the Arab and Berber armies came face to face. The date of this Battle of Meskiana is uncertain, delineated either side perhaps only by the two Arab captures of Carthage in *c*.695 and *c*.698.

The subsequent Arab defeat was said to have been so heavy that Hasan evacuated all Arab holdings in Africa, with his retreat not stopping until he was four days' march east of Tripoli at a collection of forts that became known as *Qusur Hassan*.[25] He then sent to the caliph for reinforcement, informing Abd al-Malik of the tenacity of the Berbers and possibly of the resurgence of the Romans in the form of John the Patrician's capture of Carthage and reclaiming of many fortresses in Africa. The Arab commander may have considered retreating to Barca or even Egypt, but the caliph ordered him to hold his position in Tripolitania, gather together whatever forces he still had at his disposal and await reinforcement. The various historical traditions have Hasan ejected from Africa for up to five years, but given the seeming dates of his captures of Carthage, it cannot have lasted three (if it happened at all).[26]

The subsequent actions of al-Kahina would also be somewhat at odds with the idea that the Berbers had inflicted a truly devastating defeat on the Arabs at Meskiana. Rather than build on that success, perhaps in concert with John the Patrician, the Berber queen resorted to the far more desperate measure of a scorched earth policy. This may portray al-Kahina as recognizing the power of the Arab caliphate; a portrayal perhaps invented by Muslim scholars from the benefit of hindsight to display both the long-sightedness of the Berber queen and the inevitability of Islam's victory in Africa. However, while al-Kahina's scorched earth strategy may have been to deny the Arabs supplies and even a reason to invade Africa again due to a lack of booty, it overlooked not just the proselytizing imperialism of the Arab caliphate, but also the nature of some of her own support. While her own core mountain and desert tribes would be largely unaffected, the destruction of urbanity, agriculture, foodstuffs and houses would have gravely undermined support from other parts of the African population. Romanized town and city dwellers and landowners will have been outraged at any losses they incurred, while John the Patrician and his re-established garrisons will have been deprived of resources and taxes. Perhaps worst of all for al-Kahina, her scorched earth affected some of her fellow Berbers, such as those who traded with people in towns and cities and those who lived around various oases, with the latter being targeted for spoliation in order to deprive the Arabs of their use. It should be noted that this very notion of a Berber scorched earth policy may be the invention of later Muslim writers such as Ibn Idhari, with the aim of passing the blame for the decline of North African urbanism and productivity onto the Berbers, rather than it being a centuries-long process under the Romans and Arabs.[27]

The later narrative would have it that when Hasan returned to Africa, some 12,000 Berbers had been put off fighting for al-Kahina by her destructive policies. It might be argued instead that because these 12,000 Berbers defected to the Arabs rather than just deserted the Berber queen, it was religious proselytizing on the back of the governmental framework gradually introduced by Uqba, Zuhayr and Hasan that was bearing fruit for the Arabs. Had they just been angry at al-Kahina, these Berbers were more likely to have just stayed out of the war or joined the more urban-minded Romans. Instead, they may have been sufficiently Islamified to see their future inside the Arab system rather than against it.

Bolstered by reinforcements both from Abd al-Malik and the Berbers, Hasan likely reinvaded Africa in 697/698. His first target was al-Kahina, whom he defeated at Gabes and drove back into the Aures Mountains. The chronology is again confused, but it seems that the climactic battle between Hasan and al-Kahina was perhaps up to five years after the Arab victory at Gabes. This may be because rather than chase after the Berber queen, Hasan turned his attention to the reclamation of Carthage. It would seem that with al-Kahina corralled in the Aures, John the Patrician's expeditionary force was now the biggest threat posed to the Arabs. Furthermore, if the Romans had reclaimed many fortresses in Africa, Hasan would need them to establish a militarily-secure, urban-based administration going forward.

The Roman record regarding the confrontation between Hasan and John would suggest that it was a one-off battle to decide the fate of Carthage and essentially the African exarchate as a whole.[28] However, Muslim chroniclers like al-Maliki and al-Nuwayri suggest that there was a little more to this last Romano-Arab war over Africa. As well as the battle for Carthage, Hasan also had to capture a series of forts along the north coast, such as Vaga and Hippo Regius.[29] It could well be that there were other Roman-held forts to the south of Carthage that Hasan either had to capture first or bypass *en route* to his showdown with John. This suggests that even with his expedition facing an existential threat in the face of a reinforced Hasan, John failed to bring together all of the forces available to him to defend Carthage.

When it came, the Battle of Carthage in 698 may have encapsulated two separate parts: a battle outside the city and then an Arab assault to claim control of the city walls and then the harbour. It is the Muslim tradition that suggests this potential dual aspect of the confrontation, with Ibn Idhari proposing that when Hasan approached Carthage, 'he slew its cavalry and its soldiers, [and] those who survived in it decided that they should escape'.[30] If John did lead his forces out from the city and meet Hasan head-on, the superior Arab numbers likely overcame any initial surprise or shock. The Roman commander may have taken the risk of such a battle in the open because he felt that the Carthaginian defences and the control of the sea offered by his fleet and the harbour would allow him to retreat safely should the battle go poorly. As it was, Arab numbers and preparation not only defeated the Romans in any pitched battle, they also saw Hasan's men scale the walls with ladders, force their way into Carthage and then win the battle for control of the harbour. For the second and definitive time, Carthage was in the hands of Islam.

The Usurpation of Apsimar

Defeated in battle and street fighting, John and his commanders fled to their ships and withdrew completely from Africa, not stopping until they reached Crete, a direction of retreat that seemed to suggest that they had no intention of immediately returning to contest Hasan's victory. If they had, surely a retreat to Sicily would have been more appropriate, unless there was some thought to cut Hasan's supply lines through a repeat of the successful raids against Cyrenaica. Theophanes does suggest that John was returning east because 'he wanted to get reinforcements from the emperor',[31] which he would only want to continue the fight. Circumstances were to see any plan for counter-attack forgotten as intrigue, paranoia and panic overtook what was left of John the Patrician's expedition.

On Crete, dissension in the expeditionary ranks burst into the open. The soldiers and officers were reportedly in fear of the punishment they would receive from Leontios for their failure in Africa,[32] something which might seem like a hangover from the violent reactions accredited (perhaps wrongly) to Justinian II. Rather than face that music, the officers 'turned to a wicked plot',[33] throwing off their allegiance to Leontios and declaring one of their own as emperor. Their choice fell on Apsimar, the *droungarius* of the Cibyrrhaeot regiment from Cilician Korykos. In the process of this rebellion, John the Patrician and likely other officers who remained loyal to him or Leontios were murdered. Apsimar then gathered the expeditionary force stationed in

Crete and sailed for Constantinople to press his claim to the throne. Landing at Sykai on the opposite side of the Golden Horn to the capital, the usurper's forces attempted to put the city under some kind of siege or blockade.[34]

These usurping forces were not the only danger to reach Leontios' capital by sea in 698. Originating in Syria and Iraq, where it would rage throughout 698–700, plague arrived in Constantinople along the trade routes and spent four months ravaging the capital.[35] As already mentioned, plague should not be overlooked as an important contributor to the developments of the seventh and eighth centuries. Outbreaks could damage armies and their manpower resources, which in turn would affect the aims and strategies of caliphs and emperors. After the massive bubonic outbreak under Justinian I, plague had continued to reappear at regular intervals. There are at least eleven known outbreaks in the Muslim Near East post-626, with several more in other regions, such as China in 626–628, Rome in 680 and Constantinople in 698, before a major pandemic between 743 and 750. The latter ravaged North Africa before moving east to Syria, Mesopotamia and Iraq, and north to Italy, where it was contracted by Roman military forces, which brought it through Greece, the Aegean and ultimately to Constantinople again by the spring of 747, where it would rage for a year.[36] Therefore, throughout the reigns of Justinian II, the years of military anarchy and the reigns of Leo III and Constantine V, plague was likely a constant obstacle for the Roman army and economy. Of course, plague was indiscriminate, so Roman enemies may have been equally affected; indeed, Arab, Bulgar and Slav populations with less exposure to plague than their 'Roman' neighbours may have been more drastically hit than the empire.

Leontios was therefore faced with an attempted usurpation at a time when plague had 'destroyed a great number of people in four months',[37] no doubt including the military forces available to him. It might be expected that a plague-ravaged Constantinople would not be able to resist the rebel blockade for long. However, the forces of Leontios were able to successfully hold out for several months. The likelihood is that this was mostly because the mammoth size and defences of Constantinople made it impossible for Apsimar's forces to enact a full siege or blockade. One might ask how an army unable to defend Carthage could be able to take Constantinople. Of course, there needed to be some willingness to defend the walls and take on the hardships involved in even a limited blockade. There must therefore have been some loyalty to Leontios within the city and from its garrison forces. The population may also have feared an armed takeover, even from fellow

Romans. Somewhat contrarily, the plague may have enabled the city to resist longer. Word of the pestilence could have caused some reticence in the attackers, and while a lowered population within the city might have a lesser fighting strength, it will also have reduced the mouths to feed, allowing resources to stretch further.

It is worth noting though that if Leontios did resist successfully for months, no attempted relief from any of the thematic armies is recorded, although neither is there any suggestion that they tried to back Apsimar. Such a potential wait-and-see approach from Roman forces in the face of rebellion and civil war was not a new development of the themes. Procopius recalls similar reticence to get involved during the *Nika* riots of 532:

> 'Then all of the soldiers, and the others who were stationed around the emperor's court, neither favoured the emperor nor wished to take a position in the fighting, but waited to see what would be the future outcome ... the soldiers decided to aid neither one, until one had clearly won the victory.' (*BP* I.24.39, 45)

While this may suggest that Roman armies might be less 'prone to rebellion and to violent discharge'[38] than usually thought, it does show that they could be capable of cynical self-preservation, even to the extent of not carrying out their sworn duty to protect the emperor and the imperial capital.

Apsimar likely realized that once the city did not capitulate immediately upon his arrival in the Golden Horn, he was going to have to rely on help from inside in order to gain entry. It may have taken several months, but eventually that betrayal came. The exact form it took is not entirely clear from the sources. Theophanes claims that 'foreign officers' stationed at Blachernae, who 'had been entrusted with the keys of the land wall because of their frightful oath at the holy table',[39] carried out a plot to give Apsimar's men access to the city. Nikephoros is slightly different in that he presents the guards and officers on the Blachernae walls as having been bribed by Apsimar.[40] Such soldiers are likely to have been part of the Opsikion thematic army.[41] According to the anonymous *Anecdota Bruxellensia*, Apsimar also received help from the Green faction; so much so that 'he owed as much to the help of the Greens as his predecessor had done to the Blues'.[42]

Whatever the circumstances, once inside, Apsimar's men rampaged through the city, stripping the inhabitants of their possessions as if Constantinople was an enemy settlement.[43] In short order, any resistance collapsed and Leontios fell into the hands of Apsimar. The lack of fight put up by the garrison once the rebels were inside the walls and the straightforward capture of Leontios might suggest that the imperial guard had a similar wait-and-see or cynical self-preservation approach that the garrison had during the *Nika* riots. It could be that Justinian II was captured in similar circumstances. After just three years, Leontios' reign was at an end. Once in the hands of the rebels, Leontios faced a similarly horrendous punishment to that he had inflicted on Justinian: *rhinokopia*. With his nose cut off, the deposed emperor was confined to the Psamathion monastery in Constantinople, rather than an island or a distant imperial province. That Apsimar kept Leontios in the capital would suggest that he expected mutilation to prevent any latent support for Leontios. Apsimar also went to some lengths to present Leontios in a poor light and therefore justify his own usurpation:

'Just as Justinian because of his mismanagement of the Roman empire, especially for pillaging Cyprus and breaking the peace with the Arabs, thus ruining many Roman lands, and other such things, was deprived of rule, so Leontios, though he had been enthroned for being one of the great men, has been cast out for lapsing into similar folly.' (Theophilus of Edessa, *Chronicle* 192)

With Leontios deposed and confined, Apsimar was then crowned emperor, with patriarch Kallinikos once more carrying out the ceremony. Part of that imperial crowning involved Apsimar taking a new name. Similar to Leontios, Apsimar suffered from a lack of legitimacy as a military usurper and having a problematic name. However, unlike his noseless monastic predecessor, whose name was shared with a previous imperial usurper, the new emperor's name had the issue of looking and sounding distinctly un-Roman. Exactly what kind of 'un-Roman' is not completely clear. It was long accepted that 'Apsimar' was a name of Germanic origin, but there have been suggestions that it had Slavic or even Turkic origins.[44] The lack of source record of Apsimar's life before his service as a Cibyrrhaeot *droungarius* in Africa further hinders any identification of the root of his name. It must be remembered though that having a non-Roman-sounding name does not mean that Apsimar himself was not of at least partial Roman origin.

Apsimar's choice of regnal name was 'Tiberius'. As with other emperors of repeated regnal names, Apsimar will have ruled merely as the emperor 'Tiberius', rather than have a regnal number. However, through modern conventions, he is numbered most frequently as 'Tiberius III', although some excluded the original Julio-Claudian Tiberius from the regnal count, leaving Apsimar to be 'Tiberius II'. He is also frequently listed as 'Tiberius III Apsimar' or even just 'Tiberius Apsimar'. Again, much like Leontios, he will have chosen this name because it had an established imperial pedigree and neither of the previous imperial rulers of that name had been usurpers or been usurped. It is possible that Apsimar chose 'Tiberius' specifically because as of 698, Tiberius II (reigned 578–582) was the last non-Heraclian emperor to escape deposition.

The reign of Tiberius III gets overlooked for being similarly brief and inconsequential as Leontios; just another of the line of military usurpers taking advantage of the lack of authority projected by the imperial throne at the turn of the eighth century. This is somewhat unfair. While he would not have a reign the length of virtually any of the Heraclians, he would still sit on the imperial throne for up to seven years. And although the historical record remained patchy during that period, it was a reign that involved plenty of incident and was not devoid of achievement.

Tiberius inherited an empire in disarray, although it must be said that he had something to do with that disarray. The plague ravaging parts of the empire and the capital might not have been his fault, but he shared some of the blame for the failure to reclaim Africa and, of course, for being the man who had just attacked and plundered the imperial capital and deposed the reigning *basileus*. His need to stamp his authority on the imperial hierarchies had all the hallmarks for furthering this disarray. As Leontios had been popular with many of the military officers (although not enough for some outside Constantinople to come to his rescue), Tiberius had many of them removed from office, beaten, exiled and their property confiscated.[45] Not only did he lose experienced commanders at a time of military crisis, Tiberius then appointed his own brother, Herakleios, to the position of *monostrategos*, who was to have command over all the other *strategoi*, at least in Anatolia. This looks as much an attempt to keep the themes under control as it does a bid to defend Roman territory from the Arabs.

Such nepotistic, internal policing rarely goes well, but perhaps against expectation, Herakleios turned out to be 'quite competent'.[46] He was likely helped in this regard by the apparent quiet on the Anatolian frontier during 698 and 699. This would seem a little surprising, as Arab raids into Roman territory had been largely an annual occurrence since the outbreak of war in 692. Furthermore, another bout of military revolt at the heart of the Roman Empire would seem like the perfect opportunity for the forces of Abd al-

Malik to make more ambitious attacks. However, while Constantinople was dealing with the replacing of Leontios with Tiberius III, the Umayyads were faced with the rebellion of Abd al-Rahman against the attempts of al-Hajjaj to instil discipline in the Iraqi and Iranian provinces.[47] The Umayyad response was to detach Muhammad, who had led the Arab campaigns into Roman territory, from the Anatolian front and send him to join al-Hajjaj in reclaiming the Iranian provinces from Abd al-Rahman.[48] Such a rebellion, along with the plague, may explain why Theophanes records no Anatolian Romano-Arab fighting in 698/699 or 699/700.[49]

It seems that Herakleios took advantage of this respite to not only secure his own position in the *strategos* hierarchy, but also to strike into Umayyad territory. In 700/701, a Roman army invaded Syria. The exact direction of this attack is disputed in the sources, with Theophanes suggesting it reached as far as Samosata, while al-Tabari has it attacking Antioch.[50] Even though there was no permanent conquest, the Romans raided far and wide, taking a lot of prisoners and booty and reputedly killing up to 200,000 Arabs. However, by tagging on something of a disclaimer with 'as they say', Theophanes himself seems to doubt this figure. Michael the Syrian gives a much more modest 5,000 Arab casualties.[51]

Despite this 'bad scare',[52] the Umayyads were quick to respond, with Abdallah, son of the caliph, leading an attack on Roman territory in 701/702. He targeted Taranta, a fortress in the region of Melitene and possibly a position that Herakleios' forces advanced through, given that he is recorded as having been sent by Tiberius III to Cappadocia.[53] Abdallah was unable to make much headway against Taranta's walls and soon retreated 'without having accomplished anything'.[54] However, before returning to Syria, he did oversee the rebuilding and garrisoning of Mopsuestia in Cilicia, so in terms of territorial reclamation, the caliph's son may have achieved more than the emperor's brother.[55]

The combination of the rebellion of Abd al-Rahman, the plague, the Roman attack on Syria and Abdallah's riposte destabilized the Romano-Umayyad frontier. With the Lazican revolt of Sergios in 697/698 still somewhat fresh in the memory, the fickleness of the Armenians and Caucasians again became an issue for both the Romans and the Umayyads. In 702/703, Baanes Heptadaimon – 'Vahan Seven Devils' – took Fourth Armenia, also known as Sophene, over to the Arabs. Seemingly Umayyad overtures and the impact of Abdallah's invasion in neighbouring Melitene was enough to let the inhabitants of Sophene forget that in 695/696, Muhammad had raided their lands.[56] However, the rest of Armenia was not so forgiving of Arab oppression. In 703/704, the Armenian *nakharars* rebelled against the Umayyads, killed their Arab garrisons and asked for Roman support. Tiberius III responded by sending troops, likely from the Armeniac theme. This rebellion and Roman assistance drew the returned Muhammad into a counter-invasion of Armenia. The Arab commander succeeded in driving out the Roman forces and subjugating the Armenian *nakharars*, gathering together many of the rebel leaders and burning them alive.[57]

This Armenian flashpoint and the drawing in of Muhammad caused Herakleios to respond with military action of his own. His focus fell on Cilicia, where an Arab army was operating. Theophanes seems a little confused regarding Herakleios' Cilician campaign. He suggests that in 703/704, while Muhammad subdued Armenia, Herakleios defeated a 10,000-strong Umayyad force under a certain Azar, killing most of the Arabs and sending the rest as prisoners to Tiberius.[58] The succeeding year, Theophanes records Herakleios defeating another Arab army of 12,000 men, this time under the command of Yazid b. Hunain. There is no other record of 'Azar' in the sources, while there is some backing from al-Tabari for a campaign involving Yazid,[59] so it would seem that Theophanes has accidentally replicated a single campaign. Perhaps the confusion was caused by Theophanes' sources overlapping and using different dating systems.

That is not to say that there are not issues with the record of Herakleios' seeming victory over Yazid between Theophanes and al-Tabari. While they share a geographic location – al-Tabari's Susanah is Theophanes' Sision – the Muslim chronicler has 'Yazid b. Jubayr' serving in Cilicia under the command of Abd al-Malik's son, Maslamah. He also places this campaign in 705/706, which is too late as Herakleios would be deposed by then. It is noteworthy and almost certainly telling that al-Tabari gives no mention as to the result of the battle, which surely lends credence to Theophanes' record of a substantial Arab defeat at the hands of Herakleios. It would seem that Yazid was dispatched by Maslamah in 704/705 to capture the fort of Sision, which held a strategic position at the entrance to a pass through the Taurus Mountains. To have suffered such a devastating defeat, Yazid's men were likely caught fully engaged in a siege or even attack against the walls of Sision by the sudden arrival of Herakleios' army.[60]

It is clear that throughout Tiberius III's reign, the Romano-Umayyad frontier was a hotbed of military action between the empire, the caliphate and the various Armenian princelings. However, this did not prevent some negotiations taking place between Tiberius and Abd al-Malik. The subject of this negotiation was the island of Cyprus and its inhabitants, or more accurately, its lack of inhabitants. Justinian II's removal of Cypriots from their homeland to populate his new colony at Cyzicus-Nea Justinianopolis had been a point of contention between the emperor and caliph, with Abd al-Malik complaining that such a move took away tax revenue due to the caliphate via the terms of the 'treaty of 688'. When he received no restitution, the caliph responded with not only filing this rebuke away as part of his *casus belli* for the war of 692, but also removing some Cypriots to his own lands.

It would seem that it was Tiberius III who negotiated the rectifying of this sticking point between Constantinople and Damascus. Within just 'seven years'[61] of their transfer to Cyzicus, the Cypriot colonists were repatriated to their island homeland in *c.*699. While painted by Constantine VII as being an imperial initiative that gained Umayyad acceptance, this repatriation was an agreement between Tiberius and Abd al-Malik to restore the Cypriot condominium, with both caliph and emperor returning the Cypriots taken as colonists. The caliph's willingness to return to this part of the 'treaty of 688' may reflect the continued naval strength of the Romans, although it is possible that Abd al-Malik also persuaded Tiberius to remove some more Mardaites from the Taurus highlands to Cyprus, bolstering its garrison and tax revenue.[62] Whatever the exact ins and outs of this agreement, the restoration of the condominium of Cyprus provided the island with a secure position between the Roman Empire and the Umayyad Caliphate for many decades to come.[63] Conversely, the repatriation of the Cypriot colonists saw Nea Justinianopolis essentially abandoned, but there was a strange hangover from their brief colonizing of Cyzicus. The Cypriot metropolitan, who played such a prominent role in getting Justinian involved with the island and benefitted from the emperor's promotion of Nea Justinianopolis at the Quinisext Council, retained the title of 'Archbishop of Nova Justiniana and all Cyprus'.[64]

Nothing is known of Tiberius' religious policies, but his interaction with Italy and the Ravennate exarchate hints at him doing something to anger the Italians. The *Liber Pontificalis* records 'the soldiery of the whole of Italy'[65] rising up in 701 to support the new pope, John VI, in the face of what seemed a threatening move by the exarch, Theophylactos, recently appointed by Tiberius. Not long after his own promotion, Theophylactos had set out from Sicily and marched on Rome. It has been suggested that the exarch had been ordered to 'pressurise the pontiff into accepting the Quinisext decrees'[66] or to just generally 'cause trouble for the pontiff',[67] but the historical sources give no direct reason for this episode. The timing, with both pope and exarch fresh on their thrones, might suggest that Theophylactos was looking to impose some exarchate influence over John VI, or at least remind him of the emperor's reach. The *Liber Pontificalis* does highlight some members of the exarch's entourage attempting to frame prominent Roman citizens so Theophylactos would have a reason 'to strip them of what they owned'.[68] Whatever the reason for the exarch's journey to Rome, the soldiery and citizenry felt that there was something untoward about it and 'riotously forgathered in this city of Rome, meaning to cause the exarch trouble'.[69] Recognizing that any violence towards the exarch might bring down a more brutal imperial response, John VI interjected personally and calmed the mob before they could harm Theophylactos and his entourage.[70] This was not the only Italian trouble to blight Tiberius' reign. In around 705 or earlier, Gisulf I, Lombard duke of Benevento, launched an invasion of Campania, capturing the towns of Sora, Arce and Arpinum, the birthplace of Cicero. The duke is said to have reached as far as Horrea, although exactly where this was is not clear.[71] 'Since there was no one who could resist him',[72] the pope sent ambassadors and gifts to dissuade Gisulf from further plundering. John VI only succeeded in buying off the duke by agreeing to ransom all of the captives the Lombards had taken during their Campanian incursion.

Other aspects of Tiberius III's reign contain even less detail than these Anatolian, Cypriot or Italian episodes, but they show that his was not a reign of inactivity. At some point during his career, Tiberius may have had some military success in the Balkans against the Slavs.[73] It could be opined that a reigning emperor being active in the Balkans could have encouraged the likes of the Bulgars and the Slavs to support any opposition against the emperor, particularly in the form of a deposed *basileus* soon to appear along the Danube from the east. Tiberius is also thought to have carried on the expansion of the theme system and its intendent military organization. He may have been involved in the further establishing of the Cibyrrhaeots as a separate naval theme, and may have played a part in the creation of two new themes in the West. Tiberius may have completed the separation of Sicily from the Exarchate of Ravenna, forming a Sicilian theme. The second seems to have been a conglomeration of many of the other western Mediterranean islands still in Roman hands into what is listed as the Sardinian theme.[74] Such is the difficulty in dating thematic developments that these Sicilian and Sardinian themes could have been the work of any of the emperors of the late seventh/early eighth century. The Sardinian theme almost certainly did not come into being until after the final loss of Carthage in 698. Tiberius is also recorded repairing the sea walls of Constantinople because 'before him they had been completely neglected'.[75] It should be pointed out that even in a 'neglected' state, the Constantinopolitan sea walls had kept Tiberius' forces out in 698. The cynic might suggest that the reason they were in somewhat poor condition was due to damage Tiberius' own men did to them during their attempts to take the capital and their subsequent pillaging.

One political development that took place under Tiberius III, which was to have some future impact, involved the son of an Armenian colonist at Pergamum. The colonist in question was the *patricius*, Nikephoros, and his son the future emperor Philippikos Bardanes. At a time of such uncertainty, it is unsurprising that Tiberius would react to any reputed portent. Such was the case with Bardanes, who in around 702/703 claimed to have had a dream in which an eagle – a symbol of Roman imperium – had shaded his head. The reading of dreams was still popular in Constantinople, and this was taken to mean that Bardanes would soon be emperor. Foolishly, he made his dream known, and when it reached the ear of Tiberius, he had Bardanes exiled to the island of Cephalonia.[76] This would not be the last time that suspicion of imperial pretensions would fall on the son of Nikephoros.

While certainly not the complete non-event as emperor he can be made out to be, there was one (former) region of the empire where Tiberius III was perhaps much less active than might have been expected: Africa. Despite some limited Roman resistance after John the Patrician's ousting from Carthage and the continued presence of al-Kahina as a possible ally, Tiberius was unable to act on any inclination he had to try to reclaim North Africa beyond his possible establishment of the Sardinian theme. Not that Hasan b. al-Nu'man was to know that at the time of his second capture of Carthage in 698. The trouble caused by John the Patrician's expedition made the Arab commander wary of the position of Carthage as a staging point for future Roman intervention. He decided therefore to make it a far less useful prospect, even if it deprived Arab Africa of a prominent urban centre. Carthage's mighty walls were torn down, its water supply cut, its farm land ruined, its magnificent harbours rendered unusable and its buildings dismantled as material for the development of Kairouan and Tunis. However, much like the previous Roman 'destruction' of Carthage in 146 BC, this was not the complete razing to the ground it is sometimes portrayed as. Archaeology suggests that the town of Carthage continued to be occupied after Hasan's demolitions.[77] The eleventh-century physician and Benedictine monk at Monte Cassino, Constantine the African, was said to have been born and lived in Carthage, while the fortress of Carthage was still in use in the thirteenth century, being captured in 1270 by the forces of the French king Louis IX during the Eighth Crusade.

While his demolition of Carthage demonstrated that Hasan thought that the Romans would return, no repeat of John the Patrician's expedition was forthcoming. This left the Arab commander free to mop up the isolated and largely leaderless Roman remnants, such as Vaga and Hippo Regius, and then turn his attention to a final confrontation with al-Kahina and her Berbers. It was in around 703 that this climactic battle took place. Perhaps using intelligence provided by spies in the Berber camp, Hasan penetrated the Aures Mountains and brought al-Kahina to battle somewhere near the northern stretch of the border between Tunisia and Algeria, with places such as Tobna, Setif and Tabraka all suggested as the vicinity. In-keeping with her reputation as a seer, al-Kahina is said to have sent away her sons for fear of the upcoming battle. That al-Kahina expected defeat may suggest that she had been unable to use the intervening years to rebuild her manpower base. The evacuation by the Romans, the legacy of her scorched earth and the growing Islamification of some Berber tribes will have made it hard for her to gather an army in any way capable of resisting the reinforced Hasan. As it was, the great seer queen of the Berbers was correct one last time. The Arabs easily overpowered the understrength Berber coalition and al-Kahina died, either in the fighting or by taking poison once the day was lost.[78]

While poor sources continue to cloud the Arab advance across North Africa after the Roman evacuation and the defeat of al-Kahina, it seems that Hasan oversaw the rapid integration of much of what had been Roman Numidia and Mauretania into the Arab province of Ifriqiya. It could be that the damage done by the previous western campaign of Uqba had never been recovered from, aiding the rapidity of these conquests. Hasan was also responsible for the introduction of effective Umayyad administration from the provincial capital at Kairouan. He formed a centralized bureaucracy to collect tax, pay soldiers and help incorporate newly Islamified Berbers into the provincial and military set-up. To replace Carthage, he refounded Tunis as an Arab city, connecting it to the Gulf of Tunis via a canal to enable its use as a naval base.

Despite all he had done for the Arab province of Ifriqiya, Hasan b. al-Nu'man was not to oversee its final victories. Unsurprisingly, such a successful and transformative tenure roused jealousy and opposition. His strict application of Umayyad/Muslim laws may have helped establish Ifriqiya, but also galvanized opposition amongst the non-Islamified Berbers. This meant that large parts of nominally subjected North Africa remained restless. Hasan also failed to complete the conquest of the North African coastal cities still in Roman hands, such as Tingi and Septem, and made little headway against the Roman naval forces operating along the African coast from the various western Mediterranean islands, likely the bedrock of the Sardinian theme. Hasan's tenure would have survived these limited setbacks had it not been for the political aspirations of the governor of Egypt, Abd al-Aziz. The establishment of Ifriqiya as a province in its own right reduced the area under the direct authority of the Egyptian governor, so Abd al-Aziz sought a way to expand his influence across North Africa. He no doubt succeeded in this by pointing out Hasan's failures in western Mauretania, amongst the Berbers and against the Roman navy. This saw Hasan removed as governor in 704 and replaced by Musa b. Nusayr, a partisan of Abd al-Aziz.[79]

Musa renewed the attacks on the Berbers, but coupled them with diplomatic outreach, respecting some Berber traditions whilst encouraging them to convert to Islam. As the newly converted Berbers continued to prove willing soldiers, this provided an impetus to Umayyad armies that may have been waning somewhat after three generations of unbroken warfare. The injection of new martial blood allowed Musa to complete the conquest of Morocco that had eluded Hasan, capturing Tingi and occupying the Sous. By building on Hasan's foundation of the likes of Tunis, Musa also put a sizeable Umayyad fleet into western Mediterranean waters, conquering the Balaerics and sending raids to Sicily and Sardinia.

By 709, the Arab conquest of North Africa was complete, aside from perhaps the city of Septem (modern Ceuta). Such is the paucity of the source record that the exact allegiance of this city is unclear. Much like al-Kahina, Septem's commander, the *comes* Julian, became something of a legendary figure, with Roman, Berber and Gothic origin and/or allegiance ascribed to him by different sources, ancient and modern. 'Count Julian' may have repulsed Musa's forces from Septem, but, recognizing the futility of further resistance, came to some political accord with Musa, which allowed him to retain control of the city in return for some recognition of Umayyad suzerainty. It could also be that Julian redirected Umayyad aggression away from the walls of his fortress by encouraging Musa and his senior Berber general, Tariq b. Ziyad, to become embroiled in the ongoing Gothic civil war in Spain, between the supporters of the dead king Wittiza and his reputed assassin, Roderic. With a replenished army thirsty for conquest, Musa likely needed little persuading.[80] Umayyad raids on the Iberian Peninsula in 710 quickly turned into an invasion by Tariq in 711, possibly using ships provided by Julian and the Goths.

As Roderic was campaigning against the Basques at the time, Gothic resistance was limited. Tariq had perhaps taken several large settlements such as Seville, Malaga, Granada and Cordoba before the Gothic army could intervene. When Tariq and Roderic did meet in battle in mid-711, the result was decisive.[81] The Umayyad cavalry took full advantage of divisions in the Gothic ranks, leaving Tariq not just in command of the battlefield, but most of the Iberian Peninsula once Musa arrived with reinforcements. The only bright sparks for Christianity in the Iberian Peninsula were the ability of the Basques to remain largely unsubdued and the emergence of the Kingdom of Asturias in the north-west. Having thrown off an initial Umayyad conquest, Pelagius of Asturias defeated an Umayyad army at the Battle of Covadonga in either 718 or 722, a victory remembered as the catalyst of the *Reconquista*.

While portions of the Arab conquest of North Africa and then much of Iberia took place after his reign, the actions of Tiberius III, both in his usurpation overtaking John the Patrician's expedition at Crete and his lack of attempt to recover Africa, had a significant impact on the future of the western Mediterranean. Of course, his immediate successors must bear some of that blame as well, for none of those who ruled Constantinople in the period up to Covadonga made any concerted effort to reclaim or even halt the Arab advance in North Africa. The reign of Tiberius III may have 'made the loss of Carthage and the rest of Africa to the Arabs irrevocable',[82] but this should not be the only thing to be remembered about his reign. He had shown interest in all of the areas of the empire – the western islands, Africa, Sicily, Italy, the Balkans, Anatolia and Constantinople; his forces even winning some useful victories against the Slavs and the Umayyads.

But even with these significant actions on various frontiers, they do not perhaps represent the most important actions for the longevity of Tiberius' reign. Those actions were taking place in distant Cherson, and involved a barbarian incursion of a different kind and the unquenched ambitions of a certain noseless ex-*basileus*.

Chapter 11

Justinian's Exile and Restoration: Chersonites, Khazars and Bulgars

'I know how men in exile feed on dreams of hope.'

Aeschylus, *Agamemnon* line 1668

Chersonite Exile and Khazarian Dealings

While there continued to be strife at the centre and on the frontiers of the empire, there was another storm brewing in imperial territory. The noseless, tongue-slit Justinian II had refused to let his mutilation and exile remove him from the game of thrones. Not that there seemed like there was much he could do to further those ambitions in his current location. Founded in the fifth century BC by Dorian Greeks from Heraclea Pontica in Bithynia, Cherson was situated in the south-western Crimea on a site with access to deep water for use as a harbour. The ancient site of Cherson – *Chersonesos* meaning 'peninsula' – is now part of the modern Sevastopol. Under a mixture of democratic and oligarchic governments, Cherson took advantage of its strategic position to expand its own influence north, founding its own colony at Kerkinitida, near present-day Yevpatoria. By the first century BC, Cherson and its holdings had been absorbed into the Bosphoran Kingdom, which was in turn taken over by the Pontic kingdom of Mithridates VI, but then more permanently by the Roman Empire.

While located in a position with strong trade links and agricultural production, Cherson was also something of an island of civilization in a barbarian sea. Not only were the native Taurians considered to live 'by plundering and war',[1] but the Crimean Peninsula was frequently a target for the various peoples to occupy the Ukrainian steppe, including Scythians, Sarmatians, Jazyges, Roxolani and Alans. By the late fourth century, a combination of Gothic and Hunnic invasion had swept away the Bosphoran Kingdom, but some Roman foothold likely remained in the cities of the Crimea, probably including Cherson itself. Alongside this Roman foothold, the post-Hunnic peninsula hosted a group of Crimean Goths.[2] Indeed, Cherson itself would be regarded by later Russian and Georgian sources as 'a city of the Goths, where savage and pagan people dwelt'.[3] The breaking of Hunnic dominance on the Ukrainian steppe would also have seen Cherson confronted with Avar and then Bulgar pressure in the sixth and seventh centuries.

The involvement of various barbarian groups, together with the distance and difficulty of communication with other Roman provinces, had a considerable influence on the type of government prevalent in the Crimea. Rather than a single provincial administration, the territory that still owed allegiance to the empire was governed by a series of what were essentially city-states. Furthermore, the lack of firm control from Constantinople offered the same kind of semi-autonomy that the western exarchates had enjoyed. Therefore, 'the Chersonites managed their affairs with the fierce spirit of local independence that had characterised the city-states of ancient Greece'.[4] This Crimean 'otherness' in terms of geography, politics and barbarity not only made Cherson one of the last frontiers of the Roman Empire, but also a favoured destination for the empire's exiles. The potential bleakness of existence in Cherson is borne out in the letters of Pope Martin I, who was exiled there by Constans II – perhaps somewhat melodramatically, Pope Martin writes of how bread was often about but never seen.[5]

Such a barbarian setting does not seem like the place for a former Roman emperor to thrive; and initially, it would seem that Justinian did not do very much in his Crimean exile, at least not enough to come to the attention of the sources. Whilst in Cherson, 'he was not a prisoner in the strict sense of the word, for he had freedom to roam about the town and apparently to talk to whomever he pleased'.[6] He must have been something of a local celebrity as a deposed emperor who was still in the prime of life. That celebrity brought Justinian a following amongst Chersonite adventurers and young men, who were drawn in by the former emperor's person and no doubt became even more attached upon hearing the stories of his reign and family.

Along with these young adventurers, Justinian was joined by an abbot called Cyrus. Bede suggests that Cyrus was from Pontus and looked after Justinian during his exile,[7] while Nikephoros and Theophanes propose that he was from Amastris on the south coast of the Black Sea. This would mean that he either transferred to Cherson to join Justinian or that he had already moved to Cherson to serve as abbot. Perhaps the most important part of Cyrus' support was that he predicted that Justinian would recover the imperial throne.[8] Cyrus would later be rewarded for his faith in Justinian by being elevated to the patriarchate of Constantinople. Talking with these young adventurers, hangers-on and Cyrus may have helped keep the imperial fire alive in Justinian long enough for word of Leontios' own deposition at the hands of Tiberius III to reach Cherson. The continued instability at the core of the empire and amongst its military forces must have encouraged Justinian to view his deposition as merely temporary.[9] After all, while his enemies could remove his nose, they could not remove his Heraclian bloodline, and it was from that which he ultimately drew his right to rule.

Whatever the catalyst, Justinian was soon openly planning his own return to power. Could it even be that he had some kind of proclamation of his retaking of the imperial title, or did Justinian feel that there was no need for him to do so as he had never stopped being the emperor? The deposed *basileus* became so forward with his plans that the government of Cherson was worried that he would bring disaster to the Crimea. It could also be that the agents of Leontios and then Tiberius III were just looking for a reason to alter the arrangement of his exile or to do away with the deposed *basileus* once and for all. They therefore decided that Justinian should either be killed or sent back to Constantinople to live under strict imprisonment.[10] That the landowning oligarchs of Cherson could think about targeting Justinian in such a way would not only suggest that they were not a source of support for the deposed emperor, but also that the cadre of supporters Justinian had been able to surround himself with was of a limited size.

Before the Chersonites could carry out this plan, Justinian got word of the threat to his safety and fled north to the Crimean Gothic fortress of Doros.[11] Now a fugitive, Justinian needed to find support merely to ensure his own survival, rather than to further his ambition of retaking the imperial throne. The most immediate source of manpower would be the Crimean Goths, whom he was now amongst at Doros. Justinian may well have asked these Goths, only to find that they suffered from a lack of a sufficient centralized leadership. The Crimean Goths may have been similarly divided as the city-states of the region and/or generally lacking in numbers sufficient to take on the task of overcoming Chersonite forces or an imperial army. They may have felt that there was little to gain by backing Justinian, even if he was successful, while the downside would be to potentially bring the weight of an imperial invasion on their lands. The Crimean Goths may have had little interest in getting involved in imperial politics in general. Two centuries previously, in preparation for his invasion of Italy in 488, Theoderic the

Amal had seemingly reached out to the Crimean Goths, 'but they declined to participate in the Italian venture and stayed at home'.[12] Perhaps they disliked the idea of helping the empire at all or just disliked Justinian himself.

The ruling out of local Roman provincials and the Crimean Goths as the source of sufficient military aid left Justinian with only one option. Since the break-up of Kubrat's 'Old Great Bulgaria', overlordship of the lands north of the Caucasus and onto the Ukrainian steppe had fallen increasingly into the hands of the Khazar Turks. They were certainly in a position to field an army capable of penetrating into Roman territory, even with the distance between the northern Caucasus and Constantinople. Therefore, from his refuge at Doros, in around 704, Justinian reached out to the Khazar khagan, asking for sanctuary and aid in restoring him to the imperial throne. The exact name of the khagan is unclear from the surviving material. Many sources like Theophanes and Nikephoros merely relate to him by his title – khagan/chagan. The *Parastaseis Syntomoi Chronokai* records it as Ibouzeros Gliabanos, which could be a Hellenized form of the unrecorded Turkic original, speculated as Busir or Ibuzir-Glavan.[13]

Whatever his name, the Khazar khagan leapt at the chance to befriend the deposed emperor of the Romans, who was also a member of a dynasty with which the Khazars had enjoyed good relations in the past. Where exactly the subsequent meeting took place between Busir and Justinian is not known. The Khazar capital at the turn of the eighth century was at Balanjar in the eastern Caucasus, north of Derbent, but as the Khazars remained semi-nomadic, the likelihood is that the khagan maintained an itinerant court. This would have prevented the need for Justinian to travel across the breadth of the Caucasus to meet Busir. As the khagan was shown to be keen on making a good impression on Justinian through the honour with which he received him,[14] Busir may have moved his court close to or even into one of the settlements he controlled along the eastern shore of Lake Maeotis (Sea of Azov) and around the Cimmerian Bosporus (Taman Peninsula).

The 'imperial' visit to the khagan went well. Busir not only agreed to provide Justinian with sanctuary and support for his reclaiming of the imperial throne, but the alliance was sealed through the marriage of Justinian to Busir's sister, Theodora.[15] There is some discrepancy about the identity of Justinian's new wife; specifically, whether she was the sister or daughter of the khagan. The origin of this discrepancy is Nikephoros, who writes of Theodora's 'father' being involved in the plotting surrounding the khagan's upcoming betrayal.[16] It is more likely that this is a mistake for 'brother', but it does raise other possibilities, such as Busir's father still being alive or Justinian's bride being the khagan's half-sister. Theodora's original name is uncertain. Much later, it was suggested that it was Chikhak, a name from which the term *tzitzakia*, meaning certain state vestments, was derived;[17] however, it is not clear which Khazar empress this name refers to – it could be Justinian's wife or Irene of Khazaria, wife of Constantine V.[18] What is known is that when she married Justinian, she took the name Theodora and was baptized into the Christian faith. This, along with Justinian's staunch orthodoxy, suggests that their wedding ceremony will have been Christian in nature. It might well be imagined that Cyrus had a prominent if not even presiding role in these Heraclian nuptials. Such an imperial and indeed Heraclian marriage to a barbarian is not completely without precedent. During preparations for the climactic campaign of the last Romano-Persian War in 626, Heraclius offered his daughter, Eudoxia Epiphania, in marriage to a prominent Turkic leader, although it does not appear that this match ever actually took place.[19]

> 'One can only imagine the feelings of the young Khazar princess when informed of her brother's plan for her future. Like many nobly born women through history, she had probably realised all her life that she was destined to be a matrimonial pawn in her family's political games. Yet, she could have scarcely dreamed that the husband selected for her would be a disfigured fugitive, and if she approached the union with fear and disappointment, one could hardly blame her.' (Head, (1972), 105)

This marriage to Theodora, coupled with Justinian's orthodoxy, likely provides proof that Justinian's first wife, Eudoxia, was dead or at very least divorced from the deposed emperor. The choice of Theodora as his wife's baptismal name was also laden with significance. It was surely harkening back to Justinian I and Theodora, who had ruled the empire at a time when territories – Africa, Italy and Spain – were reincorporated into the empire: a rallying cry for the empire to enjoy a similar renaissance under a second imperial couple called Justinian and Theodora.

The newlyweds then moved to the long-established Greek, but Khazar-controlled, city of Phanagoria, the largest settlement on what is now the Taman Peninsula. That they seem to have stayed there for some time suggests that Busir was not yet ready to launch a campaign to restore Justinian to Constantinople. This would hardly be surprising given that for a steppe-dwelling people to militarily intervene in Roman territory for the purpose of regime change would require considerable preparation. Looking past the size of the army needed, whichever direction this Khazar strike chose to follow, it would be faced with significant distances and obstacles. The northern route around the Black Sea would have involved confrontations with various Bulgar and Slav groups and then any imperial forces in Thrace before reaching the walls of Constantinople. The southern route involved passing through the Caucasus, the opposition of the Caucasian kingdoms and possibly their Umayyad overlords, before crossing the territory of the Armeniac and Opsikion themes and then the Bosphorus to attack Constantinople. The most direct route, across the Black Sea, would involve the concomitant dangers of sea travel and the added expense of raising, commandeering or stealing a fleet of sufficient size to transport the military forces capable of coercing Constantinople into submission.

The size of the task facing him may have been dawning on Busir when he received another imperial visit to his court. While Justinian and Theodora enjoyed their Phanagorian 'honeymoon', word of the alliance between the ex-emperor and Khazar khagan had spread beyond the Caucasus, reaching the ears of Tiberius III at Constantinople. Rather than have to deal with a Khazar invasion, or even just the persistent threat of it, Tiberius sent an embassy to Busir, offering him great rewards 'should [he] send him Justinian alive, if not, at least his head'.[20] The khagan may have initially rejected these advances, as it took 'repeated requests',[21] but upon thinking over the situation, Busir concluded that Tiberius' goodwill and rewards were preferable to the risks involved in trying to put Justinian back on the throne. This way, he was guaranteed the goodwill of Constantinople without going to war with the Roman Empire. Within months, the alliance between the khagan and ex-emperor was at an end.

Rather than plan how he would get Justinian on the imperial throne, Busir now began to scheme how he would capture his brother-in-law. The khagan sent troops to Phanagoria, ostensibly to act as a bodyguard for Justinian 'under the pretext of preventing plots against him by men of his own nation'.[22] This was a rather understandable claim, as Justinian was sure to realize that his flight and alliance with the khagan would be reported to Constantinople and draw the attention of an imperial assassin's knife. However, amongst these 'bodyguards' were two men – a Khazar courtier/tribal leader, Papatzun, and Balgitzin, governor of the Cimmerian Bosporus – who were ordered to kill Justinian when the signal was given.[23] There seemed little reason for this plan to fail, as it provided Justinian with no suggestion of treachery. The khagan's moves seemed credibly protective; Balgitzin was the local governor charged with overseeing the security of Justinian and Theodora, while Papatzun was 'on friendly terms with Justinian'.[24]

The failure of the plan stemmed from some indiscretion within the ranks of the khagan's household. Some of his slaves not only heard of the plot against Justinian, but then passed word of that plot to Theodora. The young woman was now faced with a case of conflicted loyalty – would she stay quiet out of loyalty to her brother and khagan or would she inform and potentially save the life of her new husband? When push came to shove, Theodora chose her new husband, warning Justinian of the plan to kill him. Recognizing that his time was short, Justinian acted quickly but nonetheless calmly, so as not to give away that he knew of the plot. He set a meeting with Papatzun, who suspected nothing as he willingly met Justinian alone. The deposed emperor then sprang his own trap, attacking Papatzun and strangling him to death with a cord. Justinian then repeated the trick with Balgitzin. In two rapid strokes, the leaders of the plot against him were dead.[25]

Justinian was still in grave danger. He was caught in Khazar territory, surrounded by Khazar troops and with a Khazar khagan willing to serve him up to the emperor in Constantinople. Upon learning of the murders of his agents, the khagan would no doubt order the 'bodyguards' he had sent to Phanagoria to capture or kill Justinian immediately. Flight from Khazaria was Justinian's only option, but this raised two important questions. The first was the fate of Theodora. She was by this point pregnant with her first child, so she could not be taken along on such a dangerous journey. It was decided that she should return to the court of the khagan, where she should be safe.[26] With the first issue settled, Justinian then had to face the second problem with his latest flight – where would he go? He still had hopes of regaining the imperial throne, but Constantinople, Cherson and now Khazaria had all rejected him. It would have also dawned on Justinian that he had little chance of remaining incognito wherever he went as his mutilation made him rather conspicuous, regardless of any repair or replacement he had.

In the immediate aftermath of his murders of Papatzun and Balgitzin, Justinian's first objective will have been to remove himself from the reach of Busir. To that end, he snuck out of Phanagoria, arriving at Tomi, likely a nearby coastal landing site or a Phanagorian harbour.[27] It is unlikely that he was completely alone upon boarding ship at Tomi. The Armenian chronicler Ghevond records that Justinian's brother-in-law, Trouhegh, joined him and later died in battle outside Constantinople. The existence of another sibling of Busir cannot be corroborated and Ghevond is not the most reliable source, but perhaps there is a kernel of truth in this report, with Justinian receiving some support from amongst the Khazars, possibly even from kin of Busir.[28]

Maritime Escape to Bulgar Victory

The boat Justinian and his companions commandeered from Tomi limited their options of destination. Sticking close to the shore, they sailed south through the Cimmerian Bosporus and west around the south coast of the Crimea, which was dotted with various small and/or ruined towns such as Kimmerikon and Theodosia, the future Kaffa and modern Feodosiya.[29] Their initial destination was Symbolon (now Balaklava), near Cherson. Hugging the coast from Phanagoria to Symbolon would involve a journey of at least 350km, so depending on the weather, the size of the ship and the number of men it carried, it may have been necessary for Justinian to put in at certain points along the way. On any such stops, it would be imagined that Justinian would send his companions to collect supplies and intelligence for fear of his noseless face being recognized.

Upon reaching Symbolon, Justinian felt that he could rally some support from amongst those who had gathered around him while he resided in Cherson. He therefore sent a messenger to the city, who managed to round up a small band of followers. Between Nikephoros and Theophanes, we get a list of perhaps five new supporters for the emperor – Barasbakourios, his brother Salibas, Stephen, Moropaulos ('Stupid Paul') and Theophilos.[30] Nikephoros suggests that beyond Barasbakourios and Salibas, there were 'a number of other men',[31] which would seem to mean more than the three others listed by Theophanes. However many men Justinian rounded up at Cherson, this 'imperial retinue' soon moved on from Symbolon, sailing past Cherson. The plan was to continue following the Black Sea coast until they reached the land of the Bulgars.

This was no simple, quick journey. Following the coast from Symbolon to the mouth of the Danube, passing the Nekropela (the Karkinitic Gulf) and the mouths of both the Dnieper and Dniester rivers may have involved another 600km at sea. Given the danger involved, Nikephoros passes over this epic maritime voyage in virtual silence, merely stating that it happened. On the other hand, Theophanes records a moment of peril when the boat was sailing past the Nekropela, which Constantine VII described as 'utterly

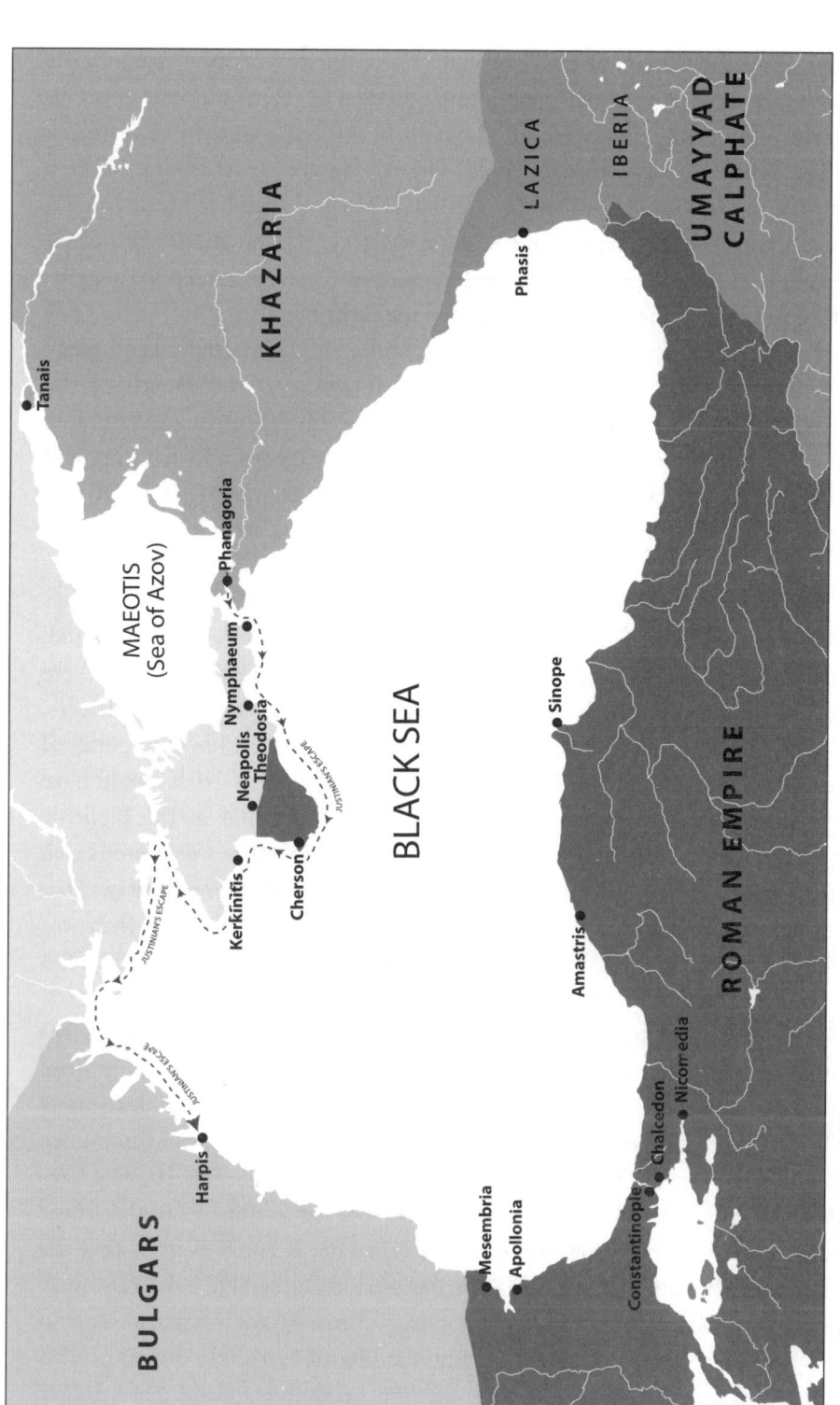

Roman Crimea and Justinian's Escape.

impossible for a man to pass through'.[32] As the sea became dangerously stormy, it seemed that the boat commandeered at Tomi was not going to survive. Thinking they were all about to be killed, a servant of Justinian called Myakes said to him, 'Behold, O lord, we are about to die. Make a promise to God for your salvation, so that, if He gives you back your empire, you will not take revenge on any of your enemies.'[33] In an answer fitting for the monster that Theophanes looked to paint Justinian as, he replied angrily, 'If I spare one of them, may God drown me right here!'[34]

The storm eventually abated, leaving Justinian and his petrified entourage to complete their 1,000km sail from Phanagoria to the mouth of the Danube. But why was this the disembarkation point for Justinian's saturated band of followers? His rejection by imperials, Crimeans and Khazars had left the deposed emperor with limited options if he was to try to involve himself in a struggle for the imperial throne. The Caucasian kingdoms were as likely to sell him to the highest bidder – Constantinople or Damascus – as they were to help him fight the Roman Empire, while his past dealings with Abd al-Malik made Umayyad backing both unlikely and unwanted. Justinian could have tried his luck with one of the thematic armies, where the Heraclian name may still have meant something to certain officers. But Justinian's treatment of Leontios will have damaged his own personal reputation with such men. Perhaps the only military forces that would have welcomed Justinian were those around Thessalonica and in the Hellenic theme; however, reaching them would have entailed either a dangerous trek through Balkan lands dotted with Bulgar and Slav raiders or taking his boat through the Bosphorus, past Constantinople, where the imperial fleet was likely to intercept him. In reality, his options were limited to just one, a people who both his father and he had had poor relations with – the Bulgars.

Since Justinian had reneged on the tribute payments agreed to by his father in the aftermath of the Oglos debacle, there had essentially been a state of war between the Romans and the Danube Bulgars. Justinian's Thessalonica campaign probably saw some Romano-Bulgar confrontations before the reverse in the Rhodope Mountains, while Tiberius III may have won a victory over Bulgars during his reign. That is not to say that these Bulgars were directly part of the Bulgar Khanate. It could even be that the peace bought by Constantine IV's tribute post-Oglos held relatively well, despite Justinian's reneging. Any lingering animosity with Asparukh could also have been set to one side following the khan's death. He was succeeded by his son, Tervel, who will have felt the need to reinforce his military leadership of the Bulgars and the other tribes that made up his khanate. The arrival of a deposed Roman emperor in his territory in perhaps late 704 provided the Bulgar khan with such an opportunity.

Sailing up the Danube, Justinian dispatched Stephen as an envoy to Tervel's court, in the hope of establishing an alliance to restore the noseless exile to Constantinople. Even if Tervel was looking to establish his military credentials, being asked to strike at the great bastion of the Roman Empire was a tall order. In their negotiations, Justinian probably played up how taking Constantinople would be more simple than it seemed, with his very presence outside the walls beside the Bulgar khan enough for the regime of Tiberius III to collapse. He also promised the khan many riches and gifts, to be topped off with the marriage of Tervel to Justinian's daughter.[35] Neither Theophanes nor Nikephoros name the daughter in question, but it must have been Eudokia's daughter, 'Anastasia'.[36] This raises the question about where Anastasia had been during her father's ten years of exile. The sources give literally no information about her whereabouts. Indeed, as an exile and now fugitive, it is unlikely that Justinian knew where she was or even if she was still alive. As the last 'eligible' member of the Heraclian dynasty, she posed a potential threat to Leontios and Tiberius III as she was capable of bestowing legitimacy upon an imperial candidate through marriage. These emperors may have considered marrying Anastasia to a member of their family, if not to themselves. If this did not happen, then Eudokia's daughter may have been confined to a nunnery, 'irrevocably committed to religious vows',[37] and therefore no use as a dynastic pawn.

Regardless of Anastasia's status in late 704, the promise of gifts, an imperial marriage and the chance to lead his army against Constantinople was enough to persuade Tervel to accept Justinian's offer of an alliance, receiving the deposed emperor at his court with honour.[38] This agreement was important enough for the Bulgars themselves to record it. An inscription at Madara in badly spelt, time-ravaged Greek lists a treaty made between Tervel and 'Rhinokopimenos'.[39] It also suggests that in building the army to take Justinian to Constantinople, Tervel reached out to other Bulgars, but they appear to have had long memories with regards to Justinian. In what seem like Tervel's own words in the Madara inscription, 'my kinsmen [literally "uncles"] in Thessaloniki did not trust the Emperor with the cut-off nose',[40] suggesting that they had fought against Justinian during his Thessalonian campaign.

Despite this snub from some Bulgars, Tervel had plenty of time to gather his army, for by the time Justinian arrived at the Danube, it was past the campaigning season of 704, negating any chance of immediate attack. Justinian was the Bulgar khan's guest through the winter of 704/705, allowing them to plan their advance and blockade of Constantinople carefully. Could it be that, while Tervel mobilized the Bulgars and Slavs under his control, Justinian used this time to reach out to potential allies in the Balkans and even the imperial capital itself? As already mentioned, he may still have had some support in Thessalonica and the Hellenic theme, while Tiberius' exiling of supporters of Leontios could have presented Justinian with some military aid. As will be seen later with Leo the Isaurian, Justinian did gain some support during his march through Thrace to Constantinople. That said, Justinian and Tervel may have decided to keep their plan as quiet as possible, in order to surprise the garrison of Constantinople, and so deferred from reaching out to Roman sources of manpower.

With the return of warm weather in 705,[41] Justinian and Tervel marched a large Bulgaro-Slav army on Constantinople – the Madara inscription mentions that Tervel gave Justinian '5,000', but of what is missing from the inscription.[42] Although 5,000 does not seem like enough to threaten Constantinople, if this was perhaps in reference to Tervel's 'royal' bodyguard, it could represent the Bulgar core of a much bigger army involving Slavs, Germans, Huns and ex-Roman provincials. Whatever the size of their army, Justinian and Tervel reached the imperial capital without having to face any opposition, which could hint at the extent of the surprise achieved, despite it being a Bulgar army led by a deposed and de-nosed emperor. It could also be that this was another instance of wait-and-see or cynical self-preservation from any Thracian forces in the field. Perhaps Tervel's force was too big for the Thracian army to contemplate challenging it, leading them to retreat to their bases or even back to Constantinople itself. Another interpretation has it that Tiberius had heard of Justinian's alliance with Tervel and recalled Herakleios from the Umayyad frontier to confront the Bulgaro-Slav army in the Balkans, only for the Bulgar khan and deposed emperor to ignore the *monostrategos*. They would surely only have done so if his army posed little threat to them in the field or while they were under the walls of Constantinople.[43]

Any benefit from surprise will have quickly worn off once Justinian and Tervel were unable to capture the city immediately upon their arrival. As had happened on many occasions before and would happen many more times in the future, the attackers were now confronted with the virtually impregnable Theodosian Walls, manned by the garrison forces of the imperial bodyguard and sections of the Opsikion army. The Bulgars and Slavs had little experience or expertise in capturing large, well-defended walled cities. Theophanes notes that the Bulgar camp covered only the section between the Gate of Charisus (modern Edirne Gate) and the Blachernae, barely a quarter of the entire length of the land walls.[44] This could suggest that Justinian and Tervel were focusing all their military power on one section of the walls, but it is perhaps more likely that they had no real intention of assaulting the walls or blockading the city into submission. Instead, they were relying on negotiation, internal betrayal or subterfuge. Justinian did engage in some discussions with the city inhabitants over the course of three days, but his demands for them to 'receive him as emperor'[45] were met with increasingly spiteful insults.[46]

With negotiation having failed and internal betrayal looking more and more unlikely, Justinian had to turn to stealth and subterfuge. This bore fruit when a breach in the walls was found, perhaps part of the Aqueduct of Valens, which entered the city near the Gate of Charisus. This aqueduct had been cut during the Avar siege in 626 and the wall there possibly not repaired until 767.[47] It could be that such a hole would only be found by someone familiar with the Theodosian Walls, possibly Justinian himself, or that someone from inside the walls showed the besiegers this way in. It was the deposed emperor who led an infiltration group of his most trusted companions through this breach into the Blachernae region. The presence of Justinian in the capital seems to have thrown the defence of the city into confusion. The infiltrators took control of Blachernae without any trouble, and the rest of the city appears to have followed with similar ease once word of Justinian's presence disseminated.

Just like that, ten years after his deposition, mutilation and exile, and perhaps no more than a year since he had to flee Phanagoria from the plotting of his Khazar brother-in-law, Justinian II was back on the imperial throne. He may not have been the first emperor to reclaim the throne after being ousted, but he was the first to return to the throne after suffering mutilation. This was supposed to be impossible. The whole point of disfigurement was to disqualify the victim from holding imperial office, but now a man perhaps wearing a fake golden nose to hide his scars sat on the imperial throne. The ease with which Justinian captured Constantinople raises significant questions about the popularity of both Tiberius III and Justinian himself. Tiberius had hardly been a poor emperor, but it could be that the inhabitants of Constantinople had not forgotten that he came to power through a prolonged attack on the city. His possible non-Roman origins may also have played against him. Furthermore, despite the insults and the presence of a Bulgar army, Justinian likely benefitted from some lingering support for the Heraclian dynasty, with the populace and garrison either refusing to help maintain the Tiberian regime or giving active aid to Justinian.

Re-establishing a Regime: Punishments and Propaganda

Justinian may have been happy to have achieved his decade-long aim to retake power, but now he had to effectively wield it. Would he learn from the mistakes which had led to his deposition, or would he make a further raft of mistakes? He certainly had a range of promises to fulfil, both of reward and revenge. There were also still some imperial opponents for him to deal with, and he had a wife and a newborn heir to bring from Khazaria to the imperial capital. It is impossible to ascertain in what order Justinian would have carried out the important issues facing him in 705. Indeed, despite using the same source, Theophanes and Nikephoros differ in their immediate order of events under the restored Justinian. Theophanes would have it that the emperor's first action was to fulfil the promises of gifts to Tervel, while Nikephoros focuses on Justinian's elimination of imperial opposition to him. A Roman emperor might not want to be seen relying on barbarians to fight Roman armies, but then Justinian had already crossed that bridge with his alliance with Tervel. It would seem more prudent for Justinian to keep the Bulgars around for a little while, just so the allegiance of the various thematic armies could be gauged and the opposition of Tiberius' regime could be dealt with. The lingering menace of the Bulgars could also be used to prevent any notion of a counter-coup in Constantinople.

Perhaps the very first measure carried out by Justinian was to inform his subjects – civil and military – that the normality of Heraclian rule had been restored. This will have included the issuing of coins both for propaganda and payment purposes. On his first coin issues after his restoration, Justinian chose to return to the Christ effigy he had innovated during his first reign and that Leontios and Tiberius had refused to use. This newer Christ does look considerably different compared to his original issues. He is now 'a young, curly-haired "Syrian" figure with a very short beard, rather than the Christ with long hair and flowing beard more familiar in the long tradition of Byzantine iconography'.[48] The reason for this change is unknown. Perhaps Justinian was trying to present a mix of continuity and change in his restored reign – he was the same but a better man. Perhaps this 'Syrian' Christ meant something specifically to Justinian himself.[49]

The reverse of his restoration coins featured the imperial portrait. It may have changed into something more stylized and even more idealized, 'but the thin, pointed face is unmistakably that of the same man'.[50] Unsurprisingly, the new portrait did not present Justinian's removed nose – the emperor must be shown as perfect, even if he physically was not.[51] As well as his thin face, beard and complete nose, Justinian wears a *loros*, a long ceremonial, jewelled scarf, and holds a large cross and orb in his hands. The orb is inscribed with '*PAX*' – 'peace' – which has been seen as a significant propaganda message from Justinian: after some years of trouble, the restored emperor was promising his people a period of peace. Justinian also innovated in his reverse inscription. Around the imperial portrait reads '*D N IVSTINIANVS MVLTVS AN*' – '*Dominus Noster Justinianus Multus Annos*', meaning 'Our Lord Justinian, for many years'.[52] Such a proclamation may demonstrate the hope Justinian had for his restored reign, but it may also be an attempt to rewrite recent history. Together with other issues, it seems that Justinian was claiming that he had never been deposed – the year 705 when he returned to Constantinople with the Bulgars was to him the twentieth year of his reign rather than the tenth;[53] 'He had always been emperor; it was as if Leontios and Tiberius Apsimar had never existed.'[54]

Despite this propagandist invention, Justinian could not help but demonstrate that these two deposed emperors did exist. He found Leontios, his fellow victim of *rhinokopia*, languishing in the Psamathion monastery, where he had been since being deposed seven years earlier. The other emperor to 'usurp' Justinian's twenty-year reign was a little harder to track down. In the face of his regime crumbling after Justinian had established himself in Blachernae, Tiberius III had managed to sneak out of Constantinople, escaping to Apollonia according to Theophanes.[55] It is not entirely clear which of the many cities called Apollonia this was, or even if it was in Europe or Asia. It certainly seems like there was a concentration of troops present in the city that Tiberius fled to, which could suggest Apollonia ad Rhyndacum in the Opsikion theme, directly south across the Propontis from Constantinople. Another suggestion, backed by Theophanes mentioning Thrace,[56] is that Tiberius fled north, either by land or sea, to Apollonia Pontica (modern Sozopol in Bulgaria), with the troops present being potentially those commanded by Herakleios and ignored by Justinian and Tervel on their march to the imperial capital.[57]

Either Apollonia provided Tiberius with a strategic site from which to cause trouble for Justinian: the European Apollonia could see him threaten Constantinople or Bulgar lands, while the Asian Apollonia ad Rhyndacum could allow him to drum up support from the major thematic armies. However, Tiberius' flight from the capital and the restoration of Justinian undermined the loyalty of the forces at Apollonia. If Tiberius and Herakleios were at Apollonia Pontica, the presence of the large Bulgar army in the field and at the side of Justinian would have further encouraged their desertion. Consequently, the forces with which Tiberius and Herakleios may have been able to lead a damaging opposition to Justinian simply melted away. The latest deposed emperor, his brother and several officers who had remained loyal were 'pursued, seized and brought to Justinian'.[58]

It may be that once Tiberius and Herakleios had been apprehended and their army neutralized, Justinian saw fit to deal with Tervel and his Bulgar army. He no longer needed the threat they posed as the thematic armies had accepted his restoration, but attempting to send Tervel and his men home meant having to make good on his promises of 'many gifts'.[59] It is here that we are met by what must have been a shocking precedent:

'[Justinian] showed many favours to the Bulgarian chief Terbelis, who was encamped outside the Blachernai wall, and finally sent for him, invested him with an imperial mantle and proclaimed him *Caesar*. He had him sit by his side and ordered the people to pay homage to them jointly, and after showering him with many gifts, sent him home.'[60]

Initially, it might be considered that Nikephoros misinterpreted the gifts Justinian gave Tervel, perhaps mistaking Theophanes' 'imperial vessels/regalia'[61] for an actual Roman imperial title, rather than overt acceptance of Tervel's regal position amongst the Bulgars. However, an official lead seal survives depicting Tervel, his monograph and the inscription Θεοτόκε βοήθει Τερβελλίου καίσαρος – 'Mother of God, lend Thy aid. [Seal of] Tervel Caesar'.[62] It would thus seem that the Bulgar khan was given the title of *Caesar* as part of his reward for aiding Justinian in reclaiming the imperial throne. There is no hint that Tervel was thought of as being part of the imperial succession, but this was a substantial break with precedent: a reigning Roman emperor bestowing an imperial title upon an undefeated, non-Roman dynast. For propaganda's sake, Justinian could claim that with Tervel as *Caesar*, the territories he ruled as Bulgar khan had been reincorporated into the Roman Empire and he himself took orders from the emperor. For the Bulgars, while not necessarily taken as an importing of Tervel into the imperial succession, it provided him and his burgeoning state with a further degree of recognition. It may not have had many long-term consequences, but for one of Justinian's first acts back on the imperial throne to be to besmirch the second-highest position in the imperial hierarchy by giving it to a barbarian khan was hardly a show of the continuity he wanted to portray.

It also must not be forgotten that Justinian had promised Tervel the hand of his daughter in marriage. There is no evidence that this marriage actually took place, with no suggestion that Kormesiy, the man to succeed Tervel as Bulgar khan and possibly his son, was also the grandson of Justinian through Anastasia. Could it be that Justinian tried to pull away from giving Anastasia to Tervel and instead offered the Bulgar khan the title of *Caesar*, however nominal? Rather than deliver part of the imperial family to a barbarian regime, Justinian may have decided to play fast and loose with imperial titles. However it played out, Tervel was seemingly happy with his reward as he broke camp and led his army back home. Even if his Heraclian bride was not to appear, an imperial title and being able to say that the emperor of Constantinople only ruled through his personal intervention, together with the riches Justinian undoubtedly gave him, galvanized his position at home and abroad.[63]

Justinian's attention then turned to his captured opponents. He might have claimed on his new coins that *PAX* was a major part of his restored reign, but if we follow Nikephoros and Theophanes, it would seem that from the moment he was deposed, mutilated and exiled, Justinian became an avatar of revenge, determined only to punish those who had wronged him while neglecting the governing of his empire once he was back on the throne. As will be seen, Justinian's restored reign was much more than that, with plenty 'to indicate his constructive statesmanship and genuine concern for his empire'.[64] However, even if it is accepted that sources like Nikephoros and Theophanes are exaggerating or even inventing Justinian's thirst for vengeance, there is no escaping that the restored emperor made a public spectacle of the execution of some who had either done him harm, usurped his authority or served those who had displaced him.

Sometime between August 705 and February 706,[65] Justinian had Leontios and Tiberius paraded in chains through the streets of the capital to the Hippodrome. In the same place where, eleven years earlier, Justinian had been the deposed emperor faced with losing his nose and tongue, the restored emperor could get his revenge on the man responsible for his mutilation. Of course, he could not have complete revenge on Leontios as his nose had already been removed. While he presided over celebratory races from his throne, Justinian had his two imperial captives thrown at his feet. Throughout the first race, he symbolically and actually stood on the necks of the two prostrate prisoners, showing to all those in attendance that he was supreme amongst all of those alive to have claimed the imperial throne. Theophanes records that this public performance of ultimate supremacy and submission sparked a biblical memory in the crowd, who chanted Psalm 91.13:

> 'Thou hast trodden on the asp and the basilisk;
> The lion and the dragon thou hast trampled underfoot.'

Such a connection was laden with puns: 'asp' (ἀσπίδα) for Apsimar and 'lion' (λέοντα) for Leontios, while 'basilisk' (βασιλίσκον) was not only a dragon-like beast of Greek myth, but also used to mean a petty king. It was also making use of the popular late antique scene of Christ treading on beasts, which may account for the crowd's recognition. For example, the Archiepiscopal Chapel to St Andrew in Ravenna contains a late fifth/early sixth-century mosaic depicting Christ as a soldier standing on an asp and a lion. Many in Constantinople may have taken this scene as the fulfilment of this biblical passage, almost as if it was prophetic, something which along with his Heraclian heritage will have helped people accept the restoration of the mutilated Justinian.

With this spectacle having served its purpose, Justinian saw to it that neither Leontios nor Tiberius were to follow in his footsteps of proving that deposition, imprisonment, exile and even mutilation were not insurmountable obstacles to the recovery of imperial power. There was only one permanent exclusion from imperial consideration – death. To that end, Leontios and Tiberius were taken to the Kynegion, an amphitheatre at the easternmost point of Constantinople, a popular execution point, where the two deposed emperors were beheaded. Their bodies were then thrown into the sea, only to later be recovered and reputedly buried in a church on the island of Prote.[66]

They were not the only victims of Justinian's return to the throne: various high-ranking nobles and officials faced execution for their perceived opposition to Justinian or support of either Leontios or Tiberius III. The latter's brother, Herakleios, and the officers who had supported him at Apollonia were all hanged from the walls of Constantinople.[67] The restored emperor then sent his own loyal officers to the provinces to root out any opposition, real or imagined. Through such vengeful dealings, 'Justinian destroyed an uncountable number of political and military figures.'[68] Some were invited to an imperial banquet, enjoyed the festivities and were then marched off to their execution. Others were tied up in sacks with rocks and thrown into the sea. Theophanes in particular highlights the sheer number of victims and that they included people from almost all levels of Roman society – soldiers, nobles, normal citizens: 'In brief, he treated his subjects with great cruelty and a savage disposition.'[69]

Another high-profile victim was the patriarch of Constantinople, Kallinikos. His willingness to support the deposition of Justinian and crown both Leontios and Tiberius III sealed his fate. That said, there was some restraint shown by Justinian with regards to Kallinikos. As a traitor to the emperor, even a patriarch would expect to lose his life, but Justinian settled for deposition and the admittedly horrific punishment of blinding. Much like *rhinokopia*, the putting out of eyes could be fatal, but the emperor could say that he had not tried to execute the patriarch. Any subsequent demise would be seen as judgement from God. Kallinikos did survive his blinding and was banished to Rome to live out his days.[70] It has been suggested that Justinian chose to send Kallinikos to Rome to present a warning to Pope John VII over the Quinisext canons; however, while this is an interesting conjecture, it is without historical backing.

Of course, this record of Justinian's brutality towards past emperors, patriarchs, army officers, officials and ordinary members of the public relies heavily on Nikephoros and Theophanes. A comparison with other sources, such as the *Liber Pontificalis* and Bede, can highlight some potential eastern exaggeration. These two western sources focus solely on the executions of 'Leo and Tiberius' and the punishment of patriarch Kallinikos, mentioning no expansive purge. This does not rule out any such purge but does suggest that the proposed extent presented by Nikephoros and Theophanes is overstated. It also does not mean that anti-Justinian bias was the sole preserve of the eastern historical tradition. Paul the Deacon's *Historia Langobardorum*, written nearly a century after the reign of Justinian, presents some ugly detail of Justinian's bloodthirstiness upon his restoration:

'Leo in banishing him [Justinian] cut off his nostrils and he, after he had assumed the sovereignty, as often as he wiped off his hand flowing with a drop of rheum, almost so often did he order some one of those who had been against him to be slain.'[71]

It is not clear where Paul got this anecdote from as it does not appear in any surviving Roman material – perhaps 'it is suggestive of a growing anti-Justinian legend'.[72] Certain figures in Italy would have reason for a lack of love for Justinian due to his dealings with Rome and Ravenna. If a historian or a regional historical tradition was going to make something up about Justinian, focusing on his mutilated face would be an easy target. Indeed, this brief paragraph sees Paul highlight perhaps four reasons why Justinian was not worthy of the imperial throne: his banishment, mutilation, poor etiquette and bloodthirstiness.

Other eastern sources highlight that Justinian allowed his reputed anti-aristocratic policies from his first reign to colour who he targeted in this so-called purge. Michael the Syrian records that he executed 'many of the great ones'[73] and sent many more into exile. If this was the case, it appears that Justinian had failed to learn one of the lessons of his first reign. A focused attack on the upper classes would again explain the poorer historical reception of Justinian, as it was these literate and leisured classes, along with clergy, who wrote the sources. That said, the presence of numerous patricians in prominent positions later in Justinian's reign suggests that any aristocratic purge was far from all-encompassing. Rather than targeting all aristocrats, it may just be that a majority of those targeted were aristocrats, not because they were aristocrats, but because they were prominent opponents of Justinian or supporters of Leontios or Tiberius III.

A clear example of how Justinian's purge may not have been as brutal or widespread as some of the sources suggest comes in the list of people who survived. There were not only some prominent aristocrats and generals, but also the one person who could cause dynastic trouble for Justinian: Theodosius, son of Tiberius III. The hostile chroniclers mention nothing of the survival of an imperial son after Justinian's restoration; indeed, it is only recorded later when Theodosius reappears in imperial politics as an iconoclastic ally of Constantine V.[74] By this point, in 753/754, Theodosius was the bishop of Ephesus (he probably had been since at least 729) and would preside over the iconoclastic Council of Hieria in 754. There has even been a theory that this Theodosius, son of Tiberius III, was the same person as Theodosius III, emperor from 715–717, the connection being that they were both bishop of Ephesus in the first half of the eighth century.[75] Such an identification would require Theodosius III to survive for nearly forty years after his abdication in 717 and it would be peculiar for Theophanes to record him as the 'son of Apsimaros',[76] rather than as a deposed *basileus*. It is also very difficult to square the perception of Theodosius III's post-imperial career as being of such outstanding piety that his grave worked miracles with the iconoclastic son of Tiberius III.[77]

While such a personal connection between these two Theodosians is unlikely, it does show that Justinian spared the son of Tiberius, so long as he took religious vows and joined the Church. This 'is in striking disharmony with the accounts that portray Justinian slaying all his enemies, real and imagined, with careless abandon'.[78] However, even if it is correct to doubt the extent of the post-restoration purge in the pages of Nikephoros and Theophanes, it does not absolve Justinian entirely. While he may have felt justified in removing various officials and officers who had supported Leontios or Tiberius, particularly any who had taken part in his deposition, it was to reflect badly upon him in the historical sources. Worse still was that Justinian, similarly to Tiberius, was removing a cadre of capable men from important positions within the civilian and military hierarchies, likely replacing them with men loyal to him but of little to no appropriate administrative or martial experience at a time when the empire faced considerable challenges.[79]

While the sources are keen to point out (and perhaps exaggerate) the extent of the punishments Justinian doled out upon his restoration, they are perhaps less keen to highlight the rewards he gave out to those who had helped him regain the throne. We have already seen his rewarding of Tervel, but there were others. With Kallinikos' deposition and blinding, the patriarchate was now vacant. Justinian used this to reward Cyrus, the monk from Amastris, for his support during his exile in Cherson and for predicting his restoration to the throne.[80] Tervel and Cyrus are the only two whom sources single out for their rewarding by Justinian, but there were more that can be suggested from other comments. Those who accompanied him in the dangerous sea voyage from the Crimea to the Danube must have received personal and professional reward. If Barasbakourios is the Georgian prince Varaz-Bakur, his support of Justinian likely saw him elevated to patrician, given the consulship/proconsulship and promoted to *comes* of the Opsikion. A certain Stephen Askemitos, who might be the same Stephen to join Justinian and act as his ambassador to Tervel in 704, is later recorded as both a patrician and a military commander. In 710, the Theophilos recorded as a patrician and *strategos* of the Karabisianoi could be the same Theophilos who took ship with Justinian. It could well be imagined that other occupants of the boat to make its way from Tomi to the Danube via Symbolon may have been rewarded with similar positions, such as patrician or membership of Justinian's advisors or bodyguards, particularly as the 'restored emperor had deposed and killed a number of officials and officers.[81]

Another person to whom Justinian showed his gratitude was the woman who had saved his life in Phanagoria –Theodora. Even in hostile sources, Justinian comes across as deeply devoted to his Khazar wife. While such spousal loyalty is to be applauded, in Constantinople and in the sources it may have reflected badly on Justinian. Regardless of how much he loved her and how loyal, fertile and interesting she might be, Theodora was a barbarian. With this barbaric heritage and the treachery of her brother Busir, it would not have been surprising to see Justinian repudiate her. Instead, he sent for Theodora almost immediately upon his restoration. His months of separation from his wife may have left Justinian ill-informed about her circumstances. Had she and her child survived childbirth? If they did, would Busir let them leave Khazaria to join Justinian in Constantinople? Worry over Busir's cooperation probably played into why Justinian sent a large fleet to fetch Theodora.[82] If necessary, the fleet could be a show of force; a reminder to Busir that Justinian had not forgotten the khagan's betrayal and a demonstration that Khazaria was not out of the reach of Roman forces. If the khagan was cooperative, the fleet was merely a ceremonial squadron to convey an empress and the imperial heir to Constantinople. However, this fleet was struck by a powerful storm, causing significant damage and casualties; enough for the remainder to not make it to Khazaria. Upon hearing of this destruction, Busir wrote a stinging rebuke to Justinian: 'O fool! Should you not have sent just two or three ships to fetch your wife and not killed such a multitude? Or did you think you would have to take her by force?'[83] The Khazar khagan finished his letter by providing Justinian with a dynastic update: 'Behold, a son is born to you. Now send and take them both.'[84]

This may have been the first direct news that Justinian had regarding his wife and child since Theodora had been packed off to the Khazar court after saving his life. Now, the emperor heard that not only had his wife and child survived the birth, but he had a son and heir. It could be that this news encouraged Justinian to not respond angrily to any such letter from Busir, dispatching a small retinue under the *cubicularius*, Theophylaktos. The Khazar khagan was good to his word, and soon the *cubicularius* returned to Constantinople with the empress Theodora and the new imperial heir.[85]

While an exact age is difficult to ascertain, Theodora's son must have been felt old enough to survive the potentially perilous journey across the

Black Sea. He was certainly born after Justinian departed Tomi, but even if Justinian's recapture of Constantinople happened in the spring of 705[86] and his apparent eagerness to have Theodora by his side is accepted, there is little concrete to date these events and therefore surmise what kind of age Justinian's son was when he arrived at Constantinople. The destruction of the first fleet sent to collect Theodora and son could suggest that it was still early in the sailing season, perhaps in the 'dangerous' period of 10 March to 15 May.[87] This may have made Justinian more cautious about the lives of his wife and son, leaving the journey of Theophylaktos to a more sedate, better-planned and safer time of the summer. The combination of his coins bearing a 'XX' and the *Necrologium* could suggest that Justinian had associated his son with his imperial rule before 10 July 705,[88] which would imply that Theodora had arrived in Constantinople before that date; however, this is based on the not universally accepted idea that Justinian became emperor on 10 July 685.

It should also not be overlooked that the travel time involved in getting Theodora to Constantinople would have added up. It involved four journeys across the Black Sea of about fifteen days each: the curtailed journey of the large fleet and word of its demise reaching Busir, the khagan's letter making its way to Justinian, Theophylaktos setting out for the Khazar court and then returning to Constantinople. Travel alone would thus have taken at least two months, before taking into account the time involved in decision-making, communicating and organizing these various trips, particularly the sailing of a large fleet. It could therefore have been the best part of three months from when Justinian first sent for Theodora to when she and her son arrived in the imperial capital, if not much longer. If Justinian left Phanagoria in the autumn of 704 and Theodora was likely pregnant enough to not join him on his flight, there is a good chance that she gave birth before the end of 704. This would mean that when he arrived in Constantinople in the summer of 705, Justinian's son was at least six months old.

There have been a few eyebrows raised about the name of Justinian's son and heir – Tiberius. Of course, it was a name with an imperial heritage and even some connection to the Heraclian dynasty, but both of these points bring what would be significant negatives to such a name. While there had been the emperor Tiberius (AD 14–37) and Tiberius II (574–582), the most recent imperial Tiberius had been the man whom Justinian II had displaced to reclaim the throne, Tiberius III. Furthermore, the most recent Heraclian Tiberius had been Justinian's uncle, and his fate at the hands of Constantine IV would not seem to make him worthy of such a memorial, unless he had been a favourite uncle and the emperor had not been particularly happy with the actions of his father towards Heraclius and Tiberius. It could be that it was Theodora who had chosen her son's name, although it still leaves questions about why she would have done so. Upon the birth of Tiberius, it could be that Theodora felt that Justinian was never going to return for her – his exit in a small boat for barbarian territory across the dangerous waters of the Black Sea would not have bred confidence. But if she thought that, why not give the boy a more obviously Khazar name? Was it loyalty to her husband? Could it be that the name 'Tiberius' meant something in Caucasia? Was Tiberius II popular there? Or did Theodora have her son's survival in mind? Even if Justinian had been given up as a lost cause on the high seas and the lands of the Bulgars by the winter of 704/705, the sheer fact that Theodora had just given birth to his son and heir made them a target in the eyes of Constantinople. Perhaps Theodora chose her son's name as a tribute to Tiberius III, hoping it would make them safer. None of these questions have answers; however, what is clear is that whoever chose the name Tiberius and why, Justinian accepted it.

Even with (or perhaps because of) having a wife of non-Roman origin and a half-barbarian son, Justinian moved quickly to have them appointed as empress and heir respectively. Almost immediately upon their arrival in Constantinople, Theodora and Tiberius were crowned.[89] Justinian himself oversaw this twin coronation, placing the crowns on the heads of his wife and infant son. More importantly, Tiberius was not just recognized as his father's son and imperial heir; he was officially proclaimed as co-emperor with Justinian. This kind of co-rulership was not unknown during the Heraclian dynasty, but it was rare for such a young infant to be established as *Augustus*. This likely demonstrates some insecurity in Justinian. For all of his propaganda about having never lost his throne, he will have realized that he was not exactly secure in power. He had been forced from his capital, marched a foreign army against that capital and supposedly been disqualified from rule by his mutilation. Promoting his son to co-ruler at least gave the impression of some dynastic security. The promotion may also have been looking ahead to the eventual reign of Tiberius. A half-Khazar coming to the throne may have caused trouble when Justinian was no longer around to protect him, so the emperor may have decided to have Tiberius share in imperial power early; by the time he came to rule by himself, people would be used to him holding an imperial position. Such thinking may be demonstrated on the coins issued after Tiberius' elevation. Despite his youth, the young *basileus* is portrayed as every inch the equal of this father – similarly dressed, both wearing crowns and together holding a large cross.[90]

While we can see the imperial portrayal of young Tiberius, Theodora is largely invisible, despite her having made the transition from barbarian princess to Roman empress.[91] One of the few mentions of her comes with regard to Romano-Khazar relations in the aftermath of Justinian's restoration. During his state visit to Constantinople, the Khazar khagan reputedly sat before a statue of his imperial sister.[92] The very presence of Busir in Constantinople after his betrayal of Justinian once more shows that the restored emperor was far from the vengeful monster the likes of Nikephoros and Theophanes would have it believed. This willingness to welcome a traitor to his capital also again demonstrates some of the insecurity and inherent weakness in Justinian's position post-restoration. One could well imagine that had Justinian been more secure, he would have not only been less accommodating towards Busir, but may even have been far more belligerent, perhaps threatening the Khazar footholds in the Black Sea. But in 705, freshly restored to the throne, Justinian required allies, and his attempts to garner them became an important part of his second reign. These attempts to find them may not have borne much long-term benefit to the empire, but the fact that he tried it at all is 'a sign of concerned statesmanship'[93] that Nikephoros and Theophanes would like to ignore. For Justinian to resort to some such diplomacy shows that he recognized the dangerous position in which the Roman Empire still found itself; a position that it was not going to struggle its way out of through sheer bloody-minded warfare. There would need to be some subtlety, willingness to compromise, resourcefulness and patience, alongside ruthlessness and aggression. In his battle to regain the throne, Justinian had shown all of those qualities. Now, he had to show that he could use them while in power.

Chapter 12

On the Warpath? The Restored Justinian in the Balkans and the East

'I believe in being everlastingly on the warpath.'
speech by American activist Carrie Nation

Ungrateful Emperor or Misidentification? The Battle of Anchialus, 708

After the executions of Leontios and Tiberius III and the arrival and crowning of Theodora and her son in Constantinople, there is a gap in the source record. Theophanes has no Roman activity for 707/708, focusing on the caliph's interference with a church in Damascus and some other anti-Christian actions,[1] while Nikephoros merely jumps from the crowning of Theodora and Tiberius to the next outbreak of war in the Balkans in 708. This could perhaps see a period of over two years, between early 706 and late 708, largely overlooked when it comes to Roman activity in the main sources. Yet it would not be surprising if, after his recovery of the throne and removal of enemies within, Justinian looked to consolidate his reign. Taking to the battlefield immediately upon his restoration would risk opposition rising in the capital or in the themes, particularly if he should be unsuccessful.

It could be that, in terms of foreign policy, Justinian used the months immediately after his restoration to build some alliances or at least reduce the number of enemies the empire had to face. While it seems to have included some military posturing from Justinian and a tetchy epistolary response from Busir, it could be that the negotiations involved in sending Theodora and Tiberius to Constantinople were more cordial than Theophanes portrays. It is worth noting that while Theophanes records these negotiations with an adversarial tone, Nikephoros merely states that the empress and the imperial heir were brought to the capital on Justinian's initiative, with no hint of any confrontation with the khagan. This might be Nikephoros removing detail from the source he shared with Theophanes or Theophanes having another source with more information, but it cannot be completely ruled out that Theophanes posited a Romano-Khazar confrontation where there was none. The very fact that Justinian accepted his Khazar wife and half-Khazar son will have reflected well on Busir's khaganate and improved relations between Constantinople and Khazaria. With Theodora and Tiberius now at the heart of the imperial regime, further improving of those relations seem to have taken place; enough for the khagan to make a state visit to Constantinople.[2]

Busir was not Justinian's only barbarian ally to visit the imperial capital. While his army had not been needed to force entry into Constantinople, as part of his reward from Justinian, Tervel the Bulgar was presented to the populace alongside the emperor. As with Busir, Tervel had played host to Justinian and promised him military aid; unlike Busir, Tervel had not tried to betray his imperial visitor and had followed through successfully on his promise. Thus, even with the marriage between Justinian and Theodora, the Bulgar khan seemed a more likely long-term ally than the Khazar khagan. And yet, while the sending of a large fleet into the Black Sea might be a hint of less than positive Romano-Khazar relations, it was against the Bulgars that Justinian waged war after his restoration. This would have included a rather dramatic falling out between emperor and khan since their cordial, even friendly relations in 705. However, there is some question over whether or not the Bulgars that Justinian squared up to in 708 were those of Tervel.[3]

Theophanes would have it that Justinian betrayed the Bulgar khan, breaking the treaty by attacking Bulgar-held territory,[4] but while Nikephoros also mentions the emperor's treaty-breaking, he does not mention Tervel at all with regard to the Bulgars whom Justinian fought in 708.[5] Could it be that Theophanes and to a lesser extent Nikephoros bought into the idea of the Bulgar khan being in control of all Bulgars south of the Danube? Or were they projecting the situation from their own time in the early ninth century, when the Bulgar Khanate was a much more well-established entity with more control in areas of northern Thrace, back to the early eighth century? As has already been seen, there were various groups of Bulgars in and around Roman territory by the turn of the eighth century, with Tervel leading only some of them. The khan had 'uncles' settled near Thessalonica, probably linked to the Bulgars who had migrated with Kuber, as might the Bulgars who helped ambush Justinian on his return from Thessalonica in 688/689. The limited source material places this Romano-Bulgar conflict south of the lands under Tervel's direct control. This could mean that either Tervel was the aggressor, taking Roman territory for Justinian to try to reclaim, or the emperor was not fighting Tervel's Bulgars.

The influence of the campaign of 688/689 should not be overlooked for this action in 708. Justinian may have seen it as a fitting twenty-year anniversary to win another Balkan triumph and gain revenge on some of the Bulgars who had ambushed him all those years previously. Could it even be that Justinian's Bulgar campaign of 708 had the tacit agreement of Tervel? Were Justinian's foes Bulgars who had refused to accept the rule of the khan, and Tervel now agreed to look the other way while Justinian attacked these renegades? Their cowing would not only give Justinian a victory to reinforce his restoration and perhaps see Tervel strengthen his rule over the remainder, but would also remove a potential flashpoint between the khanate and the empire, paving the way for further good relations. That such good relations continued is seen in 711, when Justinian asked for and received military aid from Tervel. If Justinian had fought Tervel, this would require a rapid falling out, war and then a restoration of good relations.[6] The Proto-Bulgar inscriptions at Madara contain an ill-timed break in their text, as they record '… they broke the treaty', but exactly who 'they' were is missing.[7] It could be taken as confirmation of Theophanes' claim of war between Justinian and Tervel, but with their working together again in 711, it could just as easily be a broken treaty in the aftermath of Justinian's death, with one of his successors perhaps being the man who 'broke the treaty'.[8] The likelihood is perhaps more in favour of this alliance being maintained and the Romans fighting other Bulgars in c.708 in something of an extension of Justinian's campaigning along the *Via Egnatia* and around Thessalonica two decades earlier.

If it was the Bulgars of Tervel whom Justinian went to war with in 708, there does not have to be much searching for reasons for such an attack. The Roman emperor could easily have felt that it was beneath his station to be in the military debt of a barbarian chieftain. There was also the matter of the title of *Caesar* he had bestowed upon Tervel: could Justinian have quickly come to regret such a precedent? It should also not be overlooked that Tervel himself might have had a hand in the breaking of the treaty. While making strides towards establishing a state, the Bulgar Khanate still contained many semi-nomadic peoples. Tervel may have been unable or unwilling to rein in these raiders, with Roman territory suffering. His role in installing the Roman emperor on his throne and his own title of *Caesar* – he thought enough of it to have it put on his seal – could have bred more ambition in the Bulgar khan. Perhaps he felt that he was the equal of Justinian and was emboldened to prove it through raiding or warfare. The Bulgar khan may have been presenting his new title, lands and large quantities of gold, silver, weapons and silk as not just rewards for the efforts of his men in restoring Justinian, but perhaps even something akin to a tribute payment. Such a presentation would have drawn the ire of Justinian, and defeating the khan's forces in battle could have been seen as restoring the natural order, demonstrating Roman superiority and reclaiming any ceded lands.

There was also the matter of the promised marriage to Anastasia. Such is the lack of information about Anastasia that several reasons for the failure of her organized marriage to Tervel could be suggested. Indeed, in the winter of 704, Justinian himself would have had little or no information about the whereabouts and circumstances of his daughter when he promised her to the Bulgar khan. She could easily have been confined to a convent by Leontios or Tiberius III, with the emperor, khan or Anastasia herself not wishing to go back on the religious vows she would have taken. More generally, could Anastasia have still been too young to marry Tervel in 705? The historical record gives no suggestion of when she might have been born, and while it might be assumed that it was early in Justinian's reign – perhaps within a year of his marriage to Eudokia – the only 'definite' date that can be ascertained is that Anastasia had to have been born by mid-696, nine months after Justinian's deposition and exile. It does seem that Justinian and Eudokia married early in his reign, so by 705, Anastasia could have been any age from 9 to 19, with the first section of that age bracket making her too young. Such is the dearth of information that Justinian might have found his daughter dead when he returned to Constantinople. For the failure of this promise of marriage to be a *casus belli* on the part of either the emperor or the khan, Anastasia would need to have been available for the marriage to take place, with Justinian refusing to sanction the match now that he was back on the imperial throne. Tervel could therefore have pushed for war to force through this marriage, or maybe Justinian went on the warpath to back up his rejection.

With the decision made to strike against the Bulgars resident in northern Thrace, Justinian mobilized 'a great army'.[9] Theophanes has the emperor deploying the thematic cavalry into Thrace, while overlooking the infantry that were involved. Indeed, speaking of 'thematic cavalry' could be something of an anachronism for the late seventh/early eighth century, with it becoming a more specific group within the army to face off against semi-nomadic enemies like the Bulgars. It must be imagined that this expeditionary force was mostly made up of units from the Opsikion and Thracian armies, with maybe some allied Slavs and Bulgars. Another major part of it was the navy, which was to transport a significant section of the 'great army' to northern Thrace. This in itself hints at the strategic aims of the campaign. Whereas in 688, Justinian had looked to clear the lines of land communication to northern Greece, now he was seeking to reinstate Roman control of the Black Sea coast, which would allow for later reconquest of northern Thrace. It could also be argued – if he was not the opponent of this campaign – that part of the aim of the 708 campaign was to secure land and sea communications with Tervel along the Danube. In another repeat of 688, Justinian was going to lead this expedition in person, which for all his propagandizing over how his reign had never ended, looks like a new emperor looking to stamp his authority on his reign.

If Justinian was trying to build on his earlier success along the *Via Egnatia* and into Macedonia and northern Greece, he was to be very disappointed. Rather than a repeat of his triumphal entry into Thessalonica, he got a replay of the Bulgar disaster faced by his father at Oglos. It started off well, with Justinian leading his large army and navy along the coast of Thrace to the stronghold of Anchialus (modern Pomorie in Bulgaria). In the face of such a formidable Roman land and sea host, any Bulgar forces that were present in the fortress either surrendered or were overcome in short order. As the Romans still held Apollonia Pontica to the south, establishing a tight hold of Anchialus (if they did not have it already) gave them control of the Bay of Anchialus/Burgas. From this base, Justinian's forces could have driven further north to the coastal cities of Mesembria and Odessus, and then perhaps inland to Marcianopolis. Alternatively, they could have driven west inland to Diopolis, Beroe/Augusta Traiana and Philippopolis, perhaps to force these renegade Bulgars back beyond the Haemus Mountains.

The ease with which Anchialus had been established as a base for the expedition seems to have bred complacency in the Roman ranks. With the fleet anchored in the bay and Anchialus occupied, the cavalry was sent to camp before Anchialus and then dispersed through the hinterland to forage for supplies. This was not irregular, but the complacency came in the form of the cavalry leaving the security of their camp and the cover offered by Anchialus without scouting the uplands first. Even a cursory investigation may have found that there was a sizeable conglomeration of Bulgars looking

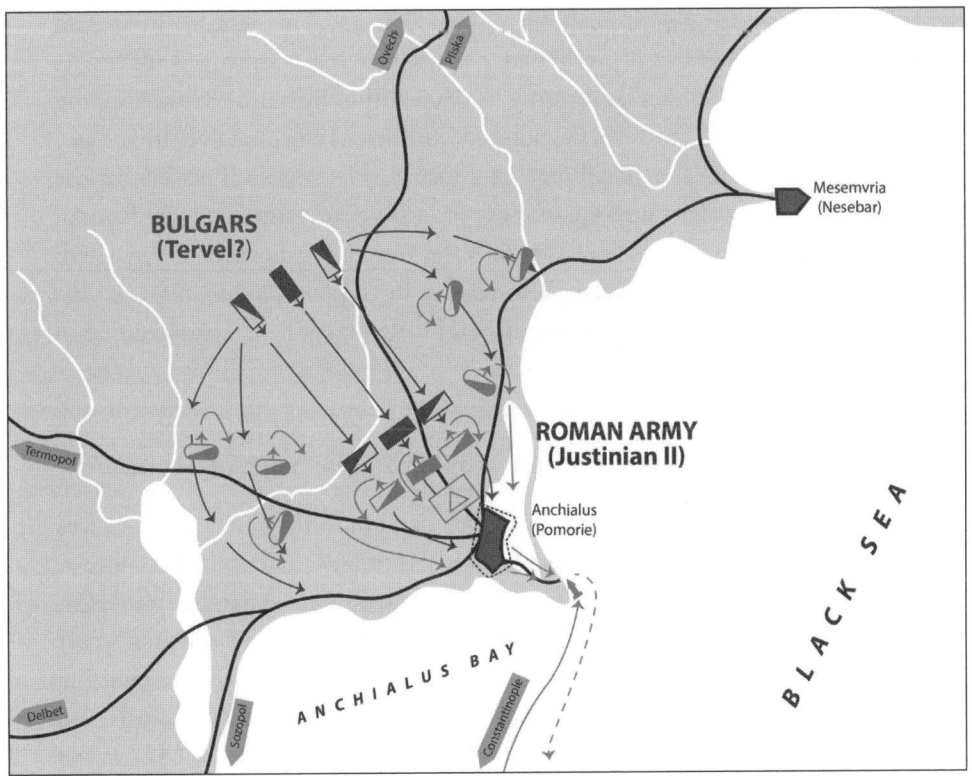

Battle of Anchialus.

down on the Roman forces. Unlike their 'civilized' opponents, these barbarians were paying close attention to the deployments outside Anchialus, with spies and scouts bringing word of the 'thoughtless behaviour'[10] of the dispersed Roman cavalry foragers. The Bulgar commanders, whether Tervel or not, decided to take advantage of this Roman recklessness: 'They came together like wild beasts and made a sudden, strong attack which destroyed the Roman flock. Besides the Romans who were killed, they took many prisoners, horses, and weapons.'[11]

This one sneak attack had shorn Justinian's army of a large proportion of its striking power. Many of the infantry might have been unscathed in camp or in Anchialus, but in a region where Bulgar raiders roamed, the loss of so many cavalry largely limited the expedition to the Black Sea coastal regions. However, it was about to get worse, dooming the expedition to ignominious failure. Egged on by their success against the Roman cavalry and possibly knowing of the emperor's presence, the Bulgars did not simply return to their homes. Instead, they moved against the Roman position at Anchialus, cutting the land routes in and out of the fortress. This left Justinian and his remaining forces in a precarious position, facing a landward blockade. Suddenly, any thought of continuing the expedition through coastal hopping from various Black Sea forts evaporated, and over the course of three days, the emperor faced the possibility of capture. He was only saved by the combination of Bulgar unpreparedness for a blockade/siege and the Roman control of the seas. After hamstringing the remaining horses to deny them to the Bulgars and posting trophies on the fortress walls, Justinian led his men under cover of night to the ships and sailed back to Constantinople in humiliation.[12]

New Arab Caliph, Same Roman Problems: The Siege of Tyana, 709

While this was not the best military restart to Justinian's reign, circumstances on his eastern frontier were going to provide another opportunity for success. Once again, an Umayyad army was driving into Roman Anatolia. However, while this had been a common occurrence in the 690s and the first years of the eighth century, the frequency seems to have dropped off around the time of Justinian's restoration. Rather than be anything to do with Justinian himself, any reduction was due to developments at the centre of the Umayyad caliphate. Just before he records Justinian approaching Constantinople alongside Tervel and his Bulgars in 705, Theophanes noted that 'in this year Abd al-Malik, the Arab ruler, died and his son al-Walid came to power'.[13] The specific date of the caliph's demise is usually given as 9 October 705.

There should be no overlooking the importance of Abd al-Malik's reign to the caliphate and much of the wider Muslim and non-Muslim world. After his victory in the Second Fitna, which had been by no means a foregone conclusion, Abd al-Malik made numerous infrastructural and administrative changes to the Umayyad caliphate, all of which made it a much more centralized and cohesive unit. He also encouraged the caliphate to have its own Arabic and Islamic identity. This involved the moving away from reliance on Roman and Persian coins with the introduction of the aniconic dinar and dirham and the establishing of Arabic as the state language. His great architectural achievement, the Dome of the Rock in Jerusalem, demonstrates the developing confidence of not just Umayyad architecture but of Islamic culture as a whole. This growing strength of culture and religion made Islam more appealing to potential converts, such as the Berbers in North Africa, and more of a unifying force within the caliphate. The centralization increased governmental revenues from taxation, which were in turn used for roads, the postal service and the establishing of an increasingly professional army. Moving away from the 'tribal mass', pay was to be for active soldiers and the hierarchies of power were made more meritocratic. This organization, backed by a centralized government with a clear Islamic message, enabled significant territorial expansion, with the conquest of Carthage and the absorption of Caucasia setting the stage for even more spectacular advances under his sons.

Given the success of Abd al-Malik's reign, it was perhaps no surprise that when his son, al-Walid I, succeeded him, he continued the policies of centralization and expansion, riding that wave to perhaps the peak of Umayyad success. Such continuity might suggest that the succession had been straightforward, and while by the time of Abd al-Malik's death in 705 it largely was, this hides some political and dynastic machinations within the Umayyad family. The initial plan had been for Abd al-Aziz to succeed his brother as caliph, only for Abd al-Malik to support the accession of his son. As governor of Egypt and 'overlord' of Ifriqiya and Barca, Abd al-Aziz was likely to have established his own people in the highest governorships of the caliphate. It would come as no surprise that the governor of Iran and Iraq, al-Hajjaj, encouraged Abd al-Malik to rewrite the succession plan. As it was, some potential dynastic ugliness was avoided when Abd al-Aziz died a few months before his older brother, leaving al-Walid I to succeed to the caliphate without opposition.[14]

The continuity of governmental policy under al-Walid was not just due to the success of Abd al-Malik. It also reflected the growing and perhaps even overshadowing role of al-Hajjaj during al-Walid's caliphate. While his father had used al-Hajjaj as a formidable and successful administrator, under al-Walid, al-Hajjaj grew even more powerful, becoming more than governor of Iran and Iraq and caliphal adviser. Although the success of al-Walid's reign was in no small part due to al-Hajjaj's guidance and continuing the numismatic, linguistic, infrastructural, cultural and religious policies of Abd al-Malik, his position as something of an Umayyad vizier was not popular within certain hierarchical circles and was to cause trouble for the Umayyads down the line.

In the meantime, from his position in Iraq and through careful choices of commanders, al-Hajjaj oversaw extensive conquests in the east under al-Walid. From Khurasan, Qutayba b. Muslim took control of sections of modern Turkmenistan, Afghanistan, Uzbekistan, Kazakhstan and Tajikistan. This brought the Umayyads into contact with the Turkic Turgesh and the western reaches of Tang China. Indeed, within two years of the deaths of al-Walid and Qutayba in 715, Umayyad Arab and Tang Chinese forces faced off at the Battle of Aksu, with the latter victorious, driving the Arabs out of northern Transoxiana. Further south, from 708/709, al-Hajjaj empowered his nephew Muhammad b. Qasim to expand into north-western India. By the time he was recalled after the deaths of al-Hajjaj and al-Walid, Muhammad had consolidated Umayyad control in Sind, expanded into the Punjab, curtailed some Hindu rulers and was planning a further campaign of conquest. While having nothing to do with al-Hajjaj, it was under the auspices of al-Walid that Musa b. Nusayr, as governor of Ifriqiya, brought about the definitive Arab conquest of North Africa and the Iberian Peninsula.

The massive spoils produced by these conquests in Central Asia, northern India and the Iberian Peninsula, together with the revenue brought in by further development of his father's taxation, allowed al-Walid's reign to encompass the largest programme of social welfare and public works the caliphate had yet seen. He provided financial relief for the poor and servants to assist the handicapped, while land reclamation, irrigation and canals were undertaken to expand the caliphate's agricultural capacity. Infrastructure projects saw the building of roads, way-stations, wells and street-lighting, while al-Walid sponsored or encouraged the building or restoration of several major mosques. His greatest architectural achievement was the Great Mosque of Damascus. Initially, a side-building of a cathedral to John the Baptist had been used for Muslim prayer, but as the Muslim population grew, a larger site was needed. The caliph therefore appropriated the church for Islam, converting it to a mosque and then substantially enlarging it to form the prayer hall and porticoed courtyard that still stands today. It was al-Walid's conversion of this cathedral that was included in Theophanes' only comment on Umayyad affairs between Abd al-Malik's death in late 705 and the outbreak of war with the Romans in late 709, where he accused al-Walid of having 'robbed the holy catholic church of Damascus out of the envy the sinner felt toward the Christians because of this church's surpassing beauty'.[15] Al-Walid also commissioned the expansion and beautification of Al-Masjid al-Nabawi – the Prophet's Mosque – in Medina, having it incorporate the graves of caliphs Abu Bakr and Umar and the Prophet Muhammad. He also oversaw the completion of the al-Aqsa Mosque in Jerusalem, the restoration and expansion of the Mosque of Amr b. al-As in Fustat and the Sanctuary Mosque around the Kaaba in Mecca.[16]

By the time he died in early 715, the conquests and building works carried out in his name earned al-Walid a place in a leadership triumvirate with Abd al-Malik and al-Hajjaj that oversaw the zenith of the Umayyad dynasty. On the surface, it appears difficult to disagree with the foreign success, domestic peace and prosperity achieved during his reign. However, it could well be that al-Walid received more credit than he personally deserved. Rather than providing any direction through his own leadership, al-Walid may have simply reaped the rewards of Abd al-Malik's careful stewardship of the caliphate. His main contribution to the general success and stability of the Umayyad caliphate between 705 and 715 might have been to let his father's appointees, such as Musa b. Nusayr and in particular al-Hajjaj, continue to follow his father's policies. It could be argued that Umayyad fortunes started to decline after al-Walid's death, but that may be more to do with the death of al-Hajjaj in 714 and the removal of his administrative allies by al-Walid's successors, rather than due to the loss of al-Walid's leadership. It could also be that some of the rot of al-Hajjaj's prolonged tenure had already set in, with al-Walid and his successors proving incapable of fixing it without upsetting the Umayyad applecart. Just thirty-five years after the zenith of its caliphal leadership, the Umayyad dynasty would be ousted from power.[17]

With so much going on at the centre of the Umayyad caliphate, it would be unsurprising that the first four years of al-Walid's reign saw no activity on the Romano-Umayyad frontier. However, contrary to the Roman sources, al-Tabari suggests that there was some Romano-Umayyad conflict in the first years of al-Walid's reign, but some of his recorded actions are unclear in date. He places the battle at Sision/Susanah in the reign of al-Walid rather than that of Abd al-Malik, which is unlikely given the reputed involvement of Herakleios. He also posits the capture of four separate Roman fortresses – Bulaq, al-Akhram, Bulus and Qumqum – by Hisham b. Abd al-Malik in around the same period, but these fortresses have not been identified and again al-Tabari's dating of such events is unclear.[18] There are similar chronological and geographical identification problems with al-Tabari's recording of a campaign by Maslamah in c.707 against the Roman fortresses of Qustanlin, Ghazalah and al-Akhram.[19] It must also be remembered that not only was the caliphate sending considerable forces to the east and west, but the previous round of Romano-Umayyad sparring had seen something of a reversal in Umayyad fortunes against the forces of Tiberius III. Even if al-Tabari's campaigns are taken into account, they were not having it all their own way. The rebellion of Abd al-Rahman had facilitated a Roman invasion of Syria in 700/701 and a possible double success in Cilicia in 703–705. Any Umayyad triumphs such as the defection of Sophene under 'Vahan Seven Devils' in 702/703 was offset by Armenian rebellion the following year, which required the recall of Muhammad to put it down, while an attack on Taranta had failed.[20] This situation may have made al-Walid happy with an unofficial peace on the Romano-Umayyad frontier until his reign was more settled and developments on other frontiers – such as the growing conversion of the Berbers – freed up some Umayyad troops to be used in Anatolia.

Al-Walid was possibly assisted in any such 'peaceful' Anatolian endeavours by Justinian II. The restored emperor seems to have been keen to cultivate good relations with the new caliph, releasing 6,000 Arab prisoners taken during the military successes under Tiberius III.[21] This bore some fruit, as al-Tabari has al-Walid asking for help from Justinian in rebuilding the great mosque of Medina. The emperor responded by sending 100 skilled workmen, gold and forty loads of mosaic cubes.[22] It was long thought that this, without confirmation in other sources, was a fictional tale created to make it seem that the caliph could demand men and supplies from the Roman emperor. However, an excerpt from Ibn Zabala, who wrote a *History of Medina* over a century before al-Tabari, provides some confirmation. Preserved in a work of the fifteenth/sixteenth century by al-Samhudi, Ibn Zabala has it that after being asked for help by al-Walid, '[T]he king of the Greeks … sent him loads of mosaic cubes and twenty-odd workmen – but some say ten workmen, adding "I have sent you ten who are equal to a hundred" – and 80,000 dinars as a subvention for them.'[23]

It should be noted that while there is no direct record in Roman sources of this mosque-building aid from Justinian to al-Walid, there is a similar incident recorded by Theophanes. He has Justinian sending Abd al-Malik some columns in 691/692 for the construction of 'the temple at Mecca'. The emperor's motivation was reputedly to prevent the caliph from taking columns from a church in Jerusalem, although there does not appear to be any confirmation of this incident in Arab sources.[24] Could it be that Theophanes or his source have misdated or misplaced the Justinian/al-Walid negotiations to earlier? Or does Theophanes record an otherwise unknown agreement between Justinian and Abd al-Malik, which demonstrates a basis for such a later agreement with al-Walid? If Abd al-Malik had carried out restorations using Roman materials and techniques in 691/692, al-Walid may have wanted to use similar material for his expansion. A third Arab source, the ninth-century Ibn Abd al-Hakam, records that al-Walid sent

Justinian 20,000 dinars worth of pepper as a gift, perhaps also highlighting some attempts at peaceful relations.[25]

If there was a period of peace in the first years after al-Walid's accession and Justinian's restoration, it was definitely over by 709, if not 707, with Maslamah's campaign against Qustanlin, Ghazalah and al-Akhram or al-Tabari's earlier dating of the attack on Tuwanah.[26] The Roman defeat at Anchialus could have encouraged a renewal of Anatolian hostilities, while Theophanes has it that the Umayyad attack on the fortress of Tyana was launched partly in revenge for the defeat and death of Maimun the Mardaite at the hands of the Roman general Marianos during an Arab attack on Cilicia – Maslamah had been responsible for Maimun's promotion to Antiochene emir.[27] The identification of this Roman commander and his success against Maimun is unclear. As Maimun was serving as emir of Antioch, his death could have been in connection with the possible Roman invasion of Syria in 700/701. It may have been during the Cilician campaign of Yazid b. Hunain, defeated by Herakleios near Sision/Susanah, with up to 12,000 Arab casualties, or the more doubted Roman success in Cilicia against the otherwise unknown 'Azar' in 703/704. Al-Tabari places the campaign in 705/706, naming Yazid b. Jubayr in command along with Maslamah and not mentioning the outcome.[28] The chronology of the Umayyad expedition against Tyana is also unclear. Theophanes reports it under the year 709/710, but Arab sources have it in 706/707 or 707/708. The other Roman source for the conflict around Tyana, Nikephoros, gives no chronological information other than placing it after Anchialus and before Justinian's dealings with Cherson.[29] The more usual modern interpretation is to see the Umayyad invasion begin in 708 and, after wintering on Roman territory, culminate in 709. It could be that the Umayyad attack on Tyana was initiated quite late in the campaigning season. With the siege supposedly lasting nine months, al-Tabari's capitulation in May/June of the following year would represent a commencement in September/October, although Michael the Syrian suggests that the siege ended in March, which would suggest an initiation by July.[30]

There is a little more information surviving about the campaign surrounding Tyana than some of the previous Romano-Umayyad conflicts in Anatolia, Cilicia and Syria. Sources agree that the Umayyad invasion was led by Maslamah and al-Abbas b. al-Walid, brother and son of the caliph respectively, their Syrian army reinforced by 1,500 men levied from Medina.[31] The Arab army won an initial encounter near or under the walls of Tyana against what must have been its garrison, which enabled Maslamah and al-Abbas to put the city under siege. What followed was a series of assaults and sallies, with Umayyad siege engines damaging sections of the Tyanan walls, but the Arabs failed to force their way into the city. Al-Tabari suggests that at some point the Arabs suffered a reverse 'from which they thought they would never recover'.[32] This may be reflected in Nikephoros' report that despite making some headway against the walls of Tyana, the Arabs 'were unable to achieve any further success and were intending to return home'.[33] It might even be that part of the Umayyad force had retreated or moved on from Tyana, possibly as the campaigning season came to an end and due to a lack of supplies, as al-Abbas becomes more the focus of al-Tabari's account at this point by refusing to leave.

This resistance of the Tyanan garrison allowed Justinian to bring together a relief army under Theodore Karteroukas and Theophylaktos Salibas. It might be suggested that it was the arrival of this thematic relief force that was the source of the reverse suffered by the Umayyad besiegers; however, neither Theophanes nor Nikephoros are glowing about the abilities of this Roman army. Both speak of a significant section of it being less an army and more a rabble of peasants, farmers and untrained militias. To make matters worse, Theodore and Theophylaktos squabbled over leadership and tactics. For them to bicker so much, it might be presumed that these two Roman commanders were of the same rank, likely the Anatolic and Armeniac *strategoi*, and perhaps that they were ill-suited to such positions but had to be promoted above their ability due to Justinian's 'purge' of the officers corps. It could be posited that their disagreement over tactics would centre on whether they should relieve the city first, attack the Umayyad force head-on, attempt to pin it against the walls of Tyana or look to wait it out.

Such divided leadership likely led to a compromised battle-plan with more than one immediate objective. With part of the Roman army made up of new recruits and/or irregulars, such confusion proved catastrophic. Even the potentially reduced Umayyad army of al-Abbas was able to first resist the Roman attack and then turn it into an embarrassing rout – 'many thousands were destroyed, and many taken prisoner'.[34] This one failed Roman relief injected renewed vigour into the Umayyad army and any thought of retreating from Tyana was forgotten, with al-Abbas deciding to winter before its walls. Theophanes reports that the Umayyads were able to undertake this winter blockade through the capture of the baggage trains and supplies of the defeated Roman relief force.[35] After what must have been a hungry and stressful winter, the inhabitants of Tyana realized that there was no further Roman relief force about to ride to the rescue. They therefore opened negotiations with al-Abbas, again joined by Maslamah (if he ever left), and the Arab commanders agreed to let the inhabitants depart unharmed if they would surrender the city. Once Tyana was delivered into their hands, the Arabs not only sacked and razed the city, but reputedly broke their word to its former inhabitants and marched them off into servitude and slavery in Arab lands.[36]

In the immediate aftermath of Tyana's fall, 'the enemy gained complete freedom to devastate Roman lands without fear'.[37] A small contingent of Arab raiders penetrated all the way to Chrysopolis, across the Bosphorus from Constantinople, where they 'massacred the local inhabitants, and set fire to the ferry boats'.[38] The initial response to such a declaration by Nikephoros might be to suggest that he was being hyperbolic for anti-Justinianic effect; however, he was not alone in presenting Tyana as a significant development along the Romano-Umayyad frontier. His partner in anti-Justinian bias, Theophanes, also presents an intensifying of Arab raids of Roman territory post-Tyana. Al-Abbas invaded again in 710/711 and 713/714, when he plundered Pisidian Antioch. In 711/712, Umayyad control of eastern Cilicia was strengthened through Uthman's capture of several fortresses, while Kamakhon (modern Kemah in eastern Anatolia) and its surrounding area were betrayed to the Arabs. In 712/713, Maslamah took Melitene and some surrounding fortresses, then in 713/714, he struck beyond Cappadocia into Galatia. It could be this western strike by Maslamah that was involved in Nikephoros' report of Arab raiders reaching the Bosphorus.[39] It seems that the destruction of Tyana had not only encouraged the reinitiating of annual Arab raids into Roman territory, but their striking further beyond the frontier through renewed Umayyad confidence, easier traversal of the Anti-Taurus Mountains and the feeble Roman reaction following the defeat of Anatolic and Armeniac thematic forces. Reaching Chrysopolis might seem like something of an outlier, but, in reality, it and various other penetrating raids were a precursor to an existential crisis looming on the horizon for the Roman Empire. The cascade of Umayyad success in the years following Tyana was to lead to the year-long Arab siege of Constantinople in 717–718.

Clearly, any attempt at peaceful co-existence with the Arabs had failed for Justinian II. It is likely that he had not put any great hopes in a lasting peace emerging from his diplomatic dealings with Damascus, but any time he bought had not been used well. Justinian was surely shocked by the seeming feebleness of his army's response to the renewed hostilities. Of course, a significant part of that may have been his own fault, with his removal of Leontios and Tiberius III's officers and replacing them with loyal but potentially inexperienced or incapable men – Barasbakourios was perhaps *comes* of the Opsikion by this point, while it seems too much of a coincidence for there to be a Salibas on the boat that sailed from Tomi and a Theophylaktos Salibas serving as one of the generals at Tyana. A lack of experienced commanders would have had a direct impact on the discipline of Roman forces and the training standards of new recruits. With the evidence of Tyana and his own personal experience of Anchialus, Justinian may have recognized the problems his actions had caused. At the very least, the emperor would surely have noted that his army would need time to breed its next generation of strong leadership and well-trained recruits. Unfortunately for Justinian, time was one thing he was not going to get.

Leo Konon the Isaurian and Imperial Machinations in the Caucasus

It was not just in Anatolia and Armenia that Roman and Umayyad interests were clashing during Justinian's second reign. In the north-western Caucasus, the Roman presence was in danger of being completely snuffed out in the wake of the rebellion of Sergios taking Lazica over to the Umayyads in 697/698,[40] and the Abasgians were showing signs of doing the same. Justinian had to find some kind of foothold in the Caucasus, and he chose to interfere with the Abasgians.[41] The problem was that with Bulgar and Umayyad trouble, the emperor did not have the military capability with which to launch an invasion of the north-western Caucasus. It was within the striking range of Busir's Khazars, but it could be that Justinian did not feel the want to involve his erstwhile 'ally'. The emperor instead turned his attention to some of the tribes that had so far escaped Khazar domination in the region or had accepted it but retained some local autonomy – the Alans, an Aryan people resident in the Caucasus for centuries.[42] Justinian needed to employ a reliable ambassador to 'financially encourage' these Alans to attack the Abasgians and his choice fell on a certain Leo the Isaurian.

The exact date of this Caucasian episode is not clear. It stems from the record of Theophanes, who recalls it – along with the story of how Leo came to be in Justinian's service – as part of his entry for the year 716/717, but he makes it clear that he is telling a story that happened in the past during the reign of Justinian II, likely late in his second reign.[43] Theophanes' excursus on Leo's background and adventure in Caucasia is a significant difference between his history and that of Nikephoros, suggesting that the former was able to use another source that contained information on Leo. It could be that Theophanes' original source for Leo's early life was notes taken by Leo the Isaurian himself.[44]

The story of Justinian's relationship with Leo began on the former's march with Tervel against Constantinople in the spring of 705. Passing through a region of Thrace colonized by some transplanted peoples from the eastern frontier, Justinian encountered a teenager called Konon, but known to his family and friends as Leo because he was said to be as brave as a lion.[45] Leo demonstrated that bravery when the Bulgar army passed through. He made his living as a shepherd, but recognized that the passing army would likely steal much of his herd without recompense. He therefore presented his 500 sheep as a gift to Justinian. The soon-to-be restored emperor was so impressed by Leo's ingenuity that he immediately promoted him to the position of *spatharios* (aide-de-camp).[46] This could be an example of Justinian's impetuousness, although it might also reflect his lack of Roman support at the time. A clever, brave and ingenious Roman recruit would be more than welcome, and as Justinian was offering Leo the chance to escape his repetitive and dreary rural life in Thrace, the emperor would expect loyalty from his new *spatharios*. It must also have come up in the course of Leo's interview with Justinian that the young man spoke fluent Arabic from his early life on the Syrian frontier. This may have encouraged Justinian to commission Leo so quickly.

Leo joined the Bulgar army on its march on Constantinople, and it is attractive – although unprovable – to suggest that this young Roman *spatharios* joined Justinian in sneaking into the city through the uncovered tunnel. The loyalty and ability Leo showed to Justinian proved the emperor's impulse correct, but the favour the emperor showed in return saw Leo face the jealousy of his fellow officers. The rapid rise of Leo from lowly shepherd to *spatharios* with imperial favour without paying his military dues makes this jealousy understandable, although it does not seem enough for them to try to get rid of Leo. But they did try, conspiring to produce a charge of the young *spatharios* plotting to assassinate Justinian and having imperial pretensions. Such accusations could easily have been a death sentence, and upon hearing them, the emperor summoned Leo to stand trial. It soon became clear that there was no evidence of Leo being involved in any such plot, and he was subsequently acquitted, his accusers disgraced instead.

The episode highlights that the emperor was not so capricious as many painted him: 'This glimpse of Justinian's dealings with a suspect is in itself significant; his willingness to give the accused an apparently fair trial reveals a less arbitrary side of his nature than is disclosed elsewhere.'[47] However, Theophanes would have it that the seed of doubt regarding Leo's supposed imperial pretensions had been planted, and 'if, indeed, Justinian did not wish to harm Leo openly, he did begin to feel anger towards him'.[48]

Not long after his acquittal, Leo was selected by Justinian for the dangerous mission of contacting the Alans north of the Caucasus and encouraging them to attack the Abasgians on the east coast of the Black Sea. In order to succeed, Leo was provided with significant sums of money, which he deposited at the city of Phasis (modern Poti in Georgia) before moving to Apsilia, crossing the Caucasus and travelling to the lands of the Alans with a force of locals. This use of Phasis as a 'bank' seems a peculiar choice, as the region of Lazica was recorded as being under Umayyad suzerainty since the rebellion of Sergios in 697/698.[49] Perhaps this early aspect of the episode is enough to start doubting parts of the story.

Upon reaching Alania, Leo was received with all honour due to an imperial diplomat, and through his abilities and the money (and possibly Roman military aid) he could promise, he succeeded in convincing the Alans to strike at Abasgia. However, despite having achieved his aim – Theophanes even suggests erroneously that the Alans successfully 'invaded and captured Abasgia'[50] at this point – Leo's position suddenly unravelled. The Alans received an embassy from the Abasgian chief, who informed them:

'As I have found, Justinian does not have anyone else who is as big a liar as this man. The Emperor made him go off to work with you against us, your neighbours. Leo has even lied to you about his promise of money, for Justinian sent a man and took it back. Give him to us and we will pay you 3,000 *nomismata*; also, we will not break off the friendship we have always felt.' (Theophanes, *Chron.* AM6209)

Unsurprisingly, Theophanes presents this rumour of an imperial seizure of Leo's funds in Phasis as true, with Justinian's motive being that he had believed Leo had plotted against him. The emperor then decided to use the Alans to get rid of Leo rather than strike at the Abasgians, with the supposed plan being that the Alans would do so when it became clear that he would not be able to provide the monies he had promised. Theophanes even has Leo believing that this was Justinian's plan.[51]

There are serious issues with this report. Its origin, the Abasgian chief, was the party most interested in thwarting Leo's mission to the Alans. Furthermore, such an action of undermining Leo does not seem in keeping with the views of Justinian. It has already been seen that Justinian oversaw the acquittal of Leo on a charge of treason. If the emperor really harboured misgivings about his young *spatharios*, would he not have used that trial to get rid of him? Could Justinian's feelings towards Leo have soured so much since the trial that he would have employed a convoluted trap involving significant funds and two foreign tribes in order to get rid of him? Would he really have risked such money and the potential enmity of both the Abasgi and the Alans just to rid himself of a single *spatharios*? It is highly improbable: 'Such indirect methods of ridding himself of a foe are strikingly unlike Justinian's usual course of action against his enemies.'[52]

Regardless of the truth behind this rumour, it left Leo in a difficult position, attempting to fulfil his diplomatic mission while dealing with the rumoured lack of funds, the seeming foreknowledge of the Abasgi and the supposed enmity of the emperor. Worse still was the attempted bribery of the Alans. At any moment, Leo could have found himself knifed by the very allies he had just struck an agreement with. As it was, the Alans stayed true to their word, refusing to betray Leo or go back on their alliance with the empire. They told the Abagasian ambassadors: 'We do not obey him on account of money, but because of our love for the Emperor.'[53] However, the Abasgians were not to be put off. Another deputation went to Alania and offered 6,000 *nomismata* to give up Leo. This time the Alans agreed, but only as part of a ploy worked out with Leo. As the Abasgians were blocking the routes back to Roman territory, the Alans suggested, 'let us turn around and agree with them to give you up. We will send our men off with them, learn their mountain passes, and raid and devastate their land to do your service.'[54]

Sending to the Abasgians, the Alans 'agreed' to give up the *spatharios* in return for gifts of friendship and the 6,000 *nomismata* payment. After keeping Leo informed, they then delivered him to the Abasgians, with the plan being that once the Abasgians had taken Leo through the mountains, the Alans would attack the column, free Leo and then seize control of the passes. This represented an awful risk by Leo. He cannot have known what the Abasgians would do once he was in their power; he might well have been killed rather than ransomed, while he was placing his trust in the Alans to save him from captivity when they could have just as easily left him to his Abasgian fate. As it turned out, the Alans again stayed true to their word, fulfilling their part of the plan. The Abasgians took Leo and his small band of men as prisoners and headed towards Abasgia, only for the column to be overtaken and attacked by the Alan leader, Itaxes, who freed Leo. A full Alan force then marched through the mountain passes to attack Abasgia, taking 'a great number of prisoners and [wreaking] destruction on the Abasgians'.[55]

Upon hearing that Leo's initial mission had been a success in bringing the Alans into the conflict on the Roman side, Theophanes would have it that Justinian now sought to use the Abasgians to get Leo into his clutches. In reality, Justinian looked to enhance the strategic benefit of Leo's mission by coercing the Abasgians into defecting to the Romans with the threat of further Alan raids, as well as get his diplomat back unscathed. He assured the Abasgian chief, '[I]f you escort our *spatharios* and let him pass through your country without harm, we shall forgive you all your transgressions.'[56] The Abasgians jumped at the idea that they could get on the good side of the Roman emperor at a time when he had the Alans willing to do his military bidding. They sent to the Alans once more, offering to give them child hostages, if they sent Leo to them so they could assist him in returning to Constantinople in order to be seen cooperating with Justinian's demand. However, Leo refused, saying, 'May God open me a gate so I can go away, as I will not do so through Abasgia',[57] because he did not trust the Abasgians or the emperor's motives.

Leo's refusal to accept Abasgian hospitality led to something of an impasse, with the *spatharios* unable to take a ship back to the imperial capital and the Abasgians unable to demonstrate their acceptance of Justinian's offer. If he had had nothing to do with any disappearance of Leo's funds from Phasis or knew nothing of the Abasgian rumour-spreading, Justinian would have had to come to other conclusions about the failure of Leo to return to Constantinople. He could have interpreted this lack of movement to repatriate Leo as a rejection of the terms of friendship he had offered to the Abasgians. He may even have thought that something untoward had happened to his diplomat. Could it be that Justinian's fear that the Caucasians had failed to adhere to the sacrosanctity of his diplomat led him to send an army into the region, or was military intervention part of the overall strategic plan for the north-western Caucasus from the start? While there might have been some time between Leo's rejection of Abasgian transport and the arrival of Roman forces in Lazica, the latter seems more likely.

The imperial force that appeared in Lazica was what Theophanes calls 'a force of Romans and Armenians',[58] but could perhaps be part of the Armeniac army. It attacked the city of Archaiopolis (modern Nokalakevi in Georgia), with perhaps the objective of marching north towards Apsilia, joining up with the Alans to isolate Abasgia further and then resist any Umayyad counter-attack. If that was the plan, the siege of Archaiopolis took too long or the Umayyad response was much quicker than predicted. Not wanting to be caught under the walls of Archaiopolis or in enemy territory, upon hearing of the approach of an Umayyad force, the Roman army lifted the siege and retreated towards Phasis, likely with the intention of taking ship for imperial territory. It had been another poor showing from Roman military forces under the restored Justinian.

So hasty was the Roman retreat to Phasis that 200 men, who were either raiding or foraging to the north of Archaiopolis, were first left behind and then cut off from the main group by the rapid arrival of Arab forces in Lazica. These men were left to take to the mountains and survive through raiding Apsilia and the Caucasus passes. The exploits of these Roman brigands attracted the attention of the Alans, who thought that this small group was the vanguard of a large Roman army in the region, rather than its remnant. They encouraged Leo to make contact with this force, and with fifty Alans, the *spatharios* set out across the snowy peaks of the Caucasus. Despite such an ordeal, Leo was soon disappointed upon finding these Romano-Armenian brigands. Not only did they explain that the army they had been part of had already withdrawn back to Roman territory, but also that the region was now overrun by Umayyad forces. This again left Leo with no obvious escape route.

The focus of the Caucasian episode then switched to the fortress of Sideron, in the lowlands of Apsilia and the borderlands between Abasgia and Lazica (linked to modern Tzibile in Abkhazia). Theophanes states that its commander, a certain Pharasmanios, was on good terms with the Armenians, despite his having accepted Umayyad hegemony. It is not completely clear from Theophanes as to who these 'Armenians' were: the Armeniac theme, Armenia in general or specifically the brigands operating in the area? Given them having raided Apsilia, it would seem more likely that Theophanes is referring to the 200 brigands having come to some agreement with Pharasmanios about leaving Sideron alone.

Such an existing connection between Pharasmanios and the brigands encouraged Leo to reach out to the fortress commander. The *spatharios* entreated him to extend his peace with the brigands to include Leo and ultimately the Roman Empire: 'Since you are at peace with the Armenians, make peace with me too, and become subject to the emperor. Help us go down to the sea and cross over to Trebizond.'[59] Gaining access to Sideron and the help of its governor may have allowed Leo and his new brigand friends to travel to one of the major settlements on the Black Sea coast, such as Sebastopolis (modern Sukhumi), where there could have been some remaining Roman influence preserved by the imperial fleet. When Pharasmanios refused to go back on his Umayyad allegiance, Leo decided that only military action would get him back to Roman territory. He sent some of his Romano-Armenian-Alan force to lie in ambush around Sideron, with orders to attack the fortress gates when they were opened to let the garrison out to work. This plan succeeded, with Leo's men capturing the gates and taking many prisoners. However, Pharasmanios was holed up in the fortress citadel; even though he had only a few men to defend it, the strength of its position meant that Leo could not capture it, nor could diplomatic overtures induce it to surrender.

This stand-off at Sideron was only resolved through the intervention of Marinos, leader of the Apsilians. He learned that Sideron was under attack and, fearing that this was only the beginning of a Romano-Alan assault on the region (and perhaps wary of a large-scale Umayyad response), Marinos dispatched 300 men to escort Leo to the coast. Seeing the opportunity to rid himself of the *spatharios* (or perhaps wary of the Apsilians), Pharasmanios now tried to treat with Leo, agreeing to serve the empire and give up one of his children as a hostage. As he now held the strategic upper hand, Leo refused to countenance negotiating with a supposed servant of the empire while he was still shut up behind the walls of a citadel. Leo promised that he would treat Pharasmanios justly and that he would only enter the citadel with thirty men. However, despite receiving Pharasmanios' word, Leo quickly broke his own, ordering an attack on the citadel gates which allowed the rest of his force to storm in. Having taken control of the fortress, Leo then had his men raze it to the ground. The *spatharios*, presumably with what remained of the brigands, then met up with Marinos and travelled first to Apsilia itself, where Leo was received with great honour, before heading to the coast to take ship for Roman territory.

Such is the lack of dating information about this Caucasian episode that it is unclear when Leo returned to Roman territory and whether or not he returned to Constantinople before the end of Justinian's reign. Theophanes would seem to suggest that he did, but there are doubts over the accuracy of this passage. If he did not, was it because he feared the reception he would receive from Justinian, or did the expedition take so long that by the time Leo was able to extricate himself, Justinian was already dead? There has been some suggestion that Leo did not return until c.713, which would involve the reign of either Philippikos Bardanes or Anastasius II.[60] Zonaras firmly states that Leo did not return during Justinian's reign, although as he was using Theophanes as a source, it could be that Zonaras has altered the story because it did not fit in with the reputation of Justinian or his supposed ill-feeling towards Leo.[61] If Theophanes is right and Leo did return to Justinian in Constantinople, the emperor did not take any drastic action against the *spatharios* despite the rumours surrounding the money at Phasis. This would be further evidence that Justinian's reputation for ruthlessly despatching perceived enemies is exaggerated, and may even 'indicate that Leo's fears about the emperor's ill-will toward him were groundless from the start'.[62]

The fact that Leo seems to have thought that the emperor was plotting against him would prove to have a significant impact on the reception of Justinian, even if no such plotting took place. This is because the reign of Leo as Leo III (717–741) was a period when many of the sources used by Nikephoros and Theophanes were compiled. An angry Leo, holding what he perceived as his poor treatment against his erstwhile mentor, may have coloured the depiction of Justinian in Leo's writings and propaganda, laying the foundation for the severe blackening of Justinian's name and reputation in Roman historical sources and public memory.

There could also be a religious reason behind Leo III's promotion of a poor depiction of Justinian II. Leo had introduced the policy of Iconoclasm – the 'breaking of icons' – and it was a very useful propagandist tool to depict the iconodule Justinian in as poor a light as possible as it reflected badly on Leo's opponents. Furthermore, Leo III's reign was beset by reports of pretenders claiming to be Justinian's son, Tiberius.[63] These pretenders were no real threat to Leo's regime, but the sheer fact that some Romans and even the Arabs, who sponsored one such pretender, made the attempt suggests that there was at least some notional latent loyalty to the Heraclian dynasty. Leo III 'may well have felt that anti-Justinian propaganda was a helpful measure in squelching the aspirations of anyone who might claim the throne as the fallen monarch's heir'.[64] However, even if it is attractive and supported by some circumstantial evidence, this Leonid origin of much anti-Justinian propaganda remains a largely unprovable theory.

Even if one of its long-term consequences was linked to the idea that Justinian had used it to rid himself of Leo the Isaurian, the reality of this Caucasian episode is far different. Rather than view it through an anti-Justinian lens, it should be seen as the north-western Caucasus theatre of the Romano-Umayyad war. Instead of some convoluted scheme to get rid of a single mistrusted *spatharios*, Justinian was trying to overturn Umayyad hegemony that had spread in the wake of the Lazican revolt of Sergios in 697/698. He aimed to do so by using a combination of diplomacy and bribery to pave the way for a military expedition. Buying the Alan entrance into the conflict and using them against the Abasgians simultaneously increased the number of Roman allies in the area and decreased the number of active opponents. Certain aspects of this plan worked well. Leo proved an able diplomat when dealing with the Alans and then a ruthless leader in the field in dealing with the Abasgians and Pharasmanios. The Leo-induced Alan raid saw the Abasgian chief eager to buy peace with the empire, while the presence of a Romano-Alan force at Sideron encouraged Marinos, leader of the Apsilians, to offer his services to Leo. The major aspects in the ultimate failure of this expedition therefore rest with the actions of the 'force of Romans and Armenians'[65] entrusted to undertake the military invasion. They failed to take Archaiopolis, retreated in the face of the Arabs and left up to 200 men behind in the process. This smacks of poor leadership and planning, underestimating the resolve of some Lazicans and the rapidity of movement the Umayyad garrisons were capable of. This in turn may reflect the damage done by Justinian in his replacing of the army leadership. Despite this failure, it should not have been overlooked by the Romans that the combination of diplomacy, bribery, military raids and the threat of greater military action had reaped some benefit in Caucasia amongst the Alans, Apsilians and Abasgians. Certainly, Leo the Isaurian would use parts of this combination in his subsequent military career in Anatolia and then on the imperial throne.

In his military dealings post-restoration, Justinian demonstrated some valuable strategic insights in his choices of target, as well as willingness to use diplomacy and bribery to the empire's military or political benefit. The alliances with Tervel and Busir may have been uneasy, with the former possibly even broken and then patched up regarding the events surrounding Anchialus, but they were potentially useful pacts. The Khazars could have been distracting raiders of the Umayyad's Caucasian dependencies, while friendship with the Bulgar khan could have been used to secure control over parts of the Balkans and would reap substantial reward for the empire in 717–718. Leo's machinations in the Caucasus brought about or strengthened a Romano-Alan alliance, made some headway with the Apsilians and saw to the Alan raid of Abasgia. Justinian may also have taken advantage of previous victories and a new Umayyad regime to perhaps bring about some limited peace in Anatolia.

Ultimately, however, all of Justinian's military operations post-restoration were blighted by poor performance in the field, and perhaps more specifically by repeated poor leadership of various thematic groups. Overconfidence and a lack of reconnaissance saw Anchialus rapidly descend from the first step in perhaps a wider reclamation of northern Thrace into an embarrassing disaster which put the emperor's life at risk. In Caucasia, the headway made by Leo's diplomacy, bribery and Alan raid was rendered largely moot as Abasgia, Apsilia and Lazica remained under Umayyad suzerainty because the 'force of Romans and Armenians'[66] that invaded Lazica failed to achieve anything. Then at Tyana, dissension between Theodore and Theophylaktos and a poorly trained army turned what could have been a battlefield success against al-Abbas and Maslamah into a strategic disaster worse than Sebastopolis, as Arab raiders streamed through the Anti-Taurus into central and even western Anatolia with increasing impunity.

Even if it is accepted that there was no significant 'purge' of the officer corps and *strategoi* upon his restoration, Justinian must shoulder some of the blame for this string of repeated leadership failures within the army. Tiberius III had also removed officers loyal or friendly to Leontios, but he had replaced them with men like Herakleios, whose personal ability in the field may have rubbed off on other officers in his role as *monostrategos*. Aside from Leo the Isaurian, who only became a *strategos* after Justinian's death, none of the men chosen by Justinian seem particularly capable of inspiring discipline, demonstrating good practice or dynamic leadership. This left Justinian's second reign punctuated with similar military setbacks to his first – defeats by Bulgars and Arabs – but with the minor achievements in Abasgia and Apsilia paling in comparison to his earlier victories over the Slavs and Arabs.

Chapter 13

Rome and Ravenna: Justinian's Revenge and Reconciliation

'If there is to be reconciliation, first there must be truth.'
Timothy B. Tyson, *Blood Done Sign My Name:*
A True Story (2004)

A 'Byzantine Papacy'?

It was not just in the eastern and northern reaches of his empire that the restored Justinian was deploying a more well-rounded, mature and diplomatic approach to his political dealings. In the west, the emperor looked to come to an accommodation with the papacy after the Quinisext-inspired debacle of his first reign. Romano-Constantinopolitan relations had not necessarily improved following the deposition of Justinian. While Quinisext was likely left to one side, Tiberius III had confronted Pope John VI through his new exarch, Theophylactos; a confrontation that had nearly come to open fighting outside Rome.[1] John VI and the citizens of Rome can also not have been happy with the failure of imperial forces to prevent the invasion of Campania by Gisulf I of Benevento. Past relations, both under himself and his second predecessor, likely made Justinian much more wary when addressing the pope and peoples of Italy in his second reign.

The eastern Roman sources completely ignore Justinian's dealings with the papacy, either because they reflected well on an emperor they were otherwise wanting to besmirch or because they cared little for the goings-on in the West. Fortunately, the *Liber Pontificalis* provides some useful information about East-West religious relations.[2] It has already been useful in presenting the disagreement between Justinian and Pope Sergius I, and almost as soon as he had retaken the throne, the emperor looked to revisit Quinisext. This aim was helped by the fact that his implacable papal foe of ten years previous had been dead since 701. Indeed, his successor, John VI (701–705), had also died after a pontificate of just over three years, so when Justinian looked to revisit the Quinisext canons, the pope was John VII.

A native of Rossano in Calabria, John VII was of Greek descent; his father was called Plato and had served as the imperial *cura palatii Urbis Romae*. This heritage is said to have made John not just the first pope to be the son of an eastern Roman official, but also a patron of the 'Byzantine' iconographic style. His pontificate 'witnessed a lavish program of artistic productivity that was fully within the mainstream of forms and styles then being fashioned in Constantinople'.[3] This artistic influence from the East has been used to suggest that John VII was also following some of the tenets of Quinisext. The decorations of churches such as Santa Maria Antiqua show more focus on the cross than on depicting Christ as a lamb. Indeed, his depiction of Jesus was similar to the numismatic depiction of Christ on Justinian's coins.[4] Such perceived acquiescence to Quinisext tenets may have led the decidedly anti-Quinisext *Liber Pontificalis* to consider John VII as 'a man of great learning and eloquence ... [but] terrified in his human weakness'[5] when it came to dealing with Justinian. This seeming accusation that John VII was tacitly giving in to aspects of Quinisext feeds into the idea that large sections of Rome's clergy and influential laity were being 'easternized', with a series of 'Greek' popes coming under the political and doctrinal influence of the emperor in Constantinople as part of the so-called 'Byzantine Papacy'.[6]

However, in the case of John VII, just below his very 'Justinianic' Jesus in Santa Maria Antiqua, there were some prominent figures which show that the pope had not given in over Quinisext. Along with himself, there were depictions of Pope Leo I, Pope Martin and probably Pope Agatho. These choices were very carefully made to send a message to Constantinople. Pope Leo I was a champion of the Council of Chalcedon and had presented a *Tome* that had supported the doctrine of Christ's two natures in the face of Monophysitism. Pope Martin had stood up to Constans II at the Lateran Council of 649, and had been arrested, deposed and exiled for it. Pope Agatho had been the spiritual father of the Sixth Ecumenical Council and represented the healing of the rift between East and West over Monothelitism. These embellishments at Santa Maria Antiqua and the messages they contain suggest that John VII was 'far less pusillanimous and irresolute a pontiff than the *Liber Pontificalis* portrays him ... [using an] adroit fusion of images simultaneously proclaiming Rome's obedience to Byzantium while asserting that the Roman church would remain inflexibly orthodox in matters of faith'.[7] When it came to the actual negotiations over Quinisext, the scathing tone of the *Liber Pontificalis* and its determination that John VII was scared of dealing with Justinian should be set aside for at the very least an 'unusually subtle and astute'[8] depiction of the pope.

Those negotiations began when Justinian sent two metropolitans to Rome with a copy of the problematic Quinisext *Tome* and an imperial letter called a *sacra*. It might be expected that the emperor would demand that the pope simply sign up to the canons; however, instead Justinian showed that he had learned from the failure of his uncompromising stance towards Sergius. Rather than demanding papal obedience to imperially backed decisions, Justinian was much more conciliatory, asking John to convene a synod in order to decide which of the canons were acceptable to him and his western colleagues. In response, the pope demonstrated what must be his anti-Quinisext leanings by refusing to hold a synod and sending the *Tome* back to Constantinople undiscussed, unchanged and unsigned. Such a rejection of Justinian's reasonable approach does not seem all that subtle. It appears a rather resounding 'no', following the Sergian hardline against Quinisext's 'various chapters in opposition to the Roman church'.[9] The only other potential explanation for what was 'a surprising response given the substantial concessions offered by Justinian'[10] would be to fully embrace the *Liber Pontificalis'* notion of John VII's 'human frailty'[11] in the face of the emperor. Could it be that the pope was wary of Justinian's reaction – particularly following his blinding, deposition and banishing of Kallinikos – to whatever he did, so he decided to do nothing?[12]

It seems there was little time for Justinian to react to this rebuff, either through more forceful means or taking advantage of any perceived weakness in the pope, as John VII died on 18 October 707. This led to a break in negotiations over Quinisext as the papal court went into election mode for the next three months. This produced another Syrian pope in the form of Sisinnius, but whether he was more open to Quinisext compromise than his predecessors or another Sergian hardliner is unknown. Indeed, next to nothing is known about his politics, because at the time of his election, 'this man was so crippled by a gouty humour that he could not take his food with his own hands'.[13] Even if he had a 'resolute mind'[14] and initiated some restoration of Rome's walls, it could be that the election of a potential stop-gap like an ailing Sisinnius demonstrates a lack of strong characters in the papal *curia* or even a significant divide amongst its members. Whatever the background to his election, Sisinnius ensured a further delay to negotiations by dying after just twenty days on the papal throne. This led to another *sede vacante* of two months, before the curial election produced yet another Syrian, Pope Constantine, on 25 March 708.[15]

This succession of two Syrian, Greek-speakers to the papacy in 707/708 at a time of negotiations with Constantinople has raised some concern over potential interference by Justinian's agents in the *curia*.[16] It could explain the election of Sisinnius, with the emperor thinking that he could readily influence or pressurise an ill Syrian Greek. Men of eastern origin like Sisinnius and Constantine may have been seen as less likely to oppose the Quinisext canons, which targeted some facets of western Church practice they may not have had much personal support for. The character of Pope Constantine is perhaps even more intriguing. Due to his upbringing, he could have been 'fully at ease in the oriental milieu of the early-eighth-century Byzantine court'.[17] He had already been to Constantinople twice by the time he was elected – he had served as a papal legate to the Third Ecumenical Council in 680/681 and delivered a letter from Pope Leo II to Constantine IV in 682.[18] Perhaps most importantly, during these capital visits, it is said that Constantine met and got to know the young Justinian. If this is true, then it does make Constantine's election in 708 a little more suspicious.

Blinding an Archbishop: Revenge or Rebellion at Ravenna

However, before Justinian could broach the subject of Quinisext with the new pope, both men were faced with another long-term problem that had politico-religious dimensions in Roman Italy: the recalcitrance of Ravenna. Neither Nikephoros nor Theophanes mention these Ravennate issues, which is somewhat surprising as Justinian's involvement could easily have been construed to further blacken his name. Yet there is a source for this incident, the ninth-century chronicler, Agnellus of Ravenna. In terms similar to Nikephoros and Theophanes, Agnellus records an attack by the forces of Justinian on Ravenna itself.[19] He claims that the motive was revenge for the role that several leading citizens of Ravenna played in Justinian's deposition and *rhinokopia*.

In this Agnellan guise, Justinian was willing to punish an entire city for the supposed actions of a few of its inhabitants, suggesting that his 'black legend' was well-established by the ninth century. It could be that Agnellus was a descendant of a victim of Justinian's intervention at Ravenna – Johannicus – and when writing a century later he was looking for a reason to explain Justinian's attack on the city that did not involve it being Ravenna's fault. The most famous thing about Justinian II was that he had been deposed and had his nose cut off, something which he would be eager to avenge. This makes it prime fodder for rumour, with Agnellus expanding on it 'with lively imagination and frequent echoes of Vergil's *Aeneid*'.[20] He had Justinian lying awake at night, thinking about what he would do to Ravenna. It could also be that Agnellus' connections to Ravenna may have given him access to some source material that otherwise does not survive, such as Ravenna's ecclesiastical archives, although such sources may not be entirely unbiased.[21]

Before we start tearing Agnellus apart for falling for this 'black legend', the *Liber Pontificalis* corroborates the record of an imperial attack on Ravenna during the second reign of Justinian.[22] However, the *Liber Pontificalis* lays out a far more substantial motive than Agnellus' claim of revenge. It says the basis for this violent imperial action against Ravenna lay in the pre-existing rivalry between Rome and Ravenna, which was itself centred on Ravenna's increased status as capital of the Italian exarchate and the brief autocephaly of its church granted by Constans II, but rescinded by Constantine IV. This increase in prominence led to clashes with Rome over the necessity of the archbishop of Ravenna swearing obedience to the pope upon taking his position. This rivalry had sparked into fighting in the past, although by 709, 'tensions between the two cities had lain dormant'[23] for about thirty years. Or at least they seem to have. Could the actions of the exarch, Theophylactos, in 701, marching on Rome at the outset of John VI's papacy, be in some way connected to the Rome-Ravenna feud? This might seem an attractive supposition, but there is not enough information to suggest how closely aligned the interests of the Ravennate exarch and the Ravennate archbishopric were. As a political appointee of Constantinople, the exarch should be following imperial policy, but given the loosening of central control over Italy, many an exarch, bishop and pope acted in their own interests.

More overt Rome-Ravenna trouble came after the election of Constantine as pope in 708 and then of Felix as archbishop of Ravenna. While Constantine oversaw the ordination of Felix, the new archbishop was quick to assert his independence from Rome. Felix refused to sign up to the customary official document – the *cautio episcopi* – which promised not to do anything that would compromise Church unity or the safety of the empire. He then compounded this move by producing his own version of this agreement which removed Ravenna from the purview of the papacy. Pope Constantine could not abide any such reduction of his authority, especially within Italy, rejecting Felix's attempted rewriting of the agreement. Constantine decried that this Ravennate-made document had been 'placed … in the holy *confessio* of St Peter the apostle, but after a few days it was found to be grimy as if charred by fire'.[24]

The growing dispute between pope and archbishop attracted the attention of Justinian. He may have felt that by standing up to the pope, archbishop Felix was also challenging the emperor, especially at a time when Constantine and Justinian were making some progress in imperial-papal relations. In widening the Rome-Ravenna divide, Felix was also sowing division in the empire, an action that could easily be seen as treason. Dealing with a recalcitrant Ravennate archbishop may also have been seen as a favour to the pope, making him more willing to compromise with Justinian; however, it will also not have escaped the pope's notice that the emperor was willing to use military methods to deal with what might be construed as a religious matter. Perhaps Justinian was providing Constantine with a veiled warning of the extent he was willing to go to not only to keep the peace in Italy but also to maintain religious unity.

Yet there seems to be even more to the imperial intervention at Ravenna than a dispute over primacy between the pope and archbishop. The whole episode is tinged with an 'air of intrigue'.[25] Agnellus sticks to the notion that Justinian sought revenge for some Ravennate involvement in his mutilation, but even with the blackening of his name, it would be a substantial leap for Justinian to launch a purely vengeful expedition against Ravenna. While it focuses on the religious dimension, the *Liber Pontificalis* does give some hints of political trouble, with Felix having the support of much of the local government at Ravenna.[26] This could include both civilian and military hierarchies, alongside the clergy, although there is no hint about what role, if any, the Ravennate exarch, Theophylactos, played in this episode. It has been suggested that the Ravenna garrison made an attempt on Theophylactos' life in 701,[27] which demonstrates problems between not just the exarch and Ravenna forces, but perhaps also between Ravenna and the central imperial government.

Could the root of the unrest be a more general resentment at the diminishing position of Ravenna and its exarchate as a whole? Not only was there the loss of ecclesiastical autonomy from Rome, but there could also have been the growing recognition that the territorial losses to the Lombard king and dukes were permanent. Another important administrative aspect to any disgruntlement within Ravenna and the exarchate was its declining authority over Sicily. In the last fifteen years of the seventh century, Sicily had been established as a theme in its own right, with a *strategos* commanding from Syracuse. This in turn saw many of the regions still under Roman and officially exarchate control in southern Italy increasingly look to the Sicilian *strategos* for leadership and protection. Such losses of prestige and power could easily have seen military and civilian officials band together in an effort to reinstate Ravenna's previous lofty position. This could mean that the imperial naval force sent to the city was not just there to demand ecclesiastical obedience to Pope Constantine in a show of force, but to compel obedience to the emperor, the pope and the empire as a whole by subduing an incipient insurrection. It is worth noting that while certainly not an unbiased source, the *Liber Ponitificalis* considered that 'the citizens of Ravenna were punished for their haughtiness with the vengeance they deserved'[28] and referred to many of them as 'rebels'.

Despite the contrasting reasons they give for Justinian's attack on Ravenna, the general layout of Agnellus' account has significant similarities to that of the *Liber Pontificalis*, enough for it to be suggested that Agnellus used the 'Book of Pontiffs' as a source.[29] Suitably perturbed by the actions of Felix and the local government of Ravenna, the emperor launched a fleet under the command of the patrician Theodore, *strategos* of Sicily. That Justinian did not charge the exarch with such a mission might seem a little odd, but while it could hint at some imperial doubt in Theophylactos' loyalty or ability, there is no proof of either. If there had been an attempt on the exarch's life by Ravennate forces, that could also explain why Justinian did not employ Theophylactos against Ravenna – he had already lost control of the men under his command. Furthermore, that the Sicilian *strategos* was charged with leading the expedition does not prove that there was any animosity between Ravenna and Syracuse. With the exarch deemed unreliable or unavailable, the Sicilian *strategos* was the only other imperial official of sufficient rank to lead such an expedition in the western Mediterranean.

Theodore's plan appears to have been two-pronged: target the military, civilian and religious leadership of Ravenna first and then deal with any rebellious reaction with more direct military action. The *strategos* arrived at Ravenna with his fleet, seemingly giving no impression of imperial displeasure. He then held a large banquet for various leading local dignitaries. When they arrived, they were conducted to the general's tent, where they were arrested in preparation for transport to Constantinople, to face imperial judgement. That Theodore could expect to carry out such a plan would suggest that any Ravennate rebellion was still in the planning stages, if not completely overstated in its existence. The plan went off without a hitch and a large section of the leadership of the city, including archbishop Felix, was taken prisoner and sailed to the imperial capital.[30]

When the Ravenna prisoners arrived at Constantinople, they were brought before Justinian: 'Agnellus, whose writing is full of vivid details, describes Justinian seated upon a gold and emerald throne and wearing a headdress of gold and pearls fashioned for him by his empress.'[31] His noseless imperial majesty initially planned to have all of the prisoners executed, only for a vision or dream to demand that he spare archbishop Felix.[32] This appears to be Agnellus again looking to explain an action of Justinian when the real reason does not fit his narrative depiction of the emperor: rather than it being the emperor's own choice to spare Felix out of religious respect, it must be divine intervention encouraging Justinian to act against his natural, violent proclivities. As it was, Felix was seemingly the only Ravennate prisoner to be spared execution – 'those who had disobeyed the apostolic see died a bitter death'.[33] That is not to say that the archbishop escaped scot-free; he was to be banished to Pontus on the south coast of the Black Sea. Before he was sent there, Felix was blinded. Agnellus records the rather peculiar method – a silver dish was heated to the point of incandescence and filled with vinegar, then the archbishop was forced to stare into the steaming vinegar until it destroyed his sight.[34] If such a method was used, it may have been so that Justinian could claim that he had not spilt the blood of an ordained archbishop, although there is no suggestion of such a bloodless but horrific method being used on Kallinikos.

These arrests were not the end of the matter. The imperial army of Theodore then forced its way into Ravenna and essentially sacked the city, looting the wealth of those imprisoned. Whatever Justinian's reason for the attack, he was determined that it was to be a lesson Ravenna was not going to forget. Agnellus would have it that this combination of Theodoran plot, Ravennate sack, imperial executions and archbishop-blinding sparked further rebellion in Ravenna rather than quelling it. The civilians and soldiers of Ravenna proclaimed a certain George, son of Johannicus, as emperor. It would be attractive to see this Johannicus not only as a victim of Justinian's executions, but also an ancestor of Agnellus, making this usurper a potential ancestor of the Ravennate historian. It might also explain why Agnellus attributes some rousing speeches, full of Vergilian quotations, to George.[35]

With regards to this usurpation, could it be that Agnellus has his chronology wrong? Rather than the usurpation coming after the sack by Theodore's forces, might it be that George was proclaimed emperor after the duplicitous banquet? Could it even be that the usurpation was the catalyst for Theodore's expedition in the first place? Such an order of events, with a rebellion coming before the sack or even initiating the Theodoran expedition, might fit in better with the brief report in the *Liber Pontificalis*: '[H]e captured Ravenna, arrested and confined that presumptuous archbishop on a ship, put all the rebels he could find there in shackles, seized their wealth, and sent them to Constantinople.'[36] However, even with their anti-Justinian stance, surely Nikephoros and Theophanes would have recorded an overt rebellion by the seat of the Italian exarch?

Details of the actions of the rebellion are scant, even though it may have continued in some form beyond the reign of Justinian II. Could it be that the exarch Theophylactos was a victim of these rebels, or perhaps he was one of them, sent to Constantinople or killed by Theodore's attack on Ravenna? Whatever his fate, Theophylactos was no longer exarch by late 710, for his successor, John III Rizokopos, was in the role in time to cross from Sicily to meet Pope Constantine at Naples. This appearance of Rizokopos in the record around the time of Ravenna's supposed insurrection raises further political questions. This is because the *Liber Pontificalis*, the only source to highlight Rizokopos' movements, has the new exarch march north to Rome from his Neapolitan meeting with the pope. There, Rizokopos 'cut the throats of the deacon [and *vicedominus*] Saiulus, the *arcarius* Peter, Sergius the abbot and priest, and Sergius the *ordinator*'.[37] It is not known why the exarch carried out the murders of these senior papal officials. Was he following the orders of Justinian, or could he even have been acting on advice shared by Pope Constantine in Naples? Given his desire to build on the cordial relations he seemingly already had with Constantine, it seems unlikely that Justinian would send his exarch to remove papal officials without the consent of the pope. But why might the pope have sanctioned the execution of four of his more senior officials? Perhaps they opposed any rapprochement with Justinian over Quinisext so vehemently that Constantine thought they would attempt something drastic in his absence.[38] It could be that 'the inclusion of the papal steward and the papal treasurer among the victims suggests a bid to empty the papal treasury'.[39]

This only looks at the potential motives of the emperor and the pope. What about the exarch himself? Could it be that Rizokopos had thrown in his lot with the Ravennate rebels? Killing the leading papal authorities in Italy may have been a way for him to remove religious opponents to George and Ravenna. The *Liber Pontificalis* speaks of how Rizokopos then marched to Ravenna, where he met 'an ignominious death'.[40] The automatic assumption in a time of rebellion might be to think that the exarch's forces were defeated by those of George, with Rizokopos being killed in the process. However, the *Liber Pontificalis* records Rizokopos' death in similar terms to those used regarding the deaths of the Ravenna dignitaries executed by Justinian – there was a divine punishment behind their demises: '[H]e went on to Ravenna where by God's judgment on his atrocious deeds he died an ignominious death.'[41] Unfortunately, this does little to resolve the mystery of the exarch's loyalties, because the *Liber Pontificalis* could judge him worthy of such 'an ignominious death' either for his killing of the papal officials or any siding with the Ravennate rebels, which meant siding against the pope. It is also noteworthy that the *Liber Pontificalis* does not say that Rizokopos was killed in battle or murdered; 'indeed, the fact that his death is described as *turpissima* may hint that it was the result of some foul disease.'[42]

The actions and demises of successive exarchs, Theophylactos and Rizokopos, do not provide enough information to come to any clear conclusions about a planned Ravennate insurrection or even a usurpation under George, son of Johannicus. However, they do suggest that there was considerable political turmoil within what remained of Roman Italy. This was further demonstrated by the fact that following Rizokopos' death – however it came about – there was an *interregnum* within the exarchate for well over a year. Indeed, by the time Scholasticus was appointed exarch in 713 and sent west with a letter declaring the emperor's orthodoxy, there had been significant developments at Constantinople. The inhabitant of the imperial throne had changed twice.

Bowing to a Papal Compromise?

If Justinian had influenced the western bishops to elevate Constantine to the papal throne and then intervened with Ravenna to gain papal support, he was to be somewhat disappointed in the lack of immediate papal quiescence. Pope Constantine might have been a moderate Syrian, but he was also 'a distinctly skilled politician'[43] who would prove anything but an imperial 'yes' man in his dealings with the Quinisext of Justinian II and the Monothelitism of Philippikos Bardanes. This alone was seen in how by 710, the Quinisext canons remained unsigned. Further delay, on top of the rebuff by John VII, the non-event of Sisinnius and his cowing of Ravenna and its recalcitrant bishop, led Justinian to send an *iussio* to the pope, demanding that he come to Constantinople to carry out negotiations in person.[44] This imperial missive made it 'obvious that the relentless emperor meant to settle once and for all the issue of Rome's acceptance of the Trullan decrees'.[45]

Previous popes had been similarly 'invited' to the imperial capital, but had usually ignored the summons or found an excuse not to go. Constantine is sure to have known that he would face considerable imperial pressure to compromise his stance over Quinisext. In spite of this, perhaps he felt he could work with his imperial friend, or maybe the tone of Justinian's *iussio* made it clear that this 'invitation' was not to be ignored. Politically, Constantine may also have had little choice. In the early eighth century, the papacy was not in much of a position to risk a break with Constantinople. The threat of the Lombards, the continued obstinacy of Ravenna, the spreading power of Islam into the western Mediterranean and the potential for rebellious imperial forces throughout the exarchate made the support of Constantinople increasingly necessary.[46] It would also not do to be seen being rather ungrateful for the help Justinian and his Sicilian *strategos* had provided against Felix and Ravenna. Any loss of prestige or imperial favour could tip the balance of power in Italy in a negative direction.

Justinian's *iussio* likely arrived in Rome by early autumn 710. This left Constantine time to gather a fleet and choose his retinue for the journey east once he had decided to go. The list of men who joined Constantine in heading to the imperial capital demonstrates the possible changing ethnicity of the papal court and perhaps much of the Roman/Italian Church. Of the thirteen names recorded by the *Liber Pontificalis*, eleven were of eastern provenance – Niketas, bishop of Silva Candida; Georgios, bishop of Portus; priests called Michael, Paulus and Georgios; the *secundicerius* Georgios; Ioannes, chief of the *defensores*; Cosmas the *sakellarios*; the *nomenclator* Sisinnius; Sergius the *scriniarius*; and a subdeacon called Dorotheos. The only recorded Latin names were a subdeacon called Julian and a deacon called Gregory, the future Pope Gregory II. The entourage was bigger than this list, but of the other 'few clerics from the remaining ranks of the church',[47] none are named. Not only does the *Liber Pontificalis* preserve this list of the members of the papal entourage, but it also records much of the papal itinerary for the journey to Constantinople.[48] There are hints too of the organization undertaken not just by the papal court, but by the imperial chancery.

His fleet prepared and retinue chosen, Constantine departed Rome through the Portus Romanus on 5 October 710. The fact that Pope Constantine set off for the eastern capital in October suggests that he was wary of appearing to ignore Justinian. It was late in the year for such a sea journey. It seems that the weather did hinder the advance of the papal retinue, with it having to spend considerable time in several places. Putting in at Naples, the pope met the Ravennate exarch, John Rizokopos. It was after this meeting that the exarch marched north and unceremoniously executed four papal officials. The possibility that Constantine knew or at least heard of these executions as he continued east, but did not interrupt his journey, suggests that he welcomed them to some extent or did not think them drastic enough to not keep his imperial 'invitation'. That the priest Georgios remained in Naples, possibly with Rizokopos, after the papal meeting with the exarch might seem a little suspicious.[49]

The next papal stop was in Sicily where he met the *strategos*, Theodore, 'conqueror' of Ravenna. The exact meeting place is not recorded, but the fact that the pope then went through Rhegium would suggest Messana just across the straits from Rhegium, unless the papal fleet went back on itself by going through the Straits of Messina, down to the thematic capital at Syracuse and back north to Rhegium. It might be that Theodore undertook the journey north from his capital to Messana because he was 'weakened by illness'.[50] By showing the pope welcome and reverence, he was said to be cured.[51] From Rhegium, the papal fleet rounded the Italian toe to Croton and then crossed the Gulf of Taranto to Gallipoli in Apulia, where Bishop Niketas died. The fleet then rounded the Italian heel to spend the winter in Otranto. Word reached Justinian of the pope's departure from Rome, and perhaps also of his slow progress. The emperor therefore sent the *regionarius*, Theophanios, to present the pope with a *sighillion*, which contained the order that every Roman officer who met the pope on his journey was to treat him as if he was the emperor and render any support they could.[52] It could be imagined that the emperor sent similar messages to the various imperial officials, towns and cities along the proposed papal route to have them ready for their visitor.

When the sailing season began again, Constantine crossed to Greece, probably putting in on some of the larger islands – Corfu, Cephalonia, Cythera – before entering the Aegean Sea. The only island he is recorded as visiting is Chios, where he was met by Theophilos, patrician and *strategos* of the Karabisianoi theme.[53] Theophilos received the pope 'with the highest honour'[54] and escorted him to Constantinople. The wintry weather meant that it was likely well into the spring of 711 before Constantine approached the imperial capital. Having landed in the harbour of Hebdomon, the pope was met at the 7-mile marker by a ceremonial delegation of patricians, nobles, clergy and ordinary citizens from the city, led by patriarch Cyrus and the now 6-year-old co-emperor, Tiberius. All those greeting the pope were lavishly dressed, their horses bedecked in impressive saddles, gilded bridles and rich fabrics. As word of the pope's arrival spread, more ordinary people poured out of the city to join what took on the appearance of an imperial *adventus* ('arrival'). Entering through the Golden Gate, the procession then travelled down the Mese, the central avenue of Constantinople, 'through the very heart of the city, with its colonnaded squares, triumphal arches and columns, porticoes and statues which truly conveyed the idea of the late antique "Roman façade" of Constantinople'.[55] It eventually arrived at the Palace of Placidia, which had become the customary residence of any visiting papal dignitaries. But this would be the last time a pope visited Constantinople until Pope Paul VI went to Istanbul in 1967.

The one thing missing from this lavish display was the emperor himself, who was in Nicaea. Is there anything to be read into this imperial absence from the capital at a time when he knew the pope would soon be arriving? Might Justinian not have wanted a public display of submission to the pope in the imperial capital, or was it that Justinian's attention was needed in Asia Minor, perhaps due to Arab raids following the fall of Tyana? Whatever the case, upon hearing of the papal arrival in the capital, Justinian reacted with great joy. He urged the pope to cross to Asia Minor and meet him at Nicomedia; an invitation that Constantine duly accepted. The eventual meeting between pope and emperor was accompanied by more lavish ceremony, with Justinian reputedly bowing to kiss the pope's feet.[56] Was such a show of imperial *proskynesis* likely? The *Liber Pontificalis* records other emperors prostrating themselves before popes, such as Justin I meeting Pope John I and Justinian I meeting Pope Agapitus.[57] But while there might be recorded precedent for Justinian II showing such deference to Constantine, it comes from western sources, who would be keen to present various emperors of Constantinople showing themselves and their position as inferior to that of the Bishop of Rome. Could it be that the likes of the *Liber Pontificalis* have created a tradition of imperial deference to the pope out of exchanges of mutual respect, including a similar showing between Justinian and Constantine in Nicomedia in 711?[58]

Conversely, any disbelief that Justinian II would 'compromise the higher regard in which he held himself and his imperial position by grovelling before the bishop of Rome'[59] in any such tradition of imperial *proskynesis* may be to play into the negative portrayal of him in various sources. The *Liber Pontificalis* also has it that the emperor and pope shared a 'mutual embrace',[60] which does seem possible if they were well-acquainted from Constantine's previous visits to Constantinople. This was seen as a positive sign of the emperor's humility, which was met by the joy of the people.[61] Pope Constantine then celebrated Mass in the presence of the emperor in Nicomedia. Justinian received communion from the pope and asked him to pray for a pardon for his imperial sins.[62] This may be a general practice for Roman emperors, as their position involved doing many things that would be considered sinful, even if they were in the name of the empire's safety. However, one cannot help think that perhaps Justinian and even Constantine himself had something specific regarding Ravenna in mind; a move to maintain imperial and Church unity that had involved sin.

Business could then turn to what was the main cause of this papal visit to the East: the Quinisext canons. Due to its author's dislike of Quinisext, the *Liber Pontificalis* does not give as much attention to the papal-imperial negotiations on the canons as it does to the ceremony and pageantry involved. It states that Justinian simply 'renewed all the church's privileges'.[63] This likely involved restating the primacy of Rome, its authority over Ravenna and the previous tax exemptions given out by Constantine IV and expanded by Justinian himself. Nothing specific is said about Quinisext at this point. It does seem that there was some kind of conference between the imperial and papal parties, which led to an agreement acceptable to both sides; however, what that agreement was is difficult to ascertain. It seems likely that the pope agreed to sign up to the Quinisext Council if the emperor released the western church from those canons Rome had found so objectionable.[64] It may be doubted that the usually strong-willed Justinian would agree to such a compromise, but the tone he had struck in religious terms since his restoration does hint at a spirit of accommodation. The limited evidence suggests that Justinian had given way on some aspects. There is no known full copy of the Quinisext canons which carry a papal ratification, while Bede records the Quinisext Council as *erratica*, which he is unlikely to have done had the pope agreed to the entire *Tome*.[65] As already seen, the *Liber*

Pontificalis condemned sections of the canons,[66] which it may not have dared to do if the pope had agreed to them fully.

It appears then that Justinian did compromise, and the *Liber Pontificalis* gives the kudos for providing the solution to the deacon, Gregory: 'When the prince Justinian inquired of him about certain chapters his excellent reply solved every disputed point.'[67] This claim is more than a little suspect, with the suspicion being that the *Liber Pontificalis* is building up Gregory's stature in order to help present his subsequent defiance of Leo III over Iconoclasm in the best possible light. It could be argued that something similar is happening with the presentation of Justinian in more pleasant terms at this point. The highlighting of his humility, deference to the pope and willingness to bow to proper doctrinal belief over Quinisext contrasts his orthodoxy with the heresy of his successor Philippikos Bardanes. Rather than some miraculous persuasion by Gregory, Justinian likely recognized that attempting to force the pope to accept all of the canons was doomed to failure. He may also have acknowledged that confrontation with the papacy would have been ill-timed in 711, and may even have felt that his previous set-to with Sergius had played some role in his deposition in 695. The renewal of privileges recorded by the *Liber Pontificalis* may further represent this spirit of compromise. This negotiating Justinian is very much at odds with his portrayal by hostile chroniclers, appearing here as a more 'responsible clear-headed sovereign, determined to undo some of the harm caused by the mistakes of his earlier years'.[68]

Pope Constantine likely did not get all he wanted in this trade-off. Perhaps the pope had to provide obvious public adherence to Quinisext in general, while keeping overt dislike of the 'anti-Roman' canons to a minimum. It must also be remembered that the pope had already made the significant compromise of going east in the first place. His absence from Rome may have encouraged the trouble John Rizocopos faced there, while the journey not only claimed the life of Niketas, but the return almost cost the pope his as well:

'After leaving the city of Nicomedia, the pontiff was worn down by frequent bouts of illness, but the Lord granted him recovery and finally he reached the port of [Gaeta] in safety; there he found the *sacerdotes* and the greater part of the Roman people. On the 24th day of October in the 10th indiction [711] he entered Rome, and all the people rejoiced and were glad.'[69]

There is some contemporary inference that Pope Constantine had faced personal pressure from Justinian II to accept aspects of Quinisext he otherwise would not have. This comes from the correspondence between Constantine and patriarch John VI of Constantinople, when the former was warning the latter about flirting with the Monothelitism of Philippikos Bardanes. John's response included the reminder that 'you know from your own experience that in the face of force it is not so easy to resist with too much intensity. You need to exercise some skill and intelligence.'[70] This hints at Constantine's dealings with Justinian and possibly that the pope did not get all he wanted in the 'Compromise of Nicomedia'.[71] It seems that Justinian had got enough out of his negotiations with Constantine to claim backing for his Quinisext canons and the attempts at canonical reform they encapsulated. The emperor could also point to the fact that he had demanded and obtained the presence of the pope in the East.[72] Of course, Constantine could claim he had signed up to canonical reform and kept a reputedly hot-headed emperor happy without compromising the practices of the Roman Church.

A more cynical approach might be to suggest that all this talk of canonical compromise, renewal of privilege and restored authority is merely a smokescreen. The cold reality may instead be that there had been no agreement reached over the offending Quinisext canons, with the entire problem 'diplomatically skirted'[73] once it became clear that actual compromise was unlikely. Rome and Constantinople had agreed to disagree for the good of the empire. The hollowness of the supposed 'Compromise of Nicomedia' may be seen in how divergence and disagreement regarding certain practices highlighted in Quinisext continued to rumble on after 711. By 872/873, Pope John VIII was announcing 'that the Roman church agreed to adopt those canons that were not in opposition to the true faith and to the traditions and decrees of the church of Rome'.[74] This seems no less vague than the papal response to Quinisext under John VII and Constantine.

While Justinian may have succeeded in reaching a rapprochement with the papacy over Quinisext through 'conciliation and compromise rather than brute force',[75] part of that rapprochement may have helped enflame turmoil within Roman Italy. Openly siding with the pope against the archbishop of Ravenna, blinding and exiling that archbishop, executing the leadership of the exarchate capital and then having his Sicilian *strategos* sack a former imperial capital undermined unity. This growing turmoil, alongside the advances of the Lombards and the distraction of Constantinople with internal matters, further increased the ability of the pope to act independently. The remaining Roman imperial officials were increasingly left to tend to their own internal and external struggles, largely to the detriment of the imperial presence in Italy.

With this political independence came a greater degree of papal religious freedom from the emperor at Constantinople, which was perhaps best seen in the comparison of reactions to religious controversies. In 653, Constans II had been able to forcibly remove Pope Martin I from the papacy when he had dared condemn Monothelitism. Meanwhile, the forces of Justinian II and Tiberius III demonstrated that Rome was still not beyond the reach of the Roman emperor in the last years of the seventh century, and Justinian could point to Pope Constantine accepting his 'invitation' to the East. However, Pope Sergius' ability to resist Quinisext, followed by the 'Compromise of Nicomedia', shows a downward trend in imperial influence over the papacy, even in the midst of the supposed 'Byzantine' papacy. When Leo III took drastic action to prevent the over-veneration of religious icons, initiating the first period of Iconoclasm, Pope Gregory II responded in 730 by excommunicating all 'those who broke icons', including the patriarch of Constantinople and the emperor himself. Such was the strength of papal and even Italian opposition in general, that once his planned expedition was thwarted by a storm, the only response open to Leo was an ineffective transfer of the 'imperial' territories under the religious jurisdiction of the pope to the patriarch. How the mighty had fallen.

Chapter 14

Cherson, Khazars and the Revolt of Bardanes: The End of the Heraclians

'Off with his head!'
The Queen of Hearts in Lewis Carroll's
Alice's Adventures in Wonderland

The Trouble with Cherson

By the time the papal visit to Constantinople came to an end with Pope Constantine's return to Rome on 24 October 711, it might seem that the second imperial tenure of Justinian II was established on a firm footing. It had seen the repairing of relations with the pope, dealing with the opposition of Ravenna, some limited headway in the Caucasus and cordial relations with the Bulgar khan and Khazar khagan. However, Justinian had less than two months to live. For all those limited successes, Justinian's second reign had been littered with incidents that could have bred his ultimate demise. He had fought unsuccessful wars with Bulgars and Arabs and shown a continuing willingness to put himself in harm's way, leading the army defeated at Anchialus and crossing to Nicaea at a time when the city was within reach of Umayyad raiders. His interventions in Caucasia and Ravenna also lengthened the list of potential opponents. Such unsuccessful wars will also have further soured the already poor relations Justinian had with members of the upper classes and military hierarchies. The Quinisext canons and his treatment of Kallinikos will have roused some opposition in religious circles too. But it was none of these that produced the action to deprive Justinian of his throne – and his head. That focus instead fell on one of the empire's isolated outposts, but an outpost that Justinian II knew well: Cherson.

Both Theophanes and Nikephoros explain this reappearance of Cherson at the forefront of imperial politics as a repercussion of Justinian's thirst for revenge on anyone he felt had wronged him in the past. In this scenario, the crime of the Chersonites was that they had attempted to sell out Justinian to Tiberius III.[1] As we have seen with his treatment of the pope, Khazar khagan and Ravenna, Justinian was by no means the avatar of vengeance he was depicted as. Unfortunately, there is no alternative source – such as the *Liber Pontificalis* was to Agnellus – with which to contrast the hostility of Nikephoros and Theophanes. Their accounts are very similar and contain much more detail than previous sections. This reflects their shared source and its possible contemporaneousness with the events it describes, although the likelihood of manipulation of Justinian's depiction through the propagandist influence of his successors must be kept in mind.[2]

Even if vengeance played some role in Justinian's willingness to get dragged into Crimean politics (and it would be folly to completely ignore that factor), there are indications from even the biased source material that there were other motives in play. As with Ravenna, if Justinian was so keen for revenge on the Chersonites, why did he take so many years to act upon that thirst? Whether they realized it or not, Nikephoros, Theophanes and their source provide hints at a much more acceptable reason for Justinian to choose now to get involved with Cherson: the machinations of Busir, the Khazar khagan and imperial brother-in-law. It seems that, possibly under cover of imperial distractions with Bulgars, Arabs and Italy, the khagan had installed a *tudun* – a Khazar official – in Cherson. This development had occurred since Justinian's exile, because there had been no Khazar official for him to go to in the city; he had to travel to Doros instead to make contact with the khagan. Early editions of the Roman chronicles listed *tudun* as a proper name, but it has been demonstrated that it was a Khazar title.[3] It may even be that *tudun* is best translated as 'governor', rather than something less intrusive like 'ambassador' or 'diplomat'.

It is worth noting that the Khazars had not been shy in throwing their diplomatic and military weight around. We have already seen Busir involving himself in Roman imperial politics over Justinian's flight from Cherson, but his raiders had also been active in various directions. In *c.*685, a significant Khazar raid through the Caucasus had led to the deaths of Iberian and Armenian leaders, and perhaps such raids had continued in the early years of the eighth century. The Umayyad general, Maslamah, is recorded having to retake several towns and forts in Azerbaijan and then march on Derbent to prevent Khazars and their Hunnic subjects from raiding Umayyad territory in 707/713. There was a definite Khazar strike into Azerbaijan in 717, which was eventually defeated by Hatim b. al-Numan. This served as a prelude to the Second Arab-Khazar War, which rumbled on into the 740s.[4] This all suggests that the Khazars had no fear of escalating conflict with the Umayyad caliphate, so any Crimean incursion against the interests of the Roman Empire would not be a stretch.

Any such Khazar attempt to assume control of Cherson would have been an egregious act of encroachment on Roman territory by Busir, and thus a perfectly legitimate reason for an imperial expedition to the Crimea. It seems unlikely that even the biased Nikephoros and Theophanes would ignore such an outrageous barbarian incursion, so the fact that they managed to do so might shift blame onto their shared source, specifically the propaganda prevalent at the time of its writing in the decade after the event.[5] As the man to most benefit from Justinian's fall and Busir's role in that drama, Philippikos Bardanes could not present the khagan as an enemy of the Roman state, even if it was clear that 'the khagan's expansionist ambition was indeed the crucial factor in setting into action Justinian's expeditions against Cherson'.[6]

In early 711, an expeditionary force was dispatched to the Crimea. It is claimed by Nikephoros to have numbered 100,000 men 'recruited from the army registers as well as among farmers and artisans and from the senate and the population of the City'.[7] Theophanes focuses more on the make-up of the fleet, listing 'every kind of ship – *dromones*, triremes, transports, fishing boats, and even *chelandia*'.[8] More importantly, when Theophanes records the involvement of 'the senators, artisans, ordinary people, and all the officials that lived in the City'[9] in the outfitting of this expeditionary fleet, he refers to them providing the various ships through 'contributions' or 'requisitions', rather than the manpower.

As for Nikephoros' suggestion that the expedition involved 100,000 men, this would seem like a drastic exaggeration. The Roman Empire of 711 was likely still capable of fielding so many men, but those forces were deployed across the various themes. Even a vengeful Justinian was not going to strip the thematic armies and fleets down to the bare bones at a time when the Arabs were raiding deeply into Asia Minor just to quench his thirst against the Chersonites or to oust the Khazars from a minor frontier settlement. It could be that Nikephoros' figure included all of those sent on the expedition, such as support staff and the sailors used to man what would have been a significant number of ships. This would still not preclude the idea that this number of 100,000 was exaggerated, but nevertheless, there could have been a significant number of personnel sent to the Crimea in 711.

Command of this expedition was given to Stephen Askemitos and Mauros, with the *spatharios* Helias to be installed as governor of Cherson, once the Khazar *tudun* and any collaborating Chersonites had been removed. It is likely that this Stephen Askemitos was the same Stephen who had joined Justinian in his flight from the Crimea and served as his ambassador to Tervel when they arrived at the mouth of the Danube. The identification of Mauros is a little more difficult. While he is described as a Bessian Thracian, he has also been identified with a Bulgar chieftain of the same name. This chieftain had been involved in the attempts of Kuber's Bulgars and Slavs to capture Thessalonica in the decade before Justinian's intervention there in 688. Having failed in these attacks, Mauros the Bulgar defected to the Romans with those under his direct command and was given a title by Constantine IV. A contemporary seal records him as 'Mauros the patrician, chief of the Sermesiani [men of Sirmium] and Bulgarians'. Aside from the potential gap of up to thirty years, the main drawback to an identification of Justinian's expeditionary commander in 711 with this previous Mauros the Bulgar is that the latter was deprived of his titles and command for his role in the plot against Thessalonica. It would certainly be strange for Justinian II to reinstate a man who had plotted against a city he held in such high regard.[10]

Helias was unknown to the historical record before his joining of the expedition, but as a *spatharios*, he must have impressed Justinian at some point. Theophanes does suggest that Helias was somehow in Justinian's debt.[11] It might be that his being sent to Cherson to act as its governor was an indication that Justinian was looking to remove Helias from his presence, either out of personal or professional considerations. Nikephoros claims that the Cherson expedition was used as an avenue to remove characters of questionable ability or loyalty, with the Armenian Bardanes being sent along with it to be left there 'in banishment'.[12] A similar motive could have been in play with regard to Helias. Circumstances would show that any doubt Justinian had for the loyalty of these two men had some foundation, or maybe that his paranoid actions fostered their eventual disloyalty.

Perhaps recalling the reported order that the emperor gave regarding the populace of Constantinople before his deposition in 695, both Nikephoros and Theophanes present the orders given to Stephen and Mauros in not only vengeful but essentially genocidal terms: 'put to the sword all the people of Cherson and Bosporus and the other principalities'.[13] Such a reputed order is 'manifestly absurd',[14] not just due to the sheer scope of such an action, but also because even the hostile sources contain contrary information. The sending of Helias on the initial expedition with the plan for him to become governor of Cherson would be a peculiar appointment if all the Chersonites had been killed. Who exactly was he to govern if the order to 'leave no one alive'[15] was carried out? The mention of the Bosporus by Nikephoros may also betray the true, non-genocidal nature of Justinian's Cherson expedition. The Cimmerian Bosporus was controlled by the Khazars, and as already seen, Busir had recently established a Khazar official in Cherson. This could suggest that the expedition was more targeted at the Khazar presence in the region, including a punitive attack on Khazar territory. It could even be that in speaking of 'other principalities' or κλιματα/*klimata* (regions or districts),[16] Nikephoros and Theophanes may hint at Justinian aiming to not only reclaim territory impinged on by the Khazars, but even to expand Roman control in the Crimea.

The expedition of Stephen and Mauros met with success throughout the campaigning season of 711. Arriving at and then landing in the Crimea without incident, the Roman forces set about reimposing imperial supremacy over the southern Crimea. However, rather than emphasize this military success, any possible victories over the Khazars or coercing other Crimeans into accepting imperial overlordship, the chronicles focus almost completely on the supposed punishments meted out to those who were thought to be enemies of the emperor. Nikephoros and Theophanes have Stephen and Mauros going to some lengths to fulfil Justinian's reputed genocidal order, putting everyone in Cherson and its surrounding forts to death, except children, who were to be sold into slavery. As already suggested, the idea of a genocidal order is absurd, but it is likely that there is some kernel of truth behind these outrageous claims. Particular focus falls on the treatment of civic leaders in Cherson. These may have been the men who tried to betray Justinian to Tiberius III, or perhaps more likely, those who had been involved in inviting and delivering the city into the hands of the Khazars. Therefore, instead of a general massacre of the population, it is much more likely that there was an imperial order to arrest and execute certain Chersonite leaders and deliver others to the imperial court. Such lethality in dealing with what was treason is to be expected in the Roman Empire, but even then, the sources record Stephen and Mauros using some horrific methods of execution:

'[S]even distinguished men of Cherson they affixed to wooden spits and roasted them over the fire; and another twenty they bound with their arms behind their backs and, after tying them to the oar-straps of a *chelandion*, filled it with stones and sank it in the sea.'[17]

This combination of immolation and drowning for Chersonite civic leaders would seem to reflect badly on Justinian, but could these methods of execution reflect more on the commanders of the expedition than the emperor himself? If Mauros was a Bulgar, perhaps they display his barbaric origin. As for Stephen, could his victims have been personal enemies of his from the time he spent in Cherson? It should also not be overlooked that such methods of execution seem as much like warnings as they do punishments. Cherson and other imperial lands in the region had at the very least been flirting with treason, their actions demanding that the emperor and his commanders provide an example to others. Such a drastic lesson would also betray that there was still someone left to potentially learn from it, rather than a smouldering, depopulated ruin of a city or region.

Besides these executions and beyond the aforementioned children, there were a significant number of Chersonite leaders taken prisoner. A group of forty men – including a certain Zoilos, seemingly the leading Chersonite civilian, and the Khazar *tudun* – were shipped off to the imperial capital with their families.[18] This taking of prisoners may also undermine the idea that Justinian ordered a Chersonite genocide, although the sources suggest that Justinian was furious at Stephen for showing such mercy. So angry was the emperor that, even with the apparent success of the campaign, he ordered the entire expedition to return to Constantinople immediately.[19]

By this point it was October, not the best time of year to cross the Black Sea; yet Stephen and his officers had no choice but to obey this imperial summons lest it be their neck on the block. Might there be a more logical explanation for this dangerously out-of-season naval voyage, beyond Justinian's apparent increasing mania or a historiographical choice to replay Justinian's Black Sea folly with regard to the transporting of Theodora and Tiberius in 705? Even if it is accepted that the Cherson expedition did not involve the redeployment of 100,000 men, it would need to have used troops and naval forces from somewhere. This leaves the question of whether Justinian dispatched an entire single thematic force and fleet or gathered an expeditionary force from various land and naval themes. Either scenario would have left the region or regions deprived of some of their forces for the majority of 711. It seems likely that the forces were gathered from Thrace,

Constantinople and Asia Minor, but this was a period when even these core provinces were requiring the presence of all of their forces. Thrace may have faced some pressure from the Bulgars victorious at Anchialus, while all thematic forces in Asia Minor, including those centred in or near Constantinople, were vulnerable to Umayyad raids following the defeat at Tyana. So even with the previous example of the first fleet sent to collect Theodora and Tiberius, the autumn crossing of the Black Sea may have been deemed necessary because the expeditionary forces were needed back in their own themes.

Whatever the reason behind the need for the expeditionary force to return, it did not lessen the threat posed by crossing the Black Sea late in the year. Sure enough, poor weather hit the fleet, sinking a large proportion of it, with bodies washing up all along the southern and western coasts of the Black Sea. The chroniclers claim that 73,000 lives were lost. As well as playing into the largely discounted notion that Justinian had sent 100,000 men to Cherson, this exaggeration seems to be using some historiographic trickery. Is it just a coincidence that these numbers match the casualties suffered by Rome at the Battle of Cannae in 216 BC? Was the shared source of Theophanes and Nikephoros looking to paint Justinian as suffering a defeat as bad as any Rome had ever endured? The ability to send out another fleet not long after this supposed destruction would suggest that if the initial expeditionary force had been faced with a Black Sea storm, it had not suffered the level of casualties the chroniclers suggest. Such a disaster would have hobbled the imperial ability to dispatch any kind of expedition for the immediate future. It must also be pointed out that in claiming so many casualties, the anti-Justinian sources provide evidence that rather than acting on a whim upon hearing of Stephen's mercy towards the children of Cherson, Justinian had ordered the majority of the expeditionary force home. He is unlikely to have done so if he felt it had not done its job; a job which, therefore, did not involve genocide because 'Cherson remained full of Chersonites'.[20] The likelihood is then that Stephen and Mauros' expedition succeeded in its objectives and was ordered home late in the year for necessary redeployment, only for a storm to cause some damage, but not enough to prevent the dispatching of another fleet to Cherson when circumstances changed.

Another reason to doubt the reports of the chroniclers regarding the destruction of the Cherson expedition at sea is the reaction they attribute to Justinian. Rather than shock, dismay or even anger, the emperor supposedly greeted the loss of so many men with joy. This scarcely makes sense, but then the chroniclers would claim that it was not supposed to make sense because the emperor 'was now at the peak of his madness'.[21] Could it be that this source tradition viewed Justinian II as having a similar breakdown in his mental health at news of the loss of the Cherson expedition as Justin II did upon hearing of the reverses his forces had suffered against the Persians in 573/574?[22]

If Justinian had decided that his troops had achieved his aims for the initial Cherson campaign, and therefore brought a sizeable portion of the expeditionary force home (only to have some of it wrecked at sea), the emperor soon had reason to fit out another fleet. Unsurprisingly, Nikephoros and Theophanes claim that Justinian's reason for sending another fleet to the Crimea was that the emperor had not had enough revenge: '[H]e threatened with loud cries that he would send another fleet and mow everyone down to the ground, to the last man that pissed against the wall.'[23] However, once more they also present a much more realistic reason for a second bout of imperial military intervention – the Chersonites, far from being suitably chastened (or exterminated) by Stephen's expedition, had asked the Khazar khagan for help. The opportunistic Busir had once more chosen to interfere in Roman territory, with Khazar troops arriving in Cherson itself. Again, foreign intervention in Roman territory would be a more than acceptable reason for Justinian to launch a second Crimean expedition.

The hostile sources might argue over the chronology of such events, with the Chersonite invitation and the Khazar move further into the Crimea coming *after* Justinian's second expedition had been organized. Having been warned about the increasing instability of the emperor, the people of Cherson were seeking to defend themselves, while the Khazars had a grievance over the treatment of their *tudun*. This seems unlikely, but there could be some element of truth behind such a claim. Any losses suffered in the reconquest of Cherson and then during the storm on the return journey would have to be replaced in order to bring whatever thematic forces they were detached from back up to full strength. If the expeditionary force of Stephen and Mauros had come from the core provinces, and especially from forces of the Opsikion theme, then any such recruiting drive would have been obvious to the populace and those who would eventually record it. Reports of continued Cherson opposition and even Khazar intervention in the Crimea may have seen Justinian immediately dispatching another expeditionary force to bolster the garrison forces left behind by the first expedition. In the hands of hostile sources, such developments – especially a rapid imperial response to a worsening Crimean situation on the back of a recruitment drive – could easily have been construed as a bloodthirsty Justinian looking to 'continue' his genocidal campaign against Cherson.

Before Justinian could send any sizeable second expeditionary force, a significant change occurred in the strategic position in Cherson, one that was to have a devastating effect on the longevity of Justinian's second reign. The Khazars were not the only source of military aid the Chersonites had been appealing to in the wake of the departure of the majority of the Roman expeditionary force. They had also spoken with the new governor of Cherson, Helias. This pressure and the arrival of any Khazar forces tipped Helias into throwing in his lot with the Chersonites and the khagan. In terms of political importance going forward, a more significant defection at this time was that of the exiled general Bardanes; but strategically, Helias' defection likely brought what remained of the first expeditionary force of Stephen over to the Chersonite rebels.

The loss of this military foothold in Cherson altered Justinian's strategic thinking; instead of going forward with his second expedition to the Crimea, the emperor attempted some diplomacy to quell this growing problem. Zoilos and the Khazar *tudun* were released from their Constantinopolitan imprisonment (proving that at least some of Stephen's fleet made it to the capital) and sent back to Cherson with an honour guard of 300 Roman soldiers. This guard was headed by the patrician George Syros, John the Prefect and Christopher, the Thrakesian *turmarch*,[24] who were to convey Justinian's apologies to the khagan and try to restore the *status quo*. That said, the new allies of the khagan and the Chersonites, the turncoats Helias and Bardanes, were to be arrested and sent back to Constantinople.

This attempted diplomacy proved too late: the Chersonites had become firmly rooted in their opposition to Justinian. Upon arriving in the Crimea, George, John and Christopher found them unwilling to talk. Only after at least a day did the Chersonites agree to meet the imperial representatives and even then, they would only do so if the envoys entered the city without any armed accompaniment. Accepting such a demand proved a fatal miscalculation. The imperial officers were quickly arrested and the city gates closed to prevent any immediate retaliation from their escort. To compound this gross breach of ambassadorial etiquette, George Syros and John the Prefect were put to death immediately. Their 300-man escort was then persuaded to surrender, through the military intervention of Chersonite and/or Khazar forces. Christopher, the *tudun*, Zoilos and the 300 Roman soldiers were then sent off to the khagan. It could even be that Christopher, to whom command of the small imperial force fell, was persuaded to fulfil his diplomatic duty regarding the *tudun* and escort him to Khazar territory.

To further compound the diplomatic disaster this whole sorry situation was becoming, on the journey east, Christopher and his 300 men were executed. Nikephoros records it merely as 'the Khazars killed them on the way',[25] while Theophanes may hint at something more than a vengeful execution. He has the *tudun* die *en route* to Khazaria, so the Khazars 'in his honour killed the *turmarch* along with the 300 soldiers'.[26] This could suggest that Christopher and his men were killed as part of a Khazar funeral rite, along with revenge for the *tudun*'s treatment by the Romans. It also highlights that the *turmarch* and his escort had found themselves in the custody of Khazar forces.

Local Revolt to Imperial Usurpation: Justinian Loses His Head

Executing imperial officers and facilitating the deaths of imperial soldiers, who were all acting under diplomatic auspices, set the seal on the revolt of Cherson. There was no going back now. They could not expect much quarter from the supposedly mad emperor. Therefore, they took the final step in renouncing their allegiance to Justinian II by proclaiming an emperor of their own. Their choice fell upon the Armenian officer, Bardanes. How he came to be in Cherson is not completely clear. Before the first Cherson expedition, we last saw him in exile on Cephalonia after his portentous dream tarring him with imperial pretensions was brought to the attention of Tiberius III. It is unclear if he received some sort of short-lived recall by Justinian only to face exile once more, or was being moved to Cherson to continue his life 'in banishment'[27] on the fringes of the Roman world, rather than on an island in the heart of the Mediterranean. Nikephoros would have it that the Chersonites proclaimed Bardanes as emperor in his absence in Khazaria, although this seems like a chronological mistake created by Nikephoros' epitomizing of his source material.[28]

Besides some military experience and supposed ambition, Bardanes comes across as a relatively mild and popular officer; perhaps a prime candidate for the imperial figurehead of a usurpation. It was initially not considered an issue amongst the Chersonites and the military forces that backed him that Bardanes was a Monothelite, although it would later become a significant problem. What was considered an issue at the time was his name. 'Bardanes' or 'Vardan' was very obviously an Armenian name and not one considered appropriate for a Roman emperor. Therefore, much as Apsimar had done, Bardanes adopted a new appellation, aiming to rule as the emperor 'Philippikos'. While this was a good classical name, it was not a name with imperial heritage. Perhaps that was the point with his name, representing a new start under his leadership unburdened by previous legacy and actions. That said, given the 'anarchic' and even illegitimate surroundings of his reign and perhaps following the increasing trend for emperors to be remembered by a 'surname' or sobriquet, again much like 'Tiberius Apsimar', the emperor Philippikos would be frequently recorded as 'Philippikos Bardanes'.

Word of this elevation of local revolt to an imperial usurpation in Cherson by an exile reputedly raised a murderous rage in Justinian. As well as the direct challenge to his rightful imperial position, might it be that the emperor recognized too much of himself in Bardanes' usurpation? After all, Justinian himself had been an exile in Cherson who announced his intention to (re-) take the imperial throne. Madder than ever, Justinian supposedly took his anger out on the family of Helias: the emperor had the Chersonite governor's children snatched from the care of their mother and murdered. He then 'obliged her to marry her own cook, who was an Indian'.[29] This merely reads like another attempt to portray the emperor as poorly as possible.

A more definite response from Justinian was to prepare and send another expedition against Bardanes, Cherson and their Khazar allies under the command of Mauros, who had evidently also survived the storm that struck the first expedition. As Mauros made for the Crimea, Justinian's orders 'to destroy the walls of Cherson and the entire town, and not to leave a single soul alive',[30] as well as warnings about what would happen should he fail, must have been ringing in his ears. Perhaps showing Justinian's growing mistrust of some of his officers, Mauros was also told to stay in regular contact with Constantinople over the progress of his campaigning.[31] Aside from being equipped with rams, catapults and other siege engines, there is no record of what forces Mauros was sent against Cherson with. Given that this was meant to be an imperial attempt to crush a usurpation, it might be imagined that this second expedition was at least as large as the first, with detachments from the core thematic armies or specifically the Opsikion once more.

Whatever its make-up or specific orders, Mauros' expedition not only achieved landfall in the Crimea, but also managed to bottle up the rebel forces in Cherson. Mauros sent his siege engines against the city walls, breaking through the gate and towers of the Kentenaresion and the Wild Boar. Cherson looked set to fall and possibly be subjected to the horror of Justinian's latest genocidal order. However, before Mauros could complete any victory, the Chersonite diplomatic offensive bore substantial and potentially life-saving fruit. With the imperial army fully deployed against the Cherson walls, a Khazar force arrived. Unwilling to fight a battle on two fronts, which perhaps hints that his army was not overwhelmingly superior to the combined Chersonite-Khazar forces, Mauros agreed to some sort of truce.

What seemed like a brief interlude in military proceedings became the final catalyst for the demise of the Heraclian dynasty when Philipikos Bardanes managed to escape Cherson and make for the court of the Khazar khagan. The flight of the usurper and his meeting up with Busir compounded Mauros' failure to force the rapid surrender of Cherson. It could well be imagined that Helias and the Chersonites were pointing out to Mauros and his men that while they would be allowed to retire unhindered by the Chersonite-Khazar forces, Justinian's growing instability made any return to Constantinople potentially fatal. Having been present in the capital for any exactions Justinian had carried out on the family of Helias, and possibly remembering any warnings the emperor had given him, Mauros and his army soon decided that they had a better chance of survival by throwing in their lot with the Chersonites and their Khazar-backed, Armenian usurper. It must also be remembered that if this Mauros and Mauros the Bulgar were one and the same, then the commander of the second Cherson expedition already had a history of changing sides.

This sudden defection by an imperial expedition and its commander was no doubt greeted with joy in Cherson and the ranks of the army backing the usurper, but there was one man who appears somewhat doubtful of this latest move: the Khazar khagan himself. In renouncing Justinian and acclaiming Philippikos Bardanes as their emperor, Mauros' men sent to Busir for Philippikos to return to Cherson to take personal command of the usurpation. The khagan's wariness of potential duplicity – perhaps a reflection of his own willingness to use betrayal as a weapon when it suited him – saw him imposing an oath of allegiance to Philippikos. Each man of Mauros' army was to promise to maintain their loyalty to the usurper and to pay one *nomisma* each to the khagan. Only once they had agreed to this pledge did Philippikos Bardanes move back to Cherson to take command of his growing army. The combination of Chersonites, Khazars and defectors from two expeditionary forces presented the usurper with a force big enough to contemplate taking the offensive against Justinian – but where would he strike?

Back in Constantinople, both Nikephoros and Theophanes report that Justinian recognized the lack of communication from Mauros for what it was – further defection. They then have the emperor gathering a force from the Opsikion and Thrakesian themes, as well as seemingly a Bulgar contingent of 3,000 men from Tervel.[32] None of this seems out of the ordinary, but it is what they record Justinian doing with this army that is somewhat perplexing. Rather than have it defend Constantinople from any impending attack or even cross the Black Sea to confront Philippikos directly, it marched out of the capital, crossed to Asia Minor and headed for the Pontic port of Sinope. Stranger still, Justinian himself was at the head of this army, leaving his Constantinopolitan bastion at a time of usurpation.

This raises considerable questions over what Justinian was doing at such a pivotal time. If his aim was to move to Sinope to confirm his suspicions about the lack of communication from his second Cherson expedition and possibly the aims of Bardanes, this would seem strong evidence that he no longer trusted his generals to carry out such a task. But if Justinian so doubted the loyalty of his own men, leaving the safety of Constantinople's defences was the last thing he should have been doing. He also seems to have left a sizeable part of the Opsikion, Thrakesian and Bulgar force to camp at Damatrys,[33] about 20 miles east of Chalcedon, while he himself led a detachment towards Sinope. Surely he would not have done such a thing if he truly feared for the loyalty of his men?

Rather than specifically a reconnaissance mission, it could be that Justinian had a more military reason for leaving his capital and marching east. If he had already received word of Mauros' defection, Justinian could have sought to move along the southern coast of the Black Sea to secure its loyalty in the face of a potential landing by Bardanes. This could explain the emperor's move towards the important port of Sinope, reaching the coastal village of Gingilissos.[34] Another military reason for Justinian's move east was a rebellion in parts of Armenia still under imperial control. It has been suggested that Justinian connected these troubles in Armenia with the usurpation of Bardanes, with the emperor perhaps trying to second guess the usurper by striking at his homeland.[35] Such an idea may be bolstered by a potential religious connotation to the trouble, with Justinian having patriarch Cyrus anathematize the Armenians, almost certainly for their Monothelitism. This would connect to Bardanes, as he too was a Monothelite. This Armenian revolt and any possible Arab involvement could have been considered dangerous enough for the emperor to confront the rebels in person. While this is an attractive connection to make, the rebellion in Armenia was adequate reason in itself for imperial intervention, rather than needing any connection to the usurper. Furthermore, Bardanes himself was a colonist from Pergamum, so any loyalty he might look to foster in Armenia should be somewhat downplayed, particularly when he is recorded in 712/713 as having to drive off Armenian invaders from imperial lands.[36] That this Armenian trouble survived to hinder an Armenian emperor demonstrates that Justinian had been able to do little about it and is testament to the disaster that was about to overtake him.

If, as Nikephoros and Theophanes suggest, the emperor had already discerned what had occurred with Mauros in Cherson, it seems incredibly foolish for Justinian to leave Constantinople. So foolish that it perhaps raises the possibility that Justinian was actually unaware of the extent of the diplomatic and military calamity the second Cherson expedition had become, with it expanding the capabilities of Bardanes. If the report that Justinian knew of the defection of Mauros or at least suspected it is discounted, then perhaps the emperor felt that matters were in hand at Cherson. After all, it could be that Mauros' last dispatch from the field informed Justinian that the walls of Cherson were crumbling under the assault of his battering rams. If that was the case, the emperor's move east could be viewed as an attempt to win a military victory to shore up the loyalty of much of the army and the empire.

There were plenty of options for Justinian to win a military victory. Not only was there the brewing trouble with the Armenians, but the raiding of Umayyad forces continued unabated. Theophanes has Maslamah active in Armenia in 712/713. This is backed up by al-Tabari,[37] who also records annual Arab attacks on parts of Roman Asia Minor, which are only infrequently identifiable throughout the first years of the 710s.[38] Gathering a force of the Opsikion, Thrakesion and Bulgar auxiliaries to serve alongside the frontier thematic forces of the Anatolikon and Armeniakon could have easily seen Justinian win a valuable victory. Perhaps he was in the first moves of such a proposed campaign when he received word of the full extent of his Cherson problem at Sinope.

Whatever the reason behind it, Justinian's departure from Constantinople was quickly transformed into a 'serious tactical error';[39] and ultimately a fatal one. While at Sinope, the emperor learned that the usurper had embarked a sizeable portion of his forces onto what had been Mauros' ships and set sail across the Black Sea. Both Theophanes and Nikephoros even state that from his position near Sinope, Justinian was able to see the rebel fleet and discern its target – Constantinople itself.[40] Not only had Justinian failed to anticipate what Philippikos Bardanes and his allies would do next, but he had left himself open to disaster. Sinope was at least 500km from the capital and it would take a Herculean effort from Justinian to get back to Constantinople before Bardanes arrived. 'Charging forward like a lion',[41] Justinian rushed back west across northern Asia Minor towards his capital. Except when he finally got there, he found that it was no longer *his* capital … Justinian was too late.

Whether taking advantage of intelligence reports or benefitting from some great good fortune, Philippikos Bardanes' opportunistic strike had not only seen him reach Constantinople in Justinian's absence, but also land his troops and enter the capital without a fight. This lack of resistance could demonstrate how denuded Justinian had left the city through his Cherson expeditions and his gathering of troops at Damatrys. However, it could also reflect a lack of loyalty felt for Justinian in the capital, particularly in the face of a usurping army. This could even be another example of the wait-and-see/cynical self-preservation already seen from Roman armies of this era, including the Constantinopolitan garrison. Or could Philippikos' success have been due to some subterfuge on the part of his fleet? If word of Mauros' defection had not yet reached Constantinople, the appearance of his ships could easily have been interpreted as a loyal and victorious general returning to his emperor. They would then be given entry into the Golden Horn, its massive chain lowered, and once they had put in at one of the many harbours, entrance into the city would have been granted. Such a situation of finding an enemy amongst them before they knew it could also explain the lack of fight from the imperial garrison as much as any latent dislike of Justinian II.

The loss of Constantinople was a disaster for Justinian, but all was not yet lost. He still had a loyal army of some size in camp at Damatrys. If he could make his way back to these forces, he could resist Bardanes long enough for support for the usurper to collapse. There were also some hints of loyalty for Justinian, with Barasbakourios, chief patrician and *comes* of the

Opsikion, becoming a target for Bardanes. However, perhaps for the good of the Roman Empire, it was spared a potentially destructive civil war by a mixture of rapid, ruthless and clement actions by Bardanes. The usurper sent forces under Helias to keep the emperor cooped up at Damatrys by mounting raids on the loyalist camp. But rather than rely solely on military action, Bardanes had also charged Helias with leading a diplomatic charm offensive. The governor of Cherson made contact with the Opsikions and Thrakesians of Justinian's army, offering a general amnesty to any who would desert the emperor.

Justinian quickly found that his unpopularity with certain parts of society, especially the upper and landowning classes, and the desperate position he found himself in, particularly with the loss of Constantinople, had severely undermined the loyalty of his army at Damatrys. In the face of Philippikos' offer of amnesty, many of these men likely wondered why they should fight and likely have to attack the immense walls of Constantinople for a chance at peace, when peace was being offered to them for not fighting. With that, what had been a sizeable force of thematic regulars and Bulgar auxiliaries with which Justinian might have expected to challenge Bardanes simply melted away, defecting to the usurper.

Left virtually alone, Justinian was then seized by Helias and his men. Gripped by the need for revenge against the man who had reputedly heaped humiliation and massacre on his family, Helias decided not to take any chances with this emperor, who had survived the loss of his throne, the loss of his nose, the mutilation of his tongue, betrayals by his Chersonite hosts and his Khazar brother-in-law, a treacherous sea journey, negotiations with Tervel and military reverses against the Bulgars and Arabs. No one would dare think it impossible that he would return to challenge for power and prominence once more. Helias therefore made this second removal of Justinian II from the throne a permanent one by removing the emperor's head from his shoulders, possibly on 4 November 711. No amount of ornamental covering or plastic surgery was going to allow Justinian to recover from that.[42]

Having carried out the execution himself, Helias sent this cranial proof to Bardanes via the *spatharios* Romanos, who was then tasked with taking the head through the western provinces to announce the final demise of the noseless emperor. The rest of Justinian's body was seemingly not accorded a Christian burial, 'his headless corpse ... tossed into the sea'.[43] In Ravenna, Agnellus records that this grim trophy was received with great glee, including by one old woman, a sister of a Ravennate rebel executed on the order of

Justinian. She had reputedly declared that she would die happy if she lived to see Justinian dead. She got her wish as she watched Justinian's head being paraded through the city. Satisfied, she then dropped dead.[44]

This proof of Justinian's demise received a far different reception in Rome, where the pope had recently become a staunch ally. Amongst the mourners in January 712, the author of the *Liber Pontificalis* recorded the 'melancholy tidings that Justinian, the most Christian and orthodox Emperor, was murdered'.[45] The focus on Justinian's orthodoxy may again be telling, as the papacy would have problems with Bardanes and his Monothelitism. Even within a short period of time, the heresy of the new emperor may have been enhancing the reputation of the old one, even though Justinian had spent a good part of his time on the throne at loggerheads with the pope over Quinisext. That said, much had changed since Justinian's dealings with Sergius. The papal and imperial thrones had changed hands several times, and following his restoration, Justinian had made great strides in patching up relations between Rome and Constantinople (aided by a rebellious Ravenna), so there may have been 'sincerity [in] the dismay felt in Rome when the city learned of his death'.[46]

Death of the Dynasty

The murder of Justinian II was not the only action taken to bring about the end of his regime and dynasty. Possibly before Helias' fatal sword strike at Damatrys, the aforementioned Barasbakourios and other loyalist officials had to be hunted down and executed by the agents of Bardanes.[47] More importantly, Bardanes also ordered the execution of the only other male member of the imperial family. Perhaps also before Helias swung his sword at the imperial neck, Bardanes' agents were searching through Constantinople for the young co-emperor, Tiberius. He had been left in the care of his grandmother, Anastasia, when Justinian left the capital for his ill-thought-out move east. Events in and around Constantinople progressed so quickly that Anastasia was unable to get her grandson out of the capital. Instead, they fled to the Church of the Theotokos at Blachernae in the hope of finding sanctuary.

Philippikos Bardanes charged Mauros and the *spatharios* John Strouthos – 'the Sparrow/Ostrich' – with dealing with this last male member of the Heraclian line. They found Anastasia keeping watch over the little emperor outside the sanctuary, likely because women were not allowed inside.

Recognizing what was about to happen, Anastasia threw herself at Mauros' feet and begged him to spare Tiberius. Meanwhile, Strouthos entered the sanctuary where the little emperor stood clinging to the altar with one hand, while holding relics from the True Cross in the other, and wearing several protective amulets and relics around his neck.

Comment has been made about how Theophanes highlights Tiberius' wearing of holy relics for protection. This could suggest that Anastasia believed in their effectiveness and/or felt that, despite there being examples of young heirs, co-emperors and even emperors being allowed to survive their deposition, there was going to be little chance of this clemency being extended to her grandson. Alternatively, it could reflect the tendency of the East Roman source tradition – and perhaps Theophanes specifically – to attribute such protective abilities to relics.[48] But if the historiographical focus on the protection provided by these relics had some iconodule motive, it was not deployed at a particularly opportune moment as that supposed protection was about to fail utterly. Perhaps a more 'useful' religious message regarding the fate of Tiberius would have been to see it as an example of the horrific actions that take place under a Monothelite heretic, with his agents violating the sanctuary of a church and ignoring the pleas of a grandmother and the symbolism of holy relics in order to butcher the young son of an orthodox emperor.

For this was how it was to play out. While Anastasia continued to remonstrate with Mauros, John Strouthos seized hold of Tiberius, placing the True Cross relics on the altar and taking the reliquary around his own neck – was he looking for some divine forgiveness for what he was about to do? The Sparrow then carried Tiberius out of the church, stripped the 6-year-old co-emperor of his clothes (perhaps his imperial vestments) and then, 'stretching him out on the door-sill, cut his throat as if he were a sheep'.[49] The young co-emperor was then buried in the church of the Anargyroi – 'those who take no money', a nickname for Saints Cosmas and Damian due to their unwillingness to take fees for their healing.

So ended the main line of the Heraclian dynasty, but there were still perhaps three surviving prominent females connected to Justinian: his mother Anastasia, his wife Theodora and possibly his daughter. The sources do not record the fate of Anastasia. It might be expected that if she shared her grandson's fate near the Blachernae, it would be recorded in the sources, particularly within those which wished to highlight the horrific treatment of an orthodox woman at the hands of a Monothelite regime. It was rare for imperial women to share the punishment of their male relatives, with confinement to a convent much more frequent. There is a good chance that if Anastasia did survive the overthrow of her family, she ended her days as a nun in or around the imperial capital. Whenever and wherever Anastasia passed away, she was accorded the honour of a burial in the tomb of her husband, Constantine IV.[50]

As little that is recorded about Justinian's mother, there is even less about his second wife, Theodora. The lack of mention of her in the chronicles, and the fact that Tiberius was in the care of his grandmother rather than his mother at the fall of Constantinople to Bardanes, could suggest that Theodora was already dead. However, some kind of record of her imperial burial would be expected, but there is none. In purely political terms, given the role of her brother, the Khazar khagan, in helping Bardanes take the imperial throne, if she was still alive at the demise of Justinian, surely she would have been treated with the respect due not just to a Roman empress, but also a Khazar princess, even if the new emperor had been responsible for the death of her son. With her connections to the Roman world gone and the new emperor indebted to the khagan, Theodora is likely to have been returned to Khazaria, rather than be confined to a convent. Unfortunately, all that can be said 'with certainty is that the Khazar lady simply disappears from history'.[51] The last potential female survivor of the downfall of the Heraclians is similarly lost to history. As already mentioned, so little is known about 'Anastasia', daughter of Justinian, that it is impossible to assert any date of death for her beyond her father's exile to Cherson in 695. If she was still alive to see his second deposition in 711, the fact that she did not marry Tervel the Bulgar might suggest that she had been committed to a nunnery, a state of affairs that would also have prevented her usage by the likes of Bardanes as a source of imperial legitimacy.

Of course, similar arguments could be applied to other members of the Heraclian dynasty due to the lack of clear information about their ultimate fates. Upon the murder of Justinian II and his young son, could there still have been a member of the male Heraclian line alive somewhere in imperial territory? Despite it being thirty years since their deposition, Justinian's uncles, Heraclius and Tiberius, could well have still been alive if they had been exiled or confined to a monastery. The same could be said of Justinian's younger brother, Heraclius. It seems likely that Constantine IV, Justinian II and their various non-Heraclian successors had made sure that there were no other imperial candidates to be dragged out of obscurity. Even if there were still some surviving, much like Justinian's daughter, mother and Khazar wife, they were to play no further role in the dynastic politics of the Roman Empire.

The Heraclian dynasty was dead.

Anarchy – Five Emperors in Seven Years

The murders of Justinian II and Tiberius may have represented the end of a dynasty, but if the likes of Bardanes, Helias, Mauros and John the Sparrow thought that this meant an end to the military anarchy that was consuming the upper echelons of the Roman Empire, they were to be gravely mistaken. Philippikos Bardanes proved unable to bring any stability to imperial proceedings. In military terms, Bardanes' failures were not necessarily his fault. His brief reign (711–713) brought word of the final Umayyad conquest of North Africa, with the last Roman outpost, Septem (if it even recognized Roman control by this point), falling at the initiation of the Muslim invasion of Spain. The assassination of Justinian had also been taken by Tervel as a *raison de guerre* to raid Roman territory right up to the walls of Constantinople in 712. Bardanes attempted to deal with this Bulgar incursion by transferring Opsikion forces to Europe, but this decisive move to deal with one threat merely stoked up another, with al-Walid I increasing the Arab raids on Anatolia.

However, it was in the realm of religion where Bardanes stirred up the most opposition. He was a follower of Monothelitism, condemned as heresy by the Sixth Ecumenical Council in 680/681. Straightaway, this was a sizeable obstacle to the perceived legitimacy of Bardanes amongst the orthodox inhabitants of the empire. The emperor only exacerbated this problem by targeting the orthodox patriarch, Cyrus, within months – even weeks – of his accession. He had Cyrus deposed and replaced by John VI, a committed Monothelite. The emperor and his new patriarch then went further by calling a council of eastern bishops to abolish the decisions and canons of the Sixth Ecumenical Council. As a result, the papacy withheld its recognition of both Bardanes and John VI.

This combination of religious opposition and military setback caused the reign of Philippikos Bardanes to fall apart after just nineteen months. In late May 713, the Opsikion army he had transferred to Thrace to deal with the Bulgars rebelled. Several officers travelled to Constantinople, stole into the city and attacked and blinded Bardanes while he was in the Hippodrome.

The fact that these men could take hold of the emperor in such a public setting, depose and then blind him without much opposition would seem to suggest that there was little public support for this Monothelite emperor. Bardanes was dead before 713 was out, suggesting that his blinding had done for him, either through its messiness, shock or infection.

The man who succeeded Bardanes on the throne did not last much longer. The choice of the rebellious Opsikion officers had fallen upon the blinded emperor's principal secretary, Artemius. Ruling as Anastasius II (713–715), the latest new emperor attempted to fix the problems caused by his predecessors. He deposed John VI, replacing him with the orthodox Germanus in 715 and re-established the canons of the Sixth Ecumenical Council, which ended the short-lived schism with Rome. Anastasius also attempted to halt the advances of the Umayyads into Anatolia through diplomacy, and when this failed, he ordered the restoration of the walls and fleet of Constantinople. He tried to disrupt the Arab preparations for a grand invasion by dispatching Leo the Isaurian, now Anatolic *strategos*, to invade Syria and the imperial navy to Rhodes to raid Umayyad stores and hinder any advance by the Arab fleet.

This seems like a strong and decisive start to the reign of Anastasius II, but he had made one drastic error. Almost immediately upon his accession, the emperor attempted to impose discipline on the army, specifically on the Opsikion. The officers who had blinded Bardanes were executed. These strict disciplinary measures and the reaction to this imperial ingratitude led to further mutiny. They murdered the admiral John and declared a low-born tax-collector, Theodosius, as their candidate to replace the ungrateful Anastasius. For the next six months, Constantinople became the scene of a contest between the forces loyal to Anastasius II and the Opsikion troops backing Theodosius III (715–717). This siege/blockade eventually saw Constantinople fall to the Opsikions, but not before Anastasius was able to flee to Nicaea. A year later, in 716, he would submit to Theodosius III and enter a monastery in Thessalonica. He would re-emerge during the reign of Leo III with Bulgar support, only to face total defeat and execution. But if it was to be Leo III who would see to the final defeat and demise of Anastasius II in 719, what had happened to Theodosius III in the meantime?

In short, Theodosius' heart never seems to have been in the imperial game. When the Opsikions had decided to elevate him in opposition to Anastasius in 715, he reputedly fled to a forest near Adramyttium – this seems a little beyond the traditional, deferential show of reluctance to accept

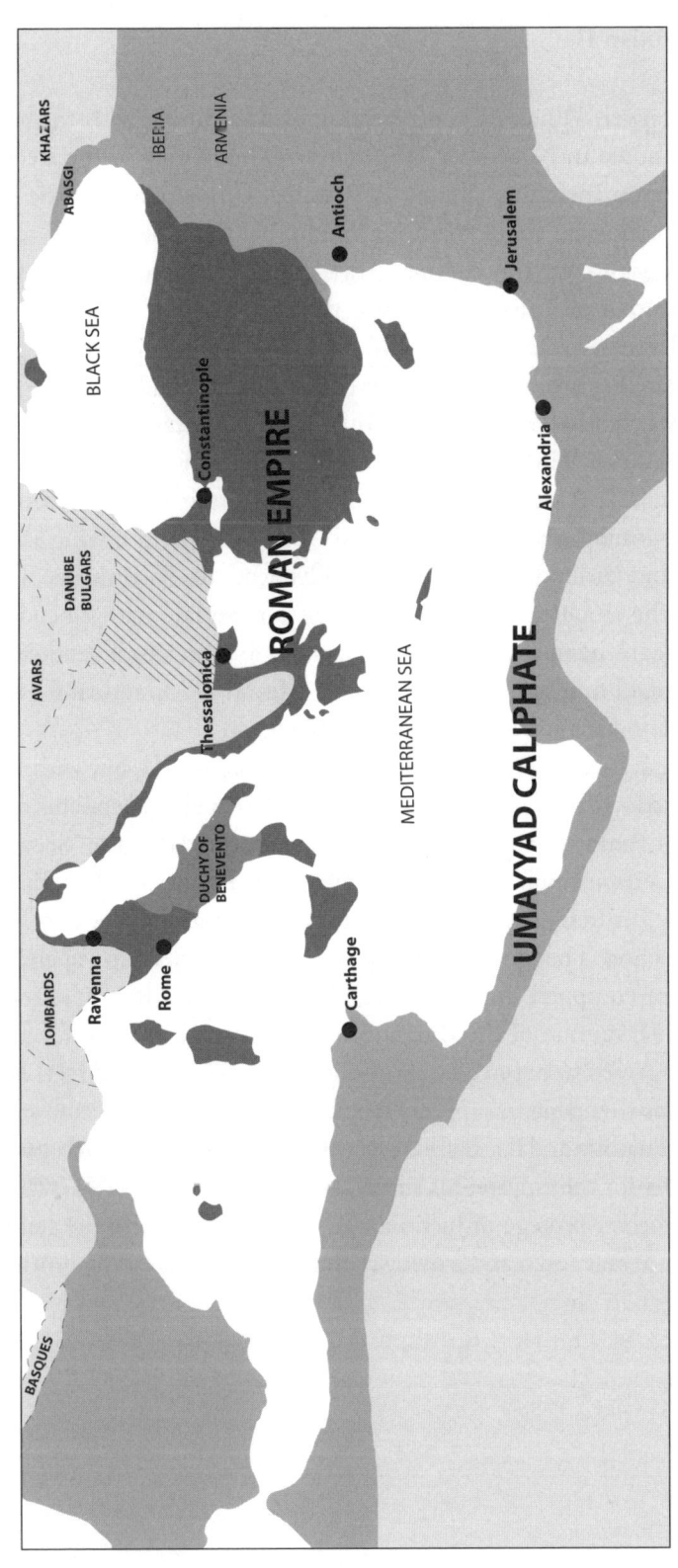

The Umayyad Caliphate and Roman Empire c.750.

imperial power. When he was placed upon the throne with the capture of Constantinople in November 715, he proved moderate in the treatment of his opponents, including sparing Anastasius. Unfortunately, little is known about Theodosius' short reign. It might be thought that he continued the preparations for the coming Arab grand invasion. Most importantly, along with that of Justinian II, it was the diplomacy of Theodosius III that produced a treaty with Tervel in 716, which brought Bulgar help against the Arabs, even if it involved significant concessions of land.

But it was not to be Theodosius III who led the defence of Constantinople in 717/718. Proclaiming his support for Anastasius II, Leo the Isaurian rebelled in 717. Aided by his Armeniac ally, Artabasdos, and a reputation built on outmanoeuvring various Arab commanders in buying the empire time in and around Amorion, Leo advanced to Nicomedia. There, he captured the emperor's son and used him to negotiate with Theodosius III. Perhaps again demonstrating his reluctance for the job, Theodosius rather swiftly agreed to resign the throne on 25 March 717 in return for the safety of himself and his son as they entered the clergy.

Leo the Isaurian therefore took the throne as Leo III, but within months he was faced with a crisis which would seem destined to curtail his reign even more than those of Anastasius II and Theodosius III – the 'Second' Arab Siege of Constantinople of 717/718. However, Leo was to benefit from the diplomatic, military, naval and structural preparations made by Justinian, Anastasius and Theodosius. On top of his own leadership capabilities, the Greek Fire-equipped imperial fleet, the restored walls of Constantinople and the intervention of the Bulgars enabled Leo III to resist for a full year before the Arabs were forced to abandon the siege. Bolstered by this success, Leo III was then able to suppress rebellions, win further success against the Arabs in Anatolia and build alliances with the Khazars and Georgians. Most importantly for the empire, his survival of the Arab siege in 717/718 enabled Leo, the former protégé of Justinian II, to give the empire the stability of a twenty-four-year reign and a dynasty that was to last into the ninth century.

Conclusions

From Tyrant to Tyrant?
The Heraclian Cycle is Complete

'Justinian of Byzantium, born to the purple, imperious, hot-tempered, wilful, sometimes cruel, yet indisputably brave and intelligent and above all possessed of invincible determination to overcome adversity.'

Head (1972), 4

For the male line of the Heraclian dynasty to end with an infant being butchered 'like a senseless animal'[1] and a noseless head being paraded around the provinces as proof of death seems unjust. They had dragged the Roman Empire back from the abyss, not once, not twice, but three times during the seventh century. It had begun by freeing Constantinople from the grip of a supposed tyrant, snatching ultimate victory from the jaws of defeat against the Persians and then showing considerable fortitude in cobbling together some kind of defence against what looked like an irresistible Arab onslaught. These achievements did engender some lasting loyalty to the Heraclians; somewhat contrariwise, this was best demonstrated in the reaction to the military catastrophe that overtook the Roman Empire on the Heraclians' watch. As the empire suffered repeated defeat and territorial loss on an immense scale, it is not surprising to find that all of the Heraclians who sat on the imperial throne faced attempts to unseat them – John Athalarichos, Valentinus, Gregory the Patrician, Mezizios, Saborius. And yet, until Justinian II, none of these revolts came anywhere near succeeding. Even the assassination of Constans II, fuelled by his unpopularity, was more a personal endeavour and the subsequent military revolt fell flat in the face of Constantine IV's leadership. While various circumstances affected this lack of success, there must have been some notion of the Heraclians being able to command the loyalty of enough of the empire, despite the desperate circumstances it found itself in with the Arab, Slav, Bulgar and Lombard invasions.

So, what was different about the reign of Justinian II for revolt to be successful against him (twice) and not against his familial predecessors?

The source tradition of Theophanes and Nikephoros would have it that it was because Justinian was a monster: an attacker of the established order of things in his 'purges' of the aristocratic and military hierarchies in his first reign, and then an avatar of bloody revenge upon his restoration. Such tyrannical reigns signalled the necessary and somewhat cyclical end of the dynasty. The Heraclians both won and ultimately lost imperial power through a provincial usurpation against a seemingly unpopular emperor – the African revolt of Heraclius against Phocas and the Cherson revolt of Bardanes against Justinian II. Of course, as has been mentioned throughout this work and in virtually anything written about Justinian, care has to be taken in dealing with his depiction by the source material. Indeed, both Phocas and Justinian II saw their reputations significantly and possibly unfairly ruined by hostile sources marshalled by the regimes of their immediate successors.

While this 'intensified historiographical hostility'[2] leaves everything we know about Justinian's actions and motives tinged with doubt, there must have been some basis for this hostility beyond the chroniclers of Leo III and the Isaurian dynasty feeling the need to build up a 'big bad emperor'. Indeed, given that Leo III did not take the throne from Justinian II, it might be wondered why, if Justinian did not breed some actual unpopularity in himself during his lifetime, Leo III did not have his historians play up his connection to Justinian and therefore the Heraclians as a source of legitimacy? There may have been some personal dislike due to the Caucasian mission, but Leo would surely have overcome that if there was some usefulness to be garnered from a connection to Justinian II.

It must be highlighted that the prevailing circumstances facing the Roman Empire in the seventh century made it easy for even largely successful emperors to be portrayed in a poor light. The loss of territory and repeated internal discord were an ever-ready stick to beat any emperor with, particularly when he found another way to make himself unpopular. Military failure was surely held against Phocas, adding to any rumours of tyrannical behaviour. Despite doing much to save the empire in the 620s, Heraclius made himself unpopular with his support of Monothelitism, something doubled-down on by Constans II with not only Monothelitism but his consideration of moving the imperial capital from Constantinople. The impact of the poor state of the empire on the reputation of an emperor might be best seen in the treatment of Tiberius III, who actually seems to have overseen some military success against Bulgars and Umayyads, but his seven-year reign gets completely overlooked. Could it be that some of the historical traditions were affected by his attack on Constantinople and allowing his soldiers to plunder parts of the city?

Even looking past the exaggeration of the sources, there are certainly aspects of Justinian II's policies which bred opposition. That said, there was nothing radical about any of his agrarian, tax or administrative policies, with many merely the next logical and necessary step following his Heraclian predecessors. They may even be part of a recognition that many of the now centuries-old systems would no longer work in the Roman Empire of the late seventh century. This may be seen in his extension of the themes to include Hellas, Sicily and perhaps Sardinia, as well as laying the foundations of an exclusively naval theme in the Cibyrrhaeots. Indeed, it could be that it was under Justinian that the *themata* were fully realized as a 'system', rather than just a series of necessary but unplanned developments. The tax and land reforms encapsulated in the *Nomos Georgikos* may have been conceived to protect small landowners – an increasingly important class in the new thematic empire – while his colonial policy was something emperors had done for centuries.

Nevertheless, logical and necessary reforms do not equate to popular reforms. With such finite resources, reforming the empire was always going to see certain groups losing out on incomes and privileges they had previously enjoyed. For Justinian, even if he did not target them specifically or vindictively, that group was frequently the aristocracy. Undermining the power, wealth and influence of the aristocrats might not have been a problem had he attained or maintained the support of other groups. Unfortunately, even those who may have benefitted from some of Justinian's policies might also have missed out through others. An increasing meritocracy could have fostered a loyal cadre of military officers, but over-reliance on these few men may have raised the ire of the officer corps as a whole. The military colonies might have provided new sources of recruitment and tax, but they may also have removed land from certain local landowners, while the reduction of taxes on some will have seen taxes raised on others. It was a difficult balancing act; one which it would seem Justinian was not entirely successful in achieving. When these groups showed even the slightest hint of disaffection with Justinian's actions and policies, he perhaps gave further rein to potentially unscrupulous officials like Stephen and Theodotus, with their stonings, whippings, eight-year imprisonments and roasting of feet exacerbating opposition to Justinian's policies, reign and person.

Despite setting himself up as a champion of orthodoxy, Justinian managed to spark some opposition in religious spheres as well. In the East, and particularly in and around Constantinople itself, his actions towards Kallinikos will have roused some disquiet. He pressured the patriarch into giving up a church in the imperial palace for a fountain/meeting place, and to innovate (something the Church was loathe to do) a prayer for the deconsecration. Even with his building of a replacement at Petrion, the tearing down of a church cannot have gone down well with the faithful. This will have been exacerbated by his deposition, blinding and exile of Kallinikos after his restoration in 705. Even if these actions were seen by some as appropriate given the patriarch's backing of the rebellion against Justinian in 695 and his crowning of both Leontios and Tiberius III, any harsh action against a religious man will have reflected badly.

In the West, it was Quinisext and the reactions over it that were the most important for Justinian's depiction. Indeed, the papal-imperial arguments over Quinisext show various sides of Justinian II. We see the champion of orthodoxy, following in his father's and illustrious namesake's footsteps, backing the Church against heresy and improper practices. However, when his Quinisext canons met papal opposition, we see the irascible character who would lash out at those who opposed his will, following the less pious footsteps of his grandfather, Constans II, in trying to have the pope arrested. But while many of the sources would want it believed that it was that impious emperor who predominated, in his dealings with Pope Constantine, Justinian proved that even when he continued to uphold the imperial majesty of his position in presenting himself able to demand the pope's presence in the East, he was capable of negotiation and learning from his past mistakes.

The good relations between Justinian and Pope Constantine, despite the so-called 'Byzantine Papacy', were soon to seem more and more like an outlier in imperial-papal relations rather than the norm. The coming Iconoclasm of Leo III and Constantine V would have a drastic effect on those relations throughout the eighth century. This was to be exacerbated by Ravenna falling out of the imperial orbit with its conquest by the Lombards in 751, while the papacy looked increasingly to the kingdom of the Franks for temporal protection, culminating in the crowning of Charlemagne as the 'Emperor of the Romans' by Pope Leo III in 800.

Justinian's Quinisext lingered on for a century and might even have had some impact on the outbreak of Iconoclasm with its focusing of attention on the depiction of Christ, a significant aspect of Christian iconography. The more definitive impact made by Justinian's Christ iconography came in imperial numismatics and Christian art throughout the Mediterranean world and beyond. While there was an Iconoclasm-sized gap between Justinian's Christ coinage and it becoming the definitive design for Roman imperial *solidi/nomismata* under Michael III post-843, this does not undermine the fact that the most prevalent depiction of Christ on Roman coins and in Christian art owes it form to the precedent set by Justinian II.

Perhaps it was less what Justinian II was attempting to do with his reforms in various social, political, military and religious settings, and more how he went about it that stoked such opposition. He seems to have lacked the finesse displayed by his father, relying instead on force of character and the majesty of his imperial position, rather than making any attempt at building some consensus; or at least making some show of it. Falling back on the autocratic nature of his position to impose change, however necessary or fair, and compounding it by reacting poorly to any opposition to those changes or his means will have exacerbated opposition. In that, Justinian II could again be seen more as the successor of his grandfather Constans II in terms of temperament. This lack of finesse may also be reflected in the breadth of areas he attempted to reform at a time when the empire was under territorial strain. The combination of some religious and aristocratic opposition not only affected Justinian's reign at the time, but also in the pages of history as clergy and the educated elite were the men who would be writing and embellishing the story of Justinian for posterity.

But why did the revolts against Justinian succeed when they had failed against his forebears? On both occasions, despite the growth of the themes and the power of the various *strategoi*, the removals of Justinian II demonstrated the importance of Constantinople itself as an imperial residence and military bastion. Unlike all the other revolts against Heraclian emperors, that of Leontios took place within the capital itself. This put the emperor within striking distance of the rebels and left him at the whim of the 'wait-and-see/cynical self-preservation' instincts of the army. Once Leontios and his men got within reach of Justinian, the regime crumbled. As for the revolt of Bardanes, it was perhaps only successful due to Justinian's ill-conceived departure from the city for Sinope/Armenia. Had he stayed put in the imperial palace, this usurpation could easily have broken against the walls of the capital.

Both these revolts also involved some unfortunate choices by Justinian. That of Leontios encompassed the poor treatment of Leontios himself, other military officials and members of the aristocracy. Keeping so many of them imprisoned in Constantinople provided not only a focus of opposition, but also a cadre of manpower when Leontios was persuaded to revolt by his monastic friends. While the involvement of rebels and Khazars undermined the Chersonite expeditions, Justinian's choices of commanders, possible treatment of these commanders and their families and supposed aims for the expeditions reflect poorly on his strategic sense. It is a reflection only worsened by his move out of the capital at the crucial point of Bardanes' revolt. While this might have seemed like a clever, proactive move against Armenian rebels, in reality it was a grave and ultimately fatal error.

Such actions play into the chronicle attempts to portray Justinian as hot-headed and of reckless ill-judgement; however, there is plenty of evidence to suggest that the emperor could be far more measured in his actions, diplomacy and policies. He is seen trying to build more peaceful relations with the Umayyads; he showed a willingness to look past Roman prejudices to build good relations with the Khazars and Bulgars; and he proved willing to compromise with the papacy over the Quinisext canons despite his bitter falling out with Sergius. Even in the face of treachery from his Khazar brother-in-law, Justinian proved capable of restraint.

Even the sack of Ravenna and the expeditions against Cherson, both drastic events and presented as the results of Justinian's thirst for bloody vengeance, may have been completely valid imperial responses rather than a raft of punitive attacks. With possible rebellion from both the Church and hierarchy of Ravenna, and foreign intervention in Cherson in the form of the *tudun* and a Khazar army, no emperor could be expected to allow rebellion and invasion to go unanswered when he was in a position to act. One wonders what Justinian might have planned for Busir had he remained on the throne longer, even with his Khazar wife by his side and his half-Khazar son and heir. If circumstances had permitted, it could well have been that Justinian would have used Busir's repeated treachery to attack the Khazars more definitively, ejecting them from the Crimea and perhaps using his new Alan allies in the Caucasus and Bulgar contacts to strike more directly at the Khazar Khaganate.

While Justinian had proven that the Crimea was within his military grasp, for him to achieve success in any such Khazar expedition would require a significant turnaround in his military fortunes. To call the military record of Justinian's reigns 'mixed' might even be a bit generous. He certainly had his successes, particularly early in his rule. The eastern campaign led by Leontios quickly proved to the Umayyads that the new regime of Justinian II was going to be as proactive as that of his father, winning an improved treaty in the process. While seemingly of immense success, driving into northern Iraq, Leontios' Armenian campaign could also be said to reflect more the internal distractions of the Umayyad caliphate than the abilities of Justinian's forces. His own personal campaign to Thessalonica may have saved the city and allowed for the establishment of the Hellas theme, some later military colonies and other governmental apparatus on the Greek peninsula. Ultimately, this was his most lasting military success, but even that was possibly tinged by a reverse suffered on the return journey east.

The cowing of Ravenna was perhaps his only other success of note, but it may highlight that most of Justinian's military achievements provided only limited benefit to the empire in the long run. The Ravennate strike of Theodore, the Sicilian *strategos*, seems more an achievement of pre-emptive action, rather than strength of arms, and it was, of course, an internal problem for the empire rather than dealing a blow to its external enemies. Virtually none of the other military successes won in Justinian's name had any long-term positives for the empire. The machinations of Leo the Isaurian amongst the Abasgi and Alans may have had some limited diplomatic benefit, but failed to create a bloc of Christian states aligned with Constantinople or to dislodge Umayyad influence from the western Caucasus.[3] The military successes in the initial stages of the Cherson expeditions were completely undone by the political developments that followed in their wake, with revolt, foreign invasion and usurpation.

Against these limited, ethereal successes were some significant losses for Justinian and the forces of the empire. In the Balkans, while Justinian's expedition to Thessalonica and his alliance with Tervel may have improved the empire's strategic position, he suffered two reverses that undermined those benefits. The check he suffered on his return east from Thessalonica may have undone much of the intimidatory impact on the local Slavs and Bulgars achieved by his march west along the *Via Egnatia*. The more decisive reverse at Anchialus, even if it did not involve Tervel's Bulgars, may have similarly overturned any strategic gain made by the Balkan campaign of Tiberius III and stunted any attempts to cow those non-khanate Bulgars still raiding Roman Thrace.

Worse still were the reverses suffered in Anatolia. Despite the strategic effectiveness of taking advantage of the caliphate's distractions, the disaster at Sebastopolis in 692 overturned the achievements of Constantine IV and Justinian himself. Through this battlefield proof that the Roman successes of the 670s and the distraction of the Second Fitna had not led to a definitive shift in power along the Romano-Umayyad frontier, Abd al-Malik was able to resume the annual Umayyad raids of Roman territory. This may have been aided by the damage done to the thematic armies at Sebastopolis, which was also perhaps the original catalyst for the revolt of Leontios. This was a situation only worsened by the destruction of Tyana in 708, which confirmed the loss of eastern Cilicia to the empire and that the Taurus Mountains were no longer a significant barrier to Umayyad raids. Justinian's inability to give more attention to Anatolia allowed the Arabs to become more brazen in their raiding, reaching the Bosphorus and paving the way for the great Arab land and sea advances that would culminate in the year-long siege of Constantinople in 717–718.

On top of these defeats and their consequences where Justinian took military action, there were also the military reverses faced by the empire where Justinian could not or would not send more troops. While it collapsed during his exile, Justinian provided little help to the crumbling African exarchate and made no attempt to reclaim it once he was back on the throne, beyond the establishing of themes in the western Mediterranean. Similarly, in Italy, aside from these thematic promotions, there is little to suggest that Justinian made any attempt to build up imperial forces there against the Lombards. Even the attack on Ravenna did not represent a bolstering of the imperial position in Italy as it was undertaken by forces already present in Sicily. Of course, such a failure does not necessarily reflect poorly on Justinian himself, but more on the growing inability of the core imperial provinces to provide sufficient manpower to look after themselves and aid other imperial territories. It might even be argued that the establishing of local Sicilian and Sardinian administrations represented something of a tacit recognition by the central government at Constantinople that those regions would have to look after themselves. This slackening of central control over Italy also increased Pope Sergius I's ability to resist imperial pressure over the Quinisext canons.

What does all of this say about the character and personage of Justinian II? From the outset of his reign, he must have felt the weight of history on his then young shoulders from various outlets: there was the reputation of his family to live up to; the expectation that came with his imperial name; and the position of the empire both in terms of the ongoing military crisis and the achievements of his father in not only stemming the Arab tide, but even taking the fight to Umayyad territory. Being a Heraclian and a Justinian, the young emperor would have felt the pressure to repeat Heraclius' defeat of the Persians, Constantine IV's successes against the Arabs and Justinian I's reclaiming of many western territories in the mid-sixth century.

Having such grand expectations to live up to affected the character of Justinian II in both a positive and negative way. It made him an ambitious man of energy, determination and ability sufficient to recognize the needs of his empire, understand how to fulfil many of those needs and achieve some success in each of the areas of socio-political, military and religious reform he undertook. The extent of these reforms and the mess the Roman Empire found itself in forced him to be innovative in some of his policies. In the process, he may have proven more far-sighted than many of his contemporaries, seemingly to his detriment as many might not have seen the benefits in his reforms, misinterpreting them as moves against sections of the political and ruling classes. The determination, possibly even obstinacy, bred in him also saw Justinian overcome staggering odds. Few would have given the mutilated, hunted, virtually friendless exile a chance at survival when he took to the seas in that small boat near Phanagoria. And yet, within mere months, Justinian II was back on the imperial throne.

While it does seem that Justinian's reputation has been unfairly ruined by hostile sources, in trying to restore balance to his portrayal, we must be careful not to go too far the other way and present Justinian as more of a paragon of imperial rule than he deserves. It is very difficult for sources to completely invent negative stories about an emperor and have them accepted, particularly when those sources are being written during a time when many of the populace could still remember that emperor. So while we must question the hostile, misleading or even unintentionally forgetful source material, it could be that rather than completely inventing the ill-repute of Justinian II, they may be exaggerating negative actions and personal flaws to paint a horrendous picture of an already somewhat ugly character.

His ambition, expectation and what he saw as the needs of his empire may have led him to overreach, trying too much too soon, at the wrong time or in the wrong way by running roughshod over 'entrenched traditions'.[4] His faith in his right to rule and his own ability to recognize and achieve what was needed may have blinded him to the wants, needs and even the power of his subjects. By failing to grasp the potential internal dangers of such rapid reform, coupled with a mixed military record – which itself could have been bred of overconfidence in his imperial status – Justinian made a rod for his own back.

For all the strength he drew from his belief in the sanctity of his imperial office, it also made Justinian adverse to any opposition or failure from his subordinates. His poor response to criticism and frustration with unwilling, unable or misunderstanding subordinates exposed him to hostile sources emphasizing his temper. The sources were also keen to portray Justinian as unforgiving, using the repeated attacks on Cherson and the blinding of Kallinikos as evidence of the emperor holding a grudge. This sort of skewing of the historical record may have led to the invention of a Ravennate connection to Justinian's initial deposition to explain the sack of Ravenna in the ugliest, most vengeful terms possible. Any such unforgiving nature could have been born of faith in himself and a recognition of the dire straits the empire found itself in, leading to an overreliance on officials and commanders who had shown some ability in fulfilling their roles, or more accurately, in fulfilling Justinian's orders. Such potential favouritism or long-term employment of certain officials may be the root of the reputed ill-behaviour of the likes of Stephen and Theodotus – prolonged tenures providing plenty of examples of harsh exactions and of jealousy from those other upper-class men seeking high office. Such a depiction of his officials, whether right or wrong, would then reflect poorly on Justinian, who had appointed, empowered and either ignored or encouraged them in their activities.

While Justinian may not have been too keen to pardon those who had wronged him, Kallinikos had betrayed the emperor, as had Cherson (more than once) and Ravenna. There are even prominent examples of Justinian's eventual clemency coming back to bite him in the form of the two men to succeed him on the throne. Leontios might have been unfairly imprisoned for his failure at Sebastopolis, but he was forgiven enough to be released and appointed as *strategos* of Hellas, a pardon that Leontios quickly repaid with rebellion and the deposition, mutilation and exile of Justinian. Furthermore, when the prophetic dream of Bardanes regarding his future imperial power came to the attention of Justinian, he followed the example of Tiberius III in exiling rather than imprisoning him. This was eventually repaid with deposition and murder.

It is entirely plausible that any such negative personality traits were exacerbated by Justinian's deposition, exile and mutilation. The violence of his *rhinokopia* stayed with him throughout his life, a constant reminder of the challenging and overturning of his Heraclian right to rule, not to mention the mental damage done by such physical trauma. The potential for Justinian's policies to be reasonable and even good for the empire can only have increased the indignation he felt at his deposition, mutilation and exile; a bitterness which may not have needed much stoking due to the pride he placed in his imperial heritage. It would also not be surprising if his experiences between 695 and 705 had bred a paranoid streak in Justinian. It had been proven through the revolt of Leontios, the willingness of the Chersonites to give him up to Tiberius III and the betrayal by Busir that people he was supposed to be able to trust – hosts, friends and family – had turned their back on him. That said, the record does show that post-restoration Justinian II was capable of negotiation with someone who refused to follow his orders in the form of Pope Constantine and the ongoing Quinisext controversy.

But even if it is accepted that the trauma inflicted on Justinian may have affected his decision-making, it does not exonerate him from some of his brutal actions. While some of those actions – Ravenna and Cherson – may have been perfectly reasonable responses to rebellion and invasion, along with the vengeance doled out to Leontios and Tiberius III, these military expeditions do help provide the bedrock for the accusations of his brutality in other areas. Was it really such a step to think that an emperor capable of pre-emptive action against a former imperial capital, however necessary, or the grisly, vengeful mutilation and execution of imperial rivals, could have also plotted to have Leo the Isaurian killed in the Caucasus? What of employing Stephen and Theodotus to torture and imprison any and all opposition, rather than just those who failed to pay their fair share of tax? Or targeting Helias' family for humiliation and execution? Or ordering the extermination of the populations of Cherson and Constantinople?

Is it really likely that all of this is completely false? The sources could certainly be imaginative, but it is unlikely that they invented every poor action. It may well be that attempting to extrapolate the 'truth' of Justinian II, cutting through the negativity of the source tradition of Nikephoros and Theophanes, does not necessarily present a much more palatable individual. The quiet of non-eastern sources might make us think twice about following the outrage of the *History to 720*, but then they also do not provide much information to balance out any underlying negativity that has been exaggerated in the portrayal of a nefarious and later mutilated madman.

This conundrum of a dual depiction of Justinian could perhaps only require the simplest of solutions: that Justinian II can be portrayed in such a mixed manner because he was a Roman emperor. This might seem *too* simplistic, but ultimately, he was an autocratic ruler faced with an empire not only in administrative, military and economic transition, but also facing a lingering existential crisis. Such a conglomeration of challenges almost certainly required not just Justinian II but all of the emperors of the previous century to be capable of the many facets of imperial rule, good and bad. Much like other Roman emperors, Justinian could well have been guilty of some of the outrages attributed to him, and even if some of them were perfectly understandable responses to the challenges he faced, they provided hostile sources with a credible basis for a believable portrayal as someone capable of the whole gamut of atrocities. Perhaps in the case of Justinian II, we have another example of a Roman emperor – like Domitian and Constantius II – who required a good publicist or court historian to counter the smearing of his reputation after his reign saw the end of a dynasty.

In the hands of a skilled historian, Justinian II's time on the imperial throne could have received some appropriate credit. From the age of just 16, he faced internal discord, barbarian incursions, war and ongoing doctrinal issues at a time when the Roman Empire was still going through the initial stages of a transformation from Mediterranean-spanning realm into an Early Medieval state centred on the border of Europe and Asia, with new provincial and economic structures to administer. A fair historical judge might recognize that as a policy-maker and strategian, Justinian II navigated this ever-changing landscape rather well. Indeed, if he could have tempered his reforming zeal, frustration and perhaps brought more of the ruling classes along with him, his determination and abilities may have seen the empire achieve more in the last years of the seventh and on into the eighth century.

If the Justinian of 685–695 had shown the willingness to compromise that the Justinian of 710 had done with Pope Constantine, the power of the Roman imperial reputation could have forged agreements with the willing Khazars and Bulgars without the need for the emperor to place his own personal safety in their hands. The same more-experienced Justinian might have recognized that a mad dash to confront the Umayyads before the manpower benefits of the Thessalonian campaign could be fully integrated into the Roman army was an unnecessary risk. Indeed, the continued Umayyad distraction with the Second Fitna may have been seen as less an opportunity to strike into Syria and more a chance to concentrate further effort on the Balkans. A more concerted campaign against the Slavs and non-Tervel Bulgars may have seen more of Greece, Macedonia and Thrace recovered for the empire. This in turn could have provided more manpower to challenge the Umayyads. The strengthening of Justinian's position in Anatolia may then have enabled him to make more concrete progress in the strategically sound plan to build an alliance with the Christian peoples of the Caucasus. This seems like going too far down the road of 'what if' counter-factual history, but Justinian II did show that he had the abilities – strategic foresight, administrative innovation, diplomatic skill and unyielding determination – to achieve such potential success. If only he had been a little less zealous in his reforming and prideful of his position.

Ultimately, for someone so keen to uphold the imperial majesty of his Heraclian dynasty and live up to the examples and achievements of his forefathers, Justinian II played a decisive role in the destruction of his family. Even accepting that Justinian is poorly treated by the sources, he must have done plenty to arouse such enmity or at least apathy at the heart of the empire to see him deposed twice. Various sections of the Roman populace surely would not have accepted the removal of the Heraclian dynasty, which had saved it from both Persians and Arabs in the seventh century, without its incumbent emperor bringing disfavour down upon himself. In Justinian II, that disfavour seems to have come from the assumptions he had made about his position as emperor: that his position gave him the right to not have his policies questioned, of the right to carry out those policies however he wanted, of the right to dictate doctrine to the Church, of the freedom from the consequences of a mixed military record and of the right to deal with opposition however he wanted. All of those presumptions saw him face the ignominy of being one of the few Roman emperors to be deposed more than once. Not only did they lose him his throne, they lost him his nose and eventually his head, thereby ending the dynasty in which he had so much pride.

Notes

Introduction

1. Head (1972), x, 4.
2. *Ibid.*, ix.
3. *Ibid*, 4; Howard-Johnston (2010), 517.
4. Head (1972), x.
5. Howard-Johnston (2010), 306–307; Treadgold in Bumazhnov *et al.* (2011), 595; Afinogenov (2002), 11–22.
6. *Suda* T901; a seal listing 'Trajan the Consul' could be the same man, although there is little to place this man's career in the late seventh century, apart from the seal appearing seventh-century in style; *PmbZ* no.8511; *PLRE* IIIb.1335; Treadgold in Bumazhnov *et al.* (2011) extrapolates a potential career outline for Trajan the Patrician.
7. Mango (1990), 16–17; Afinogenov (2002).
8. Forrest in Jankowiak and Montinaro (2015), 444.
9. Howard-Johnston (2010), 306; Forrest in Jankowiak and Montinaro (2015), 418.
10. Howard-Johnston (2010), 307.
11. Head (1972), 16; cf. Orosz (1948), 3–12.
12. Forrest in Jankowiak and Montinaro (2015), 418 n.4; Head (1972), 15–17.
13. Mango (1990), 15.
14. Brooks (1915), 42.
15. Head (1972), 16.
16. Mango and Scott (1997), lv.
17. Forrest in Jankowiak and Montinaro (2015), 418; Treadgold in Bumazhnov *et al.* (2011), 589.
18. Mango (1990), 12; Breckenridge (1959), 4.
19. Head (1972), 16.
20. Mango and Scott (1997), lxxxviii; Forrest in Jankowiak and Montinaro (2015), 418.
21. Brooks (1906), 578–587; Proudfoot (1974), 400–427; Conrad in Cameron and Conrad (1992), 317–401; Howard-Johnston (2010), 295–299; Woods (2011); Hoyland in Jankowiak and Montinaro (2015), 355–364; Debié in Jankowiak and Montinaro (2015), 365–382; Conterno in Jankowiak and Montinaro (2015), 383–400.
22. Howard-Johnston (2010), 305.
23. *Ibid.*
24. Brooks (1915), 42.
25. Hoyland (1997), 425; Woods (2011), n.10.
26. Conrad (1998), 63; Koscielniak (2004), 10–11.
27. Hunger (1978), I.393–394.
28. Brooks (1915), 42; Chabot (1899), XXIII–XXXVII; Weltecke (2009), 112–116.
29. Agile (2005), 87–107; Takahashi (2005), 1–117; Weltecke (2009), 123–129; Teule (2003), 22–23.

30. Howard-Johnston (2010), 518.
31. *Ibid.*
32. Franklin (2017).
33. Heath (2017).
34. Head (1972), 96.
35. Pizarro (1995).
36. Treadgold (1990), 203; cf. Ostrogorsky (1968), 129–146, 152–156.
37. Treadgold (1990), 225.
38. Howard-Johnston (2010), 265.

Chapter 1: The Roman Empire of 668

1. Crawford (2013) on the events of the seventh century between the Romans, Persians and Arabs.
2. Crawford (2013), 224.
3. Brown (2006), 189.
4. This 'departure' or *Hijra* was such an important event in early Islamic history that it became the foundation date of the Muslim calendar, equating to 9 September 622.
5. McEvedy (1992), 32.
6. He had served prominently during the Romano-Persian War of 572–591, saving the Roman armies at Chlomaron and Sisarbanon, before being promoted to *magister militum per Armeniam* in 595; Theophylactus Simocatta, *Hist.* III.1.1; Sebeos, *History* ch.6–7.
7. Kaegi (2003) on the life and reign of Heraclius.
8. Nikephoros, *Brev.* 29 records how the animosity between Heraclius Constantine III and Martina was enough for Heraclius to deposit money with the patriarch 'on behalf of Empress Martina so she would not be lacking funds if she were driven out of the palace by her stepson'. This money would be appropriated by Heraclius Constantine and used to buy support for him and his son.
9. Constans was born and baptized as Herakleios, only to then rule as Constantine.
10. Theophanes, *Chron.* AM6146 has Constans having a poorly omened dream, which promised victory to his opponents before the engagement.
11. O'Sullivan (2004); Theophanes, *Chron.* AM6146 suggests that the Arab naval expeditions of the late 640s and early 650s were intended as a prelude to an attack on Constantinople.
12. Theophanes, *Chron.* AM6150 on Muawiyah agreeing to pay the Romans '1,000 *nomismata*, a horse and a slave per day'.
13. Theophanes, *Chron.* AM6153.
14. The six years that Constans II had spent in Italy and Sicily was perhaps the longest Constantinople had gone without the presence of a ruling *Augustus* since the first half of the fourth century.
15. Constans II's religious policy seems to have rankled with the Armenians, leading them to accept Arab suzerainty in return for limited autonomy, although they and their Caucasian neighbours in Iberia and Lazica would frequently rebel when Arab rule became heavy-handed. It was only with a more ruthless crackdown and the imposition of an Arab governor in the 730s that Arab control became definitive.
16. Theophanes, *Chron.* AM6153; the word used by Theophanes to describe the murder weapon – κάδιον – translated by Mango and Scott (1997), 491 as 'bucket' is translated by Turtledove (1982), 51 as 'soap dish'.
17. Head (1972), 4.

18. Mauricius, *Strat.* VII, XII; Fabian (2015), 571–577.
19. Mousourakis (2003), 402–403 would have it that this transition away from the Latin legal codices to Greek compilations and summaries marked a weakening in imperial legal standards and scholarship.
20. Head (1972), 5.
21. *Ibid.*
22. They encapsulated areas in and around Rome, Venetia, Calabria, Naples, Perugia, Pentapolis, Lucania, Liguria and Umbria.
23. Such a reintegration of civilian and military powers had already appeared in several areas of the empire under Justinian I. Certain governors in Asia Minor had been given military authority to deal with brigands. The diocese of Egypt had been reformed with a *dux* at its head with civilian and military authority, while the military-civilian position of *quaestura exercitus* – 'quaestor of the army' – had been created in the Danube provinces.
24. Africa Proconsularis, Byzacena, Tripolitania (which would be attached to Egypt later), Numidia, Mauretania Caesariensis and Mauretania Sitifensis (as they dwindled in size, the Mauretanias were combined into one). There was some Roman presence in territory that had once been Mauretania Tingitania, but that really only extend to the city of Septem (modern Ceuta), on the Africa shore opposite Gibraltar, and perhaps not even there.
25. *PLRE* IIIa.554.
26. That said, even after its demise in 751, the Romans did not give up on the idea of an 'exarch' style commander in Italy. In the late tenth century, after a resurgence of Roman power in southern Italy had seen the creation of several new themes, the *strategos* of Bari was elevated to κατεπάνω (*katepano* – 'foremost'), which survived until the Norman conquest of southern Italy in the late eleventh century. This idea of a 'catepanate' appears in other parts of the empire where territory was reclaimed – Serbia, Iberia, Armenia, Antioch, Mesopotamia and Chaldea.
27. Kaegi (1967), 39–54.
28. Treadgold (1995), 23–24.
29. Haldon (1990), 215 n.27; Louth in Shepard (2008), 239–240, 266.
30. Theophanes, *Chron.* AM6113.
31. Ostrogorsky (1997), 101 n.1; Shahid (1987), 391–403; (1989), 208–243 on potential evidence of thematic terminology and organization in Syria before the Arab conquest; *contra* Haldon in Cameron (1995), 379–423.
32. Haldon (1990), 214–215; Louth in Shepard (2008), 239–240.
33. Head (1972), 81; Kaegi (1967), 39; Charanis (1963), 74–75.
34. Haldon (1993), 1–67; (1999), 71–74; Treadgold (1995), 24–25; Teall (1971), 47–48 and Oikonomides (1975), 1–8 both support Heraclius being the thematic originator; Toynbee (1973), 224–238, Lilie (1976), 287–338, Haldon (1975), 81–82, 96–107, Kaegi (1981), 174; Pertusi (1958), 1–40 and Karayannopoulos (1959) all follow the gradual evolution approach.
35. Lilie (1977), 7–47; Haldon (1997), 212–214.
36. Haldon (1990), 216; (1999), 87. A separate Thracian *strategos* is not clearly referenced in the sources until 742.
37. The name derives from the Greek κάραβις, meaning 'ship'.
38. Pryor and Jeffreys (2006), 35; Cosentino (2008), 602.
39. Ahrweiler (1966), 22–23.
40. Treadgold (1997), 315; Pryor and Jeffreys (2006), 25.
41. Ahrweiler (1966), 23–25.

42. Treadgold (1997), 73 vs Haldon (1999), 74; although Ahrweiler (1966), 12 regards such origin claims as merely hypothetical.
43. This is by no means certain, with Rhodes, Keos and Samos also suggested as the base of the Karabisiani *strategos*.
44. Ahrweiler (1966), 24–25.
45. Head (1972), 82.
46. Haldon (2016), 165; Winkelmann (1987).
47. Possibly only Ctesiphon and later Baghdad were in the same kind of size bracket – claiming Constantinople being in the range of 1 million residents by *c.*700 might be over reach; Morris (2010); Modelski (2003); Chandler (1987).
48. This outer wall could be a slightly later addition to the initial inner 'Theodosian' wall, but this has been doubted: Meyer-Plath and Schneider (1943), 4; Bardill (2004), 123; Philippides and Hanak (2011), 299–302.
49. Woods in Lewin and Pellegrini (2007) on plague having a significant effect on the Roman army defeated at Yarmuk in 636.
50. Donner (1981), 3, Hoyland (2014), 93.
51. Although not to the pope, who was not officially styled *pontifex maximus* until the Renaissance; Cameron (2007), 341–384 suggests that Gratian kept the title and that Theodosius I may also have used it.
52. Head (1972), 6; this could arguably be a continuation of the presence of pagan altars, shrines and items in or near all houses under the pagan Roman Empire.
53. Optatus, *Against the Donatists* III.3.
54. Under the guidance of their patriarch at Tiberias, the Jews represented a rather large proportion of the Roman population – Noethlichs (1996), 10, 151–153 n.64–68 on the estimates of Jewish population in the Empire; Wasserstein (1996), 309–314 against the usual total of nearly 7 million. The Diaspora and the Christianization of the Empire saw the Jews treated with a suspicion that was to become all too common and unjustified as the centuries wore on. Influenced by past revolts, Romans saw these Jewish communities as a potential 'fifth column' always on the verge of rebellion and one that 'openly rejoiced at the calamities of the empire'; Jones (1964), 950. As a result of both this political and religious suspicion, Jews were not allowed to marry Christians, make a will, inherit, testify in court, were 'barred from seeking entrance to the imperial service' (*CTh* XVI.8.24[418]) and there is some evidence of forced conversion on a local level. However, in the late seventh century, the Romans did have some justification for their wariness towards the Jewish community. While the insidious nature of the Diaspora was illusionary, the potential trouble posed by those Jews who remained in Palestine was not. They had invited the Persians to take Palestine, joined them in the siege of Jerusalem and later welcomed the Muslims.

Chapter 2: Imperial Opponents: Arabs, Avars, Lombards, Slavs, Bulgars, and Khazars

1. Madelung (1997).
2. Mecca (Arabia), Medina (Arabia), Basra (Iraq), Kufa (Iraq), Jazira in the upper Tigris and Euphrates, Syria, Aylya (Palestine), Ramlah (Palestine), Upper Egypt, Lower Egypt, Azerbaijan (Persia), Fars (Persia) and Khurasan (Persia). There were also some semi-autonomous regions such as Armenia.
3. Pourshanti (2008); Akram (2009).
4. Al-Tabari, 2816–2817; cf. Al-Ma'sumi (1964), 97–102.
5. Diehl (1896), 559–560.
6. Madelung (1997), 80; Uthman's foster-brother Abdullah b. Saad was made governor of Egypt; his half-brother, al-Walid b. Uqba, governor of Kufa; his

maternal cousin, Abdallah b. Amir, governor of Basra, while Syria was in the hands of Muawiyah. When al-Walid had to be deposed from the Kufa governorship due to misconduct, he was succeeded by another Umayyad, Sa'id b. al-As.

7. The caliph did something similar for Abdallah b. Amir in Basra, expanding his province to take in Oman and Bahrain and giving him direct command of their garrisons.

8. Madelung (1997), 80; Kennedy (2004), 75.

9. Madelung (1997), 80–81.

10. *Ibid.*, 113–140.

11. *Ibid.*, 140.

12. The exact timeline and motives of individuals involved in the aftermath of Uthman's assassination and Ali's election is not completely clear.

13. Madelung (1997), 148–149.

14. *Ibid.*, 267–269; 293–307.

15. Holland (2012), 399.

16. One of Muawiyah's closest advisers was Sergius, son of Mansur, father of St John Chrysorrhoas of Damascus.

17. Kaegi (1992), 185; 244–245, 247; Kennedy (2004), 87; Jankowiak (2013), 273.

18. The name 'Avar' appears in the fifth-century *History* of Priscus of Panium, who records the forward movement of the Saragur, Onogur and Ogur Huns as being caused by the advances of the Sabirs, who had in turn been driven west by the 'Avars' (Priscus fr.40; Maenchen-Helfen (1973), 436). However, it has been suggested that these fifth-century 'Avars' are not the same people called Avars in the 550s (Sinor (1946–1947), 35).

19. Menander Protector fr.43.

20. The Avars seem to have driven west into Germania in the early 560s, so deeply that they came into contact with the Franks in Thuringia.

21. Pohl (2002), 158.

22. Fredegar, *Chronicle* IV.48; Constantine VII, *de adm. imp.* 30–31.

23. Barford (2001), 78–79; Curta (2004); (2006), 92–93.

24. It is worth noting that the Lombards were not the only Germans to retreat in the face of the Avar advance. The Franks pulled out of Thuringia, the Bavarians evacuated Bohemia and the Saxons moved west of the Elbe. Demonstrating the lack of numbers of the Avars themselves, the lands evacuated by these Germans and incorporated into the Avar Khaganate were actually inhabited by Slavs.

25. The *Codex Gothanus*, an early ninth-century source, instead posits Lombard origins on the boundary of northern Gaul. The Lombard origin story presented by the *Codex Gothanus* is so different to that of the *Origo Gentis Langobardorum* and Paul the Deacon that Hodgkin (1896), VI.146 n.B did not attempt to find a coherent narrative by combining them, choosing instead to print the two stories separately.

26. Paul the Deacon, *HL* I.8.

27. *Origo Gentis Langobardorum* 1; cf. Paul the Deacon, *HL* I.8.

28. Priester (2004), 17; Fröhlich (1976), 19; Bruckner (1895), 30–33; other suggested etymologies focus on the Old High German root, *barta*, meaning 'axe', and börde/börd, which meant 'a fertile plain by the side of a river' and may still be seen in the names Bardengau and Bardewick, while a district near Magdeburg was called 'lange Börde'. This might see the Langobards as either 'the men of the long axes' or 'the men of the long river plain'.

29. Tacitus, *Ger.* 40.

30. Velleius II.106.
31. Tacitus, *Ann.* II.45; Strabo, *Geog.* VII.1.3.
32. Suetonius, *Claudius* 1; Dio LV.1; Tacitus, *Ann.* II.5-26; IV.44; Velleius II.104.
33. Tacitus, *Ann.* II.45, XI.16, 17.
34. Wegewitz (1964), 19; (1972), 1–29.
35. Priester (2004), 18.
36. Dio LXXI.3.
37. *Codex Gothanus* 2; Priester (2004), 14
38. Jordanes, *Getica* 116; Burns (1984), 37–38; Wolfram (1988), 86–89.
39. Some Lombards likely remained in their Lower Elbe homelands, to be absorbed by Saxon or Slav tribes; *Ravennatis Anonymi Cosmographia* I.11.
40. Paul the Deacon, *HL* I.16 records a significant defeat of the Lombards by 'Bulgarians', which for the fourth century should be read as 'Huns'.
41. Paul the Deacon, *HL* I.19.
42. Procopius, *BG* VIII.26.10–13.
43. Paul the Deacon, *HL* I.27, II.6.
44. *Ibid.*, *HL* II.7.
45. The Lombard migration to Italy will also have included significant numbers of non-Lombards. Paul the Deacon speaks of a sizeable contingent of Saxons joining Alboin and several other groups being established in 'Lombard' territory in Italy: Gepids, 'Bulgarians' (Avars), Sarmatians, 'Suebians' (probably Bavarians) and some Roman provincials from Pannonia and Noricum (Paul the Deacon, *HL* II.6). There were probably some Rugians and other tribal remnants caught up in this migration and trying to escape the Avar yoke.
46. Paul the Deacon, *HL* II.26–27.
47. *Ibid.*, *HL* II.28.
48. John of Biclaro, *Chronicle s.a.*576.
49. Paul the Deacon, *HL* IV.41.
50. Heather (2009), 386.
51. Jordanes, *Getica* V.34–35.
52. Pliny, *NH* IV.96–97; Tacitus, *Ger.* 46; Ptolemy, *Geog.* III.5.21.
53. Curta (1998), (2001), 39–43.
54. Heather (2009), 395; it should also be mentioned that the famous *Tabula Peutingeriana* from the third/fourth century depicts the *Venedi* on the northern bank of the Danube somewhat upstream of its mouth, and the *Venadi Sarmatae* along the Baltic coast; Procopius, *BG* VII.14.30 also gives the Sclaveni and the Antae a common ancestor tribe, although instead of the Venedi, he posits the Sporoi, a name meaning 'seeds' in Greek. There has been some attempt to use this as evidence of a potential connection between the Slavs and the Suebi of Tacitus, with both Jordanes and Procopius calling the Suebi 'Suavi' and the ninth-century *Bavarian Geographer* not only listing the 'Suevi' amongst his Slavic tribes but also suggesting that 'Suevi are not born, they are sown' (Metzner (2011), 321, 347).
55. Heather (2009), 388.
56. Curta (2001), 309; Geary (2003), 145.
57. Schenker (1996), 3–5.
58. Heather (2009), 398.
59. Kortlandt (1990), 4; Sussex and Cubberley (2011), 22 on 'geographical contiguity, parallel development and interaction' possibly explaining the existence of these language-group characteristics.
60. Curta (2001), 46, 60.
61. Curta (2001), 117–119, 347.

62. Heather (2009), 390–391; Heather (2009), 389–390 sums up much of this problem, displaying it on Map 17.
63. Curta (2001), 7, 11–13; Heather (2009), 391–392.
64. Curta (2001), chs 3, 6.
65. Pohl in Little and Rosenwein (1998), 20.
66. Mauricius, *Strat*. IX.3.
67. *Ibid.*, *Strat*. XI.4.
68. Procopius, *BG* V.27.1–3, VII.14.25; Mauricius, *Strat*. XI.4; Theophylactus Simocatta, *Hist*. VII.4; Curta (2001), 143 on their shared history with Sarmatians, Huns and Avars possibly being responsible for their ability as horsemen.
69. Mauricius, *Strat*. XI.4.
70. Procopius, *BG* VII.14.22.
71. Geary (2003), 145.
72. Barford (2001), 124.
73. Jordanes, *Getica* 48.247.
74. Heather (1991), 23–27.
75. Procopius, *BG* VII.40.5–6.
76. *Ibid.*, *BG* VII.29.1–3, 38, 40; Procopius, *Secret History* 18.20 suggests that the raids had become annual; Curta (2001), 75–89.
77. Procopius, *BG* VI.26.16–22, VII.14.21, 32–33, 22.3–6; John of Ephesus VI.45; Theophylactus Simocatta VIII.5.13; Curta (2001), 37, 79–81.
78. Whitby (1988), 156ff.
79. Heather (2009), 405.
80. Fredegar, *Chronicle* IV.48; Constantine VII, *de adm. imp.* 30–31.
81. Golden (1992), 103–104.
82. Maenchen-Helfen (1973), 384; Golden (1992), 104; (2011), 143.
83. Chen (2012), 92–97.
84. Simeonov (2008), 108–113; Golden (2012), n.37.
85. Nikephoros, *Brev.* 24 called the Bulgar khan, Kubrat, 'the ruler of the Unogundurs', while Theophanes, *Chron.* AM6171 connects the Bulgars settled at the mouth of the Danube in 678 directly to the Unogundurs; Golden (1992), 104; (2011), 143.
86. Procopius, *BG* VII.2.2–5; Agathias I.3.4–5; Menander VIII.4.13, 5.23, 18.18.
87. Michael the Syrian, *Chronicle* 117.
88. Golden (1992), 99; (2011), 140.
89. Keramopulos (1953), 334–336; Detschev (1927), 199–216; Maenchen-Helfen (1973), 384.
90. *Chronology of 354, liber generationis II*, 77; Movses Khorenatsi 55–56; Paul the Deacon, *HL* I.16–17; II.26; Dimitrov (1987).
91. Priscus fr.30.5.
92. Mauricius, *Strat*. XIIb.1.
93. Wiita (1977), 122.
94. Mauricius, *Strat*. XI.2, II.1.
95. John of Antioch fr. 214.7, 303; Malchus fr.22; Zacharias, *HE* III.27; Ennodius, *Pan.* 19 on Theoderic the Amal reputedly killing the Bulgar leader in single combat; Paul the Deacon, *HR* XV.15.
96. Maenchen-Helfen (1973), 164.
97. John of Antioch fr.211.4.
98. Marcellinus Comes *s.a.* 493, 499; Jordanes, *Rom.* 356; cf. Zonaras III.137.
99. Marcellinus Comes *s.a.* 502.1.
100. Malalas XVIII.36 (who refers to Huns); Theophanes, *Chron.* AM6031, 6032; Kedrenos I.651; Curta in Istvan and Karatay (2015), 76.

101. Marcellinus Comes *s.a.* 505; Malalas XVI.16.
102. Golden (1992), 104.
103. *Ibid.*, 100.
104. Jordanes, *Get.* V.37 on the 'Bulgari'; Ps-Zacharias Rhetor, *HE* XII.7 on the 'Burgars'.
105. Reflecting the issues already presented on the identity and origins of the Bulgars, Kubrat's name and origin is recorded in various forms – Krobatos, Kubratos, Cubratus, Kuvrat, Qubrat, Qobrat, Xubraat – and he is referred to as 'king of the Onogundur Huns', 'lord of the Onuğundur', 'ruler of the Onuğundur-Bulğars', 'chief of the Huns', 'Onogur', 'Oğuro-Bulğar', 'Bulgar Hunnic/Hunnic Bulgar' and various others; Golden (1992), 244–245, 252; Kim (2013), 16, 101, 138; Hupchick (2017), 8.
106. Jordanes, *Get.* 270–271; Priscus fr.28, 37; Sidonius, *Carm.* II.223–226.
107. Sophoulis (2011), 111.
108. John of Nikiu, CXX.47–49.
109. It has been suggested by Mingazov (2012) that while translating the *Chronicle* of John of Nikiu from Ge'ez/Classical Ethiopian into French in 1883, Hermann Zotenberg changed the name 'Qetrades' to 'Kubrat', perhaps intentionally. This would make the whole hostage of the future Bulgar leader a misconception.
110. This Bulgar 'state' is also recorded as *Patria Onoguria* in the *Ravenna Cosmography*; Nikephoros, *Brev.* 22, who suggests that Heraclius honoured Kubrat with the title of patrician; Golden (2011), 145.
111. Theophanes, *Chron.* AM6171.
112. *Ibid.*, *Chron.* AM6171.
113. Somogyi (2008), 104.
114. Aibabin in Zuckermann (2006), 53; Somogyi (2008), 128.
115. Theophanes, *Chron.* AM6171; Nikephoros, *Brev.* 36.
116. Golden (1992), 103, 236–237; (2011), 144 suggests that the war between the Khazars and Bulgars in the wake of Kubrat's death could have had an aspect of the tribal politics of the West Turkic Khaganate to it, with it being as much a fight between the leading Ashina clan of the Khazars and the Bulgar Dulo clan.
117. Other historians such as Brook (2018), 15 call him 'Bayan', which may highlight connections to the Avars as two Avar khans were of that name.
118. Theophanes, *Chron.* AM6171.
119. Golden (1992), 245, 253–258.
120. Theophanes, *Chron.* AM6171.
121. Curta (2006), 106.
122. The inscription of the Madara Rider seemingly speaks of Tervel's 'uncles at Thessalonica'; Petkov (2008), 5.
123. Theophanes, *Chron.* AM6171.
124. Paul the Deacon, *HL* V.29; perhaps the difference in these stories reflects the development of Lombard control of the Italian peninsula between the time of Alcek's arrival and Paul the Deacon's writing a century later; Belcastro and Faccini (2001) on seventh-century horse burials, which may be linked to the Bulgars, in the Molise region of Italy.
125. Golden (1992), 246.
126. Turtledove (1982), 56 n.125, with the Latin *'angulus'*, the Slavic *o(n)gl* – 'angle, corner' or the Turkic *agyl* – 'yard' all suggested.
127. Fiedler in Curta and Kovalev (2008), 152.
128. Theophanes, *Chron.* AM6171.

129. Golden (1992), 247 on the recording of some tribal names – Čakarar, Kubiar, Küriger – and clan names such as Dulo, Ukil/Vokil, Ermiyar, Ugain and Duar.
130. Golden (2011), 145; Fiedler in Curta and Kovalev (2008), 151, 154.
131. Head (1972), 103.
132. ibn-Sa'id al-Maghribi I.874 fol.71; cf. Dunlop (1954), 11.
133. Golden (2007a), 53 vs Zuckerman (2007), 404 on the potential leadership role of the Ashina clan in the formation of the Khazar Khaganate.
134. Golden (2006), 86; (2007a), 40–41; (2007b), 78; Brook (2018), 4.
135. Noonan (2001), 77; Dunlop (1954), 96 on the tenth-century Muslim geographer al-Istakhri's differing descriptions of White and Black Khazars; Brook (2018), 3–4.
136. Dunlop (1954), 39, 92–93; Erdal (2007), 75; Golden (2006), 91; (2007a), 13–14.
137. Dunlop (1954), 34–40; Shirota (2005), 235, 248; Golden (2007a), 15–17; Brook (2018), 5.
138. Gil (2011) and Stampfer (2013) doubt the conversion, while Dunlop (1954), 130 and Golden (2007b), 145–146 support the authenticity of the *Khazar Correspondence.*
139. Turtledove (1982), 55 n.124.
140. Golden (2007b), 124, 135.
141. Constantine VII, *de adm. imp.* 69–73.
142. Golden (2006), 89.
143. Nikephoros, *Brev.* 12 speaks of Turks, while Theophanes, *Chron.* AM 6117 calls them Khazars; Moses Dasxuranci, *Hist.* II.12; Eutychios, *Hist.* 104.
144. Theophanes, *Chron.* AM 6117; Moses Dasxuranci, *Hist.* II.12; Nikephoros, *Brev.* 12.
145. Moses Dasxuranci, *Hist.* II.14.
146. *Ibid., Hist.* II.16.
147. Golden in Reyerson, Stavrou and Tracy (2006), 11–13.
148. Zuckerman in Golden, *Ben*-Shammai *and* Róna-Tas (2007), 417.
149. Golden (2007b), 155–156.
150. Dunlop (1954), 97, 112; Noonan (2001), 77; Golden (2007b), 133–134.
151. Golden (2007b), 138; (2006), 79–80, 88; Olsson (2013), 495, 507; Noonan (2007), 211, 217; Koestler (1977), 18.
152. Noonan (2007), 211–214; Golden (2011), 64.
153. Dunlop (1954), 50–60; Brook (2018), 126–127; Wasserstein (2007), 375; Mako (2010), 45.
154. Paul the Deacon, *HL* II.26.
155. Haldon (2016).

Chapter 3: Before Power: The Early Life of Justinian II

1. Anna Komnene, *Alexiad* 151.
2. Ostrogorsky and Stein (1932), 199; cf. John of Ephesus, *HE* III.5.14; cf. Constantine VII, *de caer.* II.21.
3. Theophanes, *Chron.* AM6152.
4. Constantine VII, *de adm. imp.* 224–225.
5. Theophanes, *Chron.* AM6140.
6. Head (1972), 19.
7. Grant (1998), 32
8. Head (1972), 19; Arcadius' wife, Aelia Eudoxia, was the daughter of a Romanized Frank called Bauto; Theodosius II's wife, Aelia Eudocia, was born in Athens,

daughter of a philosopher/pagan; Verina was seemingly of similar Bessian/Thracian origin to her husband Leo I. This Bessian/Thracian union produced Ariadne, empress of both Zeno and Anastasius I. Justin I's wife, Euphemia, is spoken about in disparaging terms due to her supposed slave/barbarian origins; Justinian I's wife, Theodora, was infamously an 'actress', with Sophia, wife of Justin II, reputedly Theodora's niece; Tiberius II's wife, Ino Anastasia, was seemingly born on the Bithynian island of Daphnousia and her first marriage had been to a lowly *optio*; Mauricius' wife, Constantina, was the daughter of Tiberius II and Ino Anastasia. Little is known of Phocas' wife, Leontia, but she may have shared the relatively lowly status of her husband before his successful revolt. Neither of Heraclius' wives were of Constantinopolitan nobility, with Eudokia the daughter of an African landowner and Martina sharing the same heritage as her uncle/husband. Heraclius Constantine III's wife, Gregoria, was also part of the Heraclian family. Constans II's wife, Fausta, shared the Armenian origins of her father, Valentinus.

9. Head (1972), 20.
10. *Ibid.*
11. Justinian and Constantine were not the only 'great' imperial names utilized by the Heraclian dynasty. Heraclius Constantine III called his second son Theodosius, while at least three Heraclians would be called Tiberius: a son of Heraclius, Constans II's third son and Justinian's only son. Head (1972), 20 n.2 on the naming practices regarding Heraclius Constantine and Constans II. She suggests that while he is normally recorded as 'Heraclius Constantine III', the eldest son of Heraclius (610–641) 'used both names officially'. In turn, while his son was 'usually called by the diminutive "Constans"', his official name was Constantine, which was ever-present on his coinage. He should therefore more rightly be listed as Constantine IV, with his son (Justinian's father) in turn being Constantine V (discounting the Constantine III, the British usurper of 407–411, who was recognized as legitimate by the western government of Honorius from 409, but not by the eastern government). However, it has become even more usual since Head was writing in 1972 to list these emperors as 'Heraclius Constantine III' and 'Constans II', so for the sake of clarity those are the identifiers I will use any time they are mentioned.
12. Delbruck (1914).
13. *Parastaseis Syntomoi Chronokai* 58.
14. Cameron and Herrin (1984), 265–266.
15. Head (1972), 28.
16. *Ibid.*, 24.
17. Fredegar, *Chronicle* IV.65.
18. Leo Grammatikos, *Hist.* 147.
19. Head (1972), 28.
20. *Ibid.*, 29.
21. This was the first time in Roman imperial history that so many blood relatives had succeeded each other. The five generations of the Julio-Claudians may have shared some blood, but also relied on adoption; the six generations of the 'Good Emperors' were all adoptive successions, except for the last one when Commodus succeeded his father Marcus Aurelius; while the five Justinianic emperors were also a mixture of blood and adoption, without any father–son successions.
22. Head (1972), 29.
23. *Ibid.*

24. Theophanes, *Chron.* AM6119.
25. Head (1972), 28.
26. Theophanes, *Chron.* AM6159.
27. *Ibid.*, *Chron.* AM6160.
28. Ps.-Gregory, *Ep. ad Leonem Isaurum imp.* I, 295, 251–253 (*BHG* 1387d); Michael the Syrian II.451, 455; *Chron. ad 1234* 139; Toumanoff (1971), 149 n.20 suggests Mezizios was from the royal Gnuni family.
29. Michael the Syrian II.451.
30. Theophanes, *Chron.* AM6161.
31. Michael the Syrian II.455 on Mezizios' son John rebelling against Constantine in Sicily a decade later, but he was also defeated after seven months.
32. Theophanes, *Chron.* AM6161.
33. Theophanes, *Chron.* AM6154–6160; Theophanes refers to the Arabs striking into 'Romania', which means Roman territory in general.
34. O'Sullivan (2004) and Cosentino (2008) on Muawiyah initiating an attempt on Constantinople in the aftermath of the Battle of Phoenix/the Masts in 654, using the account of the Armenian historian Sebeos.
35. Theophanes, *Chron.* AM6162.
36. *Ibid.*, *Chron.* AM6163–6164.
37. *Ibid.*, *Chron.* AM6165.
38. George Kedrenos records that Kallinikos came from Heliopolis in Egypt, which was followed by Gibbon, but most scholars reject this as an error; Forbes (1959), 80.
39. Roland (1992), 655.
40. Constantine VII, *de adm. imp.* 13.
41. *Ibid.*, *de adm. imp.* 13.
42. Theophanes, *Chron.* AM6164.
43. Haldon (1990), 64; Treadgold (1997), 325.
44. Theophanes, *Chron.* AM6165; Michael the Syrian II.455 has the Roman commanders as three unnamed patricians.
45. Theophanes has this 'First Siege' lasting seven years, a figure which likely involves counting inclusively from the outset of the expedition in 672 to the Arab retreat from Cyzicus in 678, or perhaps from the initial attack in *c.*674 through to the withdrawal of other Arab forces from their forward bases in Anatolia in 680.
46. Olster (1995), 23–28.
47. Jankowiak in Zuckerman (2013), 240–241, 239; cf. *ACO*, ser. sec II.612–614; Fischer (1884), 289; Howard-Johnston (2010), 492–493 n.13, who, while following Jankowiak in doubting the seven-year outline to the 'siege' in Theophanes and Nikephoros, digresses on the blockade dates rendered through the unreliable patriarchal chronology.
48. Jankowiak in Zuckerman (2013), 273.
49. Kennedy (2001), 12 n.74; Bosworth (1996) doubts many of the claims of Umayyad attacks on Rhodes; one Arab intercession in Rhodes in 653/654 is said to have seen the selling off of the ruins of the Colossus of Rhodes: Theophanes, *Chron.* AM6145; Conrad (1996); Woods (2016).
50. Howard-Johnston (2010), 492–494 posits a more involved, strategic game surrounding the blockade of Constantinople under Muawiyah, involving Constantine IV travelling west, an elaborate Arab feint on Africa and a demonstration against Constantinople by Fudhala, only to be thwarted by the return of Constantine's imperial fleet by mid/late 671; Jankowiak in Zuckerman (2013) connects the Arab

attempt on Constantinople to the aftermath of the revolt of Saborius, where Fudhala and Yazid reached Chalcedon, positing an attempt on the imperial capital in the spring/summer of 668, which was broken off by June of that year.

51. Jankowiak (2013), 278–279, 316; Stratos (1978), IV.46.
52. Howard-Johnston (2010), 303–304; Jankowiak in Zuckerman (2013), 242–243, 316.
53. Howard-Johnston (2010), 303–304.
54. Jankowiak in Zuckerman (2013), 309.
55. Stratos (1978), 84–87; Treadgold (1997), 326–327.
56. Theophanes, *Chron.* AM6169.
57. Madelung (1997), 339–340.
58. Madelung (1997), 311–355 on the establishment of Muawiyah's caliphate and the Umayyad dynasty.
59. Al-Tabari XVIII.173.
60. The Kharijites remained a potent force in the lands either side of the Persian Gulf and deep into the Arabian Peninsula.
61. Upon his arrival in Kufa, Mukhtar had tried to prevent the Tawwabin from marching out to their fatal absolution upon Umayyad spears, arguing that together they could take control of Kufa and ultimately the caliphate.
62. Theophanes, *Chron.* AM6174 on Mukhtar 'the Liar' in 682/683, who styled himself as a prophet.
63. This is despite an arrangement agreed in 684 that other branches of the Umayyad family would succeed him, namely Amr b. Said and Yazid's son, Khalid.
64. On the Second Fitna, Dixon (1971), 34–35, 73–75, 104–110; Hawting (2000), 48–49; Kennedy (2016), 76–80.
65. Theophanes, *Chron.* AM6169.
66. *Ibid., Chron.* AM6171.
67. *Ibid.*
68. *Ibid.*
69. Head (1972), 32.
70. Theophanes, *Chron.* AM6171.
71. *Ibid.*
72. *Ibid.*.
73. *Ibid.*
74. It must be remembered that Constans II was not only the grandson of the great Heraclius, his actual name was Constantine, so supposing any need or want to live up to their illustrious names for Constantine IV and Justinian II must also be suggested for Constans II.
75. It should be noted that despite them usually being recorded as something of a duo – Heraclius and Tiberius – there is no evidence that they were twins.
76. Theophanes, *Chron.* AM6161.
77. *Ibid.*
78. *Ibid., Chron.* AM6173.
79. Brooks (1915), 49.
80. *Ibid.*, 46.
81. *Ibid.*, 42; 42–44, 46–47 on issues with Theophanes' records of Heraclius and Tiberius and attempts to fix the problems.
82. Brooks (1915), 44.
83. There was an imperial precedent for such an imperial 'trinity', as the sons of Constantine I – Constantine II, Constantius II and Constans – removed all

opposition and had themselves declared as *Augusti* in the aftermath of their father's death in 337.

84. Michael the Syrian XI.13.
85. *Ibid.*; Agapius of Hierapolis, *Patr. Orient.* VIII.494.
86. The reign of Constantine IV (668–685) encompassed the Ravennate bishoprics of three men, Maurus (*c.*644–*c.*671), Reparatus (*c.*671–*c.*677) and Theodore (*c.*677–*c.*691).
87. Mansi, *Concilia* XI.624, 697, 712.
88. Brooks (1915), 50.
89. *Ibid.*, 48.
90. Kaegi (1981), 167.
91 Theophanes, *Chron.* AM6173.
92. Mansi, *Concilia* XI.737, 738.
93. Head (1972), 26.
94. *Ibid.*; *Liber Pontificalis* I.363; this section of the *Liber Pontificalis* appears to be contemporaneous with the reigns of Constantine IV and Justinian II.
95. It might be thought that this was an example of a specifically imperial ceremony in its relations with the papacy; however, the *Liber Pontificalis* I.364 records a similar practice taking place between Charles Martel, leader of the Franks, and Liutprand, king of the Lombards, when the former gave a lock of his son Pepin's hair to the latter.
96. Theophanes, *Chron.* AM6151, who records the brother of Constans II as 'Theodore', rather than Theodosius.
97. *Ibid.*, *Chron.* AM6177.
98. *Ibid.*, *Chron.* AM6102; John of Nikiu, *Chron.* 110.9; Nikephoros, *Brev.* 2; Kaegi (2003), 51.
99. Constantine VII, *de caer.* I.91, 94, although it could be that the more intricate ceremony recorded by *De Caermoniis* may reflect a ceremony specific to the elevation of a *Caesar* to *Augustus*, which Justinian was not.
100. Theophanes, *Chron.* AM6102 on Heraclius marrying Eudokia and having her crowned *Augusta* straight after his own crowning.
101. Grierson, Mango and Sevcenko (1962), 30–32; Downey (1959), 35.

Chapter 4: Justinian's First War with the Umayyads

1. Head (1972), 30.
2. Haldon (2016), 46 on the Second Fitna allowing Constantine IV to make some useful inroads against the caliphate – a foray into Cilicia, retaking Mopsuetia; destroying the fortress of Germanikeia; the brief recovery of Pisidian Antioch; and the imperial fleet launching raids on Ascalon, Caesarea, Acre and Tyre, all to be added to the activities of the Mardaites.
3. Theophanes, *Chron.* AM6176.
4. *Ibid.*, *Chron.* AM6178.
5. *Ibid.*, *Chron.* AM6169.
6. *Ibid.*, *Chron.* AM6178; while Boukania could be a corruption of the Armenian province of Vaspurakan or 'the canton of Bukha south of Tayk' (Mango and Scott (1997), 507 n.4), it is more likely that it is the region of Moukania/Mukan in modern Azerbaijan, especially as the next region mentioned as being targeted by these Roman attacks was further east in Media, modern north-western Iran. However, it has also been suggested that Theophanes has inserted Iberia instead of Gurzan, a region which might make more sense as it links Media Atropatene and Armenia.

7. *Liber Pontificalis* I.366–367; Diehl (1896), 581–582.
8. Theophanes, *Chron.* AM6178.
9. Brooks (1898), 189; Theophanes, *Chron.* AM6176, 6178.
10. It could be that some negotiations were taking place between Constantine and Abd al-Malik at the time of the former's death, with Justinian choosing war rather than a treaty immediately upon his accession.
11. *Chronicle of 741* 29.
12. Conrad in Cameron and Conrad (1992); Woods (2011).
13. Al-Tabari XXI.796; Brooks (1898), 189.
14. McEvedy (1992), 32.
15. Theophanes, *Chron.* AM6178; Howard-Johnston in Goodwin (2012), 35 n.36 on other sources like Agapius and Michael the Syrian suggesting that Roman sovereignty over Armenia and Iberia was complete through the treaty between Justinian and Abd al-Malik, rather than a joint condominium.
16. Zavagno (2011–2012), 154.
17. *Ibid.*, 154–155.
18. Jenkins in Mylonas and Raymond (1953) on the real worth of the Cypriot condominium; Zavagno (2011–2012), 121–155 raises significant questions about the potential poor state of the Cypriot economy.
19. Head (1972), 34.
20. Palmer (1993), 195 n.478; Hoyland (2011), 170 n.441; Woods (2011).
21. Conterno (2014), 12.
22. Howard-Johnston in Goodwin (2012), 32; Theophanes, *Chron.* AM6169; Hoyland (2011), 169–70.
23. Howard-Johnston in Goodwin (2012), 33.
24. Theophanes, *Chron.* AM6178. It should be noted that 12,000 seems to be something of a go-to figure for Roman, Syriac and Arabic sources when it comes to the size of military groups in this period; Theophanes, *Chron.* AM6196 on Tiberius III's brother Herakleios defeating and killing 12,000 Arabs at Sision in 703/704; Theophanes, *Chron.* AM6236 and *Chron. 1234* I.317 on Marwan II defeating a rebel army of 12,000 in *c.*744; al-Baladhuri, *Futūh al-buldān* 153 had Muawiayh I settling 12,000 soldiers on Cyprus in *c.*653; Haldon (2000), 249, n.45 on there being 12,300 Mardaites in the Cibyrrhaeot theme by 911, but warning against any direct connecting to the 12,000 taken in by Justinian II.
25. Theophanes, *Chron.* AM6179.
26. Woods (2011).
27. Constantine VII, *de adm. imp.* 50.169–221; *de caer.* I.654.
28. cf. Howard-Johnston in Goodwin (2012), 33.
29. Theophanes, *Chron.* AM6159.
30. *Ibid., Chron.* AM6156.
31. Theophanes, *Chron.* AM6156 has these Slavic defectors 'settled in the village of Seleukobolos near Apamea'.
32. Michael the Syrian XI.15.
33. *Chron. 741* 29.
34. Woods (2011).
35. Woods (2011) on the comparison between the Coptic crews of the Arab navy and the potential Mardaite crews of the Romans, and how the validity of such a comparison stems from Constans II imitating Arab naval recruitment; Zuckerman (2005), 79–135.

36. Woods (2011); cf. Treadgold (1992), 115–121; The *Chronicle of 1234* also presents the Mardaites in a naval setting, having them be the result of a Roman amphibious assault on the coast of Tyre and Sidon in *c*.676.
37. *Chron. 1234* I.288; cf. Agapius 232–33; Michael the Syrian XI.13.
38. Theophanes, *Chron.* AM6169.
39. Woods (2011).
40. Woods (2011) also pertinently asks, if the Mardaites had been so successful, why would they choose to disappear into the isolated mountains rather than focus their power on the Phoenician ports to keep communications with the Romans open?
41. cf. George of Cyprus V.871, 873.
42. Woods (2011).
43. Woods (2011) suggests that the sources, if not merely a misidentification of Amanus for Lebanon, may again be projecting events from a later time back onto that of the seventh century, with a certain Theodore leading a Lebanese rebellion against the Arabs in *c*.760 (Theophanes. *Chron.* AM6252).
44. Moosa (1969), 597–608.
45. Theophanes, *Chron.* AM6178.
46. The Romans were known to have employed national groups as units in their army, such as the Isaurians, which might be a rather apt comparison as both resided in the mountains of Cilicia/northern Syria and both were frequently inferred to be mountain brigands.
47. Theophanes, *Chron.* AM6201; this may have been during the Cilician campaign of Yazid b. Hunain, who laid siege to the fortress of Sision, only to be defeated by Herakleios, brother of Tiberius III, with up to 12,000 Arab casualties. Al-Tabari XX.1185 places the campaign in 705/706, naming Yazid b. Jubayr in command along with Maslamah and not mentioning the outcome; cf. Brooks (1898), 191; Caetani, *Chron.* 1022 suggests 704/705, which is the same as Theophanes, *Chron.* AM6196.
48. Woods (2011).
49. Theophanes, *Chron.* AM6178.
50. Michael the Syrian II.469.
51. Woods (2011); cf. Michael the Syrian XI.15.
52. Howard-Johnston in Goodwin (2012), 34; Greenwood (2008), 245; Zuckerman in Golden, Ben-Shammai and Róna-Tas (2007), 430–431.

Chapter 5: Saving the Second City: Justinian in Thessalonica
1. Fine (1983), 31.
2. Head (1972), 36.
3. Theophanes, *Chron.* AM6179.
4. Theodosius issued his *Cunctos Populos* (*CTh* XVI.1.2), which established Trinitarianism as the 'catholic' Church, from the city, giving it the name the 'Edict of Thessalonica'.
5. Delehaye (1909), 106–108; cf. Woods (2000), 224.
6. Head (1972), 37; Ostrogorsky (1963–1964), 3–4.
7. Barford (2001), 61.
8. Fine (1983), 41, 44.
9. Pohl (1988), 241–243.
10. Zonaras III.316; Stratos in Laiou (1986), 48–55.
11. Theophanes, *Chron.* AM6149.
12. Curta (2001), 61–62.

13 It does appear that not all Slavic tribes in the area took up arms against Thessalonica. Some like the Belegezitai sided with the Romans and provided help to the city.

14. Curta (2001), 112.

15. Stratos (1978), 84–88; Lemerle (1981), 111–128; Curta (2001), 61–62, 112 on the Slav siege of Thessalonica.

16. Theophanes, *Chron*. AM6146–6149.

17. Stratos (1978), 88–90 collects the ideas surrounding this major Slav attack on Thessalonica.

18. Lemerle (1981), 128–132, with Stratos (1978), 90–92 postulating the precursor events involving Perboundos in 672 and the attacks on Thessalonica beginning in 675.

19. Head (1972), 8.

20. Ekonomou (2009), 123.

21. Theophanes, *Chron*. AM6179.

22. *Ibid.*, *Chron*. AM6180.

23. *Ibid.*, *Chron*. AM6179.

24. *Ibid.*, *Chron*. AM6180.

25. Head (1972), 41.

26. Jenkins (1966), 52.

27. Head (1972), 42.

28. Jenkins (1966), 56.

29. Kantorowicz (1944), 216; Vacalopoulis (1963); Vasiliev (1947)

30. Breckenridge (1955), 116–122 suggests that the figure is an otherwise unidentified saint.

31. Vasiliev (1947), 364.

32. Head (1972), 38.

33. Vasiliev (1950), 32.

34. Head (1972), 39.

35. *Ibid*.

36. *Ibid*.

37. Papageorgiou (1908) 354–360; Vasiliev (1943), 1–13 made some textual amendments and included an English translation and commentary.

38. Vasiliev (1943), 3.

39. *Ibid.*, 10; Gregoire (1944–1945), 120–121.

40. Vasiliev (1943), 6.

41. *Ibid*.

42. Theophanes, *Chron*. AM6180.

43. Head (1972), 8.

44. Nikephoros, *Brev*. 43; Theophanes, *Chron*. AM6200.

45. Theophanes, *Chron*. AM6180.

Chapter 6: A 'War of Images' all about the Money? The Romano-Umayyad War of 692

1. Theophanes, *Chron*. AM6181.

2. Dixon (1971), 126–129.

3. Al-Tabari XXI.783–789.

4. Theophanes, *Chron*. AM6178; Michael the Syrian II.469.

5. Al-Tabari XXI.807.

6. *Ibid*. XXI.805–806.

7. *Ibid*. XXI.804–813.

8. Al-Baladhuri, *Futūh al-buldān* V.341–342 has Muslim mortally wounded and carried from the field, surviving long enough to obtain a guarantee of safety for his children from Abd al-Malik. His son, Qutayba b. Muslim, would be a loyal and dependable Umayyad general, conquering significant territories in Central Asia.
9. *Ibid.* V.338.
10. Al-Tabari XXI.807.
11. *Ibid.* XXI.808.
12. *Ibid.* XXI.808-809.
13. *Ibid.* XXI.809; al-Baladhuri, *Futūh al-buldān* V.333 claims that Ubayd Allah later said that 'Never have I regretted anything as much as I regret not having cut off Abd al-Malik's head at that time, thereby giving people relief. I would have killed the two kings of the Arabs in a single day.'
14. Abd al-Malik would replace al-Muhallab as commander against the Kharijites, but would later rebuke his replacements for not taking advantage of al-Muhallab's experience and ability. By 693, al-Muhallab was back in command against the Kharijites and formed a solid partnership with al-Hajjaj b. Yusuf, governor of Kufa and Basra. By the end of 694, al-Muhallab had secured a lasting victory against the Kharijites in Fars and Kerman.
15. Dixon (1971), 301.
16. *Ibid.* (1969), 139.
17. Al-Tabari XI.829, 852–853.
18. The Umayyad rebuilding of the Kaaba involved an interesting aside on Romano-Arab relations at this point. In the repairs at Mecca, Abd al-Malik proposed to use materials, specifically pillars, from the Garden of Gethsemane in Jerusalem. Unsurprisingly, this raised opposition amongst local Christians, with their leaders, Patricius Klausus and Sergius, son of Mansur, asking Abd al-Malik not to undertake such an act. Fortunately for Gethsemane, Sergius was serving as a public finance minister for the Umayyads and as a result was an acquaintance of the caliph. Through this channel, Sergius and Klausus encouraged Abd al-Malik to contact Justinian II and ask the emperor in the name of the leaders of the Palestinian church for other columns, which he agreed to (Theophanes, *Chron.* AM6183).
19. Abd al-Malik regretted this decision later in his life, wishing he had restored the Kaaba in the form al-Zubayr had rebuilt it. This was not a unanimous opinion, with some continuing to applaud the decision, such as the poet Jarir, who wrote of Abd al-Malik: 'You restored the house of God as it was at the time of the Prophet, you corrected what the sons of al-Zubair had corrupted'; Abu Ubayda, *Naqa'id Jarir wa-al-Farazdaq* I.486; Dixon (1969), 54.
20. One thing that Abd al-Malik and his Umayyad successors failed to fix were the growing tribal tensions within the caliphate, with the Qays/Mudar vs Yemeni feud playing a significant role in the Umayyad downfall during the Third Fitna in 744–750.
21. Head (1972), 45.
22. Nikephoros, *Brev.* 38; Theophanes, *Chron.* AM6183, 6184.
23. Theophanes, *Chron.* AM6184; Nikephoros, *Brev.* 38.
24. Theophanes, *Chron.* AM6149.
25. *Ibid.*, *Chron.* AM6156.
26. Haldon (2016), 239; the importance of these settlers is shown in the seals of the officials appointed to look after them – Seibt and Theodoridis (1999); Brandes (2002a), 351–365; Brandes (2005); Brubakker and Haldon (2011), 685 n.67.
27. Mansi, *Concilia* XI.996E.

28. Constantine VII, *de adm. imp.* 32.7–12.
29. Theophanes, *Chron.* AM6183.
30. Constantine VII, *de adm. imp.* 48.
31. *Ibid.* 48.
32. Theophanes, *Chron.* AM6183.
33. Constantine VII, *de adm. imp.* 48.
34. Head (1972), 47 n.6; Hefele (1896), V.229; Hackett (1901), 41–42.
35. Head (1972), 48.
36. Theophanes, *Chron.* AM6183.
37. *Ibid.*
38. *Ibid.*
39. *Ibid.*
40. Breckenridge (1959), 75; Head (1972), 50.
41. Bellinger (1950), 108.
42. Head (1972), 54; Grierson (1966), II.516.
43. Head (1972), 55.
44. Grierson (1966), II.589, 590. Head (1972), 55 points out how despite being the same name, the ciphers of Justinian II look nothing like the cipher of Justinian I.
45. Breckenridge (1959), 1 n.1; Hunterian Collection; MacDonald (1905), 233–235, pl. IX; the emperor Marcian appeared in armour on the obverse, while the reverse has Marcian and Pulcheria together with Christ between and behind them, placing a hand on their shoulders, celebrating their marriage with the legend 'FELICITER NUBTIIS'. It was an altered version of a coin of 437, celebrating the wedding of Valentinian III and Eudoxia, where it was Theodosius II placing his hands on their shoulders.
46. Humphreys (2013), 232.
47. *Ibid.*; Head (1972), 56.
48. Breckenridge (1959), 66 mentions this idea, but ultimately rejects it; Elsner (2012), 374.
49. Elsner (2012), 374.
50. Head (1972), 57–58.
51. *Ibid.*, 55–56; Galavaris (1958), 106–109; Breckenridge (1959), 18–27, 51, 63–68.
52. Head (1972), 58.
53. Humphreys (2013), 233.
54. *Ibid.*, 234 n.23; Breckenridge (1959), 78–87; Grierson (1966), II.2; Bates (1986), 253.
55. Haldon (2016), 153.
56. Nordhagen (1967), 390.
57. Grabar (1936); Ladner (1940); (1953); Kitzinger (1954).
58. Breckenridge (1959), 3.
59. Humphreys (2013), 234; Grierson and Blackburn (1986), 51–52, 448 no.267.
60. Humphreys (2013), 234.
61. The consular office would survive in some form until consular dating was formally abolished during the reign of Leo VI (886–912), with his *Novel* 94.
62. Nordhagen (1967), 389–390; for other aspects of the *Adoration*, see Folgerø (2009).
63. Nordhagen (1967), 389; Breckenridge (1959), 26 on these Christ coins being minted in Italy.
64. Breckenridge (1959), 1, 46; Kitzinger (1963), 191–192.
65. Humphreys (2013), 234 n.23; Breckenridge (1959), 78–87; Grierson (1966), II.2.
66. Hahn, *MIB* III.48.
67. Humphreys (2013), 235; Zacos and Veglery (1972), 3.

68. Zacos and Veglery (1972), no.167.
69. *Ibid.*, no.165.
70. Humphreys (2013), 235.
71. *Ibid.*, 236–237 shows how the career of Georgios and his seals demonstrate the spread of the new imperial image and therefore the Christ *solidus* through the empire's Asian provinces before the Battle of Sebastopolis in 692.
72. Theophanes, *Chron.* AM6303.
73. Humphreys (2013), 238.
74. Humphreys in Sarris *et al.* (2011), 155–160; Breckenridge (1959), 35–45 on the connection of the *loros* to Easter in the *Book of Ceremonies*; Justinian's holding of the *akakia*, a bag of dust representing man's earthly origins, may also be linked to Christ at Easter – death, life and triumph; Humphreys (2013), 238.
75. Humphreys (2013), 231.
76. Heidemann in Neuwirth *et al.* (2010), 157.
77. *Ibid.*, 153.
78. *Ibid.*, 150.
79. *Ibid.*, 158.
80. *Ibid.*, 159.
81. *Ibid.*, 180; cf. Jamil in Johns (1999).
82. Miles (1952), 165; (1959).
83. Heidemann in Neuwirth *et al.* (2010), 159.
84. *Ibid.*, 160 n.40; cf. Moorhead (1985), 178, 184.
85. Heidemann in Neuwirth *et al.* (2010), 161–169; Humphreys (2013), 241.
86. Miles (1967), nos 6–11; Foss (2002), 361–362; Schulze in Oddy (2011); Heidemann in Oddy (2011).
87. Foss (2003), 24–34.
88. Goodwin (2012), 91–92; Foss (2003), 66–74; Hoyland (2007), 581–602.
89. Miles (1967), 215–217; Goodwin (2012), 91–93.
90. Treadwell (2009), 357.
91. Heidemann in Neuwirth *et al.* (2010), 170.
92. Hendy (1985), 168–171 on 365,000 *nomismata* representing perhaps 20 per cent of annual imperial revenue under Justinian II, which would put 52,000 *nomismata* at just under 3 per cent.
93. Foss in Haldon (2010), 90 suggests that Muawiyah I, a stable and powerful caliph, could only extract 600,000 dinars per annum from Egypt.
94. Humphreys (2013), 240 n.64 compiles the potential revenue available to the Umayyads, suggesting the tribute due to Constantinople was anything between 14 and 23 per cent of Umayyad annual revenue based on the figure of 365,000 *solidi*. At a time of civil war and in a state where the majority of monies were taken up by a small elite and the Syrian army, even a constant drain of 2–3 per cent of Umayyad cash would have been felt.
95. Humphreys (2013), 240.
96. Abd al-Malik completely overhauled the caliphate tax system and took a census of the population under his rule; Reinink in Cameron and Conrad (1992), 149–187 on this census rousing Apocalyptic literature in some Christian populations within the caliphate
97. Lopez (1943), 24; Grierson (1960), 243; Heidemann in Neuwirth *et al.* (2010), 170.
98. Breckenridge (1959), 71–73.
99. Humphreys (2013), 244.
100. Treadwell (2009), 379.

101. Heidemann in Neuwirth *et al.* (2010), 185; Elsner (2012), 374.
102. Grierson (1999), 13–14.
103. Treadwell (2009), 379.
104. Heidemann in Neuwirth *et al.* (2010), 184.
105. Treadwell (2009), 379.
106. Elsner (2012), 374.
107. Heidemann in Neuwirth *et al.* (2010), 188.
108. Head (1972), 48.
109. Theophanes, *Chron.* AM6183.
110. *Ibid.*
111. Al-Baladhuri, *Futuh al-Buldan* 383–384.
112. Wellhausen (1927), 217; Lopez (1943), 24.
113. Humphreys (2013), 229; cf. Breckenridge (1959), 69–77.
114. Heidemann in Meuwirth *et al.* (2010), 150.
115. Theophanes, *Chron.* AM6184.
116. *Ibid.*, cf. AM6183.
117. Haldon (2016), 255; Prigent (2014), 192–195.
118. Haldon (2016), 327 n.80.
119. Head (1972), 49; Breckenridge (1959), 74.
120. Haldon (2016), 310–311, n.68.
121. Theophanes, *Chron.* AM6184.
122. Bury (1889), II.328; Breckenridge (1959), 12; Head (1972), 92.
123. Nikephoros, *Brev.* 37; Theophanes, *Chron.* AM6184.
124. Theophanes, *Chron.* AM6184.
125. *Ibid.*; that Muhammad paid Neboulos with *nomismata* shows that there was still some Roman gold in the hands of the Umayyads.
126. Procopius, *BG* VII.14.22.
127. Could part of the Slav willingness to defect be that they had been put in considerable danger by Justinian, with this 20,000 representing all that was left of the original 30,000? Thinning out a barbarian herd by using them against other imperial opponents was a long-established Roman stratagem.
128. Theophanes, *Chron.* AM6156.
129. Head (1972), 42.
130. *Ibid.*, 43.
131. Nikephoros, *Brev.* 38; Michael the Syrian XI.470; al-Tabari XXII.853; Al-Baladhuri, *Futuh al-Buldan* 188.
132. Schlumberger (1903), 277; Ostrogorsky (1968), 130 n.4.
133. Maricq (1952), 348–349; cf. Charanis (1960–1961), 143.
134. Haldon (1997a), 247 n.118; Anagnostakes (2001); Vryonis (1961); the early ninth-century rebel Roman commander Thomas the Slav was reputedly born at Gazuria in Pontus, suggesting that he might have been a descendant of Justinian's Slav settlers in Asia Minor; however, the tenth-century chronicler Genesios calls him 'Thomas from Lake Gouzourou, of the Armenian race', with his sobriquet of 'the Slav' a modern development.
135. Michael the Syrian XI.15; Woods (2011).
136. Hoyland (1997), 123.
137. Theophanes, *Chron.* AM6185, 6186, 6187.
138. *Ibid.*, *Chron.* AM6185; Gregoire (1946), 18.
139. Al-Baladhuri, *Futuh al-Buldan* 188–189, 206.
140. *Ibid.* 188–189.

Chapter 7: Justinian, The Orthodox Champion?

1. Head (1972), 4.
2. The 'Three Chapters' controversy did linger on in Italy for some considerable time. It hindered the Catholicizing of the Lombards and only ended with the reconciliation of the bishop of Aquileia in 698.
3. Ostrogorsky (1968), 127.
4. He may well have returned to the Constantinopolitan patriarchate in 686–697, which suggests that he had accepted Dyothelitism.
5. Bede, *Historia ecclesiastica gentis Anglorum* IV.17.
6. Theophanes, *Chron.* AM6172 recorded 289 'bishops and fathers'.
7. Bury (1889), II.317.
8. *Liber Pontificalis* I.363; cf. Ekonomou (2009), 215.
9. Ekonomou (2009), 217; *Liber Pontificalis* I.363; cf. Paul the Deacon, *HL* VI.53.
10. *Liber Pontificalis* I.366.
11. Ekonomou (2009), 217.
12. *Ibid.*, 215 n.158.
13. *Ibid.*, 211–215.
14. Llewellyn (1976), 120–126; Ekonomou (2009), 238 n.162 suggests that Constans burned so many bridges with his conduct in Italy and his treatment of Pope Martin I that he had few contacts in the city post-663.
15. Head (1972), 58.
16. Breckenridge (1959), 10–11; Fliche and Martin (1930), V.192–193.
17. Mansi, *Concilia* XI.737–738.
18. Head (1972), 62.
19. Gorres (1908), 437, who supports it being from the pen of an imperial scribe rather than from the papal court.
20. It might conjure up ideas of a papal *legatus*, but this may be too imprecise.
21. Mansi, *Concilia* XI.737–738.
22. Haldon (2016), 48.
23. Gorres (1908) 439–440.
24. *Liber Pontificalis* I.368.
25. *Ibid.* I.368.19–369.2; Mann (1925), 46; Head (1972), 62; cf. Noye (2015), 346–361, 366–367; Calabria was a useful source of grain, wine, wool, manpower, copper, silver and gold; Noye (2015), 346–348, 354–358 on sources for Calabria.
26. Head (1972), 61 n.4.
27. Kelly (1978), 115–119; Rochow (1978), 282–283; Justinian's time will also have seen other heretical groups, such as the Montanists – Theophanes, *Chron.* 401.22–27; *Ekloga* 17.52; Rochow (1978), 271–274 – although there is no record of him dealing directly with them.
28. Haldon (2016), 185; Ekonomou (2009), 219.
29. Petrus Siculus, *Historia Manichaeorum* mistakenly calls Justinian 'Justin reigning after Heraclius'; Garsoian (1967), 55–64 demonstrates that Petrus' work is likely a composite of earlier sources.
30. Petrus Siculus, *Historia Manichaeorum* 1281–1282; cf. Garsoian (1967), 117–118; Runciman (1947), 35–38.
31. Garsoian (1967), 231–233; Theophanes, *Chron.* AM6247 records them as troublesome for Constantine V in 755/756. In 810/811, he uses Nikephoros I's supposed support for Manichaeans/Paulicians as an insult against him and the following year, Michael I's persecution of these heretics now in Phrygia was a sign of his piety (Theophanes, *Chron.* AM6303, 6304). Persecution of the Paulicians

drove them into a quasi-alliance with the Arabs, who used them as a buffer against Roman territory. By the ninth century, the Paulicians had become even more of a problem, raiding across Asia Minor, hence Basil's crushing victory. However, even then the Paulicians were not finished, as some of the survivors were transplanted to the Balkans, where they were still causing problems for Alexios I (Anna Komnene, *Alexiad* XV.9). They may also have influenced other neo-Manichaean/Gnostic sects such as the Bogomils, Cathars and Albigensians.

32. Head (1972), 59.
33. Hefele (1896), V.222–223; Humphreys (2015), 39–80 on Quinisext.
34. Haldon (2016), 127.
35. *Ibid.*, 91.
36. *Ibid.*, 127.
37. Head (1972), 67.
38. *Ibid.*, 65; Mansi, *Concilia* XI. 921–1006; Hefele (1896), V.221–242; Fliche and Martin (1930), 194–197; https://www.newadvent.org/fathers/3814.htm.
39. Head (1972), 66.
40. *Ibid.*, 67–68.
41. *Ibid.*, 69.
42. Ekonomou (2009), 220.
43. *Ibid.*, 221.
44. Hefele (1896), V.221.
45. Head (1972), 70.
46. Theophanes, *Chron.* AM6177.
47. Head (1972), 71; Holweck (1924), 577; Fortescue (1908), 104.
48. Head (1972), 71.
49. That the emperor's signature was in red was mentioned on some of the manuscript copies; the importance of there being six copies would seem to be because they were meant for the emperor, pope and each of the four patriarchs – Constantinople, Alexandria, Antioch and Jerusalem – Duchesne, *Liber Pontificalis* I.378n.
50. *Liber Pontificalis* I.372.
51. *Ibid.* I.371.
52. Ekonomou (2009), 216–217
53. *Liber Pontificalis* I.372.
54. Ekonomou (2009), 222–223 dissects the canons in order to suggest which may or not have angered the pope.
55. Gorres (1908), 444.
56. Ekonomou (2009), 222.
57. Head (1972), 69; canons 3–6, 12–13, 26, 30, 44, 47–48, 53–54, 87, 93 and 98, with 3, 6, 13, 30, 44 and 48 all mentioning the marriage of clerics.
58. Head (1972), 76.
59. *CTh* XVI.2.44; Fliche and Martin (1930), V.196; Schaff and Wace (1900), XIV.365–368 on the differences between clerical marriages.
60. *Liber Pontificalis* I.376, 375.
61. Breckenridge (1959), 83–86.
62. Re-enacting an edict of Theodosius II; Breckenridge (1959), 82.
63. Head (1972), 77; Kitzinger (1954), 120.
64. Samuelson (2016), 63.
65. Head (1972), 77; Breckenridge (1959), 83–86; Samuelson (2016), 84; other censure of western practice included canon 55, which denounced fasting on Lentan Saturdays, a popular Roman practice, on pain of clerical deposition and lay

excommunication, while canon 67 prohibited the consumption of blood and meat from strangled animals, based on a biblical injunction and against the teachings of St Augustine, which the West rejected as only a 'temporary measure' – Head (1972), 77 n.12; *Acts* 15.29; Hefele (1896), V.232 n.3.

66. Ekonomou (2009), 222.
67. *Liber Pontificalis* I.372.
68. Hefele (1896), V.238; Mann (1925), I.290.
69. Head (1972), 74.
70. Mansi, *Concilia* XI.990.
71. Head (1972), 75.
72. Hefele (1896), V.238 on how Crete belonged to the Roman patriarchate and how it is not impossible that Sergius did deputize Basil to attend Quinisext.
73. Bede, *De temporum ratione*, 66, s.a. 4649; Paul the Deacon, *HL* VI.11.
74. Collins (1989), 19.
75. While Constans' arrest, imprisonment, exile and ill-treatment of Pope Martin I, leading to his demise in Cherson, was fresher in the mind, it must also be remembered that Justinian I had had Pope Vigilius brought to Constantinople in 545 after disagreements over Monophysitism and the 'Three Chapters' controversy. Vigilius would spend eight years as a 'guest' in the imperial capital before being allowed to return west after finally accepting the decisions of the Second Council of Constantinople, only to then die in Syracuse on his way back to Rome; Gorres (1908), 440–451; Fliche and Martin (1930), V.195–197; Hefele (1896), V.237–240; Mann (1925), 87–92.
76. *Liber Pontificalis* I.373.
77. *Ibid.*
78. Head (1972), 78 n.19; *Liber Pontificalis* I.378n.
79. Head (1972), 79; *Liber Pontificalis* I.373–374.
80. Noble (1984), 17–18.
81. Ekonomou (2009), 224; Noble (1984), 188.
82. Ekonomou (2009), 224.
83. Noble (1984), 188; cf. Ekonomou (2009), 224.
84. Ekonomou (2009), 222.
85. *Ibid.*, 225; *Liber Pontificalis* I.374–375.
86. Haldon (2016), 292.

Chapter 8: Administering an Empire in Transition: Forces, Furrows and Finances
1. Head (1972), 82; Kaegi (1967), 39–54.
2. Mansi, *Concilia* XI.737–738.
3. Head (1972), 82.
4. Nesbitt and Oikonomides (1994), 22.
5. Zacos and Veglery (1972), n.2918, 2919.
6. Prigent and Nichanian (2003), 98–99.
7. *PLRE* IIIb.1333, 1108; Cassiodorus, *Var.* IX.16, 17.
8. Prigent and Nichanian (2003), 99; Brown (1984), 27–30.
9. Prigent and Nichanian (2003), 99–101.
10. Oikonomides (1972), 351.
11. Brown in Shepard (2008), 457–459.
12. Head (1972), 82; Diehl (1905), 285; Antoniadis-Bibicou (1966), 63–68.
13. Ahrweiler (1966), 50–51.
14. Theophanes, *Chron.* AM6190; Nikephoros, *Brev.* 41, with Nikephoros mentioning a contingent of Cibyrrhaeots from Korykos.

15. Treadgold (1995), 72.
16. Ahrweiler (1966), 26.
17. *Ibid.*, 26–31; Kaegi (1981), 207; Whittow (1996), 167; Treadgold (1997), 352; Pryor and Jeffreys (2006), 32.
18. Treadgold (1995), 72.
19. Kaegi (1981), 198.
20. Theophanes, *Chron.* AM6126.
21. Kaegi (1981), 202.
22. *Ibid.*, 201.
23. *Ibid.*, 201.
24. Sebeos XXI; Michael the Syrian X.25; Theophanes, *Chron.* AM6095–6097.
25. Evagrius VI.4; Theophylactus Simocatta, *Hist.* III.1, VI.7; Procopius, *BG* VII.40.39–40; Kaegi (1965); (1981).
26. Kaegi (1981), 170.
27. Theophanes, *Chron.* AM6190; Kaegi (1981), 189 lists this Heraclius as Tiberius' son, although this is a minority view and may be an error.
28. Theophanes, *Chron.* AM6190.
29. Haldon (2016), 165; Winkelmann (1987).
30. Haldon (2016), 165–166.
31. Kaegi (1981), 180.
32. *Ibid.*, 168.
33. Nikephoros, *Brev.* 39.
34. Kaegi (1981), 186.
35. Nikephoros, *Brev.* 37–38; Theophanes, *Chron.* AM6187.
36. Head (1972), 89–91, citing Levcenko (1947), 182–183 and Ostrogorsky (1968), 139–140, but Kaegi (1981), 188 n.6 highlights a lack of documentation.
37. Haldon (2016), 152.
38. Kaegi (1981), 190; Theophanes, *Chron.* AM6203; Nikephoros, *Brev.* 47.
39. Haldon (2016), 153.
40. *Ibid.*, 152; *Ekloga* 18.1.
41. Charanis (1960–1961), 140–143; Ostrogorsky (1968), 130ff; De Ste Croix (1981), Appendix III provides a long list of imperial settlements of non-Romans on Roman territory.
42. Head (1972), 83; Ostrogorsky (1959), 45–47; (1968), 132–137; Cheynet (2006), 152.
43. Charanis (1963) surveys the arguments; Kaegi (1967), 40–43.
44. Head (1972), 84; Lemerle (1954), 265–308; (1958), 63–65 on the arguments over the role of Slavic infiltration of Roman territory on agricultural changes.
45. Head (1972), 84.
46. Head (1972), 85; Ashburner (1910); (1912).
47. Vernadskij (1925), 172–173; Ostrogorsky (1968), 90–91; Jenkins (1966), 53 considered that the 'Farmer's Law' was 'almost universally attributed' to Justinian II; *contra* Dolger (1944–1945), II.21–48; Lemerle (1958) 49–55; Karayannopoulos (1958), 357–373; Ostrogorsky (1968), 90–91, while Medvedev (1984) considers it to be a composition of the sixth century.
48. Head (1972), 86; Vernadskij (1925), 172; Setton (1953), 233–234.
49. Ostrogorsky (1959), 108; (1968), 90–91; Dolger (1944–1945), 48; Lemerle (1958), 54; Toševa-Nikolovska (2008), 209.
50. Head (1972), 87.
51. Ashburner (1912), 68–71 records and refutes attempts to attribute the 'Farmer's Law' to Leo III and Constantine V.

52. Nikephoros, *Brev.* 37; Theophanes, *Chron.* AM6186.
53. Bury (1889), II.330 sees a parallel with Justinian I and his immensely powerful praetorian prefect John the Cappadocian.
54. Nikephoros, *Brev.* 39.
55. Theophanes, *Chron.* AM6186.
56. *Ibid.*
57. Nikephoros, *Brev.* 39.
58. Theophanes, *Chron.* AM6187; Nikephoros, *Brev.* 40.
59. Nikephoros, *Brev.* 39.
60. Theophanes, *Chron.* AM6186.
61. Hodgkin (1896), VI.359; Mango (1990), 95 n.27 omits a translation of *en schemati* because they 'do not appear to yield any satisfactory sense'.
62. Theophanes, *Chron.* AM6186.
63. Nikephoros, *Brev.* 39.
64. Theophanes, *Chron.* AM6186; cf. Michael the Syrian II.473 on Justinian's actions towards 'the nobility and great men'.
65. Theophanes, *Chron.* AM6187; Nikephoros, *Brev.* 40.
66. Brooks (1936), 409.
67. Theophanes, *Chron.* AM6205; Nikephoros, *Brev.* 49.
68. Stein (1928); Ostrogorsky (1931), 229240; Ostrogorsky (1968), 137; Setton (1953), 225–259.
69. *Liber Pontificalis* I.369.
70. Ostrogorsky (1931), 237–240.
71. Head (1972), 91.
72. *Ibid.*, 52.
73. *Ibid.*, 52.
74. Constantine VII, *de caer.* I.268; Bury (1912), 219–221.
75. Theophanes, *Chron.* AM6186.
76. This mention of the Blues is rare in the pages of Theophanes and Nikephoros, with neither seemingly willing to admit that these circus factions were politically active.
77. Theophanes, *Chron.* AM6186.
78. *Ibid.*
79. Head (1972), 54.
80. Grabar (1957), 49, 55.
81. Herrin (2008), 29; Trilling (1989) on the arguments over who was behind the mosaics in the imperial palace.

Chapter 9: Mutilation and Exile: The Revolt of Leontios

1. Nikephoros, *Brev.* 40
2. *Chronicle of 1234*, 151; a previous fifth-century usurper called Leontios (484–488) was also listed as being from Isauria, specifically Dalisandus (John of Antioch fr.306), although his family origin is listed as Syrian (Theophanes, *Chron.* AM5972) and Thracian (Malalas XV.13).
3. Bury (1889), II.328; Breckenridge (1959), 12.
4. Nikephoros, *Brev.* 40.
5. Theophanes, *Chron.* AM6187.
6. cf. Kaegi (1981), 203.
7. Nikepohoros, *Brev.* 40.
8. Theophanes, *Chron.* AM6187.
9. *Ibid.*

10. *Ibid.*
11. *Ibid.*
12. *Ibid.*
13. Theophanes, *Chron.* AM6187 and Nikephoros, *Brev.* 40 have Kallinikos make the same pronouncement.
14. Theophanes, *Chron.* AM6187; a curse akin to 'down with Justinian!' – Turtledove (1982), 67 n.138.
15. Nikephoros, *Brev.* 40; Bury (1889), II.329.
16. Head (1972), 94.
17. George Monachos, *Chronicon breve* III.1816–1825; cf. Maricq (1949), 66–67.
18. Cameron (1976) on the circus factions.
19. Ostrogorsky (1968), 67.
20. Nikephoros, *Brev.* 39.
21. Theophanes, *Chron.* AM6187.
22. Code of Hammurabi (L.W. King trans., https://avalon.law.yale.edu/ancient/hamframe.asp, 2008).
23. Sperati (2009), 44.
24. Mavroforou, Malizos, Karachalios, Chatzitheofilou and Giannoukas (2014) and Sperati (2009) demonstrate the preponderance of mutilation throughout history and across various parts of the world; Mazzola (1987), 4 and Yalamanchili *et al.* (2008), 3 on Indian reconstructive surgery being of ancient origin – first millennium BC/sixth century BC.
25. Velez (1912); Lastres (1943); Friedmann (1972); Pardal (1998), although Checa (2010) highlights some examples of possible medical amputations in the Museo Arqueológico Rafael Larco Herrera in Lima, Peru.
26. Martial, *Epig.* II.83 – *Trunci naribus*; III.85 – *Quis tibi persuasit naris abscidere moecho?*
27. Head (1972), 26.
28. Cf. *NJ* 134.
29. Stumpf (2017), 48.
30. Toševa-Nikolovska (2018), 217.
31. Gregory of Tours, *HF* X.18; Medvedev (1984), 137.
32. Xenophon, *Hell.* 3.3.3; Plutarch, *Agesilaus* 3.3, 30.1; Suetonius, *Cla.* 3.2.
33. John Chrysostom, *Hom. ad Philipp.* 15; *ad vid. iun.* 4; McGill, Sogno and Watts (2010), 245.
34. Orosius, *Hist. adv. Pag.* 7.42.9; Marcell. com. 412; Olympiodorus frag. 13; Procopius, *BV* III.3.9.
35. Theophanes, *Chron.* AM6132.
36. John of Nikiu, CXX.54.
37. *Ibid.*, CXX.52, 54; Theophanes, *Chron.* AM6133. While there is no definitive record, it is thought that Heraklonas died before the end of 642, an early death likely linked either to the politics behind his deposition or as a result of his mutilation. Martina does not appear in the sources again, suggesting that she never left her Rhodian exile.
38. Theophanes, *Chron.* AM6151; Michael the Syrian II.446; Kedrenos I.762; Zonaras XIV.19.
39. Theophanes, *Chron.* AM6161, 6173.
40. Stumpf (2017), 46–54 on the frequency of mutilation and the changing of punishments like fashion.
41. Agnellus, *Lib. Pont. Ecc. Rav.* 137; Nikephoros, *Brev.* 39; Theophanes, *Chron.* AM6187.

42. Agnellus, *Lib. Pont. Ecc. Rav.* 137.
43. Head (1972), 100.
44. Delbruck (1914).
45. Mazzola (1987), 4; Yalamanchili *et al.* (2008), 3.
46. Agnellus, *Lib. Pont. Ecc. Rav.* 137.
47. *Ibid.*
48. Head (1972), 96.

Chapter 10: The Lion and the Snake: The Reigns of Leontios and Tiberius III

1. Theophanes, *Chron.* AM6188.
2. Head (1972), 96.
3. Kent (1954), 217–218.
4. Crawford (2019), 194–202.
5. Head (1972), 97 n.11.
6. Theophanes, *Chron.* AM6187.
7. Al-Tabari XXII.881–939; 941–979; 979–1003.
8. Theophanes, *Chron.* AM6189.
9. Kaegi (2015) on the Muslim conquest of North Africa.
10. Theophanes, *Chron.* AM6138; Michael the Syrian II.440; al-Tabari XV.2818; Kaegi (1981), 159–160; Gregory the Patrician seems to have usurped the imperial title, with Muslim sources calling him 'Gregory *Augustus*' and having him mint coins in his own name. Gregory was perhaps a son of Niketas, cousin of Heraclius. Niketas' daughter was called Gregoria, creating a possible name link. Demonstrating how closely tied Gregory might have been to the imperial throne and how deep the feelings of political and religious abandonment might have run for him to rebel against Constans II, Gregoria was the empress of Heraclius Constantine III and therefore the mother of Constans. If Gregory was Niketas' son, he was also Constans II's uncle…
11. Al-Tabari XV.2818.
12. Maximus the Confessor, *Relatio Motionis* 112C–113C.
13. Kaegi (1981), 160.
14. Theophanes, *Chron.* AM6139; Michael the Syrian II.445; Syriac sources record that Gregory survived this defeat at Sufetula, travelled to Constantinople and was reconciled with his family; Al-Ma'sumi (1964) on a supposed invasion of Spain under Uthman.
15. Diehl (1896), 560–562.
16. Theophanes, *Chron.* AM6155.
17. Brunschvig (1975), Modéran (2005) and Benabbès (2005) vs Siraj (1995) regarding support for the ninth-century tradition of Ibn 'Abd al-Hakam, al-Baladhuri and Khalifah b. Khayyat over the twelfth-century tradition from Kairouan centred on Ibrahim b. Raqiq and followed by Ibn Idhari, Ibn Khaldun and al-Nuwayri.
18. *Liber Pontificalis* I.366.
19. Kennedy (2007), 216; it is worth noting that Hasan was a member of the Ghassanid tribe, which had long been an ally of the Roman Empire in its wars with the Sassanid Persians. This long service as Roman auxiliaries had not been transformed into a position at the forefront of the conquests of the Arab armies.
20. Kennedy (2007), 217.
21. Theophanes, *Chron.* AM6190; Nikephoros, *Brev.* 41.
22. Nikephoros, *Brev.* 41; Theophanes, *Chron.* AM6190.
23. Theophanes, *Chron.* AM6190; Nikephoros, *Brev.* 41.
24. Kennedy (2007), 220.

25. *Ibid.*
26. *Ibid.*
27. Taibi (1971); Kennedy (2007), 220–221.
28. Theophanes, *Chron.* AM6190; Nikephoros, *Brev.* 41.
29. Al-Maliki, *Riyad* 49; al-Nuwayri, *Nihaya* XXIV.35; Nikephoros, *Brev.* 41 does mention how Hasan 'reoccupied ... all the towns round about' Carthage, perhaps without much military action needed.
30. Ibn Idhari, *Bayan* I.35.
31. Theophanes, *Chron.* AM6190.
32. Nikephoros, *Brev.* 41; Theophanes, *Chron.* AM6190; could it be that any such trouble amongst the expeditionary officers hindered John's defence of Carthage?
33. Theophanes, *Chron.* AM6190.
34. *Ibid.*; Nikephoros, *Brev.* 41.
35. Theophanes, *Chron.* AM6190; Nikephoros, *Brev.* 41; Al-Tabari XXI.1036 records plague in Syria between March 698 and March 699.
36. Stathakopoulos in Little (2007), 104; Theophanes, *Chron.* AM6238; Nikephoros, *Brev.* 67.
37. Theophanes, *Chron.* AM6190.
38. Kaegi (1981), 42.
39. Theophanes, *Chron.* AM6190.
40. Nikephoros, *Brev.* 41.
41. Haldon (1984), 197ff.
42. Ostrogorsky (1968), 141; *Anecdota Bruxellensia* I.30, although this is a thirteenth-century manuscript; Maricq (1949), 67–68.
43. Theophanes, *Chron.* AM6190; Nikephoros, *Brev.* 41.
44. Bryer and Herrin (1977), 16 on Slavic; Brubaker and Haldon (2011), 72 on Turkic.
45. Theophanes, *Chron.* AM6190.
46. *Ibid.*
47. Al-Tabari XXII.881–939; 941–979; 979–1003.
48. Theophanes, *Chron.* AM6192; al-Tabari XXIII.1086–1125.
49. Theophanes, *Chron.* AM6191.
50. *Ibid.*; al-Tabari XXII.1036.
51. Theophanes, *Chron.* AM6192; Michael the Syrian, II.473–474.
52. Theophanes, *Chron.* AM6192.
53. *Ibid., Chron.* AM6190.
54. *Ibid., Chron.* AM6192.
55. *Ibid., Chron.* AM6193.
56. *Ibid., Chron.* AM6194.
57. Greenwood (2008), 345–346; Theophanes, *Chron.* AM6195.
58. Theophanes, *Chron.* AM6195.
59. Al-Tabari XXIII.1185.
60. Theophanes, *Chron.* AM6196.
61. Constantine VII, *de adm. imp.* 47.
62. Bury (1889), 356.
63. Jenkins in Mylonas and Raymond (1953), 1013–1014.
64. Constantine VII, *de adm. imp.* 47; Hill (1940), 290; Hackett (1901) 44, 260–261.
65. *Liber Pontificalis* 87.1.
66. Brown in Shepard (2019), 437.
67. Ekonomou (2009), 270.
68. *Liber Pontificalis* 87.2.
69. *Ibid.* 87.1.

70. *Ibid.*
71. *Ibid.* 87.2; Paul the Deacon, *HL* XXVII; this 'Horrea' could be Puteoli on the coast or a marker along the *Via Latina*.
72. *Liber Pontificalis* 87.2.
73. Kaegi (1981), 189.
74. Bury (1889), 356; Treadgold (1995), 26.
75. *Parastaseis Syntomoi Chronokai* 3.
76. Theophanes, *Chron.* AM6194; was this exile or was Bardanes stationed there with the island's burgeoning and future thematic naval garrison?
77. Leone (2007), 179–186.
78. Kennedy (2007), 221; Taibi (1971).
79. Kennedy (2007), 221–222.
80. Perhaps there were some in the Umayyad ranks who remembered that Wittiza and his father Ergica had sent aid to the Romans defending Carthage in 698.
81. The result is the only thing known decisively about this confrontation between Tariq and Roderic. Its dating and location are disputed; it may have not taken place until 712. The lack of consensus on what to call the battle highlights the issues of where it took place. It is known as either the Battle of Guadalete, the Battle of La Janda, the Battle of the Rio Barbate or the Battle of the Transductine Promontories. There is also a lack of consensus on the size of the forces involved.
82. Kaegi (1981), 299.

Chapter 11: Justinian's Exile and Restoration: Chersonites, Khazars and Bulgars
1. Herodotus IV.103.
2. Vasiliev (1936).
3. *Ibid.*, 79.
4. Head (1972), 99.
5. Vasiliev (1936), 77–78; (1952), 224.
6. Head (1972), 100.
7. Bede, *De Sex. Aetatibus* 317.
8. Nikephoros, *Brev.* 42; Theophanes, *Chron.* AM6198.
9. Head (1972), 101.
10. Nikephoros, *Brev.* 42; Theophanes, *Chron.* AM6196.
11. Vasiliev (1936), 47–56, 81.
12. Wolfram (1988), 279.
13. *Parastaseis Syntomoi Chronokai* 678; Dunlop (1954), 171; Artamonov (1962), 196.
14. Theophanes, *Chron.* AM6196; Nikephoros, *Brev.* 42.
15. Theophanes, *Chron.* AM6196; Nikephoros, *Brev.* 42.
16. Nikephoros, *Brev.* 42.
17. Constantine VII, *de caer.* I.32, II.126–127.
18. Dunlop (1954), 177.
19. Nikephoros, *Brev.* 12.
20. Theophanes, *Chron.* AM6196; Nikephoros, *Brev.* 42.
21. Nikephoros, *Brev.* 42.
22. Theophanes, *Chron.* AM6196.
23. Nikephoros, *Brev.* 42; Theophanes, *Chron.* AM6196; it is only Theophanes who records the names of Busir's agents; Dunlop (1954), 172 suggests that 'Balgitzin' was a Khazar title meaning 'governor'.
24. Nikephoros, *Brev.* 42.
25. *Ibid.*; Theophanes, *Chron.* AM6196.
26. Theophanes, *Chron.* AM6196; Nikephoros, *Brev.* 42.

27. Grégoire (1952), 288–292, argues that *Τομή*, meaning something akin to 'cutting', became the name 'Taman' and that Τομή[ν] τάριχα became 'Tmutarakan', the name of another town on the peninsula.
28. Artamonov (1962), 197; Head (1972), 107.
29. Theophanes, *Chron.* AM6196 mentions the ship passing by 'Assada', which is otherwise unidentified.
30. Nikephoros, *Brev.* 42; Theophanes, *Chron.* AM6196; Toumanoff (1963), 421–427 on Barasbakourios likely being the Georgian prince Varaz-Bakur described as ex-consul/proconsul and patrician; Turtledove (1982) suggests that Salibas and Stephen were two names of the one person, Barasbakourios' brother.
31. Nikephoros, *Brev.* 42.
32. Constantine VII, *de adm. imp.* 42.
33. Theophanes, *Chron.* AM6196.
34. *Ibid.*
35. *Ibid.*; Nikephoros, *Brev.* 42.
36. Head (1972), 110 n.7; cf. Hodgkin (1896), VI.367 on how even before knowledge of Justinian's previous marriage came to the fore, it was doubted that it was Theodora's child who was promised to Tervel.
37. Head (1972), 110.
38. Theophanes, *Chron.* AM6196.
39. Besevliev (1963), 97–107; cf. Cankova-Petkova (1963), 43–44.
40. Besevliev (1963), 97; Head (1972), 110.
41. Head (1969), 104–107.
42. Petkov (2008), 5.
43. Treadgold (1997), 340.
44. Theophanes, *Chron.* AM6197.
45. Nikephoros, *Brev.* 42.
46. Theophanes, *Chron.* AM6197; Nikephoros, *Brev.* 42.
47. Mango in Mango and Dagron (1995), 17 on it being hard to believe that the entire water system centred on the Aqueduct of Valens could have been out of action for nearly 150 years. More likely that some specific damage was done by the Avars and a more thorough repair was not carried out until the reign of Constantine V, but its ability to provide water to the city was restored.
48. Head (1972), 112; Breckenridge (1959); Grierson (1966) II.569, 645; Bellinger (1950), 109–110; Kitzinger (1963) 190–192.
49. Breckenridge (1959), 97–100.
50. Head (1972), 113.
51. Grabar (1936), 10.
52. Breckenridge (1959) 23, 63, 102; he also highlights that '*multus*' is a spelling error for '*multos*'.
53. Bellinger (1966), 122; Grierson (1966), II.644, 654–658.
54. Head (1972), 114.
55. Theophanes, *Chron.* AM6198.
56. *Ibid.*
57. Treadgold (1997), 340.
58. Theophanes, *Chron.* AM6198.
59. *Ibid.*, *Chron.* AM6196; Nikephoros, *Brev.* 42.
60. Nikephoros, *Brev.* 42.
61. Theophanes, *Chron.* AM6198.
62. Zacos and Veglery (1972), no.2672; Oikonomides (1986), no.26, who noted the resemblance of Tervel's portrait to that of Constantine IV on *solidi*.

63. Tervel may also have been given some territory in northern Thrace, specifically a region called Zagora; however, while this region did come into the possession of the Bulgars in the early eighth century, it would seem to been part of the treaty of 716 between Theodosius III and Tervel.
64. Head (1972), 115
65. On 15 February, according to *Chr. Alt.* 108; Grierson, Mango and Sevcenko (1962), 51.
66. *Chr. Alt.* 108.
67. Nikephoros, *Brev.* 42; Theophanes, *Chron.* AM6198; for the latter, Mango and Scott (1997), 523 suggests that Herakleios and the officers were 'impaled on the walls'.
68. Theophanes, *Chron.* AM6198.
69. Nikephoros, *Brev.* 42.
70. *Ibid.*; Theophanes, *Chron.* AM6198; Bede, *De Sex Aetatius* 317.
71. Paul the Deacon, *HL* VI.32.
72. Head (1972), 117.
73. Michael the Syrian II.478; cf. Gregorius Abu'l Faraj I.105; *Chronicon ad Anno Domino 846 Pertinens* 175; Levcenko (1947), 182.
74. Theophanes, *Chron.* AM6245; Mansi, *Concilia* XII col.967–968.
75. Sumner (1976), 292; *Chr. Alt.* 109; Theophanes, *Chron.* AM6245.
76. Theophanes, *Chron.* AM6245.
77. *Chr. Alt.* 109; *Synaxarium ecclesiae Constantinopolitanae* 828.25; Mango and Scott (1997), 537 n.6.
78. Head (1972), 118.
79. *Ibid.*
80. Nikephoros, *Brev.* 42; Theophanes, *Chron.* AM6198.
81. Toumanoff (1963), 421–427; Theophanes, *Chron.* AM6203; Nikephoros, *Brev.* 45; *Liber Pontificalis* I.390.
82. Theophanes, *Chron.* AM6198.
83. *Ibid.*
84. *Ibid.*; Michael the Syrian II.478; Nikephoros, *Brev.* 42.
85. Theophanes, *Chron.* AM6198; Nikephoros, *Brev.* 42.
86. Head (1969), 106 – 'Justinian II's hasty temperament was scarcely likely to have waited until summer to have launched his campaign of reconquest.'
87. A law of Gratian in 380 (*CTh* XIII.9.3) listed the sailing season as 13 April to 15 October, while Vegetius, *Epitome* IV.39.7 noted that the safest sailing began on 27 May and ended on 14 September; from 14 September to 11 November was potentially dangerous; from 11 November to 10 March 'the seas are closed' and remain dangerous up to 15 May.
88. Head (1969), 107.
89. Theophanes, *Chron.* AM6198; Nikephoros, *Brev.* 42.
90. Grierson (1966), II.43–44.
91. Ostrogorsky (1959), 18; Canard (1956), 49–72 shows a distorted version of the story of Justinian and Theodora amongst the Bulgars.
92. This report also states that not only was there a statue of Justinian with that of Theodora, there was also an unexplained statue of an elephant between them – *Parastaseis Syntomoi Chronokai* 678–679; cf. Dunlop (1954), 173.
93. Head (1972), 123.

Chapter 12: On the Warpath? The Restored Justinian in the Balkans and the East
1. Theophanes, *Chron.* AM6199.
2. *Parastaseis Syntomoi Chronokai* 678–679; cf. Dunlop (1954), 173.

3. The date of 708 relies on Theophanes, *Chron.* AM6200, for while Nikephoros, *Brev.* 43 records a Romano-Bulgar conflict under the restored Justinian, he gives no date.

4. Theophanes, *Chron.* AM6200.

5. Nikephoros, *Brev.* 43.

6. *Ibid.* 45.

7. Besevliev (1963), 99.

8. *Ibid.*, 116–117; Cankova-Petkova (1963), 44.

9. Nikephoros, *Brev.* 43.

10. Theophanes, *Chron.* AM6200.

11. *Ibid.*

12. *Ibid.*; Nikephoros, *Brev.* 43.

13. Theophanes, *Chron.* AM6197; cf. Michael the Syrian II.478.

14. Al-Tabari XXIII.1164–1171; four of Abd al-Malik's sons would eventually be caliph – Al-Walid I, Sulayman, Yazid II and Hisham – which sees him called the 'father of kings' in some Muslim sources. It has also seen it suggested that while '[Muawiyah] may have introduced the principle of dynastic succession into the ruling tradition of early Islam, … Abd al-Malik made it work'; Robinson (2005), 124. It is worth noting that Abd al-Aziz's son, Umar II, would be caliph, while Muhammad b. Marwan's son, Marwan II, would be the last Umayyad caliph in the East when he was ousted by the Abbasids in 750.

15. Theophanes, *Chron.* AM6199.

16. Blankinship (1994), 82, 94–95; Bachrach in *Necpoğlu* (1996), 30; Kennedy (2004), 90–91.

17. Hawting (2000), 58; Kennedy (2004), 90.

18. Al-Tabari XXIII.1185.

19. *Ibid.* XXIII.1194.

20. Theophanes, *Chron.* AM6192, 6194, 6195, 6196; cf. al-Tabari XXIII.1185.

21. Michael the Syrian II.478; Gregorius Abu'l Faraj I.105; Gibb (1958), 225.

22. Al-Tabari XXIII.1194.

23. Ibn Zabala, *History of Medina* in al-Samhudi, *Wafa al-Wafa bi akhbar Dar al-Mustafa* I.367; Gibb (1958), 231.

24. Theophanes, *Chron.* AM6183; Gibb (1958), 229.

25. Gibb (1958), 231.

26. Al-Tabari XXIII.1191–1192, 1194.

27. Theophanes, *Chron.* AM6201.

28. *Ibid.* AM6192, AM6196; al-Tabari XXIII.1185; cf. Brooks (1898), 191; Caetani, *Chron.* 1022 suggests 704/705, which is the same as Theophanes, *Chron.* AM6196.

29. Theophanes, *Chron.* AM6201; al-Tabari XXIII.1191–1192; Nikephoros, *Brev.* 44.

30. Al-Tabari XXIII.1192; Michael the Syrian II.478.

31. Theophanes, *Chron.* AM6201; al-Tabari XXIII.1192; Nikephoros, *Brev.* 44.

32. Al-Tabari XXIII.1192.

33. Nikephoros, *Brev.* 44.

34. Theophanes, *Chron.* AM6201.

35. *Ibid.*

36. Theophanes, *Chron.* AM6201; Nikephoros, *Brev.* 44.

37. Nikephoros, *Brev.* 44.

38. *Ibid.*

39. Theophanes, *Chron.* AM6202–6206; Nikephoros, *Brev.* 44; Michael the Syrian II.479; Lilie (1976), 118.

40. Theophanes, *Chron.* AM6189.
41. Bury (1889), II.374–375 suggests that Justinian II targeted Abasgia for reconquest because it had been Justinian I who had conquered the region.
42. Many are still there today as the Ossetians.
43. Theophanes, *Chron.* AM6209.
44. Bury (1889) II.375, 381.
45. Leo would become known as 'Leo the Isaurian', with some suggestion that this stems from a later confusion of him with Leontios, who was from Isauria and ruled under the name 'Leo'; Head (1971), 105ff. However, Theophanes, *Chron.* AM6209 says that he 'derived from Germanikeia [modern Kahramanmaraş], but actually from Isauria' and was transplanted to Mesembria during the first reign of Justinian II. *Parastaseis Syntomoi Chronokai* 20.1 also records him as 'Isaurian', and being written (at least partly) in the eighth century, would suggest that it was an early designation; Anastasius the Librarian considered him a Syrian; Schenk (1896), 296ff.
46. An alternative tradition, recorded by George Monachus, *Chronicon*, 737, has Leo made *spatharios* by Theodosius III and dispatched to Italy with a naval expedition before he was proclaimed emperor.
47. Head (1972), 129.
48. Theophanes, *Chron.* AM6209.
49. *Ibid.* AM6189.
50. *Ibid.* AM6209.
51. *Ibid.* AM6209.
52. Head (1972), 130.
53. Theophanes, *Chron.* AM6209.
54. *Ibid.*
55. *Ibid.*
56. *Ibid.*
57. *Ibid.*
58. *Ibid.*
59. *Ibid.*
60. Kulakovskij (1912–1915), III.324; Canard (1971), 353–357.
61. Bury (1889), II.395.
62. Head (1972), 131.
63. Bar Hebraeus I.110.
64. Head (1972), 18.
65. Theophanes, *Chron.* AM6209.
66. *Ibid.*

Chapter 13: Rome and Ravenna: Justinian's Revenge and Reconciliation

1. *Liber Pontificalis* I.383.
2. *Ibid.* I.385–391; Fliche and Martin (1930), V.198–200; Gorres (1908), 451–453; Hodgkin (1896), VI.369–378.
3. Ekonomou (2009), 266; *Liber Pontificalis* I.385; Kitzinger (1995), 119.
4. Ekonomou (2009), 267; Nordhagen (1968), 53.
5. *Liber Pontificalis* I.88.1, 5.
6. Llewellyn (1976), 120–126.
7. Ekonomou (2009), 268; cf. *Liber Pontificalis* I.385–386.
8. Ekonomou (2009), 268.
9. *Liber Pontificalis* I.88.5.
10. Haldon (2016), 50.

11. *Liber Pontificalis* I.88.5.
12. Ohme (1990), 63.
13. *Liber Pontificalis* I.89.1.
14. *Ibid.*
15. Williams (2004), 10 suggests that due to their shared Syrian heritage and abilities in Greek, the popes Sisinnius and Constantine were brothers.
16. cf. Mann (1925), I.2.126.
17. Ekonomou (2009), 271.
18. *Ibid.*
19. Agnellus, *Lib. Pont. Ecc. Rav.* 366–371.
20. Head (1972), 139.
21. *Ibid.*; cf. Fliche and Martin (1930).
22. *Liber Pontificalis* I.389–390.
23. Head (1972), 138.
24. *Liber Pontificalis* I.90.2; Head (1972), 138.
25. Head (1972), 139
26. *Liber Pontificalis* I.389.
27. Brown (1979), 25.
28. *Liber Pontificalis* I.90.2.
29. Head (1972), 139.
30. *Liber Pontificalis* I.90.2.
31. Head (1972), 140.
32. cf. Haldon (2016), 200–201 on Justinian's rule being associated with a dream/prophecy regarding its success/failure.
33. *Liber Pontificalis* I.90.2.
34. Agnellus, *Lib. Pont. Ecc. Rav.* 367–369; *Liber Pontificalis* I.389.
35. *Ibid.* 366–371.
36. *Liber Pontificalis* I.90.2.
37. *Ibid.* I.90.4.
38. Head (1970), 25.
39. Richards (1979), 212; Sansterre (1984), 10–11; Ekonomou (2009), 271.
40. *Liber Pontificalis* I.90.4.
41. *Ibid.*
42. Head (1972), 141.
43. Taddei (2013), 55.
44. *Liber Pontificalis* I.389; Bede, *Anglo Saxonis Chronicon* 201; Paul the Deacon, *HL* 225.
45. Ekonomou (2009), 270.
46. cf. *Liber Pontificalis* I.392–393.
47. *Liber Pontificalis* I.90.3; cf. Richards (1979), 275.
48. *Liber Pontificalis* I.389–391.
49. *Ibid.* I.90.4.
50. *Ibid.* I.90.4.
51. *Ibid.* I.90.4.
52. *Ibid.* I.390.
53. *Ibid.* I.390.
54. *Ibid.* I.390.
55. Taddei (2013), 61.
56. *Liber Pontificalis* I.391; Bede, *Anglo Saxonis Chronicon* 202; Paul the Deacon, *HL* 226.
57. *Liber Pontificalis* I.275, 288; Ekonomou (2009), 296 n.260.

58. Sansterre (1984), 12–13.
59. Ekonomou (2009), 272.
60. *Liber Pontificalis* I.90.6.
61. *Ibid.*
62. *Ibid.*
63. *Ibid.*
64. cf. Gorres (1908), 453.
65. Hefele (1896), V.242; Bede, *De Sex. Aetatibus* 316.
66. *Liber Pontificalis* I.88.5.
67. *Ibid.* II.91.1.
68. Head (1972), 136.
69. *Liber Pontificalis* I.90.7.
70. Mansi, *Concilia* XII.200; *PG* 96.1421–1424.
71. Ekonomou (2009), 297 n.263.
72. *Ibid.*, 272.
73. *Ibid.*, 272.
74. *Ibid.*, 296 n.262.
75. *Ibid.*, 270, rather against the tone of Justinian's portrayal elsewhere in the section, Ekonomou buys into the horrors of Justinian II recorded by Theophanes and Nikephoros: dinner guests slain, others thrown into the sea, officials appointed, deposed and executed in a matter of days.

Chapter 14: Cherson, Khazars and the Revolt of Bardanes: The End of the Heraclians
1. Nikephoros, *Brev.* 45; Theophanes, *Chron.* AM6203; could it be that Agnellus got his idea that Justinian targeted Ravenna out of revenge from the similar story of his attacking Cherson?
2. Head (1972), 142.
3. Dunlop (1954), 174.
4. Dunlop (1954), 59–61.
5. Head (1972), 143.
6. *Ibid.*
7. Nikephoros, *Brev.* 45.
8. Theophanes, *Chron.* AM6203.
9. *Ibid.*
10. *Miracula S. Demetrii* II.5; Zacos and Veglery (1972), no.934.
11. Theophanes, *Chron.* AM6203.
12. Nikephoros, *Brev.* 45.
13. *Ibid.*; Theophanes, *Chron.* AM6203.
14. Head (1972), 144.
15. Theophanes, *Chron.* AM6203.
16. Nikephoros, *Brev.* 45; Theophanes, *Chron.* AM6203.
17. Theophanes, *Chron.* AM6203; cf. Nikephoros, *Brev.* 45.
18. Hodgkin (1896), VI.380 on Theophanes' text being heavily corrupted at this point and seems to say that the *tudun* and Zoilos were executed here, but this is an error given that they reappear in the text not long later; Head (1972), 144.
19. Theophanes, *Chron.* AM6203; Nikephoros, *Brev.* 45.
20. Head (1972), 145.
21. Theophanes, *Chron.* AM6203.
22. *Ibid.* AM6066.
23. *Ibid.* AM6203; the term 'pissed against the wall' is Biblical, used in conjunction with killing of all of the males in a particular group; cf. 1 Samuel 25: 22, 34; 1 Kings 12: 24, 14:10, 16: 20: 21.

24. Theophanes, *Chron.* AM6203; George Syros was γενικόν λογοθεσιον, an official in the state treasury in charge of taxation. Might he have been a successor of Theodotus?
25. Nikephoros, *Brev.* 45.
26. Theophanes, *Chron.* AM6203.
27. Nikephoros, *Brev.* 45.
28. *Ibid.*
29. Theophanes, *Chron.* AM6203.
30. *Ibid.*
31. *Ibid.*
32. Nikephoros, *Brev.* 45.
33. Possibly modern Samandra, opposite Istanbul in Asia.
34. Kaegi (1981), 190; Nikephoros, *Brev.* 45.
35. Breckenridge (1959), 16; cf. Ghevond 34.
36. Theophanes, *Chron.* AM6204.
37. *Ibid.*; al-Tabari XXIII.1236, which has Maslamah conquering Masah (Amaseia), Hisn al-Hadid, Ghazalah and Taramah in the region around Malatya/Melitene.
38. During this period, al-Abbas b. al-Walid reputedly conquered Samastiyyah (Mistheia), Antakyah (Pisidian Antioch) and the fortresses of Tulus, al-Marzbanayn and Hiraqlah, while Marwan b. al-Walid reached Khanjarah (Gangra), Abd al-Aziz b. al-Walid reached Ghazalah, al-Walid b. Hisham al-Mu'ayti reached the land of Burj al-Hamam (possibly near Melitene) and Yazid b. Abi Kabshah reached the land of Suriyah; al-Tabari XXIII.1236, 1255–1256, 1266–1267; Brooks (1898); Lilie (1976), 121.
39. Head (1972), 146.
40. Theophanes, *Chron.* AM6203; Nikephoros, *Brev.* 45.
41. Theophanes, *Chron.* AM6203.
42. While *Chr. Alt.* 108 gives Justinian's death as occurring on 24 November, it has been suggested by Grierson, Mango and Sevcenko (1962), 62 that the original Greek document has 4 November. Head (1972), 148 suggests, without listing her source, that Justinian did not make it back to Damatrys after finding Constantinople in the hands of Bardanes. Rather, he was overtaken in his flight back to his army by a troop of men under Helias at the 12-mile marker from the capital, with the vengeful governor of Cherson executing Justinian without much of a thought.
43. Head (1972), 148; Grierson, Mango and Sevcenko (1962), 50–51.
44. Agnellus, *Lib. Pont. Ecc. Rav.* 371.
45. *Liber Pontificalis* I.391.
46. Head (1972), 149.
47. Nikephoros, *Chron.* 45.
48. Magoulias (1967), 251.
49. Theophanes, *Chron.* AM6203.
50. Grierson, Mango and Sevcenko (1962), 32.
51. Head (1972), 150.

Conclusions: From Tyrant to Tyrant? The Heraclian Cycle is Complete
1. Nikephoros, *Brev.* 45.
2. Head (1972), 151.
3. Howard-Johnston (2011), 207.
4. Head (1972), 13.

Bibliography

Abbreviations

ACO	*Acta Conciliorum Oecumenicorum*
CJ	*Codex Justinianus*
CTh	*Codex Theodosianus*
NJ	*Novels of Justinian*
PLRE	*Prosopography of the Late Roman Empire*
PmbZ	*Prosopographie der mittelbyzantinischen Zeit Online*

Primary

Abu Ubayda, *Naqa'id Jarir wa-al-Farazdaq* (Bevan, A.A. edition, 1905–1912).
Acta Conciliorum Oecumenicorum (Schwartz, E. and Straub, J. edition, 1914–1940).
Aeschylus, *Oresteia* (Fagles, R. trans., Penguin Classics, 1979).
Agapius, *Kitab al-Unvan* (Vasiliev, A.A. trans., 1910–1912).
Agathias, *De imperio et rebus gestis Iustiniani* (Frendo, J.D. trans., 1975).
Agnellus, *Liber Pontificalis Ecclesiae Ravennatis (Mauskopf, D. trans., 2004).*
Al-Baladhuri, *Futūh al-buldān* (de Goeje, M.J. trans., 1866).
Al-Nuwayri, *Nihāyat al-arab fī funūn al-adab* (Maktabah al-'Arabīyah edition, 1964).
Al-Samhudi, *Wafa al-Wafa bi akhbar Dar al-Mustafa* (Al-Samarrai, Q. edition, 2001).
Al-Tabari (Yar-Shater, E. trans., 1985–1999).
Anecdota Bruxellensia (Cumont, F. edition, 1896).
Anna Komnena, *Alexiad* (Sewter, E.R.A. trans., Penguin, 2009).
Bede, *The Complete Works of Venerable Bede (Volume 6)* (Giles, J.A. edition, 1843).
Bede, *Ecclesiastical History of the English People* (Colgrave, B. and Mynors, R.A.B. edition, 1991 reprint).
Bede, *De temporum ratione*, (Wallis, Faith trans., 1999).
Cassiodorus, *Variae* (Barnish, S.J.B trans., Translated Texts for Historians, 1992).
Cassius Dio, *Historia Romana* (Cary, E. trans., Loeb Classical Library, 1914–1927).
Cedrenus, *Historiarium Compendium* (Bekker, I. edition, 1838).
Chronicle of 741 (Hoyland, R. trans., 1997).
Chronicle of 846 (Brooks, E.W. trans., 1897).
Chronicon ad annum Christi 1234 pertinens (Chabot, J-B. trans., 1920).
Chronicon Altinate (Cessi, R. edition, 1933).
Chronology of 354 (Mommsen, T. edition, *Chronica Minora* 1892).
Code of Hammurabi (King, L.W. trans., https://avalon.law.yale.edu/ancient/hamframe.asp, 2008).
Codex Gothanus (Hodgkin, T. trans., 1896).
Codex Iustinianus (Krueger, P. trans., 1914).
Codex Theodosianus (Pharr, C. trans., 1952).
Constantine VII Porphyrogenitus, *De Administrando Imperio* (Jenkins, R.J.H. trans., 1967).
Constantine VII Porphyrogenitus, *De Caerimoniis* (Reiske, J.J. trans., 1828).
Ekloga (Humphreys, M. trans., 2017).

Ennodius, *Panegyricus dictus Theoderico regi* (Vogel, F. edition, 1885).

Eutychius, *Annals* (Breydy, M. trans., 1985).

Evagrius Scholasticus, *Historia Ecclesiastica* (Whitby, M. trans., Translated Texts for Historians, 2000).

Fredegar, *Chronicle* (Wallace-Hadrill, J.W. trans., 1960).

George Monachos, *Chronicon Breve* (de Boor, C. edition, 1905).

George of Cyprus, *Descriptio Orbis Romani* (Cuntz, O. edition, 1929).

Ghevond, *History of the Wars and Conquests of the Arabs in Armenia* (Arzoumanian, Z. trans., 2007).

Gregorius Abu'l Faraj/Bar Hebraeus (Wallis Budge, E.A. trans., 1932).

Gregory of Tours, *Historia Francorum* (Thorpe, L. trans., Penguin Classics, 1974).

Herodotus, *Histories* (de Selincourt, A. and Marincola, J. trans., 2003).

Ibn Idhari, *Al-Bayan al-Mughrib* (Levtzion, N. and Hopkins, J.F.P. edition, 1981).

Ibn Sa'id al-Maghribi (Arberry, A.J. trans., 2001)

Ibn Zabala, *History of Medina* in Al-Samhudi, *Wafa al-Wafa bi akhbar Dar al-Mustafa* (Al-Samarrai, Q. edition, 2001).

John Chrysostom, *In epistulam ad Philippenses argumentum et homiliae* (Allen, P. trans., 2013).

John Chrysostom, *Tractatus ad viduam iuniorem* (Stephens, W.R.W. trans., NPNF, 1889).

John of Antioch (Mariev, S. trans., 2008).

John of Biclaro, *Chronicle* (Ferry, J.R. trans., 1990).

John of Ephesus, *Historia Ecclesiastica* (Payne-Smith, R. trans., 1860).

John of Nikiu, *Chronicle* (Charles, R.H. trans., 1916).

Jordanes, *Getica* (Mierow, C.C. trans., 1915).

Jordanes, *Romana* (Mommsen, T. edition, Teubner, 1882).

Leo Grammatikos, *Chronographia* (Bekkeri, I. edition, 1842).

Liber Pontificalis (Davis, R. trans., 1989).

Malalas, John, *Chronographia* (Jeffreys, E., Jeffreys, M. and Scott, R. trans., 1986).

Malchus, *Historia* (Blockley, R.C. trans., *The Fragmentary Classicising Historians of the Later Roman Empire*, 1981).

Marcellinus Comes, *Chronicon* (Croke, B. trans., 1995).

Martial, *Epigrams* (anonymous trans., Bohn Classical Library, 1897).

Mauricius, *Strategikon* (Dennis, G.T. trans., 1983).

Maximus the Confessor, *Relatio Motionis* (Allen, P. and Neil, B. trans., 2002).

Menander Protector, *Historia* (Blockley, R.C. trans., 1985).

Michael the Syrian, *Chronicle* (Palmer, A. trans., Translated Texts for Historians, 1993).

Miracula S. Demetrii (Lemerle, P. edition, 1979–1981).

Moses Dasxuranci, *History of Albania* (Dowsett, C.J.F. trans., 1961).

Movses Khorenantsi, *History of Armenia* (Thomson, R.W. trans., 2006).

Nikephoros, *Breviarum* (Mango, C. trans., 1990).

Novels of Justinian (Scott, S.P. trans., 1932).

Olympiodorus (Blockley, R.C. trans., *The Fragmentary Classicising Historians of the Later Roman Empire*, 1981).

Optatus Milevitanus, *Against Parmenian* (Edwards, M. trans., Translated Texts for Historians, 1998).

Origo Gentis Langobardorum (Foulke, W.D. trans., 1907).

Orosius, *Historiae adversum paganos* (Deferrari, R.J. trans., 1964).

Parastaseis syntomoi chronikai (Cameron, A. and Herrin, J. trans., 1984).

Paul the Deacon, *Historia Langobardorum* (Foulke, W.D. trans., 1906).

Paul the Deacon, *Historia Romana* (Crivellucci, A. trans., 1914).

Petrus Siculus, *Historia Manichaeorum* (Gieseler, J.C.L. edition, 1846).
Pliny the Elder, *Natural History* (Bostock, J. and Riley, H.T. trans., 1855).
Plutarch, *Lives* (Perrin, B. trans., Loeb Classical Library, 1923).
Priscus (Blockley, R.C. trans., *The Fragmentary Classicising Historians of the Later Roman Empire*, 1981; Given, J. trans., 2014).
Procopius, *Anecdota* (Williamson, G.A. trans., Penguin Classics, 1967).
Procopius, *De Bello Gothico* (Dewing, H.B. trans., Loeb Classical Library, 1919).
Procopius, *De Bello Vandalico* (Dewing, H.B. trans., Loeb Classical Library, 1916).
Ps-Gregory, *Epistula ad Leonem Isaurum imp.* (Goulliard, J. edition, 1968).
Ps-Zacharias Rhetor, *Historia ecclesiastica* (Hamilton, F.J. and Brooks, E.W. trans., 1899).
Ptolemy, *Geographia* (Lennart Berggren, J. and Jones, A. trans., 2001).
Ravennatis Anonymi Cosmographia (Pinder, M. and Partheny, G. edition, 1860).
Sacrorum conciliorum: nova et amplissima collectio (Mansi, J.D. edition, 1755; Schaff, P. and Wace, H. trans., 1900)
Sebeos, *History* (Thomson, R.W. trans., 1999).
Sidonius Apollinaris, *Carmina* (Anderson, W.B. trans., Loeb Classical Library, 1936).
Strabo, *Geography* (Jones, H.L. trans., Loeb Classical Library, 1917–1932).
Suetonius, *Twelve Caesars* (Graves, R. and Grant, M. trans., Penguin Classics, 1979).
Synaxarium ecclesiae Constantinopolitanae (Delehaye, H. edition, 1902).
Tacitus, *Annales* (Grant, M. trans., Penguin Classics, 1957).
Tacitus, *Germania* (Mattingly, H. and Handford, S.A. trans., Penguin Classics, 1970).
Theophanes, *Chronographia* (Mango, C. and Scott, R. trans., 1997).
Theophylactus Simocatta, *Historiae* (Whitby, M. and Whitby, M. trans., 1986).
Vegetius, *De rei militari* (Milner, N.P. trans., 1993; Reeve, M.D. trans., 2004).
Velleius Paterculus, *Roman History* (Shipley, F.W. trans., Loeb Classical Library, 1924).
Xenophon, *Hellenica* (Cawkwell, G. trans., Penguin Classics, 1979).
Zacharias of Mytilene, *Historia ecclesiastica* (Brooks, E.W. trans., 1899).
Zonaras, *Epitome* (Banchich, T.M. and Lane, E.N. trans., 2009).

Secondary

Afinogenov, D., 'The Source of Theophanes' *Chronography* and Nikephoros' *Breviarium* for the Years 685–717', *Hristiansky Vostok* 4 (2002), 11–22
Afinogenov, D., 'The history of Justinian and Leo', in Zuckerman, C. (ed.), *La Crimée entre Byzance et le khaganat khazar* (Paris, 2006), 181–200.
Agile, D., 'Bar Hebraeus et son public a travers ses chroniques en syriaque et en arbe', *Le Museon* 118 (2005), 87–107.
Ahrweiler, H. *Byzance et la mer* (Paris, 1966).
Ahrweiler, H. and Laiou, A.E., *Studies on the Internal Diaspora of the Byzantine Empire* (Washington DC, 1998).
Aibabin, A., 'Early Khazar Archaeological Monuments in Crimea and to the North of the Black Sea', in Zuckermann, C. (ed.), *La Crimée entre Byzance et le Khaganat Khazar* (Paris, 2006), 31–65.
Akram, A.I., *The Muslim Conquest of Persia* (Birmingham, 2009).
Alexander, P.J., *The Patriarch Nicephorus of Constantinople: Ecclesiastical Policy and Image Worship in the Byzantine State* (Oxford, 1958).
Alexander, P.J., 'The Strength and Empire and Capital as seen through Byzantine eyes', *Speculum* 37 (1962), 339–357.
Allen, P., 'The "Justinianic" Plague', *Byzantion* 49 (1979), 5–20.
Allen, P., *Sophronius of Jerusalem and Seventh-Century Heresy: The Synodical Letter and Other Documents* (Oxford, 2009).

Allen, P. and Jefferys, E. (eds.), *The Sixth Century: End of Beginning?* (Brisbane, 1996).

Allen, P. and Neil, B., *Maximus the Confessor and His Companions: Documents from Exile* (Oxford, 2002).

Allen, P. and Neil, B. (eds.), *The Oxford Handbook of Maximus the Confessor* (Oxford, 2015).

Al-Ma'sumi, M.S.H., 'The Earliest Muslim Invasion of Spain', *Islamic Studies* 3 (1964), 97–102.

Alston, R., 'Managing the Frontiers: Supplying the Frontier Troops in the Sixth and Seventh Centuries', in Erdkamp, P. (ed.), *The Roman Army and the Economy* (Amsterdam, 2002), 398–419.

Anagnostakes, E., 'Περιουσιος λαος', in Kountoura-Galake, E. (ed.), *The Dark Centuries of Byzantium* (Athens, 2001), 325–345.

Anastos, M.V., 'The Transfer of Illyricum, Calabria and Sicily to the jurisdiction of the patriarch of Constantinople in 732–733', *Studi Bizantini e Neoellenici in Onore di S.G.Mercati* (Rome, 1957), 14–31.

Anastos, M.V., 'Iconoclasm and the Imperial Rule 717–842', in Hussey, J.M. (ed.), *Cambridge Medieval History IV.1: The Byzantine Empire* (Cambridge, 1966), 61–104.

Anastos, M.V., 'Leo III's Edict Against the Images in the Year 726–27 and Italo-Byzantine Relations Between 726 and 730', *Polychordia: Festschrift Franz Dolger zum 75* (Amsterdam, 1968), III.5–41.

Antoniadis-Bibicou, H., *Etudes d'histoire maritime a Byzance, a propos du Theme des Caravisiens* (Bibliotheque Generale de l'Ecole Pratique des Hautes Etudes, VIe section, Paris, 1966).

Antonopoulos, P., 'Emperor Constans II's Intervention in Italy and its Ideological Significance', in Koder, J. and Stouraitis, I. (eds.), *Byzantine War Ideology Between Roman Imperial Concept and Christian Religion* (Vienna, 2012), 27–32.

Artamonov, M.I., *The History of the Khazars* (St Petersburg, 1962).

Artun, T., 'The Miracles of St. Theodore Teron: An eighth century source?', *JOB* 5 (2008), 1–11.

Ashburner, W., 'The Farmer's Law,' *JHS* 30 (1910), 85–108.

Ashburner, W., 'The Farmer's Law Continued', *JHS* 32 (1912), 68–95.

Ashburner, W., 'The Byzantine Mutiny Act', *JHS* 46 (1926), 80–109.

Asutay-Effenberger, N., *Die Landmauer von Konstantinopel-Istanbul: Historisch-topographische und baugeschichtliche Untersuchungen* (Berlin, 2007).

Athamina, K., 'Non-Arab Regiments and Private Militias during the Umayyad Period', *Arabica* 45 (1998), 347–375.

Bacharach, J.L., 'Marwanid Umayyad Building Activities: Speculations on Patronage', in Necpoğlu, G. (ed.), *Muqarnas: An Annual on the Visual Culture of the Islamic World, Volume 13* (Leiden, 1996), 27–44.

Bacharach, J.L., 'Signs of Sovereignty: The "Shahāda", the Qur'anic Verses, and the Coinage of Abd al-Malik', *Muqarnas Online* 27 (2010), 1–30.

Bagnall, R.S. (ed.), *Egypt in the Byzantine World 300–700* (Cambridge, 2007).

Baird, D., 'Settlement Expansion on the Konya Plain, Anatolia: 5th–7th Centuries AD', in Bowden, W., Lavan, L. and Machado, C. (eds.), *Recent Research on the Late Antique Countryside* (Leiden, 2004), 219–246.

Ball, W., *Rome in the East: the transformation of an empire* (London, 2000).

Banaji, J., *Agrarian Change in Late Antiquity: Gold, Labour and Aristocratic Dominance* (Oxford, 2001).

Bardill, J., *Brickstamps of Constantinople, Volume I: Text* (Oxford, 2004).

Barford, P.M., *The Early Slavs: Culture and Society in Early Medieval Eastern Europe* (Ithaca, 2001).

Bashear, S., 'Apocalyptic and other materials on early Muslim-Byzantine wars: A review of Arabic sources', *JRAS* 1 (1991), 173–207.

Bates, M., 'Constans II or Heraclonas? An analysis of the Constantinopolitan folles of Constans II', *ANSMN* 17 (1971), 141–161.

Bates, M., 'History, Geography and Numismatics in the First Century of Islamic Coinage', *Revue Suisse de Numismatique* 65 (1986), 231–262.

Batty, R., *Rome and the Nomads: The Pontic and Danubian Realm in Antiquity* (Oxford, 2007).

Baynes, N.H., 'The Date of the Avar Surprise: A Chronological Study', *BZ* 21 (1912), 110–128.

Becker, A.H. and Reed, A.Y., *The Ways That Never Parted: Jews and Christians in Late Antiquity and the Early Middle Ages* (Tübingen, 2003).

Belcastro, M.G. and Faccini, F., 'Anthropological and cultural features of a skeletal sample of horsemen from the medieval necropolis of Vicenne-Campochiaro (Molise, Italy)', *Collegium antropologicum* 25 (2001), 387–401.

Bellinger, A.R., 'The Gold Coins of Justinian II', *Archaeology* 8 (1950), 107–111.

Bellinger, A.R., 'The Copper of the Second Reign of Justinian II', *American Numismatic Society Museum Notes* 12 (1966), 122–124.

Bellinger, A.R., *Catalogue of Byzantine Coins in the Dumbarton Oaks Collection and in the Whittemore Collection I: Anastasius to Maurice, 491–602* (Washington DC, 1966).

Benabbès, A., 'Les premiers raids arabes en Numidie Byzantine: questions toponymiques', in Briand-Ponsar, C. (ed.), *Identités et Cultures dans l'Algérie Antique* (University of Rouen, 2005), 459–492.

Besevliev, V., 'On the Question of the Reward Received by Tervel from Justinian II in 705', *Vizantiiskii Vremenik* 16 (1959), 12–13.

Besevliev, V., *Die protobulgarischen Inschriften* (Berliner byzantinistische Arbeiten 23. Berlin, 1963).

Bjornlie, M.S., *Politics and Tradition Between Rome, Ravenna and Constantinople: A Study of Cassiodorus and the Variae 527–554* (New York, 2013).

Blankinship, K.Y., *The End of the Jihad State: The Reign of Hisham B. 'Abd Al-Malik and the Collapse of the Umayyads* (Albany, 1994).

Bodon, G., 'Testa detta 'del Carmagnola', *Il Museo di San Marco* (Venice, 2003), 194.

Bone, H., *The Administration of Umayyad Syria: The Evidence of the Copper Coins*, PhD dissertation (Princeton, 2000).

Bonner, M., 'Some Observations Concerning the Early Development of jihad on the Arab-Byzantine Frontier', *Studica Islamica* 75 (1992), 5–31.

Bonner, M., *Aristocratic Violence and Holy War: Studies in the Jihad and the Arab-Byzantine Frontier* (New Haven, 1996).

Bonner, M. (ed.), *Arab-Byzantine Relations in Early Islamic Times* (Aldershot, 2005).

Booth, P., *Crisis of Empire: Doctrine and Dissent at the End of Late Antiquity* (London, 2014).

Borrut, A., 'Entre tradition et histoire: genre et diffusion de l'image de Umar II', *Melanges de L'Universite Saint-Joseph* 58 (2005), 329–378.

Bosworth, C.E., 'Arab Attacks on Rhodes in the Pre-Ottoman Period', *Journal of the Royal Asiatic Society* 6 (1996), 157–164.

Bosworth, C.E., *The Arabs, Byzantium and Iran: Studies in Early Islamic History and Culture* (Aldershot, 1996).

Bosworth, C.E., 'Byzantium and the Syrian Frontier in the Early Abbasid Period', in Bosworth, C.E., *The Arabs, Byzantium and Iran: Studies in Early Islamic History and Culture* (Aldershot, 1996), ch.XII.

Bowden, W., Gutteridge, A. and Machado, C. (eds.), *Social and Political Life in Late Antiquity* (Leiden, 2006).

Bowden, W., Lavan, L. and Machado, C. (eds.), *Recent Research on the Late Antique Countryside* (Leiden, 2004).

Bowersock, G.W., *Studies on the Eastern Roman Empire: Social, Economic and Administrative History, Religion, Historiography* (Goldbach, 1994).

Brandes, W., *Die Staadt Kleinasiens in 7 un 8. Jahrhundert* (*BBA* 56) (Berlin, 1989).

Brandes, W., 'Byzantine Towns in the Seventh and Eighth Century – Different Sources, Different Histories?', in Brogiolo, G.P. and Ward-Perkins, B. (eds.), *The Idea and Ideal of the Town between Late Antiquity and the Early Middle Ages* (Leiden, 1999), 25–57.

Brandes, W., *Finanzverwaltung in Krisenzeiten. Untersuchungen zur byzantinischen Administration im6-9 Jahrhundert* (Frankfurt am Main, 2002).

Brandes, W., 'Orthodoxy and Heresy in the Seventh Century: Prosopographical Observations on Monotheletism', in Cameron, Av. (ed.), *Fifty Years of Prosopography: The Later Roman Empire and Beyond* (Oxford, 2003), 103–118.

Brandes, W., 'Georgios απο υπατων und die Kommerkiariersiegel', in Ludwig, C. (ed.), *Siegel Und Siegler: Akten Des 8. Internationalen Symposions Fuer Byzantinische Sigillographie* (Berliner Byzantinistische Studien, Frankfurt am Main, 2005), 31–47.

Brandes, W. and Haldon, J.F., 'Towns, Tax and Transformation: State, Cities and Their Hinterlands in the East Roman World, *ca.* 500–800', in Gauthier, N. (ed.), *Towns and Their Hinterlands between Late Antiquity and the Early Middle Ages* (Leiden, 2000), 141–172.

Breckenridge, J.D., 'The Long Siege of Thessalonika: Its Date and Iconography', *BZ* 48 (1955), 116–122.

Breckenridge, J.D., *The Numismatic Iconography of Justinian II* (New York, 1959).

Breckenridge, J.D., 'Evidence for the Nature of Relations between Pope John VII and the Byzantine Emperor Justinian II', *BZ* 65 (1972), 364–374.

Breckenridge, J.D., 'Again the "Carmagnola"', *Gesta* 20/21 (1981), 1–7.

Brett, M., 'The Arab Conquest and the Rise of Islam in N. Africa', *CHA* 2 (Cambridge, 1978), 490–555.

Briand-Ponsar, C. (ed.), *Identités et Cultures dans l'Algérie Antique* (University of Rouen, 2005).

Brock, S.P., 'An early Syriac life of Maximus the Confessor', *AB* 91 (1973a), 299–346.

Brock, S.P., 'A Syriac fragment on the sixth council', *Oriens Christianus* 57 (1973b), 63–71.

Brock, S.P., 'Syriac Sources for Seventh-Century History', *BMGS* 2 (1976), 17–36.

Brogiolo, G.P. and Ward-Perkins, B. (eds.), *The Idea and Ideal of the Town between Late Antiquity and the Early Middle Age* (Leiden, 1999).

Brook, K.A., *The Jews of Khazaria* (Lanham, 2018).

Brooks, E.W., 'The Arabs in Asia Minor (641–750) from Arabic Sources', *JHS* 18 (1898), 182–208.

Brooks, E.W., 'The Campaign of 716–718, from Arabic sources', *JHS* 19 (1899), 19–31.

Brooks, E.W., 'Arabic Lists of the Byzantine Themes', *JHS* 21 (1901), 67–77.

Brooks, E.W., 'The sources of Theophanes and the Syriac chroniclers', *BZ* 15 (1906), 578–587.

Brooks, E.W., 'The Sicilian Expedition of Constantine IV', *BZ* 17 (1908), 455–459.

Brooks, E.W., 'The Brothers of the Emperor Constantine IV', *EHR* 30 (1915), 42–51.

Brooks, E.W., 'The Successors of Heraclius', in Gwatkin, H.M. and Whitney, J.P. (eds.), *Cambridge Medieval History Vol. II: The Rise of the Saracens and the Foundation of the Western Empire* (Cambridge, 1936), 391–417.

Brown, P.R.L., 'The rise and function of the holy man in Late Antiquity', *JRS* 61 (1971), 80–101.

Brown, P.R.L., 'A Dark-Age Crisis: Aspects of the Iconoclastic Controversy', *EHR* 88 (1973), 1–34.

Brown, P.R.L., 'The study of elites in Late Antiquity', in Rapp, C. and Salzman, M. (eds.), *Elites in Late Antiquity. Arethusa* 33 (2000), 321–346.

Brown, P.R.L., *The World of Late Antiquity* (London, 2006).

Brown, T.S., 'The Church of Ravenna and the Imperial Administration in the Seventh Century', *EHR* 94 (1979), 1–28.

Brown, T.S., *Gentleman and Officers: Imperial Administration and Aristocratic Power in Byzantine Italy AD 554–800* (London, 1984).

Brown, T.S., 'Justinian II and Ravenna', *BSI* 61 (1995), 29–36.

Brown, T.S., 'Byzantine Italy (680–876)', in Shepard, J. (ed.), *Cambridge History of Byzantine Empire ca. 500–1492* (Cambridge, 2019), 433–464.

Brown, T.S., Bryer, A. and Winfield, D., 'Cities of Heraclius', *BMGS* 4 (1978), 15–38.

Brubaker, L. (ed.), *Byzantium in the Ninth Century: Dead or Alive?* (Aldershot, 1998).

Brubaker, L., *Inventing Byzantine Iconoclasm* (London, 2012).

Brubaker, L. and Cunningham, M. (eds.), *The Cult of the Mother of God in Byzantium: Text and Images* (Farnham, 2011).

Brubaker, L. and Haldon, J.F., *Byzantium in the Iconoclast Era (ca. 680–850): The Sources: An Annotated Survey* (Aldershot, 2001).

Brubaker, L. and Haldon, J.F., *Byzantium in the Iconoclast Era, c. 680–850: A History* (Cambridge, 2015).

Bruckner, W., *Die Sprache der Langobarden, Quellen und Forschungen zur Sprach- und Culturgeschichte der germanischen Völker* (Strassburg, 1895).

Brunschvig, R., 'Ibn Abd al-Hakam et la conquête de l'Afrique du Nord par les arabes', *Al-Andalus* 40 (1975), 129–179.

Bryer, A. and Herrin, J., *Iconoclasm: Papers Given at the Ninth Spring Symposium of Byzantine Studies, University of Birmingham, March 1975* (Centre for Byzantine Studies, Birmingham, 1977).

Bumazhnov, D., Grypeou, E., Sailors, T.B. and Toepel, A. (eds.), *Bibel, Byzanz und Christlicher Orient: Festschrift für Stephen Gerö zum 65. Geburtstag* (Orientalia Lovaniensia Analecta 187. Leuven/Paris/Walpole, 2011).

Burns, T.S., *The History of the Ostrogoths* (Bloomington, 1984).

Bury, J.B., *A History of the Later Roman Empire from Arcadius to Irene, 395 A.D. to 800 A.D.*, 2 Vols (London, 1889).

Bury, J.B., 'The Great Palace', *BZ* 21 (1912), 210–225.

Caetani, L., *Annali dell' Islam*, 10 vols (Milan, 1905–1926).

Cameron, Al., *Circus Factions: Blues and Greens at Rome and Constantinople* (Oxford, 1976).

Cameron, Al., 'The Imperial Pontifex', *Harvard Studies in Classical Philology* 103 (2007), 341–384.

Cameron, Av., 'The Theotokos in Sixth-Century Constantinople: A City Finds Its Symbol', *JTS* 29 (1978), 79–108.

Cameron, Av., 'Images of Authority: Elites and Icons in Late Sixth-Century Constantinople', *Past and Present* 84 (1979), 3–35.

Cameron, Av., 'New Themes and Styles in Greek Literature: Seventh-Eighth Centuries', in Cameron, A. and Conrad L.I. (eds.), *The Byzantine and Early Islamic Near East I: Problems in the Literary Source Material* (Princeton, 1992), 81–105.

Cameron, Av. (ed.), *The Byzantine and Early Islamic Near East III: States, Resources and Armies* (Princeton, 1995).

Cameron, Av., 'Byzantines and Jews: Some recent work on early Byzantium', *BMGS* 20 (1996), 249–274.

Cameron, Av. (ed.), *Fifty Years of Prosopography: The Later Roman Empire and Beyond* (Oxford, 2003).

Cameron, Av., 'Enforcing Orthodoxy in Byzantium', in Cooper, K. and Gregory, J. (eds.), *Discipline and Diversity* (Woodridge, 2007), 1–24.

Cameron, Av., *The Cost of Orthodoxy* (Leiden, 2012).

Cameron, Av. and Conrad L.I. (eds.), *The Byzantine and Early Islamic Near East I: Problems in the Literary Source Material* (Princeton, 1992).

Cameron, Av. and Herrin, J., *Constantinople in the Early Eighth Century: The Parastaseis Syntomoi Chronikai: Introduction, Translation, and Commentary* (Leiden, 1984).

Canard, M., 'Les Aventures d'un prisonnier arabe et d'un patrice byzantine a l'epoque des guerres bulgaro-byzantines', *DOP* 9–10 (1956), 49–72.

Canard, M., 'L'aventure caucasienne du spathaire Léon, le futur empereur Léon III', *RE Arm* NS 8 (1971), 353–357.

Cankova-Petkova, G., 'Bulgarians and Byzantium during the First Decades after the foundation of the Bulgarian state', *ByzSl* 24 (1963), 41–53.

Carey, B.T., *Road to Manzikert: Byzantine and Islamic Warfare 527–1071* (Barnsley, 2012).

Casey, P.J., 'Justinian, the *Limitanei* and Arab-Byzantine Relations in the Sixth Century', *JRA* 9 (1996), 214–222.

Chabot, J-B., *Chronique de Michel le Syrien: Patrarche Jacobite d'Antioche (1166–1198)* (Paris, 1899).

Chadwick, H., *East and West: The Making of a Rift in the Church from Apostolic Times until the Council of Florence* (Oxford, 2003).

Chandler, T., *Four Thousand Years of Urban Growth: An Historical Census* (Lewiston, 1987).

Charanis, P., 'The Slavic Element in Byzantine Asia Minor', *Byzantion* 18 (1948), 69–83.

Charanis, P., 'Ethnic Changes in the Byzantine Empire in the Seventh Century', *DOP* 13 (1959), 25–44.

Charanis, P., 'The Transfer of Population as a Policy in the Byzantine Empire', *Comparative Studies in Society and History* 3 (1960–1961), 140–154.

Charanis, P., 'The Armenians in Byzantine Empire', *ByzSl* 22 (1961a), 196–240.

Charanis, P., 'The transfer of population as a policy in the Byzantine Empire', *Vizantoloskog Instituta Zbornik radova* 8.1 (1961b), 71–76.

Charanis, P., *The Armenians in the Byzantine Empire* (Lisbon, 1963).

Charanis, P., 'Kouver, the Chronology of his Activities and their Ethnic Effects on the Regions around Thessalonica', *Balkan Studies* 11 (1970), 229–247.

Charanis, P., *Studies in the Demography of the Byzantine Empire* (London, 1972).

Charanis, P., 'Cultural diversity and the breakdown of Byzantine power in Asia Minor', *DOP* 29 (1975), 1–20.

Checa, A., 'Evidences of rheumatic disorders and orthopedic practices in Moche art', *Rheumatol Int.* 30 (2010), 419–421.

Chen, S., *Multicultural China in the Early Middle Ages* (Philadelphia, 2012).

Cheynet, J-Cl., 'The Byzantine aristocracy (8th–13th centuries)', in Cheynet, J-Cl., *The Byzantine Aristocracy and its Military Function* (Aldershot, 2006), I.1–43.

Cheynet, J-Cl., *The Byzantine Aristocracy and Its Military Functions* (Aldershot, 2006).

Christides, V., 'The Second Arab Siege of Constantinople (717–718?): Logistics and Naval Power', in Bumazhnov, D., Grypeou, E., Sailors, T.B. and Toepel, A. (eds.),

Bibel, Byzanz und Christlicher Orient: Festschrift für Stephen Gerö zum 65. Geburtstag. Orientalia Lovaniensia Analecta 187 (Leuven/Paris/Walpole, 2011), 511–534.

Christie, N., *The Lombards: The Ancient Langobards* (Oxford, 1995).

Christie, N., *From Constantine to Charlemagne: An Archaeology of Italy AD 300–800* (Aldershot, 2006).

Christie, N. and Loseby, S.T. (eds.), *Towns in Transition: Urban Evolution in Late Antiquity and the Early Middle Ages* (Aldershot, 1996).

Chrysos, E., 'The Roman, Political Identity in Late and Antiquity and Early Byzantium', in Fledelius, K. and Schreiner, P. (ed.), *Byzantium: Identity, Image, Influence. Major Papers from the XIX International Congress of Byzantine Studies, University of Copenhagen* (Copenhagen, 1996), 7–16.

Clucas, L. (ed.), *The Byzantine Legacy in Eastern Europe* (New York, 1988).

Collins, R., *The Arab Conquest of Spain, 710–97* (Oxford, 1989).

Conant, J., *Staying Roman: Conquest and Identity in Africa and the Mediterranean, 439–700* (Cambridge, 2012).

Conrad, L.I., *The Plague in the Early Medieval Near East* (PhD thesis, Princeton, 1981).

Conrad, L.I., 'The Conquest of Arwad: A Source-Critical Study in the Historiography of the Early Medieval Near East', in Cameron, A. and Conrad L.I. (eds.), *The Byzantine and Early Islamic Near East I: Problems in the Literary Source Material* (Princeton, 1992), 317–401.

Conrad, L.I., *History and Historiography in Early Islamic Times: Studies in Perspective* (Princeton, 1994).

Conrad, L.I., 'The Arabs and the Colossus', *Journal of the Royal Asiatic Society* 6 (1996), 165–187.

Conrad, L.I., 'Agapius', in Meisami, J.S. and Starkey, P. (eds.), *Encyclopedia of Arabic Literature* (London, 1998), 211.

Constantelos, D.J., 'The Moslem Conquests of the Near East as Revealed in the Greek Sources of the Seventh and Eighth Centuries', *Byzantion* 42 (1972), 325–357.

Conterno, M., '"Storytelling" and "History writing" in Seventh-Century Near East', *Working Papers de la Fondation Maison des Science de l'Homme* (2014), halshs-01063730.

Conterno, M., 'Theophilos, "the more likely candidate"? Towards a reappraisal of the question of Theophanes' "Oriental source(s)"', in Jankowiak, M. and Montinaro, F. (eds.), *Studies in Theophanes. Travaux et Memoires* 19 (Paris, 2015), 383–400.

Conybeare, F.C., *The Key of Truth: A Manual of the Paulician Church of Armenia* (London, 1896).

Cooper, K. and Gregory, J. (eds.), *Discipline and Diversity* (Woodridge, 2007).

Cosentino, S., 'Constans II and the Byzantine navy', *BZ* 100 (2008), 577–603.

Cosentino, S. (ed.), *L'Italia Bizantina: una Prospettiva Economica. Cahiers de recherches medievales et humanistes* 28 (Paris, 2015).

Crawford, P.T., *The War of Three Gods: Romans, Persians and the Rise of Islam* (Barnsley, 2013).

Crawford, P.T., *The Emperor Zeno: The Perils of Fifth Century Power Politics in Constantinople* (Barnsley, 2019).

Crone, P., 'Islam, Judaeo-Christianity and Byzantine iconoclasm', in Bonner, M. (ed.), *Arab-Byzantine Relations in Early Islamic Times* (Aldershot, 2005), 361–397.

Crosby, A.W., *Throwing Fire: Projectile Technology Through History* (Cambridge, 2002).

Crostini, B. and La Porta, S. (eds.), *Negotiating Co-Existence: Communities, Cultures and Convivencia in Byzantine Society* (Trier, 2013).

Cunningham, M., *Wider than Heaven: Eighth-Century Homilies on the Mother of God* (Crestwood, 2008).

Curta, F., *Making an Early Medieval Ethnie: The Case of the Early Slavs (Sixth to Seventh Century A.D.)* (PhD thesis, Kalamazoo, 1998).

Curta, F., *The Making of the Slavs: History and Archaeology of the Lower Danube Region, c. 500–700* (Cambridge, 2001).

Curta, F., 'The Slavic Lingua Franca. Linguistic Notes of an Archaeologist Turned Historian', *East Central Europe* 31 (2004), 125–148.

Curta, F., 'Byzantium in dark-age Greece (the numismatic evidence in its Balkan context)', *BMGS* 29 (2005), 113–146.

Curta, F., *Southeastern Europe in the Middle Ages 500–1200* (Cambridge, 2006).

Curta, F., 'Avar Blitzkrieg, Slavic and Bulgar raiders, and Roman special ops: mobile warriors in the 6th-century Balkans', in István, Z. and Karatay, O. (eds.), *Eurasia in the Middle Ages. Studies in Honour of Peter B. Golden* (Wiesbaden, 2015), 69–89.

Curta, F. and Kovalev, R. (eds.), *The Other Europe in the Middle Ages: Avars, Bulgars, Khazars and Cumans* (Leiden, 2008).

Cvetkovic, M., 'The settlement of the Mardaites and their military-administrative position in the themata of the West: A chronology', *Zbornik radova Vizantoloskog instituta* 54 (2017), 65–83.

Dagron, G., *Emperor and Priest: The Imperial Office in Byzantium* (Cambridge, 2003).

Dal Santo, M., 'The God-Protected Empire? Scepticism towards the Cult of Saints in Early Byzantium', in Sarris, P., Dal Santo, M. and Booth, P., *An Age of Saints? Power, Conflict and Dissent in Early Medieval Christianity* (Leiden, 2011), 129–149.

De Ste Croix, G.E.M., *The Class Struggle in the Ancient Greek World: from the Archaic Age to the Arab Conquests* (London, 1981).

Debié, M., 'Theophanes' "Oriental source": what can we learn from Syriac historiography?', in Jankowiak, M. and Montinaro, F. (eds.), *Studies in Theophanes. Travaux et Memoires* 19 (Paris, 2015), 365–382.

Decker, M., *Tilling the Hateful Earth: Agricultural Production and Trade in the Late Antique East* (Oxford, 2009).

Delbruck, R., 'Carmagnola', *Mitteilungen des Kaiserlich Deutschen Archäologischen Instituts, Römische Mitteilungen* 29 (Berlin, 1914), 71–84.

Delbruck, R., *Antike Porphyrwerke. Studien zur spätantiken Kunstgeschichte, vol. 6* (Berlin, 1932).

Delehaye, H., *Les légendes grecques des saints militaires* (Paris, 1909).

Dennis, G., 'Byzantine Heavy Artillery: The Helepolis', *Greek, Roman, and Byzantine Studies* 39 (1998), 99–115.

Dennis, G., 'Defenders of the Christian People: Holy War in Byzantium', in Laiou, A.E. and Mottahedeh, R.P., *The Crusades from the Perspective of Byzantium and the Muslim World* (Washington, 2001), 31–39.

Detschev, D., 'Der germanische Ursprung des bulgarischen Volksnamens', *Zeitschr. f. Ortsnamenforschung* 2 (1927), 199–216.

Diehl, C., *L'Afrique byzantine: histoire de la domination byzantine en Afrique (533–709)* (Paris, 1896).

Diehl, C., *Etudes byzantines* (Paris, 1905).

Diehl, C., 'L'Empereur au nez coupé', *Revue de Paris* 30 (1923), 71–94.

Dimitrov, D., *Prabylgarite po severnoto i zapadnoto Chernomorie* (Varna, 1987).

Dixon, A.A., *The Umayyad Caliphate 65–86/684–705 (A Political Study)* (London, 1971).

Dobrovits, M., '"They called themselves Avar" – Considering the pseudo-Avar question in the work of Theophylaktos', in Compareti, M., Raffetta, P. and Scarcia, G. (eds.), *Ērān ud Anērān: Studies presented to Boris Il'ic Marsak on the occasion of his 70th birthday* (Venice, 2006).

Dolger, F., 'Ist der Nomos Georgikos ein Gesetz des Kaisers Justinian II?', *Festschrift fur Leopold Wenger* (Munich, 2 vols, 1944–1945).

Dols, M.W., 'Plague in Early Islamic History', *Journal of the American Oriental Society* 94 (1974), 371–383.

Donner, F.M., *The Early Islamic Conquests* (Princeton, 1981).

Donner, F.M., 'The formation of the Islamic state', *JAOS* 106 (1986), 283–295.

Donner, F.M., 'Centralized Authority and Military Autonomy in the Early Islamic Conquests', in Cameron, Averil (ed.), *The Byzantine and Early Islamic Near East III: States, Resources and Armies* (Princeton, 1995), 337–360.

Donner, F.M., *Narratives of Islamic Origins: The Beginnings of Islamic Historical Writing* (Princeton, 1998).

Downey, G., 'The Tombs of the Byzantine Emperors at the Church of the Holy Apostles in Constantinople', *JHS* 79 (1959), 27–51.

Dunlap, J.E., *The Office of Grand Chamberlain in the Later Roman and Byzantine Empires* (New York, 1924).

Dunlop, D.M., *The History of the Jewish Khazars* (Princeton, 1954).

Dunn, G.D. and Mayer, W. (eds.), *Christians Shaping Identity from the Roman Empire to Byzantium: Studies inspired by Pauline Allen* (Leiden, 2015).

Dura, N., 'The Ecumenicity of the Council in Trullo: Witnesses of the Canonical Tradition in East and West', in Nedungatt, G. and Featherstone, M. (eds.), *The Council in Trullo Revisited* (Rome, 1995), 229–262.

Duri, A., *Early Islamic Institutions: Administration and Taxation from the Caliphate to the Umayyads and 'Abbāsids*, trans. Razia Ali (London, 2011).

Dvornik, F., *Early Christian and Byzantine Political Philosophy* (Washington DC, 1966).

Eger, A., *The Islamic-Byzantine Frontier: Interaction and Exchange among Muslim and Christian Communities* (New York, 2015).

Eisner, M., 'Killing Kings. Patterns of Regicide in Europe, AD 600–1800', *British Journal of Criminology* 51 (2011), 556–577.

Ekonomou, A., *Byzantine Rome and the Greek Popes: Eastern Influences on Rome and the Papacy from Gregory the Great to Zacharias AD 590–752* (Lanham, 2009).

Elsner, J., 'Iconoclasm as Discourse from Antiquity to Byzantium', *Art Bulletin* 94 (2012), 368–394.

Erdal, M., 'The Khazar Language', *in* Golden, P.B., Ben-Shammai, H. and Róna-Tas, A. (eds.), *The World of the Khazars: New Perspectives. Selected Papers from the Jerusalem 1999 International Khazar Colloquium* (Handbook of Oriental Studies, Section 8 Uralic & Central Asian Studies) (Leiden, *2007), 75–108.*

Every, G., *The Byzantine Patriarchate (451–1204)* (London, 1947).

Fabian, I., 'Strategikon by Mauricius: Eastern military philosophy in Europe?', *The Proceedings of the 'European Integration – Between Tradition and Modernity' Congress* 6 (2015), 571–577.

Fergus, R.C., 'The Influence of the Eighteenth Novel of Justinian II', *Yale Law Journal* 7 (1897), 67–74.

Fiala-Fürst, I. and Czmero, J. (eds.), *Amici amico III: Festschrift für Ludvík E. Václavek* (Olomouc, 2011).

Fiedler, U., 'Bulgars in the Lower Danube region: A survey of the archaeological evidence and of the state of current research', in Curta, F. and Kovalev, R. (eds.), *The Other Europe in the Middle Ages: Avars, Bulgars, Khazars and Cumans* (Leiden, 2008), 151–236.

Fine, J.V.A., *The Early Medieval Balkans: A Critical Survey from the Sixth to the Late Twelfth Century* (Ann Arbor, 1983).

Fischer, F., *De patriarcharum Constantinopolitanorum catalogis* (Lipsiae, 1884).

Fisher, G., *Between the Empires: Arabs, Romans and Sasanians in Late Antiquity* (Oxford, 2011).

Fledelius, K. (ed.), *Byzantium: Identity, Image, Influence. XIX Int. Congress of Byzantine Studies* (Copenhagen, 1996).

Fliche, A. and Martin, V. (eds.), *Histoire de L'Eglise*, 5 vols (Paris, 1930).

Folgerø, O., 'The Lowest, Lost Zone in the *Adoration of the Crucified* Scene in S. Maria Antiqua in Rome: A New Conjecture', *Journal of the Warburg and Courtauld Institutes* 72 (2009), 207–219.

Forbes, R.J., *More Studies in Early Petroleum History 1860–1880* (Leiden, 1959).

Forrest, S., 'Theophanes' Byzantine source for the late seventh and early eighth centuries, c. AD 668–716', in Jankowiak, M. and Montinaro, F. (eds.), *Studies in Theophanes. Travaux et Memoires* 19 (Paris, 2015), 417–444.

Fortescue, A., *The Orthodox Eastern Church* (London, 1908).

Foss, C., *Cities, Fortresses, Villages of Byzantine Asia Minor* (Aldershot, 1996).

Foss, C., 'A Syrian coinage of Mu'awiya?', *RN* 158 (2002), 353–366.

Foss, C., 'The two-caliph bronze of 'Abd al-Malik', *ONSN* 171 (2003), 24–34.

Foss, C., *Arab-Byzantine Coins: An Introduction, with a Catalogue of the Dumbarton Oaks Collection* (Washington DC, 2008).

Foss, C., 'Mu'awiya's State', in Haldon, J.F. (ed.), *Money, Power and Politics in Early Islamic Syria* (Farnham, 2010), 75–96.

Franklin, C.V., 'Reading the Popes: The Liber pontificalis and Its Editors', *Speculum* 92 (2017), 607–629.

Frazee, C.A., 'Late Roman and Byzantine Legislation on the Monastic Life from the Fourth to the Eighth Centuries', *CH* 51 (1982), 263–279.

Frendo, J.D., 'The Miracles of St. Demetrius and the Capture of Thessaloniki', *Byzantinoslavica* 58 (1997), 205–224.

Friedmann. L.W., 'Amputations and prostheses in primitive cultures', *Bull Prosthet Res* (1972), 105–138.

Fröhlich, H., 'Zur Herkunft der Langobarden', *QFIAB* 55/56 (1976), 1–21.

Frye, R.N., *The Golden Age of Persia: the Arabs in the East* (London, 1993).

Fueg, F., *Corpus of the Nomismata from Anastasius II to John I in Constantinople 717–976: Structure of the Issues, Corpus of Coin Finds, Contribution to the Iconographic and Monetary History* (Lancaster, 2007).

Galavaris, G.P., 'The Symbolism of the Imperial Costume as Displayed on Byzantine Coins', *American Numismatic Society Museum Notes* 8 (1958), 106–109.

Gandila, A., 'Early Byzantine Coins Circulation in the Eastern Provinces: a Comparative Statistical Approach', *AJN* 21 (2009), 151–226.

Garland, L., *Byzantine Empresses: Women and Power in Byzantium AD 527–1204* (London, 1999).

Garsoian, N.G., *The Paulician Heresy: A Study of the Origin and Development of Paulicianism in Armenia and the Eastern Provinces of the Byzantine Empire* (The Hague, 1967).

Gauthier, N. (ed.), *Towns and Their Hinterlands between Late Antiquity and the Early Middle Ages* (Leiden, 2000).

Geary, P., *Myth of Nations: The Medieval Origins of Europe* (Princeton, 2003).

Gero, S., *Byzantine Iconoclasm during the Reign of Leo III* (Louvain, 1973).

Gero, S., 'Notes on Byzantine Iconoclasm in the Eighth Century', *Byzantion* 44 (1974), 23–42.

Gero, S., 'Armenians in Byzantium: Some reconsiderations', *JAS* 2 (1985), 13–26.

Gibb, H.A.R., 'Arab-Byzantine Relations under the Umayyad Caliphate', *DOP* 12 (1958), 219–233.

Gil, M., 'Did the Khazars Convert to Judaism?', *Revue des Études Juives 170 (2011)*, 429–441.

Golden, P.B., *An Introduction to the History of the Turkic Peoples: Ethnogenesis and State Formation in Medieval and Early Modern Eurasia and the Middle East* (Wiesbaden, 1992).

Golden, P.B., 'The Khazar Sacral Kingship', in Reyerson, K.V., Stavrou, T.G. and Tracy, J.D. (eds.), *Pre-modern Russia and its world: Essays in Honour of Thomas S. Noonan* (Wiesbaden, 2006), 79–102.

Golden, P.B., 'Khazar Studies: Achievements and Perspectives', *in* Golden, P.B., Ben-Shammai, H. and Róna-Tas, A. (eds.), *The World of the Khazars: New Perspectives. Selected Papers from the Jerusalem 1999 International Khazar Colloquium* (Handbook of Oriental Studies, Section 8 Uralic & Central Asian Studies) (Leiden, *2007a)*, 7–57.

Golden, P.B., 'The Conversion of the Khazars to Judaism', *in* Golden, P.B., Ben-Shammai, H. and Róna-Tas, A. (eds.), *The World of the Khazars: New Perspectives. Selected Papers from the Jerusalem 1999 International Khazar Colloquium* (Handbook of Oriental Studies, Section 8 Uralic & Central Asian Studies) (Leiden, *2007b)*, 123–161.

Golden, P.B., 'Nomads of the western Eurasian steppes: Ogurs, Onogurs and Khazars', in Golden, P.B. (ed.), *Studies on the Peoples and Cultures of the Eurasian Steppes.* (Bucharest, 2011), 135–162.

Golden, P.B. (ed.), *Studies on the Peoples and Cultures of the Eurasian Steppes* (Bucharest, 2011).

Golden, P.B., 'Oq and Oğur~Oğuz', *Turkic Languages* 16 (2012), 155–199.

Golden, P.B., Ben-Shammai, H. and Róna-Tas, A. (eds.), *The World of the Khazars: New Perspectives. Selected Papers from the Jerusalem 1999 International Khazar Colloquium* (Handbook of Oriental Studies, Section 8 Uralic & Central Asian Studies) (Leiden, *2007*).

Goodchild, R., 'Byzantines, Berbers and Arabs in seventh-century Libya', in Reynolds, J. (ed.), *Libyan Studies* (London, 1976), 255–268.

Goodwin, T. (ed.), *Arab-Byzantine Coins and History* (London, 2012).

Görres, F., 'Justinian II und das römische Papsttum', *BZ* 17 (1908), 432–454.

Grabar, A., *L'empereur dans l'art Byzantin: recherches sur l'art officiel de l'empire d'Orient* (Paris, 1936).

Grabar, A., *L'Iconoclasme Byzantin: dossier archéologique* (Paris, 1957).

Grant, M., *From Rome to Byzantium: The Fifth Century* (London, 1998).

Gray, P., 'The Legacy of Chalcedon: Christological Problems and Their Significance', in Maas, M. (ed.), *The Cambridge Companion to the Age of Justinian* (Cambridge, 2005), 215–238.

Gray, P.T.R., 'Theological Discourse in the Seventh Century: The Heritage from the Sixth Century', *BF* 26 (2000), 219–228.

Greenwood, J., 'Armenian Neighbours (600–1045)', in Shepard, J. (ed.), *Cambridge History of Byzantine Empire ca 500–1492* (Cambridge, 2019), 333–364.

Greenwood, T.W., *A History of Armenia in the Seventh and Eighth Centuries* (unpublished PhD thesis, Oxford, 2000).

Greenwood, T.W., '"New Light from the East": Chronography and Ecclesiastical History through a Late Seventh-Century Armenian Source', *JECS* 16 (2008), 197–254.

Gregoire, H., 'Un edit de l'empereur Justinien II', *Byzantion* 17 (1944–1945), 120–121.

Gregoire, H., 'An Armenian Dynasty on the Byzantine Throne', *Armenian Quarterly* 1 (1946), 4–21.

Grégoire, H., 'Le nom de la ville de Tmutarakan', *Nouvelle Clio* 4 (1952), 288–292.

Grierson, P., 'Commerce in the Dark Ages: A Critique of Evidence', *TRHS* 5 (1959), 123–140.

Grierson, P., 'The Monetary Reforms of Abd al-Malik', *JESHO* 3 (1960), 241–264.

Grierson, P., *Catalogue of the Byzantine Coins in the Dumbarton Oaks Collection and in the Whittemore Collection*, 2 vols (Washington, 1966).

Grierson, P., *Catalogue of the Coins in the Dumbarton Oaks Collection and in the Whittemore Collection II: Phocas to Theodosius III, 602–717* (Washington DC, 1968).

Grierson, P., *Catalogue of the Coins in the Dumbarton Oaks Collection and in the Whittemore Collection, Leo III to Nicephorus III, 717–1081* (Washington DC, 1973).

Grierson, P., *Numismatics* (London, 1975).

Grierson, P., *Byzantine Coinage* (Washington DC, 1999).

Grierson, P. and Blackburn, M., *Medieval European Coinage I: The Early Middle Ages (5th–10th centuries)* (Cambridge, 1986).

Grierson, P., Mango, C. and Sevcenko, I., 'The Tombs and Obits of the Byzantine Emperors (337–1042); With an Additional Note', *DOP* 16 (1962), 3–63.

Griffith, S., 'What Has Constantinople to Do With Jerusalem? Palestine in the Ninth Century: Byzantine Orthodoxy in the World of Islam', in Brubaker, L. (ed.), *Byzantium in the Ninth Century: Dead or Alive?* (Aldershot, 1998), 181–194.

Gwatkin, H.M. and Whitney, J.P. (eds.), *Cambridge Medieval History Vol. II: The Rise of the Saracens and the Foundation of the Western Empire* (Cambridge, 1936).

Gyuzelev, V., *The Proto-Bulgarians* (Sofia, 1979).

Hackett, J., *A History of the Orthodox Church of Cyprus* (London, 1901).

Hahn, W., *Moneta Imperii Byzantini: Von Heraclius bis Leo III. Alleinregierung (610–720)*, Vol. III (Vienna, 1981).

Hahn, W. and Metcalf, W.E. (eds.), *Studies in Early Byzantine Gold Coinage* (New York, 1988).

Haldon, J.F., 'Aspects of Byzantine Military Administration: the Elite Corps, the Opsikion, and the Imperial Tagmata from the Sixth to the Ninth Century', unpublished Diss. (University of Birmingham, 1975a).

Haldon, J.F., 'Some Aspects of Byzantine Military Technology from the Sixth to the Tenth Centuries', *BMGS* 1 (1975b), 11–47.

Haldon, J.F., 'Some Remarks on the Background to the Iconoclast Controversy', *ByzSl* 38 (1977), 161–184.

Haldon, J.F., *Recruitment and Conscription in the Byzantine Army c.550–950: A Study on the Origins of the Stratiotika Ktemata* (Vienna, 1979).

Haldon, J.F., *Byzantine Praetorians: An Administrative, Institutional and Social Survey of the Opsikion and Tagmata c. 580–900* (Bonn, 1984).

Haldon, J.F., 'Ideology and social change in the seventh century: Military discontent as a barometer', *Klio* 68 (1986), 139–190.

Haldon, J.F., *Byzantium in the Seventh Century: the transformation of a culture* (Cambridge, 1990).

Haldon, J.F., 'Constantine or Justinian? Crisis and Identity in Imperial Propaganda in the Seventh Century', in Magdalino, P. (ed.), *New Constantines: The Theme of Imperial Renewal in Byzantium* (London, 1993), 95–107.

Haldon, J.F., 'Military service, military lands and the status of soldiers: Current problems and interpretations', *DOP* 47 (1993), 1–67.

Haldon, J.F., 'Seventh-Century Continuities: the *Ajnad* and the Thematic Myth', in Cameron, A. (ed.), *States, Resources and Armies: Papers of the Third Workshop on Antiquity and Early Islam* (Princeton, 1995), 379–423.

Haldon, J.F., *State, Army and Society in Byzantium: approaches to military, social and administrative history 6th–12th centuries* (Aldershot, 1995).

Haldon, J.F., *Byzantium in the Seventh Century: The Transformation of a Culture* (Cambridge, 1997).

Haldon, J.F., *Warfare, State and Society in the Byzantine World 565–1204* (London, 1999).

Haldon, J.F., 'Theory and Practice in Tenth-Century Military Administration', *Travaux et Mémoires* 13 (2000), 201–352.

Haldon, J.F., 'The Byzantine World', in Raaflaub, K.A. and Rosenstein, N. (eds.), *War and Society in the Ancient and Medieval Worlds: Asia, The Mediterranean, Europe, and Mesoamerica* (Cambridge, 2001), 241–270.

Haldon, J.F., 'Greek Fire Revisited: Recent and Current Research', in Jeffreys, E. (ed.), *Byzantine Style, Religion and Civilisation: In Honour of Sir Steven Runciman* (Cambridge, 2006), 290–325.

Haldon, J.F., *The Byzantine Wars* (Stroud, 2008).

Haldon, J.F. (ed.), *Money, Power and Politics in Early Islamic Syria* (Farnham, 2010).

Haldon, J.F., 'Commerce and Exchange in the Seventh and Eighth Centuries: Regional Trade and the Movement of Goods', in Morrison, C. (ed.), *Trade and Markets in Byzantium* (Washington DC, 2012), 99–122.

Haldon, J.F., *The Empire That Would Not Die: The Paradox of Eastern Roman Survival, 640–740* (London, 2016).

Haldon, J. and Byrne, M., 'A Possible Solution to the Problem of Greek Fire', *BZ* 70 (1977), 91–99.

Haldon, J.F., Elton, H. and Newhard, J., *Euchaita: A Late Roman and Byzantine City in Anatolia* (Cambridge, 2016).

Haldon, J.F. and Kennedy, H., 'The Arab-Byzantine Frontier in the Eighth and Ninth Centuries: Military Organisation and Society in the Borderlands', *Zbornik Radova Visantoloskog Instituta* 19 (1980), 79–116.

Haldon, J.F. and Kennedy, H., 'Regional Identities and Military Power: Byzantium and Islam ca. 600–750', in Pohl, W., Gantner, C. and Payne, R. (eds.), *Visions of Community in the Post-Roman World, the West, Byzantium and the Islamic World 300–1100* (Farnham, 2012), 317–353.

Halkin, F., *The First Dynasty of Islam: The Umayyad Caliphate AD 661–750* (London, 2000).

Hatlie, P., *The Monks and Monasteries of Constantinople ca. 350–850* (Cambridge).

Hawting, G.R., *The First Dynasty of Islam: The Umayyad Caliphate AD 661–750* (London, 2000).

Head, C., 'On the date of Justinian II's restoration', *Byzantion* 39 (1969), 104–107.

Head, C., 'Towards a Reinterpretation of the Second Reign of Justinian II', *Byzantion* 40 (1970), 14–32.

Head, C., 'Who was the real Leo the Isaurian?', *Byzantion* 4 (1971), 105–108.

Head, C., *Justinian II of Byzantium* (London, 1972).

Head, C., 'Physical descriptions of emperors in Byzantine historical writing', *Byzantion* 50 (1980), 226–240.

Heath, C., *The Narrative Worlds of Paul the Deacon: Between Empires and Identities in Lombard Italy* (Amsterdam, 2017).

Heather, P., *Goths and Romans 332–489* (Oxford, 1991).

Heather, P., 'New Men for New Constantines? Creating an Imperial Elite in the Eastern Mediterranean', in Magdalino, P. (ed.), *New Constantines: The Theme of Imperial Renewal in Byzantium* (London, 1993), 11–33.

Heather, P., *Empire and Barbarians: Migration, Development and the Birth of Europe* (London, 2009).

Hefele, C.J., *A History of the Councils of the Church from the Original Documents* (Edinburgh, 1896).

Heidemann, S., 'The Evolving Representation in the Early Islamic Empire and its Religion on Coin Imagery', in Neuwirth, A., Sinai, N. and Marx, M. (eds.), *The Qur'an in Context: Historical and Literacy Investigations into the Qur'anic Milieu* (Leiden, 2010), 149–196.

Heidemann, S., 'The Standing Caliph type – the object on the reverse', in Oddy, A. (ed.), *Coinage and History in the Seventh-Century Near East* (Oxford, 2010), 23–34.

Hendy, M., *Studies in the Byzantine Monetary Economy c.300–1450* (Cambridge, 1985).

Henning, J. (ed.), *Post-Roman Towns, Trade and Settlement in Europe and Byzantium II: Byzantium, Pliska and the Balkans* (New York, 2007).

Herrin, J., *The Formation of Christendom* (Princeton, 1987).

Herrin, J., *Byzantium: The Surprising Life of a Medieval Empire* (London, 2008).

Herrin, J., *Margins and Metropolis: Authority across the Byzantine Empire* (Princeton, 2013).

Hill, D.R., *The Termination of Hostilities in the Early Arab Conquests AD 634–656* (London, 1971).

Hill, G.F., *A History of Cyprus* (Cambridge, 1940).

Hinds, G.M., *Studies in Early Islamic History* (Princeton, 1996).

Hitti, P.K., *History of the Arabs* (London, 2002).

Hodgkin, T., *Italy and Her Invaders*, 8 vols (Oxford, 1896).

Holland, T., *In The Shadow Of The Sword: The Battle for Global Empire and the End of the Ancient World* (London, 2012).

Hollingsworth, P.A., 'Justinian II', in Kazhdan, A.P., *Oxford Dictionary of Byzantium* (New York, 1991), 1084–1085.

Holweck, F.G., *A Biographical Dictionary of the Saints* (St Louis, 1924).

Hopkins, K., 'Elite mobility in the Roman Empire', *Past and Present* 32 (1965), 12–36.

Hovorun, C., *Will, Action and Freedom: Christological Controversies in the Seventh Century* (Leiden, 2008).

Howard-Johnston, J.D., *East Rome, Sasanian Persia and the End of Antiquity: Historiographical and Historical Sources* (Aldershot, 2006).

Howard-Johnston, J.D., 'The Rise of Islam and Byzantium's Response', in Oddy, A. (ed.), *Coinage and History in the Seventh Century Near East* (Oxford, 2010), 1–9.

Howard-Johnston, J.D., *Witnesses to a World Crisis: Historians and Histories of the Middle East in the Seventh Century* (Oxford, 2010).

Howard-Johnston, J.D., 'The Mardaites', in Goodwin, T. (ed.), *Arab-Byzantine Coins and History* (London, 2012), 27–38.

Hoyland, R.G., *Seeing Islam as Others Saw It: A Survey and Evaluation of Christian, Jewish and Zoroastrian Writing* (Princeton, 1997).

Hoyland, R.G., 'Writing the biography of the Prophet Muhammad: problems and sources', *History Compass* 5 (2007), 581–602.

Hoyland, R.G., *Theophilus of Edessa's Chronicle and the Circulation of Historical Knowledge in Late Antiquity and Early Islam*, TTH 57 (Liverpool, 2011).

Hoyland, R.G., *In God's Path: the Arab Conquests and the Creation of an Islamic Empire* (New York, 2014).

Hoyland, R.G., 'Agapius, Theophilus and Muslim sources', in Jankowiak, M. and Montinaro, F. (eds.), *Studies in Theophanes*, Travaux et Memoires 19 (Paris, 2015), 355–364.

Hudson, J. and Rodriguez, A. (eds.), *Diverging Paths? The Shapes of Power and Institutions in Medieval Christendom and Islam* (Leiden, 2014).

Humphreys, M., 'Images of Authority? Imperial Patronage of Icons from Justinian II and Leo III', in Sarris, P., Dal Santo, M. and Booth, P. (eds.), *An Age of Saints? Power, Conflict and Dissent in Early Medieval Christianity* (Boston, 2011), 150–168.

Humphreys, M., 'The War of Images Revisited: Justinian II's Coinage Reform and the Caliphate', *NC* 173 (2013), 229–244.

Humphreys, M., *Law, Power and Imperial Ideology in the Iconoclast Era c. 680–850* (Oxford, 2015).

Hupchick, D.P., *The Bulgarian-Byzantine Wars for Early Medieval Balkan Hegemony: Silver-Lined Skulls and Blinded Armies (London, 2017).*

István, Z. and Karatay, O. (eds.), *Eurasia in the Middle Ages. Studies in Honour of Peter B. Golden* (Wiesbaden, 2015).

Izdebski, A., 'Why did agriculture flourish in the late antique east? The role of climate fluctuations in the development and contraction of agriculture in Asia Minor and the Middle East from the 4th till the 7th c. AD', *Millennium* 8 (2011), 291–312.

Jamil, N., 'Caliph and Quṭb. Poetry as a Source for Interpreting the Transformation of the Byzantine Cross on Steps on Umayyad Coinage', in Johns, J. (ed.), *Bayt al-Maqdis: Jerusalem and Early Islam*, Oxford Studies in Islamic Art IX.2 (Oxford, 1999), 11–57.

Jandora, J.W., 'Developments in Islamic Warfare: The Early Conquests', *SI* 66 (1986), 101–113.

Jankowiak, M., 'Travelling Across Borders: a Church Historian's Perspective on Contacts Between Byzantium and Syria in the Second Half of the 7th Century', in Goodwin, T. (ed.), *Arab-Byzantine Coins and History* (London, 2012), 13–25.

Jankowiak, M., 'The First Arab siege of Constantinople', in Zuckerman, C. (ed.), *Constructing the Seventh Century*, Travaux et Memoires 17 (Paris, 2013a), 237–320.

Jankowiak, M., 'The *Notitia* I and the impact of Arab invasions on Asia Minor', *Millennium* 10 (2013b), 435–461.

Jankowiak, M. and Montinaro, F. (eds.), *Studies in Theophanes*, Travaux et Memoires 19 (Paris, 2015).

Jeffreys, E. (ed.), *Byzantine Style, Religion and Civilisation: In Honour of Sir Steven Runciman* (Cambridge, 2006).

Jenkins, R.J.H., 'Cyprus between Byzantium and Islam, A.D. 688–965', in Mylonas, G.E. and Raymond, D. (eds.), *Studies Presented to David Moore Robinson*, 2 vols (St Louis, 1953), II.1006–1014.

Jenkins, R.J.H., *Byzantium: The Imperial Centuries* (New York, 1966).

Johns, J. (ed.), *Bayt al-Maqdis: Jerusalem and Early Islam*, Oxford Studies in Islamic Art IX.2 (Oxford, 1999).

Johns, J., 'Archaeology and the History of Early Islam: The First Seventy Years', *JESHO* 46 (2003), 411–436.

Jones, A.H.M., *Later Roman Empire 284–602* (Oxford, 1964).

Kaegi, W.E., 'Arianism and the Byzantine Army in Africa 533–546', *Traditio* 21 (1965), 27–53.

Kaegi, W.E., 'The Byzantine Armies and Iconoclasm', *Byzantioslavica* 22 (1966), 48–70.

Kaegi, W.E., 'Some Reconsiderations on the Themes (Seventh–Ninth Centuries)', *JOB* 16 (1967), 39–53.

Kaegi, W.F., 'Al-Baladhuri and the Armeniak theme', *Byzantion* 38 (1968), 273–277.

Kaegi, W.E., 'Initial Byzantine reactions to the Arab conquests', *Church History* 38 (1969a), 139–149.

Kaegi, W.E., 'Some Perspectives on the Middle Byzantine Period', *Balkan Studies* 10 (1969b), 293–298.

Kaegi, W.E., 'The First Arab Expedition against Amorium', *BMGS* 3 (1977), 19–22.

Kaegi, W.E., *Byzantine Military Unrest, 471–843: An Interpretation* (Amsterdam, 1981).

Kaegi, W.E., *Some Thoughts on Byzantine Military Strategy* (Brookline, 1983).

Kaegi, W.E., *Byzantium and the Early Islamic Conquests* (Cambridge, 1992).

Kaegi, W.E., *Heraclius, Emperor of Byzantium* (Cambridge, 2003).

Kaegi, W.E., 'The Interrelationship of Seventh-Century Muslim Raids into Anatolia with the Struggle for North Africa', *BF* 28 (2004), 21–43.

Kaegi, W.E., *Muslim Expansion and Byzantine Collapse in North Africa* (Cambridge, 2010).

Kaegi, W.E., 'The Heraclians and Holy War', in Koder, J. and Stouraitis, I. (eds.), *Byzantine War Ideology Between Roman Imperial Concept and Christian Religion* (Vienna, 2012), 33–40.

Kaegi, W.E., 'Confronting Islam: Emperors vs Caliphs (641–c.850)', in Shepard, J. (ed.), *Cambridge History of Byzantine Empire ca. 500–1492* (Cambridge, 2019), 365–394.

Kaldellis, A., *The Byzantine Republic: People and Power in New Rome* (London, 2015).

Kantorowicz, E.H., '"The King's Advent" and the Enigmatic Panels in the Doors of Santa Sabina', *The Art Bulletin* 26 (1944), 207–231.

Karayannopoulos, J., 'Contribution au probleme des themes byzantins', *Hellenisme contemporain* 10 (1956), 455–502.

Karayannopoulos, J., *Des Finanzwesen des fruhbyzantinischen Staates* (Munich, 1958).

Karayannopoulos, J., *Die Entstehung der Byzantinischen Themeordnung* (Munich, 1959).

Kazhdan, A.P., *Oxford Dictionary of Byzantium* (New York, 1991).

Kazhdan, A.P., 'The Notion of Byzantine Diplomacy', in Shepard, J. and Franklin, S. (eds.), *Byzantine Diplomacy* (Aldershot, 1992), 3–21.

Kelly, J.N.D., *Early Christian Doctrines* (San Francisco, 1978).

Kennedy, H., 'Byzantine-Arab Diplomacy in the Near East from the Islamic Conquests to the Mid Eleventh Century', in Shepard, J. and Franklin, S. (eds.), *Byzantine Diplomacy* (Aldershot, 1992), 133–143.

Kennedy, H., 'The Financing of the Military in the Early Islamic State', in Cameron, A. (ed.), *The Byzantine and Early Islamic Near East III: States, Resources and Armies* (Princeton, 1995), 361–378.

Kennedy, H., *The Armies of the Caliphs: military and society in the early Islamic state* (London, 2001).

Kennedy, H., *The Prophet and the Age of the Caliphates: The Islamic Near East from the Sixth to the Eleventh Century* (Harlow, 2004).

Kennedy, H., *The Great Arab Conquests: How the Spread of Islam Changed the World We Live In* (Philadelphia, 2007).

Kennedy, H., *The Prophet and the Age of the Caliphates: The Islamic Near East from the 6th to the 11th Century* (Oxford and New York, 2016).

Kent, J.P.C., 'The Mystery of Leontius II', *Numismatic Chronicle* VI.14 (1954), 217–218.

Keramopoulos, A., *Πρόσφορα εἰς Στ.Κυριαχίδην* (Thessalonica, 1953).

Kim, H.J., *The Huns, Rome and the Birth of Europe* (Cambridge, 2013).

King, G.R.D. and Cameron, A. (eds.), *The Byzantine and Early Islamic Near East II: Land Use and Settlement Patterns* (Princeton, 1994).

Kitzinger, E., 'The Cult of Images in the Age before Iconoclasm', *DOP* 8 (1954), 83–150.

Kitzinger, E., 'On Some Icons of the Seventh Century', in *Late Classical and Mediaeval Studies in Honor of Albert Mathias Friend Jr* (Princeton, 1955), 132–150.

Kitzinger, E., 'Some Reflections on Portraiture in Byzantine Art', *Vizantoloskog instituta Zbornik radova* 8.1 (1963), 185–193.

Kitzinger, E., *Byzantine Art in the Making* (Cambridge, 1995).

Koder, J., 'Regional Networks in Asia Minor during the Middle Byzantine Period, Seventh–Eleventh Centuries: An Approach', in Morrison, C. (ed.), *Trade and Markets in Byzantium* (Washington DC, 2012), 147–175.

Koder, J. and Stouraitis, I. (eds.), *Byzantine War Ideology Between Roman Imperial Concept and Christian Religion* (Vienna, 2012).

Koestler, A., *The Thirteenth Tribe: The Khazar Empire and Its Heritage* (London, 1977).

Kolbaba, T., 'Fighting for Christianity: Holy War in the Byzantine Empire', *Byzantion* 68 (1998), 194–221.

Komatina, P., 'Settlement of the Slavs in Asia Minor during the Rule of Justinian II and the Bishopric ΤΩΝ ΓΟΡΔΟΣΕΡΒΩΝ', *Belgrade Historical Review* 5 (2014), 33–40.

Kontoura-Galake, E. (ed.), *The Dark Centuries of Byzantium (7th–9th c.)* (Athens, 2001).

Kortlandt, F., 'The spread of the Indo-Europeans', *Journal of Indo-European Studies* 18 (1990), 131–140.

Kościelniak, K., *Greeks and Arabs. The History of the Melkite (Catholic) Church in the lands conquered by the Muslims (634–1516)* (Krakow, 2004).

Kulakovskij, J., *Istorija Vizantii*, 3 vols (Kiev, 1912–1915).

Ladner, G.B., 'Origin and Significance of the Byzantine Iconoclastic Controversy', *Mediaeval Studies* 2 (1940), 127–149.

Ladner, G.B., 'The Concept of the Image in the Greek Fathers and the Byzantine Iconoclastic Controversy', *DOP* 7 (1953), 1–34.

Laiou, A.E. (ed.), *The Economic History of Byzantium from the Seventh through the Fifteenth Century* (Washington DC, 2002).

Laiou, A.E. and Morrison, C. (eds.), *The Byzantine Economy* (Cambridge, 2007).

Lampsidis, O., 'The Penalty of Blinding by the Byzantines', unpublished dissertation (Athens, 1949).

Lastres, J.B., *Peruvian Aboriginal Medicine* (Lima, 1943).

Lefort, J., 'The Rural Economy, Seventh–Twelfth Centuries', in Laiou, A.E. (ed.), *The Economic History of Byzantium from the Seventh through the Fifteenth Century* (Washington DC, 2002), 231–310.

Leicester, H.M., *The Historical Background of Chemistry* (New York, 1956).

Lemerle, P., 'Invasions et migrations dans les Balkans depuis la fin de l'epoque romaine jusqu'au VIIIe siècle', *Revue historique* 211 (1954), 265–308.

Lemerle, P., 'Esquisse pour une histoire agraire de Byzance', *Revue historique* 219 (1958), 32–74, 254–284.

Lemerle, P., *The Agrarian History of Byzantium from the Origins to the Twelfth Century: the Sources and the Problems* (Galway, 1979).

Lemerle, P., *Les plus anciens recueils des miracles de saint Démétrius et la pénétration des Slaves dans les Balkans (Paris, 1981)*.

Leone, A., *Changing Townscapes in North Africa from Late Antiquity to the Arab Conquest* (Bari, 2007).

Lev, Y. (ed.), *War and Society in the Eastern Mediterranean 7th–15th Centuries* (New York, 1997).

Levcenko, M.V., 'Blues and Greens in Byzantium in the Fifth to Seventh Centuries', *Vizantiiskii Vremenik* 1 (1947), 164–183.

Lightfoot, C., 'Byzantine Anatolia: reassessing the numismatic evidence', *RN* 158 (2002), 229–239.

Lilie, R.J., *Die Byzantinische Reaktion auf die Ausbreitung der Araber* (Munich, 1976).

Lilie, R.J., 'Thrakien und Thrakesion. Zur byzantinischen Provinzorganisation am Ende des 7. Jahrhunderts', *Jahrbuch der österreichischen Byzantinistik* 26 (1977), 7–47.

Lilie, R.J., Ludwig, C., Pratsch, T., Zielke, B. *et al.*, *Prosopographie der mittelbyzantinischen Zeit, Erste Abteilung (641–867)* (Berlin, 2001).

Little, L.K. (ed.), *Plague and the End of Antiquity: The Pandemic of 541–750* (Cambridge, 2007).

Llewellyn, R.A.B., 'Constans II and the Roman Church: A Possible Instance of Imperial Pressure', *Byzantion* 46 (1976), 120–126.

Lopez, R.S., 'Mohammed and Charlemagne: A Revision', *Speculum* 8 (1943), 14–38.

Louth, A., *Greek East and Latin West: The Church AD 681–1071* (Crestwood, 2007).

Louth, A., 'Byzantium Transforming (600–700)', in Shepard, J. (ed.), *Cambridge History of Byzantine Empire ca 500–1492* (Cambridge, 2008), 221–248.

Ludwig, C. (ed.), *Siegel Und Siegler: Akten Des 8. Internationalen Symposions Fuer Byzantinische Sigillographie*, Berliner Byzantinistische Studien (Frankfurt am Main, 2005).

Luttwak, E.N., *Grand Strategy of the Byzantine Empire* (Cambridge, 2009).

Maas, M. (ed.), *The Cambridge Companion to the Age of Justinian* (Cambridge, 2005).

Macdonald, G., *Coin Types, Their Origin and Development* (Glasgow, 1905).

Madelung, W., *The Succession to Muhammad: A Study of the Early Caliphate* (Cambridge, 1997).

Maenchen-Helfen, O.J., *The World of the Huns: Studies in Their History and Culture* (Berkeley, 1973).

Magdalino, P. (ed.), *New Constantines: The Theme of Imperial Renewal in Byzantium* (London, 1993).

Magdalino, P. and Nelson, R. (eds.), *The Old Testament in Byzantium* (Washington DC, 2010).

Magoulias, H.J., 'The lives of Byzantine saints as sources of data for the history of magic in the sixth and seventh centuries A.D.: Sorcery, relics, and icons', *Byzantion* 37 (1967), 228–269.

Mako, G., 'The Possible Reasons for the Arab–Khazar Wars', *Archivum Eurasiae Medii Aevi* 17 (2010), 45–57.

Malter, J.L., *Byzantine Numismatic Bibliography 1966–1994* (Encino, 1995).

Mango, C., 'The *Breviarium* of the Patriarch Nicephoros', in *Byzantium: A Tribute to Andreas N. Stratos* (Athens, 1986), II.539–552.

Mango C., *Le développement urbain de Constantinople (IV–VII siècles)* (Paris, 2nd edn, 1990).

Mango, C., 'The water supply of Constantinople', in Mango, C. and Dagron, G. (eds.), *Constantinople and its Hinterlands: Papers from the Twenty-seventh Spring Symposium of Byzantine Studies, Oxford, April 1993* (Aldershot, 1995), 9–18.

Mango, C., 'The Triumphal Way of Constantinople and the Golden Gate', *DOP* 54 (2000), 173–188.

Mango, C. and Dagron, G. (eds.), *Constantinople and its Hinterlands: Papers from the Twenty-seventh Spring Symposium of Byzantine Studies, Oxford, April 1993* (Aldershot, 1995).

Mann, H.K., *The Lives of the Popes in the Early Middle Ages* (London, 1925).

Maricq, A., 'La Duree du regime des partis populaires a Constantinople', *Bulletin de la Classe des Lettres et des Sciences Morales et Politiques* 35 (Brussels, 1949), 63–74.

Maricq, A., 'Notes sur les Slaves dans le Peloponnese et en Bithynie et sur l'emploi de "Slave" comme appellative', *Byzantion* 22 (1952), 337–356.

Martin, E.J., *History of the Iconoclastic Controversy* (London, 1930).

Martindale, J.R. (ed.), *Prosopography of the Later Roman Empire: AD 395–527 Volume IIIa* (Cambridge, 1992).

Martindale, J.R. (ed.), *Prosopography of the Later Roman Empire: AD 395–527 Volume IIIb* (Cambridge, 1992).

Mavroforou, A., Malizos, K., Karachalios, T., Chatzitheofilou, K. and Giannoukas, A.D., 'Punitive Limb Amputation', *Clin Orthop Relat Res* 472 (2014), 3102–3106.

Mazzola, R.F., 'History of Nasal Reconstruction. A Brief Survey', *Handchirurgie – Mikrochirurgie – Plastische Chirurgie* 19 (1987), 4–6.

McCormick, M., 'The Imperial Edge: Italo-Byzantine Identity, Movement and Integration AD 650–950', in Ahrweiler, H. and Laiou, A.E., *Studies on the Internal Diaspora of the Byzantine Empire* (Washington, 1998), 17–52.

McEvedy, C., *The New Penguin Atlas of Medieval History* (London, 1992).

McEvoy, M., *Child Emperor Rule in the Late Roman West AD 367–455* (Oxford, 2013).

McGill, S., Sogno, C. and Watts, E. (eds.), *From the Tetrarchs to the Theodosians: Later Roman History and Culture, 284–450 CE* (Cambridge, 2010).

McNeill, W.H., *Plagues and Peoples* (New York, 1976).

Medvedev, I.P., *Vizantiĭskiĭ zemledel'cheskiĭ zakon* (Leningrad, 1984).

Meier, M., 'Ostrom-Byzanz Spatantike-Mittelalter. Uberlegung zum "Ende" der Antike im Osten des romischen Reiches', *Millennium* 9 (2012), 187–253.

Metcalf, D.M., 'Avar and Slav invasions into the Balkan peninsula (c.575–625); the nature of the numismatic evidence', *JRA* 4 (1991), 140–148.

Metcalf, D.M., 'Monetary recession in the middle Byzantine period: the numismatic evidence', *NC* 161 (2001), 111–155.

Metcalf, D.M., 'An Imperial Initiative in the time of Tiberius III (698–705): *apo hypaton* and *apo eparhon*', in Papaefthymiou, E.G. and Touratsoglou, I.P. (eds.), *Studies in Byzantine Numismatics and Sigillography in Memory of Petro Protoriotarios* (Athens, 2013), 167–172.

Metzner, E.E., 'Textgestützte Nachträge zu Namen und Abkunft der "Böhmer" und "Mährer" und der zweierlei "Baiern" des frühen Mittelalters – Die sprachliche, politische und religiöse Grenzerfahrung und Brückenfunktion alteuropäischer Gesellschaften nördlich und südlich der Donau', in Fiala-Fürst, I. and Czmero, J. (eds.), *Amici amico III: Festschrift für Ludvík E. Václavek* (Olomouc, 2011), *321–350*.

Meyendorff, J., 'Byzantine views of Islam', *DOP* 18 (1964), 115–132.

Meyer-Plath, B. and Schneider, A.M., *Die Landmauer von Konstantinopel* (Berlin, 1943).

Miles, G.C., 'Miḥrāb and Anazah. A Study in Early Islamic Iconography', in Miles, G.C. (ed.), *Archaeoligia Orientalia in Memoriam Ernst Herzfeld* (Locust Valley, 1952), 156–171.

Miles, G.C. (ed.), *Archaeoligia Orientalia in Memoriam Ernst Herzfeld* (Locust Valley, 1952).

Miles, G.C., 'The Iconography of Umayyad Coinage', *Ars Orientalis* 3 (1959), 207–213.

Miles, G.C., 'The Earliest Arab Gold Coinage', *American Numismatic Society Museum Notes* 13 (1967), 205–229.

Mingazov, S., *Kubrat – the Ruler of Great Bulgaria and Qetrades – the character of John, Bishop of Nikiu* (Kazan, 2012).

Modelski, G., *World Cities: -3000 to 2000* (Washington DC, 2003).

Modéran, Y., 'Kusayla, l'Afrique et les Arabes', in Briand-Ponsar, C. (ed.), *Identités et Cultures dans l'Algérie Antique* (University of Rouen, 2005), 423–457.

Moorhead, J., 'Iconoclasm, the Cross and the Imperial Image', *Byzantion* 45 (1985), 165–179.

Moosa, M., 'The Relation of the Maronites of Lebanon to the Mardaites and the al-Jarajima', *Speculum* 44 (1969), 597–608.

Morris, I., *Why the West Rules – For Now* (New York, 2010).

Morris, J.T., 'Byzantine Foreign Policy During the Reign of Constans II', unpublished diss. (University of Central Florida, 2014).

Morrison, C. (ed.), *Trade and Markets in Byzantium* (Washington DC, 2012).

Mosshammer, A., *The Chronicle of Eusebius and Greek Chronographic Tradition* (Lewisburg, 1979).

Mousourakis, G., *The Historical and Institutional Context of Roman Law* (Farnham, 2003).

Mylonas, G.E. and Raymond, D. (eds.), *Studies Presented to David Moore Robinson*, 2 vols (St Louis, 1953).

Necpoğlu, G. (ed.), *Muqarnas: An Annual on the Visual Culture of the Islamic World, Volume 13* (Leiden, 1996).

Nedungatt, G. and Featherstone, M. (eds.), *The Council in Trullo Revisited* (Rome, 1995).

Nesbitt, J.W. and Oikonomides, N. (eds.), *Catalogue of Byzantine Seals at Dumbarton Oaks and in the Fogg Museum of Art, Volume 2: South of the Balkans, the Islands, South of Asia Minor* (Washington DC, 1994).

Neuwirth, A., Sinai, N. and Marx, M. (eds.), *The Qur'an in Context: Historical and Literacy Investigations into the Qur'anic Milieu* (Leiden, 2010).

Noble, T.F.X., *The Republic of St. Peter* (Philadelphia, 1984).

Noethlichs, K.L., *Das Judentum und der römische Staat: Minderheitenpolitik im antiken Rom. Wissenschaftliche Buchgesellschaft* (Darmstadt, 1996).

Noonan, T.S., 'The Khazar Qaghanate and its impact on the early Rus' state: the Translatio Imperii from Itil to Kiev', in Khazanov, A.M. and Wink, A. (eds.), *Nomads in the Sedentary World* (London, 2001), 76–102.

Noonan, T.S., 'The Economy of the Khazar Khaganate', in Golden, P.B., Ben-Shammai, H. and Róna-Tas, A. (eds.), *The World of the Khazars: New Perspectives. Selected Papers from the Jerusalem 1999 International Khazar Colloquium* (Handbook of Oriental Studies, Section 8 Uralic & Central Asian Studies) (Leiden, 2007), 207–244.

Nordhagen, P.J., 'John VII's *Adoration of the Cross* in S. Maria Anitqua', *Journal of the Warburg and Courtauld Institutes* 30 (1967), 388–390.

Nordhagen, P.J., *The Frescoes of John VII (A.D. 705–707) in S. Maria Antiqua in Rome* (Rome, 1968).

Noth, A. and Conrad, L.I., *The Early Islamic Historical Traditions: A Source Critical Study* (Princeton, 1994).

Noye, G., 'L'economie de la Calabre de la fin du Vie au VIIIe siècle', in Cosentino, S. (ed.), *L'Italia Bizantina: una Prospettiva Economica. Cahiers de recherches medievales et humanistes* 28 (Paris, 2015), 323–388.

Obolensky, D., *Byzantium and the Slavs* (New York, 1994).

Oddy, W.A., 'The Debasement of the Provincial Byzantine Gold Coinage from the Seventh to Ninth Centuries', in Hahn, W. and Metcalf, W.E. (eds.), *Studies in Early Byzantine Gold Coinage* (New York, 1988), 135–142.

Oddy, W.A., 'Arab Imagery on Early Umayyad Coins in Syria and Palestine: Evidence for Falconry', *NC* 151 (1991), 59–66.

Oddy, W.A. (ed.), *Coinage and History in the Seventh-Century Near East* (Oxford, 2010).

Ohme, H., *Das Concilium Quinisextum und seine Bischofsliste: Studien zum Konstantinopler Konzil von 692* (Berlin, 1990).

Oikonomides, N., *Les listes de préséance byzantines des IXe et Xe siècles (Paris, 1972).*

Oikonomides, N., 'Les premieres mentions des themes dans la *Chronique* de Theophane', *ZRVI* 16 (1975), 1–8.

Oikonomides, N., *Dated Byzantine Lead Seals* (Washington, 1986).

Olsson, J.T., 'Coup d'état, Coronation and Conversion: Some Reflections on the Adoption of Judaism by the Khazar Khaganate', *Journal of the Royal Asiatic Society* 23 (2013), 495–526.

Olster, D.M., *The Politics of Usurpation in the Seventh Century: Rhetoric and Revolution in Byzantium* (Amsterdam, 1993).

Olster, D.M., *Roman Defeat, Christian Response and the Literary Construction of the Jew* (Philadelphia, 1994).

Olster, D., 'Theodosius Grammaticus and the Arab Siege of 674–78', *Byzantinoslavica* 56 (1995), 23–28.

Olster, D.M., 'Justinian II's Odd Note to Pope John V', in Bumazhnov, D., Grypeou, E., Sailors, T.B. and Toepel, A. (eds.), *Bibel, Byzanz und Christlicher Orient: Festschrift für Stephen Gerö zum 65. Geburtstag*, Orientalia Lovaniensia Analecta 187 (Leuven/Paris/Walpole, 2011), 559–570.

Orosz, L., *The London Manuscript of Nikephoros' 'Breviarium'* (Budapest, 1948).

Ostrogorsky, G., 'Les debuts de la querelle des images', *Melanges Charles Diehl* (Paris, 1930), I.235–255.

Ostrogorsky, G., 'Das Steuersystem im byzantinischen Altertum und Mittelalter', *Byzantion* 6 (1931), 229–240.

Ostrogorsky, G., 'Sur la date de la composition du Livre des Themes et sur l'epoque de la constitution des premiers themes d'Asie mineure', *Byzantion* 23 (1953), 31–66.

Ostrogorsky, G., 'The Byzantine Empire in the World of the Seventh Century', *DOP* 13 (1959a), 1–21.

Ostrogorsky, G., 'Byzantine Cities in the Early Middle Ages', *DOP* 13 (1959b), 45–66.

Ostrogorsky, G., *Geschichte des byzantischen Staates* (Munich, 1963).

Ostrogorsky, G., 'Byzantium and the South Slavs', *The Slavonic and East European Review* 42 (1963–1964), 1–14.

Ostrogorsky, G., *History of the Byzantine State* (Oxford, 1968).

Ostrogorsky, G., 'Observations on the Aristocracy in Byzantium', *DOP* 25 (1972), 3–32.

Ostrogorsky, G. and Stein, E., 'Die Kroenungsordnungen des Zeremonienbuches: chronologische und verfassungsgeschichtliche Bemerkungen', *Byzantion* 7 (1932), 185–233.

O'Sullivan, S., 'Sebeos' account of an Arab attack on Constantinople in 654', *BMGS* 28 (2004), 67–88.

Palmer, A., *The Seventh Century in the West-Syrian Chronicles* (Liverpool, 1993).

Papaefthymiou, E.G. and Touratsoglou, I.P. (eds.), *Studies in Byzantine Numismatics and Sigillography in Memory of Petro Protoriotarios* (Athens, 2013).

Papageorgiou, P.N., 'Μνημεῖα τῆς ἐν Θεσσαλονίκη λατρείας τοῦ μεγαλομάρτυρος ἁγίου Δημητρίου', *BZ* 17 (1908), 321–381.

Parani, M.G., *Reconstructing the Reality of Images: Byzantine Material Culture and Religious Iconography (11th–15th Centuries)* (Leiden, 2003).

Pardal, R., *American Aboriginal Medicine* (Buenos Aires, 1998).

Partington, J.R., *A History of Greek Fire and Gunpowder* (Baltimore, 1999).

Pertusi, A., 'La formation des themes byzantins', *Berichte zum XI Internationalen Byzantinisten-Kongress* (Munich, 1958), 1–40.

Petkov, K., *The Voices of Medieval Bulgaria, Seventh-Fifteenth Century: The Records of a Bygone Culture* (Leiden, 2008).

Philippides, M. and Hanak, W.K., *The Siege and the Fall of Constantinople in 1453: Historiography, Topography, and Military Studies* (London, 2011).

Phillips, M. and Goodwin, A., 'A seventh-century Syrian hoard of Byzantine and imitative copper coins', *NC* 157 (1997), 61–87.

Pizarro, J.M., *Writing Ravenna: The Liber Pontificalis of Andreas Agnellus* (Ann Arbor, 1995).

Pohl, W., 'Conceptions of ethnicity in Early Medieval Studies', in Rosenwein, B. and Little, L.K. (eds.), *Debating the Middle Ages: Issues and Readings* (Oxford, 1998), 15–24.

Pohl, W., *Die Awaren: ein Steppenvolk im Mitteleuropa, 567–822 n. Chr.* (Munich, 2002).

Pohl, W., Ganter, C. and Payne, R. (eds.), *Visions of Community in the Post-Roman World: The West, Byzantium and the Islamic World 300–1100* (Aldershot, 2012).

Potesta, G.L., 'The *Vaticinium of Constans*. Genesis and original purposes of the legend of the Last World Emperor', *Millennium* 8 (2011), 271–289.

Pourshariati, P., *Decline and Fall of the Sasanian Empire: the Sasanian-Parthian Confederacy and the Arab Conquest of Iran* (London, 2009).

Price, R., Booth, P. and Cubitt, C., *The Acts of the Lateran Synod of 649* (Liverpool, 2014).

Priester, K., *Geschichte der Langobarden: Gesellschaft – Kultur – Altagsleben* (Stuttgart, 2004).

Prigent, V., 'The Mobilisation of Fiscal Resources in the Byzantine Empire (Eighth to Eleventh Centuries)', in Hudson, J. and Rodriguez, A. (eds.), *Diverging Paths? The Shapes of Power and Institutions in Medieval Christendom and Islam* (Leiden, 2014), 182–229.

Prigent, V., 'The Mobilisation of Fiscal Resources in the Byzantine Empire (Eighth to Eleventh Centuries)', in Hudson, J. and Rodriguez, A. (eds.), *Diverging Paths? The Shapes of Power and Institutions in Medieval Christendom and Islam* (Leiden, 2015a), 182–229.

Prigent, V., 'Un confesseur de mauvaise foi. Notes sur les exactions financieres de l'empereur Leon III en Italie du Sud', in Cosentino, S. (ed.), *L'Italia Bizantina: una Prospettiva Economica. Cahiers de recherches medievales et humanistes* 28 (Paris, (2015b), 279–304.

Prigent, V. and Nichanian, M., 'Les stratèges de Sicile. De la naissance du thème au règne de Léon V', *Revue des études byzantines* (2003), 97–141.

Pringle, D., *The Defence of Byzantine Africa from Justinian to the Arab Conquest: An Account of the Military History and Archaeology of the African Provinces in the Sixth and Seventh Century* (Oxford, 1981).

Proudfoot, A., 'The sources of Theophanes for the Heraclian dynasty', *Byzantion* 44 (1974), 400–427.

Pryor, J.H. and Jeffreys, E.M., *The Age of the ΔΡΟΜΩΝ: The Byzantine Navy ca. 500–1204* (Leiden and Boston, 2006).

Purton, P., *A History of the Early Medieval Siege c.450–1200* (Woodbridge, 2009).

Raaflaub, K.A. and Rosenstein, N. (eds.), *War and Society in the Ancient and Medieval Worlds: Asia, The Mediterranean, Europe, and Mesoamerica* (Cambridge, 2001).

Rapp, C., 'Old Testament Models for Emperors in Early Byzantium', in Magdalino, P. and Nelson, R. (eds.), *The Old Testament in Byzantium* (Washington DC, 2010), 175–197.

Rapp, C. and Salzman, M. (eds.), *Elites in Late Antiquity. Arethusa* 33 (2000).

Reinink, G., 'Ps-Methodius: A Concept of History in Response to the rise of Islam', in Cameron, Av. and Conrad L.I. (eds.), *The Byzantine and Early Islamic Near East I: Problems in the Literary Source Material* (Princeton, 1992), 149–187.

Reyerson, K.V., Stavrou, T.G. and Tracy, J.D. (eds.), *Pre-modern Russia and its world: Essays in Honour of Thomas S. Noonan* (Wiesbaden, 2006).

Reynolds, J. (ed.), *Libyan Studies* (London, 1976).

Richards, J., *The Popes and the Papacy in the Early Middle Ages, 476–752* (London, 1979).

Rio, A. (ed.), *Law, Custom and Justice in Late Antiquity and the Early Middle Ages* (London, 2011).

Robinson, C.F., *Abd al-Malik* (Oxford, 2005).

Robinson, C.F., 'The Rise of Islam, 600–705', in Robinson, C.F. (ed.), *The New Cambridge History of Islam I: The Formation of the Islamic World, Sixth to Eleventh Centuries* (Cambridge, 2010), 173–225.

Rochow, I., 'Zu einigen oppositionellen religiosen Stromungen', *Byzanz im 7. Jahrhundert. Untersuchungen zur Heraushildung des* Feudalismus (Berlin, 1978), 225–288.

Rodd, F., 'Kahena, Queen of the Berbers: A Sketch of the Arab Invasion of Ifriqiya in the First Century of the Hijra', *Bulletin of the School of Oriental Studies* 3 (1925), 731–732.

Roland, A., 'Secrecy, Technology, and War: Greek Fire and the Defense of Byzantium, 678–1204', *Technology and Culture* 33 (1992), 655–679.

Rosenwein, B. and Little, L.K. (eds.), *Debating the Middle Ages: Issues and Readings* (Oxford, 1998).

Runciman, S., *History of the First Bulgarian Empire* (London, 1930).

Runciman, S., *The Medieval Manichee* (Cambridge, 1947).

Samuelson, C., 'Iconography after the Quinisext Council (c. 680–720)', unpublished diss. (Darwin College, Cambridge, 2016).

Sansterre, J.M., 'Le Pape Constantin Ier (708–715) et la politique religieuse des Empereurs Justinien II et Philippikos', *Archivum Historiae Pontificae* 22 (1984), 7–29.

Sarris, P., 'The Justinianic Plague: origins and effects', *Continuity and Change* 17 (2002), 175–179.

Sarris, P., *Empires of Faith: The Fall of Rome to the Rise of Islam, 500–700* (Oxford, 2010).

Sarris, P., 'Law and Custom in the Byzantine Countryside from Justinian I to Basil II (c. 500–1000)', in Rio, A. (ed.), *Law, Custom and Justice in Late Antiquity and the Early Middle Ages* (London, 2011a), 49–61.

Sarris, P., 'Restless Peasants and Scornful Lords: Lay Hostility to Holy Men and the Church in Late Antiquity and the Early Middle Ages', in Sarris, P., Dal Santo, M. and Booth, P. (eds.), *An Age of Saints? Power, Conflict and Dissent in Early Medieval Christianity* (Boston, 2011b), 1–10.

Sarris, P., Dal Santo, M. and Booth, P. (eds.), *An Age of Saints? Power, Conflict and Dissent in Early Medieval Christianity* (Boston, 2011).

Schaff, P. and Wace, H., *The Seven Ecumenical Councils* (A Select Library of the Nicene and Post-Nicene Fathers of the Christian Church, Second Series) (Edinburgh, 1900).

Schenk, K., 'Kaiser Leons III Walten im Innern', *BZ* 5 (1896), 257–301.

Schenker, A.M., *The Dawn of Slavic: An Introduction to Slavic Philology* (New Haven, 1996).

Schlumberger, G., 'Sceau des enclaves (mercenaires) slaves de l'eparchie de Bithynie', *BZ* 12 (1903), 277.

Schulze, I. and Schulze, W., 'The Standing Caliph coins of al-Jazira: some problems and suggestions', *NC* 170 (2010), 331–353.

Schulze, W., 'Symbolism on the Syrian Standing Caliph copper coins: A Contribution to the Discussion', in Oddy, A. (ed.), *Coinage and History in the Seventh-Century Near East* (Oxford, 2011), 11–22.

Seibt, W. and Theodoridis, D., 'Das Rätsel der Andrapoda-Siegel im ausgehenden 7. Jh. Waren mehr Slawen oder mehr Armenier Opfer dieser Staatsaktion?', *ByzSl* 60 (1999), 400–406.

Settipani, C., 'The Seventh-Century Bagratids between Armenia and Byzantium', *TM*17 (2013), 559–578.

Setton, K.M., 'On the Importance of Land Tenure and Agrarian Taxation in the Byzantine Empire, from the Fourth Century to the Fourth Crusade', *AJPh* 74 (1953), 225–259.

Shaban, M.A., *Islamic History: A New Interpretation I: AD 600–750 (AHI32)* (Cambridge, 1971).

Shahid, I., 'Heraclius and the Theme System: New Light from the Arabic', *Byzantion* 57 (1987), 391–403.

Shahid, I., 'Heraclius and the Theme System: Further Observations', *Byzantion* 69 (1989), 208–243.

Shahid, I., *Byzantium and the Arabs in the Sixth Century* (Washington DC, 1995).

Shepard, J. (ed.), *Cambridge History of Byzantine Empire ca 500–1492* (Cambridge, 2019).

Shepard, J. and Franklin, S. (eds.), *Byzantine Diplomacy* (Aldershot, 1992).

Shirota, S., 'The Chinese Chroniclers of the Khazars: Notes on Khazaria in Tang Period Texts', *Archivum Eurasiae Medii Aevi* 14 (2005), 231–261.

Simeonov, B., *Prabülgarska onomastika* (Plovdiv, 2008).

Sinor, D., 'Atour d'une migration des peuples au Vᵉ siècle', *Journal Asiatique* 1946–47 (Paris, 1948), 1–77.

Siraj, A., *L'Image de la Tingitane. L'historiographie arabe medievale et l'Antiquite nordafricaine* (Paris, 1995).

Smith, W., *Dictionary of Greek and Roman Geography, illustrated by numerous engravings on wood* (London, 1854).

Somogyi, P., 'New remarks on the flow of Byzantine coins in Avaria and Walachia during the second half of the seventh century', in Curta, F. and Kovalev, R. (eds.), *The Other Europe in the Middle Ages: Avars, Bulgars, Khazars and Cumans* (Leiden, 2008), 83–150.

Sophoulis, P., *Byzantium and Bulgaria, 775–831* (Leiden, 2011).

Spears, W.H. Jr, *Greek Fire: The Fabulous Secret Weapon That Saved Europe* (New York, 1969).

Speck, P., *Kaiser Leon III, die Geschichtswerke des Nikephoros und des Theophanes und der Liber Pontificalis* (Bonn, 2003).

Sperati, G., 'Amputation of the Nose throughout History', *Acta Otorhinolaryngol Italica* 29 (2009), 44–50.

Stampfer, S., 'Did the Khazars Convert to Judaism?', *Jewish Social Studies: History, Culture, Society* 19 (2013), 1–72.

Stathakopoulos, D., *Famine and Pestilence in the Late Roman and Early Byzantine Empire: A Systematic Survey of Subsistence Crises and Epidemics* (Aldershot, 2004).

Stathakopoulos, D., 'Crime and Punishment: The Plague in the Byzantine Empire, 541–749', in Little, L.K. (ed.), *Plague and the End of Antiquity: The Pandemic of 541–750* (Cambridge, 2007), 99–118.

Stein, E., *Geschichte des spätrömischen Reiches. Band I. Vom römischen zum byzantinischen Staate (284–476 n. Chr.)* (Vienna, 1928); Palanque, J.R., French trans. (Paris, 1959).

Stolte, B.H., 'Is Byzantine Law Roman Law?', *Acta Byzantina Fennica* 2 (Helsinki, 2005).

Stouraitis, I., 'Roman Identity in Byzantium: a critical approach', *BZ* 107 (2014), 175–220.

Stratos, A.N., *Byzantium in the Seventh Century*, 6 vols (Amsterdam, 1968–1980).

Stratos, A.N., 'The Naval Engagement at Phoenix', in Laiou, A.E. (ed.), *Charanis Studies: Essays in Honour of Peter Charanis* (New Brunswick, 1986), 48–55.

Stumpf, J.A., 'On the Mutilation and Blinding of Byzantine Emperors from the Reign of Heraclius I until the Fall of Constantinople', *Journal of Ancient History and Archaeology* 4 (2017), 46–54.

Sumner, G.V., 'Philippicus, Anastasius II and Theodosius III', *GRBS* 17 (1976), 287–294.

Sussex, R. and Cubberley, P., *The Slavic Languages* (Cambridge, 2011).

Taddei, A., 'Some topographical remarks of Pope Constantine's journey to Constantinople (710-711)', *Eurasian Studies* 11 (2013), 53–78.

Tagliaferri, A., *Problemi della civilita e dell'economia Longobarda: Scritti in memoria di Gian Piero Bognetti* (Milan, 1964).

Takahashi, H., *Barhebraeus. A Bio-Bibliography* (Piscataway, 2005).

Talbi, M., 'Un nouveau fragment de l'histoire de l'Occident musulman (62–196/682–812): l'épopée d'al Kahina', *Cahiers de Tunisie* 19 (1971), 19–52.

Teall, J.L., 'The grain supply of the Byzantine Empire', *DOP* 13 (1959), 87–139.

Teall, J.L., 'The Byzantine Agricultural Traditions', *DOP* 25 (1971), 33–59.

Teule, H., 'Gregory Barhebraeus and his Time. The Syrian Renaissance', *Journal of the Canadian Society for Syriac Studies* 3 (2003), 21–42.

Thomson, R.W., *Rewriting Caucasian History: The Medieval Armenian Adaptation of the Georgian Chronicles* (Oxford, 1996).

Toševa-Nikolovska, D., 'Some Observations on the *Nomos Georgikos*', *Colloquia Humanistica* 7 (2018), 205–226.

Toumanoff, C., *Studies in Christian Caucasian History* (Washington DC, 1963).

Toumanoff, C., 'Caucasia and Byzantium', *Traditio* 27 (1971), 111–158.

Toynbee, A.J., *Constantine Porphyrogenitus* (Oxford, 1973).

Treadgold, W., *The Byzantine State Finances in the Eighth and Ninth Centuries* (New York, 1982).

Treadgold, W., *The Byzantine Revival 780–842* (Stanford, 1988).

Treadgold, W., 'Seven Byzantine Revolutions and the Chronology of Theophanes', *GRBS* 31 (1990), 203–227.

Treadgold, W., 'The Army in the Works of Constantine Porphyrogenitus', *Rivista di Studi Bizantini e Neoellenici* 29 (1992), 77–162.

Treadgold, W., *Byzantium and its Army 284–1081* (Stanford, 1995).

Treadgold, W., *A History of the Byzantine State and Society* (Stanford, 1997).

Treadgold, W., *The Early Byzantine Historians* (London, 2007).

Treadgold, W., 'The Darkness of the Seventh-Century Near East', *International Journal of the Classical Tradition* 18 (2011), 579–592.

Treadgold, W., 'Trajan the Patrician, Nicephorus, and Theophanes', in Bumazhnov, D., Grypeou, E., Sailors, T.B. and Toepel, A. (eds.), *Bibel, Byzanz und Christlicher Orient: Festschrift für Stephen Gerö zum 65. Geburtstag*. Orientalia Lovaniensia Analecta 187. (Leuven/Paris/Walpole, 2011), 589–621.

Treadgold, W., 'Opposition to Iconoclasm as Grounds for Civil War', in Koder, J. and Stouraitis, I. (eds.), *Byzantine War Ideology Between Roman Imperial Concept and Christian Religion* (Vienna, 2012), 17–26.

Treadwell, L.W., *The Chronology of the Pre-Reform Copper Coinage of Early Islamic Syria* (London, 2000).

Treadwell, L.W., 'Abd al-Malik's Coinage Reforms: the Role of the Damascus Mint', *Revue Numismatique* 165 (2009), 357–381.

Treadwell, L.W., 'Byzantium and Islam in the Late 7th Century AD: A Numismatic War of Images?', in Goodwin, T. (ed.), *Arab-Byzantine Coins and History* (London, 2012), 145–155.

Trilling, J., 'The Soul of the Empire: Style and Meaning in the Mosaic Pavement of the Byzantine Imperial Palace in Constantinople', *DOP* 43 (1989), 27–72.

Trombley, F., 'The Arab Wintering Raid against Euchaita in 663/4', in *Abstracts of the Fifteenth Annual Byzantine Studies Conference 1989* (Amherst, 1989), 5–6.

Turner, D., 'The Trouble with the Trinity: The Context of a Slogan During the Reign of Constantine IV (668–85)', *BMGS* 27 (2003), 68–119.

Vacalopoulis, A.P., *A History of Thessaloniki* (Thessaloniki, 1963).

Vachkova, V., 'Danube Bulgaria and Khazaria as part of the Byzantine oikoumene', *in* Curta, F. and Kovalev, R. (eds.), *The Other Europe in the Middle Ages: Avars, Bulgars, Khazars and Cumans* (Leiden, 2008), *339–362.*

Vasiliev, A.A., *The Goths in the Crimea* (Cambridge, 1936).

Vasiliev, A.A., 'An Edict of the Emperor Justinian II, September 688', *Speculum* 18 (1943), 1–13.

Vasiliev, A.A., 'L'entrée triomphale de l'empereur Justinien II a Thessalonique en 688', *Orientalia Christiana Periodica* 13 (1947), 355–368.

Vasiliev, A.A., 'The Historical Significance of the Mosaic of Saint Demetrius at Sassaferrato', *DOP* 5 (1950), 31–39.

Vasiliev, A.A., *History of the Byzantine Empire* (Madison, 1952).

Velez Lopez, L.R., 'Las mutilaciones en los vasos antropomorfos del antiguo Peru', *International Congress of Americanists. Proceedings of the XVIII session, Londres, 1912* (London, 1913), 267–275.

Vernadsky, G., 'Sur l'origine de la loi agraire', *Byzantion* 2 (1925), 169–180.

Vernadsky, G., 'On the Origins of the Antae', *Journal of the American Oriental Society* 59 (1939), 56–66.

Vryonis, S., 'St Ioannicius the Great and the "Slavs" of Bithynia', *Byzantion* 31 (1961), 245–248.

Vryonis, S., 'An Attic Hoard of Byzantine Gold Coins (668–741) from the Thomas Whittemore Collection and the Numismatic Evidence for the Urban History of Byzantium', *Recueil des travaux de l'Institut d'Études byzantines* 8 (1963), 291–300.

Wagschal, D., *Law and Legality in the Greek East: The Byzantine Canonical Tradition, 381–883* (Oxford, 2015).

Wasserstein, A., 'The Number and Provenance of Jews in Graeco-Roman Antiquity: A Note on Population Statistics', in Katzoff, R. (ed.), *Classical Studies in Honor of David Sohlberg* (Ramat Gan., 1996), 307–317.

Wasserstein, D.J., 'The Khazars and the World of Islam', in Golden, P.B., Ben-Shammai, H. and Rona-Tas, A. (eds.), *The World of the Khazars: New Perspectives* (Leiden, 1997), 373–386.

Wegewitz, W., 'Stand der Langobardenforschung im Gebiet der Niederelbe', in Tagliaferri, A., *Problemi della civilta e dell'economia Longobarda: Scritti in memoria di Gian Piero Bognetti* (Milan, 1964), 19–51.

Wegewitz, W., *Das langobardische Brandgräberfeld von Putensen* (Hildesheim, 1972).

Wellhausen, L., *The Arab Kingdom and Its Fall* (Calcutta, 1927).

Wells, P.S., *Barbarians to Angels: The Dark Ages Reconsidered* (New York, 2008).

Weltecke, D., 'Les trois grandes chroniques syro-orthodoxes des XIIe et XIIIe siècles', in Debie, M. (ed.), *L'historiographie syriaque* (Paris, 2009), 107–135.

Whitby, M., *The Emperor Maurice and his Historian: Theophylact Simocatta on Persian and Balkan Warfare* (Oxford, 1988).

Whittow, M., 'Ruling the late Roman and Byzantine city: a continuous history', *Past and Present* 129 (1990), 3–29.

Wickham, C., *The Inheritance of Rome: Illuminating the Dark Ages 400–1000* (London, 2009).

Wiita, J.E., 'The Ethnika in Byzantine Military Treatises', Ph.D. Thesis (University of Minnesota, 1977).

Williams, G.L., *Papal Geneaology: The Families and Descendants of the Popes* (Jefferson, 2004).

Winkelmann, F., *Quellenstudien zur herrschenden Klasse von Byzanz im 8. Und 9. Jahrhundert* (Berlin, 1987).

Wolfram, H., *History of the Goths* (Berkeley, 1988).

Woods, D., 'Thessalonica's Patron: Saint Demetrius or Emeterius?', *Harvard Theological Review* 93 (2000), 221–234.

Woods, D., 'Jews, Rats and the Battle of Yarmuk', in Lewin, A.S. and Pellegrini, P. (eds.), *The Late Roman Army in the Near East from Diocletian to the Arab Conquest* (Oxford, 2007), 367–376.

Woods, D., 'Corruption and Mistranslation: The Common Syriac Source on the Origin of the Mardaites', American Foundation for Syriac Studies (2011).

Woods, D., 'Maslama and the Alleged Construction of the First Mosque in Constantinople c.718', in Crostini, B. and La Porta, S. (eds.), *Negotiating Co-Existence: Communities, Cultures and Convivencia in Byzantine Society* (Trier, 2013), 19–30.

Woods, D., 'On the Alleged Arab Destruction of the Colossus of Rhodes c. 653', *Byzantion* 86 (2016), 441–451.

Yalamanchili, H., Sclafani, A.P., Schaefer, S.D. and Presti, P., 'The Path of Nasal Reconstruction: From Ancient India to the Present', *Facial Plastic Surgery* 24 (2008), 3–10.

Zacos, G. and Veglery, A., *Byzantine Lead Seals* (Basel, 1972).

Zavagno, L., 'At the Edge of Two Empires: The Economy of Cyprus between Late Antiquity and the Early Middle Ages (650s–800s CE)', *DOP* 65/66 (2011–2012), 121–155.

Zuckerman, C., 'The reign of Constantine V in the miracles of St. Theodore the Recruit (*BHG* 1764)', *REB* 46 (1988), 191–210.

Zuckerman, C. 'Learning from the Enemy and More: Studies in "Dark Centuries" Byzantium', *Millennium* 2 (2005), 79–135.

Zuckerman, C. (ed.), *La Crimée entre Byzance et le khaganat khazar* (Paris, 2006).

Zuckerman, C., 'Learning from the enemy and more: Studies in "Dark Centuries" Byzantium', *Millennium* 2 (2006), 79–135.

Zuckerman, C., 'The Khazars and Byzantium: the First Encounter', in Golden, P.B., Ben-Shammai, H. and Rona-Tas, A. (eds.), *The World of the Khazars: New Perspectives – Selected Papers from the Jerusalem 1999 International Colloquium* (Leiden, 2007), 399–432.

Zuckerman, C. (ed.), *Constructing the Seventh Century*. Travaux et Memoires 17 (Paris, 2013).

Index